T0326722

Hellenic Studies 22

PLATO'S *SYMPOSIUM*

ISSUES IN INTERPRETATION AND RECEPTION

PLATO'S *SYMPOSIUM*

ISSUES IN INTERPRETATION AND RECEPTION

Edited by

J. H. LESHER
DEBRA NAILS

and

FRISBEE C. C. SHEFFIELD

CENTER FOR HELLENIC STUDIES
TRUSTEES FOR HARVARD UNIVERSITY
WASHINGTON, DC
DISTRIBUTED BY HARVARD UNIVERSITY PRESS
CAMBRIDGE, MASSACHUSETTS, AND LONDON, ENGLAND
2006

Plato's *Symposium*: issues in interpretation and reception, edited by J. H.
Lesher, Debra Nails, and Frisbee C. C. Sheffield

Published by Center for Hellenic Studies, Trustees for Harvard University,
Washington, DC
Distributed by Harvard University Press, Cambridge, Massachusetts, and
London, England
Volume Editor: Casey Dué
Production Editor: Ivy Livingston
Cover Design and Illustration: Joni Godlove

LIBRARY OF CONGRESS CATALOGING-IN-PUBLICATION DATA

Plato's *Symposium*: issues in interpretation and reception / edited by J. H.
Lesher, Debra Nails, and Frisbee C. C. Sheffield.
     p. cm. — (Hellenic studies ; 22)
Includes bibliographical references and index.
ISBN 0-674-02375-7
1. Plato. *Symposium*. 2. Socrates. 3. Love—Early works to 1800. I. Lesher, J. H.
(James H.). II. Nails, Debra, 1950–. III. Sheffield, Frisbee C. C. (Frisbee Candida
Cheyenne). IV. Title. V. Series.
B385.P58 2006
184—dc22

               2006037295

To our students
past, present, and future

Contents

Diagrams and Illustrations

Acknowledgments

E ACH OF THE ESSAYS INCLUDED IN THIS VOLUME was presented at a conference held at the Center for Hellenic Studies in Washington, DC, in August of 2005. On behalf of all the conference participants we would like to thank the Director of the Center, Professor Gregory Nagy, Associate Director Douglas Frame, Programs Officer Jennifer Reilly, Executive Assistant Abby Porter, and staff members Adam Briscoe, Sylvia Henderson, Zoie Lafis, Jill Curry Robbins, Ruth Taylor, and Temple Wright. Our conference on Plato's *Symposium* represents only one of the many outreach initiatives recently undertaken by the Center to foster greater understanding and appreciation of our Hellenic heritage.

One of the requirements established by the Center was that copies of the conference papers be made available to all participants well in advance of the event. Lori Keleher of the University of Maryland and two members of the Center's publications staff, Mark Tomasko and Professor Leonard Muellner, converted the documents into the required electronic format. Once the conference had taken place, the papers were made available to the general public through electronic publication on the Center's Web site.

In preparation for the appearance of the papers in book form, two anonymous external readers were engaged by the Center whom the participants also wish to thank. Zoie Lafis provided the handsome image of Diotima and Socrates that appears on the cover, and Jill Curry Robbins obtained the many permissions required for the use of visual materials. Professor Leonard Muellner provided technical support, and Chet McLeskey of Michigan State University assisted with copy-editing and indexing the volume in its final stages.

J. H. L.

D. N.

F. C. C. S.

Introduction

IN HIS *SYMPOSIUM* Plato crafted a set of speeches in praise of love that has attracted the interest of philosophers, theologians, poets, and artists from antiquity down to the present day. In the third century CE, Plotinus drew on aspects of the *Symposium* to fashion an account of the nature of the twin processes of emanation and return to "the One." Following Plotinus' lead, a number of early Christian writers elected to read the dialogue's "ascent passage" as a thinly veiled description of the soul's ascent to heaven. Ficino's commentary on Plato's *Symposium* introduced Plotinus' view of love and beauty to the poets and artists of Renaissance Europe and brought the phrase "Platonic love" into common speech. Ideas and images drawn from the *Symposium* appear in Thomas Mann's *Death In Venice*, E. M. Forster's *Maurice*, T. S. Eliot's *The Cocktail Party*, Virginia Woolf's *To the Lighthouse*, and Yukio Mishima's *Forbidden Colors*. Scenes and characters depicted in the dialogue appear in paintings or sketches by Peter Paul Rubens, Pietro Testa, Asmus Jakob Karstens, Jacques-Louis David, Anselm Feuerbach, and John La Farge, among others, as well as in musical compositions by Erik Satie and Leonard Bernstein. The 1969 BBC production of *The Drinking Party*, the musical *All about Love*, and the rock musical *Hedwig and the Angry Inch* all testify to the dialogue's enduring appeal. Sigmund Freud looked back to Plato's understanding of *erōs* or "passionate desire" as the model for his concept of the libido, and the dialogue's view of love as "desire for eternal possession of the good" is still of great philosophical interest in its own right. Nevertheless, for all the interest shown in the *Symposium* over the centuries, questions remain concerning the meaning of individual passages, the relationship between the *Symposium* and views Plato presented in other dialogues, and the nature of the dialogue's influence on later artists and writers. The present volume offers a set of perspectives on each of these topics.

Part I: The *Symposium* and Plato's Philosophy

The *Symposium* has traditionally been seen as a "middle period" dialogue which moves away from certain characteristic features of the Socratic dialogues towards the grand theorizing of the *Republic*. Yet, as Christopher Rowe argues in "The *Symposium* as a Socratic Dialogue," the *Symposium* does not fit neatly into such a categorization in so far as it appears to embrace Socratic psychology on the one hand and Platonic metaphysics on the other. In his paper, Rowe addresses this apparent tension. After arguing against various interpretative strategies (those of Price, Vlastos, and Irwin, in particular), Rowe argues that there is, in fact, no necessary connection between Platonic Forms and Platonic psychology. The presence of the one feature (Platonic Forms) should not lead us to anticipate the other (Platonic psychology). Rowe moves on to present a case for viewing the *Symposium* as a Socratic dialogue, and explores the philosophical ramifications of such a view.

A further interpretative issue related to the reading of the *Symposium* concerns the relationship between the parts of the dialogue itself. The *Symposium* is a curiously constructed work, which has divided scholars who wish their philosophy and literature to be served up separately. Why did Plato offer such an array of speeches on the topic at hand? And what is the relationship between the account of the philosopher Socrates and those of his (non-philosophical) peers? In "The Role of the Earlier Speeches in the *Symposium*: Plato's Endoxic Method?" Frisbee Sheffield considers whether Plato operated "endoxically," that is, whether he used "views accepted by most people, or the wise," as the basis for his philosophical inquiry into the nature of *erōs*. After assessing the contributions made to Socrates' speech by each of the previous speakers, Sheffield shows how Socrates transforms, rejects, or (quite commonly) preserves a grain of truth embedded in each of the accounts. Sheffield proceeds to consider whether agreement among the speakers carries any philosophical or evidential weight, and concludes that although the speeches play an important role in prompting fruitful investigation of the topic, there is insufficient reason to accord them the status of Aristotelian *endoxa*.

In "A Platonic Reading of Plato's *Symposium*," Lloyd Gerson argues that whether the "unitarians" or the "developmentalists" are right in their reading of the *Symposium*, one needs to look beyond the dialogue itself to resolve its interpretative puzzles. Gerson presents a case for adopting Platonism, or more specifically the thought of Plotinus, as the basis for a fruitful reading strategy.

Plotinus' account, which expresses most concisely the central elements of Gerson's Platonism, is argued for in the bulk of the paper, and shown to resolve numerous interpretative difficulties. Gerson further argues that this suggests a larger thesis, namely that that there is a philosophy called Platonism in the dialogues which is needed to interpret them successfully.

Part II: Interpreting Plato's *Symposium*

In "Medicine, Magic, and Religion in Plato's *Symposium*," Mark McPherran argues that these three themes serve to link Eryximachus' speech with the speeches given by Aristophanes, Agathon, and ultimately the account of *erōs* put forward by Socrates based on the instruction given to him by the Arcadian priestess Diotima. In sharp contrast with the common view of Eyrixmachus' speech as the superficial observations of a boring pedant, on McPherran's account Plato chose to incorporate the remarks of a noted physician in order to appropriate and extend the scientific and religious conventions of his own time in the service of the new and superior enterprise of philosophy.

The role played by beauty in the experience of *erōs* is a central theme in many of the speeches in the dialogue. In "Permanent Beauty and Becoming Happy in Plato's *Symposium*" Gabriel Richardson Lear explores the value of beauty and addresses the vexed question of its relationship to the good. Lear argues that we value beauty in part because we honor beautiful creations, which endow their producers with an afterlife in human memory. When we perceive good things as beautiful this arouses our desire to possess happiness eternally. The encounter with beauty generates creative activity because it is intimately related to the immortality we crave. Lear argues that beauty is "a shining forth of stability and self-sufficiency" and that such a good is valued by all erotically disposed human beings.

Socrates' own status in relation to beauty and goodness is a controversial issue on which the papers by Ruby Blondell and C. D. C. Reeve offer different perspectives. In "A Study in Violets: Alcibiades in the *Symposium*," Reeve draws on Alcibiades' references to the *agalmata*—"statues" or "images"—of virtue inside Socrates in order to clarify how far, or how little, Socrates' friends and associates were able to understand him. Reeve examines the various senses of *agalmata* in order to determine the sense in which Socrates can be seen to have such *agalmata* inside him. Beginning with a substantive construal of *agalmata* as statues of the gods, which seems implied by Alcibiades' use of the term at various points, Reeve argues that this is incompatible with Socrates' disavowal of knowledge and his portrait in the dialogue at large. Alcibiades has ultimately misunderstood the nature and status of the philosopher. Nonetheless, *agalmata* is an appropriate term for what the philosopher does have inside. For an *agalma* originally conveyed the idea of a bridge to the divine. So the real nature of the philosopher, misconstrued by Alcibiades, is not that of a complete divine nature, whose goods can be transferred to another person, but rather of one who can motivate others towards the divine life of philosophical inquiry.

In "Where is Socrates on the 'Ladder of Love'?" Ruby Blondell considers whether Socrates has attained true virtue or merely approached it. Plato presents an ambiguous picture of the philosopher. On the one hand he is presented as the eager seeker after wisdom, lacking and desirous of the goodness he lacks; on the other he is a paradigm of achieved virtue. Blondell provides an account of each step of the ascent and assesses the degree to which Socrates may be considered to have occupied each of them. She concludes that Plato places him on all of them, not in an orderly sequence but in an impressionistic manner that frustrates our desire to pin Socrates down.

Debra Nails' "Tragedy Off-Stage" takes its start from the curious thesis defended by Socrates in the dialogue's final scene to the effect that "the same man should be capable of writing both tragedy and comedy" (223d2–5). When we apply Socrates' thesis to the *Symposium* itself we are required to consider whether and in what respects the dialogue might have dealt in both tragedy and comedy. Nails argues that the tragic-comic distinction has little relevance to the contents or "internals" of the *Symposium*. The real tragedy of the dialogue, she argues, lay "off-stage" in the real lives of the persons whom Plato chose to portray in the *Symposium*.

In "The Virtues of Platonic Love" Gabriela Carone asks how, if at all, the account of *erōs* Socrates presents is supposed to help us to understand the nature of love as we encounter it in our daily lives. Taking up a series of objections often raised against Plato's view, Carone argues that Plato's account has both a descriptive and a normative aspect. While his theory of *erōs* draws upon and thereby captures some aspects of our experience of love it also seeks to explain how a person can fail to understand the nature of his or her love as well as its true object.

Part III: The *Symposium*, Sex, and Gender

Plato's *Symposium* has contributed significantly to our understanding of ancient sexuality and the construction of gender in the classical world. The papers by Luc Brisson, Angela Hobbs and Jeffrey Carnes shed new light on the nature of *paiderastia* (Brisson), the use of female imagery in a largely homo-erotic context (Hobbs), and the influence of the *Symposium*'s views about homosexuality on modern legal theory (Carnes). In "Agathon, Pausanias, and Diotima in Plato's *Symposium: Paiderastia* and *Philosophia*," Brisson clarifies the practice of sexual relationships between males in Greece as a necessary back-ground to the *Symposium*. He argues that Plato critiques the institution of *paiderastia* in relation to the quest for knowledge, *philosophia*. Diotima's speech is crucial to the critique, replacing the image of transmission with that of preg-nancy, and replacing physical with incorporeal beauty.

In "Female Imagery in Plato" Angela Hobbs proposes that our under-standing of the image of the pregnant philosopher is enriched by placing it in the context of Plato's use of "female" and "male" imagery throughout the corpus. She argues against a popular feminist reading according to which Plato appropriates and ultimately obscures the female. Once a certain level of understanding has been reached, Plato is equally happy for the philosopher to appear as male or female, as gender is not central to the higher rungs of his philosophical project. Plato is not specifically negating the role of the female in his text, but employing both male and female images to illustrate that ulti-mately we should liberate ourselves from "irrelevant ... cultural constraints."

In "Plato in the Courtroom: The Surprising Influence of the *Symposium* on Legal Theory," Jeffrey Carnes reviews a number of recent controversial court cases relating to homosexuality (*Romer v. Evans*, *Bowers v. Hardwick*, and *Lawrence v. Texas*). He places his discussion within the constructionist versus essentialist theories of homosexuality which often underlie such cases, and assesses the degree to which this is an appropriate legacy for the *Symposium*.

Part IV: The Reception of Plato's *Symposium*

This final section explores the influence of Plato's *Symposium* on later artists and writers. In "Plato's *Symposium* and the Traditions of Ancient Fiction," Richard Hunter argues for an intimate relationship between the *Symposium* and the development of the novel. He makes the case for such a relationship by exploring the ways in which ancient novels appropriated, or parodied, themes from the *Symposium*. Hunter argues that Plato's work foreshadows later devel-opments in both the form and content of the ancient novel.

In "Some Notable Afterimages of Plato's *Symposium*" James Lesher identi-fies and describes many of the works of art inspired by Plato's masterpiece, and asks why, of all of Plato's dialogues, the *Symposium* alone inspired such a rich visual response. Chief among the factors he identifies are the universal appeal of the topic of love, the dialogue's many dramatic qualities, the vivacity of its portraits of Socrates and Alcibiades, and the absence of a clear and dominant philosophical message that would have served to narrow the scope of its appeal.

In "The Hangover of Plato's *Symposium* in the Italian Renaissance from Bruni (1435) to Castiglione (1528)," Diskin Clay offers a *tour de force* of the ways in which the *Symposium* informed Renaissance art and literature. Clay focuses on Pietro Bembo's *Gli Asolini*, Ficino's commentary on the *Symposium*, commonly known as the *De Amore*, and Castiglione's *Il Cortegiano*, and shows how each of these works was influenced by, and transformed, its Platonic template.

David O'Connor's "Platonic Selves in Shelley and Stevens" explores the reception of the *Symposium* in the poetry of the English Romantics and their heirs. O'Connor argues that in "Alastor" (1815) Shelley anticipated aspects of the translation of the *Symposium* he would produce three years later. O'Connor then uses these two texts to explain some central features of Socrates' speech. The notion of love as involving elements of "narcissistic projection," a key Romantic notion, can be seen in Socrates' emphasis on the creative power of *erōs*. O'Connor also explores the theme of narcissism in connection with Wallace Stevens' commitment to Platonism and finds that theme expressed in some of Stevens' most characteristic poems. Shelley and Stevens are thus seen to be careful readers and critics of the *Symposium* who valued the Platonic ascent but valued their freedom more.

J. H. L.

D. N.

F. C. C. S.

Part One

THE *SYMPOSIUM* AND PLATO'S PHILOSOPHY

One

The *Symposium* as a Socratic Dialogue

Christopher Rowe

T HIS ESSAY WILL MAKE ONE VERY SPECIFIC CLAIM: that the *Symposium* is properly to be treated as a Socratic dialogue. In one way it will of course be quite uncontroversial to describe the *Symposium* as "Socratic": Socrates is on any account the focus of the whole dialogue, which ends as it begins, with a celebration of particular features of his, and includes a kind of *tableau vivant* in the middle with the great man as Eros. The *Symposium* is a kind of repertory of details of the character and life of the Platonic Socrates (whatever the relationship between this Socrates and the real, historical Socrates).[1]

What will concern me in the present essay, however, is rather the *philosophical* aspect of the dialogue: whether, or to what extent, the *philosophy* of the *Symposium* is "Socratic." In the first place, given the recent tradition of modern Anglo-American scholarship, this will mean asking whether the dialogue is closer, philosophically, to the dialogues we modern Anglophones have come to label as "Socratic," or "early," or whether it is, rather, closer to—what are called—the "middle" dialogues. To that question, the answer is apparently simple and straightforward: by the criteria enunciated by that great modern Platonist Gregory Vlastos,[2] whose lead the majority of modern English-speaking readers of Plato follow, and encourage others to follow, the *Symposium* is a quintessentially "middle" dialogue, above all because it not only contains but ultimately pivots on those special Platonic metaphysical entities, the Forms, of which—allegedly—Socrates never dreamed. Never

---

[1] As it happens, I believe that there is a close connection between the two Socrateses, but nothing much hangs on this in the present context. [I wish to thank the participants at the *Symposium* conference at the Center for Hellenic Studies in August of 2005, especially Frisbee Sheffield and the anonymous readers, for their comments on the earlier version of this paper.]

[2] Vlastos 1991:47–49.

mind that, in stylistic terms (as Charles Kahn has reminded us),[3] the dialogue actually belongs to a very large group of dialogues that includes not only the "Socratic," metaphysically innocent, dialogues but also *Phaedo* and *Cratylus*; few modern readers hesitate to associate *Symposium* with the *Republic* and the *Phaedrus*. (Again, I refer primarily to Anglophone readers: for example, "early/middle/late" as a way of dividing up the dialogues, is—as I have discovered from experience—difficult to translate into French, or into Italian, except by way of reference to Anglo-Saxon habits.)

That the *Symposium* should be so treated, however, is rather odd. Witness the following passage from one of the most brilliant and illuminating of contemporary writers on the *Symposium*, Anthony Price:

> A remarkable aspect of the *Symposium* is its loyalty to the Socratic psychology of the *Lysis* ... Agathon throws out the truism that love (*erōs*) is of beauty (197b5). Socrates elicits the thesis that its object is one's own happiness by a brisk inference: the lover loves beautiful things to have them for himself; to love beautiful things is to love good things, and to have good things is to be happy; hence the lover desires to be happy (204d5–e7). Happiness is a final end; we need not ask why anyone wishes to be happy (205a2–3). This is not yet decisive, for it might apply to love, but not to desire universally. Even in its broadest sense, a man's *loves* might be what we may call his *projects* (whether these be poetic, chrematistic, gymnastic, philosophic, or erotic, cf. 205a8–d8), but not his natural appetites or incidental inclinations. What I love may be altogether a function of the sort of life I wish to lead and the sort of man I wish to be, whereas what I desire may in part ride free of such central evaluations. It might be that, while all love and desire is for things that one lacks (200a9, e2–9), only all love is ultimately for happiness. *However, it serves Socrates' present purpose, which is to say nothing against erotic desire, that he gives no hint of any divergence or conflict of the kind that serves in the Republic to distinguish rational and irrational desires (IV 436b8–441c2).* And there is a sequence of particular indications that he is placing *all* desires within a eudaimonist perspective. He argues unqualifiedly that personified Love is a pauper: loving and lacking beautiful things, it must also lack all goods, for goods are beautiful (201a9–c5, cf. *Lysis* 216d2). Yet if its loves were only its projects, it would not have to lack any natural or incidental goods that did not

---

[3] Kahn 1996:42–48.

fall within those. Further, even involuntary genital responses, male and female, are taken to express love (206d3–e1). Finally, love is taken to be evidenced by the behaviour of brutes (207a6–b6), and human physiological processes (c9–e1); yet if we were to extend the term "project" beyond personal ideals to desires that are funda-mental though unthinking, it would draw a line that was never Platonic. Rather, we must take the background assumption to be Socratic: happiness is the ultimate goal of all desire, animal as well as human. Erotic desire has then to be accommodated as a special mode of desiring that which all desire desires; its definition is a theorem derived from a Socratic axiom.[4]

What is particularly interesting (and complex) about Price's position here is that he holds that the Plato of the *Symposium* has actually *abandoned* "the Socratic psychology of the *Lysis*"; he employs it, keeps it on, as it were (so I take Price to be saying), in this dialogue just because *"it serves Socrates' present purpose, which is to say nothing against erotic desire."* Desire in general, according to that *Lysis* account, will always be innocent, always aimed at what really is good (for us): if anything goes wrong, whether in our relationships or in our lives and actions in general, the culprits will be our beliefs, which are the only things that *can* go wrong. Price claims to find confirmation of his proposal, i.e. that Plato had already abandoned the psychology of the *Lysis* by the time of writing of the *Symposium*, in the analysis of (some kinds of) human relationships that finally emerges from the larger and allegedly later dialogue (i.e. the *Symposium*), which he takes to show a singular advance over the more limited, and ultimately disappointing, analysis of the *Lysis*. (Disappointing, that is, to Price, not to me. I am therefore not particularly impressed by the form of Price's confirmation of his thesis. However, little will hang on this if, as I claim, Price in fact has no success in showing that the analysis of personal relationships offered in the *Symposium* is significantly different from what we are offered in the *Lysis*.)[5]

Many of the detailed issues involved here I shall leave to one side for reasons of space. I introduce the passage from Price not only because it is so clear and useful a statement of what is, for my purposes, and in general, a central feature of the *Symposium* (its Socratic-style psychology), but because

---

[4] Price 1997:254–255 (my emphasis); Price admits in a footnote that "[t]his view was barely advanced [in the first edition, of 1989]."

[5] For what is, *inter alia*, a defence of the *Lysis*'s treatment of relationships between *philoi*, "friends" of all kinds, and the theory of desire and action on which it is based, see Penner and Rowe 2005, especially part II.

it illustrates the abiding influence of what I may call the "Vlastosian" paradigm of Platonic interpretation. I do not claim that Anthony Price thinks as he does merely because he happens to believe Gregory Vlastos; indeed I have already cited a separate argument of Price's for associating *Symposium* with Plato's "middle" period (i.e. that Plato's treatment of human relationships is maturer, more developed and successful—though as I have already indicated, I dispute that claim).[6] And elsewhere[7] Price gives a lengthier explanation of his reasons for thinking that Plato has abandoned the psychology he uses to ground Socrates' eulogy of *erōs* in the *Symposium*. Yet, despite the independence of his case, Price may nevertheless still stand as an example—if a usefully complex one—of that clear majority of scholars who continue to treat *Symposium* as a "middle" dialogue. The difference between Price and others of the same persuasion is that he has recognized the nature of the situation more clearly than they have: namely that, here in the *Symposium*, we find an allegedly "middle" dialogue that nevertheless contains at its core a psychology that (a) belongs to the "Socratic" dialogues (as normally so-called) and (b) is actually, and deliberately (in its pure form), *rejected* in other "middle" dialogues, notably *Republic* and *Phaedrus*.[8] Socratic psychology, on the one hand; Platonic

---

[6] In particular, the claim seems to be based at least for the most part on speculation; Price finds gaps in the account of love given by Diotima and Socrates in the *Symposium*, and proposes a way of plugging them. But, as Penner and I spell out in Penner and Rowe 2005:300–307, Price has offered no compelling reasons why we should accept his diagnosis, let alone his cure.

[7] See Price 1995:8–14 (though I am not sure that these pages add substantially to his case).

[8] Compare and contrast Irwin (1995:303): "The conversation between Socrates and Diotima in the *Symposium* begins with the sexual aspect of *erōs*, as desire for the beautiful (204d). But this description is soon supplemented or replaced by two others: *erōs* as desire for the good and for happiness (204e), and *erōs* as the desire to "give birth in beauty" (206b7). Plato uses *erōs* not in its usual restricted sense, but to refer to the generalized desire for the good from which more specific desires are to be derived (205a–d). In doing this, Plato implies that he can explain a more specific love of persons, and in particular a more specific love of beauty, by appeal to this more general desire"—and Irwin goes on to suggest that "the *Symposium* [thus] eliminates the common conception of *erōs* in favour of the Socratic conception of desire"—which he thinks of as abolishing the distinction between different kinds of *erōs*, and its connection with the common notion of *erōs*. (I think it right to say that Irwin, at least, has a different view of "the Socratic conception of desire" from my own view of it; I shall return to that point in a moment.)

So far so good with Irwin's account, in a way. But he adds in a footnote (chap. 18n12): "If [Plato in the *Symposium*] accepts the division of the soul defended in the [*Republic*] and the [*Phaedrus*], his account of *erōs* in the [*Symposium*] will not apply to spirited and appetitive desires. In the [*Symposium*] he neither endorses nor rejects this division of the soul, since he neither affirms nor denies psychological eudaemonism." Price seems to me to have shown sufficiently clearly that the latter claim is false: the Socrates of the *Symposium* unmistakably shows his allegiance to (what Irwin calls) "psychological eudaemonism"—even if that allegiance, according to Price himself, is only temporary, and adopted for ulterior reasons. Irwin's

Forms on the other. How are we to explain the mix? This is exactly the question Anthony Price raises.[9] However, the answer I shall give will be radically different from Price's.

One immediate, and surely correct, response will be to point out—as Price points out—that there is no clear or necessary connection between Platonic Forms and a Platonic psychology (even though, as we shall see, some have constructed a link between them in at least one context).[10] Roughly speaking, Platonic psychology allows, as its (so-called) Socratic counterpart does not, that we may desire bad things while knowing them to be bad; even more importantly, it allows that our desires for things we know to be bad may actually cause us to act even as we recognize them to be bad, and therefore contrary both to our nature as reasoning beings and to the desire that belongs to us because we are such beings, namely, again, our desire for the good. This diagnosis of human action, and of the human condition, like the Socratic one (whether we call that "rationalist," "intellectualist," or whatever label we may prefer), will be entirely unaffected by the range of entities we, or Plato or Socrates, happen to believe in; that is, whether those entities include Platonic-style Forms or not.[11]

So, let us suppose that the *Symposium* is "Socratic" in psychology, "Platonic" in metaphysics: according to the standard view, the dialogue will still count as "middle," because it is Plato's *metaphysical* turn, according to the same standard view, that is the decisive moment in the dialogues, the one that marks Plato's coming of age as a philosopher—although, paradoxically (still by the standard view in question), it is his subsequent *abandonment* of "middle-period" Forms that brings him to true maturity. I refer here, of course, to that

---

case perhaps depends on the fact that it is mainly Diotima, not Socrates, who advances the Socratic concept of desire. But insofar as Socrates (a) is made to claim that Diotima is his teacher in matters of love (*Symposium* 201d), (b) represents her as endorsing "psychological eudaemonism," i.e. in his report of what she taught him, and (c) ends by asserting that he "is persuaded" of what she said (212b2), then (*pace* e.g. Price—see following note) it is hard to agree that he "neither affirms nor denies psychological eudaemonism."

[9] See Price 1995:9: "... there is no sound inference from the Platonism of the ensuing metaphysics [sc. in Diotima's account] against the Socraticism of the antecedent Socratic psychology [though Price thinks that Plato does have Socrates increasingly distance himself from aspects of what Diotima proposes]. The combination is still unexpected—which may be why it is overlooked. What could explain it?"

[10] There is a category of "transitional" dialogues, according to the Vlastos paradigm; the *Symposium* is not among them.

[11] As a matter of fact it is quite unclear what a Platonic Form is, and what believing in the existence of such things actually entails; fortunately that does not touch the immediate issues (but see further below, on Nicholas White's reading of the intersection of metaphysics and ethics in Plato).

other allegedly pivotal dialogue, the *Parmenides*, in which Plato—allegedly—has the Eleatic philosopher criticize a younger Socrates' version, or versions, of Form-theory, and find them in need at least of serious overhaul.

But now, again, it is in the "middle" dialogues—specifically in the *Republic*—that there apparently occurs the shift from a Socratic to a Platonic psychology. So either we must suppose the *Symposium* to be an early "middle" dialogue, written before Plato changed his mind about the nature of desire; or we must welcome back Price's interpretation, which has the Plato of the *Symposium* taking the Socratic psychology out of cold storage, to give it one last run before permanent retirement, because it provides him—let me here vary Price's description a little—with an account of erotic desire according to which such desire can do no wrong.[12] And what better, or at least simpler, strategy could there be for providing the kind of praise or Eros that Socrates needs to win the competition of *logoi* at the feast?

This, however, seems to me to be rather more than a rhetorical question; for the cost of such a strategy—as indeed Price himself recognizes—will be to have Socrates praising Love on the basis of a theory he no longer believes in or accepts. For his, and his author's, real views we must apparently supplement the *Symposium* with the *Phaedrus*, which contains an account of erotic love based on a *Republic*-type treatment of desire that divides it into rational and irrational—with irrational desires capable of successfully opposing the former, and causing the agent to act against what he or she believes to be best. Of course we have no way of ruling out the possibility that Plato should have adopted such a strategy—one of suppressing his real views—for the *Symposium*, which is by any account the most literary of all the dialogues.

But I for one do wonder a little: exactly what will a eulogy based on what the author takes to be false premises (or at best half-truths) be *worth*, especially when it will, apparently, leave Socrates doing less well—from the point of view of the whole truth—even, in one respect, than Pausanias? Pausanias, after all, according to Anthony Price, recognizes the distinction between good and bad love that Plato accepts and Socrates rejects.[13] Such a reading of the

---

[12] "By retaining a Socratic psychology Plato can combine what Socrates contrasts: Socrates will tell the truth as he sees it, but in Plato's eyes that will be half-truth too approving of love by half. It is striking that Socrates makes no distinction between good and bad love such as was drawn by Pausanias ... and will be recurrent in Plato [Price gives references to *Republic*, *Phaedrus*, *Laws*]. As we shall see, Socrates remains free of moral error in Plato, for his vision of love is blind to those aspects that are not proper objects of eulogy. A Socratic conception of love is an expression of innocence" (Price 1995:9).

[13] See preceding note. (Whether in fact Plato's notions of good and bad love are quite the same as Pausanias' must surely be in doubt; but still the general point holds.)

dialogue seems to me set fair to ruin its whole architecture. The ending of the *Symposium*, if not the ending of the round of speeches with the irruption of Alcibiades,[14] surely marks out Socrates as the winner of the competition: whatever anyone else present may have supposed, Socrates—thanks to Diotima—is (so the implication surely is) better informed than the rest about the nature of *erōs*. It is hard, otherwise, to make sense of the closing scene, with Socrates talking the tragic poet and his comic counterpart under the table.

So should we treat the *Symposium* as a "middle" dialogue, but just as *early-middle*—an alternative I briefly floated before? On this reading, Plato will not yet have given up on the Socratic psychology, even while he has made the crucial move to Platonic Forms. Quite why scholars have not rushed to adopt this solution, apart from their not—perhaps[15]—having seen the size of the problem, is not immediately clear. But I think that it may well be connected with a general view that the Socratic psychology is simply inadequate; that it *obviously* fails to meet the facts of human experience. Such is clearly Price's view:

> If the conception of desire in the *Symposium* remains Socratic, it is also precarious, for it is easier to suppose that desires that are rooted in the body have their own ends that are not identical to the goal of reason. In the *Phaedo*, written at about the same time as the *Symposium*,[16] Plato ascribes desires to the body itself (66d7), and aims them at "the pleasures that are through the body" (65a7). Celebrating the escape of the soul from the body, and not hymning the loves of soul and body, the *Phaedo* takes a less positive view of the body's inclinations. The *Symposium* avoids pointing soul and body in different directions: even if we say (as Socrates in fact does not) that our bodies desire what our "mortal nature" pursues (207d1), this will still be a single end desired as a result both of rational deliberation (cf. 207b6–7), and of a natural teleology that explains both animal behaviour and physiological processes. *Of course the upshot contradicts common sense, and may seem not so much innocent as myopic.*

---

[14] The reception of Socrates' *logos* by the immediate audience is noticeably somewhat lukewarm (general applause/praise [*epainos*, 212c4], as against universal, loud/uproarious applause [*pantas ... anathorubēsai*, 198a1–2] for Agathon's contribution; but then that is hardly surprising, given the strangeness of what Socrates has said, and of his transformation of *erōs*.

[15] So Price suggests (see n9 above ["which may be why it is overlooked"]).

[16] So too Kahn, with respectable stylometric opinion (cf. n3 above), except that this places both in the earliest group of dialogues, along with the so-called "Socratic" ones. Price, of course, is saying rather that the *Phaedo*, like the *Symposium*, is a "middle" dialogue.

> *Socrates owes us a redescription of the phenomena that we commonly take to constitute mental conflict.*[17]

Terry Irwin, and others,[18] understand Socrates rather as treating desire as deriving from the agent's beliefs about the good. Clearly, on this reading, Socrates' view of desire would be one that by the simple rule of charity one might want to see Plato ditching as soon as possible (much as Price wants Plato to have ditched the rather different account of desire *he*, Price, attributes to Socrates); and when better to do the ditching than at the very moment of writing the *Symposium*, when he turns his attention specifically to the subject of *erōs*? Surely, as soon as he began to think about erotic experience in all its variety, he *must* have seen the inadequacy of the Socratic treatment?

This is not, however, a particularly compelling argument, given that the *Lysis*, too, begins and (more or less) ends as a discussion of *erōs*; and no one, at least in the present context, is suggesting that Plato is not serious about his analysis, there in the *Lysis*, of *erōs* in Socratic terms. It is, it seems, just taken as read that "middle" dialogues show us the mature Plato, or at least a matur*er* Plato: a Plato who has already embarked on his ambitious metaphysical program, and must (surely?) have rid himself of that well-meaning, "innocent," but ultimately useless treatment of desire. Here is Price again:

> A more sophisticated view than is evidenced in the *Symposium* would distinguish the goal of appetite (which may just be the pleasure of the moment) from the teleological ground of having appetites: by their brute importunity these may generally serve our survival, and so happiness, better than they would do if they were less insistent; yet our happiness may not be their object, and they may trouble us even when that is not served by their satisfaction.[19]

In my own view this represents a serious underestimation of Socrates' theory of desire. The theory does not require that felt desires like hunger, or thirst, or indeed lust themselves be seen as expressions of the agent's desire for happiness. He or she may feel hungry, thirsty, or lustful, but at the same time be

---

[17] Price 1995:13–14. (I add: but that—"a redescription of the phenomena ..."—is exactly what Socrates is offering us; the redescription is just not in terms of "mental conflict." But then Socrates specifically denies that the phenomena "constitute mental conflict," or at least that model of "mental conflict" that Price represents as an incontrovertible fact of human experience.)

[18] Among whom is John Cooper: see his review of Irwin's *Gorgias* in the Clarendon Plato series: Cooper 1982; also Cooper 1999a.

[19] Price 1995:14n7 (note to the passage last cited in the text above).

mistaken about the truly best (most happy-making) objects for such appetites; in such cases, as in any other in which desire seems to lead us to the wrong (because not happy-making) outcomes, it will make sense to say that the agent "didn't want that"—even if he or she really did feel hungry, thirsty, lustful at the time. The question is about exactly what desire causes, or helps to cause, actions, and the Socratic claim is that this is the universal desire for happiness, or benefit: "if we act in response to thirst or hunger it will be acting in order to be benefited rather than harmed—that is, the desire in question [the desire that causes the action] is not desire for food, say, but desire for the good in this situation which happens to include eating."[20] In short, Socrates need not be interpreted as claiming, in the *Symposium* or anywhere else, that hunger or thirst have happiness as their object; Price's complaint here falls—as, equally, does any objection to Socratic psychology that is based on the notion that Socrates thinks beliefs (our beliefs about the good) determine our desires.[21] What Socrates thinks, and claims, is that the desire that causes our actions is always the desire for our (real) good, and that we only ever go wrong, do the wrong things, because our beliefs about what that good is are not up to scratch.

Once again, the issues are too complex to be discussed in full detail here. But I may perhaps be allowed to offer, as a hypothesis, not only that Plato was for a long time interested in what I may broadly term the Socratic theory of action, but that he had good reason to be interested in it (because it is a respectable theory).[22] Given that hypothesis, then we so far seem to have no reason for supposing that Plato disbelieved in the theory when he wrote the *Symposium* and based the dialogue on it; indeed we have considerably more

---

[20] Penner and Rowe 2005:154, commenting immediately on *Lysis* 220e6–221b3—a passage which, we think, suggests that appetites would exist even if there were no bad things that resulted from them: our appetites too, that is, in principle contribute to our overall drive towards the (real) good, and bad things result only from the misalignment of our beliefs. See in the index under "desire: supposed irrational desires" for references to a succession of passages in Penner and Rowe that progressively illuminate our view of (Socrates' view of) appetites. (Penner, it should be added, is not committed to any further interpretation of or gloss on the ideas originally expressed in Penner and Rowe 2005 that may be offered in the present essay; such interpretations or glosses, if they in any way get the book wrong, will be trumped by what is said in the book—which in any case offers the longer and more worked-out kind of reply to Price that his elegantly stated case deserves.)

[21] I refer here, once more, to the kind of interpretation of Socratic psychology proposed by (e.g.) Irwin and Cooper.

[22] In any case, even if it were a bad theory, that would hardly be a good argument for supposing that Plato abandoned it at any particular point—since he evidently entertained it, or at least wrote as if he took it seriously, for a considerable period, i.e. for at least most of that period in which he wrote so-called "Socratic" dialogues.

reason to suppose that he believed in it, i.e. because otherwise Socrates will be represented as having won the *agōn* of *logoi* about *erōs* on false pretences. One may still wish to allow the possibility that the *Symposium* represents a kind of part-historical document, showing how an "innocent," or alternatively perverse, or merely odd, not to say downright peculiar, Socratic-type defense of *erōs* could outshine more ordinary defenses, even while being built on half-truths. But that seems hardly an attractive option. Once again, the *Symposium* admittedly is more *literary* than other dialogues. However, the expectation must surely be that, in common with—so far as I understand the matter—all the other dialogues that Plato wrote, the *Symposium* will have been written somehow to persuade; if Socrates/Diotima fail to convince his/her immediate audience, nevertheless, so I assume, the purpose must be to persuade us, and it would be odd, if that were the case, that Plato should have had Socrates expound a theory of *erōs* based on other ideas that he, Plato, would have rejected as untrue to reality. The only argument I am able to construct for supposing anything of the sort would be (1) that the *Symposium* is a "middle" dialogue (because it contains Platonic Forms), (2) that the "middle" period sees Plato rejecting the Socratic psychology (i.e. in the *Republic*), and (3) that therefore (?) he must have rejected it, even if he doesn't say so, by the time he was writing the *Symposium*. That is clearly an appalling argument, insofar as not all "middle" dialogues can be expected to have exactly the same spread of features, where these are not connected: if there is no connection between Platonic Forms and a Platonic psychology, then once again the best a supporter of the *Symposium*-as-"middle-period"-dialogue thesis could do would be treat it as a kind of pre-"middle," half and half, "transitional" sort of dialogue.

For myself, I prefer a more radical solution, for I have serious doubts about the importance, for the *whole* Socratic-Platonic project, of Platonic Forms (whatever these may turn out to be). That is: not only is there no necessary connection between the hypothesis of Forms (whatever this hypothesis may amount to) and any particular kind of psychology or theory of action, but most of what Socrates and Plato care about will go through irrespective of whatever metaphysical commitments are involved in believing in (Platonic) Forms. Or, to put it another way, Plato's thinking about Forms is by way of the articulation of certain proposals about which both Socrates and he were convinced in any case, and on which they rely in any case: that there are such things as goodness and justice, things that we can investigate and have some hope of grasping; and so on. If that claim of mine were to turn out to be true, then the introduction of Platonic Forms would not be a crucial moment in the development of Platonic thought, as it has so often, in recent times and in certain parts of the world, been thought to be; or, if it is such a crucial point, it is not exactly a *turning-point*, except perhaps for metaphysicians. And that is really the crux of the matter. It is Aristotle who first fixes on Forms as the, or a, crucial distinguishing mark between Plato and Socrates;[23] and it is Aristotle for whom Forms are a real issue, just because he thinks them so bad a mistake—he wants, and requires, forms of a different sort. But there seems no particular reason why we moderns should follow Aristotle. ("Separation" is the big mistake, Aristotle says; but Socrates obviously did not set out to *deny* separation. He just didn't get that far. Some dialogues contain Forms, some do not; it may be that those that do were written later than those that do not, but that—on the view I am proposing—will have no obvious consequences for our actual *interpretation* of the dialogues. We might be able to say of a dialogue that refers to Platonic Forms that it is, to that extent, Platonic rather than Socratic, but only in virtue of that single feature; and there may well be other features of them of which the same could be said—if only we knew which these were).[24] But by the same token, the fact that the *Symposium* contains, and even proposes, a Socratic psychology also makes it Socratic rather than Platonic. And to the degree that the dialogue is about *erōs*, and about desire, I venture that the dialogue as a whole ought to be treated in the same way—that is, as Socratic rather than Platonic; although at the same time I have no desire to prejudge just how different the Platonic project is from the Socratic, if indeed we can in principle properly distinguish them at all, as opposed to marking off certain specific differences.[25] In terms of the standard ways of talking about the Platonic *oeuvre*, the *Symposium* seems to have closer connections with the so-called "Socratic" dialogues like the *Lysis*, the *Charmides*, or the *Laches* than with those other dialogues with which we have become used to associating it, i.e. the other so-called "middle" dialogues;[26] of which, in fact, two others—*Phaedo* and *Cratylus*—also belong to the earliest stylistic group.[27]

[23] See Aristotle, *Metaphysics* 1078b30–1079b11.

[24] For a longer treatment of the issues here, see Rowe 2005.

[25] Indeed, it is important to stress how close the Platonic psychology actually remains to its Socratic counterpart—something that emerges as soon as one compares Plato with Aristotle, whose position is fundamentally different from Plato's (e.g. and importantly, in that Aristotle thinks of actions done from anger or appetite as voluntary or willing, while Plato—extraordinarily—treats them as involuntary or unwilling, because contrary to the desires of reason).

[26] This is not to deny the obvious fact that the old "middle" dialogues have at least one other thing in common, over against the old "Socratic" ones: sheer scale and size. But even that is not a decisive factor; we should have to decide first what to say about *Euthydemus* and *Gorgias*, both of which are fairly large-scale productions.

[27] Kahn again (n3 above). I advert to this more or less by the way; we need not suppose that stylistic differences go hand in hand with developments in Plato's philosophical thinking.

Why does any of this matter? It matters because a *Symposium* interpreted as a close relation of the *Lysis* will tend to look very different from a *Symposium* interpreted as a close relation of the *Republic*; or so it will, at any rate, given some interpretations of the *Republic*. I refer here especially to treatments of the Form of the Good in the *Republic* as if it were something entirely different from the good that functions as the object of all desire in what I have been labeling as the Socratic theory of desire. As an example of this approach, I cite Nicholas White:

> ... there seems to me to exist no significant room to doubt that the notion that is represented in *Republic* VI and VII as "the Good itself" or the Form of the Good is the notion of non-self-referential good-ness [i.e. a goodness that at least implies thinking that "extends beyond eudaimonism"] that ... figures in the *Timaeus* and the *Laws* ... [T]his is the Form which, Plato believes, is grasped by the philoso-pher-rulers whom he puts in charge of his ideal *polis* ....[28]

This is the kind of case that I referred to, very briefly, early on in the present essay, according to which there would after all turn out to be a real conceptual link between Platonic Forms and the abandonment of the Socratic psychology; for now (at least so far as White's own argument goes) the claim, fundamental to the Socratic outlook, that "all desire is for the good" will simply evoke the question "Which good?" "The non-perspectival good (the Form), or what is good for oneself?" And the two may very well be in conflict. The outcome, White says, is not unlike "the modern [concept] that creates the distinction between self-regarding and broader aims";[29] and this already seems to allow in the very kind of mental conflict whose existence Socrates' schema denies, or, better,[30] explains in different terms. However, of this good, or Good, there is rather little sign in the *Symposium*, which is framed throughout in terms of the "perspectival" good, the good of the agent.[31] More generally, it is tempting to align true "ascent" passages of the *Symposium* with the Cave simile in the *Republic* (if only because this too involves an ascent); and

---

[28] White 2002:199–200.

[29] White 2002:211.

[30] See n17 above.

[31] I further, and more radically, propose that even the *Republic* itself should be seen as building on the outcomes of the *Lysis* and the *Symposium*, rather than overturning them: see my "The Form of the Good and the good in Plato's *Republic*," first offered in very preliminary form to the Leventis Conference held in Edinburgh in 2005, and to be published in the proceedings of that conference (ed. Penner and others).

this comparison may then take one's eye away from that very preoccupation of the *Symposium* with the good of the agent, and lead us to suppose that has a better, or different, story to tell about human relationships than the *Lysis*. In fact, I suggest, it does not: it has essentially the same story to tell. But then, as Penner and Rowe assert (i.e. in their 2005), that is after all not a bad story.

The outcome of my argument, then, is that the *Symposium* is Socratic in the sense that it shows Socrates interpreting *erōs* according to the kind of psychology which Plato allows him develop in the alleged "Socratic" dialogues (especially the *Lysis*)—and to all appearances doing so with *absolute serious-ness*. No philosophical analysis of the *Symposium*'s main argument that fails to acknowledge this—so I claim—has any real future. And such an outcome surely makes it much more difficult to treat the psychology around which its central argument revolves as something that Plato came to despise, as he emerged blinking into the light of maturity (and developed his allegedly defining, showcase, Theory of Forms).

However, my argument also has a crucial consequence for our reading of the *Symposium* as a whole, and in particular for our reading of the accounts of *erōs* given by others present at the party. It is often claimed that the *logos* of a Phaedrus, or a Pausanias, even—especially—that of an Aristophanes, is somehow meant to contribute positively towards the picture Socrates puts together from what Diotima, the fictional priestess, told him; or else some other way is found of giving at least partial validation—from Plato's perspec-tive—to other speakers' treatments of *erōs* in the dialogue. (Why else, the argu-ment tends to go, would Plato have allocated them so much space?) But if it is the case, as I have urged, that Plato wishes to recommend not merely Socrates' treatment of *erōs*, but *the theory that it is built on*—if it is the case, as indeed I propose, that it is the *theory* that Plato cares most about, along with its partic-ular application to the analysis of *erōs*, then that reading of the earlier speeches in the dialogue, as somehow cumulatively building, or building towards, the Socratic perspective, must be wrong. For none of the earlier speakers has the slightest inclination to understand things in the way that Socrates under-stands them. Socrates' perspective is just *different*, and *strange*. What is more, it comes as a package: earlier speakers may say things that sound like things that Socrates says; but they are not the same things, because the speakers lack the perspective, the whole system, to which they belong, and without which they are mere *disiecta membra*. What Plato is doing is to *contrast* the peculiar Socratic view with more ordinary views, not derive it from them—for the fact is that it cannot be derived from them. In order to appreciate fully what Socrates is saying, one has to throw away what one thought one knew, and start again. That itself, it seems to me, is the chief point of the whole dialogue: to celebrate the distance that separates Socrates from his audience, and from the rest of us.[32]

---

[32] The introduction of parts of the soul, in *Republic* IV, then marks the moment when Plato distances himself from the Socratic psychology—even while, as I have suggested, he manages to preserve some central features of it. The *Phaedrus* is, in part, his new account of *erōs*, written from a *Republic* or post-*Republic* viewpoint, and acknowledging the possibility of bad as well as good *erōs* (for which—as Anthony Price and I agree, on different grounds—the theory of the *Symposium* leaves no room). But that is another story (one told, at least in summary form, at Penner and Rowe 2005:307–312.

Two

The Role of the Earlier Speeches in the *Symposium*: Plato's Endoxic Method?

Frisbee C. C. Sheffield[1]

I T IS WELL KNOWN that there are deep and important differences between Plato and Aristotle. One of these concerns the status and role of *endoxa* in philosophical inquiry. Although Aristotle appears to find value in the *endoxa*, that is in "the things which are accepted by everyone, or by most people; or by the wise—either by all of them, or by most, or by the most famous and distinguished" (*Topics* 1.1.100b21–3), the Platonic dialogues appear quite regularly to degrade the opinions of both the majority and the so-called "wise."[2] Such views do not appear to make a constructive and positive contribution to philosophical inquiry. One may begin to question this difference on encountering the *Symposium*, however. First, the symposium as a setting for this work was, what we might call, a prime *endoxic* forum. It was a gathering of the intellectual elite of the day and it is to be expected that they will deliver reputable opinions, backed up by the authority of ancient tradition or current expertise. Agathon's banquet is no exception. As has often been noted, those present are broadly representative of a wide variety of Greek wisdom.[3] Second, Plato pres-

---

[1] I would like to thank all the participants at the *Symposium* conference in Washington for much stimulating feedback on this paper, especially Jim Lesher who provided helpful written comments. The paper has also benefited from discussions with Peter Adamson, Arif Ahmed, Charles Brittain, Ben Morison, Hendrik Lorenz, and Zena Hitz.
[2] On this contrast see, for example, Nussbaum 1986:242–243 who argues that "It is Plato who most explicitly opposes *phainomena*, and the cognitive states concerned with them, to truth and genuine understanding ... Whereas Aristotle finds his truth inside what we say, see and believe, Plato finds his 'far from the beaten path of human beings' (in Plato's words) 'out there'." See also Solmsen 1968:52: "What sets the Platonic dialectician apart from the majority of professionals is that he has resolutely turned his back on opinion; his entire concern is with reality and truth. Yet Aristotle's dialectical syllogisms draw their persuasive force from *endoxa*." Cf. also Owen 1986:155.
[3] See, for example, Bury 1932:lvii and Rowe 1998a:9.

ents us with five accounts on the topic of *erōs* before that of the philosopher, and so invites us to consider just what relationship is supposed to hold between the realm of so-called expert opinion and philosophical insight.[4] And third, as I hope to show, there is, in fact, much continuity between the two. Some account of this needs to be given, and it is the purpose of this paper to explore the nature of this continuity and to determine what philosophical reasons there might be for constructing the dialogue in this way. In so doing I hope to contribute to the controversial issue of how to read the *Symposium*, and what significance is to be assigned to each speech preceding that given by Socrates.

1. The Speeches

The aim of each speaker at Agathon's symposium is to offer an encomium to *erōs* which amounts to showing that it is a good thing and has good effects. The first task will be to outline the central claims of each speaker. This will necessarily be selective since I am concerned here with what relationship, if any, the speeches have to a philosophical account. Before exploring that relationship, though, we shall see that there is a significant degree of interplay between the previous speeches themselves.

We begin with Phaedrus (178a6–180b8), whose central claim is that *erōs* has the most power when it comes to the acquisition of virtue and happiness (178c3–d1; 179a8; 180b6–8). This power is apparently due to the fact that *erōs* can instill a feeling of shame at shameful things and a love of honor in the case of fine ones (178d1). The connection between an erotic relationship, an appreciation of the *kalon*, and a striving for virtue will prove crucial to a proper account of the benefits of *erōs*. For if it is the case that *erōs* can instill a love of the *kalon*, and it is the case that this is necessary for virtue,

---

[4] I am not here going to defend reading Socrates' speech as a piece of philosophical insight in any detail. For the purposes of this paper I note only that Socrates presents his account as one that aims for the truth and, in this respect, contrasts it with those of his peers (198–199). Further, he presents himself as an expert on "erotic matters" (198d1, cf. 177d8). One may object that Socrates also claims that his wisdom is as debatable as a dream (174e4). One way to combine these two claims is to suppose that having knowledge of erotic matters is knowing how *erōs* is best satisfied (by the attainment of knowledge and virtue in the ascent). And claiming that one knows how to become virtuous is clearly not the same as claiming that one has achieved this (i.e. that one has knowledge of the form of beauty). This, I submit, is the kind of knowledge Socrates disclaims when Agathon attempts to "lay hold" of some substantive bit of knowledge from Socrates (175d1), and not the knowledge of "erotic matters" (viz. the proper aims and activity of *erōs*) to which he elsewhere lays claim. Compare Socrates in the *Republic*: he can provide an account of an ascent to the form of the good, but disclaims knowledge of the form of the good. For further discussion of this issue see Sheffield:2006.

then it will have been shown that *erōs* has positive potential. But we have little sense at this point of how a love relationship can instill an appreciation of the *kalon*, and what beautiful things lead to virtue, rather than, say, idle staring or sex. According to Phaedrus such relationships foster a love of honor, and it is the realization of this aim in our erotic pursuits that motivates such action (178d2–d). But it is unclear what this appreciation of the *kalon* involves such that it arouses this aim, and why it is that *erōs* aims at honor, rather than at sex or wisdom, for example. We need to know just what sort of *erōs* can lead to this end in particular, and why it does so.

Pausanias' speech (180c3–185c3) builds on Phaedrus' idea that *erōs* can lead to the acquisition of virtue (cf. 185b1–c1), but argues that not all *erōs* issues in the benefits Phaedrus claimed (180c4–5). Beneficial *erōs* privileges the soul over the body (183e1). Attraction to a beautiful soul will be concerned to encourage the development of the soul and its characteristic virtues (184c3–4). Pausanias suggests that cultivating wisdom is intimately related to virtue (184d1–2) and that the best relationship occurs "when the lover is able to help the man become wiser and better, and the young man is eager to be improved by his lover" (184e). If virtue is intimately connected to wisdom (a relationship that remains to be clarified), then one can begin to grasp why *erōs* must be focused on the areas responsible for its realization: the soul. What stands in need of clarification is the nature of this wisdom and how it is best cultivated. Why Pausanias advocates a slavish model whereby a beloved should submit himself to instruction in exchange for his charms is not at all clear (184c3).

Eryximachus agrees with Phaedrus and Pausanias that the aim of *erōs* is virtue (188d5–9), and with Pausanias' distinction between *erōs* for the body and that for the soul (186a1–2). He adds that the correct lover must have an expertise. An expert lover is one with moderation and justice who embodies harmony and enables us to associate both with each other and with the gods (188d8–9). The medical art (186c5–6), music, prophecy, and astronomy (187c2–3) are cited as examples of such expertise. The connection between the harmonious order promoted by these *technai* and the development of these virtues is not so clear, however (188d5); nor are his reasons for emphasizing these *technai* in particular. We need more details about this knowledge of "*ta erōtika*" (188d2).

Aristophanes' speech "fills in," as he puts it, an important gap in the accounts thus far. In order to appreciate why *erōs* has such "healing" and beneficial effects for human beings we need an account of human nature and its needs; for *erōs* is a "doctor to our ills" (189d1). Human beings are apparently incomplete and needy creatures who strive towards a state of self-realization and happiness. If there is to be an erotic expertise, it must involve the ability to discern what these deficiencies are—what it is that we are lacking—and how they should best be remedied by finding the appropriate partner. For Aristophanes this resides in the *oikeion*, what is akin to ourselves, and it is to be found in another person. Union with the right other half will bring us *eudaimonia* (193d5). Why *eudaimonia* resides in the *oikeion* as such is unclear.

Agathon also sees an important omission thus far. The previous speakers have discussed the benefits to human beings for which *erōs* is responsible, but they have failed to explain the sort of nature responsible for those benefits (194e5–8). *Eros* is in every way supremely beautiful and virtuous (196b5); he mentions justice (195b–c), moderation (196c5), courage (d1) and wisdom (d5). Agathon "takes his turn in honoring his own expertise as Eryximachus honored his" (196e1–2) and picks out wisdom in particular, which he identifies with poetic expertise. Because *Eros* is so beautiful himself he pursues beauty and induces others to good and beautiful things, such as wisdom and virtue (196e5–6)—particularly to poetry, or some other creative endeavor (196e1–2). According to this account, then, it is the intimate relationship between *erōs* and beauty that leads to the productive effects the speakers praised. Although this will prove to be a promising idea, we have little sense at this stage why *erōs* for beauty issues in the *production* of good things, rather than in their *possession*. Further, since lovers are here characterized as already in possession of almost all the good things one can imagine, it is not clear why they should engage in such erotic-cum-creative endeavor at all. This aspect of the account is certainly inconsistent with the needy nature of desiring agents described by Aristophanes. Are we to suppose that we desire the beauty we already possess? Or (with Aristophanes) the things we lack?

Taken together these ethical reflections upon the role of *erōs* in the good life present some plausible ideas, as we shall see from their use in Socrates' account, albeit ones that are incomplete, or that require further clarification for those who would like to have a clear and consistent account.[5] Although each speaker criticizes his predecessor in some way, they also incorporate elements of their speeches and supplement certain features of their accounts. This is explicit at numerous points.[6] This manner of supplementing and building on

---

[5] And this will not, of course, be everyone. There are many merits to the speeches and other criteria they can be measured by which may not involve clarity and consistency (e.g. literary finesse, humor etc.). I am concerned here with what relationship, if any, they have to a *philosophical* account of *erōs* and that will be one in which clarity and consistency are important criteria.

[6] Eryximachus claimed that Pausanias failed to bring his speech to a close (186a), and is concerned that he, too, may "have left out many things in my praise of *erōs*, but that was certainly

one's predecessors lends itself to reading the speeches as one "intertextual web," a characteristic feature of sympotic discourse.[7] The accounts of each are incomplete, but taken together they can be see as parts of an overall picture of the role of *erōs* in the good life. Phaedrus explains that the aim of *eros* is virtue. Pausanias adds that it is *erōs* for the soul that can achieve the virtue he praised, since this is associated with some kind of wisdom, in particular. Eryximachus adds that the correct application of such *erōs* must be governed by knowledge. Aristophanes "fills in" with an account of human nature and its deficiencies which attempts to explain why *erōs* has such beneficial effects. And Agathon attempts to explain these beneficial effects as creative expressions that result from an encounter with the *kalon*, towards which *erōs* is essentially related.[8]

In addition to their incompleteness, there are many puzzles and inconsistencies for those who would like to have a clear and consistent account of *erōs*. Phaedrus presents the idea that *erōs* can lead to the acquisition of virtue by instilling a sense of shame and a striving towards the *kalon*. But he leaves us wondering just what the connection is between an erotic relationship, an appreciation of the *kalon* and a striving for virtue. Pausanias agrees that *erōs* can lead to virtue, but goes on to argue that it is only *erōs* which privileges the soul over the body and, as a consequence, is concerned to encourage the devel-

---

not my intention. If I have left anything out, it is up to you Aristophanes to fill in the gaps" (188e). After Aristophanes, there is a concern that Agathon and Socrates might be at a loss for things to say because of "the many and various things that have already been said" (193e5–7). But Agathon rises to the challenge and hopes to deliver a complete and unbeatable performance: "let me leave nothing out," he says at the start (196d5).

[7] See Stehle 1997:222, from whom I take the phrase. Commenting on sympotic discourse more generally, Stehle argues that: "All of the forms that this might take, the singing in turn, the new turn on the known song, are designed to keep the discourse collective, while at the same time highlighting each person's contribution. The participants must constantly respond to one another, but the full forms ... require the work of more than one contributor. One could say that ideally the symposium should create one intertextual web." As Rowe 1998a:8 argues, the responsiveness in this case takes the form of competitiveness, a prominent feature of encomia in the fifth and fourth centuries (on which see Nightingale 1995:117).

[8] Compare Rowe 1998a:8 who argues that: "The capping effect of the first five speeches means that they already, in a sense, represent a single whole, culminating first in the speech of Agathon ... and then in Socrates' contribution ... But we should be wary of supposing that there is, or is meant to be, any sense of a gradually developing picture of *erōs* ... with each speaker fitting new and better pieces to the jigsaw. Socrates, after all, prefaces his account with a general criticism of the others, and proceeds immediately to reduce Agathon's speech—which everyone else thought brilliant—to rubble. It is in any case hard to construct a joint account that might emerge from the sequence from Phaedrus to Agathon. All five are essentially individual contributions, with each attempting to go one better than the one before in an apparently haphazard way." The view being developed here implies that the relationship is not quite so haphazard.

opment of the soul and its characteristic virtues—particularly wisdom—that can lead to that end. But we are left wondering about the relationship between wisdom and virtue, and how a love relationship is supposed to foster that end. Eryximachus argues that the correct application of *erōs* must be governed by knowledge. But it is not clear what knowledge of *ta erotika* consists in, nor why it is associated with the particular *technai* he cites. Aristophanes' account of human nature and its deficiencies leaves us wondering why we should desire the *oikeion,* and whether there is anything particularly beneficial about being welded together with another person. And Agathon invites us to consider why *erōs* for the *kalon* is *productive* of good things, and whether (and, if so, why) it is a state of plenitude that motivates this beneficial and productive *erōs*. If lovers are already in a state of plenitude it is not clear why they should engage in such erotic endeavors at all.

Significant issues and questions relating to the role of *erōs* in the good life emerge from reflection upon this "web," which highlights where the agreements and the disagreements are on the subject of *erōs*.[9] The previous speeches seem to agree that *erōs* aims at *eudaimonia* (180b7, 188d8, 193d5, 194e6, 195a5) and that this has something to do with pursuing beauty (178d1–2, 196e4–5), and virtue (179d1–2, 184d7, 185b5, 188d4–9, 196d4–e6). The disagreements lie in their accounts of the nature of this virtue and happiness. In one account virtue is heroism on the battlefield, and related to, or identified with, honor (Phaedrus). In another, wisdom is somehow central to virtue (Pausanias). For Eryximachus, the virtues are those of the doctor or seer who can promote a harmonious order (188d). Aristophanic *erōs* aims at the *oikeion*, though he also highlights the virtues of the politician that result from that pursuit (192a7–8), and Agathon identifies virtue with poetic skill (196d5, e1). At numerous points it is suggested that *erōs*' beneficial effects are related to wisdom (182b7–c2, 184d1, 187c4–5, 184e1, 196d5–6), but this is variously construed as medical expertise and poetic skill (186c5, 196e1–2). The accounts leave it unclear why *erōs* should manifest itself in virtue and just what such virtue is supposed to be. Further disagreements are also to be found in the accounts of the aims thought to constitute *eudaimonia* (honor, the *oikeion* [poetic/medical] wisdom)? The "intertextual web" created by the speakers raises some of the difficulties and problems in need of resolution by the next speaker, in a way that is suggestive of a significant philosophical role. What needs to be clarified is whether, and how, these issues are, in fact, resolved in a philosophical account.

---

[9] This is not to make the further claim that the speakers themselves should be understood to be suggesting these specific issues and questions.

2. Socrates' Critique

Although Socrates criticizes and responds to his predecessors, he does so in such a way that some have wondered whether his account fits into their intertextual web at all. For he claims that all the speakers (note the "you" plural):

> attribute the greatest and most beautiful characteristics possible to the thing in question, whether they are true of it or not, and if they are false, well, that is of no importance. It seems that what was proposed was that each of us should appear to be offering an encomium to Eros, not that we should actually offer him one. It is for that reason, I imagine, that you rake up everything you can think of saying and attribute it to *erōs*.
>
> *Symposium* 198d7–e6, trans. Rowe

Since Socrates says that he will speak differently from his predecessors (199b2–5), in a way that privileges the truth, we may be tempted to see a sharp break in the text between the "rhetorical and poetical [and] the dialectical" (Jowett; cf. Bury1932, Dover 1980, and Rowe 1998a). If there is such a break, then does this imply that, from a philosophical perspective, the previous accounts are "fanciful performances," with little to offer to our understanding of *erōs*? Since such a break might make it difficult to entertain the possibility that Socrates' speech is continuous with those of his peers, I need to examine this critique with care.

Socrates' central claim is that the speakers have not made the truth their priority (198e1–6). He does not say that the accounts are actually false, just that the question of their truth or falsity seems to be of no importance to the speakers. This leaves room for the possibility that they may have hit upon the truth, but if they did, it would have been a happy accident since they did not aim for this goal (198e2). But Socrates does imply that the speakers have no knowledge. They have been more concerned to appear to be offering an encomium to *erōs* than with actually offering one (e4). The speakers seem more concerned with "the probable," rather than "the necessary," as Socrates puts it later (200a9; cf. 201a8). This concern with appearances rather than truth motivates the attribution of all sorts of characteristics to *erōs*, without any clarity about whether and, if so, how these characteristics actually do apply to *erōs*.

There are some substantive views about knowledge and method behind this assessment. Socrates begins to clarify these when he turns to Agathon's account next. He approves (199c) Agathon's methodological rules (195a) and the distinction it implies (201e): one should first display the character *erōs* has and then explain what it does. Socrates' approach shows that he believes that questions concerning the nature of the subject are prior to questions about its effects. As he makes more explicit elsewhere, it is only when one has correctly identified the nature of one's subject matter that one can go on to make inferences about the kind of benefits that such a character can bestow and how it can bestow them.[10] Since the other speakers have not identified *erōs'* nature, they cannot know what it is about such a nature that leads to the virtue they praise as its proper outcome.[11] That is, perhaps, why we are offered such diverse views about the nature of *erōs* and its relationship to virtue. The speakers have not begun by identifying the nature of *erōs* first and so they have no firm basis on which to infer anything about its beneficial effects. When Phaedrus attempts to settle a dispute about the status of the lover and beloved he merely cites the conflicting accounts of Aeschylus and Homer (180–181; cf. 178b, 178c for further reliance on tradition and agreement). As Socrates makes plain elsewhere, the poets could be used in support of almost anything since there is no way of determining what they mean (*Protagoras* 347e). In order to have knowledge about *erōs* one must be able to identify the nature of the thing under discussion and go on to make inferences about this nature and effects on that basis.

So, to imply that Agathon and others do not have knowledge of *erōs* is to imply that they cannot provide a clear and consistent account about *erōs* because they do not have a viable definition of *erōs* on which to ground their views about its proper functioning, and from which to infer its benefits. But this is not to say (or imply) that they have no plausible beliefs about *erōs*. The previous speakers may believe many fine things about *erōs* (and some false ones), but they will not know either that these opinions are true, or why. To know why these things are true of *erōs*, one must have a definition of *erōs* which these statements involve. And to acquire this one must adopt a method designed to lead to that end. Nothing so far, then, rules out the possibility of continuity between a philosophical account and those with no concern for the truth. The previous speakers may be like "untrained soldiers in a battle, who rush about and often strike good blows, but without science."[12]

---

[10] This manner of investigating a subject is familiar Socratic procedure; see, for example, *Meno* 71a5–b7, *Republic* 354c1–3.

[11] We can imagine Socrates saying (as he does more explicitly elsewhere): "When I do not know what *erōs* is, I shall hardly know whether or not it happens to lead to benefits, or whether or not the one having it is happy" (cf. e.g. *Laches* 190b7–c2).

[12] Aristotle *Metaphysics* 1.4.985a.

3. Continuity and Resolution?

How, then, if at all, are the speeches used in the philosophical account? I want to begin by laying out some interpretative options to navigate us through the continuity I will outline shortly. Now it could be the case that any continuity between the speeches serves a rhetorical purpose in the dialogue. There could be artistic reasons that motivate the remarkably inclusive finale of the philosopher. Although I am concerned here with whether they play any significant philosophical role, any continuity between the speeches in itself need not be indicative of that. So let us entertain the possibility of a purely rhetorical view, option (1). It could also be the case that there are deeper epistemological convictions underlying any such continuity. Plato could be indicating in the construction of this dialogue that philosophical understanding emerges ultimately through a process of working through the *endoxa*. Let us call this the endoxic view, option (2). If the latter, then this could be taken in a weak or a strong sense. It could be the case that the speeches raise the right sorts of ideas and issues to be resolved for a proper explanatory account, and so they need to be attended to and worked through as part of philosophical progress. The speeches on this view could include useful falsehoods, that is views that are not true, but whose underlying puzzles prompt the inquiry in a relevant direction. But the salient point is that they are relevant and significant for a philosophical inquiry. Let us call this the weak dialectical reading (2 [a]). Rather more substantially, it may be the case that the speeches not only contain "nuggets of truth," but as such they play a role in grounding the course and nature of the inquiry. Let us call this the strong dialectical reading (2 [b]). Consider, for example, the following from Aristotle on his procedure in ethics as a possible parallel for this category:

> We must, as in all other cases, set the phenomena (*phainomena*) before us and, after first discussing the difficulties, go on to prove, if possible, the truth of all the reputable opinions about these affections or, failing this, of the greatest number and the most authoritative. For if we both resolve the difficulties and leave the reputable opinions (*endoxa*) undisturbed, we shall have proved the case sufficiently.
>
> *Nicomachean Ethics* 7.1.1145b2–7, trans. Ross

And compare

> About all these matters we must try to get conviction by arguments, using the phenomena as evidence and illustration. It would be

best that all men should clearly concur with what we are going to say, but if that is unattainable, then that all should in some way at least concur. And this if converted they will do, for every man has some contribution to make to the truth, and with this as a starting-point we must give some sort of proof about these matters. For by advancing from true but obscure judgements he will arrive at clear ones, always exchanging the usual confused statement for more real knowledge.

Eudemian Ethics 1.1.1216b26–35, trans. Solomon

There is some dispute about whether Aristotle's procedure is endoxic in a weak or strong sense and, if so, in just what works. The details of this dispute will not concern me here.[13] The above passages from the ethical treatises certainly suggest a rather strong view. Reputable views or appearances ground the course of the inquiry: "*with this as a starting-point* we must give some sort of proof about these matters," and "if we both resolve the difficulties and leave the reputable opinions (*endoxa*) undisturbed, *we shall have proved the case sufficiently*." At any rate, we can use this to demarcate a third position, which gives the most substantive role to *endoxa*. On such a view, one aims to create as little disturbance for the *endoxa* as possible. Such views are seen to carry a certain evidential status, and it is as such that they are employed in a philosophical account.[14] In the following I will offer a brief and rather dogmatic sketch of Socrates' speech with an eye on how the things said previously are employed in that account.

Socrates begins by subjecting Agathon to an elenchus (199c3), designed to scrutinize Agathon's proposed characterization of *erōs* as a beautiful god. Although this elenchus ends with Agathon's frank admission that he did not know any of the things which he said then, as he puts it (201b10), this should not be thought to introduce a sharp break between Socrates and his peers. For it is by clarifying certain views from Agathon's account—in particular, the precise nature of *erōs'* relationship to beauty—that Socrates locates an issue of crucial importance for the development of his own account, and aids the formulation of a viable definition of *erōs*.[15] Agathon had claimed that

---

[13] On this issue see Irwin:1988 and the references in n1.

[14] For the epistemological basis behind such a procedure, see Bolton:1990.

[15] Agathon's speech may have been selected for such attention because his speech, at least, attempts to clarify the nature of the subject before making inferences about its beneficial effects. If one must begin an investigation with an identification of the subject matter, then examining Agathon's speech will be the best place to start. Agathon's speech is, in this respect, an improvement (199c). One might compare here the similar difference between Lysias' speech

erōs' nature is beautiful and that *erōs* desires beauty (197b). On reflection, he is shown to believe that *erōs* lacks what it desires (200e1–5). These opinions are inconsistent. For if *erōs* desires beauty, and lacks what it desires, then *erōs* cannot possess beauty. Either *erōs* does not, in fact, desire beauty, or *erōs* lacks the beauty it desires. Both Agathon and Socrates preserve the view that *erōs* desires beauty, which leads to the preliminary conclusion that *erōs'* nature is such that it lacks the beauty it desires (202d1–3). Agathon did not propose a viable account of *erōs'* nature (as a beautiful god) on which to base his account of its beneficial effects. But this is not to say that Agathon's speech is nonsense. Socrates goes on to show that Agathon is right that *erōs* has some relationship both to beauty and to divinity; he is muddled about the precise nature of those relationships. This is a muddle to which Socrates himself, apparently, was subject, before he met the mysterious Diotima (201e3–7). Indeed, Socrates presents his own account as a repeat performance of this meeting because he used to say things similar to those said by Agathon. He goes on to show how his own account developed *on the basis of things agreed* between himself and Agathon, and, on that previous occasion, Diotima and the young Socrates (201d5).

Let us examine the details of this apparent continuity between Socrates' account and Agathon's. Socrates starts from the claim agreed to by Agathon that *erōs* lacks what it desires. He explains how his initial reaction to this was to assume that whatever is not good and beautiful must be the opposite (201e8–9, 202b1–2). On reflection, he came to realize (perhaps through similar elenctic scrutiny with Diotima) that there is a realm of intermediates between the opposites good and bad, beautiful and ugly (202a1–e1) and wisdom and ignorance (202a5–9). But he now has difficulty with the belief that Eros is a great god and that the gods possess all good things, such as wisdom (as Agathon and Phaedrus had held), and at the same time that Eros has an intermediate status in relation to these things. These opinions are inconsistent. Diotima/Socrates points out to Socrates/Agathon that he himself does not believe that Eros is a god (202c1–4) by which must be meant, as the following goes on to make plain, that this belief is at odds with other views he has agreed upon. Socrates comes to realize that, given that he has agreed that Eros lacks what he desires (202d1–3 which repeats Agathon's agreement at 201a–b), and that the gods possess good things (202c6–8), Eros cannot be a god (202d5), but a great spirit in between the two realms (202d13–e1). Herewith a definition of *erōs*. Now,

---

and Socrates' first speech in the *Phaedrus*: although Socrates' first speech is misguided, it is nonetheless methodologically sounder than that of Lysias.

after Socrates has answered both the *ti esti* and the *poios tis* questions central to a philosophical account, there is a clear back reference to Agathon's mistaken characterization of *erōs* as perfect and beautiful. In answer to the first we have the claim that Eros is an intermediate *daemon* (202e1); in answer to the second, that he is in between the needy and the resourceful (203b–204b). Agathon had, in fact, confused the lover with the beloved (204c which picks up on Agathon's encomium at 197b; cf. 180b3 where Phaedrus made a similar mistake). Since (as Stokes and Rowe have noted) the engagement with Agathon's speech (albeit in the guise of what Diotima said to Socrates) does not end until 204b–c when we are well into the positive section of Socrates' account, we can see a degree of continuity between Socrates' account and that of one of his peers, at least.[16] Socrates preserves a grain of truth in Agathon's account: *erōs* does have some relationship both to beauty and to divinity, but these views required critical modification. There was some confusion about the nature of this relationship which led Agathon to believe that *erōs* was in possession of the things he strives towards. Clarifying the precise nature of *erōs'* relationship to beauty and divinity led to Socrates retaining some ideas and rejecting others as inconsistent with them, as we have seen. For example, he retains the idea that *erōs* desires beauty, and rejects the ideas that Eros is himself beautiful, and a god, both of which are inconsistent with the first—preserved—opinion. But although he rejects these specific notions, it seems reasonable to take it that Socrates spends so much time with Agathon's account because he also got things partially right: *erōs* does have some relationship to beauty and to divinity. It is for this reason that the speech can be used to clarify the precise nature of those relationships and lead well into the positive section of Socrates' account.

Only when a viable definition of *erōs* is reached does Socrates proceed to build up his account and move on to the aims and activity of *erōs*. Socrates considers what follows from this proposed definition: If *erōs'* nature is intermediate, then what use is *erōs* for human beings (204c6–7)? What does *erōs* aim to achieve in this deficient, yet resourceful, state (204d1–206a12)? Now, the needy nature of *erōs* was a central feature of Aristophanes' account. Because *erōs* had a needy nature Aristophanes inferred that *erōs* was after the pursuit of the whole: the *oikeion*. Although Socrates does not engage Aristophanes in an elenchus, he explicitly refers to this view and uses it to argue towards a clarification of the aim of *erōs* (205d10–206a1). The claim that *erōs* desires the *oikeion* is rejected when a further premise is introduced: that we are happy to relinquish diseased limbs (e3–5). If we are happy to relinquish diseased

---

[16] See, for example, Stokes 1986:130, 146 and Rowe 1998a:173.

limbs, it cannot be the *oikeion* as such that attracts. If we want only to possess *healthy* limbs (implicit), then there must be a connection between our desires and our good. Unless the *oikeion* and the *agathon* are the same, we will not aim to replenish a lack of the *oikeion* as such, but the good (206a1). For it is by the possession of good things that we are made happy, and we all want *that* (205a1–7). Aristophanes had given the wrong account of what it is that we are lacking, but since it is true that *erōs* desires what it lacks, and Socrates provides additional arguments for this claim, this seems to be a useful falsehood. Constructive dialectical work is being undertaken here, too, and notice that in this instance, we can see a view being modified on the basis of a further—and perhaps more basic—view also held by the speaker in question: that *erōs* has a connection to *eudaimonia* (193d5, cf. 180b7, 188d8, 194e6, 195a5 for the same view in the other accounts).

Socrates moves on from the aim of *erōs* to its activity. Phaedrus and Agathon had claimed that good things (e.g. the virtues) arise from the love of beautiful things (178d1–2, 196e4–5), but their accounts left the relationship between *erōs'* characteristic pursuit of beauty and this goal unclear. Socrates considers this next in the account. The desire for good things manifests itself in the pursuit of beauty (206b1), because it is in the pursuit of beauty that we can be productive of the good and beautiful things we value (206c1–2), as Agathon had held (197b8–9; cf. Phaedrus at 178d1–4). There is a nugget of truth here. And we now have an answer to why the pursuit of beauty is typically creative. Desiring agents are not in the abundant state Agathon envisaged; we are, in fact, needy creatures subject to flux and change who require productive work to attain anything at all. Unlike the divine, human beings cannot possess things in any straightforward way (207d5–208b5). Production is the mortal approximation to a state of divine possession (208b5). So *erōs* manifests itself in creativity as the distinctively mortal way in which we can possess good things. Agathon was right that creative activity is central to *erōs*, but wrong that this issues from a state of divine abundance.

Socrates then considers the kinds of creative activity that are, in fact, productive of the happiness that we desire. We pursue beauty because beauty arouses us to realize ourselves in certain ways and to make manifest whatever good we take to be central to our happiness (206c1–207a5). Phaedrus was right that some desiring agents, but not all, manifest this productive tendency in a love of honor (178c5; cf. 197a3–6 with 208c5–e3). These are the lovers of the lesser mysteries among whom are mentioned Admetus and Achilles and Patroclus (208d3), examples taken from Phaedrus' speech (179b5–7, e1–5). If the desired good end is honor (208c3), then desiring agents will pursue beautiful cities and souls in which they can realize themselves as honorable law-makers, poets, educators and craftsmen (209a1-e4), all activities cited in the previous accounts as expressions of *erōs* (182a7, 186d5, 197a-b).

The love of honor *is* a manifestation of *erōs* (Phaedrus was right about *that*), but it is not the only (or the best) one. Both the having of children and the procurement of a name for oneself by poetic production are unstable goods (*eidola*, 212a1-6) that will not satisfy the desire for the sort of good around which one's happiness can revolve. For the desire for *eudaimonia* is a desire for a stable and enduring good (206a12). But such productive activities depend on whether or not one's children turn out well, or one's books are well received; for only so can one secure honor for oneself. Virtue is, in fact, the real end of the desire for good things and happiness, this is not dependent on cults or shrines set up in one's honor (cf. 209d6-e4), but is a good of one's own soul, not dependent on any further event for its acquisition. The goods of the soul are desired for their own sake and not for the sake of a further end, just as the beautiful object that occasions such a good is chosen for its own sake (210e5-6). Again in this case Socrates preserves the view expressed by many speakers that *eudaimonia* is an end of *erōs* (180b7, 188d8, 193d5, 194e6, 195a5, 205a1), and virtue its proper outcome (179d1-2, 184d7, 185b5, 188d4-9, 196d4-e6). It is his account of the nature of these things that differs, and which grounds his arguments against the claim that honor is the privileged value.

According to Socrates to be able to produce genuine virtue is to know and love the cause of all beauty: true virtue is, in fact, knowledge of beauty (212a1-6). Pausanias had already suggested that there was a connection between virtue and wisdom (184d7-e1), and he was evidently right about *that*, though the slavish nature of his educational model suggested a misguided conception of this wisdom and virtue. If wisdom is required for virtue, then we need a method to achieve this end (viz. the ascent to the form), an expertise (*technē*) of the sort mentioned by Eryximachus as required for the proper expression of *erōs*. Pausanias' claim that *erōs* can only achieve virtue if it is focused on the soul and not the body (210c1-2) is also employed by Socrates. But the account of that *erōs* will, again, be different. The love of soul is important because it encourages one to turn to other bearers of beauty—those things that are responsible for the creation of beautiful souls—and so to continue searching into the nature of beauty (210c5-6). For if one is interested in the beauty of soul one will be interested in the kinds of things that are responsible for the creation of beautiful souls: laws, practices and knowledge. This expansive encounter with different kinds of beauty encourages reflection upon the nature of beauty in a wide variety of cases. And if one is to produce something beautiful oneself (*kaloi logoi* about virtue, or true virtue itself), then one must understand the cause of all beauty in the world: the form of beauty.

So, if a relationship is to lead to the virtue previously praised, it must be one that leads to the form. In the contemplation of the form of beauty a desiring agent will no longer see an individual as the ultimate source of value—so that he is ready "to stop eating and drinking and just gaze at them and be with them" (211d5–e1), like Aristophanes' copulating lovers. But, as Aristophanes suggested, he will at last find a *paidika* in accordance with his *nous* (cf. 193c7–8): the form. This union issues in the creativity praised by Agathon (196d7–e2 with 212a4), and this time not for the sake of fame, as Phaedrus and Agathon claimed (197a3–6), but for its own sake. If what we want is a good whose possession delivers *eudaimonia* (205a1–3 with 180b7, 188d8, 193d5, 194e6, 195a5, 205a1), this is found, above all, in the life of contemplation—of the beautiful (211d1–3 with 212a1–5). This is the best human life (211d1–3), and a god-like life, which issues in friendship between gods and men, as Eryximachus had rightly claimed (188c1–d1 with 212a6).

This brief survey of Socrates' speech should suffice to show that there is a great deal of continuity between the philosophical account and the previous speeches. We have seen many cases where things said by the previous speakers are taken up as they stand. Consider, for example, the following claims: that *erōs* desires what it lacks (191a5–6); that *erōs* is of beauty (197b8); that *erōs* for the soul is more valuable than *erōs* for the body (184a1); that good things arise from the love of beautiful things (197b8–9); that *erōs* aims at virtue (178c5–6, 179a8, 180b7–8, 188d5–6, 178c5–6, 179a8, d1–2, 180b7–8, 184d7, 185b5, 188d4–9, 196d4–e6), the good (188d5) and happiness (180b7, 188d8, 193d5, 194e6, 195a5); that *erōs* must be governed by knowledge (188d1–2; cf. 184d1–e1); that it has some intimate relationship to *phronēsis* (182b7–c2, 184d1) *epistēmē* (187c4–5) *sophia* (196d5–6), and that *erōs* brings together the human and the divine (188d8–9). The inclusion of such views in an account that professes to "speak the truth" suggests that these are indeed "nuggets of truth."

As we have seen, the speakers have differing conceptions of what constitutes *eudaimonia*, or wisdom, for example. It is partly because of such differing, and often inconsistent, accounts of virtue, or *erōs*' relationship to beauty and wisdom, that many things said previously appear in a substantially modified form. For example, Phaedrus was right that *erōs* aims at virtue, though wrong that the pursuit of honor is the only, or best, way to achieve it. Pausanias was right that there is an intimate relationship between wisdom and virtue, though wrong about the slavish transmission of wisdom and virtue. Eryximachus, though right that expertise is essential to the proper activity of *erōs*, mistakenly identified this with the medical art, and music, prophecy and astronomy. Aristophanes was right that *erōs* pursues what it lacks, but wrong that this is the *oikeion*. And Agathon was right that *erōs* has an intimate relationship to beauty, though wrong about the details of this relationship.

Although it seems to be the case that much said previously is employed in some shape or form, one can also find cases where a specific view is disregarded, and cases where there is no attempt to preserve a grain of truth in the view in question. For example, Eryximachus' claim that the medical art best characterizes erotic expertise is neither employed nor refuted, but it is in tension with Socrates' argument that philosophy is the best expression of *erōs*; it is philosophy that establishes the relationship between the human and the divine that Eryximachus praised (212a1–6 with 188d8–9). But rather more charitably perhaps, such a case could be seen as one which is modified (wrong identification of expertise), though preserved (expertise of a certain kind is central). Such nuances of classification will depend ultimately on how charitable one wants to be. But the above should be sufficient to show that many of the speakers' most central views are either subjected to critical re-figuration on the basis of further arguments, or otherwise employed in some shape or form. There is no sharp separation between the things said by the previous speakers—what they say about *erōs* in a muddled or incomplete form—and Socrates' account. Furthermore, many of the puzzles and inconsistencies are clarified by Socrates' account and put on a more plausible rational foundation.

One might raise the following objection, however. Since the speakers have such different conceptions of what is *kalon*, or the nature of virtue and wisdom, for example, to what extent can one claim that it is the same *belief* employed in the philosophical account? If one cannot establish this claim then, does that not undermine the further claim that there is continuity between the accounts?[17] One might say that it is the same belief employed by philosophers and non-philosophers (e.g. the *erōs* has a relationship to wisdom and virtue), but the accounts also exhibit different related beliefs (e.g. about what constitutes wisdom and virtue). Or, one might say that the speakers hold different original beliefs because of their different related beliefs (e.g. about what constitutes wisdom). On this latter view the related beliefs make the original beliefs mean something so different that it no longer makes sense to consider the original beliefs to be the same beliefs at all. There are clearly important issues underlying such an objection. There is some evidence to suggest that Plato considered the important thing to be what the speakers

---

[17] I thank Christopher Rowe for this objection.

are referring to by the words they use and not what is in the heads of individual speakers, or even what is determined by the meaning of their words
(e.g. from the *Cratylus*). If so, then we can indeed consider the speakers to be
referring, albeit dimly, to the same thing, though they hold widely divergent
views about it. And insofar as they are still beliefs about the same thing, then
there is continuity between the accounts in this work.[18]

There is a further point of clarification required at this stage. Any continuity between Socrates and his peers is dramatically signposted as fictional.
Socrates (rather uncharacteristically) is presented as an expert on erotic
matters, who visited Diotima *before* this symposium. If so, then this undermines the potential philosophical significance of any apparent continuity
outright. Let me make it clear that I am concerned here with *Plato's* composition of the dialogue and why he constructs such continuity between the
accounts. Socrates' visit to Diotima, and his apparent expertise on erotic
matters, does nothing to undermine that fact, though it may be relevant to an
interpretation of how such continuity is to be explained, as we shall see.[19]

4. Endoxic Method?

I hope to have shown so far that the previous speeches provide more than just
a survey of current views on the topic of *erōs*. Their ample use in Socrates'
speech—one that aims for the truth—indicates that they raise the right sorts
of issues and puzzles that an explanatory account needs to address. So much
continuity and resolution, in fact, emerges with the philosophical account that
it is very tempting to compare this account with Aristotle. And note that, as
many have argued, the speeches are reflective of broad intellectual undercur-
rents operative in Plato's contemporary culture. In other Platonic dialogues
some of those present are linked to famous wise men. Phaedrus is linked to
Hippias in the *Protagoras* (315c) and to Lysias in the *Phaedrus* (228a). Pausanias
is linked to Prodicus in the *Protagoras* (315d). Eryximachus' speech relates him
to Hippocrates, Aristophanes needs no introduction and Agathon is linked
to Gorgias (*Symposium* 198c). Such links suggest that the things said by the
previous speakers are not just things that struck Plato as possibly plausible
things to say about *erōs*, but are views that are related, albeit roughly, to views

---

[18] Agathon and Socrates must also mean something similar when they discuss *erōs* and the *kalon*,
for example, otherwise how would any discussion get off the ground at all, let alone make the
progress that we see in the elenctic encounter between these two? I thank C. D. C. Reeve for
helpful discussion of this issue.
[19] I thank David Sedley for discussion of this issue.

current at the time, in much the same way as Socrates' speech is related to the sorts of Platonic concerns that occur time and again in the dialogues. This is important to bear in mind if we are to entertain an endoxic reading of an Aristotelian sort, and return to the interpretative options above.[20]

We are familiar with Aristotle's procedure of laying out the views of his predecessors, and showing where the agreements and disagreements lie before going on to offer the beacon of philosophical resolution. And in this dialogue the presentation of the speeches seems to do just that: it sets out the appearances, shows where the puzzles are, and prepares the ground for the philosophical account to work through. Further, Socrates' account employs many of the previous views in some shape or form, and seems to preserve some of the most basic things said from the previous accounts. It might appear then that each speaker "has some contribution to make to the truth" (see *Eudemian Ethics* as cited above). Now, this raises the question of just how significant and substantive a role we are to ascribe to the previous views in the development of a philosophical understanding. If we return to the interpretative options above, are we to conclude that the speeches contribute philosophically (option 2) in a weak (a), or a strong (b), dialectical sense? If we are to consider the latter option then we need some evidence that the *endoxa* have more than pragmatic utility in directing the mind towards possibly promising theories. We need to entertain the idea that they have a role to play in the discovery of philosophical truth, and in the justification of the results of philosophical inquiry. The *endoxa* might perform this role if they are seen to be endowed with a certain evidential status and thereby seen to be authoritative.[21] In order to clarify whether the *legomena* in the *Symposium* have the status of Aristotelian *endoxa*, then, we need evidence that Plato is trying to preserve the truth of the greatest number, or at least "the most authoritative" because proceeding in this way will be a mark of truth. Do the agreements among the speakers carry any philosophical weight? Are there any indications that at least some of the previous views, at least—those preserved in the philosophical account—are seen to be authoritative?

There are considerations that do not sit comfortably with supposing that the previous views, or some sub-set of them, have such status. For Aristotle, ethics is something we are all supposed to know something about in some

---

[20] I thank Zena Hitz for pressing me on this point.
[21] Cf. Barnes 1981:495 on Aristotle: Aristotle "announces time and again that the way to truth is through the study of reputable opinions [i.e. through dialectic]." Cf. Burnyeat 1986, though compare Irwin 1988 for a more cautious view. I thank Ben Morison and Hendrik Lorenz for useful discussion of this issue.

way; ethical knowledge reflects the accumulative wisdom of generations of intelligent people. This does not sound very Platonic, at least if we suppose that Plato (at the time of writing the *Symposium*) held similar views to those expressed in the *Republic*. For there ethical knowledge is an axiomatized deductive system grounded in knowledge of the form of the Good. It is not clear whether we should bring such considerations to bear on the *Symposium*. But there is little evidence internal to the text that the speeches are taken up because they are reputable and seen to be authoritative. There is no explicit statement, for example, to the effect that a good theory of *erōs* must respect and preserve ordinary, or reputable, views about *erōs*. Nor is Socrates' account littered with "we all believe that p" statements that serve as authoritative grounds for his arguments.

The most suggestive piece of evidence for the stronger reading emerges from consideration of the elenchus of Agathon. The philosophical account is advertised as one that "aims for the truth" (199b1), and yet it would appear that the account is presented as developing dialectically, in part, by means of engagement with the views of Agathon, as we have seen. Recall that it is by clarifying the precise nature of Agathon's beliefs about *erōs* and beauty and their relationship to other beliefs (e.g. that *erōs* lacks what it desires) that Socrates seems to generate the central premises on which his own account relies.[22] If it is the case that the proposed definition of *erōs* as an intermediary being is deduced from views expressed and clarified from previous accounts, then this is puzzling. In reaching this idea one does not know why certain views are retained and others rejected as inconsistent with them. Are these views widely accepted? Or are they the results of repeated *elenchi*?[23] Two views, in particular, play a crucial role here: that *erōs* desires beauty (from Agathon's speech), and that it lacks the thing it desires (from Aristophanes' speech and endorsed by Agathon on reflection). It may be the case that all Socrates needs for an *ad hominem* examination of Agathon are beliefs held by Agathon, but the nature of *erōs* is clarified in his own account *on the basis of things agreed*

---

[22] Cf. Stokes 1986:146: "In the talks as recorded Socrates takes over the part of Agathon and Diotima that of Socrates. The *Socrates* of the story has accepted exactly the same propositions (201e) as the Agathon of the *Symposium*; and Diotima, although she has naturally not heard Agathon's encomium and the ensuing discussion, bases her arguments on Agathon's admissions and implications, or occasionally corrects them." He argues further that "every question Socrates has asked has been explanatory of Agathon's original encomium. In each question Socrates either extracts from Agathon a relatively clear inference or he asks for a resolution of a difficulty or ambiguity"; see Stokes 1986:130; cf. 114.

[23] The elenchus of Agathon is presented as a repeat performance of *elenchi* which took place between Socrates and Diotima on numerous occasions (201e3–7; 206b5–6; 207a5–6).

between himself and Agathon, as he says explicitly (201d6), and as back reference to Agathon's speech after the *ti esti/poios tis* questions are answered indicates. What justifies the presentation of that account as aiming at the truth if it is a continuation of views which have been critically re-figured and clarified from at least one previous account (199a7)? We are given plenty of evidence to show that the accounts present conflicting views. Why suppose that one has the right starting points if one proceeds in this way? It does not seem plausible to suppose that Socrates is not committed to the truth of the account of *erōs*, but is simply exploring the view of his peers. Although nothing in my account commits me to the claim that Socrates' speech is a full exposition of the truth, it is clearly presented as one that aims for the truth (199b1).

It seems reasonable to think that the clarification of the two conflicting beliefs that *erōs* desires beauty, and that it lacks what it desires, are ones which are not only most commonly held, but also ones which elenctic experience has proven to be most viable. The former is taken to be axiomatic by most speakers, though the latter is only explicit in Aristophanes' account and resurfaces in the elenchus of Agathon.[24] When the latter claim resurfaces it is given further argumentative support and put on a better rational foundation. The present is necessary, and so everyone who desires must desire something not yet available to him (200a10–e10). If so, then it is not the case that these beliefs are adopted simply on the grounds that they are common views. But it may be the case that beliefs are tested in relation to what is most commonly held (e.g. that *erōs* desires beauty, and *eudaimonia*),[25] and that these beliefs are also ones

---

[24] One reason why Agathon and Aristophanes may have been picked out for special attention in this section of his account is that their speeches discuss the nature of *erōs* and are therefore of special relevance to a definition of *erōs*. If one is committed to the centrality of definitional questions, then one will focus on those accounts most relevant to that. Recall that Aristophanes focused on the needy nature of *erōs*. He emphasized its distinctively human character and expressed concern that *erōs* stay in its proper (mortal) place and avoid a hubristic ascent to the divine (190c8). Agathon, by contrast, claimed that Eros was a great god and lovers in a divine state of abundance (195a5, 197a1). Socrates' account explains that the real nature of *erōs* is in between a state of lack and possession, the mortal and the divine. This is also relevant to the conversation with Agathon and Aristophanes about comedy and tragedy at the end of the dialogue (223d2–5). Since *erōs* has such a nature, one who understands it must know that it is not just a deficient state fitting for Aristophanic portrayal, not just an abundant state of communion with the divine, fitting for a tragedian to portray. The nature of *erōs* is a needy, yet productive, aspiration to the divine and best captured by a combination of the low and the high, the mortal and the divine, the comic and the tragic. And if that is the case, then we can see why Aristophanes and Agathon are particularly relevant here, too.

[25] We can see an example of this in the rejection of Aristophanes' claim that *erōs* pursues the *oikeion*. This claim is rejected when two further premises are introduced: that we are happy to relinquish diseased limbs, and that we all desire *eudaimonia* (205d10–206a1).

which elenctic experience has repeatedly shown to be viable ones, perhaps because asserting their contrary leads to absurdity.[26] But even so, why suppose that this will deliver a truthful, rather than just a consistent, account? One thing that might ground such confidence is precisely if such views did have some status and authority, as the strong dialectical reading above would have it.

An argument in favor of an endoxic reading of this strength would need support of the sort that is not readily available in this text. For Aristotle, for example, his confidence in our capacity to know the world and its capacity to reveal itself in the *phainomena* provide much of the driving force behind his method.[27] As Bolton has argued, "it is not because certain beliefs are widely accepted by us that the belief in question is justified by reference to them. Rather it is because those beliefs bear a special relation to the data of experience" (Bolton 1990:235–236). And herewith the nub of the difference between such views and Plato. For the Socrates of the *Symposium* knowledge is of separately existing forms, and these are not to be grasped in the appearances of the world. Since the privileged "special relation" between one's cognitive states and the world is not that between our views about things and the readily accessible appearances, but that between the mind and the forms, no philosophical theory is going to be justified with reference to such views. That is not to say that the world of non-philosophers is cognitively sterile, however. The sensible world is an imperfect reflection of the real nature of things and, *as a reflection*, is continuous with the real nature of things. The problem with the sensible world is often presented as a very specific one: appearances present things as "confounded" (*Republic* 524c), that is, they ascribe opposite properties to the same object thus making it difficult to consider the real nature of the thing. Grounding one's beliefs in such objects leads to a corresponding compresence of opposites in one's beliefs, which is a problem if knowledge entails truth.[28]

---

[26] On one occasion when Socrates was "using the very arguments" he was using with Agathon, he asserted that *erōs* was neither beautiful nor good, a claim which was rejected since it led to absurdity (201e10).

[27] See *Eudemian Ethics* 1.1.1216b26–35, *Rhetoric* 1.1.1355a14–18, *Nicomachean Ethics* 1.8.1098b27–29. In certain places a connection is established between what is most deeply held and what is based on experience, or perceptual data (cf. *Topics* 6.4.142a2; *Physics* 1.1.184a16–26; *De Insomniis* 462b14–16). This relationship between what is most *endoxon* and experience provides a further reason for confidence on Aristotle's part. On this issue, see Bolton 1990:235–236. This accounts for the fact that when perceptual data are in conflict with the *endoxa* they have priority (cf. *De Caelo* 3.4.303a20–23 with 3.7.306a3–17 and *Generation of Animals* 3.10.760b27–33), and account for those passages where Aristotle stresses his desire to accommodate both *phainomena* and *endoxa* in scientific inquiry (*De Caelo* 3.4.303a20–23 and *Physics* 4.4.211a7–11).

[28] On this issue, see Fine 2003b.

For some of these may be true, and some false, and that is why, as the argument against the Sight-lovers in *Republic* V tried to show, knowledge of the real natures of things cannot be grounded in the appearances, or ultimately justified with reference to beliefs about them.

But perhaps the strongest reason against the strong dialectical reading is the following. Socrates' critique of his peers (considered above) was an explicit statement to the effect that the previous speeches did not aim for truth (*Symposium* 198d7–e6). This suggests that any nuggets of truth found therein cannot be preserved because they are considered to carry a certain evidential status, or authority. They may happen to be true, but this is just a happy accident. So, even if Socrates, or rather, Plato, happens to agree with such views, there is little sense (and evidence to the contrary) that he does so because the speakers said such a thing. This perhaps explains why there are independent arguments provided for many of the claims that are preserved (e.g. for Aristophanes' claim that *erōs* desires what it lacks: 200a1–e10, or Agathon's claim that *erōs* issues in creativity: 207c5–208b5). It also explains why Socrates' account also employs views we do not see emerging dialectically, e.g. ones involving a conception of human nature and its potentialities (206b1), and the nature of knowledge (211–212). The account as a whole remains dialectical in the sense that Socrates explains some of their most central beliefs about *erōs* by showing how they can be understood in light of a certain conception of human nature, and knowledge and so on, but it is not ultimately accountable to them. There is little to suggest that the previous views provide "some proof" of the veracity of the account.[29]

But we need not opt for the strong reading in order to see the philosophical value in the previous accounts. So far I have argued the following. The speeches are more than just a sequence of equally arbitrary claims that provide a rough and ready survey of how people discuss the topic at hand. The central claims of each speech are reasonable, and the disputes worth solving. The evidence for this is that many of the ideas are, in fact, taken up, and the disputes resolved, in the account of the philosopher. After all, as Apollodorus

---

[29] Further, at the end of his speech Socrates claims that the account is a matter of which he is persuaded, not something he knows to be true (212a6–7). Since the account of the ascent to the form of beauty indicates that more is required for knowledge proper, we might suppose that the account is not yet grounded at all. Although there are no indications of a form of *erōs*, it could be the case that an account of *erōs* needs to be grounded in an account of the *kalon*, towards which it is essentially related. Once we know the nature of the relevant form, then this will provide the proper grounds of an account of *erōs*. Such knowledge will not be attained by dialectical work of the sort that drives Socrates' inquiry alone, though it may still contribute to the emergence of such knowledge.

said at the start of the dialogue, the speeches at Agathon's banquet that were preserved were those "worthy of mention" (178a4). The speeches are worthy of inclusion in the dialogue, not because they justify the results of the inquiry (the strong dialectical reading), but because they are a useful tool towards those results (the weak dialectical reading). The detailed speeches provide the opportunity to examine a variety of puzzles and issues arising from the topic, and this enables one to discern more clearly where the resolutions might lie. The speeches lay out the issues that a philosophical account needs to, and does in fact, explain.

One might still like to know what grounds Plato's confidence in even this. What ensures that the direction in which the speeches take us is a relevant one? What guarantees that a consideration of such mixed views can play a useful role in an inquiry that aims towards the truth? In the *Symposium*, as in the *Meno* and the *Phaedo*, Plato seems to assume that one will end up with the right starting points for further inquiry because there is something about the nature of the mind that ensures such progress is possible. All human beings are pregnant with wisdom and virtue, albeit to varying degrees, and when we reach a certain age we naturally desire to express this in actions and productions of various kinds (206c1–3, 209a3). Human beings, we might say, are naturally knowers (albeit to varying degrees, 209a3), and this ability naturally develops as we mature as human beings (206c3–4).[30] If we engage in proper reflection on the *endoxa* then we are such as to be able to favor truth over falsehoods, as one scholar has put it, and so to make progress towards the truth.[31]

Whatever the ultimate grounds of such an account turn out to be, we can nonetheless conclude that Plato finds value in the things said by non-philosophers, and some *philosophical* value in particular. It could also be the case, of course, that including the previous views in the philosophical account serves a pedagogical, or rhetorical function. Such a procedure not only aids clarity, but also advertises the superior value of philosophy by appropriating and perfecting the insights of others. But I have argued that there is a deeper epistemological conviction at work here. Philosophical understanding emerges

---

[30] There is, of course, variation in the degree to which human beings develop over time, as the contrast between the desiring agents of the lower and higher mysteries of his speech indicates (212a1–6 with 209a3). This variation in epistemic performance will depend in part on external factors, like having the proper method (of the ascent). But insofar as our souls are pregnant with wisdom and virtue we are perhaps to suppose that we are fitted by nature to reach this specific end and are naturally inclined towards the truth. If so, then perhaps this is the optimistic assumption behind the more constructive slant of the Socrates of the *Symposium*. I argue this point more fully in Sheffield 2001a.

[31] E.g. Fine 2003b commenting on the *Meno*.

from a process of working through the *endoxa*. Unlike Aristotle, Plato presents these in detailed accounts delivered by richly developed characters. This surely serves to remind us of the sorts of lives that were constructed as a result of adopting the beliefs and values espoused by the individual speakers.[32] However they are presented, the accounts of Socrates' peers will be for the sake of our philosophical education, in much the same way as the lower mysteries were taught to Socrates for the sake of his grasp of the higher (210a6–7). In fact, the striking parallels between the desiring agents of the lower mysteries and the symposiasts strongly support such a reading.[33] We can nonetheless conclude, then, that Plato does find value in the things said by non-philosophers. The shared wreath of wisdom given by Alcibiades to Socrates *and* the symposiasts' greatest representative (i.e. Agathon) is richly deserved (213e1–5). And this, after all, reflects not only the epistemic value of dialectic as a shared enterprise, but also the value of the symposium as a place in which the truth may be sought as part of a communal enterprise—and when properly conducted— discovered.[34]

---

[32] On this issue see further O'Connor forthcoming, Nehamas 1998, and Sheffield 2006.

[33] Such types included lawmakers, poets and craftsmen (209a5), many of which were celebrated by the symposiasts in their speeches. They value the life of the soul over the body (209c with 176e4–10) and were characterized by a love of honor (208c3 with 198d7–e6). Further, the desiring agents of the lower mysteries were, after all, meant to be familiar to Socrates in his role play with Diotima (209e5); in other words, they are supposed to be familiar to Agathon and his peers as types of character they would recognize. For further arguments for this claim, see Sheffield 2006.

[34] On this role for symposia generally, see Rösler 1995.

Three

A Platonic Reading of Plato's *Symposium*

Lloyd P. Gerson

1.

THE AMERICAN POET AND CRITIC John Jay Chapman (1862–1933) wrote,

> ... to the historical student, to the man who not only knows some-
> thing of books, but something of the world, the *Symposium* of Plato
> is seen to have been in every age since Plato the most effective plea
> for evil that one can point to or recall. The moral disease which it
> inculcates is apt to break out in any age and to poison the young.
> The *Symposium* has always been the *vade mecum* of those who accept
> and continue the practice which it celebrates. To them it is a sort of
> lurid devotional book—the sulphurous breviary of the pederast.

This is not a view of the dialogue to which scholars today generally subscribe.[1]
Why not? What precisely are the grounds on which we can confidently or even
reasonably eliminate any particular interpretation of a Platonic dialogue?
Some would say, indeed, that there are no grounds for eliminating any interpretation. Let a thousand flowers bloom. If "interpretation" here means,
roughly, "what the dialogue has inspired me to think" or "what I learned from
the dialogue," then it is difficult to argue with this approach. Most, though,
would use "interpretation" more narrowly, based on some sort of criteria for
interpretation. This is where things get interesting. Because now we can ask
the question, "what sort of criteria and assumptions must we bring to our
reading of the dialogue?" I say "must" and not "can" because I am myself
assuming that these criteria and assumptions are supposed to be the right
ones, or at least criteria and assumptions which are such that, at the end of

---

[1] Though it is an interpretation implicit in the culture that, say, produced *Brideshead Revisited*.

the day, statements beginning "this dialogue teaches that ..." or "Plato in this dialogue claims ..." are not purely arbitrary.

Regarding *Symposium*, interpretation is at least in part inspired by some of the extraordinary claims made by the interlocutors. Here are some of the claims found in Diotima's speech in *Symposium* as reported by Socrates. Diotima picks up Socrates' assertion that love is the desire to possess beautiful things (204d–e). She replies, "What will one have who has beautiful things?" Socrates cannot answer and she says, "Suppose someone changes the question using 'good' in place of 'beautiful' and asks, "What is it that the lover of good things loves?" Socrates now confidently replies that he will have good things. In reply to the next question, "What is it he has who has good things?" Socrates says, "This is an easier question; he'll have happiness." So, "this wanting [good for oneself] *is* what this love is" (205a5). Later on, Diotima formulates a definition of love: "love is [desire for] the possession of the good forever" (206a11–12).[2] And its 'work' (ἔργον) is "birth in beauty in the body and the soul" (206b3–8). This birth in beauty or reproduction is "what mortals have in place of immortality" (206e7–8). It is the replacement for immortality (207d1-208b6). Birth in beauty is of two sorts: bodily and spiritual or intellectual (208e1-209a3). But it is clear that the latter is superior to the former (209c7–d1).

When Diotima turns to the "higher" mysteries of love, she proceeds to explain an ascent or progression or 'right order' (ἐφεξῆς τε καὶ ὀρθῶς) of spiritual or intellectual love, from individual beautiful bodies, to all beautiful bodies, to beautiful practices and laws, to beautiful areas of knowledge, to, finally, beauty "by itself" (210a4-211d1). It is only when the lover has reached this goal that he is able to give birth, not to 'images' (εἴδωλα) of virtue, but to true virtue, because he is in touch with true beauty (212a4–5). And thus he will attain immortality, if any human being may.

These passages are puzzling precisely because we are unsure what tools to bring to their interpretation. The apparent denigration of the individual as love object, the casual conflation of the beautiful with the good, the claim for the ubiquity of love as a psychic phenomenon aimed at the good, the distinction between bodily and spiritual beauty and love, the imitation of immortality, the superiority of the spiritual to the bodily and the further superiority of one who produces "true virtue" as opposed to one who, presumably, produces mere images of it, and, finally, the very idea of an "ascent" or "right order" of ascent to the vision of a separate Form—all of these "mysterious"

---

[2] Ἔστιν ἄρα συλλήβδην, ἔφη, ὁ ἔρως τοῦ τὸ ἀγαθὸν αὑτῷ εἶναι ἀεί, picking up ἐπιθυμία from 205d2.

statements have evoked in readers the awe and wonder Socrates reports that he felt himself when Diotima uttered them. If one takes these claims seriously, it is certainly possible to *question* them. Why, for example, should we believe that there is a "right order" to the ascent or even that there *is* an ascent? Or what reason have we for agreeing that spiritual beauty is superior to bodily beauty or that true virtue is produced only by one having experienced philosophical knowledge of beauty itself? Indeed, why should we accept that goodness has anything to do with beauty at all?

One familiar reply—typically, tacitly assumed rather than defended—is that there is no reason to accept Plato's "vision" because Plato does not explicitly argue for it.[3] We can, nevertheless, appreciate its poetic splendor alongside of and perhaps even above those of other "visions" of love, including those of the previous speakers in the dialogue. Another reply—equally familiar—is that every single one of Diotima's claims is expatiated upon elsewhere in the Platonic canon. So, for example, we can refer to *Meno* and *Gorgias* to understand why "all desire the good;" we can refer to *Apology* and *Lysis* to illuminate Diotima's account of what a philosopher is; we can refer to *Phaedrus* and *Timaeus* to make the distinction between the quasi-immortality of the 'human being' (ἄνθρωπος) and the *real* immortality of the immortal part of our soul, that which *Laws* calls "the true self;" we can refer to *Philebus* to understand the relationship between the good and the beautiful, and we can refer to *Republic* to understand the notion of a hierarchical ascent to the intellectual world, including the 'origin' (ἀρχή) of the hierarchy; and, finally, we can refer to *Phaedo* to understand the difference between "images" of virtue and true virtue.[4]

The former view holds that since every dialogue can be shown to stand on its own two feet dramatically, so it must be assumed to stand on its own two feet philosophically.[5] And if the cues or concepts necessary to clarify the philosophical views expressed are not already imbedded in the individual dialogue, then those views must remain fragmentary probes or aperçus. On this view, the only tools needed to interpret a Platonic dialogue are knowledge of Attic Greek and perhaps some knowledge of the historical context of the work. By

---

[3] See, e.g. Press 1995:133–152.

[4] Such a view is the contradictory of the rarely maintained position that Diotima's speech contains an anti-Platonic doctrine of love. See Neumann 1965:33–59.

[5] A stellar example of this mode of interpretation is Tejera 2000. A different and more interesting example is Shorey 1933, who believes that Plato's philosophy is a unity and that that entire philosophy has to be adduced in order to understand each dialogue. Yet, his account of each dialogue fairly consistently refuses the adduction of material from elsewhere.

contrast, the latter view maintains that the proper context for the interpretation of any dialogue of Plato is Platonism itself. Such a view invites disbelief,
owing to the not unreasonable suspicion that it is hopelessly entangled in a
form of Meno's paradox. How can we know what Platonism is without mining
the dialogues? But if we do that in a way that does not already presuppose
what Platonism is, then we are never going to be in a position to construct
Platonism out of the individual building blocks, the dialogues themselves.

Owing to such difficulties, a "middle" position is sometimes sought.
One middle position asserts that *some* material from other dialogues can be
licitly used to interpret any one. The principle of selection is almost inevitably developmentalist in some way. Thus, if we can distinguish, say, early,
middle, and late Platonic dialogues on philosophical grounds (whether we
identify the first with Socratic philosophy or not), we can use material from
one period of development to interpret dialogues from the same period, but
not from any other. According to most proponents of this view, material from
Phaedo, Republic, Gorgias, Lysis, and *Meno* would probably be eligible for use in
interpreting *Symposium,* but material from *Philebus, Timaeus,* and *Laws* would
not.[6] But surely, apart from the inherent and well canvassed problems with
developmentalism as such, this principle of selection as stated is too strong.[7]
For proponents of its use would in fact want to exclude only those dialogues
or their parts which maintain a view contrary to the one maintained in
Symposium. And here the problem is determining the view being expressed
in *Symposium* so that one could maintain that what is being expressed in, say,
Timaeus is contrary to *that.* For example, it is often supposed that *Symposium*
does not acknowledge or maintain *real* immortality, but rather only the *quasi-*
immortality possible in reproduction, whether physical or "spiritual." If this is
the case, it is incorrect to suppose that the immortality proclaimed in *Timaeus*
and *Laws* can be read back into *Symposium.* Two things are wrong with this:
(1) *Republic,* a dialogue that on this view may be adduced on behalf of interpreting *Symposium,* maintains a view of immortality that at least appears to be
pretty close to *Timaeus,* and (2) *Timaeus* does not maintain the immortality of

---

[6] Cornford 1971:119–131, provides an excellent example of a very vigorous, though selective,
use of *Republic* in interpreting *Symposium* (especially in the application of the doctrine of the
tripartite soul to the higher mysteries, along with a reluctance to allow that genuine immortality is present in *Symposium*), but a disinclination to use much of anything else.

[7] The mere possibility of Plato having a large philosophical vision that is variously expressed in
the dialogues itself always trumps developmentalism. That is, Plato might be *developing* in the
sense of unfolding the expression of Platonism. There is no space here to enter into the developmentalism vs. unitarianism debate. But I take the above possibility to render it unnecessary
that I do so.

the human being any more than does *Symposium*, if the human being is understood as the composite of the immortal part of the soul plus the *mortal* parts
of the soul plus the body. Only if we insist on identifying the person or true
self with the human being would there seem to be any opposition between
Symposium and *Timaeus*.[8] But to hold that the former dialogue so identifies the
person would be to put it into conflict with the view directly implied in, for
example, *Phaedo*, a dialogue supposedly usable for interpreting *Symposium*.

Another middle position eschews developmentalism in favor of a strictly
circumscribed type of Platonism as a device for interpreting the dialogues.
Typically, this approach rejects the indirect tradition—including Aristotle's
testimony—as relevant to reconstructing Platonism. Among its most adept
practitioners—scholars such as Harold Cherniss—this rejection itself requires
limitations on the extraction of doctrine from the dialogues.[9] For example,
separate Forms are asserted but the superordinate status of the Idea of the
good is disallowed. It is difficult to see the justification for this approach
beyond the unwillingness to have Plato say anything that the scholar regards
as embarrassingly silly.[10] Hence, Plato "lite."[11]

---

[8] See Corrigan and Glazov-Corrigan 2004:224–234, for some perceptive remarks on how *Symposium* must be understood to be focusing on the soul-body composite or the embodied person,
not the true, immortal self.

[9] Cherniss 1944 and 1945 is the mirror image of Robin 1908. Often the rule seems to be: "if I can't
understand the argument or if the argument seems silly to me, then Plato could not have held
the doctrine whose expression is the conclusion of the argument."

[10] Strauss 2001 provides an elegant example of the pitfalls of combining the principle of "reading
Plato dialogue by dialogue" and yet bringing to the dialogues a mitigated Platonism. Strauss,
200, declares that in Diotima's speech, the good is not identical with the beautiful and then,
238, Strauss says that the beautiful is the good. Strauss's way of dealing with such absurdi-
ties is to proclaim that what we have in Diotima's speech (and in the dialogue as a whole) is a
"poetic presentation of philosophy." In such a presentation, there is no compelling need for
consistency.

[11] Kahn 1996 elaborates what I regard as the least objectionable form of this interpretation. On
Kahn's view, all the dialogues prior to *Republic* should be read "proleptically," that is, as antici-
pating or pointing to that work. Kahn, however, cannot explain why *all* the dialogues, including
Republic, are not proleptic to Platonism itself. The limitation to *Republic* seems arbitrary. A
similar problem is faced by Allen 1991:85, who thinks that in *Symposium* beauty and good are
"equivalent" and "at the same level" because this dialogue "looks forward" to *Republic*. Neither
of the specific passages that are what *Symposium* supposedly looks forward to (507b4, 532b1)
say precisely this about beauty and good. The first passage just says that there is a αὐτὸ καλόν
and a αὐτὸ ἀγαθόν. The second passage just says that αὐτὸ ὅ ἐστιν ἀγαθόν has to be grasped in
order to grasp the being of each thing. Better passages for Allen's case might be 509a6 where
Glaucon says that the good is ἀμήχανον κάλλος and 508e5 where Socrates says that the good
is κάλλιον than knowledge and truth, though the use of the comparative in the latter passage
tells us at least, I take it, that τὸ καλόν is not being treated like an ordinary Form. Indeed,
one might reply that the Idea of the good is no ordinary Form either. It is not clear why Allen

Recoiling from the entanglements of developmentalism and the philo-sophical insubstantiality of mitigated Platonism, various sophisticated forms of the first position—what I would term principled hermeneutical Alzheimer's disease—have been proposed. I have no quarrel with these ways of reading *Symposium* unless they purport to seek out and defend philosophical claims. Even the view that the structure of the dialogue, including the succession of speeches, and the Alcibiadean farce at the end, have a philosophical point is one that I believe is not available to one who holds this position consistently. And here I include the idea that the dialogues have principally a protreptic function among the philosophical claims that this view is in no position to make.[12] This is so because *Symposium* does not come supplied with an instruc-tion sheet that states: read this dialogue protreptically. In order to get to the protreptic conclusion, one has to appeal to dialogues like *Phaedo*, for example, and to its remarks about philosophy and *logos*. And I say, "If you can use *Phaedo*, then I can use *Philebus*." And if you say, "I renounce *Phaedo* and therefore forbid you *Philebus*," I reply, "that's fine if you don't want to explicate Plato's philosophy but are interested in something else. But if you do want to expli-cate Plato's philosophy, then in order to understand *Symposium*'s contribution to that, we need *Philebus and Phaedo*, and much else besides."[13]

What is the basis for supposing that Platonism is more than just the empirically arrived at collection of claims—whether consistent or inconsis-tent—in the dialogues? One sort of evidentiary consideration is, of course, Aristotle's testimony in regard to Plato's unwritten teaching. I don't discount this or intend to belittle it, though I do believe that this testimony—except in

---

thinks that *Symposium* does not look forward to *Philebus* 64e5–65a5 where beauty is treated as an aspect of good, not literally identical with it. Allen does add that "beauty is ... the sensuous aspect of goodness," though what this means in the context of his assertion that beauty is identified with that which is beyond being I have no idea. Surely, it is not just the sensuous aspect if laws and institutions can be called "beautiful." In my view, what underlies the inter-pretations of both Kahn and Allen is a reluctance to face squarely full-blown Platonism.

[12] Whether the protreptic aimed at drawing readers to the philosophical life generally or to "enrolment" in the Academy, I have never understood why it is supposed that a protreptic precludes a heavy dose of doctrine. For example, the explicit protreptic function of Thomas Aquinas' *Summa Contra Gentiles* is intended to depend entirely upon the force and extent of the argument therein. Ancient Platonists like Proclus reasonably enough took the prologues to dialogues like *Symposium* and *Timaeus* to anticipate the dialogue's main theme. But *Symposium* was classified by all the ancient Platonists as a "theological" dialogue, that is, one whose central theme was the intelligible world. The connection between the contents of the prologue of that dialogue and the theological theme is itself dependent on bringing to that dialogue the wider framework of Platonism.

[13] A nice summary of the elements from later dialogues needed to illuminate *Symposium* can be found in Corrigan and Glazov-Corrigan 2004:236 and n119.

certain crucial details—mostly confirms what is present in the dialogues rather than adds anything new.[14] More significant, I believe, is that there was any oral teaching at all. Plato was evidently not just a writer of dialogues. The relevant context for interpreting the dialogues must include ongoing Academic discussions.[15] This fact alone renders for me hollow the claim that Plato is forever occluded for us by his authorial mask.[16]

A different sort of evidentiary consideration is the analysis of the position that arises when one takes together the contradictories of the philosophical positions of Plato's predecessors rejected in the dialogues. By "Platonism" I mean, as a starting point, roughly, what results if you reject Eleaticism and its implicit nominalism, the materialism of the "giants" in *Sophist*, Protagorean epistemological relativism, extreme Heracliteanism, the doctrine that the soul is a *harmonia* of bodily parts, and the hedonism of the "subtle thinkers" in *Philebus*. I realize that many find a certain tentativeness or equivocation in many positive doctrines expressed in the dialogues. I find no such tentativeness in the arguments offered on behalf of rejecting the above positions. If you add to the Aristotelian testimony the position that emerges from the conjunction of the negation of the above rejected views, then that is basically what Platonism is.[17] There is an additional and highly controversial potential adumbration of this position. That includes whatever is entailed by this position whether Plato endorsed the entailment or not or even whether he was aware of it or not. So, for example, Plato endorses some consequences of the rejection of nominalism, like the possibility that two things, though they be self-identical, can be the same, though he does not explicitly consider other implications of the rejection of nominalism, like the equivocity of being. Such a contentious adumbration of Platonism allows for the possibility of *varieties* of Platonism, depending on how many implications you can figure out and how many you embrace.[18]

---

[14] Cf. especially Miller 1995:225–244.

[15] See Miller 1995:239–243.

[16] This is, incidentally, why the analogy of Shakespeare's plays adduced on behalf of the view that Plato's dialogues are to be read non-doctrinally is false. We have no evidence of Shakespeare having a view of literature or of life other than that which we find in each individual play. So, we can safely ignore his "real" intention and avoid what aesthetic theoreticians have long recognized as "the intentional fallacy." For the interpretation of all the dialogues as plays, see Arieti 1991.

[17] Perhaps more precisely, Aristotle's testimony indicates his interpretation of one version of Platonism which is just the position that emerges from rejecting the above mentioned competing philosophies.

[18] See Gerson 2005b for a much fuller exposition of Platonism positively and negatively conceived. I do not mean to suggest that Platonism is to be understood exclusively as consisting of the

Let us take for granted the fact that if Plato believes A, and A entails B, it does not follow that Plato believes B.[19] But someone who is more interested in Platonism that in the working of Plato's own cognitive apparatus is probably going to be more interested in whether or not A actually entails B than in whether or not Plato believed that it did. Disciples will differ here. For example, they might differ on whether Plato's commitment to the immortality of the soul is necessarily a commitment to personal immortality, however this may be defined. Or they may agree that a commitment to the immortality of the soul does entail a commitment to personal immortality, though they might differ as to whether or how moral deserts have any meaning for the immortal person.

I believe it is both the case that Plato was a Platonist and that his disciples embraced varieties of Platonism. By this I mean simply that Plato was the exponent of a distinctive philosophical position that later disciples identified as "true philosophy" or "wisdom" or "Platonism."[20] In the dialogues, and for reasons that need not be rehearsed here, Plato does not address, or address unequivocally, a lot of the implications of his basic position. I have argued at some length recently that Aristotle was a dissident Platonist, embracing most of the elements of Platonism, but not enough to preclude his dissidence.[21] In this paper, I am interested in how Platonism illuminates *Symposium*, in particular, Diotima's speech. The best argument I can come up with for my interpretation of *Symposium* is that Platonism *does* illuminate it better than anything else. If applying Platonism removes our puzzles, and nothing else does, what better argument could there be for this interpretation?

I am henceforth going to ignore interpretation of the role of the earlier speeches in the dialogue, principally because they have never been supposed to be constitutive of Platonism. This fact—if it is a fact—does not obviate the need for an answer to the question of how, if at all, the speeches support the delivery of the Platonic message. A very brief answer to this question, along

---

conjunction of the contradictions of all the positions refuted in the dialogues. On the contrary, I believe that there is an abundance of evidence in the dialogues that positively supports the position here sketched.

[19] But we might, with Sedley 2004:chap. 1, expect to find in Plato's later works efforts to "reclaim his Socratic heritage" by locating Socratic philosophy within a Platonic embrace, that is, we would find him drawing out some of the implications of the Socratic inspiration.

[20] Proclus *Platonic Theology* 1.6.19 (S–W), calls Plotinus and others "exegetes of the Platonic revelation" (τοὺς τῆς Πλατωνικῆς ἐποπτείας ἐξηγητάς). Proclus goes on to make clear that Plato was not the first or only vehicle of this divine revelation. The justification for distinguishing Platonism from *what Plato says* is that Plato is himself articulating or expressing an "ancient tradition." We call what Plato says "Platonism" because he was the greatest exponent of this tradition.

[21] See Gerson 2005a.

the lines of the above construction of Platonism through a *via negativa* is that these speeches all reveal inadequate conceptions of love—inadequate because they are not expressions of Platonism. And yet their inadequacies, paradoxically, reveal the depth of the Platonic doctrine because no one, Platonist or anti-Platonist, is completely unacquainted with or oblivious to various expressions of love or beauty or goodness.[22] As Aristotle would say, the truth is broad enough for no one to have missed it completely.[23]

2.

When Proclus at the beginning of his *Platonic Theology* singled out Plotinus, along with Porphyry, Iamblichus, and Theodore of Asine as great "exegetes of the Platonic revelation," he was acknowledging the consensus (which actually antedates Plotinus) that there was a coherent and distinctive philosophical position to which those who called themselves "Platonists" generally adhered. It is this general position that provides the framework for interpreting any dialogue or any part therein. Plotinus would have decisively rejected the eighteenth-century characterization of him as a "founder of Neoplatonism;" on the contrary, he would have insisted on being understood as nothing more than a "paleo" Platonist. He stands out among Platonists as absorbed with understanding what Plato has to say about *erōs* in the light of Platonism. It is not merely that he wrote a treatise (3.5 [50]) devoted to the topic, but he endeavored to integrate the concept of *erōs* fully into Platonic metaphysics and psychology. Most remarkably, he employs Plato's concept of *erōs* in his characterization of the One or the Good, the first principle of all, as a "lover of itself."[24] This is remarkable because, as we know, *erōs* in *Symposium* at any rate, is a concept from which connotations of "lack" or "deficiency" are seemingly inseparable.[25] Yet the absolutely first principle of all is without limitation or

---

[22] I believe that this interpretation is at least consistent with a central element of that of Rowe 1998b:246–247; 258, namely, that the central desire of the lover is for the good. Rowe holds that Diotima transforms this into a desire for quasi-immortality. I would prefer to say that the latter is an expression of the former rather than its transformation. Cf. Allen 1991:77 who concisely catalogues the ways in which Diotima's speech corrects the claims of all the previous interlocutors. Also, Buchner 1965:16 who argues that Diotima's speech provides a "criterion" by which the truth in each of the previous speeches can be judged.

[23] See *Metaphysics* 2.1.993a30–b11.

[24] *Enneads* 6.8 [39] 15, 1–2: Καὶ ἐράσμιον καὶ ἔρως ὁ αὐτὸς καὶ αὑτοῦ ἔρως, ἄτε οὐκ ἄλλως καλὸς ἢ παρ' αὑτοῦ καὶ ἐν αὑτῷ. Square brackets indicate the chronological ordering of Porphyry's edition of Plotinus.

[25] Plotinus *Enneads* 3.5 [50] 7, 9–15; 19–24, acknowledges this feature in his interpretation of the myth of the birth of ἔρως.

imperfection of any kind. How can this be? Why does Plotinus take from Plato the appropriateness of applying the concept of *erōs* to the One?

Let us begin with Plotinus' interpretation of the lover in *Symposium*. Plotinus assumes that the life of the human being, the life of the body-soul composite is held by Plato to be inferior to the life of the real person.[26] Plotinus seems justified in interpreting Plato in this way if he is also justified in assuming that what Plato says in *Alcibiades, Phaedrus, Phaedo, Republic, Timaeus,* and *Laws* can be legitimately adduced on behalf of understanding the qualified immortality to which a human being may aspire.[27] So, the happiness attendant upon the possession of good things will vary according to whether we are talking about the happiness of the "composite" or the happiness of the real person.[28]

If this makes good sense, we can perhaps next resolve an ambiguity in the contrast between the higher and lower mysteries. When in the higher mysteries, the lover attains his goal, he gives birth to true virtue, not its images. What is true virtue here supposed to be and what are its images? How does the offspring that is true virtue differ from the offspring of the spiritual or intellectual love in the lower mysteries? I cannot fathom how anyone could understand what Plato means by "images" of true virtue without adducing what is said in other dialogues.[29] In addition, I cannot fathom what the reason

---

[26] See ibid., 1.4 [46] 16, 9–13: Οὐκ ἔστιν οὖν ἐν τῷ κοινῷ [i.e. the composite of body and soul] εὐδαιμόνως ζῆν. Ὀρθῶς γὰρ καὶ Πλάτων ἐκεῖθεν ἄνωθεν τὸ ἀγαθὸν ἀξιοῖ λαμβάνειν καὶ πρὸς ἐέκεῖνο βλέπειν τὸν μέλλοντα σοφὸν καὶ εὐδαίμονα ἔσεσθαι καὶ ἐκείνῳ ὁμοιοῦσθαι καὶ κατ' ἐκεῖνο ζῆν. Plotinus is here referring to *Symposium* 212a as well as to *Theaetetus* 176b1.

[27] O'Brien 1984:185–205 argues that the immortality attained by one engaged in contemplating the Form of beauty and in thereby becoming virtuous is genuine immortality. It is a gift of the gods, like that awarded to epic heroes. Cf. 212a. This is in contrast to the quasi-immortality of the lower mysteries. O'Brien is followed, though without attribution, by Dyson 1986:67, who argues that philosophers—those who are privy to the higher mysteries—experience the "personal survival of the ephemeral soul" owing to their having pleased the gods.

[28] See Gerson 2004:217–248, where I argue that Aristotle similarly distinguishes between the happiness of the composite and the happiness of "that which we are especially," namely, intellects. I adduce Aristotle here because Plotinus was bolstered in his interpretation of Plato by finding the same distinction in Aristotle. Porphyry, Plotinus' pupil, tells us that Plotinus' teacher, Ammonius Saccas, was one of the first to show that Aristotle was a Platonist.

[29] At *Lysis* 219d2–5 Socrates argues that things that are dear for the sake of the 'primary dear' (πρῶτον φίλον) are only 'images' (εἴδωλα) of the "true" dear, namely, the first. Although he does proceed to argue that the good is dear (220b7), it is not clear that it would appropriate to read back into *Lysis* what is said about the Idea of the good in, say, *Republic*. On the other hand, the logic of the *Lysis* argument provides the framework for its application to the *Symposium* argument. There are, of course, several big inferential steps from: when each of us loves or desires some concrete good (e.g. health), anything we pursue for the sake of that we do not truly love to: there is one thing (the Idea of the good) that we all truly love. Note also that

would be for *not* adducing other dialogues, given that the material for an answer to these questions is readily available there. One may indeed suppose that the offspring that is true virtue do not differ at all from the offspring of spiritual love and that the images referred to are a rhetorical flourish on Plato's part. Yet, the offspring of spiritual love are *logoi* about virtue (209b8).[30] The offspring of contact with the good or intelligible beauty is true virtue, not *logoi* about it.[31] As Plotinus argues elsewhere, the images of true virtue are identical with the "popular and political" virtues of *Phaedo*.[32] One could, I suppose, take the images of true virtue as *deceptive* images or *counterfeits* of virtue. But only one who is reading *Symposium* in the light of the Platonism as expressed in the other dialogues would realize that, for Plato, not all images are deceptive.

According to Plotinus, the true virtue itself is the virtue attained by the philosopher in contrast to popular and political virtue.[33] The latter is identical with the virtue produced by those who are pregnant from spiritual love (209a–b). True virtue is the virtue of the "aristocratic" human being in books VIII and IX of *Republic* in contrast to the virtue available to all members of the state, as described in book IV. It is the virtue that constitutes "assimilation to the divine" (ὁμοίωσις θεῷ).[34] This assimilation is the process by which a human being *achieves* immortality, not its simulacrum. The achievement is to identify oneself with the "human being within the human being."[35] This is, of course,

---

whereas in *Symposium* it is the product or the ἔργον of love that is the image, in *Lysis* it is the putative object of love that turns out to be the image.

[30] Cf. 210a7–8 where the first step on the ascent within the higher mysteries is love of one beautiful body which produces καλοὶ λόγοι.

[31] See *Cratylus* 439a–b where Socrates contrasts learning about things "through themselves" and learning about them through 'names' (ὀνόματα). Previously, at 425a, he describes a λόγος as consisting of names plus 'verbs' (ῥήματα). Cf. *Sophist* 262e. The point is not, I think, that the addition of verbs turns the image of the thing into something else.

[32] See *Enneads* 1.2 [19] on the grades of virtue. The "popular and political" virtues are described in *Phaedo* 82a10–b3. Cf. 69b6–7, where this sort of virtue is called an 'illusory façade' (σκιαγραφία), fit for slaves. Cf. *Protagoras* 323a7, b2; 324a1 where Protagoras uses the term "political virtue" in the same way without of course the pejorative Platonic overtones. Cf. *Republic* II 365c3–4 and VI 500d8 with VII 518d3–519a6 where the "popular" virtues are identified as the "so-called virtues of the soul" and especially 619c7–d1 for participation in virtue by 'habit' (ἔθει) "without philosophy." At 430c3, courage is characterized as "political." At 443c10–d1, characterizing justice, Plato contrasts "external" behavior with "internal" virtue, which is concerned with what is "truly oneself and one's own" (ἀληθῶς περὶ ἑαυτὸν καὶ τὰ ἑαυτοῦ).

[33] Cp. *Phaedo* 82b1 ἐπιτετηδευκότες; *Symposium* 209c1 ἐπιτηδεύειν.

[34] *Theaetetus* 176b.

[35] *Republic* IX 589a7–b1. As Price 1989:30, points out, both *Phaedrus* (245c5–246a2, 276e5–277a4) and *Laws* (721b7–c6, 895e10–896e2) recognize both quasi-immortality and real immortality in the same dialogues.

the soul, or, more accurately, the immortal or rational part of the soul.[36] The achievement is thus naturally contrasted with the *endowment* of immortality for anyone with a human soul.

One who achieves immortality insofar as this is possible for a mortal human being produces true virtue rather than images of it because he is "in touch with true beauty" (212a5). The contrast then is not just between the products of the one who follows the higher mysteries and the one who follows the lower, but also between intelligible reality, on the one hand, and images of it, on the other. All of the objects of *erōs* other than the true beauty are images, including all of the objects loved by the practitioners of the lower mysteries.[37] The sublation of the individual love object as the focus of the account of *erōs* is thus inseparable from the whole point of the ascent.[38] That ascent aims at self-transformation via assimilation to the divine. This assimilation is impossible without the ascent because focusing on any love object other than beauty itself stops the assimilation. The love of images will enable production—since that is the work of *erōs* in any case—but it will not result in self-transformation.

To see this point clearly it is essential that the relation between beauty and the good be understood. The simple reading of the text has Diotima conflate beauty with the good.[39] If these two are not virtually identical, then it remains obscure or even scandalous (as in the view of Gregory Vlastos) why the pursuit of the beautiful wherever one finds it is not sufficient for the achievement of immortality.[40] Indeed, one can either suppose that *real*

---

[36] See *Timaeus* 41c-d, 69c5-6, e1, 90a, c1-3. Cf. *Republic* X 611b9-612a6: *Laws* IV 713b8, XII 959b3-4. That *Symposium* is denying immortality to the ἄνθρωπος and not to the rational or divine part of the soul that is identical with the real person was seen long ago by Luce 1952:137-141, refuting Hackforth 1950:43-45. Cf. 208b1-4 for the explicit contrast between the participation in 'immortality' (ἀθανασίας) by that which is 'mortal' (τὸ θνῆτον) and by that which is 'immortal' (ἀθάνατον).

[37] See *Enneads* 6.9 [9] 9, 41-43: ... καὶ ὅτι ταῦτα μὲν τὰ ἐρώμενα θνητὰ καὶ βλαβερὰ καὶ εἰδώλων ἔρωτες καὶ μεταπίπτει, ὅτι οὐκ ἦν τὸ ὄντως ἐρώμενον οὐδὲ τὸ ἀγαθὸν ἡμῶν οὐδ' ὃ ζητοῦμεν.

[38] Cf. Price 1989:48-49, who disagrees and takes the true virtue to be identical with the products of spiritual love and so to require interpersonal relations.

[39] For example, Robin 1964:9, just assumes that '*belle*' and '*bon*' are synonymous, though in his concluding remarks (183-189), he does adduce *Philebus* 64e-65a on behalf of understanding the relationship between good and beautiful. Cf. Grube 1935:21, 30. One motive for the conflation is, I suspect, the assumption that if beauty and good are *not* conflated, then Plato's own argument in *Symposium* is actually refuted by an argument in *Philebus*, an argument against Eudoxus' conflation of pleasure with the good on the grounds that there are goods other than pleasure. See *Philebus* 20e-22e; 60b-61b. If, however, beauty is not conflated with good, then a similar argument can be made adducing goods that are not beautiful.

[40] See Vlastos 1973b. Vlastos complains about the denigration of the individual as love object in *Symposium*. Cf. Neumann 1965:41, who makes the same complaint, referring to scholars going

immortality is not part of this story, in which case it is hard to see why anyone should privilege the immortality gained by spiritual love over physical love except one who prefers that sort of love. Or, again supposing the separation of the beautiful and the good, it is hard to see why "good" cannot be a property univocally predicable of anything beautiful. So, on this interpretation we bid farewell to hierarchy or ascent.[41] Such was the approach of Epicurus, for example, who, identifying the good with pleasure, infamously proclaimed, "I spit on the beautiful if it does not bring pleasure."[42]

If, however, the good is in fact a reference to the Idea of the good and, as Plotinus assumes—basing himself on *Philebus* (among other texts)—the beautiful is that Idea in its attractive aspect, there is a hierarchical, Platonically based, difference between the good and any image participating in it.[43] What everyone *really* desires is the good itself, not an image of it.[44] The fact that people will settle for images of beauty, when they will never settle for images of good, is owing to their belief that images of beauty can be something other than just images of good; they can be really good. If, however, beauty and good

---

back to Wilamowitz who share this view. Vlastos is well answered by Levy 1979:285–291. As Levy argues, Vlastos's definition of love—"wishing good things for someone for that person's sake"—is neither necessary nor sufficient for love. Only, though, if one gets the relation between beauty and good right, can the charge of egocentrism in the pursuit of the beloved be dismissed. Cf. Warner 1979 for a different sort of response based on a defense of the claim that qualities not persons are the objects of love. Mahoney 1996 argues that love is egoistic at the "lower levels" but non-egoistic at the "highest level." This seems to me to presuppose a false dichotomy if in fact everyone desires the good for themselves. Allen 1991:95–98, brings out very clearly the specious contrast of ἔρως and ἀγάπη used to fuel the dichotomy egoistic/selfless love. Indeed, this interpretation also rests heavily on the mistaken idea that the ἔργον of love is its purpose such that one reproduces in order to get something for oneself, in this case quasi-immortality.

[41] Nussbaum 1986:176–184, thinks the gradations in the ascent can be preserved despite univocity if the grades are grades of increasing quantity. But on this view, the "vast sea of beauty" should be "higher" in the scale than the Form of beauty, though in fact it is not

[42] Cf. Tolstoy's remark in *What is Art?* "What a strange illusion it is to suppose that beauty is goodness."

[43] *Enneads*, 6.7 [38] 30, 29–39 alluding to *Philebus* 64e5–65a5. Cf. *Republic* VI 517c2–3 and *Phaedrus* 250e which stresses the easy accessibility of beauty to our senses. At 1.6 [1] 9, Plotinus explains in one sense the intelligible world is primarily beautiful, in which case, the good has beauty προβεβλημένον ... πρὸ αὐτῆς. In another sense, the good is itself the "primal beauty" because it is virtually what the intelligible world is. Cf. Murdoch 1970:41–2, 59–60, 92-5, who expresses a similar view.

[44] Cf. White 1989:152–157 for a criticism of the view that (a) love is of the beautiful and (b) the beautiful is identical with the good. White, though, 155–156, misinterprets *Philebus* as maintaining the identity of the beautiful and the good. Since White thinks that *Symposium* denies this, he rejects the relevance of the *Philebus* passage here. But see n19 for a concession that "good" and "beautiful" may be "co-extensive."

are inseparable as Plotinus holds and as Plotinus believes Plato holds, then a devotion to real good entails a devotion to real beauty and to the psychological inevitability of the ascent beyond images, individual or otherwise.[45]

More than psychological inevitability, there is ontological necessity. For sensible images of beauty, though they be real cases of beauty, are not really real.[46] Moreover, though souls are more beautiful or higher up in the scale than are bodies, they are themselves images and inferior to the model. In fact, (a) "beautiful" is, on Platonic metaphysics, univocally predicable of all that it is predicable, and (b) the inferiority of beautiful bodies is owing to the bodily, while souls are not inferior in this way. The possibility of understanding the inferiority of the beauty of souls over against the model depends upon there being some additional criterion for ranking beauties. I mean some criterion other than intelligible vs. sensible.[47] *Timaeus* gives us just such a criterion, since there soul is composed of a mixture of indivisible and divisible *ousia*.[48] Without adducing *Republic*, the inferiority of bodily beauty to psychic beauty is unexplained; without adducing *Timaeus*, the complex superiority/inferiority of psychic beauty is not explained either.

It is common for the relation between beauty and good in Diotima's speech to be understood as follows. When Diotima 'shifts' (μεταβαλών, 204e) from asking "what will one have when one has the beautiful" to "what will one have when one has the good," she is generalizing, treating "beautiful" as but one example of "good."[49] So, on this view, what one really desires is the good, which one supposes is achieved by "possession" of the beautiful.[50] Apart

---

[45] See *Republic* VI 505d5–9; *Enneads* 5.5 [32] 12, 19–25.

[46] Cf. *Republic* V 479e7–480a13. Rosen 1968:270, maintains that "Diotima's description of beauty does not presuppose the theory of Ideas." Yet, the diminished reality of the sensible world and its description as that which is "not really real" is a direct inference from the separation of the really real, that is, of the Ideas.

[47] Price 1989:40, puzzlingly, claims that the recognition that beauty is beauty wherever it is found (210c4–5) "confirms a reduced valuation of, and commitment to, an inferior object, whether individual physical beauty (b5–6), physical beauty in general (c5–6), or any individual beauty (d1–3)."

[48] See *Timaeus* 35a with 41d–e. Plotinus generally treats the myth of the birth of ἔρως as an allegory of the creation of a property of soul; hence, Πόρος and Πενία stand for indivisible οὐσία and divisible οὐσία respectively. See especially 3.5 [50] 5–9. Cf. 3.6 [26] 14, 10–12.

[49] See e.g. Gould 1963:46: "The beautiful is but a special, electrifying example of the good that which, when possessed, will make us happy." By contrast, Bloom (Benardete 1993:134–135), apparently completely unfettered by textual scruples, goes from "Diotima insists on a distinction between beautiful and good" to this distinction indicating "the conflict between the aesthetic and utilitarian ways of life." As it turns out, though (151), Diotima is really confused about the relation between beauty and good, unlike Socrates in *Republic*.

[50] Cf. *Meno* 78b5; *Gorgias* 468a7–8. See Price 1989:16. who thinks that "beauty" and "good" are interchangeable, though not synonymous. But Price goes on to analyze their connection in a way

from the obvious objection that the beautiful would seem to be an instance of beauty itself, not of the good, there is the more profound objection that treating the beautiful as an instance of the good makes utterly obscure the motive for affirming a hierarchy of beauty, of love, and of the products of love. No one instance or beautiful example of good is more of an example than another. Perhaps it will be replied that the beautiful is not here being considered as an example of the good, but as a means to it or an instrument of it. But if we take the beautiful as a putative means to the good, like money or power or the way that Epicurus takes the beautiful as a possible means to the good conceived of as pleasure, and say that just as one desires the latter because they are thought to be a means to the good or happiness, so that is why one desires to possess beautiful things, it still remains obscure why this should produce a hierarchy; why, for example, true virtue should result from loving and possessing beauty itself but not from loving and possessing beautiful bodies or even other beautiful souls.[51]

There are three principal requirements for keeping beauty and good united within a framework that allows for hierarchical ascent. One requirement is that real immortality is an implicit part of the story.[52] Without this, not only is there no way to privilege one type of lover over another, there is no way (or almost no way) to distinguish the real and the apparent or the "higher" and the "lower" good. For instance, on what basis could one argue that the ἔργον of a love that produces human babies is inferior to the ἔργον of a love that produces epic poetry?[53] There must be a standard against which

---

that makes hierarchy unintelligible. He takes the ascent as one of increasing generalization rather than gradation in being. Cf. 38–42.

[51] That the beautiful and the good are habitually related by Plato is clear from *Lysis* 216d2: λέγω γὰρ τἀγαθὸν καλὸν εἶναι; *Protagoras* 360b3: εἰ καλά, καὶ ἀγαθά; *Hippias Major* 297b2–3: εἰ ἄρα τὸ καλόν ἐστιν αἴτιον ἀγαθοῦ, γίγνοιτ᾽ ἂν ὑπὸ τοῦ καλοῦ τὸ ἀγαθόν. In none of these passages, however, is hierarchy implied. Cf. *Alcibiades* I 115a–116e, where Socrates tries to persuade Alcibiades that something καλόν, since it is good, could not also be bad. Even if we endorse Socrates' argument, there are no grounds here for hierarchy. Indeed, since the argument maintains that something is good *just insofar* as it is καλόν (see 116a–b), hierarchy would seem to be precluded.

[52] Ferrari 1992:253 and n14, recognizes that the hierarchy is not explained in *Symposium*. Ferrari thinks, though, that the tripartite soul of *Republic* provides the relevant basis for the hierarchy.

[53] Cornford 1971:127, for example, sees nothing problematic in saying that one type of beauty is "above" another. When at *Symposium* 206c3–4 Diotima says: τίκτειν ἐπιθυμεῖ ἡμῶν ἡ φύσις these words do not indicate an alternative to the good that all desire. It is *because* humans desire the good that they desire to reproduce. So, the effect of the primary desire is a secondary desire, secondary only in the sense that it is the desire of the composite human not the desire of the real person. Cf. Dover 1980:146–147, who remarks that "since on most occasions people have sexual intercourse for its own sake and not as a means to procreation ... the argument

such judgments can be made. And, granted that everyone desires the real good and immortality, without *real* immortality, one's *own* evaluation always trumps an objective standard.[54] I mean that one has to be shown that, given that one thing is really good and another only an image or illusion of good, one has no rational option but to aim for the former.

There is apparently one textually based reason for resisting this approach. This is that the ultimate vision revealed in the higher mysteries is of the Form of beauty itself, not of the entire intelligible realm, taken by Plotinus as an aspect of the Idea of the good.[55] Beauty is in this passage characterized as 'uniform' (μονοειδές) and 'itself by itself with itself' (αυτὸ καθ᾽ αὐτὸ μεθ᾽ αὑτοῦ), 'simple' (εἰλικρινές), 'pure' (καθαρόν), and 'unmixed' (ἄμεικτον). How can these be referenced to the entire realm of intelligible reality as opposed to just the Form of beauty? Well, for one thing, if the ultimate vision is of a single Form of beauty, then why is it that the *ergon* of *this* vision is birth in true virtue? We might just as easily suppose that the vision of a Form of a virtue or of a Form of virtue itself would produce such a birth. It would seem that on this interpretation, good drops out of the picture. The previous conflation of beauty and good is ignored. For another thing, if the ultimate vision is of the Form of beauty, then the penultimate vision of "the sea of beauty," can hardly be a vision of *other* Forms. For the product of this vision is "many and beautiful *logoi* and 'thoughts' (διανοήματα)" (210d4–5), whereas the product of the vision of beauty is true virtue. It does not make sense that the vision of one class of Forms (including, presumably, Forms of the virtues) produces *logoi* whereas the vision of beauty produces virtue.[56]

If, however, the penultimate vision is not of Forms but of multiple propositional truths about all intelligible reality, then it is even more unlikely that

---

requires the assumption that humans, like animals, are impelled by forces of which they are not aware."

[54] At 210b7, the beauty of souls is said to be more 'honorable' (τιμιώτερον) than the beauty of bodies. Though one might build an objective standard on "honorable," how exactly within the context of *Symposium* alone is this to be done? See Gerson 1997:1–11. Cf. *Crito* 47e6–48a3; *Gorgias* 512a5; *Protagoras* 313a6; *Republic* III 415a9; *Laws* V 727d8 on the superiority of soul to body. But in all these passages, the superiority is owing to the fact that soul identifies us more than body, which is essentially a possession. This could not be the reason for gradation throughout the ascent.

[55] Ibid., 1.6 [1] 9, 35–36: τὸ κάλλος τοῦτο εἶναι, τὰς ἰδέας. Cf. 5.8 [31] 9, 40–42: Διὸ καὶ τὸ εἶναι ποθεινόν ἐστιν, ὅτι ταὐτὸν τῷ καλῷ, καὶ τὸ καλὸν ἐράσμιον, ὅτι τὸ εἶναι. Πότερον δὲ ποτέρου αἴτιον τί χρὴ ζητεῖν οὔσης τῆς φύσεως μιᾶς.

[56] Dancy 2004:287–290, confuses the ultimate stage of the ascent with the penultimate stage. He identifies the ultimate state with the vision of the "sea of beauty" and claims that the product of this vision is additional λόγος rather than true virtue.

the ultimate vision is of just a Form of beauty. For in this case, the hierarchy would make no sense. Assume that beauty is a distinct *ousia*. Then, seeing the beauty in true *logoi* is no different from seeing the beauty in 'laws' (νόμοι) or in 'practices' (ἐπιτηδεύματα) or, indeed, in beautiful bodies. In addition, if happiness is the result of the possession of the good, and the possession of the good is just the possession of beauty, it is not at all clear why *this* Form as opposed to any other is supposed to render one happy. It is more plausible that "possession" of a Form is the knowledge of it, and, if happiness is supposed to result from this possession, it is with the knowledge of *all* the Forms that it arises.[57]

The penultimate vision in fact seems to correspond to the bottom section of the top half of the divided line in *Republic*.[58] This mode of cognition, namely, 'discursive reasoning' (διάνοια) is a type of 'understanding' (νόησις) as *Republic* later adds, and is inferior to the mode of cognition that is most properly called 'knowledge' (ἐπιστήμη).[59] The one who cognizes the "sea of beauty" is, in fact, on any reading of the text, gazing upon kinds of science, not just the beauty of each. It is the content of each that is expressed in the beautiful *logoi*. Thus, the ultimate vision would seem to correspond to the top section of the top half of the divided line where cognition is of the Forms in the light of the first principle of all, the Idea of the good.[60]

By contrast with this approach, Plotinus maintains that the Idea of the good is virtually all the Forms analogous to the same way that white light is virtually all the colors of the spectrum. Beauty is, as *Philebus* suggests, an aspect of the good, namely, the good as attractive to us. That is, if the good were not attractive, we would not seek it. But goodness is more than attractiveness.[61]

---

[57] Cf. *Republic* VI 490a8–b7 where the achievement of the ἔρως of the philosopher is a vision of all the Forms and a "birth" in understanding and truth. Allen 1991:80, thinks that the hierarchy is based on grades of universality, though there is nothing in the text to indicate this. At the same time, his correct observation that the beauty of souls is not the same thing as the beauty of bodies undercuts his argument for a single Form of beauty.

[58] See *Republic* VI 510d–511a. So Moravcsik 1971:295; Sier 1997:151–153.

[59] See *Republic* VII 533e7–534a8. This corrects what he says at 511d–e where he seems to identify understanding with knowledge alone.

[60] *Republic* VI 511b2–c1. The *Symposium* passage describing the ultimate stage of ascent (210d7–e1): κατίδῃ τινὰ ἐπιστήμην μίαν τοιαύτην, ἥ ἐστι καλοῦ τοιοῦδε, should be compared with *Phaedrus* (247e1–2): τὴν ἐν τῷ ὅ ἐστιν ὂν ὄντως ἐπιστήμην οὖσαν. The latter passage explicitly goes on to take this knowledge as being of *all* the Forms. The words in *Symposium* (212a3): ὁρῶντι ᾧ ὁρατὸν τὸ καλόν, are usually taken to refer to intellect as that by which the beautiful is seen. But it is not clear why this is not a reference to the Idea of the good, as in *Republic* VI 509b5, where the Idea is that owing to which that which is knowable is knowable.

[61] Plotinus, *Enneads* 6.7 [38] 22, 5–7: Ἔστι γὰρ ἕκαστον ὅ ἐστιν ἐφ᾽ αὑτοῦ· ἐφετὸν δὲ γίνεται ἐπιχρώσαντος αὐτὸ τοῦ ἀγαθοῦ, ὥσπερ χάριτας δόντος αὐτοῖς καὶ εἰς τὰ ἐφιέμενα ἔρωτας. So, we can cognize form, and hence beauty, without being attracted to it or without desiring

And what is maximally attractive to us as rational creatures is knowledge of all that is knowable. So, the reason why true virtue results from possession of beauty—possession of the good in the only way possible for us—is that we are with this possession imbued with the knowledge that is virtue. The ultimate vision of the ascent then refers to *all* the Forms distributively, that is, each and every Form, understood in the light of the first principle of all.[62]

A second requirement for keeping beauty and good united within a hierarchy is that the love that is for the beautiful is identical with the desire that is for the good. The latter, though, is achieved by a cognitive experience, a vision of intelligible reality. It is one thing to make the general point that when you think you desire x, you really desire y, if x is a counterfeit of y. But is it plausible to apply this general principle to the present case and say that when you think you desire heterosexual or homosexual intercourse, what you *really* desire is knowledge of Platonic Forms? Of course, it will not do to reply that the latter desire is a substitute (in the Freudian sense) for the former. If anything, it is the other way around. How can we make sense of the implicit claim that there is only one real desire and that the desire is for the knowledge of the good?

In some way or another, it must be shown that the subject of the desire for the putative counterfeit x is not the real subject. This is, not surprisingly, exactly how Plotinus understands the claim.[63] My main point, however, is not that Plotinus has interpreted Plato correctly, but that Plato himself in numerous places identifies the "real person" with the ideal knower. He does this with sufficient clarity and frequency that there is no reason to hesitate to call this doctrine a central tenet of Platonism.[64] But he does not say this in

---

it. With the recognition of form as an expression of the good, we have, once again, the basis for hierarchy. The "goodlikeness" of intelligible form is easier to discern than the "goodlikeness" of bodily form because the latter is occluded by body. If we agree that beauty is form, we certainly would need to say that we can recognize form or beauty without being attracted to it or loving it.

[62] Cf. *Republic* VII 517b7–c4 where the Idea of the good is said to be αἰτία πάντων ὀρθῶν τε καὶ καλῶν in τὸν νοητόν τόπον. Also, *Timaeus* 28a8–b2 where the demiurge produces that which is καλόν *because* he is using as a model intelligible reality; 30d2. Cf. Price 1989:43, "In effect the Form of beauty constitutes the world of Forms qua objects of love." I would say: "not just in effect."

[63] See especially *Enneads* 6.9 [9] 9, 22: Καὶ ἐκεῖ [in the intelligible world] γενομένη γίγνεται αὐτὴ [the soul, that is, real person] καὶ ὅπερ ἦν. In this chapter, Plotinus is interpreting the underlying doctrine of both *Symposium* and *Phaedrus*.

[64] It is also a central tenet of Aristotle, a fact which ought to mitigate the criticism that Plotinus is "reading his own views" into Plato. See *Nicomachean Ethics* 10.7.1177b30–1178a8. See also the line here referred to, namely, 9.8.1169a2: ὅτι μὲν οὖν τοῦθ' [intellect] ἕκαστός ἐστιν ἢ μάλιστα, οὐκ ἄδηλον ... Also, 9.4.1166a22–23; 9.8.1168b31–33. See Gerson 2004:217–248.

Symposium. One *could*, I suppose, say that Plato, when he wrote *Symposium*, had not yet figured out this part of the picture. In that case, we must prepared to say that when Plato wrote *Symposium*, though he had a view about hierarchy and its metaphysical analysis, he really had no clue how to fit the human soul into this picture. He grasped the difference between real virtue and its images, but he did not realize that subjects engaged in practicing the former were not identical with subjects engaged in practicing the latter. This is, of course, a possibility. But it would require, in addition, that we athetize *Alcibiades* I, or at least that part where Socrates clearly distinguishes between the soul and the body, and identifies the "real self" with the former.[65] We would also need to "deal with" *Gorgias* and its affirmation of personal immortality (albeit in a myth). At some point, though, one begins to lose enthusiasm for these hermeneutical epicycles. Why not simply admit that there is a philosophy called "Platonism" and that bringing it to bear on the interpretation of any dialogue enables us to resolve interpretive problems better than any other approach?

Finally, a last requirement for keeping beauty and good together within a hierarchical ascent is the manner in which we conceive of the *ergon* of the desire for the good. Treating the birth in beauty as an instrument for satisfying the desire for immortality is psychologically lame, to say the least.[66] But this seems inevitable if the desire for immortality is merely the desire for quasi-immortality. On this view, the *ergon* turns out to be the steps taken to achieve this quasi-immortality, rather than the natural *result* of the achievement of the desire for the good which is identical with the natural result of the love of the beautiful. The work of love turns out to be a peculiarity of certain people, not the necessary property of love that it is evidently supposed to be.[67] Either people really want the good itself, in which case the psychological explanation for birth in beauty is rendered null and void or else they really want, say, physical or spiritual offspring, in which case beauty and good are, once again, pried apart. The latter alternative could only appeal to one who supposes that *Symposium* can be understood on its own. The former alternative holds that in talking about the work of love, Diotima is making a metaphysical point, one which draws beauty, good, and *erōs* even closer together. The achievement of the good, that is, the knowledge of intelligible reality, necessarily results in

---

[65] See *Alcibiades* I 129b1–131a1.

[66] So Rowe 1998b:253. Rowe, though, thinks that despite the implausibility of the claim, it would appeal to the *Symposium*'s interlocutors—Phaedrus, Pausanias, and the rest. And that is why it should be taken ironically.

[67] Cf. *Republic* I 353a9–11: Νῦν δὴ οἶμαι ἄμεινον ἂν μάθοις ὃ ἄρτι ἠρώτων, πυνθανόμενος εἰ οὐ τοῦτο ἑκάστου εἴη ἔργον ὃ ἂν ἢ μόνον τι ἢ κάλλιστα τῶν ἄλλων ἀπεργάζηται.

the birth of true virtue because that knowledge is extensionally equivalent to true virtue.[68]

All three of the above requirements can be met if we adduce material from the other dialogues, as does Plotinus. If we do not seek out help from other dialogues, the association of beauty and good appears to be arbitrary and perhaps even absurdly false. What is sometimes called "the principle of charity" in the interpretation of the works of philosophers seems to suggest that we opt for the former approach.

Here is an additional consideration on behalf of this interpretation. At the beginning of *Republic* II, Glaucon, no doubt expressing a common Greek notion, says that there are three kinds of good. There is (a) a good that we desire for itself; (b) a good that we desire not in itself but only for its consequences and (c) a good that we desire both for itself and for its consequences. Socrates, of course, wants to argue that justice belongs to the third kind. If we suppose that the good desired in *Symposium* is, too, of the third kind, we can make sense of the idea that its achievement produces true virtue as a consequence. If, on the other hand, we take the products of love—the births that occur in beauty—as a means to achieving some good, namely, quasi-immortality, we deprive ourselves of an explanation for the love of offspring except as a means and of an explanation for the hierarchy of products.

Here we have finally an answer to the question regarding Plotinus' extraordinary claim that the Idea of the good has *erōs* of itself. This claim is, in effect, an abductive inference from the claim that goodness is essentially self-diffusive. And the proof that goodness is essentially self-diffusive relies upon the self-evident multiplicity of intelligible forms in the universe. That the knowledge of intelligible reality necessarily produces true virtue is one expression of the necessary production of intelligible form from the good.[69] The good must love itself if in the achievement of its desire it necessarily produces.

Meeting the above three requirements for uniting beauty and the good actually enables us to understand why the pederast embraces his "sulphurous

---

[68] Cf. *Enneads* 5.4 [7] 2, 26–28 where Plotinus introduces the principle that generation is a product of the perfection of an activity. Contra White 1989:154 who argues that "birth in beauty" is the "means" to the only sort of immortality available to mortals. On White's view, the production of true virtue is presumably another "means."

[69] The prior expression is the demiurge's production of order in the universe, *Timaeus* 29e. Because the demiurge is good, he is without φθόνος. "Being ungrudging" is a negative way of characterizing the ἔργον of love. But even in the case of the demiurge, the production is a *result* of the good that he possesses, not a constituent of it.

breviary" without delusion while at the same time meeting them enables us to understand the inadequacies of an interpretation based on that embrace. Plato, understood Platonically, has given us a way not just to acknowledge the manifest diversity of desire but to order that diversity hierarchically. One is of course free to reject the hierarchy, or even to reject its presence in the dialogue, but not I think without abandoning hope for its coherent interpretation.

Part Two

INTERPRETING PLATO'S *SYMPOSIUM*

Four

Medicine, Magic, and Religion in Plato's *Symposium*

Mark L. McPherran

IF YOU [ERYXIMACHUS] SHOW ME that you know me better than I do myself, and can foresee even my next mood, ... must I not conclude that my whole effort is puerile, that my intimate tactics vanish in the face of your entirely exterior art, which envelops my body and soul at once in a network of particular points of knowledge woven together, thereby capturing at a single stroke the universe of my person?

Socrates to Eryximachus in Paul Valéry's "Socrates and His Physician"

Plato's attention to the craft of medicine, conceived of as a paradigmatic instance of expert knowledge that lesser fields should imitate, is evident throughout his work.[1] Thus, it is natural to suppose that at least one of Plato's purposes in employing the character of the physician Eryximachus in the *Symposium* is to convey the import of his own understanding of medicine insofar as it bears on the central topic of that dialogue: *Erōs*.[2] However, this natural interpretive expectation runs up against many initial impressions and scholarly accounts of Eryximachus' role in the dialogue, which take him to be a bombastic dogmatist who serves primarily as a target of Platonic satire.

---

[1] Poulakos 1998:165; Jouanna 1998:68–69; e.g. *Gorgias* 464b–467c; *Phaedrus* 268a–270d; *Republic* 403d–410b; *Statesman* 292d–300a; *Timaeus* 64a–92c; *Laws* 889b–e. This is made particularly evident by his appeals to the analogy of soul to body, of psychic health to somatic health (e.g. *Crito* 47a–48b; *Gorgias* 463e–465d; *Phaedrus* 270a–e; *Sophist* 223e, 226e–230e) and the micro-cosmic and macro-cosmic conception of human nature found in the *Timaeus*—a conception that parallels the similar one found in the Hippocratic work *On Regimen* (Jouanna 1998:70). Indeed, some take the frequency and force of the analogy to contribute to the view that—among other things—Socrates and Plato were the inventors of "scientific verbal psychotherapy," beside whom "Gorgias and Antiphon are mere prehistory" (Entralgo 1970:137; cf. 126).

[2] In other papers of this volume, the god Eros is distinguished from *erōs*, but I deliberately preserve the ambiguity here.

Since both he and his speech are offered up as a mere caricature of the self-important physician, goes this line of thought, we need not take his speech as anything much more than a comic interlude between the self-serving oration of Pausanias on behalf of homoerotic *Erōs* and the magnificent, darkly comic speech of Aristophanes that serves to put the dialogue on the true track of *Erōs*.[3]

A corrective to this dismissive view has been available for many years, however, in the form of an impressive article on Eryximachus by the esteemed scholar of ancient medicine, Ludwig Edelstein (1945). There Edelstein makes a convincing case for the view that Eryximachus' speech "is not a caricature but rather an historically correct picture of a medical man of that time. It cannot have been Plato's intention to deride Eryximachus as a pedant, a system-monger, unduly fond of medicine" (Edelstein 1945:91).

More than this, however, Edelstein draws our attention to the fact that Eryximachus is one of the most prominent and influential speakers at the banquet, with "an important place in the economy of the dialogue" (Rowe 1998a:147). For example, Eryximachus assumes the position of *symposiarch* at the outset of the dialogue—insisting that tradition be followed with the speeches proceeding around the room from left to right—and then establishes the foundation for the whole contest of speeches with his warning against heavy drinking (176a–e).[4] Next, it is he who dismisses the distracting flute girl as soon as she appears—perhaps hoping to ensure that all the *Erōs* that follows will be entirely theoretical[5]—and it is he who sets the dialogue's agenda by proposing an evening of conversation (176e–177a). Finally, the very topic of that conversation is introduced by Eryximachus in the guise of fulfilling Phaedrus' perennial complaint that while everything from Heracles to salt has been the subject of encomia, the venerable and supremely important god *Erōs* has been neglected. Finally, in the end, it is Eryximachus who saves the conversation from complete alcoholic collapse by proposing that Alcibiades offer an encomium of Socrates instead of one on *Erōs* (213e–215a).

Given, then, that Eryximachus plays a pivotal role in the *Symposium*, it is natural that we should wonder why that role is given by Plato to a physician, and why to a physician who holds the particular views on *Erōs* Plato ascribes to him. On this issue Edelstein's essay is unhelpful, since he addresses only

---

[3] See e.g. Bury 1909:xxvii–xxix; Dover 1980:105; Edelstein 1945:85; Nehamas and Woodruff 1989: xvi; and Rosen 1987:119.

[4] Phaedrus also has some claim on the title of *symposiarch* (177a–d).

[5] In conjunction with his warning against heavy drinking (176c–e). *Erōs* threatens to becomes non-theoretical yet again with the arrival of Alcibiades on the arm of a flute girl (212c–e).

the first of these questions, and only in general and unpersuasive terms. For according to Edelstein, Plato employs a physician in his dialogue in order "to emphasize the singularity of the content of this dialogue" insofar as the physician is an authority with superior wisdom who uses *rhetorical* persuasion to apply that wisdom to the healing of his patients (Edelstein 1945:102). Hence, we are to construe all the other speeches of the *Symposium* (even that of Socrates) in line with this, understanding them to be rhetorical, non-philosophical proems that cannot convey truths. For these speeches are encomia to—hence in alliance with—the nonrational psychic power of *Erōs*. And although Diotima's final revelation of the ladder of ascent indicates that *Erōs* can drive us to a vision of the Beautiful-itself (209e–212c), *Erōs* cannot by itself deliver the epistemic apprehension of the Beautiful-itself that we are thus led to desire, since such knowledge requires the philosophical dialectic conspicuously absent from our text (Edelstein 1945:101–102).[6]

Edelstein's suggestion that Eryximachus' speech looks forward to the theories of Diotima is a useful one that I shall take up as I attempt to discover the manner in which his speech is "part of a larger plan governing the sequence of discourses throughout the dialogue" (Konstan and Young-Bruehl 1982:45n1). Nevertheless, Edelstein's account makes Plato's choice to ascribe the content of Eryximachus' speech to a physician as opposed to, say, an expert rhetorician a puzzling one in view of Edelstein's overall thesis. To solve this puzzle and to address other matters, this paper offers an interpretation of the dramatic function of Eryximachus' speech in the context of the whole dialogue—one according to which it is the three threads of medicine, magic, and piety that explain Eryximachus' role and which connect that role to Diotima's. By identifying and following these threads as they pass from Eryximachus through Aristophanes to Agathon and Diotima, we can observe how Plato uses these figures to appropriate and extend the scientific and religious conventions of his own time in the service of the new, superordinate enterprise of philosophy.[7]

The Speech of Eryximachus

After making Eryximachus physician to the conversation of the *Symposium*, so to speak, Plato introduces Eryximachus in a fashion that confirms him in that role. Plato does so through the artifice of providing the chance occurrence—or

---

[6] This, I take it, is simply because Plato's focus is on *Erōs*, not dialectic *per se*, in this dialogue.
[7] See Konstan and Young-Bruehl 1982:44 on polemical intention.

is it providence?—of Aristophanes' sudden attack of the hiccups so as to place his physician's speech before that of his poet.[8] This interjection of the power of the human physical constitution over the power of custom and reason—of *nomos* and *logos*—signals the need for an account of *Erōs* from that very viewpoint.[9] Thus, to answer that need we are provided with a general representation of the Hippocratic physician of the time in the person of Eryximachus.[10] However, Eryximachus is also cast as a somewhat atypical Hippocratic. For rather than merely spelling out the medical account of *Erōs* that we more-or-less expect from him, Eryximachus claims that his practice of medicine had led him to a universalizing account of *Erōs*—one that takes in both the realm of nature and that of the gods. Moreover, it is a theory supported by such stars of Presocratic science as Heraclitus (187a–c) (and, it seems, Empedocles [with his two principles of *philia* and *neikos*] and Alcmaeon; Gosling and Taylor 1982:23; Rosen 1987:94–95). In brief, we are told that although Pausanius' division of *Erōs* into two species of human motivational force (Heavenly Love and Common Love) was a useful one, Pausanius failed to pursue that distinction to its logical conclusion—had he done so, Pausanius would have realized that the operations of *Erōs* are to be found in animals, plants, and indeed, the entire cosmos including the realm of the divine (186a–b). In view of the particular focus of Phaedrus' and Pausanius' speeches on human *Erōs*, then, it appears as though Plato has placed his physician's speech just where he does precisely in order to turn the conversation *toward* the universal, that is, toward the philosophical.

Commentators are at odds over the form and merits of the grand theory Eryximachus proceeds to develop, but something like this minimally-modified version of Christopher Rowe's (1999:56) account seems accurate.

---

[8] The narrator Apollodorus speculates that the hiccups resulted from Aristophanes' habit of stuffing himself (185c). But since Eryximachus will go on to praise divination, and since hiccups are traditionally taken to be omens (e.g. popular lore in a variety of cultures holds that hiccups are a sign that someone is remembering you; by analogy, note that in the *Odyssey* [xvii 539–547] sneezing is a sign that an earlier wish will come true; Langholf 1990:248–254), perhaps we are to take Aristophanes' sudden attack as a divinatory sign of something or other. With this initial, odd scene, then, we may be faced with the question of how to differentiate the physical from the psychological and/or divine that Eryximachus' speech will pose, as well as the notion of divination (see below).

[9] And, again, we see Eryximachus ("belch fighter") serve as a physician to the conversation though his prescription of three hiccup cures to Aristophanes, the last of which proves successful (185d–e, 189a).

[10] For our knowledge of Eryximachus, see Nails 2002:143–144. Like Hippocrates, he comes from a medical family; for our knowledge of Eryximachus' physician-father, Acumenus, see Nails 2002:1–2. Note that Eryximachus is a close friend of Phaedrus (177a–d; cf. *Protagoras* 315c). On the identity of Hippocrates and the authorship of the texts ascribed to him, see Lloyd 1975a; and Jouanna 1998:25–38.

(i) There is a double *Erōs*, i.e. good and bad, in human bodies (186b4), because

(ii) "what is healthy in a body and what is diseased in a body are by common consent different and unlike" (b5–6); but

(iii) "what is unlike desires and loves unlike things" (b6–7);[11] so

(iv) there is one kind of *Erōs* in the case of the healthy, another in the case of the diseased (b7–8).

(v) Well (*dē*), just as Pausanias said it was *kalon* to gratify (*kharidzesthai*) the good man, *aischron* to gratify the *akolastos*, so too in the case of bodies it is *kalon* to gratify the good and healthy things in a body, and *aischron* to gratify the bad and diseased (b8–c5).

(vi) The doctor must distinguish the *kalos Erōs* from the *aiskhros* one, and implant the first while removing the second (c6–d5); *for* (*gar*)

(vii) it is his job to make the most hostile things in the body friendly to each other, and love (*eran*) each other (d5–6); and

(viii) "the 'most hostile things' are the things most opposed to each other, cold to hot, bitter to sweet, dry to wet, everything like that" (d6–e1).

(ix) Medicine consists in knowing how to implant *Erōs* and *homonoia* among these opposites (e1–3).

On this account, the "things" having either good or bad *Erōs* in (v) (and so by implication in [i], [ii], [iv], and [vi]) are the somatic opposites such as the hot and the cold, whose possession then allows us to speak of each body as having these two loves. When such opposites have good love towards one another the body possessing them is healthy and in a state of *homonoia* (162e2, 187c4), but when one or both of such a pairing become greedy for an excessive amount of their opposite, then the possessing body is in an unhealthy state (cf. 188b4).[12] We may say that healthy bodies have *Erōs*/desire for what is good for them, and sick ones have *Erōs*/desire for what is bad. This theory arguably employs a single and coherent sense of one *Erōs* (188d5) differentiated into two modes: moderating, harmonizing, Heavenly *Erōs*; and pleonexic, disharmonizing Common *Erōs*.[13] When this theory is extended to the cosmos as a

---

[11] Meaning, presumably (in view of claim [ii]), that the two unlike qualities (namely, the healthy and the diseased) each desire unlike things; that is, the things desired by what is healthy and the things desired by what is diseased are unlike each other.

[12] Rowe 1999:56–58 has the opposites loving more of *themselves* when they are healthy, which seems at odds with the text.

[13] Rosen 1987:98–101; *pace* Dover 1980:105, and Konstan and Young-Bruehl 1982:40, the latter holding that Eryximachus is working with two kinds of love: *epithumia* (desire) and *philia* (concord).

whole, natural disasters and epidemics are then understood to be caused by a lack of local harmony, of Heavenly *Erōs*. In any event, the general and systematic structure of Eryximachus' exposition testifies to a degree of "intellectual rigor ... that is incompatible with sheer parody" (Konstan and Young-Bruehl 1982:44).[14] Again, we are also no doubt supposed to see Eryximachus as practicing what he preaches—serving as physician to the conversation—insofar as he attempts in his capacity as informal *symposiarch* to keep all the speeches of the *Symposium* in order by attempting to maintain *homonoia* (e.g. with his warning against heavy drinking [176b–e] and his hiccup cures [185d–e]) and by injecting *kalos Erōs*—a desire to make beautiful speeches concerning something good (viz. *kalos Erōs*)—throughout the dialogue.

Eryximachus exhibits a good familiarity with Hippocratic medicine in the course of his speech. His definition of medicine as involving repletion (*plēsmonē*) and emptying (*kenōsis*) (186c–d), for example, has parallels in *Breaths* 1, *On the Nature of Man* 2–4, 9, *Regimen* 1.2, and *Tradition in Medicine* 16, and he shares with the author of the Hippocratic treatise *On Regimen* a sympathy for Heraclitean thought (*Symposium* 187a–b; *Regimen* 1.5, 1.11; esp. the idea that opposites attract and are in agreement [*Regimen* 1.11, 1.21]), and the notion that musical high and low notes provide an analogy relevant to the harmony of the body (*Symposium* 187b–d; *Regimen* 1.8) (Hunter 2004:55–56; Gosling and Taylor 1982:24). Eryximachus' association of the legendary patron of Hippocratic medicine, Asclepius, with his own account of medicine as being essentially a matter of reconciling opposites (186d–e) is also accepted testimony for the Hippocratic tradition (Edelstein and Edelstein 1945:182). Even Eryximachus' account of the operations of *Erōs* in human beings in terms of somatic forces finds a loose parallel in the way *Airs, Waters, Places* 22 accounts for the impotence—the damaged *Erōs*—of certain Scythians. Hence, had Eryximachus at this point merely gone on to elaborate his theory of love-medicine in respect of the human body he would have escaped much of the abuse heaped on him by generations of scholars. Instead, Plato has his doctor spend the bulk of his speech extemporizing on the extended application of his theory to poetry, music, meteorology, climatology, astronomy, and even theology—specifically, sacrificial practice, divination, and piety in general.[15] We are no doubt supposed to read all this as a parodic example of high-flying

---

[14] *Pace* Dover 1980:105, Nehamas and Woodruff 1989:xvi. However, Rowe 1999:54 thinks Konstan and Young-Bruehl "over-estimate the 'philosophical significance' of the speech," although it is "distinctly clever."

[15] Edelstein 1945:87 observes that Eryximachus' "analysis of medicine (186b–e) is shorter than his analysis of music."

medical rhetoric,[16] but at the same time we should appreciate the extent to which Eryximachus is himself merely entering into the general light-hearted sympotic spirit of things by speaking as bombastically as he does. Moreover, Hippocratic physicians at the time did take a self-conscious interest in such things as music, meteorology, and astronomy. For example, we are told that a competent physician should know what epidemics to expect on the basis of his understanding of the progress of the seasons, and this is in turn dependent on his knowledge of the rising and setting of the stars (*Airs, Waters, Places* 2; *Aphorisms* 3.2; cf. Plato *Epinomis* 976a). Finally, we have reason to suppose that Plato is knowledgeable about, sympathetic to, and even draws lessons from both Asclepian and Hippocratic medicine, so far as they go (*Philebus* 31a–33c, 44b–48b; *Phaedrus* 270a–e; *Republic* 405a–410a; *Timaeus* 81e–86b; Staden 1998; Gosling and Taylor 1982:24).[17] It is particularly important to note that Plato agrees with the Hippocratic author of *On the Sacred Disease* that epilepsy is to be explained by a physical, not a religious, account of the way that the brain is affected by phlegm (*Timaeus* 85a–b).[18] Moreover, like Eryximachus (176b–d, 187e), Plato endorses the view that we should drink wine in moderation (*Republic* 389e–390b, 403e, 571b–d, 573c), that the problem of sexual profligacy has a somatic causal explanation (*Republic* 572d–580a; *Timaeus* 86d; namely, excess moisture), and that the *Erōs* from which it springs comes paired with a noble form of *Erōs* (*Phaedrus* 253c–257a).[19]

On the other hand, Eryximachus is also clearly portrayed as an iconoclast among his fellow Hippocratics—men who would distance themselves from his effusive endorsement of sacrifice and the mantic art (*Regimen in Acute Diseases*

[16] Eryximachus' speech can be read as an parodic example of a medical *epideixis* common to the period; see e.g. Hunter 2004:53–54; and Jouanna 1998. Plato has no patience with medicine's overblown claims; *Republic* 403d–410b.

[17] On this score, it is worth noting that Plato has Socrates praise the beauty—hence, the correctness, it seems—of Eryximachus' speech at 194a. I am grateful to Mitchell Miller for pointing out Plato's use of the Hippocratic notions of repletion and emptying in the *Philebus*, and to Eric Brown for emphasizing Plato's reliance on the "method of Hippocrates" at *Phaedrus* 270a–278b; namely, that one must know the nature of the whole in order to know the soul.

[18] Plato even goes so far as to implicitly deny the popular view that epilepsy is caused by a divinity when he explains that its name 'the sacred disease' (τῆς ἱερῆς νούσου) is justly applied insofar as the disease attacks the most sacred part of us (our head) (85b). Plato also agrees with the author of *On the Sacred Disease* that divinities are not the personal causes of illness—especially those supposedly manifesting *miasma*—when he argues in the *Republic* that gods are never the causes of anything evil (376d–380c); Edelstein 1937:220. The gods are, however, responsible for certain kinds of beneficial madness, such as mantic possession (*Phaedrus* 244a–257a).

[19] Indeed, the later abrupt descent from the heights of Diotima's ladder of spiritual *Erōs* into the physical, drunken *Erōs* of Alcibiades (212c–223d) is an elliptical warning in sympathy with Eryximachus' Puritanism.

8; *Airs, Waters, Places* 22; *On Dreams* 87 [i.e. *Regimen* 4.87]; cf. *On the Sacred Disease* 1–4, 21).[20] In the case of the latter *technē*, Eryximachus even elides the distinction between prognostication and divination insisted on by the Hippocratic authors, allocating the former expertise to themselves alone, while minimizing the practice of divination and the authority of the *manteis* (Langholf 1990:246). Eryximachus would also be opposed in his grand theorizing—his philosophizing—by those many Hippocratics intent on freeing medicine from its roots in philosophy. These physicians were party to a "crisis" in medicine contemporary with the dramatic and compositional dates of the *Symposium*.[21]

Those physicians who advocated philosophical medicine maintained that medical knowledge requires a prior understanding of human nature and the elements composing it—one derived from a study of the cosmos as undertaken by natural scientists such as Anaximenes, Diogenes of Apollonia, Melissus, and Heraclitus.[22] Allying themselves with the theories and methods of natural science, these physicians were able to oppose those healers who engaged primarily in forms of magical rites and temple medicine (Lloyd 1975b:9). Thinkers who rejected this philosophical approach argued for medicine's independence from both philosophy and shamanistic healing on the grounds that prior training in scientific medicine is required to formulate an accurate account of human nature (Jouanna 1998:50–53). The author of *Tradition in Medicine*, for example, claims that

> There are some doctors and sophists who maintain that no one can understand the science of medicine unless he knows what man is; that anyone who proposes to treat men for their illnesses must first learn of such things. Their discourse then tends to philosophy, as may be seen in the writings of Empedocles and all the others who have ever written about Nature ... It is my opinion that all which has

---

[20] Plato's choice of Eryximachus—rather than some other physician (historical or not)—seems particularly designed to raise the issue of medicine's relationship to piety and popular religion, since Eryximachus, his father, and his friend Phaedrus, were all "implicated in the accusations and counter-accusations of sacrilege that preceded the Athenian invasion of Sicily in 415," Nails 2002:2. For as Halperin 2005:56 perceptively notes, "It would have been impossible for a contemporary Greek to read the *Symposium* unironically ... Readers of the *Symposium* ... [possess] a tragic knowledge [of the characters' histories] that is denied the characters at the moment of their speaking."

[21] The dramatic date of the main conversation of the *Symposium* is 416 BCE, "not long before the disastrous Athenian expedition to Sicily, in which Alcibiades played a leading part," while the date of its composition is usually placed in the second half of the 380s (Rowe 1998a:10–11).

[22] For a late example (later than 300 BCE) of such as physician, see the author of the *Decorum*, who holds that "a physician who is a philosopher is the equal of a god" (*Decorum* 5.4).

been written by doctors or sophists on Nature has more to do with painting than medicine. I do not believe that any clear knowledge of Nature can be obtained *from any source other than a study of medicine* and then only through a thorough mastery of this science.

Tradition in Medicine 20.1–14, Chadwick and Mann trans., my emphasis[23]

Given his grand theorizing and his citation of Heraclitus, Eryximachus seems very much the kind of physician targeted by this Hippocratic author. That, in turn, suggests that at least part of the role Plato has assigned to Eryximachus is for him to respond one-Hippocratic-physician-to-all-others to just this sort of view of the relationship between medicine and philosophy held by some Hippocratic physicians. This reading is supported by our natural expectation that Plato would have mounted such a reply at some point in his works because of his respect for medicine as a model *technē* and because "the fundamental methodological problem" of the time for physicians concerned their relationship with philosophy (Jouanna 1998:50). This interpretation also very much fits with Plato's constant advocacy of the idea that a proper physician must be a philosopher, since good medical treatment requires an understanding and treatment of the whole patient, and thus his or her soul, something that requires training in philosophy (e.g. *Republic* 408d–e, 591c; *Charmides* 155b–158c). Indeed, we are told that "if we are to listen to Hippocrates, Asclepius' descendent, we will not understand the body" if we do not attempt to understand the body from the perspective of the world as a whole (*Phaedrus* 270c3–5). Finally, since Plato and his Socrates approve of divination rightly conceived,[24] and Plato appears to link divination to medicine

---

[23] Cf. *On the Nature of Man* 1, *On Nature* 1.

[24] E.g. *Apology* 20e–24a; *Ion* 531b, 538e–539e; *Phaedrus* 244a–e; *Timaeus* 71e–72d; *Republic* 427a–c; cf. *Republic* 461e, 540b–c; McPherran 1996:chap. 4. Plato and his Socrates also accept the ancient view that god-given dreams can offer glimpses of the future (e.g. *Crito* 43c–44b, *Phaedo* 60c–61b). And although Plato vigorously rejects the idea that gods can be magically influenced (*Republic* 363e–367a; cf. *Laws* 885b–e, 888a–d, 905d–907b, 948b–c), he retains a role for pious, traditional-appearing religious practices. In the *Republic*, for example, there will still be sacrifices (419a) and hymns to the gods (607a), along with a form of civic religion that features temples, prayers, festivals, priests, and so on (427b–c; Burkert 1985:334). Plato also expects the children of his Kallipolis to be molded "by the rites and prayers which the priestesses and priests and the whole community pray at each wedding festival" (*Republic* 461a6–8). The *Republic* is lamentably terse on the details of all this, but that is because its Socrates is unwilling to entrust the authority of establishing these institutions to his guardians or to speculative reason ("We have no knowledge of these things"; 427b8–9). Rather, the "greatest, finest, and first of laws" (*Republic* 427b3–4; cf. 424c–425a) governing these matters will be introduced and maintained by "the ancestral guide on such things for all people": Delphic Apollo (427a–c; cf. 461e, 540b–c). Morgan 1990:106, notes that this charge to the Delphic oracle

both in its proper and improper forms (*Laws* 932e–933e), it would seem that he would want his ideal physician to respond on its behalf to any Hippocratic skepticism concerning it.[25] This, then, is the second function Plato assigns to Eryximachus by having him offer effusive approval of divination and sacrificial rites (188b–d).[26]

On this reading, we should understand Eryximachus' account of universal *Erōs* to involve a Platonically-acceptable theory of physical Nature that simultaneously rebuts Hippocratic reservations concerning divination, and this—I think—is just what we find. First, Eryximachus' vision of the world as a place of change mediated by the relations between somatic opposites is at least compatible with accounts of the sensible world found in those dialogues typically grouped with the *Symposium*—especially the *Phaedo* (70c–107a). Secondly, Eryximachus' citation and correction of Heraclitus' claim that "The one ... being at variance with itself is in agreement with itself ... like the attunement of a bow or lyre" (187a5–6; cf. fr. B51 D-K) brings to mind Plato's own Heracliteanism in respect of the realm of sensible particulars (see Irwin 1977b). Finally, there is evidence that Heraclitus' doctrine of flux and the unity of opposites did in fact play a significant role in the formulations of Hippocratic theorizing (see *Regimen* and *Nutriment*; Kihara 1998).[27]

---

is "completely normal." Plato assigns the same function to Delphi in his *Laws* (738b–d, 759a–e, 828a) and pays better attention to such details (e.g. 759a–760a, 771a–772d, 778c–d, 799a–803b, 828a–829e, 848c–e). These details are rather conventional, something we should expect, given that Plato's Athenian Stranger insists that his Cretan city will absorb and preserve unchanged the rites of the Magnesians (848d). This fact alone suggests that the ritual life of Plato's Kallipolis will—with the exception of its cult for deceased philosopher-kings (*Republic* 540b–c)—be very hard to distinguish from that of Plato's Athens. Confirmation of this occurs when we are told that the citizens of Kallipolis will "join all other Greeks in their common holy rites" (*Republic* 470e10–11 [and note the warning against innovation at 424b–c]; cf. *Laws* 848d).

[25] The author of the *Decorum* would seem to fit Plato's ideal, since from that author's perspective a physician must be a philosopher (1.5) who also acknowledges and understands the role of the gods in the curing of illness (1.6).

[26] Note, too, how Plato has Socrates draw our attention to Eryximachus' approval and possible practice of divination at the conclusion of Agathon's speech (198a).

[27] Of course, those who see Eryximachus' role as entirely parodic often claim that he badly misinterprets Heraclitus at this point in support of their view (e.g. Woodruff and Nehamas 1989: 21n24; Hunter 2004:55; cf. Rowe 1998a on 187a6–7; for a defense of Eryximachus' understanding of Heraclitus, see Kihara 2002). But whether or not that is so, on a charitable reading of this section we can understand Plato to be signaling that Eryximachus is no slave to Presocratic science—that he, like Plato, will adopt the physical views of his predecessors on the basis of his own considered view of the matter at hand. And strictly speaking, we can sympathize with Eryximachus' desire that Heraclitus' aphorism (his version of it, at any rate) should differentiate between the kind of homeostatic opposition existing between the harmonized somatic opposites (e.g. hot and cold) in a healthy person and the sort of unbalanced opposition present

The Hippocratics are often thought by modern interpreters to hold that divinities and supernatural forces have absolutely nothing to do with disease, but this involves an anachronistic reading of their material, especially *On the Sacred Disease*. A more nuanced approach reveals that rather than eliminating the influence of divinity over us, these writers followed the lead of the Ionian *phusiologoi* by implicating "divinity even more thoroughly in nature," urging physicians to think that no particular disease is more divine than any other (Martin 2004:48; see *On the Sacred Disease* 1, 21; Jouanna 1998:41; McPherran 1996:chap. 3). On this innovative view, all the forces of nature are to be found divine insofar as they each have a nature (*phusis*) that is beyond human control and regular in an impersonal fashion that allows for calculative investigation (for "all things take place through a divine necessity [δι ἀνάγκην θείην]," *Regimen* 1.5; Eijk 1990:93–105; Lloyd 1975b:5). Moreover, the intervention in these forces by the vengeful, warring gods of popular theology—gods whose baleful influence can be manipulated by the ritual purifications and incantations hawked by bogus magicians—is at odds with natural causation and must be rejected (*On the Sacred Disease* 2–4, 21; *Airs, Waters, Places* 22; DeHart 1999:353–376; Jouanna 1998:39–41; cf. *Republic* 363e–366d). Indeed, we are told that if the gods did send physical afflictions and then responded dependably to petitionary sacrifices to avert or cure them it would not be the richly sacrificing Scythians who suffer from impotence as much as they do, but the poor ones—contrary to the facts (*Airs, Waters, Places* 22 [the true cause being the frequency of horseback riding by the rich]; Jouanna 1998:40, 66–67). Thus, no god *personally* or *directly* causes a disease—for all natural forces are impersonally divine (e.g. air; see *Breaths*). Nevertheless, it is still possible to accept that the gods of traditional religion—when rightly comprehended as being thoroughly good residents of the natural cosmos—can impart purification and healing to us, though never pollution (*miasma*) or illness (*On the Sacred Disease* 4; cf. *Phaedrus* 244d–e; *Republic* 379a–380c). This is why Hippocratics are still able to recommend the ritual practices of everyday religion to their patients—generally in chronic and incurable cases (Edelstein 1937:244–246)—and presumably with no guarantees that the gods will respond to their petitions (*On the Sacred Disease* 4; *On Dreams* [*Regimen* 4] 87, 89, 90, 93).[28] However, appeals

---

in a diseased person (whose state could be likened to that of a bow or lyre that was strung too tightly or too loosely).

[28] See Eijk 1990:105–119 for discussion of the tension between the claims of *On the Sacred Disease* that all diseases are equally divine and involve natural causation and that (yet) the gods can dispense cleansings; cf. Lloyd 1979:31–32. Edelstein 1937 argues that while some Hippocratic texts should be understood as identifying the divine with nature, the greater number "acknow-

to popular forms of divination—the supposed mantic *technai* that allow us to descry the future—are another matter.

As a son of Asclepius, Hippocrates had a long-standing relationship with his illustrious forefather and his temples, but the details of that relationship are hard to ascertain.[29] Asclepius, we are told, was born to a mortal woman, but his father was Apollo, a god of healing, and hence he became a physician (both deities are invoked at the outset of the Hippocratic Oath).[30] Asclepius allegedly lost his mortal incarnation, however, after being struck down by Zeus for resurrecting one of his patients from the dead (*Republic* 408b–c). More pertinent to our concerns here, Asclepius wards off death and heals via the well-attested method of incubation—that is, dream-induction. This is the practice of spending a night in the god's temple (*Asklepieion*) with the hope of being visited by the god in a dream who then offers a prognosis, or instructions on how to be cured, or even imposes the cure itself.[31] As an Asclepiad—born on the site of one of the four major healing temple-hospitals of Asclepius (*Kos*) and claiming direct descent from Asclepius via his son Podalirius—Hippocrates would have been well acquainted with, probably even trained in, the use of this procedure.

The first appearance of professional physicians in Athens closely coincided with the entry of Asclepius and his daughter Hygieia (the personification of health) into the Piraeus in 420/19, followed by an additional installation of the cult in Athens in the year following. The fact that this latter development also coincided with the final abatement of the waves of plague Athens had suffered through (430–420 BCE) seems to have ensured the fame and success of the new god.[32] From its very foundation the Athenian cult-center and

---

ledge the divine as a factor apart from nature, which is a power of its own" (217; see e.g. *On the Sacred Disease* 4.48–50).

[29] The most complete study of Asclepius is Edelstein and Edelstein 1945.

[30] This familial and functional link between the two deities makes it natural that the Socrates of the *Apology*, *Crito*, and *Phaedo* would find a long-lasting affinity with Asclepius. As both the *Apology* (e.g. 20e–23c, 29c–31a) and *Phaedo* (84d–85b, 69d–e) make clear, Socrates is Apollo's missionary, the god's gift to Athens. The god has commanded Socrates to elenctically examine those who hubristically claim to possess divine wisdom and to urge on all and sundry the philosophical care and tendance of the soul (*Apology* 29d7–e3, 30a7–b2; Xenophon *Memorabilia* 1.2.4–5). See McPherran 1996:chap. 4.2.

[31] See Edelstein and Edelstein 1945:221–237 for a sample of incubation testimonies; see also e.g. Garland 1992:chap. 6; Mikalson 1983:55–56; Vlastos 1949:281–286; and Aristophanes *Plutus* 653–747. Clients of Apollo, Amphiaraus, and Trophonius might also have incubation recommended to them, but the method was most famously tied to Asclepius (e.g. while both Amphiaraus and Trophonius are merely local deities, "Asclepius and his sons perform the whole world over," Vlastos 1949:281n49).

[32] Parker 1996:180. The actual reason for the abatement seems to have been the sudden decrease in Athens' crowded population when the Peace of Nicias (421) allowed refugees

Asclepiad physicians also enjoyed a close and supportive bond with Delphi and, especially, with Eleusis and the celebration of its Mysteries (Garland 1992:121–124; Langholf 1990:234). The clinical work and success of the Hippocratic school, on the other hand, dates for the most part from the time *subsequent* to Hippocrates' departure from Cos and its temple (Jouanna 1998:27, 30–31). We may infer the possibility that as scientific medicine began to distinguish itself as a *technē* its own right, independent of temple-medicine, Hippocratic physicians had to take care in drawing a clear boundary between the super-seded but ongoing practices of their progenitors/competition and their own new theories and methods.[33] It is against this backdrop that *On Regimen* (esp. 4 [*On Dreams*]), *Prognosis*, and the entire Hippocratic attitude toward popular forms of *mantikē* versus their own practice of prognostication (προγνωστικόν) should be understood.[34]

The prognosis of patients "was one of the most important activities of the Hippocratic authors," and this crucial procedure had its conceptual, termi-nological, and practical roots in earlier religious forms of divination, including dream divination (Lloyd 1979:45; Langholf 1990:232, 242, 250–254; note, too, that Apollo was the god of both medicine and divination). But although *On Regimen* does initially refer to *mantikē* as a craft (1.12), its actual status as a *technē* is thrown into doubt by the opening of book 4 (*On Dreams* 86–88). Here we are told that there are two kinds of dreams. First, there are god-given dreams that contain cryptic information concerning the future of both indi-viduals and cities—the interpretation of these sorts of dreams requires special religious interpreters. Secondly, there are also diagnostic dreams experi-enced by souls during sleep as a result of somatic imbalances—and for these dreams there are also special interpreters, namely, properly trained physi-cians. However, and despite their differing origins, since both kinds of dream are brought to our attention by their unusual features, it is no surprise that

---

to return to their homes. For a description of the epidemic (leading candidates for its cause are true plague [*Yersinia pestis*], typhus, and smallpox), see Thucydides 2.47–58, 3.87.

[33] And without offending those progenitors; Lloyd 1979:45. Hippocrates, at any rate, "never broke off contact with his birthplace," and was treated as a hero of Cos into Roman times (Jouanna 1998:27; cf. 40–41). It seems that Hippocratic ire is directed more towards independent *manteis* than those associated with established institutions of healing; cf. Holowchak 2001:384–386.

[34] During Socrates' lifetime, divination (μαντική) was widely employed by both states and indi-viduals, and appeared in roughly three forms (in order of prestige): (1) divination by lots (κλῆροι) (cleromancy); (2) interpretation of signs (σημεῖα) such as thunder, the direction of flights of birds, and the reading of sacrificial entrails; (3) the production and interpretation of oral oracles by a seer (μάντις) (with these being recorded, collected, and interpreted by "oracle-mongers" [χρησμολόγοι]). See e.g. Zaidman and Pantel 1992:121–128.

the religious interpreters offer predictions on the basis of what are actually somatic dreams (Holowchak 2001:388–389, 398). But in such cases as these, their interpretations concerning the future—including whether or not a body will experience from a surfeit or depletion of humors—are often inaccurate. In either case, these religious diviners lack an account of the cause of their successes and failures. Moreover, they offer only the most general—and, thus, useless—advice on how to prepare for the future they predict, such as "Beware of taking harm!" (*On Dreams* 87), supplemented by a recommendation to pray.

The author's response to this situation is careful but fairly straightforward. While prayer is indeed a good thing, patients "should also lend a hand" (*On Dreams* 87.15–16), where "taking a hand" strongly suggests that one should avoid the approach to unusual dreams offered by the religious interpreters—whatever their source may *seem* to be. Moreover, and without saying as much, the mention of the religious interpreters' mistaken application of their alleged *technē* to an inappropriate subject-matter (somatic dreams) and the vacuity of their prescriptions suggest that we should find their professed *technē* to be entirely illegitimate. The religious approach to dreaming, then, is to be contrasted with the Hippocratic attention to the facts about dreaming. Such physicians take no stand as to what sorts of religious rites of healing ought to be performed (leaving this up to the patient's own judgment), but treat unusual dreams as resulting from a disturbance of the soul caused in turn by a *bodily* disturbance requiring treatment of that body by a physician (*On Dreams* 88). Dreams thus continue in Hippocratic medicine to offer a vital diagnostic tool (Holowchak 2001:388), but the dominant message of this text and the deafening silence on the topic of divination by other Hippocratic authors is that serious physicians are to regard religious dream divination as an ineffective non-science—one to be supplanted by a Hippocratic inquiry into the reliably predicable causal connections between somatic signs and subsequent bodily changes (Edelstein 1937:241–246).

As for other forms of forecasting the future, the Hippocratic physician is to look not to the incursions of distant divinity allegedly displayed in the spontaneous and unpredictable omens sent by gods and intermediary *daimōns* (e.g. the state of sacrificial entrails, the flights of birds) in an attempt to outdo the hereditary *manteis*. Rather, he is to engage in a professionalized prognostication informed by Hippocratic humoral theory and based on observations of the "signs" displayed by the patient's body. This attention to bodily signs tries to apprehend "not so much a future event ... but an event that had already begun in an incipient, invisible fashion—an event on the level of a humoral disequilibrium already ongoing in the body" (DeHart 1999:365). These signs, unlike those subjected to interpretation by popular forms of divination, must be taken as causal signs to some degree and so "are now to be dealt with by reckoning and discriminating ... instead of by traditional means of propitiation or sacrifice" (DeHart 1999:369; cf. 376). For although Hippocratic physicians still saw in these signs, their bodies, and the cosmos as a whole, the operations of divine power, it was a power now conceived to be "calculable and predictable and which made ritual action irrelevant to human contact with these powers," or at least largely so (DeHart 1999:377; cf. Jouanna 1998:49).

In view of the preceding, Eryximachus' endorsement of the sort of divination associated with the traditional rites of prayers and sacrifices marks a clear point at which he parts company with many if not most of his fellow Hippocratics (Jouanna 1998:48–49; *The Science of Medicine* 4–6).[35] Consider the relevant passage in full:

> ... all types of sacrifice [*thusiai*] and the whole sphere of divination [*mantikē*] (these are the ways in which gods and human interact) are wholly directed toward maintaining the proper kind of Love and curing the kind that is diseased. Every kind of impiety [*asebeia*] towards one's parents or the gods occurs when we refuse to gratify or honor and give pride of place in every action to the orderly kind of Love, and offer deference to the other sort. The task of divination is to keep watch over those whose Love is the wrong kind and to doctor them as necessary. Divination is thus the craft that produces loving affection between gods and men; it is the science [*epistamai*] of the effects of love on justice [*themis*] and piety [*eusebeia*]. Love as a whole has such great and varied power that in all cases it might be called total. But it is the Love whose nature is expressed in good actions marked by temperance and justice, at the human and divine level that provide us with happiness and good fortune, the bonds of human society, friendship [*philia*] with the gods—our superiors.
>
> *Symposium* 188b6–d3; after Gill trans.

This is a remarkable passage. For not only does it have a Hippocratic physician endorsing rather than rejecting *mantikē* (including knowledge of the rites of sacrifice), but it characterizes *mantikē* as a quasi-medical expertise concerning Heavenly *Erōs*—now conceived of Socratically as the desire for the good—

---

[35] The effectiveness of traditional rites of prayers and sacrifices directed to external deities is still in principle compatible with the principle of sufficient reason implicitly invoked by the Hippocratics, so long as those deities are conceived of as operating inside the domain of the sphere of natural causes (see n28 above).

and the virtues of piety, temperance, and justice (virtues, which, if rightly doctored, produce happiness and good fortune). In particular, a Heavenly *Erōs* guided by medical piety will result in *a loving friendship* between humans and gods, as opposed to the more mercantile relationship fostered by the *do ut des* piety of popular fifth-century Greek religion—a relationship grounded more in fear and respect than in loving affection for deity (McPherran 1996:chap. 3).[36] Naturally, we would expect Eryximachus to argue for the self-interested payoff this new form of piety and friendship with the gods might bring; e.g. in terms of an improvement to our health. But then he must also explain how his allegiance to Hippocratic physical causal theory can be made compatible with the independently existing deities of whom he speaks, and who it is that can serve as the new sort of diviner who can doctor our *Erōs* for the good via the virtues—will it be the physician, the diviner, the philosopher, or some combination of these?

Eryximachus implicitly raises these puzzles by the way he incorporates into his grand theory the sort of Socratic/Platonic response to the Hippocratics that Plato (and Xenophon, too) is elsewhere willing to credit to Socrates, according to which medicine must be supplemented by and subservient to the soul-therapy provided by philosophy (e.g. *Charmides* 156b–159a). It is also important to note that although Eryximachus forecasts friendly relations between gods and humans, they remain quite unequal partners, separated by the traditional, defining gap that divides the human from the divine in respect of power and wisdom, a gap repeatedly endorsed by the Socrates of such texts as the *Apology* (20e–23b). Eryximachus' claims that we are on friendly terms with the divine when we are pious and that happiness and good fortune are produced when the power of *Erōs* is expressed *via* the virtues of temperance and justice toward the good should put us in mind of the Socratic piety arguably latent in the second half of the *Euthyphro* (see McPherran 1996: chap. 2; note, too, that *Memorabilia* 1.4.7, for example, has Socrates characterizing the Demiurge as not only wise, but "loving"). The conception of piety at work here is thus contrary to that manifested by those Hippocratics who collapse the divine into nature—offering "a different vision of man ... in which man measures himself no longer against the gods but through his ties to the universe that surrounds him" (Jouanna 1998:42). As we will now see, the nature of the connection between *Erōs*, piety, and the other virtues becomes a running subtext of the next three speeches.

---

[36] Rowe 1998a:152 writes "... if seers are concerned with the causes of impiety, and impiety has its origin in people's desires, then seers *ought* to be involved in examining them."

In sum, Eryximachus as a Platonic construction represents (in part) Plato's attempt to join in the contemporary battle as to where and how to draw the lines among magic, medicine, religion, and philosophy. He is, in particular, Plato's response to all other physicians who would rank the craft of medicine as superior to, rather than subordinate to, the new craft of philosophy. As Plato stresses throughout his later work, this new expertise employs a rational approach to knowledge that encompasses and supersedes Presocratic science (see e.g. *Phaedo* 96a–107d) but also provides a medical *therapeia* of the soul lacking in Greek medicine—doing so by recasting the traditional forms of piety and divination in relation to deities properly reconceived (McPherran 1996:chaps. 2.2, 4, 5.3; McPherran 2004). On the one hand, then, Eryximachus is a Platonic physician because of his nominal piety, his recognition of the realm of divinity, and "his philosophical orientation and his understanding of the nature of the human body as part of the larger picture, the picture of a perfectly harmonious cosmos" (Poulakos 1998:170). These features, in turn, prepares us for Diotima's own revelation of the universality of *Erōs* and its origin in our sexual attraction to and procreation in beautiful bodies (206a–208b). But this physician proves not to be a thorough-going Platonist—for despite his talk about piety and the gods, he is fixated on the physical universe, and so his actual theory of love offers merely a thorough-going *physicalistic* conception of *Erōs* as a natural power—the *Erōs* relevant to the mediation of only our mortal nonsense, to use Diotima's scathing terminology (211e). In this, Eryximachus embodies the old anthropomorphism made newly scientific—for it seems that he conceives of what Plato understands to be very much a psychological and transcendental force as an essentially somatic phenomenon "located in a field of 'natural' (*kata phusin*), hence, dependable, processes" (DeHart 1999:353). This non-Platonic aspect of Eryximachus is best explained as providing the sort of physicalistic conception of *Erōs* that can serve as the oppositional bedrock against which the non-physicalistic account of *Erōs* and deity offered by Diotima/Plato can then be seen as making the sort of metaphysical progress that makes philosophers superior to physicians. It may even be that the lack of coherence many scholars have found in Eryximachus' physical theory is intended to turn us toward this view. But to see better how Eryximachus foreshadows Diotima, we need first to see how he also foreshadows both Aristophanes and Agathon.[37]

---

[37] Patrick Miller has made the interesting suggestion that not just Eryximachus, but all of the *Symposium*'s pre-Diotima speakers, should be understood as calling each of these craftsmen to a deeper—that is, philosophical—understanding of the significance of his/her craft.

The Speech of Aristophanes

Piety is very much at issue in the comic myth of Aristophanes. In this revisioning of the traditional tale of the battle of the Titans (after the story of Ephialtes and Otos, *Iliad* V 385, *Odyssey* xii 308),[38] we humans are said to have been originally powerful double-humans who once dared to attempt an overthrow of the gods (190b–c). In retaliation for this impiety, Zeus cut the double-humans in half (190c–e), instructing Apollo in his guise as a physician to heal the wound (190e–191a). However, since their natural form had been whole, these halves intensely desire to find their other halves. This, then, is the origin of *Erōs*: it is the longing to be healed (189d, 193d) by being made whole and complete once again (192e; cf. 191a, 191d). But whether or not this search is successful, we humans must scrupulously avoid impiety, lest we be split in half once more (190d, 193a–b).

We have been prepared for Aristophanes' account of *Erōs* as a healing power by Eryximachus' earlier disclosure that the physician aids *Erōs* to bring about an attunement of our desires (Allen 1991:28; cf. Rowe 1999:62–64). However, Aristophanes' account also marks progress over both Eryximachus' and Pausanius' viewpoints—on both his and Plato's assessment (189c–d)—since it treats *Erōs* as a uniquely human and predominant psychic force affecting both men and women. Moreover, it offers a theory of *Erōs* that still captures our romantic imaginations. Aristophanes also produces a small advance in the concept of piety—one foreshadowing the piety of Diotima.[39] For, subsequent to his tale, Aristophanes concludes that it is *Erōs* who assists us in finding our other halves (193a–b, 193c), thus helping us to procure for ourselves the greatest benefit present circumstances will allow (193b8–d2). Naturally, if we offend *Erōs* the gods will hate us (193b) and so we will thus fail to find our beloveds, but if we are pious towards the gods, *Erōs* will not only help us to find our beloveds in the here and now, but we may entertain the greatest hope for the future—namely, that *Erōs* "will establish us in our original condition and, by healing us, make us blessed and happy" (193d5–6). This last claim is initially puzzling. For given that Aristophanes has already concluded his myth and developed its practical applications for understanding *Erōs* in our actual, present human condition, it seems implausible that he would here be

---

[38] A story of the kind banned from well-conducted *symposia* by Xenophanes (fr. B1 D-K) and from well-conducted states by Plato (*Republic* II and III)

[39] Aristophanes' myth itself does, however, emphasize the kind of semi-traditional piety congenial to Eryximachus insofar as that myth urges us to avoid hubris by recognizing the fact of human inferiority in respect of the power and wisdom of the gods.

forecasting a literal return to our original double-human physical form in the future. Arguably, then, Aristophanes is in this passage hinting that piety in the here and now will lead to a union with our beloved in the afterlife. If so, Aristophanes' speech foreshadows the sort of erotic eschatology Plato draws in the *Phaedrus* (256a–e). With his portrait of *Erōs* as the soul's desire for its proper object, Aristophanes has brought us one step closer to the account of Diotima.

The Speech of Agathon

Agathon's speech transports readers from the rich Aristophantic world of mythic poetry to a Gorgian victory of style over substance (cf. 198c), concluding with an "incantation of rhythmical phrases" that "brings Greek prose as close to metrical poetry as it ever got" (Hunter 2004:73). There is, however, substantive content to be elicited from the contrived form of Agathon's encomium. One obvious contribution is noted by Socrates, who—fully in character—endorses the way Agathon inaugurates his speech by trying first to *define Erōs* before attempting to say anything substantive about *Erōs* (198c; see e.g. *Hippias Major* 304d5–e3). Another contribution—relatively unnoticed—has to do with what Agathon does and does not say about piety and the gods.

Agathon offers his fellow symposiasts a new *Theogony* in order to explain the nature of *Erōs*, one that explicitly rebuts Phaedrus' genealogy (178b) and that adds a further stage of development to the Hesiodic gods of Aristophanes. As Agathon inverts the old story, *Erōs* must be recognized as being not an ancient god, but the youngest of them all, and is now their king as well (195a–d). Prior to the birth of *Erōs*, the gods were ruled by Necessity, and as a result the gods quarreled with one another—sometimes violently (195c, 197b). But with the arrival of *Erōs*, the gods' enmities were settled, and this is because *Erōs* implanted four canonical *aretai* in the gods: justice, temperance, courage, and wisdom (196b–197c).[40] This section of Agathon's speech should thereby put us in mind of *Republic* II–IV, where Plato rejects the Homeric/Hesiodic account of the gods, argues for their complete goodness, and then adumbrates four of the cardinal virtues—justice, temperance, courage, and wisdom—but with piety conspicuously missing from the list. Here as there, then, we are thus provoked to ask why piety is not among the virtues Agathon lists. For if a god can be temperate, why not pious as well? Plato answers this question he has implicitly raised, I think, within the speech of Diotima.

---

[40] Agathon's moral theory does seem confused—as Nehamas and Woodruff 1989 point out (34nn34, 36), since justice seems incorrectly equated with nonviolence, while courage and temperance are implausibly equated with power.

The Speech of Diotima

It seems that in his youth Socrates had a penchant for not only Presocratic science (*Phaedo* 96a–100e) but Presocratic wizardry as well. From the physicians of Zalmoxis, for example, he claims to have learned the principles of holistic medicine and a particular headache cure composed of a leaf (for the body) and an incantation (for the soul).[41] Diotima of Mantinea is another figure of the same sort—like Zalmoxis, she is a physician and diviner (ἰατρομάντεις) and an especially skilled one at that.[42] For, according to Socrates, she managed to stave off the Athenian plague (430–426 BCE) for an entire decade by instructing the Athenians as to the sorts of sacrifices they should make (201d; cf. *Laws* 642d–e). By pointedly characterizing Diotima in this fashion, Plato not only establishes her credentials in anticipation of the bold, religious theory of *Erōs* of which she

[41] In the *Charmides*, Socrates endorses the view of certain successful Greek physicians who do not attempt to cure eyes by themselves, but only by means of treating the entire head (156b–d). But curing the head requires in turn that the entire body be cured. These physicians are holistic, and Socrates endorses their approach. He then explains how he will be able to cure Charmides' headache by using a treatment that extends the principle of holistic medicine to include even that aspect of us concerned with reason and speech; namely, the soul—a treatment of leaf and charm that he learned when in the army near Thrace from one of the physicians of the Thracian king Zalmoxis (156d–157c). The standard view of this passage sees Plato as engaging in a purely fictional, literary maneuver using the trope which characterizes foreign wisdom as superior to the haphazard science of the Greeks. Hence, we are to think that Socrates' encounter with these physicians of psychosomatic medicine must be entirely Plato's invention (see e.g. 'Zalmoxis' in the *OCD* [1970]:1144; and Rutherford 1995:89). However, this piece of text does not appear to be woven of purely fictional threads: Plato's original audience believed that Thracians have "special powers of music and healing" (Murphy 2000:288), "the reputation of the Geto-Dacian physicians [of Thrace] was real" (Eliade 1972:56), Socrates does appear to have been on military service near Thrace twice in his lifetime (Potidaea [431–429], Amphipolis [422]; *Apology* 28e), Zalmoxis was the deity of the Getae in Thrace, and he was connected as Plato connects him with the themes of mind-body dualism and the immortality of the soul (Herodotus 4.93–6; Morgan 1990:26). Note also Zalmoxis' reputed connection with Pythagoras, his achievement of immortality through initiatory incubation, and so on. Note, too, that Greek medicine of the time commonly assumed that the application of drugs would precede or be joined with that of charms/chants (Entralgo 1970:1–107; see also *Theaetetus* 149c–d, 157c), and that the most renowned physicians of Athens—the Hippocratics—accepted the holistic view Plato ascribes to them (Tsekourakis 1991–1993:166).

[42] Supposing that Plato invented Diotima (a name meaning "honored by Zeus"), "he may have made her Mantinean because of the resemblance of the place-name to μάντις 'seer' and its cognates" (Dover 1980:137). Despite her possibly fictional status, Plato can still use her to provide "a vision of love from a god-like, authoritative standpoint" (Gill 1999:xxix). It is to be hoped that Diotima—to the extent to which she is Plato's creature—does not attribute the origin of the Athenian plague to any deity (Apollo was thought by some Athenians to be its source). For discussion of the issue of Diotima's historicity and the relationship of her views to those expressed in other Platonic dialogues, see Waithe 1987b.

convinces Socrates, but he also puts her in league with the plague-curing god Asclepius and those Hippocratics who still approve of sacrificial rites of purification (*On the Sacred Disease* 4).[43] It seems clear that we have been prepared for this reassertion of the reality and efficacy of the divine by Eryximachus' endorsement of the rites of sacrifice and divination (cf. Rowe 1998a:152).[44]

With her authority as a woman of god in place, Plato proceeds to use Diotima to outline a radical new vision of piety—one that utterly trumps all prior accounts. First, Agathon's *Erōs* is demoted from the status of god to *daimōn* (201e–204c), and then—in rough agreement with Eryximachus—such intermediary beings are connected with the traditional piety of prayer, sacrifice, and divination (202e–203a). Here, however, Diotima offers a sharp critique that seems consciously aimed at comparing and contrasting Eryximachus with Socratic/Platonic philosophers, when she asserts that a man wise about the ways that *daimōns* interact with humans and gods—thus grasping true piety—is a spiritual man (δαιμόνιος ἀνήρ), whereas one with wisdom about the subject of a profession or craft—hence, a Hippocratic physician of the non-philosophical sort—is merely a vulgar mechanic (βάναυσος).[45] Here Diotima's descriptive phrase *daimonios anēr* harks back to the archaic shaman, described as a a man of god (θεῖος ἀνήρ)—who is also generally an *iatromanteis* (Dodds 1951:140–147; Langholf 1990:233).[46] As Diotima now proceeds to make clear, these spiritual men are none other than those who philosophize—indeed, even *Erōs* is a philosopher, caught between ignorance and knowledge, longing for beautiful things such as wisdom and goodness (203a–204b).[47] Now, at last, the

---

[43] Like most commentators, I assume here that Diotima speaks for Plato (compare e.g. what Diotima says of the true lover at 203b–212b with what is said of the true philosopher at *Republic* 490b); White 2004:366n2.

[44] The theme of piety, religious rites, and the mantic art begins at the outset of the dialogue, however, with Plato's mention of the madness (μαίνομαι; 173e2) of Apollodorus, the seeming-trance of Socrates (174d–175b), and the way the symposium began with "the whole ritual" of a libation and hymn to Dionysus (176a; cf. 174c).

[45] It is worth noting that Diotima thus tars non-philosophical physicians with the same brush used by the author of *On the Sacred Disease*, who in manuscript variant M concludes his treatise by labeling the earlier vilified "magicians, purifiers, charlatans, and quacks" μάγοι τε καὶ καθαρταὶ ἀγύρται καὶ ἀλαζόνες (*On the Sacred Disease* 2.3–4) as βαναυσίη.

[46] Empedocles is such a figure; see e.g. frr. B111 D-K and B112 D-K (Lloyd 1979:34–35).

[47] It is a commonplace that Diotima's portrayal of impoverished, barefooted *Erōs* also characterizes the impoverished barefooted Socrates as a philosopher who is also a δαιμόνιος ἀνήρ—a "genius with enchantments and potions" (203b–204b). We are prepared for this appropriation of shamanistic terminology by the new enterprise of philosophy in the dialogue through not only Eryximachus' approval of the mantic art, but by Plato's continual characterization of Socrates as a kind of *magus*. This begins at the outset of the dialogue with the unexplained trance of Socrates (175a–c) and carries on through Agathon's claim that Socrates tried to cast

most proper beautiful object of the erotic passion of these pious philosophers can be revealed (209e–212b).

Here in the ladder of ascent section of the *Symposium* we see a prime instance of the way that Plato appropriates the language of traditional myth and religion in its many forms (e.g. the Eleusinian Mysteries) to link our desire for knowledge and post-mortem happiness with the new intellectual enterprise of philosophy—one that sees the philosopher as driven by an erotic desire or a kind of madness for epistemic union with the Forms (cf. e.g. *Republic* 490a–b; *Phaedrus* 249c–253c).[48] And as Plato emphasizes here as elsewhere, one requirement for such knowledge involves the soul in becoming more like the Forms in terms of their purity, that is, their lack of sensible characteristics. Hence, for the soul this means freedom from both attachment to the body and a desire for erotic pleasure (210b). To obtain such freedom requires that the soul be purified not by traditional religious methods but by philosophical training of one's reason, which—as a "practice for death" (*Phaedo* 81a1; 89b–c, 94d–e, 95b)—releases it from the chains of bodily desire (*Phaedo* 81a–e; cf. 66d–67a, 67d). Although this purification is sometimes characterized as the turning around of the soul (e.g. *Republic* 518b–521c) or as the soul's attempt to become as much like god as possible in respect of justice and wisdom (*Symposium* 207c–209e; *Phaedrus* 248a, 252c–253c; *Republic* 613a–b; *Theaetetus* 172b–177c; *Timaeus* 90a–d; *Laws* 716c), here the soul moves up through a process of seeing the beautiful things in the correct ascending order (210e) in a fashion similar to what the initiates in the Mysteries undergo (e.g. *Phaedo* 81a)—an unveiling (*epopteia*) of those Mysteries revealed to the initiates of Eleusis.[49] What is seen

---

a spell on him (φαρμάττειν; 194a5), Socrates' claim to have forecast (μαντικῶς; 198a5) the beauty of Agathon's speech (198a), and Alcibiades' characterization of Socrates as a satyr-like, word-wizard full of godlike figures, party to the Bacchic frenzy of philosophy, *daimonios* (219c1), "strange" (221d3), and resistant to the effects of climate and strong drink (215d–222a).

[48] A partial list of text-references to Eleusinian purification (*katharsis*), initiation, and sudden revelation (*epopteia*) include *Republic* 560e, 378a; references to the Bacchic Mysteries include *Symposium* 218b, *Laws* 672b, *Phaedrus* 250b–c, 265b; Corybantic references include *Crito* 54d and *Euthydemus* 277d. Eleusinian Mystery motifs also contribute to the Myth of the Cave in *Republic* VII and the Myth of the Soul in the *Phaedrus* (244a–257b). See Morgan 1990:chaps. 3–6.

[49] Elsewhere, Plato also assimilates into philosophy the less mainstream Pythagorean, possibly Orphic, view that the body is a kind of prison for the soul which must undergo many trials of intellectual purification (*katharsis*) and initiation (*teletē*) for it to achieve liberation, a homecoming whose rewards include a final revelatory vision (*Phaedo* 62a–b, 69b–d, 79d, 82d; *Republic* 533c; *Philebus* 400b–c; Dodds 1951:chap. 7; Edmonds 2004:175–179). Here Plato allies himself with Hippocratic medicine which also rejects ritual purification in favor of scientific, medical purification (*On the Sacred Disease* 1–4).

by those initiated into the mysteries of philosophy, however, are not the sacred objects of Demeter, but the most perfect and sacred object of all: Beauty-itself (210a–212b) (Morgan 1990:chap. 4).

The trajectory of piety running from Eryximachus to Diotima is now laid bare. Plato uses Eryximachus to insist that true physicians must be philosophers who are pious by accepting the primacy of *Erōs* and the legitimacy of a divination that produces concord between gods and humans—an idea that Diotima will exploit.[50] Eryximachus' extension of *Erōs* beyond sexual desire, and his account of opposites desiring opposites, of cold needing warmth, of bitterness needing sweetness, also anticipates Diotima's revelation that *Erōs* must be a desire for something we do not yet possess (Hunter 2004:57). However, Eryximachus' piety and that which is implied in the speech of Aristophanes is still a relatively traditional one, retaining the traditional Apollonian gap separating the human from the divine in terms of wisdom and power. But then through the speech of Alcibiades we are led to accept *Erōs* as a psychic force that promotes our union with what is properly our own by nature. Agathon subsequently provides the appropriate Platonic theology of wise and good gods, and simultaneously raises the question of the place of piety in the new scheme. This question is then answered by Diotima's new vision of piety.

Appropriating a variety of ecstatic religious forms, Plato's philosophical theology now offers the hope of intimate Form-contemplation in the realm of divinity (210a–212b; cf. *Phaedo* 79c–84b; *Republic* 490a–b; *Phaedrus* 247d–e). Unlike the Socratic piety on display in the *Apology*, self-knowledge on Plato's scheme now leads not so much to an appreciation of our mortal limits as to the realization that we are ourselves capable of possessing all the knowledge there is to be had (*Meno* 81c–d; *Phaedo* 72e–77e; *Symposium* 210a–211b; cf. Sheffield 2001a). In such a scheme there is little room for the old Apollonian piety of Delphi and the Socrates of the *Apology*, since now the central task of human existence becomes less a matter of merely assisting gods who are vastly superior to us in wisdom, and more a matter of becoming as much like them as one can (e.g. *Theaetetus* 172b–177c; McPherran 1996:chap. 5.3). This fact, in addition to the more complex psychology Plato develops in *Republic* IV (427e–428a), may now help us to explain Plato's decision in that book and in Agathon's speech to no longer count piety as a cardinal virtue or as a virtue possessed by a god. For it seems that in *Republic* IV Plato came to the view that there is little *internal* difference between the knowledge of how to do what is just toward gods and

---

[50] Diotima already makes use of Eryximachus' Heracliteanism at 207c–208b.

the knowledge of how to do what is just toward mortals—as a result, piety as a form of psychic virtue seems to be nothing other than justice *simpliciter*. So although Plato continues to speak of piety and pious actions, piety as a virtue is subsumed under the virtue of justice (and wisdom) as a whole (McPherran 2000). At any rate, keeping in mind Eryximachus' account of piety, Diotima can be seen to offer an implicit explanation as to why Agathon fails to ascribe piety to his gods. None of the gods love wisdom, she asserts, since being already wise they do not love/desire it (204a). So, then, if—as Eryximachus has it—piety is a form of proper love toward the gods as preeminently wise and just beings by mortal humans who lack those qualities, only human beings and not gods can exemplify piety (188b–d).[51]

Plato, then, has in part used his symposiasts to reveal a new vision of piety through an ascending sequence of speeches—offered like the successive talismanic objects of an Eleusinian initiation—capped by Diotima's concluding protreptic :[52]

> Do you think it would be a poor life for a human being to look there [at Beauty-itself] and to behold it by that which he ought, and to be with it? Or haven't you remembered, she said, that in that life alone, when he looks at Beauty in the only way that Beauty can be seen—only then will it become possible for him to give birth not to images of virtue ... but to true virtue ... The love of the gods belongs to anyone who has given birth to true virtue and nourished it, and if any human being could become immortal, it would be he.
>
> *Symposium* 212a–b

---

[51] Insofar as Eryximachus' piety resembles the piety of the Socrates of the *Apology*—modeled as a service after the kind that human soldiers and assistants render to distant generals and craftspeople (whose chief *ergon* is beyond full human comprehension)—it is at odds with the *Republic*'s and *Symposium*'s epistemology that puts expert knowledge theoretically within the grasp of humans (McPherran 2000:322–328). White 2004:373n34 points out that although Diotima's gods cannot possess or experience *Erōs*, they can still have *philia* toward us.

[52] Alcibiades' entrance at 212d, of course, initially marks a *descent*. He appears "all of a sudden," like some kind of anti-Form, to take us away with dizzying speed from the ecstatic heights of the incorporeal, divine, and virtue-inducing world of Beauty-itself down to the fleshy but quite drunken beauty of Athens' notorious bad boy. It is here, as I noted at the outset, that Plato has his physician make a proper medical stand and affirm his role as informal *symposiarch*, by having him insist that Alcibiades not simply drain the two-quart cooling jar in silence (214b). Moreover, we see Eryximachus doctor the conversation by proposing that Alcibiades offer an encomium to Socrates in place of *Erōs*. Since Alcibiades provides the capstone speech of the entire dialogue, this therapeutic encounter of Alcibiades with Eryximachus once again supports the idea that Eryximachus serves as Plato's model of a properly philosophically-oriented physician.

Here in the piety of Diotima the equivocal piety of Eryximachus—where "Love is directed ... toward good things *whether in heaven or on earth*" (188d5–7, my emphasis)—finds its Platonic revision. Although we must inevitably begin our embodied lives with an *Erōs* that aims at the good things of this earth, the life of genuinely successful piety demands a reorientation of our *Erōs* toward the only truly good things there are—the invisible objects of Plato's new heaven. The complete physician who would bring us a return to our original wholeness, then, is no Eryximachus, but must be that rare individual who has moved beyond an expertise of bodies and become one of those wise about *daimōns*.[53]

[53] My thanks to Patrick Miller for his helpful commentary on an earlier draft of this paper, presented to the Eleventh Annual Arizona Colloquium in Ancient Philosophy, University of Arizona, Tucson, February, 2006. I am also grateful to David Halperin, James Lesher, Debra Nails, Jennifer Reid, and Lisa Rhoades for their comments on an earlier version of this paper. Finally thanks to James Lesher, Debra Nails, and Frisbee Sheffield for inviting me to write this piece for the CHS conference, for all the conferees' helpful suggestions, and to Gregory Nagy and the staff of CHS for their work on behalf of our conference.

Five

Permanent Beauty and Becoming Happy in Plato's *Symposium*

Gabriel Richardson Lear[1]

OUR FIRST ENCOUNTER WITH SOCRATES in the *Symposium* is bizarre. Aristodemus, surprised to run into Socrates fully bathed and with his sandals on, asks him where he is going "to have made himself so beautiful (*kalos*)" (174a4, Rowe trans.). Socrates replies that he is on his way to see the lovely Agathon, and so that "he has beautified himself in these ways in order to go, a beauty to a beauty (*kalos para kalon*)" (174a7–8). Why does Socrates, who in just a few moments will be lost in contemplation out on the front porch, care about being beautiful? His remark to Aristodemus is clearly in some sense ironic, but on the other hand, he really has taken unusual care with his physical appearance. Later, in his encomium to love, he will claim that beauty has this effect on lovers: the beauty of the beloved causes the lover to disdain his former way of life and "give birth" to beautiful "offspring." Is the image of the squat and snub-nosed Socrates all freshly scrubbed and kitted out a comic foreshadowing, or a debunking, of his serious speech? Does Socrates really believe in the transformative power of beauty?

One of the most alien aspects of Plato's ethical theory is that it gives a central place to beauty (*to kalon*) and erotic love. The young guardians in the *Republic* must develop *erōs* for the beautiful before they begin their training in

[1] This paper was greatly improved by comments I received in various venues. I am especially grateful for the detailed response I received from Frisbee Sheffield at the *Symposium* conference at the Center for Hellenic Studies and for the comments of all the other participants. My thanks also to my colleagues in the Chicago Area Consortium who commented on this paper, Elizabeth Asmis, Richard Kraut, Jonathan Lear, Connie Meinwald, and Martha Nussbaum, and to the audience at University of Chicago Divinity School 2006 Ethics Club conference on aesthetics and morality. Finally, thanks to James Lesher, Debra Nails, and Frisbee Sheffield for organizing that excellent conference on the *Symposium* and for bringing the fruits of our thinking to bear in this volume.

philosophy, an *erōs* first expressed in love for beautiful souls in beautiful bodies (402c–403c). And in the *Phaedrus* Socrates attributes to beauty the power to awaken the soul's erotic "madness" and thereby to liberate us from our impure, bodily existence. For some reason, Plato seems to think that receptiveness to and devotion to beauty (including physical beauty) is necessary for a rational grasp of the good and for the virtuous behavior that follows from it. This is bound to strike us as strange. We may be ready to grant that erotic love, and thus physical beauty, is ethically relevant. But why exactly does Plato think they are so ethically important? This is the question I will try to answer here in my interpretation of the *Symposium* and in particular of Socrates' speech.

The idea that beauty is central to ethical theory is, as I said, alien to us. So we should not expect an adequate interpretation of the *Symposium* to show us that this idea is, after all, one we already accept. But neither should we settle for a superficial explanation in which we get the gist, but not the details, of how beauty figures in the virtuous life. This danger is especially acute when we try to interpret Socrates' speech. He evidently believes that good things are beautiful; and we know from other dialogues that beauty depends on good-ness. Thus when he speaks about love as an urge to give birth in beauty, we may be tempted to suppose that this is merely a mysterious way of describing the fact that our desire for the good is focused and made effective when we encounter something in particular that we think is good, as if beauty *per se* did not really matter in this context. That is to say, we may be tempted to explain the ethical significance of beauty solely by appeal to the fact that, according to Plato, genuinely beautiful things are good. But we should not be too hasty. I do not want to deny that the connection between the beautiful and the good is relevant to the proper interpretation of Socrates' account of love. Indeed, as we will see, it plays a central role in explaining why lovers want to create beauty. But what is especially interesting about the *Symposium* is that it draws our attention to the fact that our response to things *qua* good is not the same as our response to them *qua* beautiful. Even if, in truth, the class of good things is coextensive with the class of beautiful things; even if a thing's beauty depends on its goodness, the experience of a thing as good plays a different role in our lives than does the experience of a thing as beautiful. This, I will argue, is something Socrates wants his audience to see. Thus if we adopt the strategy of substituting 'good' for 'beautiful' in his account of love, we will ignore and leave unexplained his overt and insistent concern with the place of beauty in human life. Perhaps worse, we will flatten out the distinction between the role of good as the *object* of love and the role of beauty as its *midwife*, a distinction that Socrates (speaking as Diotima) takes pains to make.

I will argue that, according to Socrates, what grabs the attention of the lover when he experiences someone or something as beautiful is its self-sufficiency and lack of change. That is to say, insofar as things are beautiful, their goodness strikes us as being impervious to the passage of time. The temporal dimension of our experience of beauty has not, to my knowledge, been noticed as being part of Plato's thought. It is important for two reasons, though. Once we understand it, we can better see why, in his view, we lovers who desire to be happy forever care so much about experiencing and creating beauty. This will be my focus here. But in addition, as I will suggest at the end, it helps us see how Plato can allow for that aspect of the experience of beauty which Kant called disinterestedness, while nevertheless maintaining that the pleasure we take in beauty is deeply interested. Thus, my reading of the *Symposium* will enrich our understanding of Plato's conception of beauty and, in my view, make it more plausible.

1. Phaedrus' Speech: A Paradigm and Two Problems

Before turning to Socrates' speech, let us consider for a moment the first speech of the evening, for in his speech Phaedrus praises love in terms that Socrates will basically accept.[2] According to Phaedrus, love "gives people who intend to live in a fine and beautiful way [*kalōs*] what is necessary to lead them through their whole lives ... What is this thing I mean? Shame at shameful and ugly things and ambitious striving[3] for fine and beautiful ones (*tois kalois*). For neither city nor private citizen can achieve great and beautiful [*kala*] deeds without these things" (178c5–d4). In other words, he describes lovers as responding to the beauty of their beloveds by living and acting in a way that is itself beautiful. It is this power of love to make us creative of beauty that Phaedrus praises. The remainder of the speech is a catalogue of extraordinary feats caused by love—for example, it is none other than love that inspires Homer's heroes on the field of battle.

---

[2] Phaedrus does not emphasize as much as Socrates will do that love is a response to someone beautiful. Still, it is clear that he assumes it, for instance when he argues that Achilles must have been the beloved of Patroclus because he was more beautiful (180a5). The assumption is perhaps also implicit in Phaedrus' claim that lovers are rivals in *philotimia* (179a1); the idea would be that love implants—or rather, awakens—love of honor because the beloved is *kalon* and seeing his beauty ignites a desire to outdo him in beauty. But as we will see, this is not the only possibility.

[3] Hunter's translation of *philotimia* (2004:41). Translations are mine, unless otherwise noted, but I have often consulted the translations of Rowe (1998a), and Nehamas and Woodruff (1989).

There is nothing extraordinary in the paradigm for praising love that Phaedrus introduces.[4] In fact, there is such a long tradition of praising love for its creation of beautiful poetry and acts of derring-do that it may to us seem trite. What is more interesting is that Socrates endorses both sides of Phaedrus' trope. That is to say, he claims *both* (1) that love is a response to beauty *and* (2) that love responds by creating beauty. To be sure, Socrates (or Diotima) emphasizes the first half. Lovers of all stripes are able to give birth only in beauty (206c–d, 209b–c) and the steps by which the lover-initiate ascends the ladder of love are all beauties (210e, 211c). But when they encounter beauty, lovers of the lower mysteries give birth to laws, political wisdom, poetry, and glorious deeds of justice, moderation, and the rest of virtue—all of which Socrates calls beautiful (209a6–8, 209d6–e3).[5] And since he says that these offspring are more beautiful and immortal than physical, human children (209c6–7), it is reasonable to assume that bodily lovers, too, give birth *to* beauty, albeit perhaps only to beauty that a mother could see. The situation is the same for the lovers of the higher mysteries. At the first stage, when the lover loves a single beautiful body, he generates beautiful speeches (210a7); when he reaches the "great sea of beauty" he gives birth to "many beautiful and magnificent speeches and thoughts" (210d4–5). At the apex of his journey, the lover grasps the most complete knowledge of the beautiful and gives birth to true virtue. Socrates does not say explicitly that this creation is something beautiful, but since all the earlier offspring were beautiful, and since virtue in general is usually considered to be *kalon*, it seems reasonable to assume that here, too, Socrates' lover responds to beauty with beauty. His analysis of love is far more ambitious than anything Phaedrus suggests. Still, it

---

[4] That is, I assume that Phaedrus' phenomenon is a *phainomenon* in a more Aristotelian sense, i.e. a widespread belief that any account of love must accommodate or explain away. (See Sheffield in this volume for a consideration of the claim that Plato is working with the endoxic method in the *Symposium*.) Since Phaedrus and all the other symposiasts in one way or another mention that love of a beautiful person or thing tends to promote acts of virtue, deeds that are "beautiful and good," I cannot agree with Ferrari that only lovers of the higher mysteries "establish a connection between the beautiful and the good" (1992:255). These lovers (including the other symposiasts) may not truly understand the connection, but they have noticed and reflected upon it.

[5] Diotima does not limit the beautiful offspring of these psychic lovers to *logoi*, contra Ferrari 1992:255. Even if justice and moderation are kinds of wisdom, it is natural to think that the beautiful manifestations of these virtues, particularly at the lesser level, include actions as well as speech. This is supported by Diotima's previous mention of Alcestis' self-sacrifice and by her claim that cults have been established in honor of these psychic lovers' *kala erga* (208d2–6; 209e3–4). Although there were *hiera* established for Lycurgus (a maker of political *logoi*), it is natural to think also of cult-heroes such as Heracles who were remembered more for their actions than for their words.

is fair to say that one of the principal tasks of Socrates' speech is to rethink the way beauty figures in erotic experience while nevertheless remaining true to the widespread intuition that Phaedrus expresses.

Let us return to Phaedrus, however. His speech is obviously a party set-piece (Hunter 2004:38–39 suggests that it may have been prepared in advance), so it may seem churlish to examine it for philosophical coherence. Still, for the philosophically inclined reader the speech raises more questions than it answers. First, Phaedrus takes for granted that lovers are attracted to beautiful people. But given how ethically and politically crucial the effect of love is in his view, we might well find it curious that it is *beautiful* people who set love in motion. Why is it *beauty* that has this power? Second, despite what Phaedrus claims, it is far from clear that love as he understands it will characteristically issue in great and beautiful actions. As he sees it, the beneficial power of love is due to the fact that it instills *philotimia*, love of honor. Lovers are especially ashamed to be caught by their beloved doing something shameful and so, presumably because they would like to be admired, are zealous to perform fine actions on their behalf. But it is hard to see how love of honor can explain lovers' inclination to take the most fine and beautiful risk of all, the risk of death. How will the lover enjoy the fruits of honor once he's dead? Oddly, Phaedrus himself opens the door to this objection when he criticizes Orpheus, who dared to enter Hades for the sake of his beloved, but wasn't willing to go there by the traditional, deadly route. If Orpheus' love has in fact filled him with love of honor, as Phaedrus' account requires, then his eagerness to do something fine *up to the point of actually being killed* seems utterly reasonable. What good will Eurydice's attentions do him when he's dead? (Cithara-players aren't soft (179d4); they're smart!)

Even leaving aside this extreme case, it is unlikely that *philotimia* can provide an adequate explanation of the phenomenon Phaedrus invokes it to explain. For honor is a reward not for behavior that genuinely is fine and beautiful, but for behavior conventionally assumed to be fine and beautiful. Thus, if a society admires actions that are not genuinely good, love of honor might in fact drive a Phaedran lover to actions that are shameful and ugly.[6] And indeed it soon emerges that even the Athenians encourage lovers

---

[6] The connection between love and beautiful actions is even more tenuous if it turns out that winning honor is itself desired only as a means to sexual favors. Why not pay the beloved for sex, if that is more effective? The fact that, in ancient Athens, paying a citizen for sex would not be effective (since if the beloved were known to prostitute himself he would lose his civic privileges) does not alter the philosophical point. The beauty of the lover's actions would still be merely instrumental and thus contingent.

to behave in ways whose beauty may be seriously doubted. According to Pausanias, who speaks after Phaedrus, the custom in Athens is for lovers "to beg their beloveds, swear oaths, sleep in doorways, and be willing to submit themselves to forms of slavery that no slave, even, would submit to" (Rowe modified, 183a4–7). Pausanias professes to approve of this arrangement, but as he himself says, this is the sort of behavior that the Athenians would typically reproach as obsequious, shameful, and unbecoming a free man (183b1–3). Pausanias claims that the lover's pandering and making a slave of himself (for the sake of sex, one assumes) is more admirable than comparable behavior for the sake of money (183a2), but it is hard to see why this behavior's source in erotic desire makes it any better. (It is ironic that Pausanias heightens our uncertainty about whether the connection between love and beautiful action is reliable, for he explicitly claims that he will do a better job than Phaedrus had done of praising love as the cause of fine and beautiful action [180c1–d3; 180e4–181a7].)

Phaedrus' account of love cannot ultimately be supported, therefore. He cannot explain why it is beauty to which we are especially responsive or why love properly issues in beautiful actions. If, as I said before, Socrates preserves Phaedrus' idea that love is characterized by and is valuable for its response to and creation of beauty, we ought to wonder whether his explanation fares better. Why is it *beauty* that elicits this response? And why is it good for us to create something *beautiful*?

2. The Uncertain Value of Beauty

The questions I am raising about the value of beauty are ones that Plato himself encourages us to ask. The point is not merely that Plato is admirably unsentimental about beauty, although he is unsentimental and it is worth our while to note it. For example, at 198b–199a Socrates gushes about the beauty of Agathon's speech, a speech which he also thinks is utterly untrue.[7] (He reiterates the point 201c1–2.) Socrates' own speech will be a hymn to the power of love and beauty to draw us upwards, but he is not unaware that the experience of beauty can also freeze us in place like the sight of a Gorgon's head (198c4–6).

---

[7] Perhaps Socrates is being sarcastic here. Can a speech be genuinely beautiful if it is false? The *Republic* provides clearer evidence of Plato's unsentimental attitude to beauty. Socrates claims both that training in and love of beauty are essential for moral and intellectual development (401d–402a, 403c) *and* that in certain circumstances attachment to beauty can stunt this very growth (476b–c, 479d–e; cf. 505d).

More important for the interpretation of the *Symposium*, however, Socrates actually includes a sense of confusion about the value of beauty in his very speech. Consider his conversation with Diotima. Early on, he agrees that happiness is the enduring possession of good and beautiful things—this is the divine condition (202c10–11).[8] And, like Agathon, he agrees that good things are also beautiful (201c2, 201e5–7). So it looks as though he confidently attributes the highest value to beauty. But a short while later, when Diotima asks Socrates why love wants to possess the beautiful things it desires, he does not have an answer.

> "If someone should ask us, 'Why is Love of beautiful things, Socrates and Diotima?' Or to put it more clearly, the person who loves beautiful things, loves; why does he love?"
>
> And I said, "To possess them for himself."
>
> "But that answer requires a question of this sort: what will he have when he possesses beautiful things?"
>
> And I said that I wasn't able to answer this question at all readily.
>
> *Symposium* 204d4–10

Only when Diotima substitutes 'good' for 'beautiful' is Socrates able to see that the benefit of possessing love's objects is happiness:

> "Well," she said, "answer just as you would if someone changed things and inquired using good instead of beautiful. 'So, Socrates, the person who loves good things, loves; why does he love?'"
>
> And I said, "To possess them for himself."
>
> "And what will he have when he possesses good things?"
>
> "This," I said, "I can answer more easily: He will be happy."
>
> *Symposium* 204e1–7

Diotima's substitution of 'good' for 'beautiful' is perplexing. She and Socrates agreed earlier (as did Socrates and Agathon) that all good things are beautiful, but they did not agree in addition that all beautiful things are good.

---

[8] Young Socrates is utterly conventional both in (a) associating the happy life with the beautiful life and in (b) associating the happy, beautiful life with the life of the gods. Many of Socrates' well-born interlocutors do the same, e.g. *Crito* 48b, *Meno* 77b, *Gorgias* 484a and 491e–492c, *Republic* 362e–363e, cf. Pericles' Funeral Oration, Thucydides 2.44. Of course, these interlocutors *also* have the intuition that sometimes the beautiful life is not a happy one, e.g. *Republic* 363e–364b, *Gorgias* 474c–d.

That is to say, they did not agree that the class of good things and the class of beautiful things are coextensive. Thus Diotima's substitution strikes us as being *ad hoc* and of questionable validity. We may be tempted to defend her logic by appealing to other dialogues in which Socrates claims that goodness is the cause of beauty. (As I will explain in a moment, this attempt to alleviate our discomfort is ineffective and also obscures part of the point of the passage. Nevertheless it will be worth our while to describe it in outline.) So for example in the *Republic* the good is "the cause of all that is correct and beautiful in anything" (517c; cf. 452e). Although I cannot discuss this in detail, what Socrates seems to mean is that the standard of beauty is functional goodness: "the virtue or excellence, the beauty and correctness of each manufactured item, living creature, and action is related to nothing but the use for which each is made or naturally adapted" (601d, trans. Grube/Reeve; cf. *Timaeus* 87d–e). When a thing's parts are proportioned, ordered, and made appropriate to its characteristic work (*ergon*), then it will be truly beautiful (*Republic* 420c–d, *Laws* 668b, *Timaeus* 87c–d). Beauty is linked to *moral* goodness in the human case because, in Socrates' view, the virtuous soul is one ordered to its proper (rational) activity. In addition to its connection to orderliness and proportion, beauty especially displays itself to perception and cognition (*Phaedrus* 250b) and this too may be due to its intimate connection to the good. At least in the *Republic* Socrates says that the form of the good, when considered as the cause of knowledge and truth, is the most beautiful thing there is (508e–509a). When we put these ideas together, the thought seems to be that beauty is the perceptible or cognizable—and also attractive, exciting (*Symposium* 206d; *Phaedrus* 251a–b), and pleasant (*Phaedrus* 251d; *Philebus* 65e–66a)—manifestation of goodness.[9] Thus not only are all good things beautiful, but all genuinely beautiful things (as opposed to things that are merely apparently beautiful) are good. However, it is hardly likely that the student Socrates, much less Agathon, has this sophisticated account of beauty in mind when they agree quite readily and with no explanation that good things are beautiful. And if we cannot assume some earlier (and unrecorded) acceptance by them of the sophisticated account of beauty, then it may look as if Diotima is playing a sophistical trick in her argument here at 204d4–e7. On the basis of their previous agreement that good things are beautiful she blithely substitutes 'good' for 'beautiful', a move that would be warranted only if they had agreed in addition that all beautiful things are good.[10]

---

[9] See Lear 2006 for further discussion.

[10] This is Dover's interpretation (1980:144–145). The careful way Socrates prepares for his substitution of 'good' for 'pleasure' in the *Protagoras* (353c–356c), establishing that overall pleasure is

We should not be distracted from the main point of this passage by worries that Diotima or Socrates or Plato is being slippery, however. Diotima does not in fact appeal to their earlier agreement to justify her substitution of 'good' for 'beautiful', so there is no need to accuse her of playing fast and loose with logic. Rather, what happens is that Socrates gets stuck in his investigation of the nature of love and Diotima proposes that he try another tack to see whether it will make for smoother sailing. If their earlier agreement that good things are beautiful plays any role here at all, it is to assure us that in conceiving of the object of love as good things, we are not supposing that love loves things that are ugly and *not* beautiful.[11]

And, as we have seen, the new tack does enable Socrates to make progress, for once he conceives of the objects of love as good, he can explain why love wants them. The chain of implication, then, is not from their prior agreement that (1) good things are beautiful to the claim that, therefore, (2) love is of the good; rather, the implication is from the fact that (1′) it is illuminating to conceive of love's objects as good (being assured that, as such, they are also beautiful) to the claim that (2′) we have reason to suppose that no one desires anything unless it is good (205d10–e2). Diotima supports this conclusion with an additional argument: since people reject even what is their own (e.g. their own body parts) if their own turns out to be bad (205e2–4), we must assume that people desire things only on the condition that they are good.

So there is no puzzle about why Socrates allows the substitution of 'good' for 'beautiful'. There is a puzzle, though, about why he needs this help. Why does Socrates represent himself as stumbling over what ought to be a fairly straightforward deduction? If he has already committed himself to the claim that happiness is the possession of good and beautiful things; and if he has already committed himself to the claim that all good things are beautiful;

---

both necessary and sufficient for a course of action to be good, suggests that Plato is aware of the logical problem Dover attributes to him.

[11] Rowe defends the argument in a slightly different way. He claims that since Socrates has already agreed that love is of the good, the substitution is legitimate (1998a:179 on 204e1–2). But it does not seem to me that Socrates (or rather, Agathon) has agreed to this at 201c1–2. All he has said there is that among the class of beautiful things are all the good ones. (Thus, since love is utterly deprived of beautiful things, it must lack good ones as well.) He has not indicated that the good is a proper object of love. True, Diotima goes on to describe love as "a schemer after beautiful *and good* things" (203d3–4), but the emphasis in her speech here is clearly on the beauty of love's object. If, as Rowe argues, Diotima is being careful here not to claim in her own voice that love is properly of the beautiful (1998a:176 on 203c4, 184 on 206e2–3), that only supports my reading that, while Socrates has admitted that love desires things that are good, at this point in the dialogue he still believes that, insofar as they are objects of love, they are beautiful.

why does the conclusion elude him that what love wants in desiring beautiful things is happiness?[12] This, I suggest, is the puzzling fact to which the *ad hoc* nature of Diotima's substitution is supposed to draw to our attention. I suggest that Socrates stumbles because even if, intuitively, the gods in their happiness possess good *and* beautiful things, it is not obvious to us what value the beauty of their possessions has. The benefit of beauty *per se* is not immediately clear. The problem becomes all the more acute when we realize that among the most admired of beautiful things are self-sacrificing acts of virtue. The virtuous life is beautiful, but is it, after all, happy? As the young Socrates sees things—and, I suspect, as we do too—it is the goodness of one's possessions that constitutes their contribution to happiness, whether or not they also happen to be beautiful.

Still, even though the young Socrates finds it easier to understand why we desire good things, Diotima continues to insist that love is essentially inspired by the presence of the beautiful and that love causes us to create beautiful things, in particular beautiful acts of virtue. That is to say, she remains true to Phaedrus' paradigm. And rightly so, since even if love does aim at things that are good, even if, as Diotima argues, love can desire them only on the assumption that they are good, it is their beauty that enchants us. So on the one hand, Socrates agrees with Phaedrus that it is right to praise love for making us responsive to and creative of beauty. But on the other hand, he begins his speech by making us uncertain of the value of beauty. Like the young Socrates, we are likely not to know why we want beauty. Since the *Symposium* raises the question, we may hope it will answer it, too.

What I have argued is that Plato in the *Symposium* brings our simultaneous attraction to and ambivalence about beauty to the fore in Socrates' speech. Insofar as love is intertwined with the experience and creation of beauty, beauty is something we must consider in deciding how to live. But if it is clear that beauty *does* matter, it is not at all clear why it matters. In the next section we will examine the sense in which, in Socrates' view, love is characteristically expressed in beautiful action or the creation of something beautiful. Once we understand that, we will turn in the following section to the question of the importance to the lover of his beloved's beauty.

---

[12] Does he worry perhaps that love might acquire beautiful things that are not good? This possibility should not stump Socrates so completely and I see no evidence that this is what he has in mind. But this may be a reason *we* share in Socrates' confusion and it is possible that the spectacle of Agathon's beautiful but ignorant speech (198b–199a, cited above) was intended by Plato to make us uneasy in just this way.

3. Eros for Immortality and the Creation of Beauties

In contrast to the previous speakers, Socrates (and Diotima) argue that lovers love only objects they believe to be good. In the strictest sense, therefore, the object of love is the good (206a3–4). Furthermore, insofar as we all already desire to be happy, that is, insofar as we all already desire to possess good things for ourselves permanently, we are already full of love, a condition Diotima figures as a pregnancy (205a5–8, 206c1–3). Thus Diotima begins her positive account of love by denying both that beauty is the object of love's desire and that beauty instills love. But notice that as soon as she banishes beauty from its expected roles, she reintroduces it. Curiously, she does so in a passage (206a3–13) that mirrors the one at 204d4–e7 (quoted above) where Socrates' confusion about the value of love began. Here she reminds Socrates of what they had discovered earlier: love desires good things so that it may possess them and possess them forever. Given that this is love's goal, she now asks what activity is characteristic of love (*ergon*, 206b3). Again, Socrates is stumped, so Diotima generously supplies the answer: the function of love is to "give birth in the beautiful" (206b7–8). Thus contrary to what Phaedrus (quite understandably) assumed, the role of the beautiful beloved is not to instill love, but rather to induce the lover's labor.[13] Beauty evokes a creative outburst, a procreation, that is, Diotima says, an attempt to secure immortality insofar as that is possible for a mortal human being (206e7–8). The idea that beauty unleashes a desire for immortality may seem odd—Socrates certainly portrays himself as being astonished by what Diotima says (208b7–9)—but it is in fact required by the claim that love desires happiness.[14] For, as she has already argued, happiness is the permanent possession of good and beautiful things.

---

[13] This explains how we might be confused into thinking that the experience of beauty inspires love itself. We tend to identify love with the passionate excitement that, according to Socrates, is only a mode of our standing desire for happiness caused by the presence of beauty (206b1–3, 206d7–e2).

[14] Of course it is not odd to think that people desire immortality. Homeric warriors want to be immortal like the gods; precisely because they cannot be, they strive to win glory and the quasi-immortality of fame. (See *Iliad* XII 322–328.) What strikes Socrates as odd is that this desire for immortality is characteristic of love. It is interesting to note that in epic culture the desire for immortality is also linked to beauty. (E.g. "But since men must die, why would anyone sit / in darkness and coddle a nameless old age to no use / deprived of all beautiful [*kalōn*] deeds?" Pindar *Olympian* 1.82–84, trans. Race, modified. See Vernant [2001] for this reference and a fascinating discussion.) However, in that tradition beauty is what is remembered and thus "possessed" by the warrior forever. For Diotima, beauty is also what excites the lover to this extravagant act of self-perpetuation.

We should be clear about this point: love aims to possess (a) the good (b) permanently. This is one desire, the desire for happiness.[15] If procreation is to serve as a metaphor for the expression of this universal desire,[16] then we must interpret it as involving both these aspects. Thus, we should not interpret Diotima's talk of procreation and quasi-immortality as merely concerning ways of extending our brute existence in time. Even literal immortality would be of no value if it were a life of eternal misery. What Diotima is talking about is a way, a more permanent way, of possessing the good. She makes this clear at 206e8–207a2 when she concludes, "from what we agreed before it is necessary to desire immortality *with* the good, if in fact love is of *always* having the good for oneself" (emphasis added). Love's creative activity is a mortal creature's means of grasping the good in as immortal or godlike a way as possible.

I emphasize this point for two reasons. First, it makes clear that beauty reenters Diotima's account of love precisely at the moment she begins talking about the immortal mode in which the lover desires to possess the good. Beauty is the goddess of erotic generation, the mortal form of immortality (206d1–2; 206e7–8). Thus if we want to understand why it is *beauty* to which lovers respond, we ought to explore the connections between beauty and immortality. (We will turn to this suggestion in the next section.) Second, it makes clear that the lover's progeny must be things he considers good (or in possession of the good) if they are to serve his purpose of having the good forever. In other words, by conceiving of love as an expression of the universal human desire for perfect happiness, Socrates explains why lovers tend to create things that are good.

This point is confirmed by looking at the uninitiated lovers.[17] "By having children, they supply for themselves through all time to come immortality and memory and happiness," (208e4–6). Notice that Diotima is talking about lovers

---

[15] *Contra* Ferrari 1992:255 and Santas 1988:35–36.

[16] Presumably procreation is an instantiation of the desire for happiness as well. But since the process of giving birth applies literally only to women, it must apply metaphorically to all male lovers and thus to nearly all the lovers Diotima mentions.

[17] Since bodily existence and honor and anything else pursued by lovers of the lower mysteries are not in fact the good that gives genuine happiness, their creative activity is in this sense a failure. But we should not dismiss their activity as utterly futile. Bodily existence and honor are not *the* good in Diotima's account, but it is very likely that they nevertheless participate in the good. She appears to want to give a teleological explanation of all biological reproduction, i.e. she wants to explain it in terms of its aiming at the good. If the outcome achieved by reproduction on her account is not in fact good in any way at all, but is only apparently good, then she will not have succeeded in offering a teleological explanation. For this reason we are warranted in studying the details of the lower mysteries for information about Socrates' account of the nature of love.

who are pregnant in their bodies here; living children serve the purposes of love not simply because they resemble their parents and so, in a way, extend their existence. Living children also provide future happiness for their parents, at least "as they think" (208e5). Diotima is not altogether clear about how this works, but presumably the idea is that these lovers think of bodily existence as itself being something good; in children it is possible for this good of bodily life to transcend the limits of the parents' death but nevertheless to be in some sense their own. Or consider those lovers pregnant in soul who seek honor. It looks irrational to be driven by *philotimia* to risk death unless we understand that love fills the honor-lover with a desire for a name and a glorious reputation that will last forever (208c2–d2). Presumably, for such people, their own renown is a central component of happiness. Diotima argues that, counterintuitive as it may at first seem, sacrificing your life in a noble way is an effective means of extending your possession of glory past the limits of death. You may die before your time, but it is precisely self-sacrificing actions that are remembered and celebrated. And since the glory is always linked to you in particular—it is specifically your reputation that is remembered—then the glory that survives your death is genuinely yours.[18] Since death is in any case inevitable, the honor lover who dies a beautiful death actually manages to hold on to the good, at least in a way, for much longer than he would if he lived a long and quiet life. This is something Achilles in the *Iliad* understands quite well. Diotima also mentions Alcestis (208d2–4).

Diotima's mention of Alcestis is important because it signals that she (or rather, Socrates) is directly addressing a problem that emerged in Phaedrus' speech while nevertheless preserving his principal intuition that love causes the lover to respond to beauty with fine and beautiful deeds. Recall, we worried how *philotimia* could warrant taking the risk of death. As we have just seen, Diotima solves the problem by recasting erotic *philotimia* as a desire for immortality.

Let me recapitulate Diotima's picture so far. We all have a standing desire to be happy—i.e. a desire to possess the good permanently. When we fall in love we are inspired to approximate to this godlike condition by creating an image

---

[18] In fact, a further premise is needed. For although the long-lasting reputation may be mine, we may worry that nothing essential to me survives my death. The solution would be to suppose that the essence of my self is just my appearance in the opinion of my community. (Similarly, the lovers pregnant in body would need to believe not only that bodily existence is the good but also that the body is what the self essentially is.) It seems reasonable to attribute this confused view of the self to people who pursue honor as the highest good, but I leave that issue aside.

of ourselves in association with the good or the good life as we understand it. Those who think sheer physical existence is good create human children; those who think honor is good perform actions worthy of memory; those who think political power is good write constitutions that will influence the city after their death. But in every case lovers aim to create offspring that are, in their opinion at least, possessed of the good. Unless they do create good progeny, they will not succeed in making their own grasp of the good permanent.

We are now in a position to see why, in Socrates' view, love tends toward the creation of beauty. Since all these creations are (or are apparently) good, they will be (or apparently be) beautiful. But in the case of the honor lovers it seems fair to say that the beauty of their offspring is positively desirable to them. Their ambition is to be celebrated forever. Thus they must try to act not just well, but beautifully. For it is only by acting in a genuinely beautiful way, in a way that commands the admiration of human beings across great reaches of time, that their names will be remembered and praised.

This point about the visibility of the lover's beautiful creations has broader application than we might at first notice. Diotima says in the passage from 209a1–e4 (i.e. in describing the lower mysteries) that people who are pregnant in their souls give birth in the presence of a beautiful person to beautiful poems and laws and other manifestations of beautiful wisdom. It is notable that Diotima implies that these speeches bring the lover immortality by causing him to be remembered. "Everyone would welcome engendering children of this sort more than human children, and when they look at Homer and Hesiod and all the other good poets they envy the sort of progeny they leave behind them which provide them with immortal glory and memory because they are themselves things of this sort" (209c7–d5). Likewise, Solon and Lycurgus achieved immortality by establishing laws for which they are honored (209d5–e2). In other words, these lovers do not achieve immortality merely by perpetuating their ideas in teaching, song, or lawgiving. Rather, their beautiful *logoi* are remembered and remembered as belonging to them. Given that this is so, it is reasonable to suppose that lovers of this sort consciously aim to create something beautiful. They must make their creativity conspicuous (*apophēnamenoi*, 209e2); and the more beautiful something is, the more likely it is to be remembered. (Notice, too, that when later generations remember Homer on account of the beauty of the *Iliad*, they remember him as a good poet. That is to say, he achieves a quasi-immortal possession of the good, as he understands it.)

We have discovered something about the value of living in a beautiful way: beauty allows us to be noticed and remembered as in some way or other possessing the good. We want to have the good, but given the sort of creatures we are, our possession of the good is enhanced and extended when it is recognized and celebrated by other people. Thus, there is a sense in which our interest in the beautiful is an expression of our social nature.

This explanation for why lovers desire to create beauty is more difficult to sustain when we turn to the best, philosophical lovers, however. They, presumably, do not equate being honored with being happy. Socrates does not explain why this is so in the *Symposium*, but it is reasonable to suppose that it is because philosophers do not regard their social nature as essential to their rational selves. (This seems to be the view of the *Republic*, for example.) So if beauty's tendency to be noticed and remembered is to play a role in their creation of beautiful offspring too, then we need to ask whether there is some other, higher good than honor that can be preserved by memory.

But of course the answer is yes; memory perpetuates knowledge. Indeed, Diotima says as much at 208a3–6 when she argues that the everyday experience of thinking "the same thought" from one day to the next is in fact a matter of creating a new memory to replace one that passed away by being forgotten. If, as she claims, my own process of remembering today what I understood yesterday counts as a case of achieving mortal immortality, then perhaps the same is true when other people remember what I have taught them. That is to say, perhaps my (good) thought transcends my finite ability to think it when other people remember it. Bearing this in mind we notice that at the beginning of the ascent, at least, it appears that the lover speaks in order to teach the beautiful boy who has captured his attention (210c2–3). It can be argued that, at every stage of the ascent, the lover continues to speak in order to inculcate his newfound wisdom.[19] This invites the speculation that the lover aims to make his speeches beautiful not primarily so that they will be noticed, but so that they will be especially intelligible and persuasive to others. This fits with the close association in Socrates' speech between the *kalon* and sight. (There are numerous variations of the verbs *blepein*, *theōrein*, *idein*, and *katidein* in the description of the ascent, 210a–212a.) What is visible is not just noticeable; it can also be grasped in its sensible properties. Likewise, the thought would be, insofar as beautiful things "flash out" (*Phaedrus* 250d) or are apparent to the mind, they are not just easily noticed, they are intelligible.

---

[19] This idea was suggested to me by Richard Kraut (forthcoming). I am uncertain, however, whether we should accept the idea that the lover's immortality is secured through his activity of teaching. As the lover ascends, the emphasis shifts to his being a student, someone who is led. If he continues to try to make young men better, Diotima does not say so.

I have suggested two ways that the connection between beauty and memory might explain the lover's interest in giving birth to what is beautiful. Insofar as beautiful actions and speeches are noticed and remembered, they will win fame for their authors. And insofar as beautiful speeches are easily intelligible and thus easy to remember, they will remain "alive" in the thinking of those who remember them. In both these ways, the beauty of the lover's offspring might help them outlive their author and so achieve for him a sort of immortality.[20] But these suggestions must remain merely speculative. The fact is that Socrates does not explain how the higher-mysteries lover approximates immortality with his speeches. It makes one wonder whether his quasi-immortality is not something altogether different from enduring for a very long time in the minds of others. (I'll return to this point later.)

4. The Encounter with Beauty

I want to turn now to the question why beauty is so specially attractive. Diotima says that lovers give birth only in the beautiful because only beauty harmonizes with this divine activity (206c4–d1). Beauty is in fact the goddess of childbirth (206d1–2). But the role of beauty in unleashing erotic activity is obscure. As Anthony Price quite correctly observes, the "appeal to the divine seems extraneous, and sophistical: why must something that is divine in one way (being linked to immortality) be divine in another (being linked to beauty)?" (1997:16–17).

We might be tempted once again to recall that, for Plato, beauty is closely associated with goodness. If we human beings have a standing desire for happiness, then coming into the presence of something beautiful—which seems good—will naturally excite this desire. The suggestion becomes all the more promising when we recall that this beautiful thing which excites *erōs* is, in the first instance at least, a beautiful human body or, if the lover is more elevated, a beautiful human soul. Attraction to this sort of beauty makes sense given that, by manifesting human beauty, the beautiful person seems to be in possession of the good appropriate to human beings. No doubt this appear-

---

[20] A problem: if the lover's understanding is genuine, then the account he grasps will not differ from the account of anyone else who genuinely understands. But in that case, how will his articulation of the account bring about the quasi-immortality of him rather than of anyone else who understands? After all, he will not be teaching the truth as he sees it, but simply the truth. That is to say, on this account of how the lover of the higher mysteries achieves immortality, there is a disregard not only for differences among beautiful beloveds (at each level), but also for differences among lovers.

111

ance will, to put it mildly, seem relevant to someone bursting with the desire for immortal happiness.

This suggestion is correct so far as it goes, but as I argued before, the intimate connection between beauty and goodness cannot all on its own explain beauty's role as a midwife. Diotima says that "love is not of the beautiful in the way you [Socrates] think" but is rather "of generation and giving birth in the beautiful" (206e2–5). Here she corrects young Socrates' assumption that beauty is the desirable object of love—that role goes to the good—and assigns it a different role, the role of facilitating the pursuit of the good. Now since all good things are, according to Socrates, beautiful, desirable objects of love are also in fact beautiful. But insofar as beautiful things play the role of love object, it is because they are good. On the other hand, when she emphasizes beauty's role as midwife, Diotima seems to imply that if good things help us to "give birth," they do so not insofar as they are good, but insofar as they are beautiful. If this is correct, then the goodness of beauty cannot explain the peculiar way that beauty releases the lover's pent up pregnancy. We must find some role peculiar to beauty *qua* beauty.

There is something odd in thinking that we need a property in addition to goodness to explain the activation of a standing desire for happiness. If people do have a standing desire to be happy, then the ordinary way for a person to be moved to action is to see or remember something good, which he will then pursue as an object. There seems no need for beauty to play a facilitating role. But then again, this ordinary way of being prompted to action is quite different, I take it, from the extravagant generative activity "characteristic of this zeal we call love" in which beauty plays an essential part.[21] It may help to consider a case of being moved to act by an experience of good that is not at the same time an experience of beauty. I have in mind painful or embarrassing or just tedious medical treatments. The ordinary patient does not find these treatments beautiful and may in fact be repelled by them, considered just in themselves. Even if a person chooses medical treatment because, ultimately, he wants immortal happiness, it seems thoroughly unreasonable to describe his choice as "giving birth in the beautiful." If a good thing does not strike a person as beautiful, then I cannot see how its beauty functions as a midwife. It is heartening to notice that every example Diotima mentions of giving birth in beauty is a case in which the lover is actually attracted by his beloved's beauty.[22] This suggests that Socrates thinks of giving birth in beauty

---

[21] See Appendix for a brief defense of this claim.

[22] Are animals attracted to the beauty of their mates? Well, it is at least true that they do not mate

as a special case of the universal pursuit of perfect happiness. And that, in turn, suggests that beauty is required not to facilitate the lover's pursuit of good, but to facilitate his unusual means of pursuing the good. As I said before, since beauty reenters Diotima's account as part of her explanation for how mortal creatures seek to possess the good immortally, we should concentrate on this question: how does beauty affect the lover's desire to possess the good *in an immortal way?*[23]

When we examine the lover's ascent through the higher mysteries, where Diotima especially emphasizes the phenomenology of encountering beauty, two points are notable, one concerning what the lover finds impressive in the beautiful beloved and the other concerning how his encounter with beauty affects the order of his life. I begin with the second point.

Consider how the lover experiences the form of the Beautiful. It rushes into his awareness. He "catches sight of it all of a sudden" (*exaiphnēs katopsetai,* 210e4, cf. 210d7) and it is amazing (*thaumaston,* 210e5) to behold. The sight of the Beautiful itself arrests the lover and is experienced by him as interrupting his previous activity. "There, if anywhere at all, life is worth living (*bioton*) for a human being, for one looking at the beautiful itself" (211d1–3). Diotima says, and surely the lover must recognize too, that his previous activity was just an image of virtue. In the presence of beauty itself, the lover radically reevaluates and changes his life.

It is not only the fully initiated lover who experiences the beauty of his beloved this way. Socrates suggests that all lovers are "driven out of their minds" (Rowe trans., 211d5) when they see their beloveds and go so far as to stop eating and drinking just so they can look at their beauty. At each stage the lover recognizes that something new (or more vast) is beautiful. This recognition leads him to think of his previous way of living as foolish (*pollē anoia,* 210b2); he relaxes from his previous ardor and considers it to have been

---

with the first biologically suitable animal to come along; animals can be quite choosy. Male birds in particular seem to preen for the females and female birds seem to be attracted by it. Do admirable politicians give birth in beauty? Yes; they are attracted by the beauty of their cities.

23 All lovers give birth in beauty, including those whose pregnancy is not psychic and thus is not rational, much less philosophical. Thus, we need an account of the experience of beauty that explains (a) why *all* erotic creativity is inspired by beauty of some sort or other and (b) why the intelligible Beautiful itself inspires the most successful delivery. Constraint (a) necessitates that we not begin by attributing beauty's power to its intelligibility. Although the intelligibility of beauty will explain its appeal to lovers who are already in the business of trying to understand, it will not explain its appeal to lovers in the business of trying to reproduce or to become famous.

in truth small (210b5–6). (Notice, it is his previous love he disdains, not the beloved body.) When he sees the "great sea of beauty," he thinks of his former attachment to particular people or practices as having been "slavish, ignoble, and petty" (210d2). The experience of every sort of beauty changes the lover's evaluation of his life. Interestingly, Alcibiades describes his own encounter with the beauty of Socrates in exactly the same terms. Socrates always appears to him "all of a sudden" (*exaiphnēs*, 213c1) and when he speaks, Alcibiades becomes possessed, like a Corybant. Socrates makes him think that his present life is not worth living (*bioton*) since there is so much of importance that he lacks (215d7–216a5).[24] In any case, the emphasis in Diotima's speech is overwhelmingly on the ethical effect of beauty. We could add that when the lover stands on the step of the vast sea of beauty, he grows and is strengthened (210d6), as if the metaphor of steps is intended to invoke not the ideas of trampling the beloved and using him merely as a means, but the idea of the beautiful beloved as a place where we rest and gather our strength.

So, to sum up, the experience of beauty—both the Beautiful itself and its images—is the feeling of being shaken from one's way of living, so that one feels that it is better to live in association with this beautiful thing and to alter one's whole life accordingly. Why does beauty have this effect? Diotima's description of the Beautiful itself can help:

> First, (1) it always is and does not come into being nor passes away, it does not grow or diminish; then, (2) it is not beautiful in some respect and ugly in another, not beautiful at one time and not at another, not beautiful in relation to one thing but ugly in relation to something else, not beautiful here and ugly there because it is beautiful to one person and ugly to another. (3) Nor again will it seem to him that the Beautiful is the sort of thing a certain face is or hands or any of the things partaking of body, nor is it a certain speech or knowledge, nor is it anywhere in some other thing, such as in an animal, or in earth, or in heaven, or in any other thing; but it is always itself by itself with itself one form. And all the other beautiful things partake in it in such a way that when those other things

---

[24] Alcibiades' beauty has the same effect. He enters "all of a sudden (212c6)" and immediately all the symposiasts—including Socrates—give up their way of proceeding (*pantas*, 213a3; Socrates makes a space for Alcibiades when he sees him, 213b1–2). Of course, Alcibiades' beauty causes them all to give up their orderly speech-making in favor of uproarious drinking. Whether this is a change from better to worse is beyond the scope of this paper, but it does seem significant that only in this context is Socrates free to pursue one-on-one conversation (223c6).

come into being and pass away, it does not become more or less nor
does it suffer anything.

Symposium 210e6–211b5

It is striking that the parallel description of forms in Socrates' palinode in the
Phaedrus gives more emphasis to their epistemological status as intelligible
but not sensible. He says there that all the forms, including the form of Beauty,
are without color, shape, solidity—i.e. they cannot be perceived by the senses.
They are visible only to intelligence and as such are the subject of true knowledge (*Phaedrus* 247c6–d1). *Phaedrus* 250c2–3 does describe forms as complete
(*holoklēra*), simple, unmoved, and (significantly) happy, but these qualities are
immediately linked to the fact that the forms can be clearly seen only when we
have been purified of the body (250c4–6). By contrast, the description of the
form of the Beautiful in the *Symposium* is far more interested in contrasting its
being with the *being* of lower objects. That is to say, Socrates in the *Symposium*
is interested in the *ontological* status of the Beautiful itself more than its *epistemological* status (although of course these things are related). This emphasis
is notable given that the lover of the higher mysteries is, presumably, engaged
in an epistemological ascent. That is to say, at each level he obtains a deeper
or more accurate understanding of beauty. We might expect, on the basis of
similar ascents in the *Phaedrus* and also the *Republic*, that if the lover's cognitive level has improved, the objects of his cognition have become more knowable. But although no doubt such a view is consistent with what Diotima says
and may even be something she (or Plato) has in mind, it is not something
she emphasizes or explains. Consider, for example, that once the lover moves
beyond love of bodies, every beauty he encounters is grasped by thought
rather than by sensory perception. Are souls less knowable than the practices
that improve them? Are these in turn less knowable than the special sciences?
Diotima is completely silent about this issue. Ontology, not epistemology, is
her point.[25]

Consider again the three aspects of the Beautiful Diotima describes: (1)
The Beautiful always is and never becomes; (2) not only does it not change
its being, it does not change its appearance; and (3) it is metaphysically independent of particular things—it does not partake of them, but rather, these
particular things partake of it. This is in marked contrast to the picture of

---

[25] In the world of the *Symposium* (as opposed to the *Phaedrus*), cultural practices do last longer
than souls since souls are mortal. And the sciences are more "immortal" still, not necessarily
by lasting longer in time but (in the rather different way explained below) by being associated
with atemporal objects.

mortal, human life that Diotima has developed so far. We mortal human beings are always trying to become good and beautiful (i.e. happy), but can never permanently be so; we must concern ourselves with whether our actions seem beautiful to others since what strikes one person as admirable may not impress someone else; and we are so far from being self-sufficient that our selves persist in time only in the being of our literal or metaphorical children. In other words, given the context of Diotima's speech, what is particularly notable about her description of the Beautiful and what she clearly emphasizes is that it has immortal being. She reiterates this point a few lines later: the Beautiful is "unalloyed, pure, unmixed, not infected by human flesh and colors and other great mortal nonsense, but [is] the divine, uniform Beautiful itself" (211e1–4). Whereas in the *Phaedrus* Socrates emphasizes the intelligibility of the Beautiful and the other forms by contrast with the sensibility of physical beings, in the *Symposium* he illuminates its immortality by contrast with our mortality.[26]

In saying that the Beautiful is presented as immortal, I do not mean simply that it endures through all time (although it must in some sense do this too). Rather, the point is that in so thoroughly escaping change, the Beautiful escapes being affected by the passing of time in any way at all. This is an even more perfect sort of immortality than the one we have been imagining up to this point in the dialogue, an immortality in which the approaching future is of no concern at all because it is simply impossible for any future change to make a difference.[27] How different the existence of the Beautiful is from the life of toil endured even by the happiest lover (cf. 210e6)! When the lover of the higher mysteries suddenly catches sight of the Beautiful itself, it is its stable, self-sufficient being that shines out to him and fills him with awe.

We know from other Platonic dialogues that being beyond change is not peculiar to the Beautiful. All forms have this property. Thus, presumably, if the lover caught sight of any other form at the end of his ascent, he would marvel at its unchanging character, too. But I take it that part of Socrates' point in describing the lover's encounter with the Beautiful itself is to show in a pure and unqualified light what strikes lovers as important when they experience in a similar but diminished way the beauty of their beloveds. After all, as we saw before, the experience of *all* beauties causes the lover to reevaluate what is important in his life. If this line of thought is correct then, although it is

---

[26] The difference is appropriate to the different subject matter of the two dialogues, persuasion and desire.

[27] If no change can make a difference, we may wonder whether it makes sense to think of the Beautiful as existing in time at all. Cf. *Timaeus* 37d–38b on time as an imitation of eternity.

not peculiar to the form of the Beautiful to be unchanging, it is peculiar to it that its unchanging character "shines out" in the beautiful bodies, souls, laws, and sciences that participate in it. The idea that the Beautiful manifests in its instantiations a property common to all forms has a parallel in the *Phaedrus*. There too it is not peculiar to the form of the Beautiful to be especially "visible" or intelligible; all the forms shine "in a pure bright light" (250c4) when they are seen just in themselves. But the Beautiful is especially "radiant' with the result that its splendor "flashes out" like lightening in the physical objects which participate in it (250b5–6, 250d1–3). Socrates cannot mean simply that beautiful people, unlike just people or wise people, remind us of the forms, for he insists that all speech, i.e. all use of concepts, involves recollection of the forms (249b6–c4). Rather, the point must be that when we perceive and speak about things participating in other forms, we are unaware that our cognitive activity depends on our referring these sensible objects to something radically other than their imperfect, sensible nature. By contrast, when we perceive someone as beautiful, the transcendent, intelligible nature of Beauty appears to be present in the finite, sensible object which participates in it. That is to say, unlike the other participants in other forms, participants in the Beautiful manifest transcendence. For this reason, the lover seems to perceive a god inside his beloved and immediately begins to worship him (251a; 252d–253c).[28] What I am suggesting is that just as in the *Phaedrus* beauty manifests transcendent intelligibility, in a parallel way in the *Symposium* it manifests transcendent being.

The Beautiful itself is especially overwhelming to experience, but all beautiful things participate in it and so, as we have seen, they all affect those who experience them in a similar, if diminished, way. What would it be like to experience something (other than the form) as being beautiful in the way Socrates describes it in the *Symposium*? It would be to experience a mortal thing as being or being filled with something immortal, unchanging, and unchangeable. It would be to experience the beautiful thing or person, insofar as he was beautiful, as being godlike in the stability and self-sufficiency of his

---

[28] The picture is complicated somewhat by the fact that, in the *Phaedrus*, being divine is not equated with being a form. Rather, the gods are souls who, by contrast with human souls, have permanent and easy access to the forms, including the form of the Beautiful. Socrates makes it clear at 251a, though, that the beloved seems to be divine because he is beautiful. This is consonant with the account of love found in the *Symposium*. It is beyond the scope of this paper to explain how these two dialogues describe aspects of a coherent account of love, despite apparent differences. But in general it is important to remember that while Socrates' speech in the *Phaedrus* is intended to show the benefits of *being loved* (it is a seduction speech), his speech in the *Symposium* is intended to show the benefits of *loving*.

being. This would certainly be confusing to anyone. But if we are as Diotima has described us as being, then its effect would be even more tumultuous. For according to her account, we all already long for immortal happiness. It is reasonable to expect that if we experience something beautiful *as beautiful* and yet also see it as being a perishable body or soul or city, this experience will fan the flame of our latent desire. What had once seemed a futile wish for immortality all of a sudden appears to be within reach, at least in a way.[29]

If the interpretation I have suggested is correct, we are in a position to understand why beauty is the goddess of erotic creativity. The point is not, as Price worried, that beauty and immortality both happen to be divine attributes. The divine is beautiful because it manifests its immortal possession of the good. This is why Diotima says that beauty in all things harmonizes with the divine and is the midwife of creativity. Most of the time, we go through life with our heads down, being mortal, thinking mortal thoughts. We are absorbed in ordinary prudential calculation, figuring out how to get food, and clothes, and other goods for tomorrow and the next day and the next. Beauty—the manifestation of godlike permanence and self-sufficiency—reminds us that our aspirations for happiness are of a different order. Not just long-lasting, but immortal. When we see our beautiful beloved, our desire for immortality is unleashed.

To repeat, my suggestion is that in the *Symposium* Socrates presents and makes use of a connection between beauty and immortality. Beauty appears godlike in its relationship to time and change. In fact, its manifestation of its atemporal imperviousness to change is exactly what strikes the lover as being so wonderful about beauty. I think it is good evidence in favor of this interpretation that it can make sense of why beauty facilitates erotic creativity. It also explains why the objects at each level of the ascent are more beautiful than the ones preceding it: at least, the movement from bodies to practices and from practices to sciences is a movement away from what is subject to change. (My thought is that the *epitēdeumata* are practices peculiar to a particular social time and place.) Notice also that we students of Plato would expect that the more unchanging an object is, the more knowable it is. Thus the conception of beauty I have been describing is entirely consistent with the obvious, but unexplained fact that the higher mysteries represent an epistemological ascent. In fact, since the paradigmatically beautiful object is, of necessity, something intelligible, philosophy will be vindicated as the true art of love.

---

[29] This effect is suggested in the *Phaedrus* as well. Not only does the beautiful boy remind the lover of the form of Beauty, he also reminds him of a god (251a–b, 252d–253c).

The link Plato forges between beauty and immortality has not (I believe) been much noticed, but it is not found only in the *Symposium*. According to Timaeus craft objects are beautiful only when they are accurately copied from an unchanging model. If the craftsman takes as his model something that comes-to-be, his creation will not be beautiful (*Timaeus* 28a–b). And although what the *Philebus* says about beauty is extraordinarily complicated, if not just obscure, it clearly draws a link between beauty and self-sufficiency; they are of the same "family stock (*geneas*)" (66b1–3). To the extent that something is self-sufficient though, it will be resistant to change. It is not clear why in the *Philebus* beauty is akin to self-sufficiency. At one point Socrates claims that beautiful shapes are ones whose beauty is not relative to something else (*pros ti*, 51c6–d1). Perhaps his thought is that their appearing beautiful does not depend on their being juxtaposed to something else, so that the pleasure that arises from seeing them is pure. At any rate, it seems clear that in the *Philebus* the genuineness of a shape's beauty comes—for whatever reason— from its independence. Furthermore, Socrates says that beautiful things are proportionate and symmetrical (*summetron*, 66b1). Insofar as they are proportionate, beautiful things will not lack anything—and so will be self-sufficient and stable. Finally, for what it is worth, I refer you to Aristotle's remark in the *Nicomachean Ethics*: "For the one who acts (*pepoiēkoti*), his deed endures, since the beautiful (*kalon*) is long-lasting (*polluchronion*). But for the one who is affected, the benefit passes by in time" (1168a15–17). That is, Aristotle contrasts beauty and the beneficial in terms of their relationship to time. I do not claim that beauty's transcendence of time and change is, for Plato, its most important feature. But there is a connection here that we ought to explore.

Let us return for a moment to a question I raised earlier: how does the fully initiated lover achieve immortality? The immortality of the Beautiful itself transcends unending endurance through time. It is, in itself, utterly without change. I think this should lead us to wonder whether the lover who succeeds in gazing at the beauty of this ultimately self-sufficient object does not become, as a consequence, less interested in extending his existence in time and more interested in being stable and unchangingly what he is, insofar as that is possible for a human being. I cannot pursue the possibility here, but it does seem to me that, from this vantage point, Alcibiades' Socrates looks very much like a fully initiated lover. He does not sway from his self-control when Alcibiades tries to seduce him;[30] he is not visibly affected by hunger, cold, and other hardships of military life; he remains calm even as his comrades are

---

[30] The point of this story is to show that Socrates is surpassingly temperate (216d7).

being overrun by the enemy. Perhaps it is the stability and self-sufficiency of his character that accounts for the godlike, brilliant, and beautiful statues Alcibiades sees within him (216e7–217a2; 221c4–222a6).[31]

4. Real Life Beauty

The interpretation I have just given is in a certain way satisfying. It makes use of what little Socrates says to explain why he insists repeatedly that love is a response to and creation of beauty. But it may appear less satisfying when we consider it as an interpretation of an account that is supposed to be true. (Socrates begins by saying that he, unlike Agathon, speaks only the truth, 199a7–b2.) Isn't beauty the most evanescent of qualities? Indeed, doesn't a sense of transience give beauty the power to heighten our awareness of the presentness of present experience? Furthermore, we may wonder what room there is in Plato's account of the experience of beauty for that quintessentially aesthetic attitude, disinterestedness.

The conception of beauty in the *Symposium* is certainly incomplete, but it has the resources to save these, perhaps more familiar, phenomena of aesthetic experience. First, Plato seems to agree that beauty affects the perceiver with a sense of immediacy and presence. The lover does not infer that his beloved participates in something transcendent and divine; he experiences it immediately; it startles him. But we should distinguish the kind of presence in which the present moment is a moment in flux from the presence involved in the immutable. For Plato, to experience something as beautiful is to sense in the present moment an infinite perfection. Now it might seem that this account is incompatible with the common intuition that beautiful things seem fragile. But we need not assume that they seem fragile insofar as they appear beautiful. In fact, if Plato is right that beautiful things manifest perfection, then a thing's fragility cannot be a proper part of its appearance of beauty. For it is no part of perfection to be and seem to be on the brink of decay. Rather, if beautiful things often affect us with a sense of their fleetingness, then that may well be because something about beauty heightens our awareness of every living thing's mortality, calling to our awareness how tenuous is their grasp of the good and, indeed, of beauty. The conception of beauty I have been describing, according to which beauty is a shining forth of stability and self-sufficiency makes good sense of this phenomenon. The fragility of beauty

---

[31] See Nussbaum 1986:183–184. Notice that this point is independent of the question whether Socrates achieves self-sufficiency by disassociating himself from his body.

would be a second, poignant, moment in our experience, when we reflect that this mortal thing cannot grasp the infinite perfection its beauty promises.

The pleasure and excitement aroused by this experience certainly differ from our ordinary experience of desire and prudential calculation. Usually we take as our object a good that can be possessed completely within a finite amount of time. We try to acquire some finite good, for instance a house or a car, and then seek to hold on to it for some specific length of time, for fifty years, ten years, or for tomorrow and the next day and the next. Thus, the way we normally attempt to possess the good is different from the "immortal" way beautiful things seem to have perfection. In this respect, then, Plato's account captures the intuition that when we experience something beautiful we step apart from or transcend our quotidian practical standpoint. We may believe that this phenomenon is best described by saying that aesthetic experience is disinterested. But stepping outside our ordinary, finite practical standpoint does not imply that we have stepped outside the practical standpoint altogether. For according to Plato, our desire for the good is infinite, although this is not something we ordinarily notice. Thus, it is no longer clear that we must find a disinterested aspect to proper appreciation of the beautiful.

For Plato, the ethical imperative to become lovers of beauty is a reflection of his vision of human nature as aimed towards self-transcendence. We are creatures who by nature long to be more perfect, like the gods. Must we accept Plato's view of human nature as being radically self-transcendent in order to accept his account of beauty? Perhaps not. All we must accept is that central to our practical perspective are not only finite desires—desires for objects which can be fully realized in a finite part of our lives—but also a desire that takes as its object the totality of our lives. Our desire to possess *permanent* happiness *now* is a desire to transcend our finite, temporally bounded moment and have a good that it seems no human being can have so long as he's alive and subject to change. On the Platonic account, beauty reminds us of this desire and so recalls us to ourselves, to our erotic, aspiring nature. This is something ordinary encounters with the good do not do. Even if no mortal thing can have the degree of perfection its beauty makes it seem to have, nevertheless in its beauty it gives us a glimpse of what truly perfect being is like. If this is correct, it is ethically important. In the midst of this inevitably incomplete mortal life, the lover chances on someone beautiful, living proof that it is not completely futile to aim at an ideal of happiness more perfect than anything we can literally achieve.

Appendix

It is an assumption of my interpretation that not every experience of desire is an experience of erotic desire. Or to put it more clearly, not every desire is a desire to give birth in the beautiful. This is controversial and my reasons for interpreting the *Symposium* this way are not novel. (1) I cannot see how, for example, the desire for lunch and the activity of eating it, as normally pursued, can be interpreted as giving birth in the beautiful. There might be occasions where this activity does qualify—gourmet cooking may be like this—but it is not always a creative response to beauty. Eating lunch is sometimes just a response to the pain of hunger. Likewise, I do not see how every case Diotima mentions of acting for immortality can be interpreted as giving birth in the beautiful, e.g. growing hair (207d5–e2). (2) At 206b1–3, immediately before the analysis of erotic activity as giving birth in the beautiful, Diotima indicates that she wants to talk about the activity that is "called love." I take it that she is referring back to the distinction made at 205d1–7 between *erōs* in the generic sense as desire for permanent happiness and *erōs* in the specific sense as sexual love. It is this sort of love that she analyzes as the desire to give birth in the beautiful. (*Contra* Rowe [1998b:245n15] Socrates' perplexity at 206b5–10 does not indicate that Diotima is asking about generic love. Socrates is perplexed because he cannot see how sexual activity could be an expression of desire for permanent possession of the good. Diotima's language of exertion and zeal [206b2] prompts Socrates to think of sex but, understandably enough, he cannot see how this could be the right answer to her question.) Now although in ordinary Greek and in the preceding speeches in the *Symposium* 'erōs' means sexual love, we should not think that it ordinarily connotes merely a desire for sexual pleasure. Lysias' speech in the *Phaedrus*, which portrays a non-lover trying to persuade a young boy to give him sexual favors, shows quite clearly that 'erōs' does not simply mean a desire for sex. It is precisely because *erōs* means something more that, once she has analyzed it as giving birth in the beautiful, Diotima is able to expand the meaning of 'erōs' in this specific sense to cover cases that do not involve sexual desire at all. But just because "giving birth in the beautiful" describes more than sexual *erōs* does not mean that it describes absolutely all other kinds of desire for the good.

In sum, it seems to me that Diotima describes three layers of human striving: (1) All living things aim to possess the good forever, most basically by continuing in their own existence (e.g. growing hair); (2) sometimes that striving takes the form of desiring to have the good permanently, e.g. money-making; (3) and sometimes that desire for the permanent good takes the form of desiring to give birth in the beautiful, e.g. sexual love, honor-seeking, and philosophy. (My thinking about this issue has been greatly helped by Rowe's [1998b] thorough defense of the opposite position.)

Six

A Study in Violets: Alcibiades in the *Symposium*

C. D. C. Reeve[1]

GATHON'S DRINKING-PARTY has reached its philosophical apogee in Socrates' vivid, Diotima-inspired description of the ultimate object of all love and desire, the Platonic form of beauty—the beautiful itself. All of a sudden, there is a commotion and loud knocking. Someone "very drunk and shouting loudly" is "asking, Where is Agathon? and saying, Take me to Agathon" (*Symposium* 212d5).[2] Alcibiades, the best-looking man in Athens, has arrived, "crowned with a bushy wreath of ivy and violets and a multitude of fillets on his head" (212e1–2). And what happens? The beautiful itself gets eclipsed by the beautiful body; the philosophical apogee trumped by the theatrical one. The speech Alcibiades subsequently gives is riveting, too, as dramatic as his entrance. It casts the other speeches into the shade. It is so vivid, so entertaining, so alive, in fact, that we almost forget it had any predecessors.

Alcibiades insists at the outset that he will tell the truth and invites Socrates to see that he does: "if I say anything untrue, interrupt me right in the middle, if you wish, and say that I said it falsely; for I won't willingly say anything false" (214e10–215a2). At the same time, he admits that it isn't easy for someone as drunk as he is to present things "fluently and in the correct order (*euporōs kai ephexēs*)" (215a3–4). Given the importance had by *euporia*,

---

[1] This is a revised version of the paper I gave at the conference. The revisions sufficiently changed the thrust of the paper to require a new title. I am grateful to all of the conferees, especially Ruby Blondell for reminding me (again!) about the etymology of *agalma*, Christopher Rowe for demanding more about *ta erōtika*, and Gabriel Richardson Lear for being sufficiently puzzled by some remarks about Kant that I omitted them. Helpful written comments from Frisbee Sheffield, Jim Lesher, and an anonymous referee led to further significant changes. Thanks, finally, to Jim Lesher, Debra Nails, and Frisbee Sheffield for organizing the conference and inviting me to participate, and to Gregory Nagy and the staff of CHS for hosting it in such style.

[2] Translations, sometimes silently modified in minor ways, are from Allen 1991.

its opposite *aporia*, and the idea of correct order in the preceding sections of the *Symposium*, we are duly warned to interpret Alcibiades' speech with care. I shall focus, first, on something within the speech itself, namely, the use of the term *agalmata* (singular, *agalma*), and, then, on two other terms related to correct order and its disruption, which are used to contextualize it—*epi dexia* ('from left to right') and *exaiphnēs* ('all of a sudden'). *Euporia* and *aporia* are discussed at various points throughout.

In Plato, an *agalma* (from the verb *agallein*, meaning to glorify or honor something) is a figurative statue in honor of a god or, more often, a figurative statue of any sort—the puppets which cast their shadows on the walls of the cave in *Republic* VII are *agalmata* (517d7).[3] The question is, can this be what *agalmata* are for Alcibiades? Initially, the answer seems to be yes: "I say that Socrates is exactly like those silenuses sitting in the statuary shops, the kind the craftsmen manufacture, with flutes or pipes, but when opened in the middle, they prove to have *agalmata* of the gods inside them" (215a7–b3). But though Silenuses could have been statues that, like Russian dolls, contained smaller statues inside them, "no examples have survived, nor are there any references to such a type of statue except in late passages dependent on this one" (Dover 1980:166). It has been conjectured, indeed, that what Alcibiades is referring to are not statues at all, but moulds for making them (Peters 1976; Rowe 1998a:206). According to François Rabelais, writing in 1534, they were not even moulds, but painted boxes: "a Silenus, in ancient days, was a little box, of the kind we see today in apothecaries' shops, painted on the outside with such gay, comical figures as harpies and satyrs" (Cohen 1955:37).[4] Alcibiades' supposedly helpful image of Socrates is almost as plagued by *atopia* ('strangeness'), therefore, as the man himself (215a3–4).

In the second passage, matters are unclear for a different reason:

> As to his appearance—isn't it Silenus-like. Of course it is. His outside covering is like a carved[5] Silenus, but when he is opened, gentlemen and drinking companions, can you guess how he teems with temperance within?... But he is sly and dishonest and spends his whole life

---

[3] A glance at the occurrences recorded in Brandwood 1976 will bear this out: *Charmides* 154c8, *Critias* 110b5, 116d7, e4, *Epinomis* 983e6, 984a4, 5, *Laws* 738c6, 931a1, 6, d6, e6, 956b1, *Meno* 97d6, *Philebus* 38d10, *Phaedrus* 230b8, 251a6, 252d7, *Protagoras* 322a5, *Timaeus* 37c7. *Agalmatopoios* ('sculptor' or 'statue-maker') occurs at *Protagoras* 311c7, 8, e2. More generally, though, "anything on which one *agalletai*" (Griffith 1999:243), such as a child (Aeschylus, *Agamemnon* 208) or fame (Sophocles, *Antigone* 704), can be an *agalma*.

[4] Thanks to Scott LaBarge for this reference.

[5] *Geglumenos silēnos*: *gluphein* also means to hollow out (as one might a mould).

playing with people. Yet, I don't know whether anyone else has seen the *agalmata* within when he is in earnest (*spoudasantos*) and opened up, but *I* saw them once, and I thought that they were so divine and golden, so marvelously beautiful, that whatever Socrates might bid must, in short, be done. Believing he was earnestly (*espoudakenai*) pursuing my youthful beauty, I thought it was a stroke of luck and my wonderful good fortune, because by gratifying Socrates I could hear everything he knew. For I was amazingly proud of my vernal bloom.

Symposium 216d4–217a6

We expect Alcibiades to abandon the simile at this point and tell us what it was he actually saw inside Socrates. Instead he perplexingly continues to speak in figural terms: what he saw were *agalmata*. Since these cannot literally be statues, we are left wondering what they could be. If the sileneuses were moulds, things would be a bit clearer. The *agalmata* would at least be *like* statues, since they would be likenesses of Socrates himself as some sort of model or paradigm of temperance. It is a pleasing idea, even if not one on which we can place a great deal of weight—especially once we turn to the third passage.

Confirming the suspicion aroused by the phrase "teems with temperance," it tells us that the *agalmata* inside Socrates are *agalmata* of virtue, and that they are also inside his arguments:

But the sort of man this is and his strangeness, both himself and his arguments, one couldn't come close to finding if one looked, neither among people present nor past, except perhaps if one were to compare him to those I mention—not any man, but silenuses and satyrs, him and his arguments. Actually, I left this out at first, that even his arguments are like silenuses that have been opened. For if one is willing to listen to Socrates' arguments, they'd appear quite ridiculous at first; they're wrapped around on the outside with words and phrases like the hide of an outrageous satyr. He talks about pack asses and smiths and cobblers and tanners ... but if the arguments are opened and one sees them from the inside, he will find first that they are the only arguments with any sense in them, and next that they're the most god-like and contain the most *agalmata* of virtue, and that they are relevant to most or rather to all things worth considering for one who intends to be noble and good.

Symposium 221e1–222a6

Now we are well and truly at sea, since an argument could not literally contain a statue—or a likeness of Socrates either, for that matter.

In the seduction scene, *agalmata* are again present, this time implicit in the response Socrates makes to Alcibiades' sexual overtures:

> My dear Alcibiades, you are really not to be taken lightly, if indeed what you say about me happens to be true, and there is in me some power through which you might become better; you would then see inconceivable beauty in me, even surpassing your own immense comeliness of form. But if, seeing it, you are trying to strike a bargain with me to exchange beauty for beauty, then you intend to take no slight advantage of me: on the contrary, you are trying to get possession of what is truly beautiful instead of what merely seems so, and really, you intend to trade bronze for gold.
>
> *Symposium* 218d7–219a1

The repeated "in me," the equivalence of "inconceivable beauty" and "marvelously beautiful," the use of "gold(en)" all serve to make plain that what Alcibiades expects to receive in return for his bronze body are our *agalmata*. Socrates, however, shows no inclination to endorse the claim that these exist: a cautious "if indeed what you say about me happens to be true" is as far as he will go.

How does Alcibiades imagine that these *agalmata* might become his? In the seduction scene, he seems to entertain the fantasy of acquiring them through sexual intercourse: "Believing he was earnestly (*espoudakenai*) pursuing my youthful beauty, I thought it was a stroke of luck and my wonderful good fortune, because by gratifying Socrates I could learn everything he knew" (217a2–5). It is certainly not a fantasy peculiar to him. When Socrates finally arrives at Agathon's, after a sojourn in a neighbor's porch, his host greets him by saying: "Come here, Socrates, and lie down beside me, so that by touching you I'll get the benefit of the wisdom that came to you on the porch" (175c7–d1). The simile with which Socrates responds amplifies the sexual innuendo implicit in the verbs "lie down" (*katakeisthai*) and "touch" (*haptein*):[6] "It would indeed be well, Agathon, if wisdom were the sort of thing that might flow (*rhein*) from the fuller of us into the emptier if only we touch each other, as water flows through a woolen thread from a fuller into an emptier cup. If wisdom is that way too, I value the place beside you very much indeed; for I think I will be filled from you with wisdom of great

[6] LSJ cites *Laws* 840a4 and Aristotle *Politics* 1335b40.

127

beauty" (175d4–e2). As *agalmata* of virtue are fantasized as entering Alcibiades through sexual intercourse, thereby making him "as good as possible" (218d2), so wisdom is fantasized as flowing into Agathon though sexualized contact, making him wise.

Alcibiades' use of the verb "teems" (*gemein*) at 216d7 is both consonant with this picture and helps fill it out. For though *gemein* usually just means "to be filled with," which is its most common meaning in Plato, LSJ lists *kuein* ("to be pregnant") as one of its synonyms. That, no doubt, is why "teems" seemed to R. E. Allen (1991) to be a particularly apposite translation. If Socrates is being imagined as *pregnant* with *agalmata* of virtue, however, the latter are themselves being imagined as embryo-like entities. But embryos, it goes without saying, are genuinely like figurative statues, making *agalmata* an appropriate term for Alcibiades to apply to them.

Though Alcibiades' picture of Socrates as a male pregnant with embryonic virtue is part of a fantasy, it is a fantasy with deep roots in Greek thinking about sexual reproduction. In Aeschylus, for example, Apollo claims that a female serves only as an incubator for an embryo produced exclusively by a male:

> She who is called the child's mother is not
> Its begetter, but the nurse of the newly sown conception.
> The begetter is the male, and she as a stranger for a stranger
> Preserves the offspring ...

> *Eumenides* 658–661, trans. Lloyd-Jones

We know from Aristotle's *Generation of Animals* (763b21–23) that a similar theory was advanced by Anaxagoras, who may well have been Aeschylus' source (Sommerstein 1989:206). In a later generation, Diogenes of Apollonia (D-K 64A27) and others also accepted some version of it. It is with this embryological tradition, moreover, that Diotima allies herself earlier in the *Symposium*, when she portrays reproduction as involving pregnant males seeking females in whom to beget the embryo-like entities they are carrying (208e2–3).[7]

Moreover, she develops her account of the type of psychic pregnancy involved in philosophical *paiderastia* or boy-love precisely by analogy with such males:

---

[7] The fact that she earlier claims that "all human beings (*anthrōpoi*) are pregnant in respect to both the body and the soul" (206c1–2) may mean that her allegiance is less than wholehearted. But since, in the sequel, only males are ever pregnant in soul, her expression may simply be imprecise: by *anthrōpoi* she means *male* human beings. What that means for her own odd status is another question.

Some men are pregnant in respect to their bodies, and turn more to women and are lovers in that way... Others are pregnant in respect to their soul—for there are those, she said, who are still more fertile in their souls than in their bodies with what it pertains to soul to conceive and bear. What then so pertains? Wisdom and the rest of virtue—of which, indeed, all the poets are procreators, and as many craftsmen as are said to be inventors. But the greatest and most beautiful kind of wisdom by far is that concerned with the correct ordering of cities and households, for which the name is temperance and justice. Whenever, then, one of them is pregnant of soul from youth, being divine, and reaches the age when he then desires to bear and procreate, he too, then, I think, goes about seeking the beauty in which he might beget; for he will never beget in the ugly. Now, because he is fertile, he welcomes beautiful rather than ugly bodies, and should he meet with a beautiful and naturally gifted soul, he welcomes the conjunction of the two even more, and to this person he is straightway resourceful in making arguments about virtue and trying to educate him.

Symposium 208e2–209c1

A man pregnant in respect to his soul, then, is pregnant with embryo-like virtues. What he produces when he meets a beautiful boy are arguments about virtue. And it is these that "make young men better" (210c1–3; cf. 218e1–2). In this respect, too, Alcibiades' portrait unwittingly mimics Diotima's—unwittingly, because he has not heard her speak. For when, as an out-of-order afterthought ("Actually, I left this out at first," 221d8), he also locates the *agalmata* inside Socrates' arguments, he seems to be referring back to an earlier thought in which philosophical discussion not sexual intercourse is the mode of their transmission: "I'd been bitten by something more painful, and in the most painful place one can be bitten—in the heart or soul or whatever one should name it, struck and bitten by arguments in philosophy that hold more fiercely than a serpent, when they take hold of a young and not ill-endowed soul" (218a3–7).

In the critique of writing at the end of the *Phaedrus*, Socrates himself explicitly invokes very similar ideas.[8] A written argument, he says, like the "offspring of painting," stands there "as if alive." Yet it cannot answer questions or attune itself to the needs of different audiences, and "when it is ill-treated and unjustly abused, it always needs its father to help it; for it is

---

[8] Translations are from Rowe 1986.

incapable of defending or helping itself" (275d4–e5). Its "legitimate brother," however, which is "the living and animate argument of the man who knows, of which a written argument would rightly be called a kind of phantom" is "much better and more capable" in all these departments (276a1–9). Then comes a telling contrast:

> The sensible farmer who had some seeds he cared about and wanted to bear fruit—would he sow them in earnest (*spoudēi*) during the summer in some garden of Adonis, and delight in watching it become beautiful within eight days, or would he do that for playful purposes (*paidias*) on a feast-day, when he did it at all; whereas for the purposes about which he was in earnest (*espoudaken*), he would make use of the craft of farming and sow them in appropriate soil, being content if what he sowed reached maturity in the eighth month?
>
> *Phaedrus* 276b1–8[9]

Next, based on the contrast, comes an equally telling analogy. The man who has "[seeds] of knowledge about what is just, and what is beautiful, and what is good" will have "no less sensible an attitude toward his seeds than the farmer" (276c3–5). Thus, when others "resort to other sorts of playful amusements (*paidiais*), watering themselves with symposia," he will amuse himself (*paidias*, 276d2) by writing "stories about justice and the other virtues," so as to "lay up a store of reminders both for himself, when 'he reaches a forgetful old age', and for anyone who is following the same track, and he will be pleased as he watches their tender growth" (276d1–e3). But when "he is in earnest (*spoudē*) about them," he instead, "makes use of the craft of dialectic, and taking a fitting soul plants and sows in it arguments accompanied by knowledge (*met' epistēmēs logous*), which are able to help themselves and the man who planted them, and are not without fruit but contain a seed, from which others grow in other soils, capable of rendering it forever immortal, and making the one who has it as happy as it is possible for a man to be" (276e5–277a4).[10] Living arguments (*logoi*) are now explicitly likened to seeds (*spermata*)—something on which the Stoics, with their *spermatikoi logoi* (seminal principles) will capitalize.[11]

---

[9] Many thanks to Julia Annas for correcting an oversight in my initial account of this passage.

[10] I cannot resist noticing the reference to symposia as amusements that Plato—who else?—would rather write books than attend!

[11] See e.g. SVF 1.497, 2.780, 1027, 1074, 3.141. I am grateful to David Sedley for advice on this Stoic doctrine.

Though Alcibiades is not mentioned by name in this section of the *Phaedrus*, he is, I think, lurking in the shadows of Adonis' garden.[12] As part of the *Adōnia*, the feast celebrating the love-affair of Aphrodite and Adonis, and mourning the early death of the latter, women in fifth-century Athens, "sowed seed at midsummer in broken pots and placed these on the rooftops, so that germination was rapidly followed by withering" (OCD ed. 3:12). These were the eponymous gardens. Three things connect them to Alcibiades. First, the fact that the seeds Socrates sowed in him withered quickly: "as soon as I leave [Socrates]," Alcibiades confesses, "I cave in to the honors of the crowd. So I desert him and flee" (216b4–6). Second, the fact that Alcibiades was suspected of involvement in the mutilation of the Herms—*statues* of the god Hermes—and in the profanation of the Eleusinian Mysteries, both of which occurred in midsummer, right around the *Adōnia*.[13] The use of the technical term "uninitiated" (*bebēlos*) at *Symposium* 218b6, strongly suggests that Plato had the latter scandal in mind. He uses the odd term *agalma*, I am confident, in part to memorialize the former scandal too. The third and most striking connection to Alcibiades, however, is entirely intertextual. In the *Symposium*, Alcibiades claims that Socrates, while always playing with people about matters of virtue, was in earnest with him about them (216d4–217a6). The *Phaedrus*, in which play and earnestness about such matters are obsessively contrasted, has obvious critical bearing on his claim. Someone who had "arguments accompanied by knowledge" of "what is just, fine, and good" (276c3–4), it says, would never, *except for playful purposes*, sow them in a garden of Adonis like Alcibiades, whose planting-season (adolescence) was long passed by the time Socrates entered his life (cf. *Alcibiades* I 131c5–d8). Socrates, we may infer, either did not possess the sort of knowledge-conferring *agalmata* of virtue Alcibiades describes or (which we can surely rule out) was merely playing with him too.

If, as we should, we seek the specifically social or cultural origins of *logoi* as *spermata/agalmata*, the obvious place to look is the complex ideology of Athenian *paiderastia*, which Diotima explicitly adapts to her philosophical purposes. It is an ideology that seeks to negotiate between ideals of masculinity and the somewhat conflicting reality of male desire. The salient issue is, what is it to be a man?—in the sense of who has manly control of his appetites and desires and who, like a woman or a slave, does not (Davidson 1998:139–182, 250–277). What a boy who desired to be sexually penetrated by his lover was

---

[12] As he is at *Republic* 494c4–495b7. See Adam (1902).
[13] See Thucydides 6.27.

in danger of being thought was not primarily a passive penetratee, as Michel Foucault famously argued, but a *katapugōn*, a *kinaidos*, a "sex addict" or "slut" as we might say—someone too enslaved to his appetites, too much of an unfillable or insatiably leaky vessel, to be trusted with citizenly power.[14] Hence the boy's desire had to be ideologically refigured as something more appropriate—a desire to be a slave to his lover for the sake not of sexual pleasure, but of virtue (184c2–7, 219e3–5). At the same time, the sexual desire of the lover had also to be refigured as educative rather than orgasmic or ejaculatory in intent. Boy-love became implicitly divided, as a result, into what Pausanias calls (good) Uranian love, whose object is the soul and whose aim is to instill virtue in the boy, and (bad) Pandemotic love, whose object is the body and whose aim is sexual pleasure for the lover (180c1–d7). Sexual intercourse and the inculcation of virtue thus become so metonymically related, their conceptual fields so fused, that *spermatikoi logoi* took on the aura of a natural kind.

While the strategy of getting hold of Socrates' golden *agalmata* through philosophical discussion is less an obvious fantasy than the explicitly sexual strategy we looked at earlier, it has a manifest defect. It does not immediately explain why anything statue-like should be involved in Alcibiades' conception of the process. Nonetheless, it does add something important. It explains why Alcibiades thinks there is *something* in Socrates that is virtue-relevant— something the sexual strategy allows him to characterize as he does. What generally happens to those who see him in elenctic action, Socrates tells us, is that they infer that he is wise about the subjects on which he examines others (*Apology* 23a3–5). When Alcibiades describes him as "sly and dishonest (*eirōneuomenos*)," and as spending his whole life "playing with people" (216e4– 5), he shows himself to have done precisely that. But his description is true only if he believes that Socrates is a disingenuous *eirōn*—an ironist as we riskily say[15]—because, like everyone else, he imagines that something like knowledge-conferring *agalmata* must exist in him to account for his elenctic competence. "By gratifying Socrates," he says, "I could learn everything he knew" (217a4–5).

When Socrates tacitly accepts this description by not objecting, he does so, I surmise, because he understands it as the consequent of a conditional, the antecedent of which the description itself records him as not having corrobo-

---

[14] *Problems* 4.23, attributed to Aristotle, but probably dating from the third century BCE, is revelatory in this regard. In men who have "a superfluity of semen" or whose sperm ducts are blocked, semen collects in their rectum, instead of being discharged in the natural way. Unable to find release in normal sexual intercourse, they desire "friction in the place where the semen collects." But since this doesn't result in seminal discharge "they are insatiable or unfillable (*aplēston*) just like women."

[15] See Vlastos 1991:21–44 and Nehamas 1998:19–98 for some risk assessment.

rated (218e1–2). What he tacitly accepts, then, is just this: "*if* I have *agalmata* in me, of the sort that provide me with knowledge of virtue, then I am sly and dishonest and do spend my life playing with people." That he has such knowledge of virtue, however, whether deriving from *agalmata* or not, is something he always denies:

> In fact, gentlemen, it's pretty certainly the god who is really wise, and by his oracle he meant that human wisdom is worth little or nothing. And it seems that when he refers to the Socrates here before you, and uses my name, he makes me an example, as if he were to say: "That one among you is wisest, mortals, who, like Socrates, has recognized that he's truly worthless where wisdom's concerned."
>
> *Apology* 23a5–b4

Alcibiades' sense of privilege—"I don't know whether anyone else has seen the *agalmata* within when he is in earnest and opened up, but *I* saw them once"—stands diagnosed, then, as a common illusion.

Though as hesitant to claim that he has any knowledge-conferring *agalmata* of virtue within him as that he has any knowledge of virtue itself, Socrates does make an apparently grand epistemic claim in the *Symposium*. "I claim to know nothing," he insouciantly says, "except *ta erōtika*" (177d8–9). What exactly is he claiming? Literally translated, *ta erōtika* are "the things of love." But just as *ta phusika* is "[the science of] physics" and *ta politika* is "[the art or craft of] politics," *ta erōtika* is "the craft of love" (*hē erōtikē technē*)—the one the god Eros gives to Socrates in the *Phaedrus* (257a3–9). And that raises a problem; in fact, two problems. The first is to explain how it can be true, as Socrates puts it, that "I myself honor and surpassingly devote myself to the craft of love and exhort (*parakeleuomai*) others to do the same" (212b5–7). I mean, where do we see him doing *that*? The other is to reconcile his knowing that craft with his general epistemic modesty, with his characterization of himself as wise "in neither a great nor a small way" (*Apology* 21b4–5). How can the man who has no worthwhile wisdom possibly know something as apparently important and difficult as the art or craft of love?

To these questions the *Lysis* offers appealing clues.[16] Hippothales, like a true Socratic, loves beautiful boys and philosophical arguments (203b6–204a3). But what he does to win Lysis' love is sing eulogies to him. And that, Socrates argues, no master of the craft of love would ever do:

---

[16] Translations are from Lombardo (1997).

If you make a conquest of a boy like this, then everything you've said and sung turns out to eulogize yourself as victor in having won such a boyfriend. But if he gets away, then the greater your praise of his beauty and goodness, the more you will seem to have lost and the more you will be ridiculed. That is why someone who is wise in the craft of love doesn't praise his beloved until he has him: he fears how the future may turn out. And besides, these beautiful boys get swelled heads if anyone praises them and start to think they're really somebody.

Lysis 205e2–206a4

Convinced, Hippothales turns to Socrates: "What different advice can you give me about what someone should say or do to get his prospective boyfriend to love him?" (206c1–3). Unlike in the *Symposium*, where he is laconic, Socrates goes into detail: "if you're willing to have him talk with me, I might be able to give you a demonstration (*epideixai*) of how to carry on a discussion with him" (206c4–6).[17] An elenctic examination of Lysis quickly ensues.

"This is how you should talk to your boyfriends, Hippothales," Socrates says when the examination is finished, "making them humble and drawing in their sails, instead of swelling them up and spoiling them, as you do" (210e2–5). What he goes on to say about philosophy, however, shows elenctic discussion to be much more than merely chastening (cf. *Symposium* 204a1–b5):

Those who are already wise no longer love wisdom (*philosophein*), whether they are gods or men. Neither do those who are so ignorant that they are bad, for no bad and stupid person loves wisdom. There remains only those who have this bad thing, ignorance, but have not yet been made ignorant and stupid by it. They are conscious of not knowing what they don't know.

Lysis 218a2–b1

By showing Lysis that he isn't already wise, by getting him to recognize that he doesn't know, Socrates is setting him on the right road to love—the one that leads to the love of wisdom, and so to the beautiful itself.[18] Just how that solves Hippothales' problem of getting Lysis to love *him* is another matter—one we will need Diotima's metaphysics to solve.

---

[17] "Periods of silent absorption," are not, therefore, "the closest Socrates comes to public display, or *epideixis*" (Hunter 2004:33).

[18] Cf. *Sophist* 231b3–8: "the refutation of the empty belief in one's own wisdom is nothing other than our noble sophistry."

As a philosopher himself, Socrates does not know the answers to his own questions about virtue, and so really is "wise in neither a great nor a small way." Yet, unlike those he examines, he knows that he doesn't know, that he lacks wisdom. What gives him that knowledge is the one craft he does possess—the craft of asking questions. *It* is what makes him a lover of wisdom, therefore, and so is itself the craft of (producing) love. And questioning, of course, is what we do see Socrates devoting himself to and exhorting others to practice (*Apology* 29d2–30a2,[19] 38a1–6). Socrates' claim to know the craft of love reveals a deep truth about him, therefore—so deep, in fact, that it appears to have been encoded in language itself by the possibly divine "rule-setter" who made it: "The name 'hero' (*hērōs*) is only a slightly altered form of the word 'love' (*erōs*)—the very thing from which the heroes sprang. And either this is the reason they were called 'heroes' or else because they were sophists, clever speech-makers and dialecticians, skilled at questioning (*erōtan*)" (*Cratylus* 398c5–e5). Add *eirōn* to the etymological mix, and you have Socrates—questioner, lover, philosopher hero, "ironist"—as truly a gift of the god (*Apology* 30d7–e1)!

The identification of the craft of love with that of asking questions, while compatible with Socrates' usual *modus operandi* and disavowal of wisdom, is not entirely problem free. For Diotima, as the one who taught Socrates the former craft (*Symposium* 201d5), characterizes it as leading to scientific knowledge (211b8–d1). Did Socrates really have wisdom, then, while dishonestly disavowing it? Was Alcibiades right in thinking that he had glimpsed "truly beautiful things" (219a1) within him? Perhaps, it is sufficient here to take a way out suggested by Diotima herself. Socrates, she is fairly confident, could be instructed in part of the craft of love (the so-called "lesser mysteries"), in which the philosophical lover gives birth to beautiful arguments about the virtues when he finds a boy beautiful in body and soul (209a1–c7). But about the part where scientific knowledge of the beautiful is acquired, Diotima is more circumspect: "as for those parts relating to the final revelation [of the beautiful itself], the ones for whose sake I've taught you the others [the "lesser mysteries"], I don't know whether you would be capable of being initiated into *them*" (210a1–2). It is noteworthy that Alcibiades' own characterization of the Socratic arguments he has heard as "wrapped around on the outside with words and phrases like the hide of an outrageous satyr," and as being about "pack asses and smiths and cobblers and tanners," while it fits the arguments we see Socrates giving in the so-called early dialogues, doesn't fit the sublime

---

[19] Note, especially, *parakeleuomenos* at 29d5.

lessons he learns from Diotima. Like the very fact that Socrates has had to learn them from her, this suggests, as many have argued, that they are not Socratic in provenance, but Platonic—something, as I put it elsewhere, that Plato gave birth to in the beauty of Socrates (Reeve 2004:96).

"A thing that desires, desires what it lacks," the *Lysis* tells us (221d7–e2). The *Symposium* delivers the same message yet more stridently: "what is not at hand, what is not present, what one does not have, what one is not oneself, and what one lacks—desire and Eros are of such things as these" (200e2–5). In *Republic* IX, this picture of desire gets tied explicitly to the theory of forms. Hunger, thirst, and the like, are "some sorts of emptiness related to the state of the body," while "foolishness and lack of knowledge" are "some sorts of emptiness related to the state of the soul." Nourishment fills the former; "true belief, knowledge, understanding, and, in sum, all of virtue," the latter. But these fillings are not on a par. Nourishment fills temporarily—it is soon digested or excreted; virtue fills permanently, because, as something that always is what it is, it partakes more of "pure being" than nourishment does, and so "*is* more" than it (585a8–b8). Since the things that that *are* more—that fully are (what they are)—are the Platonic forms (*Republic* 475c6–480a13), it is only when the true lover of boys reaches these—or, more particularly, the beautiful itself—that his desires are satisfied, his emptinesses truly filled, his happiness assured (*Symposium* 210e2–212a7). The elenchus is important to love in part because it reveals the presence of these emptinesses—emptinesses which, because they were concealed or occluded by the false conceit of knowledge, were erotically inert. The revelation of a hunger thereby becomes a sort of feeding: "When a man has his mouth so full of food that he is prevented from eating, and is likely to starve in consequence, does giving him food consist in stuffing still more of it in his mouth or does it consist in taking some of it away, so that he can begin to eat?" (Kierkegaard 1941:245n).[20]

A philosopher who encounters a boy with "a godlike face or some form of body which imitates beauty well," Socrates tells us in the *Phaedrus*,[21] "reveres it like a god as he looks at it, and if he were not afraid of appearing thoroughly mad would sacrifice to his beloved as if to an *agalma* of a god" (251a1–7). In this regard, he is no different from any other recently reincarnated lover who still remembers vividly the forms he glimpsed as he traversed the heavens in the chorus of his patron—because character-defining—god:

---

[20] I owe notice of this passage to J. Lear (2004:106–107), a book no student of Socratic irony can afford to miss.

[21] I am grateful to Diskin Clay for encouraging me to look again at these texts.

So each selects his love from the ranks of the beautiful according to his own disposition, and fashions and adorns him like an *agalma*, as if he were himself his god, in order to honor him and celebrate his mystic rites. And so those who belong to Zeus seek that the one they love should be someone like Zeus in respect of his soul; so they look to see whether he is naturally disposed towards philosophy, and when they have found him and fall in love they do everything to make him of such a kind. So if they have not previously set foot in this way, they undertake it now, both learning from wherever they can and finding out for themselves; and as they follow the scent from within themselves to the discovery of the nature of their own god, they find the means to it through the compulsion on them to gaze intensely on the god, and grasping him through memory, and possessed by him, they take their habits and ways from him, to the extent that it is possible for a man to share in god; and because they count their beloved responsible for these very things they love him still more, and if it is from Zeus that they draw, like Bacchants, they pour the draught over the soul of their loved one and make him as like their god as possible.

Phaedrus 252d5–253b1

Here it is the boy's face, body, and soul that are *agalmata*, and the philosopher who is drawn by them, through *anamnēsis*, to philosophy, god-likeness, and the philosophical education of his beloved. It is into him, not into the boy, that a strange fluid flows:

"nourishment ... flows in" upon him (*epirrueisēs de tēs trophēs*, 251b5); he "receives the stream of beauty in through the eyes" (*dexamenos gar tou kallous tēn aporroēn dia tōn ommatōn*, 251b1–2); and, as he gazes upon the beauty of the beloved, his soul "receives particles from there that come at him in a stream" (*ekeithen merē epionta kai rheont' ... dechomenē*, 251c).

Nightingale 2004:159

The effect of such influx is not satiation or filling up, moreover, since the name of the particles (*merē*) that come at (*epionta*) the philosopher in a stream (*rheonta*) is *himeros*—desire (251c6–7). It is these now activated desires, in turn, that eventually lead to the learning and investigation that enable the philosopher to "gaze intently" on Zeus. The fluid he draws like a draught from this divine source is what really nourishes him and what he then pours over the soul of his boyfriend (253a6–b1). If the effect of such pouring is to make the latter "as like their god as possible," we may infer, it must serve as stimulus rather than satisfier for his desires too, leading him to hunger for philosophy, Zeus, and the Platonic forms. The inversion of the description Alcibiades gives—memorialized by the use of the term *agalma*—could hardly be more complete. When he refers to "the madness and Bacchic frenzy of philosophy" (*Symposium* 218b4), therefore, we may be confident that he has in mind not the "parts of madness on the right-hand side" of the definitional division, which are identified with "divine," non-genital, philosophical love, but those of the bad madness on the left, which are identified with sexual love (*Phaedrus* 266a3–b1).

Even when a philosopher has climbed Diotima's ladder to the very top and has seen the form of the beautiful, then, *what he has in him for his beloved boy* isn't what would fill up his emptinesses, but what would activate them, turn them into effective motives to philosophical inquiry. No Platonic philosopher, one might say, no matter how wise and knowledgeable, can ever be more than a Socrates to another person! One must see the forms for oneself. For this reason, too, *agalmata* is a peculiarly appropriate term to use for what such a philosopher does have in him. For an *agalma* originally had no "relation whatsoever to the idea of resemblance or imitation, of figural representation in the strict sense." Instead, it was something the aim of which was "to construct a bridge, as it were," that would reach "toward the divine." Yet "at the same time and in the same figure," it had to "mark its distance from that domain in relation to the human world." It had to make the divine power present, yet it had also to emphasize "what is inaccessible and mysterious in divinity, its alien quality, its otherness" (Vernant 1991:152–153). Like what is in a Platonic philosopher for another, *agalmata* are a bridge to something else—an image for what is itself necessarily beyond images (*Symposium* 212a4–5).

The idea of *agalmata* as a bridge between human and divine is bound to remind us of Diotima's characterization of Eros as a *daimōn*—a being "intermediate between god and mortal" (202d11–e1). "Ever poor," "rough and hard," "unshod," "dwelling ever with want," "courageous," and "a lover of wisdom through the whole of life," Eros sounds remarkably similar to Socrates himself (203c6–d8), whom Alcibiades actually describes as a "genuine *daimōn*" (219b7–c1). But that implies that Socrates is, in the relevant respect, also remarkably similar to an *agalma*, and it to him. Like the conjecture mentioned earlier that Alcibiades' openable silenuses are really statue moulds, this has the effect of turning the *agalmata* inside Socrates into statues of himself. Though Alcibiades claims to have seen these *agalmata* before he tried to seduce Socrates, it is noteworthy that in the penultimate section of his speech, it is the figure of Socrates as a model of virtue that is front and center. Whether in resisting Alcibiades' beautiful body, or on campaign at Potidaea or Delium, *he* is the paradigm of wisdom, temperance, fortitude, and courage (219d3–221c1).

The phrase *euporei logon peri arētes* ("resourceful in making arguments about virtue"), applied by Diotima to the pregnant and properly philosophical lover of boys (209b8), finds a parallel in Alcibiades' last words about Socrates, which are also, in fact, his last words *sans phrase*: "It's the same old story ... When Socrates is around, it's impossible for anyone else to get a share of the beauties. Now, too, see how resourcefully (*euporōs*) he's found a convincing argument (*logon*) to make this fellow [Agathon] lie down beside him" (223a6–9). They are words carefully prepared for. "Was I not prophetic," Socrates says, "when I said just now that Agathon would speak wonderfully and I would be at a loss (*aporēsoimi*)." "As to you being at a loss (*aporēsein*)," Eryximachus replies, "I doubt it." "And how am I not to be at a loss (*aporein*)," Socrates responds, using the verb for the third time, "after so beautiful and so varied a speech" (198a5–b3). In Diotima's story of Poros and Penia, we discover how potentially deceptive they are:

> Because Eros is the son of Poros and Penia, this is his fortune: first, he is ever poor, and far from being delicate and beautiful, as most people suppose, he on the contrary is rough and hard and unshod, ever lying on the ground without bedding, sleeping in doorsteps and beside roads under the open sky. Because he has his mother's nature he dwells ever with lack. But on the other hand, by favor of his father, he ever plots for good and beautiful things, because he is courageous, eager and intense, and a clever hunter ever weaving some new device, desiring wisdom and capable of it, a philosopher through the whole of life, clever at enchantment, a sorcerer, and a sophist. And he is by nature neither mortal nor immortal, but sometimes on the same day he lives and flourishes, whenever he is resourceful (*euporēsei*), but then he dies and comes back to life again by reason of the nature of his father, though what is provided (*porizomenon*) ever flows away, so that Eros is never rich nor at a loss (*aporei*), and is, on the contrary, in between wisdom and ignorance. For things stand thus: no god loves wisdom or desires to become wise—for he is so; nor, if anyone else is wise, does he love wisdom. On the other hand, neither do the ignorant love wisdom nor desire to become wise; for ignorance is difficult just in this, that though

not beautiful and good, nor wise, it yet seems to itself to be sufficient. He who does not think himself in need does not desire what
he does not think he lacks.

Symposium 203c5–204a7

Just as Socrates turns Athenian *paiderastia* upside down by playing the part of
the pursued boy rather than of the pursuing older lover (222b3–4), the source
of *agalmata* rather than their recipient, so, by means of his skill at asking questions, he turns *aporia* into *euporia*, emptiness into a resource. What as a philosopher he desires, however, isn't to lie down with Agathon ("Mr. Goodman"), as
Alcibiades claims, but to have intercourse with the Platonic form that shares
his—much punned upon—name. Alcibiades' suggestion otherwise is a genuine
profanation of mysteries—not the Eleusinian this time, but the philosophical
ones Diotima has modeled on them (see Sheffield 2001b).

One might say the same, I think, about the way Alcibiades experiences
the *aporia* Socrates induces in him:

I wrapped my own cloak around him—for it was winter—and I lay
down on his threadbare coat, and I put my two arms around this
genuine *daimōn*, this wonderful man, and lay there the whole night
through. And, again, Socrates, you will not say I speak falsely. But
when I did this, he was so contemptuous of my youthful bloom that
he ridiculed and outrageously insulted it; and in that regard, at
least, I thought I was really something, gentlemen and judges—for
you are judges of the arrogance of Socrates—for know well, by gods
and by goddesses, when I arose after having slept with Socrates, it
was nothing more than if I'd slept with a father or with an elder
brother. Can you imagine my state of mind after that? I considered
myself affronted, and yet I admired his nature, his temperance and
courage, having met a man of a sort I never thought to meet in
respect to wisdom and fortitude. The result was that I could neither
get angry and be deprived of his company nor was I resourceful
enough (*ēuporoun*) to win him over. For I well knew he was far more
invulnerable to money than Ajax was to iron, and he'd escaped
me in the only way I thought he could be caught. So I was at a loss
(*ēporoun*), and went around enslaved by this man as no one ever was
by any other.

Symposium 219b5–e5

What should be experienced as a resource that can lead to the forms of the good or the beautiful is instead experienced as a genuine loss, recoupable only by gaining possession, through seduction or bribery (the only genuine resources Alcibiades seems to recognize), of Socrates himself, and the *agalmata*-based wisdom he is imagined to contain. The idea that Socrates' love could be won only through joining him in leading the philosophically examined life seems hopelessly far away.

An important passage in *Republic* VI strongly suggests that this negative interpretation of Alcibiades is very much a part of Plato's own. In it Socrates is explaining why philosophers have an undeservedly bad reputation, and what the real effect is on their souls of contemplating Platonic forms:

> The harshness of the masses towards philosophy is caused by those outsiders who do not belong and who have burst in like a *band of revelers* (*epeiskekōmakotas*), *abusing one another*, indulging their love of quarreling, and *always arguing about human beings—something that is least appropriate in philosophy* ... For surely, someone whose mind is truly directed towards the things that are has not the leisure to look down at human affairs, and be filled with malice and hatred as a result of entering into their disputes. Instead, as he looks at and contemplates things that are orderly and always the same, that neither do injustice to one another nor suffer it, being all in a rational order, he imitates them and tries to become as like them as he can. Or do you think there is any way to prevent someone from associating with something he admires without imitating it? ... Then the philosopher, by associating with what is *orderly* (*kosmiōi*) and divine becomes as divine and orderly as a human being can. Though, mind you, there is always plenty of *slander* (*diabolē*) around.
>
> *Republic* 500b1–d2

Alcibiades, notice, accuses Socrates of "abusing" him (*Symposium* 213d2), and then proceeds to give a speech entirely about human beings, which is therefore as anti-the-philosopher-Socrates as possible. No wonder, then, that it is represented by the latter as slanderous in intent: "as though you hadn't said it all to sow slander (*diaballein*) between me and Agathon" (222c7–d1; also 222d6). Finally, there is the "crowd of revelers (*kōmastas*)" that shows up at the end of the *Symposium* (223b1–2) and, finding Agathon's doors as "open" (223b3) as Alcibiades thought he had found Socrates, bursts in and puts an end to all "order (*kosmōi*)" (223b4–5). The echoes are surely too insistent to be accidental.

The order the revelers literally destroy is that established by Eryximachus in his role as master of ceremonies—"I think each of us should make as beautiful a speech as he can in praise of Eros, from left to right (*epi dexia*)" (177d1–2). When Alcibiades arrives late at the party, Eryximachus tries to impose it on him too:

> Before you came, it seemed best that each of us, from left to right (*epi dexia*) should give the most beautiful speech about Eros he could and offer an encomium. The rest of us have all spoken; but since you haven't and you've finished your drink, you ought to speak too. Once you've done so, you can prescribe for Socrates as you wish, and he for the man on his right (*epi dexia*), and so on for the rest.

> *Symposium* 214b9–c5

As we have seen, however, Alcibiades does not really follow the rule, since he speaks not about Eros, but a human being (214d2–10)—albeit one who is like Eros. Later, however, when Aristodemus wakes up, he finds order restored: "only Agathon and Aristophanes and Socrates were still awake, drinking from a large bowl, and passing it from left to right (*epi dexia*)" (223c4–5). I take this to imply that Alcibiades and the crowd of revelers—and the disorder they represent—have gone. But perhaps, like some others, they have simply gone to sleep.

This order, this movement of love (or of the *logoi* about it) around Agathon's table, is literally symposiastic, but it is also allegorical. It is related, first and most obviously, to the order discerned in love by dialectic in the *Phaedrus*, where, as we saw good philosophical love is identified with the parts of madness "on the right-hand side (*dexiai*)" of the definitional division (266a3–b1). But it is also related to "the movement of the Same," which the Demiurge in the *Timaeus* "made revolve toward the right (*epi dexia*) by way of the side" (36c5–6). For like dialectic, and the divisions and collections of which Socrates proclaims himself a lover (*Phaedrus* 266b3–4), this movement, too, is associated with philosophy: "whenever an argument concerns an object of reason, and the circle of the Same runs well (*euporos*) and reveals it, the necessary result is understanding and knowledge" (*Timaeus* 37c1–3).

What these allegorical aspects of *epi dexia* mean within the *Symposium* emerges when we turn to Diotima's philosophical demythologizing of the story of Poros and Penia discussed above. If those already filled with wisdom, and so touching all the Platonic forms, neither love nor desire anything, what happens to the philosopher who reaches the goal of education in the craft of love? Is his love wrecked by its very success? In Diotima's view, the answer is no. The philosopher's desire, like that of all lovers, isn't to possess the beautiful or the good for a moment, but to have it be his "forever" (206a3–13). Concealed in every desire or love, therefore, is "the love of immortality" (207a3–4). But the closest a mortal creature can come to gratifying *that* love is a far cry from the permanent satisfaction achieved by the gods:

> Mortal nature seeks so far as it can to exist forever and be immortal. It can do so only in this way, by giving birth, ever leaving behind a different new thing in place of the old, since even in the time in which each single living creature is said to live and be the same—for example, as a man is said to live and be the same from youth to old age—though he never has the same things in himself, he nevertheless is called the same, but he is ever becoming new while otherwise perishing, in respect to hair and flesh and bone and blood and the entire body. And not only in respect to the body but also in respect to the soul, its character and habits, opinions, desires, pleasures, pains, fears are each never present in each man as the same, but some are coming to be, others perishing. Much more extraordinary still, not only are some items of knowledge coming to be and others perishing in us, and we are never the same even in respect to items of knowledge, but also each single one among the items of knowledge is affected in the same way. For what is called practicing exists because knowledge leaves us; forgetting is departure of knowledge, but practice, by introducing a new memory in place of what departs, preserves the knowledge so that it seems to be the same. For it is in this way that all that is mortal is preserved: not by being ever completely the same, like the divine, but by leaving behind, as it departs and becomes older, a different new thing of the same sort that it was. By this device ... what is mortal has a share of immortality both body and everything else; but what is immortal by another device.[22]

> *Symposium* 207d1–208b4

---

[22] It is an interesting question whether this account applies to all parts of the human soul in all circumstances, or only, as the *Republic* suggests, to the "form it takes in human life," when, encrusted with bodily appetites, its true nature, like that of the sea-god Glaucus, is disguised (612a5–6). If, when separate from the body and the other elements present in the embodied soul, the rational element is truly immortal and divine, truly a vessel from which knowledge never leaks away, then what applies to the gods will apply also to it.

Thus, when the philosopher reaches the beautiful itself, his task, just because he is mortal, is by no means complete. To stay in touch with the beautiful, each item of knowledge that is his knowing or contemplation of it must give birth to another like it—just as, if he himself is to stay alive, each of his person-stages or time-slices, as we call them, must give birth to another.

One effect of this way of thinking, as Derek Parfit has famously argued in our own time, is to blur or soften the distinction between self and others, and with it the distinction between egoism and altruism (Parfit 1984:199–347). There is little doubt, I think, that Plato is aware of this effect and seeks to exploit it. What a philosopher begets in the true beauty of the beautiful itself, is the good thing that is his own "true virtue." And it is with the nurturing of it that he is first concerned. Since he is a changing or metabolizing creature, however, what he has to do to remain virtuous—to keep that good thing—is to give birth to a later stage of himself that is virtuous too. This later self, as a case of possessing good things himself, is also something he loves, and for the same reason as he loves his present self as such a case: when a person becomes virtuous, the *Republic* tells us, he thereby "becomes his own friend (*philon genomenon heautōi*)" (443d5).[23] Pregnant with virtue, then, and ever ready to give birth to it in true beauty, the philosopher meets a boy that he, using the beautiful itself as his standard of beauty (211d3–5), finds beautiful, and so "seeks to educate." That is, he seeks to make the boy, too, a virtuous lover of wisdom—something "of the same sort" as himself. If he succeeds, the boy will be his "offshoot" (208b4–6), and will be loved as his own future selves are loved, and for exactly the same reason—the boy stands to him (to his present self) precisely as they do. Egoism has moved closer to altruism; self-interest to something more impersonal. If we look at this from the point of view of the boy, we can see why Socrates' elenctic demonstrations do show Hermogenes how to get Lysis to love *him*. An elenchus of another is always at the same time, Socrates claims, a self-examination (*Apology* 38a4–5, *Charmides* 166c7–d2, *Gorgias* 506a3–5). Thus if Hermogenes, like Lysis, is a nascent philosopher, their elenctic conversations will make each the other's second self, every bit as much beloved as the first.[24] The true path to gaining Socrates' love is thus laid out.

"I think," says Diotima, "that in touching *tou kalou* and holding familiar intercourse *autōi*, he bears and begets what he has long since been pregnant

---

[23] Thanks to Jim Lesher for reminding me of this text.

[24] In Reeve 1992a:173–183, I argue that we should understand Aristotle's views on virtuous friends in a similar way. Such friends are each other's "second selves" in part because they help produce one another as virtuous.

with" (209c2-4). Is it the boy or the beautiful she's talking about? A happy ambiguity (*tou kalou* and *autōi* could be either masculine or neuter) allows her to superimpose on one another, as it were, what I have presented as two separate events—the philosopher's giving birth in the true beauty of the beautiful itself to *what we would all intuitively consider* to be his own later self, and his giving birth in a beautiful boy to *what Diotima's own theory of the self* invites us to see as such.

As prominent in the *Symposium* as the fourfold repetition of *epi dexia*, and as deeply associated with Alcibiades, is the fourfold repetition of *exaiphnēs* ("all of a sudden"): *exaiphnēs*, the true lover catches sight of the beautiful itself (210e4-5); *exaiphnēs*, Alcibiades arrives at Agathon's house (212c6); *exaiphnēs*, Socrates turns up in Alcibiades' life (213c1); *exaiphnēs*, the crowd of revelers burst in (223b2-6). What suddenly turns up in each case is a candidate object of love: the beautiful itself for the philosopher's love; Alcibiades for Socrates'; Socrates for Alcibiades'. As for the crowd (*pampollous*) of revelers, they are the object that successfully competes with Socrates for Alcibiades' love, since it is to "the honors of the crowd (*tōn pollōn*)" that Alcibiades caves in when not by Socrates' side (216b4-6).

For what suddenly turns up—what lands the *coup de foudre*—to be truly beautiful, however, to be what is really loved, it has to come at the right place in an order that is, first and foremost, an education-induced order in the lover's own soul. This is something on which Diotima is insistent:

> It is necessary for him who proceeds correctly in this matter to begin while still young by going to beautiful bodies; and first, if his guide guides correctly ... he who has been educated in the craft of love up to this point, beholding beautiful things in the correct order (*ephexēs*)[25] and way, will then suddenly, in an instant, proceeding at that point to the goal of the craft of love, see something marvelous, beautiful in nature.
>
> *Symposium* 210a4–e5

But the importance of proper order doesn't end there. To stay in touch with the beautiful itself, the psychological order thus acquired must be sustained. Like Socrates' own fabled orderliness it must be of a sort that neither wine, nor sexual desire, nor extremes of hot or cold, nor lack of sleep, nor normal human weakness can disrupt. Expressed figuratively as a movement, it must be that of the circle of the Same.

---

[25] The word Alcibiades uses to describe what his description of Socrates will precisely not manifest.

145

With one clear exception, prior to the arrival of Alcibiades, Eryximachus' left-to-right order is followed until all those present have spoken (214c2). The clear exception is Aristophanes.[26] He should have spoken after Pausanias, but he got the hiccups, and so yielded his turn to Eryximachus, who praises orderly, harmonious, pious, temperate love, while condemning "the Pandemotic Eros of the many-tuned Muse Polyhymnia."[27] Comedy, which Aristophanes represents, is thus presented as a backward turn, a step in as anti-philosophical a direction as the "satyr play—or rather Silenus play" of Alcibiades (222d3–4). As in real life, so in the *Symposium*, neither Aristophanes nor Alcibiades is a true friend or lover of Socrates.

I said at the beginning that Alcibiades' portrait of Socrates is the theatrical apogee of the *Symposium*. That we find it so is a measure of how interesting we find Socrates as a person, and "human affairs" more generally—how much we like laughter, intoxication, disorder. It is an interest that aligns us with the anonymous friends of Apollodorus whose desire to hear about what happened at Agathon's house results, as we are invited to suppose, in our interest being gloriously satisfied. Yet the *Symposium*, of which the story of Apollodorus and his friends is a part, diagnoses that interest as dangerously un-philosophical, as potentially an interest in the wrong things. It isn't Socrates we should be interested in, but philosophy and the forms. Alcibiades' speech is filled with human interest. There is no doubt about that. Yet, as neither *euporōs* nor *ephexēs* nor *epi dexia*, it is the work of an unreliable narrator—the product of a life which, torn between shame and the desire for the approval of the masses (216b3–6), self-confessedly does not itself run well (*ēporoun*, 219e3). In part because of the conceptual-density of the term *agalmata* and the skill with which Plato exploits it, however, there is a reading of the speech in which the image it presents of Socrates is uncannily correct. Socrates and his arguments *do* have *agalmata* of virtue in them. Just not ones that, like a randy lover's embryo-containing semen, are there for the easy taking. To get hold of *them*, you must change your life.

---

[26] The unclear case is Aristodemus, the narrator, who, because he is lying next to Eryximachus (175a3–5), should presumably have spoken after him had Aristophanes not take his turn.

[27] Note *kosmios* at 187a5, d5, 188a3, c3, 189a3.

Seven

Where is Socrates on the "Ladder of Love"?

Ruby Blondell

On the Road

WHERE IS [SOCRATES]?" Agathon asks Aristodemus, when the latter shows up at his house a couple of pages into Plato's *Symposium* (174c12). Later Alcibiades tacitly likens Socrates to Odysseus (220c), the archetypal wanderer, thus obliquely raising the question of where he is in his larger "travels."[1] Travel language runs through the *Symposium* from the first sentence (or more accurately, the second) to the last, when Socrates' intellectual and physical wanderings end at a (temporary) point of rest. Diotima's famous image of the "ladder of love" forms, as it were, the climax of this system of imagery.[2] In Greek texts generally, and Plato in particular, such images carry a complex set of associations, ranging over intellectual discovery, the sequential steps of an argument or narrative, education, the struggle for virtue (often on an uphill path), and the course of life itself.[3] Travel with

---

[1] For Plato's Socrates as a wanderer, like the Homeric Odysseus, in search of his true "home", see Blondell 2002:158–159; cf. also Montiglio 2005:151–155. Alcibiades' particular allusions, to *Odyssey* iv 242 and 271, would suggest that Socrates is far from reaching home, since they both refer to events at Troy. The first reference is particularly suggestive in the context of the *Symposium*, since it tells of Odysseus disguising himself with a beggar's ugly exterior, which only one person (Helen) can see through (*Odyssey* iv 240–250). Socrates himself alludes to the *Odyssey* at 198b–c (cf. Rosen 1987:204).

[2] On the "ladder of love" as a mystic's journey, see especially Nightingale 2004:83–86. "Love" is an inadequate translation of the Greek *erōs* (see Halperin 1985:161–163). Moreover the ascent is more like a staircase than a ladder, since it leaves room on each step for company (which suits the Socratic model of "leadership," as we shall see) and suggests ascent to a temple and thus to divinity. But the traditional phrase remains more euphonious than "staircase of passionate desire."

[3] See Montiglio 2005. As Nightingale has recently argued (2004), the theoric journey is of particular significance for philosophical inquiry. For the "path" of dialectic, cf. Nightingale 2004:108–

companions may also serve as a metaphor for various kinds of human relationship. The *Symposium's* pervasive travel imagery therefore sensitizes us to questions of metaphorical placement, intellectual or ethical progress, and philosophical relationship, questions that center especially on Socrates.

Like many Platonic dialogues the *Symposium* opens with a literal journey.[4] In the frame dialogue Apollodorus recalls his trip from home to town in the company of Glaucon (172a–173b). This journey becomes a metaphor for interpersonal relationships and the pursuit of ideas, in part by becoming an opportunity to seek out and reiterate the ideas of others, most notably Socrates. It raises all the most basic questions that one might ask of such a journey: who is in front, who behind, who is moving, who is stationary, who wants to know and who can tell him, who is interested in philosophy and, above all, who is intimate, or even "in love," with Socrates. The structure of this journey is a simple one. The follower catches up with the leader, and the two of them proceed together, the leader giving the follower a narrative of past events. There is an explicit contrast between this kind of orderly pursuit of a *telos*, which characterizes the philosophical life, and the random "running around" of the non-philosopher (172c–173a).[5]

This preliminary journey introduces the next one: Socrates' journey to the house of Agathon in the company of Aristodemus. Like Apollodorus' opening journey, but more fully and subtly, this too is a metaphor for human relationships and philosophical progress.[6] This time, since Socrates is actually present, we receive a sketch of the philosopher as fellow traveler, one that underlines his autonomy both in choosing a destination and in proceeding towards it. Thus Socrates chose not to be present at yesterday's gathering, a decision illustrating his independence from social convention (174a). Similarly, by "spoiling" the proverb about party-crashing (174b–c) he shows a light-hearted disrespect for traditional wisdom, and by bringing along an uninvited guest he challenges symposiastic exclusivity and decorum,[7] as Aristodemus' nervousness and embarrassment make clear. Socrates tries to

---

110. The "journey" of narrative is also of particular interest in the context of the *Symposium's* complex narrative structure (cf. e.g. διελθεῖν x 3 at 201d–e).

[4] Cf. Blondell 2002:64. On the opening journey of the *Symposium* and its relevance to the ascent, cf. Osborne 1994:86–90.

[5] Cf. also the "going around" and random encounters of the non-philosophical lover (209b), and Alcibiades' "going around" in a state of *aporia* after Socrates rejects him sexually (219e). On the interplay between directed travel, wandering, and rest in Plato, see Montiglio 2005:163–179.

[6] Cf. Lowenstam 1985:87; Osborne 1994:90–91, 97–98 (though their interpretations differ from mine).

[7] On which cf. Stehle 1997:218.

enroll Aristodemus in his own independent ways, suggesting that the two of them proceed autonomously (αὐτόματοι 174b5). Though he initially tells Aristodemus to "follow" him (174b2–3), he quotes Homer to suggest collaboration as equals: "going along the road together as a pair, we'll plan what we shall say" (174d2–3; note the dual). This cooperative approach to life, and discourse, is typical of Plato's Socrates.[8] Aristodemus, however, will "follow" mechanically until the very end (223d10; cf. 172c5–6). Here in the prologue he refuses to take responsibility for himself, saying he will do whatever Socrates "orders" (174b2) and warning him that he will have to take responsibility for "leading" him to Agathon's (174c7–d1). Despite his enthusiasm for things Socratic, Aristodemus lacks his idol's chutzpah and is dubious about Socratic autonomy and collaboration as equals. These character traits are echoed in his inability to follow Socrates intellectually (cf. 223c6–d1).

Despite his collaborative proposal, however, Socrates ends up obliging Aristodemus to strike out on his own, upsetting the leader-follower hierarchy by falling behind and "ordering" Aristodemus to go on ahead (174d). Aristodemus will prove laughably bad at this enforced exercise in Socratic autonomy and unwanted leadership, failing to notice that he has left Socrates behind and feeling ridiculous upon arriving without him (174d–e). When he is "led" in by a slave (174e3) Agathon asks him why he is not "leading" Socrates (174e8). Aristodemus has apparently failed as a "leader," since unbeknownst to him, Socrates is not "following" (174e10). Though "left behind," Socrates has not become a follower in the way that Aristodemus expected. Whatever role he takes, he handles the situation on his own terms, proceeding autonomously even when Aristodemus is leading the way, and at the same time "leading" Aristodemus by suggesting a destination and then encouraging him to strike out towards it on his own.

For a brief period no one knows where Socrates is—a slave must be sent to find him (174e–175a). Only then do we find out that he has been standing in a neighbor's doorway, resisting any invitation to come in (175a7–9), with his mind (*nous*) only on himself (174d). He has stopped moving, standing still on the road as he sometimes does, according to Aristodemus (175b). The situation is *atopos*, "strange," or more literally "out of place,"[9] at least in the view

---

[8] Cf. Blondell 2002:120–121. At *Protagoras* 348d–e he uses the same quotation from Homer to express both kinds of cooperation.

[9] Though *atopos* primarily means "strange"—having lost most of its spatial sense—Plato reactivates its association with (intellectual) wandering by linking it with Socrates' signature state of mental *aporia*. See further Blondell 2002:73–74; Nightingale 2004:105–107; cf. also Montiglio 2005:154–155, 170.

of Agathon, who wants to put a stop to it by sending someone (presumably a slave) to fetch him (175a10–11). Aristodemus warns that Socrates must not be "led in" by another (175a–b). He must be left to come in of his own volition. Aristodemus *thinks* he will arrive at some point (175b2–3), but cannot be certain. Nevertheless, Agathon keeps wanting to send for him (175c2–4). He wants to do away with Socrates' strangeness, his odd location, and *place* him in a conventional space and conventional set of relationships: he should be at dinner with his friends, not lurking solipsistically in doorways. When Socrates does finally arrive, in his own good time, it is half way through dinner (175c). This shows not only his general lack of interest in bodily needs and appetites, but a willingness to participate in social institutions, to follow others and respect conventional destinations, only on his own unconventional terms.

This opening scene, with its literal journey to Agathon's house, foreshadows questions that we will want to ask of Socrates in connection with the more profound, figurative journey of the "ladder of love." We will want to know not only where he is, but where he is going (and whether he will ever arrive), who (if anyone) is leading him, and whom (if anyone) he is leading. The journey to Agathon's also adumbrates answers to such questions: Socrates covers a good deal of ground, but is sometimes in an unknown (and potentially unknowable) place; he is equally capable of leading, following, collaborating and proceeding autonomously; whatever role he may take, he goes only where he pleases, and encourages others, such as Aristodemus, to do the same; in the end, he arrives; but although the location of his body can (eventually) be determined at any given moment, the location and activity of his mind or soul cannot—at least not always.

Just as Socrates plays several roles on this literal journey, he also takes on the whole range of identities associated with Diotima's ladder. The most important of these is, of course, the role of the *erastēs*—the one who proceeds "correctly" in such matters. The perfect *erastēs* is presumably to be identified with the anthropomorphized Eros, in so far as the latter is a lover, as opposed to an object of desire (204c). Diotima's Eros notoriously resembles Socrates himself,[10] thereby suggesting that he too is ascending the ladder as an ideal *erastēs*. This is clearly adumbrated in the opening scene, in which Socrates proceeds on the road towards beauty and goodness as embodied in the beautiful Agathon, whose name means "good."[11] But Socrates is also the beautiful human

---

[10] For the textual evidence, see Bury 1932:lx–lxii. The equation has been much discussed (see e.g. Robin 1908:194–196, 1958:ci–cviii; Anderson 1993:101–103; Osborne 1994:93–101; Hadot 2002:42–50). But Socrates also differs from Eros in significant respects, as we shall see.

[11] There are many puns on his name, the most overt of which is at 174b4.

object of desire. He has made himself "beautiful" by bathing and donning sandals, thus inviting comparison between his own beauty and Agathon's (174a). We even hear that on the previous day he "escaped" from Agathon, like a beloved fleeing his pursuer (174a),[12] again signaling his desirability and hinting at the reversal of erotic roles with Alcibiades that is to come.[13]

Diotima's ladder also involves a third person, the mysterious leader.[14] As we saw, Aristodemus' opening narrative dramatizes the difference between Socratic leadership and the kind that calls for a passive, dog-like follower. Socrates' attitude towards his companion there foreshadows his response to Alcibiades when the latter tries to seduce him: "planning in the time to come we shall do whatever seems best to both of us" (219a8–b2; note the dual, echoing 174d2). In contrast to the passive education exemplified by tradition and the sophists, Socrates' "leadership" is a collaborative enterprise in which the leader encourages the follower to figure things out for herself.[15] *Qua* embodiment of Eros,[16] he "leads" by means of dialectic, as exemplified in his elenchus of Agathon. This—not personal authority—is the means by which he exerts "compulsion" (216a4–5; cf. 201c, 216b3–4, b6), even on those like Alcibiades who cannot "follow" him properly (223d3–7).[17] This dialectical compulsion evokes the "compulsion" that drives the ascent (cf. 210c3). This too is collaborative. When Diotima declares that the lover will "go or be led" (211c), the "or" is not exclusive.[18] Rather, the right kind of "leading" results in "going" of one's own accord and volition, as with the combination of discipline and autonomy in the higher education of the guardians in the *Republic*.[19]

Alcibiades will speak of Socrates' resistance to being led or won over erotically (προσαγαγοίμην 219d8), and of his autonomy over his own movements in defiance of "normal" behavior (cf. 220b4), both features that we

---

[12] The diction (διέφυγον) suggests this connotation (cf. e.g. Sappho 1.21).

[13] On Socrates as the beautiful *erōmenos*, see especially Lowenstam 1985:98–100.

[14] Referred to variously as the ἡγούμενος (Step 1 in my summary below), "leader" (implied at Step 5 and in the reprise) and *paidagōgos* (Step 7, 210e3).

[15] Blondell 2002:95–101; cf. also Burnyeat 1977:9. On the Socratic character of the guide, see Sheffield 2001a:17–18.

[16] In Aristophanes' speech Eros is the ἡγεμών and στρατηγός (193b1). In Agathon's he is a leader and teacher (197a), the ἡγεμών whom we should all follow (197d–e). For Phaedrus, Eros implants the sense of shame that should lead us (178c).

[17] Alcibiades' misunderstanding of Socrates' collaborative proposal (219b) betrays an intellectual passivity that parallels that of Aristodemus: he views Socrates' advice as "ordering" (216b4, 217a2) and desires simply to "hear" his inner wisdom (217a5).

[18] *Pace* Ferrari, who thinks the leader is optional (1992:257). This seems most unlikely considering the heavy emphasis on the "leader" throughout the ascent (cf. Rowe 1998a:*ad loc.*).

[19] See Blondell 2002:214–216.

151

have seen foreshadowed in the opening scene. Yet these traits do not prevent him from himself "following" the right kind of leader in the right kind of way (cf. 210a4). He seeks out Diotima for enlightenment, just as others such as Aristodemus seek him out, impelled by *erōs* (173b; cf. 206b).[20] She adopts a bossy tone appropriate to a *paidagōgos* (esp. 204b1; also 201e10, 202a5–6). But despite her commanding style (and slightly acerbic tongue),[21] her mode of "leadership" turns out to be uncannily similar to Socrates' own pedagogical methods.[22] He even seems to have learned from her the most characteristic of those methods, as exemplified in the elenchus of Agathon (201e). She supposedly "taught" him through question and answer, showing him his own ignorance just as he shows Agathon his.[23] In another familiar Socratic move, she even places herself in the position of learner (along with Socrates), vis à vis an imaginary and more knowledgeable questioner (204d), suggesting that she has attained her exalted wisdom in part by learning from others dialectically, in the same way that Socrates learns from her, and others such as Agathon learn from him. Socrates' self-substitution for Agathon in his conversation with Diotima signals that he too is one who can both lead and be led, as he demonstrates by jauntily switching roles to suit his purpose (201d).

It seems clear enough, then, that Plato encourages us to identify Socrates with all the roles connected with the ladder, which in turn echo the relationships sketched in the literal journey to Agathon's house. But the main focus of Diotima's attention—and of Plato's—is the *erastēs*. Socrates is clearly to be identified with this figure. But just how far should we take him to have progressed in his ascent? At the time of his acquaintance with Diotima he has obviously not attained the vision of the Form of Beauty; but certain moments in his speech manifestly provoke us to speculate how far he may have proceeded in the twenty-five years between their conversations and the dinner party at which they are recalled (cf. 210a, 211d3–4, 212b).[24] In short, Plato strongly invites us to put the question of my title to his text, and scholars have not

---

[20] Note the suggestive verb φοιτάω, which can be used as a euphemism for sex (cf. e.g. *Republic* 390c).

[21] Cf. Blundell 1992:130; Rutherford 1995:192.

[22] She incorporates aspects of both the elenctic and the constructive Socrates (cf. Blundell 1992:129–130; for the terminology, see Blondell 2002:10–11).

[23] Like an elenctic victim Socrates (as "Agathon") starts with the beliefs held by "everyone" (202b) or the many (203c7).

[24] The reference to the plague (201d) seems to indicate that Diotima was in Athens around 440, from which most commentators infer that her conversations with Socrates are imagined to have taken place around that time (whether or not the relationship is entirely fictional, as I take it to be). Anton 1974 speculates on Socrates' erotic/philosophical development over this period of time.

been slow to take the bait. I therefore turn now to examine this central question in greater detail.

Room at the Top

I begin with an analysis of the steps of the ladder as outlined by Diotima at 210a–212a, with the reprise of 211b–d interwoven into the summary (and also summarized separately beneath it). I have highlighted the linguistic markers that underpin my analysis of the ladder's structure.

STEP 1 (210a4–8): The one going correctly (ὀρθῶς) towards this matter must (δεῖ) begin while young to go towards beautiful bodies, and FIRST (πρῶτον), if the one leading him (ἡγούμενος) leads correctly (ὀρθῶς), be in love with (ἐρᾶν) one body and there give birth to (γεννᾶν) beautiful λόγοι. [Reprise A: start from the beauty of one body (211c3).]

STEP 2 (210a8–b6): NEXT (ἔπειτα) he must [δεῖ] recognize (κατανοῆσαι) for himself[25] that the beauty of any body at all is twin (ἀδελφόν) to the beauty of any other body, and that if one must (δεῖ) pursue (διώκειν) what is beautiful in form (εἴδει), it is great foolishness (ἄνοια) not to consider (ἡγεῖσθαι) the beauty of all bodies to be one and the same, and realizing (ἐννοήσαντα) this, he must [δεῖ] become (καταστῆναι) an ἐραστής of all beautiful bodies, and slacken from that vehement *erōs* for a single body, despising it (καταφρονήσαντα) and considering it (ἡγησάμενον) something slight (σμικρόν). [Reprise B & C: from beauty of one body to two, and from two to many (211c3–4).]

STEP 3 (210b6–c3): AFTER THIS (μετὰ ταῦτα) he must [δεῖ] consider (ἡγήσασθαι) the beauty in souls more precious (τιμιώτερον) than that in the body, so that (ὥστε) if someone (τις) who is even reasonably attractive (ἐπιεικής) in soul has even a slight [bodily] bloom, this suffices for him and he is in love with and cares about (κήδεσθαι) [that person] and gives birth to (τίκτειν) and seeks[26] λόγοι of a kind that will make young men better (βελτίους) ... [This step absent from the reprise.]

STEP 4 (210c4–6): ... SO THAT (ἵνα) NEXT (αὖ) he may be forced (ἀναγκασθῇ) to gaze upon (θεάσασθαι) the beauty in activities and νόμοι and see (ἰδεῖν) that this is all akin (συγγενές) to itself, so that (ἵνα) he may consider (ἡγήσηται) the beauty that concerns the body to be something slight (σμικρόν). [Reprise D: from beauty of bodies to beauty of activities (211c4–5).]

---

[25] See Rowe 1998a:*ad loc.* for a defense of this interpretation of αὐτόν.
[26] For defense of the text here, see Sier 1997:276; Rowe 1998a:*ad loc.* (and cf. his note on 210d4–6).

STEP 5 (210c6–7): AFTER (μετά) activities [he] must [δεῖ] lead [him] (ἀγαγεῖν) to the [various] kinds of knowledge, so that (ἵνα) he may see NEXT (αὖ) the beauty of kinds of knowledge... [Reprise E: from beauty of activities to beauty of kinds of learning (211c5–6).]

STEP 6 (210c7–d6): ... and AT THIS POINT (ἤδη) looking towards beauty that is abundant, may no longer be worthless (φαῦλος) and petty (σμικρολόγος) in his servitude, feeling affection (ἀγαπῶν) like a slave, for the beauty of some individual boy or other person or single activity, but being turned towards the great sea of beauty and gazing at it (θεωρῶν) may give birth to (τίκτῃ) numerous beautiful and magnificent (μεγαλοπρεπεῖς) λόγοι and thoughts (διανοήματα) in unstinting philosophy ... [This step absent from the reprise.]

STEP 7 (210d6–211b5): ... UNTIL (ἕως) strengthened and increased there, he catches sight of (κατίδῃ) a certain kind of knowledge which is one, whose object is beauty of the following kind ... For whoever is guided (παιδαγωγηθῇ) until this point concerning τὰ ἐρωτικά, gazing (θεώμενος) at beautiful things in order (ἐφεξῆς) and correctly (ὀρθῶς), coming now (ἤδη) to the end/goal (τέλος) of τὰ ἐρωτικά will suddenly catch sight of (κατόψεται) something amazingly (θαυμαστόν) beautiful in its nature, the very thing for the sake of which all the previous labors [were undertaken] ...; and beauty will no longer appear to him (φαντασθήσεται) like some face or hands or anything else that the body shares in, or some λόγος or some kind of knowledge, nor as being in anything other [than itself], such as an animal, the earth or the sky, or anything else ... [This step absent from the reprise.]

STEP 8 (211b5–c1; 211c7–d1; 212a2–7): When someone going up away from these things by means of correct παιδεραστεῖν begins to see *that* beauty, the END/GOAL (τέλος) is pretty much within his grasp. For this is to approach τὰ ἐρωτικά correctly (ὀρθῶς) or be led by someone else ... [omitting reprise A–E] ... [reprise F]: from kinds of understanding to end up (τελευτῆσαι) at the kind of understanding that is the understanding of nothing other than that very beauty, so that he may understand (γνῷ) in the end (τελευτῶν) what beauty itself is ... There alone will it happen to him, seeing beauty with the kind of vision with which it is visible, to give birth (τίκτειν) not to images (εἴδωλα) of excellence, since he is not grasping an image, but to true things, since he is grasping truth; and after giving birth to (τεκόντι) true excellence and rearing it (θρεψαμένῳ) it is his to be god-loved, and himself immortal as far as any mortal can be.

REPRISE (211b7–d1)

A   One body (211c3)
B   Two bodies (211c3)
C   All bodies (211c5)
D   Activities (211c5)
E   Kinds of learning (μαθήματα) (211c6)
F   The μάθημα of beauty itself (211c6–d1)

On which of these steps does Plato envisage Socrates as standing? I shall examine each in turn, beginning with the summit (Step 8), the climactic level at which the successful lover gazes upon the Form of Beauty itself. Since the Form exists outside space and time,[27] it is not comparable to, or on a level with (κατά), beautiful objects or people (211d3–5). It is perceptible only with the mind or soul (212a3). Those who can gaze upon it by such means (θεάομαι 211d2, d7, 212a2; cf. 210c3, e3) will give birth to true *aretē*, not mere images of it, and become "god-loved" and as immortal (i.e. divine) as a human can be (212a). The successful lover is alone at the top.[28] The leader has evaporated, since the destination has been attained. The love-object is now the Form itself (cf. *Republic* 490a–b, 501d), which has replaced all previous objects of desire. The lover no longer has need of other human beings—or indeed of anything in the material world—to inspire his procreativity. The metaphor of raising a child is carried over from its initial appearance in the "lesser mysteries" (210a6; cf. 209c), but there is no longer any sign of a second human parent (or foster-parent).[29] Moreover since the lover is now producing true *aretē*, instead of mere (verbal) "images,"[30] he no longer needs anyone to listen to his words. Accordingly, there is no sign of discourse at the summit.[31] Presumably, "true" virtue is a state of soul that causes one to act virtuously with full and complete understanding of the "beauty" and excellence of one's deeds. Since the philosopher cannot exist permanently in the contemplation of the

---

[27] Cf. Rowe 1998a on 211a7–b8.

[28] I am all too aware that this claim will not meet with universal agreement. Rowe and Price, for example, believe that the individual beloved boy remains a presence all the way up the ladder to the top (Rowe 1998b:257; Price 1997:52–54). But *pace* e.g. Rowe 1998a:*ad loc.*, Price 1997:48, 259, the word παιδεραστεῖν (211b5–6) does not show the continued presence of a human love-object as such (cf. Sier 1997:150n10, 287). See further Sier 1997:149–151.

[29] The other parent, if there were one, would have to be the Form on whose beauty the lover now gazes. On the awkwardness of this, see Pender 1992:82–85. For the lover's need to "nurture" his *aretē*, see Nightingale 1993:129–130.

[30] Poets, craftsmen, and lawgivers were previously said to produce *aretē*, including *phronēsis*, in deeds as well as words (209a–c, e), but these likewise now turn out to have been mere images.

[31] Cf. e.g. Ferrari 1992:259–60.

Forms,[32] and must descend to interact with his fellow humans, such virtue will produce collateral benefits for others.[33] But any such benefits are side-effects of the successful lover's relationship with Beauty, not its purpose. The *purpose* of his affair with the Form is to generate his own virtue for his own sake, not to benefit others *qua* love-objects.

The placement of Socrates at Step 8 is by far the most popular among commentators, for a wide range of reasons.[34] Socrates' role as philosophical "leader," and his endorsement of Diotima's teachings, may suggest that, like Diotima, he has some authority deriving from a vision of the Forms. The intervening twenty-five years have given him plenty of time to develop his intellectual vision (cf. 219a). Moreover he notoriously tells us that he *knows* τὰ ἐρωτικά (ἐπίστασθαι 177d8)—a remarkably strong claim for Plato's Socrates. Perhaps this "knowledge" is equivalent to the "single knowledge" that is of the Form (210d7; cf. 211c6–d1).

Many specifics of Socrates' behavior are also strongly suggestive of the summit. His contempt for wealth and conspicuous display (216d7–e4), for example, resembles the outlook of the successful lover (211d). His *unique* indifference to the bodily effects of alcohol, food (or its lack), temperature, and other hardships (219e–220a)—not to mention sexual temptation—also suggests that he is obsessively in love with something transcending the material world (cf. 211d). The emphasis on his endurance is particularly significant, in so far as the ladder metaphor implies struggle,[35] as is his uniqueness, since it is clear that few—if any—have made it to the top. As for his virtues, they too are manifested at a level that is extraordinary to the point of uniqueness. In addition to his incredible *sōphrosunē* he deserves the *aristeia* for courage more than Alcibiades (220d–e) and the crown for *logoi* more than Agathon (213e).[36] His remarkable behavior may plausibly be understood as a manifestation of the virtue that is inside him, here expressed as actions rather than *logoi*—

---

[32] Cf. the difference between human and divine nature at 208a–b. On the impossibility of dwelling permanently in the presence of the Forms, see especially Nightingale 2004:98–100.

[33] So rightly Lowenstam 1985:94; Price 1997:50–52. But Price is wrong to identify those so benefited with "an individual ... as an object of love" (1997:53). The "object of love" is the Form of Beauty.

[34] See e.g. Robin 1908:196–198; Burnet 1928:140; Stannard 1959:125; Taylor 1960:232–233: Gagarin 1977:27–28; Lowenstam 1985:92–93; Nussbaum 1986:183–184; Price 1997:49; Gill 1990b:80; Blundell 1992:128; Lear 1998:164; Hadot 2002:48.

[35] The metaphor of an (ascending) path towards virtue standardly implies hardship and struggle (cf. e.g. *Protagoras* 340d). Compare Nightingale 2004:113–114 on the difficulty of the path of dialectic in the *Republic*. Cf. also the struggles directed towards lesser forms of immortality in the *Symposium* (207b, 208c–d).

[36] Their rivalry is also configured as a contest of *sophia* (175e8–9; cf. 212e7–8).

the real thing, not mere images. This virtue results in benefit to others, e.g. through his military courage and his continuing efforts to engage Alcibiades in philosophy (cf. 219a8–b2). But these benefits are not inspired by personal *erōs* for those benefited.[37]

As many commentators have observed,[38] Socrates actually resembles the Form of Beauty in a number of ways. Like the Form he shows up "suddenly" (213c1; 210e4). He convinces Alcibiades that his present life is not "livable"— recalling the summit of the ascent (211d1–3)—and that he should spend the rest of his life in his company (216a), as the successful lover does with the Form (cf. 211e4). Like the consistent and unchanging Form he is always the same (221e; cf. 213e4). The Form is "amazingly beautiful in its *phusis*" (210e) and brings us as close as possible to divinity (212a). Similarly, Socrates is not only ironically and externally "beautiful" on this particular occasion (174a), but himself opens the door to the possibility that he possesses a "true" and "golden" beauty, as opposed to the "bronze" of mere opinion (218e). Moreover Alcibiades asserts that he contains interior *agalmata*, sacred images of gods that are utterly beautiful (216e; cf. 215b3).[39] His words too are "most godlike" and contain *agalmata* of virtues (222a).[40] Alcibiades' admiration for his *phusis* (ἀγάμενον 219d4), may also pun on the word *agalma*.[41]

Above all, Socrates, like the Form, is "amazing" (θαυμαστός)—a key word in Alcibiades' speech.[42] Most amazing of all is his uniqueness. He cannot be compared to any human being—just as the Form is not comparable to anything in the human world (211a5–b2, d3–5)—but only to the quasi-divine satyr (221c–d), than whom Socrates is even more amazing (215b8). This strangeness makes him, like the Form, the inadvertent, detached object of other people's amazed gaze (θαυμάζω 220c6; θεάομαι 220e8, 221a6). Alcibiades' allusion to Socrates' theatrical appearance in the *Clouds* (221a) draws further attention to his body and looks, accentuating the appearance and demeanor that make him both different from ordinary people and a source of fascination to them. For many of these viewers—Alcibiades, Agathon, Aristodemus, Charmides,

---

[37] The discussion usually revolves around Alcibiades, but Laches (221b6–7) is presumably no love-object.

[38] E.g. Nussbaum 1986:195; Hunter 2004:19.

[39] The connotations of the word *agalma*, in Plato and elsewhere, have been much discussed. See most recently Nightingale 2004:163–164 (and passim).

[40] They also serve as a diagnostic test for those who stand in need of divinity (215c5–6). That Alcibiades views Socrates as bordering on divinity is further suggested by 214d.

[41] According to Chantraine the words could be connected but there is no evidence (1968:s.v.). Either way, there is probably a Platonic pun.

[42] 213e2, 215b8, 217a1, 219c1, 220a4, c6, 221c3, c6, 222e8.

Euthydemus, and other unnamed *erastai*—he is also the *telos* of erotic and/or philosophical pursuit (173b, 222b). Like his famously ugly features, his weird demeanor underlines the paradox of Socrates as love-object. This strange and ugly body, with its extraordinary magnetism for the Athenian social and intellectual elite, radiates the power of a transcendent beauty that is invisible to the physical gaze but irresistible to the eye of the soul.[43]

All this suggests that Socrates has a special kinship with the Form, reinforcing the impression that he has communed with it and given birth to the true virtue that results from such intercourse. Alcibiades is, to be sure, an unreliable witness.[44] Indeed, his fundamental error may be that he confuses Socrates with the Form as the ultimate object of desire. He treats Socrates as if he had brought "true" virtue back down from the summit to be purchased by the likes of himself with no more effort or expense than a one-night stand. There is thus good reason to be suspicious of his purported insights into Socrates' inner nature. This is not true, however, of the facts Alcibiades reports about Socrates' *behavior*, whose truth is strongly authorized by Socrates' tacit assent (cf. 214e, 217b, 219c), and corroborated in some cases by the witness of others. These facts include, most importantly, Alcibiades' account of Socrates' virtuous actions and his strangeness. We cannot see inside his soul, but we can see the visible behavior for which he deserves the *aristeia* for courage and the crown for *logoi*.

The most important evidence, however, for Socrates' arrival at the top of the ladder consists in those dramatically powerful moments when he turns inward, in solitude, abandoning the physical gaze entirely in favor of the intellectual. Intellectual perception is required on lower rungs of the ladder too, of course (cf. e.g. 210c3–5). But only when the Form itself is sighted does all need for other people for such activity—whether as participants in philosophy or as the recipients of improving *logoi*—come to a full stop. Only when his journey is at an end does the lover's relationship to the human world become utterly insignificant. Socrates' isolation from his fellow mortals at such moments is strongly marked dramatically. There is also heavy emphasis on the fact that he is standing still, as if at the *telos* of his journey (175a8, b2, 220c4, 5, 7, d3).

Those internal witnesses who interpret Socrates' mental state at these times—Agathon, Alcibiades, and the soldiers at Potidaea—assume that he is engaged in the kind of mental activity they expect from him or understand

---

[43] It is, of course, hard to attain this kind of vision. The ordinary soldiers cannot see Socrates' inner beauty, so they become hostile (220c1), foreshadowing his death.

[44] On this I completely agree with Nightingale 1993:119–127. Cf. also Belfiore 1984:141–143; Halperin 1992:115; Lear 1998:159; Hunter 2004:100.

from their own experience: grasping a transmissible piece of wisdom, seeking an answer or trying to solve a problem (175c–e, 220c).[45] But none of these people is a reliable interpreter of Socrates' inner processes.[46] And in so far as Socrates, throughout Plato's dialogues, treats philosophical inquiry as something to be undertaken through verbal interaction with other human beings, what he is doing in the doorway *cannot* be "seeking," or solving a problem, since it entails neither words nor other people. If he is no longer "seeking" then, according to Diotima, he is no longer philosophizing (cf. 204a). It seems plausible to infer that he is, instead, gazing on the Form of Beauty. The fact is, however, that we do not know what is going on in Socrates' soul when he stands in that doorway, or stands in the cold all night at Potidaea.[47] These incidents are opaque to us.

This opacity bespeaks a Platonic attempt to represent the unrepresentable by dramatic means. Plato can show us only Socrates' exterior, since Socrates cannot use *logoi* to express the state of mind at the top of the ladder without descending to the level of mere images. Accordingly, no *logoi* are produced in immediate consequence of Socrates' episode in the doorway. He avoids giving Agathon an account of what happened during that interlude, and goes out of his way to ascribe the birth of his *logoi* at the *symposion* to a different occasion, and indeed a different author. Likewise the incident at Potidaea generates no *logoi* except for a prayer to the sun (220d), a divinity clearly suggestive of the godlike Form. If Socrates has indeed been gazing on the Form of Beauty, the offspring he produces will be not *logoi*, but interior virtues. Such virtues may, however, be manifested in action. That this is true of Socrates is hinted by the artful disorder of Alcibiades' speech, in which the account of Socrates' exceptional courage, for which he deserves the *aristeia*, follows immediately on the incident at Potidaea.

All this adds up to a compelling case for placing Socrates at the very top of Diotima's ladder. Yet many have seen this placement as essentially unsocratic, owing to Socrates' strong and obvious resemblance to the personified Eros who is a seeker after wisdom but never attains it, fluctuating between

---

[45] Many commentators have followed their lead (e.g. Dover 1980:*ad loc.*; Allen 1991:86).

[46] Socrates himself repudiates Agathon's account of what happened in the doorway (175c–d). Cf. his warning regarding Alcibiades' interpretation of his inner beauty (218d–219a). Only Aristodemus is wisely cautious enough to remain an exterior observer of Socrates' behavior (175b). His inability to see past Socrates' external appearance and behavior makes him deficient as an imitator of Socrates (cf. Blondell 2002:107–109). At the same time, his respect for Socrates' exterior saves him from interpreting his interior in ways that may be quite misleading.

[47] Cf. Hunter 2004:32.

euporia and *aporia* but never becoming *sophos* (203b–204a)—an image that maps onto numerous representations of Socrates in Plato's dialogues. Much of the evidence I have discussed can be reinterpreted from this perspective. Perhaps when Socrates stood in the doorway he was engaged not in contemplation of the Form of Beauty but in an interior dialogue, as per the definition of thinking in *Theaetetus* (190a). And if Alcibiades really did see into Socrates' soul, what he saw there might have been the (potential) virtue with which Socrates was already pregnant prior to beginning the ascent, as opposed to the kind of virtue that one gives birth to and "nourishes" at the summit (212a5–6). Socrates himself casts Alcibiades' assessment of his "true" beauty into question, warning that he may actually be "nothing" (219a). As for his extraordinary claim to "know" erotics (177d; cf. 198d), this may very plausibly be taken to mean that he understands the process of philosophizing, which, paradoxically, entails understanding that one does *not* have determinate knowledge or "wisdom."[48]

Nevertheless, I do not think we are warranted in dismissing the strong case for locating Socrates on Step 8. I would argue, rather, that both aspects of the text are clearly present and should be taken equally seriously. The deeply felt disagreement among commentators reflects Plato's success in suggesting that Socrates, though in his essence a seeker, has also been to the top. He personifies the unresolved tension within the dialogue, and within Plato's works more generally, between achieved (divine) wisdom as a human aspiration and the human condition which prevents us from attaining it.[49]

This tension is perceptible in several key passages of the *Symposium*, such as Socrates' warning to Alcibiades that he may actually be "nothing" (219a). Like any mortal, Socrates is "nothing" compared to the Form, yet he may still have attained the fullest knowledge of it that is available to a mere human.[50] His wording leaves either possibility open, leaving it up to Alcibiades to look into the matter for himself (σκόπει 219a2). Similarly, his claim to "know" erotics is explicable in standard Socratic terms,[51] but *also* allows us to grant his understanding of Eros a privileged status, leaving us to figure out what he

---

[48] See Gould 1963:44; Lowenstam 1985:94–98.

[49] On this tension in the *Symposium*, see Scott and Welton 2000. The paradox becomes even more acute if we ask whether Eros himself ever reaches the top. For Eros *qua* permanent seeker, the answer must be no; for Eros *qua* ideal *erastēs*, however, and communicator with the divine, the answer would seem to be yes.

[50] In Belfiore's formulation, he may be simultaneously indispensable and unnecessary (1984:148).

[51] Elsewhere he makes similar claims, with varying degrees of strength (cf. *Theages* 128b, *Phaedrus* 257a, *Lysis* 204c; Xenophon *Memorabilia* 2.6.28).

may mean by it and assess the status of this "knowledge" in relation to the ladder and the wisdom attained at its summit. His "knowledge" of erotics may, in typically paradoxical fashion, turn out to be *both* an acknowledgment that humans are doomed to remain seekers, and *also* equivalent to the "single knowledge" (210d7) that is of the Form: to understand the Form is (in part) to understand that mortals must constantly strive to remain in its presence by means of philosophy.

The identification of Socrates with Eros the seeker is also ambiguous, for it is by no means precise or complete. For example, Socrates is not nearly as rootless and grubby as the personified Eros—especially on the present occasion. Unlike that unshod divinity, he sometimes gets cleaned up and puts on shoes to attend a party.[52] Unlike Eros, he is, on this occasion, "beautiful" (174a), and will turn out to be an *erōmenos* as well as an *erastēs*. Moreover unlike Eros (203d1) he has a home. This fact is sometimes downplayed,[53] but it should not be dismissed, since we are told in the last two words of the dialogue that he went there to rest (ἀναπαύεσθαι). This is an unusual moment of even temporary closure for a Platonic dialogue, evoking the "rest" (ἀνάπαυλα) of the philosopher who reaches the end of the dialectical journey in the *Republic* (532e).[54] To judge from Plato, Socrates' home is a place where his daily travels— both physical and philosophical—come to an end. But it is also a place where he seems to spend very little time. My point is thus not that Socrates should *not* be identified with Eros as the philosophical seeker—clearly he should—but that we should not limit ourselves to this identification or insist on disambiguating the mixed messages that Plato sends our way. As so often, Plato wants to have his cake and eat it, to situate Socrates as the philosophical seeker while simultaneously hinting that he is the wise man who has arrived.

Stairway to Heaven

If Socrates has indeed made it to Step 8, this has certain consequences that have not, to my knowledge, been addressed by the many scholars who would locate him there.[55] For Diotima emphasizes strongly that one can reach the top of the ladder only by proceeding "correctly" up all the steps in orderly sequence

---

[52] Socrates' uncharacteristic wearing of shoes in the *Symposium* has been much discussed (e.g. by Osborne 1994:96–100). Whatever else it means, it clearly distinguishes him from Diotima's Eros (cf. Gagarin 1977:26–27; Rosen 1987:234).

[53] E.g. by Osborne 1994:91.

[54] Cf. Nightingale 2004:114.

[55] Scott 2000:33 is a partial exception.

(210a2, 4, 6, e3, 211b5, 7). Even if Plato does not actually *show* Socrates to us at every level, he must at least make it seem plausible that he has trodden each step in turn on his way to the summit.[56] I therefore swoop down now to Step 1, to see if we can find any evidence that Socrates has passed that way. While the *Symposium* itself will, of course, be my primary focus, other dialogues may also be useful for establishing a supporting context.

At Step 1 a young man (νέος) is in love with a single beautiful body—or at least with one at a time[57]—and there gives birth to beautiful *logoi* (210a). It is a fact well known from *Charmides* that Plato's Socrates is not immune to strictly physical desire for the body of an extraordinarily beautiful individual (*Charmides* 154b–d, 155d).[58] Within the *Symposium* itself, obsession with the physical beauty of an individual *paidika* is a condition that Diotima attributes to Socrates, along with "many others" (211d).[59] If his conversations with Diotima are supposed to have occurred around 440, then Socrates would have been about thirty years old—a little younger than both Agathon and Alcibiades at the time of the party, and still (barely) a νέος, as the first rung of the ladder requires.[60] Socrates is, of course, situated in an Agathontic role here in relation to Diotima, who serves as his "leader." Plato may have had a number of reasons for temporarily putting him into Agathon's sandals in this fashion.[61] One such, I would argue, is that it allows us to envisage a Socrates at the very bottom of the ladder—a place from which a young and gifted Agathon,

---

[56] More generally, he must have visited all the steps below whatever step he *has* attained, and done so in sequential order. For why all the steps are necessary, see Sheffield 2001a:22–24.

[57] I see no reason to rule out serial obsession with particular individuals, provided that the lover in each instance thinks of the boy in question as the sole object of his desire. The apparent idealization of lifelong monogamy in male couples by Pausanias (181d) and Aristophanes (192d, 193b) is highly unusual (contrast Xenophon *Symposium* 8.2, where Socrates says he cannot remember a time when he was not in love with someone or other). Besides being culturally appropriate, serial obsession would also provide a natural foundation for the transition to Step 2.

[58] Cf. Patterson 1991:198. Xenophon's Socrates appears to acknowledge physical desire for a woman (*Memorabilia* 3.11.3).

[59] That this *erōs* is based on external or bodily beauty is clear from the mention of gold and clothing in the same breath as beautiful boys, plus the emphasis on gazing at the beloved. That it is directed towards an individual (at least as long as this particular infatuation lasts) is clear from the desire to be with the beloved and gaze at him forever. Cf. the obsessive desire for one's individual complement in Aristophanes' speech (esp. 191a).

[60] A man is a νέος until about the age of thirty (Garland 1990:242). Alcibiades and Agathon are probably both in their early thirties (see Nails 2002:s.vv.), but still notional "youths" because of their desirability as love-objects (cf. 198a2).

[61] The most commonly given, but scarcely sufficient, reason is that Socrates is sparing Agathon's feelings (cf. Sier 1997:9). A more significant factor is the part the substitution plays in revealing the Socratic pedigree of Diotima herself, as we saw earlier.

with all his potential for growth (175e4), might himself ascend if he proceeds "correctly."[62] If Socrates can (supposedly) see his younger self in Agathon, perhaps Agathon (and others like him) can see themselves in this imagined early-model Socrates. This playful conjuring of what he might once have been links the extraordinary Socrates—who is also the extraordinary lover of the ascent—to our ordinary (Agathontic) selves.

Many scholars take the "beautiful *logoi*" generated at Step 1 to be conventional discourses in praise of the beauty of the *erōmenos*.[63] But in so far as Eros is a philosopher, and a Socratic philosopher to boot, we would expect the "correct" lover to produce encomia of a Socratic nature, privileging moral education, as in *Lysis*, and truth, as here in the *Symposium* (198d–199a).[64] The physically gorgeous Agathon is very keen to be praised by Socrates, who in turn desires (ἐπιθυμῶ) to praise him (222e–223a). But we may surmise that this hypothetical encomium would look very different from the norm. The beauty of an individual body might also be the starting point for the Socratic "what is x?" question, which could plausibly be involved in the transition to Step 2.[65] Socrates' elenctic discourses are—notoriously—not beautiful in any ordinary sense (cf. 221e); but they are certainly *kalos*, 'fine', and Plato gives us reason to believe they are both beautiful and erotically effective in a way that trumps the superficial beauty of oratory like Agathon's.[66] Socrates has no objection to the original project of praising Eros "as beautifully as possible," and implies that he will not speak himself if he thinks this project has been successfully fulfilled (177d–e). As for his revised species of encomium, he grants that his speech will be less beautiful than Agathon's but also implies that it will be as beautiful as is consistent with the truth (198d). This may actually make it the most beautiful speech possible since it will not be marred by the ugliness of falsehood (cf. *Theaetetus* 194c).

---

[62] Agathon is the *erōmenos* of Pausanias, rather than an *erastēs*. But an attractive male of his age might be simultaneously *erastēs* and *erōmenos*, provided this was not in relationship to the same person (cf. 222c–d). (Dover [1989:1n1 and 87] cites Xenophon *Symposium* 8.2 where the person in question is Charmides, at about age twenty-four) Socrates himself embodies the fact that philosophically speaking, one may be both a lover and an object of desire.

[63] So e.g. Price 1997:41; Ferrari 1992:256. Agathon—with whom Socrates at this stage is equated—does something of the kind in praising Eros *qua erōmenos*.

[64] Cf. Patterson 1991:211–214. On *Lysis* see Nightingale 1993:114–116.

[65] Cf. Socrates' efforts to lead Hippias beyond the idea that τὸ καλόν is a beautiful girl (*Hippias Major* 287e–289d). I cannot address here the question of how one proceeds from step to step. In my view this is radically (and provocatively) underdetermined, but clearly depends on philosophical activity of a kind associated with Socrates.

[66] Cf. 213e, 215b–216a, 221e–222a, 223a, and Patterson 1991:197n3.

On to Step 2. The lover has now progressed from serial to simultaneous admiration of beautiful bodies, with a concomitant weakening of desire for any one individual. It is not difficult to see in Socrates an admirer of all beautiful bodies, and even one who regards the beauty of all such bodies as "the same." His general interest in physically attractive young men is notorious.[67] This is *not* contingent on beauty of soul. In *Charmides* he inquires after youths with beauty of body *or* wisdom, or both (153d), and claims that *all* young men of a certain age look beautiful to him (*Charmides* 154b–c; cf. *Republic* 474d–e). A similar outlook is taken for granted in the *Symposium* (cf. 194d, 213c–d). Alcibiades claims that Socrates constantly behaves like someone "in love" (ἐρωτικῶς κεῖται), that he is visibly and "always" smitten with beautiful people (216d; cf. also 192b7, 222b, 223a).[68] Socrates himself acknowledges that he desires proximity to *any* beautiful person (213c–d), and manifests this desire by flirting—successfully—with Agathon (222c–223a). Alcibiades' language (ἐκπέπληκται 216d3) suggests the intensity of Step 1—an intensity supposedly abandoned by Step 2 (210b5)—and echoes Diotima's admonishment to the untutored Socrates (ἐκπέπληξαι 211d5). But this behavior is (now) directed at *many* beautiful young men (216d, 222b). If we can believe Alcibiades—and his appeal to the assembled company as witnesses suggests that we can (216d)—then Socrates behaves like someone who has arrived at Step 2 without losing the intensity of a Step 1 lover.

Alcibiades, of course, claims that Socrates' apparent attraction to καλοί is deceptive (216d3–5). But recent scholars have argued effectively that he is wrong about this.[69] He equates Socrates' "true" indifference to the beautiful young with his lack of interest in such things as money and honor (216e1–2). But Socrates never pretends, even in play (cf. 216e4–5) that he cares about money or status, and often makes his lack of interest in them perfectly clear.[70] Alcibiades, however, thinks extremely highly of his *own* bodily beauty (217a5–6, 219c5; contrast 219a2). He is quite willing to use it as a currency comparable to money, and therefore infers that it is as contemptible as money in Socrates' eyes (though he should know better, cf. 219e1–2). Socrates' alleged "contempt"

---

[67] Cf. *Lysis* 204b, *Meno* 76c, *Phaedrus* 227c, 257a, Xenophon *Symposium* 8.2. Xenophon emphasizes the physical basis of the attraction (see Gould 1963:193n28; Vlastos 1991:38n65).

[68] καλῶν at 216d2 is of course ambiguous (it could be neuter), an ambiguity no doubt intended by Plato, but not by Alcibiades.

[69] See Vlastos 1991:40–41 and cf. Friedländer 1969a:139–142; Price 1991:297–298. I do not agree with Vlastos, however, that *Alcibiades* is using the verb εἰρωνεύω in a "modern" sense (so too Nightingale 1993:120n28).

[70] Socrates' lack of interest in money is notorious. For status cf. 174a6–7, 220e5–7.

for (Alcibiades') physical beauty clearly evokes Step 2 of the ladder (216d8, 219c4; cf. 210b5–6).[71] But Alcibiades is wrong to declare that Socrates thinks nothing of the καλοί themselves (216e2–4); rather, like the Step 2 lover, he thinks little of their bodily beauty as individuals.[72] This does not mean he does not honestly admire and seek out the company of those beautiful in body. His external behavior speaks the truth.

In fact the whole of Alcibiades' discourse regarding Socrates' "hidden" interior seems in an important sense misbegotten, since all Socrates' virtues are open to view. Alcibiades says his interior is "stuffed with *sōphrosunē*" (216d). But in what sense does his *sōphrosunē* lie concealed in his interior? His behavior is manifestly *sōphrōn* on the *outside*, and this *external* (albeit private) behavior is Alcibiades' own evidence for his alleged interior view.[73] Socrates does not actually *hide* anything.[74] Why then should his pleasure in the company of beautiful bodies be judged deceptive? Alcibiades makes this mistake because he thinks an attraction to beautiful bodies must cause one to seek sex,[75] that it is incompatible with *sōphrosunē*, and therefore that Socrates' self-control shows up his manifest attraction as a "deception" (222b). But if Socrates really does not care whether someone is physically *kalos* (216d7), then why does he habitually and notoriously hang around with people who are?

The multiple-body-lover of Step 2 will no doubt encounter some love-objects who also have beautiful souls (cf. 209b6)—perhaps those who respond well to an elenchus arising from their physical beauty—and come to realize that they are the most attractive to him. This brings him to Step 3, where a reasonably attractive (ἐπιεικής) soul outweighs even the most exceptional physical beauty, provided the body it inhabits exhibits "a slight bloom" (210b8). Beauty of soul is more precious (τιμιώτερον) than that of the body, presumably because it is less contaminated by mortal "rubbish" (cf. 211e1–4). The Step 3 lover will therefore be satisfied with only slight bodily beauty. He clearly does care personally about his object of desire.[76] But the vague τις (210b8) does not

---

[71] Cf. also 220c1, where the soldiers think Socrates has contempt for them. This time Alcibiades can see they are mistaken because it is not *his* vanity that is being challenged.

[72] Cf. Nightingale 1993:n29.

[73] Note that his vision of Socrates' interior is a mere *doxa* (216e7). He clearly has not "seen" Socrates' virtues for what they truly are, since he thinks of them as something that can be traded for sex.

[74] Xenophon insists on Socrates' openness, as Nightingale interestingly points out (1995:124–125). This defensive maneuver implies that Alcibiades was not the only one who found Socrates baffling, if not actively deceptive.

[75] Cf. Price 1991:297–298.

[76] The verb κήδεσθαι (210c1) is often used for the kind of concern that is due to family members.

rule out serial or even plural relationships,[77] and the plural νέους (210c3) is not confined to the τις in question.[78] The lover may spend considerable time at this level,[79] but there is no indication that he raises intellectual progeny in an exclusive relationship rather than developing all and any ideas in any partnership that will help him to progress to the next step. His general appreciation of beauty of souls (plural) presumably makes plural or serial relationships more likely.[80]

This broad scope well suits Plato's Socrates, with his wide interest in beautiful souls and bodies and his lack of an exclusive or committed life-long relationship with anyone—his special relationship with Alcibiades notwithstanding.[81] Most importantly, Step 3 fits Socrates' marked preference for beauty of soul over that of the body. Even the truly exceptional Charmides' physical beauty takes a back seat to his psychic charms (*Charmides* 154b–e).[82] In *Alcibiades* I Socrates claims to love Alcibiades for his burgeoning beauty of soul, despite his fading looks (131c–d).[83] And in the *Symposium* itself he makes it clear that interior beauty is "more precious" than that of the body, with his wry reference to the Homeric exchange of gold for bronze (218e; cf. 210b7). Not surprisingly, the placement of Socrates on this step is quite popular with commentators.[84]

At the same time, Socrates' interest in bodily beauty exceeds that of Step 3 by a considerable margin. His preference is not merely for the non-ugly, as per Step 3,[85] or the reasonably attractive, but for the stunningly beautiful,

---

[77] So too Rowe 1998b:256. Price argues on the basis of 210d2 and 7 that it is more exclusive (1997:39n38). But in both the passages he cites the word τις is made more exclusive by the presence of ἑνός and μίαν respectively.

[78] There is a marked contrast with the singular and lasting obsession of the non-philosophical lover when he encounters a beautiful soul in a beautiful body (209b–c). On the difference between this lover and the "correct" lover, see especially Sheffield 2001a:2–11.

[79] It is unclear how long it is supposed to take to proceed up the ladder to the top, but the *erastēs* starts as a young man and it presumably takes a good many years for the "eye of the soul" to mature (cf. 219a). Cf. the many years required to attain the vision of the Good in the *Republic*.

[80] So too Scott 2000:35–36.

[81] For the latter in Plato, see esp. *Alcibiades* I and II, *Protagoras* 309a–c, *Gorgias* 481d. It was also a fixture of the Socratic literature generally.

[82] Physical beauty, though desirable, likewise comes a distant second to excellence of soul in the fledgling guardians of the *Republic* (402c–e, 535a). Cf. also Xenophon *Symposium* 8.12.

[83] At the dramatic date of this dialogue Alcibiades is about twenty (past the ἄνθος of adolescence). But Socrates' depreciation of his physical charms should be taken with a pinch of salt. Not only is it clear that Alcibiades remained attractive for many more years (cf. *Symposium* 213c–d, 222c–d), but Socrates takes a serious interest in him while he is still at his physical prime (*Protagoras* 309a–b, *Symposium* 217b).

[84] E.g. Bury 1932:xxxviii; Wellman 1969:150–155; Reeve 1992b:113 with Blundell 1992:126.

[85] This is Rowe's interpretation of 210b8 (1998a:*ad loc.*; 1998b:256).

the supermodels of Athenian culture: the gorgeous Alcibiades and Agathon, the extraordinary Lysis, and the super-beautiful Charmides. Alcibiades adds Euthydemus son of Diocles, another conspicuous beauty,[86] to the list of Socrates' boytoys (222b). Socrates' attraction to these stunning beauties seems, on its face, to distinguish him from the Step 3 lover. Yet a continued passion for extremely beautiful bodies is presumably not *ruled out* at this level, provided the *erastēs* is fortunate enough to find well-endowed souls in the bodies of supermodels. Certainly these gorgeous youths all seem to have substantial philosophical potential as well as, and possibly in proportion to, their physical beauty.[87] We might therefore speculate that Socrates prefers to spend time with the super-beautiful in body because he thinks they are more likely to have beautiful souls. This would be entirely concordant with Greek tradition and aristocratic ideology, which tends to see physical beauty as reflecting and complementing nobility of character or soul.[88] Bodily beauty is, after all, an excellence, and the best person will have as many excellences as possible. But Socrates never makes such a claim, and even if he did, his predilection for stunning beauties would remain in tension with the main emphasis of Step 3.

Overall, Plato shows considerable ambivalence on this matter. Bodily beauty is regularly downplayed in comparison with the soul and sometimes becomes utterly insignificant. Theaetetus, who strangely resembles Socrates' notoriously ugly self, is the most beautiful in soul of all his young interlocutors (*Theaetetus* 143e, 185e), and Protagoras' wisdom is so beautiful that it eclipses the body of Alcibiades even in his prime (*Protagoras* 309b–c).[89] Clearly physical beauty is unnecessary for those beautiful in soul. But the corollary, that beautiful bodies may house ugly souls, is never acknowledged: the dialogues feature no stunningly beautiful fools. As for the *Symposium* itself, the ladder's transition away from physical beauty is remarkably discreet.[90] Diotima never

---

[86] See Nails 2002:s.v.

[87] Alcibiades, Agathon, Lysis and Charmides are all marked, in various ways, as intellectually gifted as well as extraordinarily beautiful. The same applies to Euthydemus son of Diocles, as far as we know of him from outside Plato's pages (Nails 2002:s.v.). Meno, another handsome young man (Nails 2002:s.v.) with whom Socrates flirts (*Meno* 80b–c), seems less gifted, but takes a definite interest in current intellectual trends.

[88] Blondell 2002:58–62; Patterson 1991:199–202 (though he goes too far in equating grace of deportment etc. with beauty *per se*. Aside from anything else, this undermines the paradox of Socratic ugliness, on which see further Blondell 2002:70–77).

[89] Protagoras is nearly sixty at the dramatic date of his dialogue, which rules him out as a physically attractive *erōmenos*. On Theaetetus see Blondell 2002:260–261.

[90] Cf. Rosen 1987:266–267.

speaks of preferring ugly boys of good character, as Pausanias does (182d7), or of putting up with "disharmony" in body provided the soul is harmonious, as Glaucon does, with Socrates' approval (*Republic* 402d–e), let alone of a beautiful soul making a physically ugly person beautiful, as Socrates does in *Theaetetus* (185e). There is no level at which beautiful souls, irrespective of the quality of the bodies that contain them, are the object of desire, and the reprise seems to go out of its way to avoid mentioning souls as such.

There may be various reasons for this evasiveness. Visual beauty is of great importance as the starting point for the ascent, since it is in the visual realm that beauty is most readily and commonly perceived (cf. *Phaedrus* 250b–d); clearly more beauty is always better, even if the contribution made by bodily beauty is a slight one; and the visual provides a powerful metaphor for the perception of the Form itself.[91] At the same time, Plato's conception of Socrates requires him to avoid linking beauty of soul and body unequivocally. Socrates is the iconic representative of the beautiful soul in an ugly body, the soul so beautiful that it arouses *erōs* even in the absence of the "slight" bodily beauty of Step 3. The power of this paradox is, however, parasitic on the mainstream assumption that it defies, that beauty of soul is even better when complemented by physical beauty. This assumption seems to linger not only in the ascent but in Socrates' choice of young men to spend time with.

A further reason for placing Socrates at Step 3 is the specification that the lover, like Socrates and Diotima's Eros, both seeks out and generates *logoi* beneficial to the young (210c1–3). There is an obvious (defensive) allusion here to the charges against Socrates, to be developed in the speech of Alcibiades with its insistence on the improving nature of Socrates' words (222a; cf. 218d). Alcibiades' failed seduction shows us how Socrates treats those beautiful in body and soul—the kind of improving *logoi* that they elicit from him. Though we know the content only in general terms, we do know that he persistently spends his time with them in conversation (διαλέγεσθαι 217b), and we have a pretty fair picture of what Socratic conversation with the beautiful and talented young looks like.[92]

These educational discussions presumably embrace both "activities" and "laws" (ἐπιτηδεύματα and νόμοι),[93] which leads the lover to an appre-

---

[91] Such language is also suggestive of the mysteries (O'Brien 1984:204; Nightingale 2004:83–86). On the need for bodily beauty, cf. Pender 1992:77–8.

[92] It is illustrated in the *Symposium* by his elenchus of Agathon. *Alcibiades* I shows Socrates addressing improving *logoi* to Alcibiades himself.

[93] Both are included in the improving discourses of the non-philosophical soul-body lover (209b8–c1, 209d4–7).

ciation of the beauty of such things in their own right.[94] Accordingly, he is now "compelled" to "gaze upon" their beauty, and see that it is all "akin" (συγγενές), i.e. to ascend to Step 4. At this level physical beauty generally—as opposed to the obsessive love of individual bodies[95]—is looked down upon as something slight (210c5). This is the point at which the lover leaves behind any merely human object of desire. He still needs other human beings as partners, or at least an audience, for his discourses. But their beauty—of body or even soul—is no longer required to inspire the lover to "give birth." It is preferable, of course, for all of the lover's human associates to be beautiful in soul and/or body, in so far as more beauty is always better. And a beautiful-souled partner may help one ascend the ladder more swiftly through his intellectual talents. But no such human beauty is *necessary* for the lover's further progress. His words are now stimulated by a more "purely" beautiful inhuman beloved.[96]

Do we have any reason for situating Socrates on this step? It is clear enough that he thinks of bodily beauty in general as something slight. Other things being equal he would always rather be in the presence of such beauty, but he will talk to anyone who is willing to listen to him even if they are *not* beautiful (194d)—in body or even in soul.[97] Does he also appreciate the beauty of νόμοι and ἐπιτηδεύματα as such? Between them, these words embrace laws, customs, and all kinds of human activities, behaviors, institutions and social practices.[98] Though Plato's Socrates never declares his *erōs* for such things, he does engage with many of them. In Plato's dialogues he grapples continually both with Athenian political culture (along with the associated νόμοι) and with an array of culturally central ἐπιτηδεύματα. An exceptional number of the latter are represented in the *Symposium* in particular, through the various participants with their different skills and ways of life, as reflected in their speeches. One of the most important of these is the theater, which informs the setting of the dialogue. Socrates shows ironic, but not necessarily insincere, appreciation of its charms, as he praises the brilliant beauty of Agathon's

---

[94] Cf. the *erōs* for virtuous ἐπιτηδεύματα at *Laws* 711d. Comparable ideas are expressed at *Laws* 643e (*erōs* for being a perfect citizen) and *Letter* VII 339e (*erōs* for the best life).

[95] So Bury 1932 and Rowe 1998a:*ad loc.*

[96] The degree of purity depends on the extent to which a beautiful item is or is not contaminated with "mortal rubbish" (211e).

[97] Plato shows Socrates eagerly conversing with some quite untalented people, and in general, with anyone he happens to meet (*Apology* 30a).

[98] Alcibiades' reference to Socrates' ἐπιτηδεύματα (221c) includes by implication the whole preceding account of his extraordinary *sōphrosunē*, courage, and so forth, as well as his philosophical activities. Omission of νόμοι from the reprise suggests that ἐπιτηδεύματα can stand for both. At *Laws* 793c-d the two are equated (along with ἤθη) as the glue that binds the city together. For educational ἐπιτηδεύματα, cf. also *Republic* 444e, *Gorgias* 474e, *Laches* 180a.

wisdom (175e).[99] Notoriously, Plato allows him to intervene in the dramatic contest and emerge as the ultimate victor, one who, by means of his dialectical understanding, transcends the tragic-comic divide.[100]

The theater is also strongly linked with rhetoric in this dialogue (as elsewhere), notably by means of the Gorgianic Agathon.[101] Using language that evokes the higher levels of the ascent, Socrates praises Agathon's speech as beautiful and amazing (198b), avowing that he spoke μεγαλοπρεπῶς and καλῶς (199c7). Once again, Socrates' praise is clearly ironic, but not necessarily insincere, as far as it goes. In *Phaedrus* Socrates lets it be known that he is an *erastēs* of *logoi* (*Phaedrus* 228b–c), and in the context of the ascent there is clearly nothing wrong with beautiful *logoi* as such. They are like beautiful bodies, however, in that their beauty of form comes a distant second to the beauty of their intellectual and ethical content.[102] Socrates admires Agathon's beautiful rhetoric in the same way that he admires the physical beauty of an Alcibiades—or perhaps more so, to the extent that it supplies a more promising starting point for dialectic. Even superficial physical beauty may stimulate intellectual offspring in the "correct" lover; Socrates uses Agathon's beautiful rhetoric similarly, as the starting point both for elenchus and for his own reinvention of the encomium.

The *sumposion* itself, another culturally sanctioned and informally educational social practice with clearly defined νόμοι, is a further institution that Socrates frequents,[103] critiques,[104] and reinvents on his own terms.[105] Strongly

---

[99] There is no reason to believe that Socrates' reaction is not based on his own experience of the performance, especially since he was present at the προαγών (194a–b). The criticisms of drama voiced by Plato's Socrates bespeak a general familiarity with the theater, and a number of anecdotes locate him there, especially in connection with *Clouds* (cf. Aelian *Varia Historia* 2.13, Plutarch *Moralia* 10c–d).

[100] Cf. Rowe 1998a:*ad loc.* On the theme of dramatic contest in the *Symposium*, see Bacon 1959; Friedländer 1969b:32; Clay 1975; Sider 1980; Patterson 1982.

[101] Socrates calls rhetoric an ἐπιτήδευμα (albeit a despicable one) at *Gorgias* 463a. It is perhaps through such ἐπιτηδεύματα as this that we can find a place on the ladder for beautiful *logoi* as an object of desire—one of those objects that is left behind at the summit (211a7)—despite the fact that they have previously been mentioned only as the lover's progeny.

[102] Cf. the equivalence of Socrates with his *logoi*—a point perceived, but not fully understood, by Alcibiades (221c–d).

[103] See Rutherford 1995:179–180.

[104] Tecuşan 1990.

[105] This is marked dramatically in the *Symposium* by his late arrival, bringing an uninvited guest, and changing the rules of discourse. In addition, Plato as author uses various strategies to appropriate the *sumposion* on his behalf. E.g. the *sumposion* included a libation to the Ἀγαθὸς Δαίμων, and Socrates is equated with the beneficent δαίμων Eros; Socrates surpasses all others in the *sumposion*'s test of character through drinking, which equates him with Dionysus, "the only one who can drink without danger" (Lissarague

marked as both autonomous and unconventional, Socrates would be the last person to attend such a gathering merely out of social pressure, and his presence at this particular party is clearly an active choice (cf. 174a). The attraction does not seem to be only the presence of Agathon or his beautiful friends, since they were also present at the victory party that he avoided (176a). Rather, he chooses to attend such events when they can be used to serve his agenda of testing and revising educational and ethical norms through dialectic (hence his preference for smaller gatherings). He is particularly inspired, it seems, by the social practices surrounding erotic desire which often informed symposiastic discourse, especially the carefully structured and rule-bound relationship between an *erastēs* and an *erōmenos*.[106] Plato shows him engaging with all these ἐπιτηδεύματα in his own peculiar way, evincing a critical appreciation even as he reinvents them in his own terms, and using them to generate improving discourses of his own idiosyncratic variety.

In what does their beauty consist, however? In what sense is it all "akin," as Step 4 indicates, and is this something to which Socrates can be seen to respond? The context would suggest that the beauty of laws and activities inheres in their effectiveness at fostering virtue, which in turn depends on their availability for dialectical understanding and—crucially—on their relationship to truth. We may safely assume that Socrates agrees with Diotima that *sophia* is one of the most beautiful of all things (204b3; cf. *Protagoras* 309c–d), and hence an object of desire.[107] Truth is wisdom's inseparable companion, and likewise an object of philosophical *erōs* (*Republic* 485a–b, 501d, *Philebus* 58d). As Socrates puts it to Theaetetus, truth bestows beauty upon one's opinions, in contrast to the ugliness of falsehood (*Theaetetus* 194c).[108] As for the *Symposium* itself, the intimate relationship between truth and beauty will be made clear at the summit of the ascent (212a).[109] And it is truth that underpins Socrates' various cultural reinventions, distinguishing his encomium

---

1990:37; cf. 8–9); he is equated with a satyr, a figure emblematic of the *symposion* (cf. Lissarague 1990:passim); his commitment to truth reflects the ideology of the *symposion* (Rösler 1995; for the educational significance of the *symposion*, see also Bremmer 1990).

[106] Cf. Pausanias' consuming interest in the proper νόμοι surrounding such relationships (182a–185c).

[107] *Erōs* is almost by definition a response to beauty (*Symposium* 204c, *Republic* 402d6, *Charmides* 167e; cf. also *Symposium* 196a4–b3, 197b3–5, 201a2–5, Isocrates *Helen* 55). (See further Lear's paper in this collection.)

[108] In the *Philebus* he declares the "truest" patch of white to be the most beautiful (53a–b). Cf. also Pausanias' remark that nothing is "beautiful" unless done "correctly" (181a). In the *Republic*, the Good is the cause of everything "correct and beautiful" (517c1).

[109] Cf. Stokes 1986:180.

from Agathon's (198d),[110] his rhetoric from that of Lysias.[111] Commitment to truth is thus a unifying force in his engagement with the cultural institutions of his time. It also unifies his own behavior. He will discourse upon anything, and yet, as Alcibiades declares, what he says is always the same (221e). It is all philosophy, the single activity that trumps all others,[112] with which Socrates tells us elsewhere that he is in love (*Gorgias* 481d).[113] This movement towards unity, a perception of what is shared by different kinds of intellectual and cultural activity and their common availability as grist to the philosophical mill, is illustrated at the end of the dialogue when Socrates argues that the expertise of the tragic and comic poet is one and the same (223d).

If the beauty of activities lies in their relationship to truth and wisdom, the lover who can see this is a short step from perceiving the beauty of understanding for its own sake. All that needs to be added is an appreciation of those branches of learning that are not directly concerned with moral and political improvement—presumably abstract studies like mathematics.[114] This brings us to Step 5, where the lover perceives the (shared) beauty of "kinds of knowledge" (ἐπιστῆμαι) collectively,[115] in a process that will culminate in the "single ἐπιστήμη" at the summit of the ladder (210d7). That Socrates is moving along this unifying path is indicated by the wording of that final scene, when he equates two "kinds of knowledge" (ἐπίστασθαι) that were typically viewed as mutually exclusive (223d).

Step 5 precipitates the lover's perception of the "great sea of beauty" (Step 6). All the significantly beautiful items of the human world—bodies, souls, cultural practices, intellectual attainments—have now been embraced in such a way that their common beauty can be perceived and their relative beauty properly comprehended.[116] The repudiation of an attachment to indi-

---

[110] It is lack of truth that marks the deficiency of Agathon's admittedly beautiful speech (201b-c).

[111] *Phaedrus* 277a-c; cf. 272d-273a, *Apology* 17a-c, *Gorgias* 521d-522c. Socrates' overall commitment to truth is, of course, well known (cf. e.g. *Gorgias* 458a-b).

[112] Contrast the fragmenting view of the lover who cannot see beyond a single activity (210d2-3). Philosophy transcends this particularity because it engages with what is (or is not) valuable in all other human activities.

[113] On Plato's use of erotic language for intellectual states and activities, see Halperin 1986:71-72.

[114] From a larger Platonic perspective, however, this is not a real distinction. Cf. *Republic* 501d where the word ἐπιτηδεύματα refers to the entire course of the philosopher-rulers' education, including its highly theoretical upper levels. The ethical significance of understanding as such in the *Symposium* is evident from the fact that the wisdom achieved at the summit of the ascent yields true virtue (212a).

[115] For the criteria that make something count as an ἐπιστήμη in Plato, see Patterson 1991:205-206.

[116] Some kinds of beautiful thing, such as works of art and the natural world, are not explicitly considered as objects of *erōs*, but they are implied in the repudiation of particulars of *all* kinds

vidual items at any of the previous levels is therefore reiterated (210d1–3). The lover who gazes upon the "great sea of beauty" with the eye of the mind can perceive the true degree of beauty of everything in the human world, rather in the way that an infrared sensor allows the viewer to "see" an object's temperature. The naked eye allows us to guess which items in a landscape are warmer, but the guess can be quite wrong (e.g. we often mistakenly equate heat with light). The same is true of beauty: the naked eye needs the assistance of philosophical insight (the eye of the mind) to perceive the landscape of beauty in its true intensity. A beautiful soul shines forth through an ugly body, just as an infrared sensor may reveal the hot core of a nuclear reactor in winter. Beautiful boys and individual activities are no less beautiful at Step 6 than they were at previous levels (210d2–3),[117] but they are merely a drop in the "great sea" as a whole, where the beauty of understanding outshines everything else as the sun outshines a fire-fly. The vision of this "sea" inspires the lover to produce explicitly philosophical *logoi*,[118] which are abundant, beautiful and "magnificent" (210d), like the great sea itself,[119] and filled with equally magnificent ideas.

Socrates' simultaneous ability to appreciate the beauty of bodies, souls, activities, and knowledge itself—in reverse order of importance—places him comfortably on this level. As for magnificent *logoi*, his speech in the *Symposium* itself is obviously among the most magnificent, abundant, and intellectually powerful in all of Plato's works. He is thus poised to glimpse the Form of Beauty itself, like the Step 7 lover. Step 7 differs from Step 8 only in that the lover

---

at the top of the ladder, which mentions material objects such as gold and clothing and also the natural world (211a5–b1, 211d3–4). Presumably such items are even less significant than human bodies because they do not house a soul. Thus Socrates is capable of enjoying a beautiful landscape, but this is far outweighed by his desire to be near beautiful bodies and their souls (*Phaedrus* 230b–d). As for works of art, his simultaneous *erōs* and disapproval are, in the case of poetry, legendary (*Republic* 607e–608a).

[117] Even at the summit the beauties of this world remain beautiful (211b2, 211d4). This is a broadly but weakly "inclusive" reading similar to that of Vlastos 1991:40.

[118] The mysterious phrase "in philosophy" (210d6) must refer to the lover's activity in producing these *logoi* (cf. 218a5). I am sympathetic to Pender's interpretation, whereby philosophy is the beautiful love-object (1992:81–82), and in light of the presentation of philosophy as an object of desire elsewhere in Plato it is hard not to hear such resonances. But by Pender's own criterion—the "logic" of metaphor—philosophy cannot serve here as the love-object, since it is an activity, and as such cannot simply be equated with the "great sea" of beauty that inspires the lover's discourse at Step 6 (though *qua* activity it presumably manifests a beauty that is part of the "great sea"). It is, rather, the activity that enables us to attain the ἐπιστήμη that is the object of desire.

[119] A more beautiful love-object generates more beautiful (and "more immortal") offspring (209c). The *logoi* generated at each level are thus more beautiful in proportion to the beauty that inspires them (Santas 1988:43). Similarly in the *Republic* the *erastai* of truth (501d) are also begetters of truth (490a–b).

has just *glimpsed* the unitary knowledge of the Form of Beauty, and indeed the Form itself, but not yet "grasped" it, and is therefore still proceeding on his upward path (with the continued assistance of the guide, whose presence is emphasized at this level: 210e3). Socrates' presence at this level is suggested by the fact that he claims only conviction—as opposed to knowledge—about the "mysteries" Diotima taught him (212b; cf. 198d).[120] Furthermore he describes his own wisdom as uncertain and dreamlike (175e), a familiar Platonic metaphor for belief in contrast to knowledge.[121] The difference between Socrates and Diotima is also significant here. Her mysterious, superhuman authority is contrasted with Socrates' confident but less securely grounded belief in her teachings, which he still seems to rely on as providing some kind of inspiration, if not guidance (cf. 212b). For such reasons Step 7 is favored by some interpreters.[122] Which brings us full circle.

Nowhere Man

In the *Symposium* Plato takes advantage of the symposiastic setting, with its characteristic role-playing, self-parody, story-telling and games,[123] to present Socrates in many different guises—all conjured up through several layers of narration—from the Socrates of the party itself, to the Socrates of Alcibiades' memory, to the "hypothetical Socrates" who consorts with the quasi-fictional Diotima.[124] One effect of this kaleidoscopic presentation—or so I have tried to argue—is that Socrates can be viewed more or less plausibly as occupying all of the steps on the "ladder of love."

What are we to make of this? Perhaps we should envisage Socrates as having ascended the steps in due order, occupying each in sequence over time until he stands securely and permanently at the top, having left behind the lower steps on which we temporarily glimpse him at moments in his past.[125] But it is in practice impossible to chart his position on the ladder against time in any such fashion. Alternatively one might argue—on a strongly "inclusive" reading—that his existence at the summit is somehow expressed in behaviors that only appear to belong to the lower steps. Thus, for example, his erotic

---

[120] Cf. Penwill 1978:157. I see no reason, however, to doubt Socrates' assertion that he has been convinced by Diotima (cf. Rowe 1998b:240–241; O'Brien 1984:186–190).

[121] See Gallop 1971.

[122] E.g. Penwill 1978:159.

[123] For these aspects of the *sumposion*, see Lissarague 1990. Hunter 2004 is especially useful on their relevance to Plato's dialogue.

[124] The phrase is Bury's (1932 on 210a).

[125] This seems to be Scott's view (2000:31–34), though he does not place Socrates at the very top.

response to beautiful young men may be viewed as compatible with, or even an expression of, his presence at the top.[126] But in my view this is inconsistent with the rhetoric of the ascent, with its belittling of the steps that are left behind and the shift of the lover's passionate attention to a new object at each new level.[127] This shift is marked most strongly at the transition from Step 6 to Step 7. There is a categorical leap here away from the ordinary world,[128] based on the sharp disjunction between beauty as manifested in *anything* in that world and Beauty *per se*, which is explicitly detached from all such manifestations. The "great sea" of beauty consists in the sum total of these worldly manifestations of the Form, but the lover who takes the crucial next step comes to see all such objects in their true light, as "mortal rubbish" in comparison with the Form itself (211e). As beautiful as Alcibiades' body may be, its beauty appears only in the kind of visibly beautiful surfaces—flesh and skin-color—that the successful lover now views with contempt.[129] Even his soul is a particular, and as such insignificant. The lover's gaze in its full intensity cannot rest on human bodies, souls, activities, *and* the Form of Beauty all at once. He cannot simultaneously participate in the world of eating and drinking and gaze at a vision so beautiful that it deprives him of any desire to do so (211d–e).[130] Such Beauty will surely blind the lover completely to the beauty of this world, just as the vision of the Form of the Good blinds the philosopher who returns to the cave in the *Republic*.[131] At best, Beauty's earthly manifestations can occupy no more than the periphery of the successful lover's vision.

[126] So e.g. Kosman 1976:65–67; Irwin 1977a:169 with 323n58. This issue is distinct from the question of whether he still *cares*—non-erotically—about other people. (The two seem to be confused by e.g. Irwin 1995:310.) Cf. Scott 2000, though I am not as sure as he is that rescuing Alcibiades is a sign of Socrates' special affection (2000:36). He also saves the life of Laches (221b6–7), and his courage would presumably lead him to protect any fellow-soldier in need. Possibly, however, *philia* is one of the virtues that is generated in the lover at the top of the ladder.

[127] As Allen acknowledges in passing (1991:82), a strongly inclusive reading is inconsistent with the ladder metaphor itself. The same may be said for the cave image of the *Republic*, which implies that the philosopher cannot remain in the cave while contemplating the Forms.

[128] On this point I agree with Chen 1983 (though he disregards the ladder metaphor altogether). Price resists this on the circular ground that it is necessary to avoid an "acute discontinuity" (1997:50), but the discontinuity is marked by Diotima herself. The stairway to heaven is a way to bridge this gap, not to eliminate it.

[129] This does not mean that he has contempt for Alcibiades' beauty *qua* beauty. But this kind of beauty is also, always, ugly (cf. *Republic* 479a).

[130] Diotima's point here is that even the lover of beautiful boys would gaze upon his love-object constantly without eating or drinking, *if only that were possible*. The implication is that the lover of Forms must likewise take a break from gazing in order to turn to such mundane matters as food and drink—or else he will starve.

[131] See Nightingale 2004:102–105. As has often been noted, visual language increases higher up the ladder, as if in compensation for the fact that literal (physical) vision is becoming otiose.

A third possibility is that Socrates should be construed as shimmying up and down the ladder, as Steve Lowenstam has argued.[132] I find this more plausible for a number of reasons. First, it is not possible for a human being to reside permanently at the top of the ladder. The temporarily solipsistic Socrates will soon be back in the company of his fellow mortals (cf. 175b2–3, c4–5). Even he must eat and sleep occasionally. Second, this interpretation evokes the activity of the *daimōn* Eros with whom Socrates is so strongly identified, who runs up and down between mortal and divine realms in a dynamic process of interpretation, communication, "intercourse and conversation" (ἡ ὁμιλία καὶ ἡ διάλεκτος 202e–203a). On this interpretation the ladder provides a less mythic, more systematic explanation of how mere mortals may imitate the *daimōn*, allowing for the fact that even the most philosophically exalted among us must inevitably descend from time to time. One advantage of this interpretation is that it lets us grant, for example, that Socrates has a real erotic response to Alcibiades *qua* love-object while on Step 3, while also accepting that individuals are not the objects of his *erōs* when he is at the summit. In other words, it gives us a different way of approaching the issue of "inclusiveness," allowing Socrates to embody a variety of different kinds of love-relationships at different moments in Plato's presentation without destroying the magnificent solitude of the philosopher in intercourse with the Form.

I believe this interpretation is in essence right. At the same time, Plato's complex presentation of Socrates does not correspond to a "correct" and "orderly" movement up and down the ladder of the kind required by the ascent passage. We need not worry much about how the descent occurs. Doubtless it is caused by a failure to maintain one's intellectual vision at more challenging levels. This might make one tumble all the way down to the foot of the ladder, as Socrates does momentarily when he catches a glimpse inside Charmides' clothing. But such lapses presumably require one to start climbing the ladder again "correctly," with each step in its proper order.[133] And we do not see Socrates recovering, for example, from Charmides' physical beauty in order to address himself to beauty of body collectively before moving on to souls. Nor is there any sign that the retreat into the neighboring porch, or the Potidaea episode, comes as the climax of a series of ascending steps. Indeed,

---

[132] Lowenstam 1985:94–98. But Lowenstam addresses only the vacillation between the mortal realm and the summit, not the sequence of lower steps as such.

[133] The memory of having seen the Form itself might accelerate one's progress in repeating the ascent, for example by enabling one to recognize manifestations of the Form in bodies or souls more easily, but there is no sign that it is possible to actually skip any of the steps.

the interlude in the doorway is preceded, as far as we can tell, by appreciation of a beautiful individual body, or soul-body complex (namely Agathon's, 174a), not by a discussion of the one supreme kind of knowledge or contemplation of the "great sea" of beauty.

The sense that Socrates is someone who repeatedly ascends and descends, like the *daimōn* Eros, derives, rather, from Plato's construction of an artfully impressionistic picture—or perhaps better, a cubist one, which departs from the logic of a unifying perspective to show us different aspects of its subject simultaneously from different points of view, resulting in a composite image that conveys more than verisimilitude ever could. Socrates is everywhere, and therefore nowhere. We cannot pin him down or plug him into an orderly sequence. Even when he temporarily seems to settle, it is hard to locate him securely on any one rung. If we turn our backs for a moment, what appears to be evidence for one level seems to turn into evidence for another.[134] He is *atopos*, 'placeless', a distinctive term used with special weight in the *Symposium*. Socrates' *atopia*—foreshadowed, as we saw, in the prologue—is, according to Alcibiades, his very essence: the thing that makes him who he (uniquely) is (221c–d; cf. *Alcibiades* I 106a). This mysteriousness is central to Socrates' allure as an object of desire, as Alcibiades, in his extravagant effort to solve that mystery, so clearly demonstrates.[135]

Socrates' singular (in both senses) body grounds his various identities as a receptacle of human possibilities. He is both the lens through which we perceive all the different steps of the ascent, and the paradigm by which we may judge their "correct" performance. He thus invites emulation.[136] Yet his *atopia* resists imitation.[137] The strength of the authorial invitation to place Socrates on the ladder, which I emphasized at the outset, is in itself significant here. Plato *elicits* our desire, only to frustrate it by refusing to locate Socrates securely on any one step or in an orderly sequence of steps.[138] This desire and its frustration lure us into scrutinizing Socrates' ascent, seeking traces of his passage, while at the same time preventing us from organizing those traces into a coherent set of signposts—like Internet driving directions—that we can use to follow him in any straightforward or comfortable sense. Plato deflects

[134] The same applies to the way he shifts from leader to follower, and from subject to object of desire.
[135] On Socrates' mysteriousness, see esp. Nehamas 1998:91–92; Blondell 2002:69.
[136] For the pervasive Greek assumption that one emulates literary characters, see Blondell 2002: 80–86.
[137] Cf. Blondell 2002:106–109.
[138] For the way Plato simultaneously elicits and thwarts the reader's interpretive desire by raising unanswerable questions, see Halperin 1992.

our attempts to "grasp" Socrates or his wisdom directly as Alcibiades and Agathon try to do, each in his fashion (175c–d, 219b). He prohibits us from taking him as our "leader" in the mindless manner of an Aristodemus, who is unnerved when left to forge his own path. We must start at the bottom of the ladder for ourselves (as he, putatively, once did) and respond actively to his enigmatic mode of "leadership," emulating his independence by seeking to "grasp" not Socrates, but the truth from which he insists on distinguishing himself (209c), which may allow us ultimately to "grasp" Beauty itself (211b7, 212a4–5).

The adjective θαυμαστός, 'amazing', is a leitmotif in Alcibiades' encomium of Socrates. His baffled amazement is foreshadowed in an apparently innocent usage early in the dialogue, when Aristodemus answers Agathon's opening question, "Where is Socrates?" (174e12), with the word θαυμάζω: "I too wonder where he can be" (175a1–2). Unlike Aristodemus, we are not in a position to send a slave to find Socrates for us. Consequently we are obliged to live with our wondering. And that, of course, is the beginning of philosophy.[139]

---

[139] *Theaetetus* 155d; cf. *Symposium* 205b, 208b.

Eight

Tragedy Off-Stage

Debra Nails

P LATO WEAVES STRANDS of the tragic and the comic, high seriousness and low bawdiness, into his *Symposium*; that much is uncontroversial. If someone should miss the sweep of the plot from the celebration of Agathon's prize for tragedy to the waves of drunken revelers, the *kōmos,* there is a telling reminder at the end. With snores in the background, Socrates is passing the cup with Agathon and Aristophanes, "forcing them to agree that it belongs to the same man to know how to compose comedy and tragedy, and that the person who is an expert tragic poet is also a comic poet" (223d2–5).[1] Socrates' parting comment has generated a variety of interpretations, most of which take Plato's *Symposium* to be tragedy, comedy, and philosophy in one.[2]

The *Symposium* is obviously funny, less obviously tragic, though there are precedents for identifying both what the tragedy of the *Symposium is,* and what is tragic *in* the *Symposium.* I will argue that Peter H. von Blanckenhagen (1992) was right to suggest what Jonathan Lear (1998) would later argue in detail, that the *Symposium* sets up a tragedy that occurs off-stage—though I disagree with

---

[1] Trans. Rowe. προσαναγκάζειν τὸν Σωκράτη ὁμολογεῖν αὐτοὺς τοῦ αὐτοῦ ἀνδρὸς εἶναι κωμῳδίαν καὶ τραγῳδίαν ἐπίστασθαι ποιεῖν, καὶ τὸν τέχνῃ τραγῳδοποιὸν ὄντα καὶ κωμῳδοποιὸν εἶναι, echoed in *Laws:* "it is impossible to learn the serious without the comic, or any one of a pair of contraries without the other" (VII 816d9–e1, trans. Bury). We can see with some amusement where the elenchus would go if anyone could stay awake: since neither Agathon nor Aristophanes composed plays in the other's genre, if either had agreed to Socrates' principle, he would thereby have been admitting that he was not an expert poet (Rowe 1998a:214). On the bivalence principle more generally in Plato, see *Republic* I 334a1–3 where expertise in guarding is expertise in stealing (cf. *Republic* III 409d8–10), *Charmides* 166e7–8, and *Phaedo* 97d1–5.

[2] Clay 1975:250 called it "a new form of philosophical drama which, in the object of its imitation, comprehends and transcends both tragedy and comedy"; and Wardy 2002:58, "the literary genre which at once mixes and transcends the dramatic genres." Nietzsche 1967:§13 had gone so far as to offer a maxim to bind the three together: "only the intelligible is beautiful."

them about whose mistake has tragic results and what those results are. To anticipate my conclusion, the most defensible notion of tragedy across Plato's dialogues is a fundamentally epistemological one: if we do not know the good, we increase our risk of making mistakes and of suffering what are sometimes their catastrophic consequences. Specifically, the tragedies envisioned by the *Symposium* are two, both introduced in the dialogue. Like staged tragedies of the era, however, their most dramatic events occur off-stage. Within months of Agathon's victory, half the characters who celebrated with him that night in the late winter of 416 will suffer death or exile, resulting from charges of impiety, *asebeia*; and, also for *asebeia*, Socrates will be executed in 399, weeks after the dramatic date of the frame. The cause of both calamities was the ignorance—superstition and religious hysteria—of the Athenians. Not only did the *polis* use its democracy to destroy the lives and happiness of hundreds of people through summary executions, exiles, confiscations, and disenfranchisement, they killed Socrates, the city's best friend, because they mistook him for an enemy.

Blanckenhagen's Stage and Actors Revisited

Blanckenhagen (1992:62) provided full descriptions of the characters of the *Symposium*, arguing:

> The simple fact that Plato wrote just this historical fiction means that he expected his readers to recognize the identity and character of setting and actors, and to apply that knowledge to their reading; and this in turn demands that we collect all the information, internal and external, that would have been a matter of course in Plato's time, if we wish to understand what Plato tells us.[3]

Simple ignorance of the facts would be bad enough for our interpretations of the dialogue, but two things make it worse. One is rare, the selection of

---

[3] The date of Blanckenhagen's publication is misleading not only because the publication was posthumous, based on a lecture described as given "several years ago" (1992:68), but because Blanckenhagen's views on Plato's *Symposium* had exerted a lasting influence at the University of Chicago already in 1959 when Leo Strauss gave a set of lectures not published until 2001 (Strauss 2001:vii). Blanckenhagen died on the cusp of an era when computer use would steeply increase access to such information as he considered important. So thoughtful a scholar, I assume, would wish to sift current evidence before reasserting his claims; for that reason I will not joust with his particulars here. I provide an account that differs in some details but that respects the motivation for collecting the details that he articulated so well.

ornamental biographical details from suspect sources to add poignancy to, and reinforce, existing interpretations.[4] The other is virtually unavoidable: our long-held assumptions about Socrates and the people around him are comprised in a running background narrative that silently compensates for what we don't know. Absent positive evidence to the contrary, our intellectual backdrop is the image of Socrates in the company of aristocratic youths. Even Blanckenhagen (1992:56, 61–62) defaults to it, calling Plato's dialogues "historical fiction" and assuming more poetic license on Plato's part about Socrates' companions than I can. Far less for us than for Plato's auditors and readers, but nonetheless significantly, Plato's characters are more intelligible because of what we can know about them. We have substantial independent information about most of the characters gathered at Agathon's house, some of it, I hope to show, crucial to our understanding of the tragedy of the *Symposium*.

It is necessary then to introduce the characters and setting, to add information that was inaccessible when Blanckenhagen made his influential claims.[5] There are four pairs of men celebrating Agathon's victory, expressing four different relationships,[6] all of which go back before the war began, at least sixteen years, for we met them that long ago in Plato's *Protagoras*: Pausanias and Agathon were already lovers, Eryximachus and Phaedrus were already friends, Aristophanes and Aristodemus of Cydathenaeum were already fellow-demesmen, with social as well as civic obligations to one another.[7] Socrates' favorite was Alcibiades, whose first beard was filling out, and the two of them were about a year away from being posted to Potidaea. Socrates was beginning to attract the attention of both youths and intellectuals, Protagoras' for example (*Protagoras* 361d7–e6), but he was not yet well known in the city or even in his own deme (see *Laches* 180b–181a). When Protagoras, Hippias, and Prodicus were in town auditioning for paying students, all but Socrates

---

[4] E.g. Nussbaum 1986:199 on what Alcibiades dreamed just before his death.

[5] Caveat: Plato was a child of eight in 416, so—precocious though he may have been, and attentive to Socrates' words later in life—I do not read the dialogue as history. Plato represented actual persons and their relations with some care: the more facts the archaeologists and epigraphers turn up, the more accurate Plato's accounts turn out to be. See Nails (2002:s.vv.) for the contemporaneous sources for the descriptions of the individuals, and for additional details about all of them.

[6] *Pace* Waterfield 1994:81–82.

[7] The special relationship to, and services due, one's fellow demesmen are attested in the literature and alluded to, for example, in Plato *Laches* 180b–d (cf. 187d–e), *Apology* 33e, *Phaedo* 115c3; Aristophanes *Clouds* 1206–1210, 1322, *Ecclesiazusae* (*Assemblywomen*) 1023–1024, 1114–1115, *Acharnians* 333, *Knights* 319–320, *Plutus* (*Wealth*) 253–254; and Lysias *For Mantitheus* 16.14, *Against Epicrates* 27.12.

were young enough to be considering higher education; so the rich and well-connected Callias (whose half-brothers were Pericles' sons, and whose sister would later marry Alcibiades) hosted a gathering where everyone who was anyone in Athens dropped in.

When we advance to 416, the fragile Peace of Nicias, declared in 421, has allowed some relief from the war. The characters are now mature men,[8] and at least three have married in the interim—Socrates, Alcibiades, and Aristophanes. Phaedrus of Myrrhinus, son of Pythocles, will marry his first cousin within the year. There is little money in his family or in that of Eryximachus, perhaps because the war has led to changes of fortune for so many. Eryximachus' father, the doctor Acumenus, is also a friend of Phaedrus and known to the Socratic circle (*Phaedrus* 227a5). Phaedrus is youngest of the group though he is at least twenty-nine; Agathon is at least thirty-one but looks youngest, clipping his beard very short; Eryximachus is not much over thirty-two, Aristophanes at thirty-four has been bald since his twenties, the lion Alcibiades is thirty-five, Pausanias is not yet forty, and Socrates is fifty-three.

By 416, Aristophanes had already made comedy of Agathon's friends, Socrates and Alcibiades, and seems in that very year to have abandoned a revision of the *Clouds* that he was preparing for a revival; he never brought Socrates back on stage.[9] From Plato's fourth-century perspective, however, and that of Plato's audience, Aristophanes was remarkable for later having scathingly represented the beautiful Agathon as a luxuriant Asian drag queen, obviously offensive to Athenian sensibilities, in the *Thesmophoriazusae* (Women at the Thesmophoria) in 411. That makes it peculiar that Aristophanes should be among the guests, and he is the odd man out in other ways: his speech is least compatible with that of Diotima, he conspires to speak out of order, he shushes Eryximachus, he deliberately bypasses Aristodemus,[10] and he makes an aborted complaint about Socrates' speech—in short, he's a grumpy companion, though the folktale he embellishes is marvelous.[11]

---

[8] They are young enough, nevertheless, to be mindful of the lessons of such professors as they have encountered (cf. *Symposium* 177b1–5, 185c5–6, 208c1).

[9] Henderson 1998b:3n2.

[10] See Figure 1. Aristodemus was on Eryximachus' couch, so should have spoken after Aristophanes (who had switched places with the doctor); but Aristophanes pointedly says "There are only Agathon and Socrates left" (193e2–3).

[11] Dover 1966:41–47 makes a compelling case for the lack of originality in Aristophanes' contribution to the occasion—a view that should mitigate others' perplexity that Plato should present Socrates' nemesis in a favorable light: the light is not favorable.

The tragedian, Agathon, son of Tisamenus, is by contrast courteous and accommodating, especially so to Aristodemus. He gives scant reason in Plato's dialogue to credit Aristophanes' later representation.[12] It is his victory, his invitation, his celebration, and there are no hints that he offends with any affectations. His lover, Pausanias[13] of Cerameis, a deme just outside the northwest city wall, appears faithful to the pederastic life he praises in the dialogue.

In 416, 'Socrates' is a household word, thanks to Aristophanes' *Clouds* and other comedies, and thanks perhaps also to his notorious physiognomy, exacerbated by his failure to bathe regularly or to cut his hair. His early interest in natural philosophy and his distinguished military service are behind him now. He fulfills all his civic obligations, including the religious ones, but people are becoming aware of further strangeness in Socrates—that he claims a personal *daimonion*, and that he opposes the stories of the poets that attribute injustice to the gods of the Athenians. He is a householder, but an austere one: everything he owned, including his house, was worth five *minae*—enough for a single course with the rhetorician Evenus.[14] He has recently married Xanthippe, and their first son is on the way. Her dowry was probably adequate for her basic support; the fact that their first son will be named for her presumed father, Lamprocles, rather than for his, points in that direction. Socrates maintains close ties with his childhood friends, Chaerephon of Sphettus, and Crito of Alopece. With no visible means of support, he spends his time in conversation with anyone who will join him. On this night in 416, Socrates exhibits a habit we witness only in this dialogue, he goes into one of his odd "trances" on his way to Agathon's; Alcibiades will later describe Socrates' having done so on campaign as well.

Alcibiades of Scambonidae, son of Clinias and Dinomache—from Athenian "first families" on both sides, reared in the house of Pericles (his mother's first cousin), and elected general as soon as he met the age qualification—is in 416 attractive, rich, and strong, a leader of men, at the peak of his power and influ-

---

[12] I note that he abrogates his *symposiarch* (dominant) role, and that there is something in this mature man's appearance, perhaps the close-cropped beard, that invites his being called νεανίσκος (198a2). Blanckenhagen 1992: 58–62, however, details additional ways in which Agathon is portrayed as effeminate in the dialogue, especially in his depiction of *Erōs* as a self-portrait, banter about Agathon's youthful appearance that begins at 175d and continues throughout, and most of all Agathon's inviting Socrates to his couch. Finding nothing of the sort is Bury 1932:xxxiv–xxxvi.

[13] The name 'Pausanias', like the name 'Alcibiades', is of Spartan origin.

[14] For Socrates' net worth, see Xenophon *Oeconomicus* 2.3.4–5; for Evenus' fee, see Plato *Apology* 20b9–c1. By implication, the fine Socrates says he is willing to pay (38b8) with help from friends is considerable, six times his net worth.

ence; but he is spoiled, arrogant, and dissolute. He is rarely seen without his hangers-on—cousins, fellow demesmen, and men related by marriage—some of whose names are known to us,[15] so it would be odd to absent them from among the revelers in Alcibiades' entourage at Agathon's. Alcibiades was married to Callias' sister, and is the father of two children, but his wife has recently died, probably at the time of giving birth to their second child, now an infant. He had long since run through Hipparete's huge dowry. Diotima could be describing Alcibiades when she says of the lovers of honors and glory, "for the sake of that they're ready to run all risks, even more than they are for their children—they'll spend money, undergo any suffering you like, die for it" (208c6–d2). There was always controversy about what Alcibiades' relationship with Socrates really was,[16] but there is no question that Alcibiades had a larger-than-life, heroic (if bad-boy), popular reputation by the time of the early Academy.

Another in the list of characters of 416 is Diotima of Mantinea though, given what is said about her postponing Athens' plague, Socrates would have been acquainted with her when he was about thirty. We meet her in a flashback. Perhaps she is one of those "priests and priestesses" from whom Socrates occasionally says he has heard things (*Meno* 81a9), but most scholars consider her a wholly fictitious character. No matter. Diotima is a priestess, religious, who counts prophecy and magic among the branches of knowledge (*Symposium* 202e7–203a1). Thus, even if what she offers is beauty itself, or the good itself, she offers something less than what the philosopher seeks, less than what is to be found at the top of the divided line, for example: the fundamental, unhypothetical principle of the all (*Republic* VI 511b5–6).[17] She is a mystagogue who has been initiated into the higher Eleusinian mysteries, where she says she is not sure Socrates can follow (209e5–210a2).[18] I submit that he did not follow. Mystery religions, like rhetoric, like mathematics or

---

[15] Alcibiades of Phegous, Adeimantus of Scambonidae, and Axiochus of Scambonidae (see Figure 2 below) are known from a number of inscriptions, from comic poets, forensic speeches, and historians. See Nails 2002:s.vv.

[16] Although Xenophon (*Memorabilia* 1.2.47) was a critic of Alcibiades, and Isocrates a supporter (*Busiris* 11.4), both say he sought to use Socrates for his own advancement.

[17] τοῦ ἀνυποθέτου ἐπὶ τὴν τοῦ παντὸς ἀρχὴν (cf. VI 510b6–7)—not to be confused with the form of the good, despite the near unanimity of the confusion, and *pace* Lloyd Gerson's contribution to this volume. See also *Republic* VII 533c8–9 contrasted with 534b8. The good, while the cause of what is correct and good in all things (VII 517b4–c7, 527b–c), is not the cause of everything—not the cause, for example, of what is bad in things (cf. II 379b3–16), and not the cause of the form of the bad (cf. V 476a5–8). I have argued this in greater detail elsewhere (Nails 2001), but my argument in this paper does not depend on the distinction.

[18] Cf. Socrates' remark to Glaucon at *Republic* VII 533a1.

fine poetry, are at best stepping stones to philosophy, and we expect too much of Diotima, who is neither Socrates nor Plato, if we expect profound philosophy from her.[19]

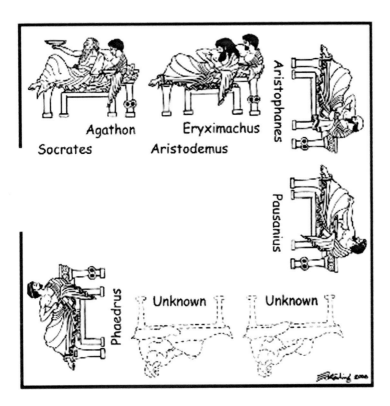

Figure 1. Seating arrangement of the guests at Agathon's *symposion*, assuming the standard configuration of seven couches in a square room, and at least two unknown guests.

We know something about the setting of the dialogue as well. In the fifth century, large private dining rooms were unusual, but the seating arrangement in the *Symposium* implies that there were probably seven couches (see

---

[19] I will return to Diotima below. Ruby Blondell's contribution to this volume, emphasizing the rigidity of the order of the steps in the process of initiation described by the priestess, has added to my mistrust of the mysteries as a path to truth, beauty, wisdom, and excellence.

Figure 1) because there were at least two additional guests whose encomia were not memorable (180c1-2). The arrangement in a square with the couches on a slightly raised platform was standard, so the number of couches, usually either seven or eleven, was always odd, to accommodate the door.[20] Lighting was provided by oil lamps along the wall behind the diners. The men's dining area was usually centrally located in the houses of the period, so the female relatives with whom Agathon lived (176e8) and who are noted as sequestered elsewhere, were most likely in an adjacent room with no common door. It is important to note that, by 416, the war's widows and orphans had been reassigned to *kurioi* under a highly regulated system, and the city was feeling the effects of the increased proportion of women. One finds evidence of it in the female-dominated plays of Aristophanes;[21] when Aristarchus complains to Socrates that the war has so increased the number of women in his house that he cannot feed them all (Xenophon *Memorabilia* 2.7); and when the Athenians pass a wartime decree permitting men to have legitimate children by women other than their wives. All of this is in the wartime background of the dramatic date of the dialogue's interior story.[22]

There is another social issue of relevance to understanding the dialogue: Athenian citizen males did not marry until they were at least thirty, and the period of being an *erōmenos* was very short—adolescence to first beard. *Then* what for the next dozen years or more? Nice Athenian girls were locked away, and, as Kenneth Dover (1989:88) says, "Purchased sex ... could never give him what he needed emotionally, the experience of being valued and welcomed for his own sake." Whatever disapproval was expressed by a young man's parents or the laws, sexual relations between young men were an appropriate extension of the *erōmenos* stage.[23] The age difference in homosexual couples, if

---

[20] I am grateful to Terry Echterling for producing Figure 1 from my embarrassing attempt to draw the layout of Agathon's dining room for my Plato seminar in 2005. Bergquist 1990:37 traces dining rooms from the pre-archaic to the Hellenistic period, and I have used her observations for the room's dimensions: it has walls of about 4.5 meters, with a diagonal of about 6.4 meters (it is roughly 20 meters square). There may have been more than two guests who failed to give memorable speeches, suggesting double occupancy on other couches as well.

[21] *Lysistrata* and *Thesmophoriazusae*, both produced in 411, and *Ecclesiazusae*, produced in 392 or 391.

[22] The decree is known from Diogenes Laertius 2.26, Athenaeus 556a, and Aulus Gellius *Noctes Atticae* 15.20.6; but the original criteria for legitimacy had been restored by the fourth century, so it was not in effect for long. It is, however, a part of the persistent myth that Socrates took a second wife, Myrto. See Nails 2002:209–210. For a more insightful view of Plato's use of female imagery in the *Symposium*, see Angie Hobbs' contribution to this volume.

[23] The literature on heavy penalties for a citizen's allowing himself to be penetrated, and the hypothesis of intercrural sex (e.g. Dover 1989:103–105, Halperin 1986, 1990:94–99) is not fully

any, was probably not more than a few years (1989:86), and was likely to have involved physical pleasure for the *erōmenos* as well as the *erastēs* (1989:204). The view sometimes entertained that there was a generation's difference between Pausanias and Agathon runs into trouble with Plato's texts: Callias' guests in the *Protagoras* seem to be young men, born in the late 450s and early 440s—except Socrates and Critias, both of whom keep their distance from the individuals seeking paying students. It is Agathon's beauty and youth, not his companion's relative seniority, that merits comment (315d7–e3). Vases showing mature men with smaller adolescents, according to Dover (1989:204), were highly conventional, and did not reflect actual practice. Further, Agathon and Pausanias cannot be assumed to have cohabited in Athens (though cohabitation may have been a motivation for their joining the Macedonians): the *oikos* was a trans-generational institution that put civic obligations on an adult male, even if he was in a permanent erotic relationship with another male; so Agathon's celebration took place in his own house, which was not Pausanias' house.[24]

In Search of the Tragic

No one needs to be persuaded that Plato could write scenes that are tear-jerkers or side-splitters: the death of Socrates in the *Phaedo*, and the Stesilaus story in the *Laches* are proof enough of that claim. Equally, we have adequate evidence that Plato sometimes conceived tragedy broadly as encompassing serious subjects, and took trifling matters to be comic (cf. *Republic* X 595c1–2, *Laws* VII 817a2–b5). I want to see how far we can progress toward accommodating *Symposium* 223d2–5 with these modest claims. Without waxing technical, we might begin with Christopher Gill's minimalist judgment that the comment at 223d2–5 "seems to highlight Plato's own skill in combining both comic and serious drama in the service of philosophy" (1999:xxxix).[25] This asks less than the logical necessity Socrates invoked,[26] and mentions knowledge

---

persuasive about actual practice because the probability of being caught and charged appears to have been very low, and because the evidence in Old Comedy is more dispositive than that from the courts (Dover 1989:204).

[24] For a contrasting interpretation of the relationship between Agathon and Pausanias, and a different account of their circumstances, see the contribution by Luc Brisson to this volume.

[25] Cf. Arieti 1991:110, Nightingale 1995:2.

[26] The 1989 Nehamas-Woodruff translation of 223d2–5 ("authors should be able ... tragic dramatist should also be ...") is thus misleading, but the weaker sense they give the Greek has been taken up by Nightingale 1995:2, Corrigan 1997:54–64, et al.

(ἐπιστήμη) not at all, but it nevertheless already excludes the explanations of a few commentators who have weighed in on 223d2–5.[27]

The bounty of comic elements from the *Symposium* that support Gill's minimalism has been spectacular and delightful: dirt and food and boisterous drunks, slaves in charge, musical chairs, rules broken, seemliness made unseemly, and the order of things upset at every turn.[28] In a rare role-switch, Socrates-in-sandals (clean for a change) invites an uninvited guest, the dirty and barefoot runt, Aristodemus of Cydathenaeum. Plato also throws in some of his best slapstick scenes: the uninvited guest's arrival without the invited guest; the doctor's straight-laced speech with his patient in the background hiccoughing loudly, holding his breath and then gasping for air, gargling, and sneezing—trying out each of the doctor's remedies in succession until cured, just in time to follow the straight man with a stand-up comic's re-told tale; and Alcibiades, drunkenly acting out his story on a Socrates who sits like Patience on a monument.

Solemn (σπουδαῖος) content does not flow so freely. Scholars have not been as successful at identifying tragic elements—except in relief against the comic, or as serious subjects given a light touch. Mystery religions, for example, are a constant running theme of the dialogue both in the vocabulary of initiation and revelation, and in actions represented, as others have pointed

---

[27] Murray 1996:107–108 denies that poetry is a skill (τέχνη) although "a practitioner of a τέχνη will have knowledge of the whole of a given subject area." The knowledge facilitates accurate judgments about poetry but falls short of guaranteeing that one can compose comedy or tragedy, so Murray twice refers to the comment at 223d2–5 as "hypothetical" (1996:107, 174, cf. Shorey 1937:233n395a on poetry as inspiration, and Schein 1974). She concludes, "If composing poetry were indeed a τέχνη, then it would be the case that the same poet could compose both tragedy and comedy. Since no such poet exists, we are left to infer that poetry is not in fact a τέχνη." This argument has the same form, and the same flaw, as the *Meno* argument (98d10–e9) that if excellence is teachable, then there must be teachers of it; since there are no teachers of it, excellence cannot be taught. Gill's minimal formulation also excludes Strauss 2001:285–286 and Rosen 1968:326, who interpret the remark as revealing something about Socrates. Only by "natural gift," they say, could a man compose both tragedy and comedy (d3–4); by art, a man who can compose tragedies can compose comedies (d4–5), but not the reverse, as confirmed by Aristophanes' falling asleep before Agathon (d6–7). We are to learn from this, they tell us, that Socrates could compose comedies but not tragedies, and therefore wrote nothing. They make identical claims about the text, and Rosen credits Strauss with being πατὴρ τοῦ ἐμοῦ λόγου.

[28] Wardy 2002 accounts systematically for twenty-nine significant sets of opposites introduced in the dialogue and provides asides on others. He analyzes these "polarities" by the degree to which they remain or collapse under examination. Although he does not claim his list is comprehensive, it comes close: I miss only democratic and hierarchic, a pair with historical significance for comedy and tragedy, respectively (Aristotle *Poetics* 1448a28–b2) and which feature in the structure of the *Symposium* as well.

out in detail.[29] The Athenian democracy is another. A *symposion*, in contrast to a *hetaireia* or a *sunōmosia*, was a democratic institution with no fixed membership or oaths sworn, but also in its deliberate emphasis on equal portions in the distribution of food and mixed wine, shared entertainment, taking one's turn, and preserving left to right order.[30] Plato adds other democratic allusions to the dialogue. He uses demotics more than patronymics, for example, beginning with Apollodorus' being hailed simply as "Phalerian" (172a4).[31] There is no permanent *symposiarch* for the evening. Rather, the guests are to drink as they please. And there is no hierarchy, so different men at different times make proposals for conduct, sometimes peppered with phrases appropriate to the Assembly (e.g. 176e4–177e8) or the courts (e.g. 219c3–6). Alcibiades arrives crowned in ivy and violets, where violets are the symbol for Athens (Pindar fr. 76 Bergk),[32] and ivy is associated with Dionysus. Besides positive and neutral references, some are negative, e.g. Agathon's "to an intelligent person a few sensible people are more frightening than a lot of stupid ones" (194b7–8); Diotima's similar distinction between everyone and the knowledgeable among them (202b8–9, cf. 208c2–d2); and Alcibiades' use of the adage, "a medical man is worth as much as many other men together" (214b7). In each case, knowledge is valued above numbers. There is other serious subject matter in the dialogue, mostly spoken by Diotima: the beautiful and the good, the best life for a human being, the human portion of immortality, the method illustrated in Socrates' elenchus with Agathon. All these are weighty matters, but they do not rise to the level of the tragic—in case that should be the expectation aroused by 223d2–5.

I turn now to authors who have no quarrel with the notion that the tragedy of the *Symposium* is played out off-stage, but who take *Alcibiades* to be the tragic figure of the dialogue. After his attempted seduction of Socrates failed, he turned away from philosophy and squandered his promise and great talents, turning traitor to Athens. An important insight of Dover's—that raised Aristophanes' stakes and diminished Diotima's—ignited what is now a widely held view, so I begin there.[33]

---

[29] See Bury 1932, des Places 1964:17–18, des Vries 1973, Maraguianou 1985:248–251.

[30] Schmitt-Pantel 1990:19, Wecowski 2002.

[31] Although Eryximachus is introduced with his patronymic (176b5), that brings to mind Acumenus, the doctor known to those present who will share their fate in the months ahead. See Sider 2002:260–262 for Φαληρεύς.

[32] Cited by Nussbaum 1986:193.

[33] There are far more issues, perspectives, and complications than the ones relevant to the epistemologically-based interpretation I pursue below; see Vlastos 1973b, Erde 1976:164–167; Kosman 1976, Gagarin 1977, Patterson 1982, Price 1981, 1991, Rowe 1990, 1998a, Scott 2000, and

Dover argued (1966, 1980) that Aristophanes gives "the only speech in the *Symposium* which strikes a modern reader as founded on observable realities" (1980:113) and, because "homosexual response was the most powerful emotional experience known to most of the people for whom he [Plato] was writing" (1980:5), the ancients too would have found Aristophanes' account more realistic than Diotima's. Dover points beyond *erōs* as desire for orgasm to what he calls "preference" for a single, unique, other person who complements oneself and for whom one's *erōs* persists regardless of seemingly more attractive potential partners, regardless of one's attraction even to the infinitely beautiful; this he sees as Aristophanes' position against Diotima's (1966:47–50). Her account excludes exactly the personal and subjective element in the object of *erōs*, so Dover declares her position formally incompatible with that of Aristophanes.

Martha Nussbaum (1986:197–199), acknowledging Dover's general incompatibility argument, but with her attention on human action, applies it to particular individuals. No one, by her lights, can *prefer* another person in Dover's sense and simultaneously prefer absolute knowledge.[34] The one is "unique passion" for another person, e.g. Alcibiades' desire for Socrates; and the other is "stable rationality" of the Socratic sort that Diotima's way is said to provide.[35] "We see two kinds of value, two kinds of knowledge; and we see that we must choose. One sort of understanding blocks out the other."[36] And, "You have to blind yourself to something." In Nussbaum's view, "philosophy is not fully human; but we are terrified of humanity and what it leads to. It

---

Penner and Rowe 2005:300–307, all of whom are concerned in different ways with Plato's views on interpersonal relations.

[34] That follows trivially from one sense of 'prefer', but her claim is based on more than that. See also Vlastos 1973b.

[35] In support of the view that personal and objective knowledge are incompatible, Nussbaum 1986:198 notes, "Socrates was serious when he spoke of two mutually exclusive varieties of vision"; but Socrates makes *no such pronouncement* in the dialogue. Nussbaum may be referring loosely to the vision of the beautiful that appears "all at once" (ἐξαίφνης, 210e4) together with her own description of that process as a "change in vision" (1986:182–183), but let us for now withhold judgment on whether it was Socrates who advocated the experience of the higher mysteries.

[36] Although the *Symposium* is free of the tripartite psyche, one may be reminded of Freud's early hydraulic model of the psyche, similar to Plato's stream of *Republic* VI 485d; given a finite quantity of psychic energy, an increase in one streamlet causes a proportional decrease in the others. Or, to borrow the metaphor from *Republic* IX 588c7–589a10, gratification of lust "feeds the beast," drains psychic energy away from the intellect. Even these metaphors, however, fall short of Nussbaum's blocking out or blinding. Three millennia of human history argue for the usefulness of tripartition, but I nevertheless take Plato's several representations of the psyche as useful metaphors, not doctrine.

is *our* tragedy: it floods us with light and takes away action." In the dialogue, it is "movingly displayed to us in the person and the story of Alcibiades." Nussbaum's Plato's *Symposium* offers the vulnerable, passionate Alcibiades as an alternative to the "rational stone" Socrates whom she describes as, "in his ascent towards the form ... very like a form—hard, indivisible, cold" (1986:195). Nussbaum concludes that the reader must choose between Alcibiades and Socrates, between poetry and philosophy, between pursuits of personal and objective knowledge.

She cannot be right. Either (a) there really are two distinct and incompatible kinds of knowledge (ἐπιστήμη), as Nussbaum says, one personal, one objective; or (b) human beings (i.e. all of us, for it is, she says, "our" tragedy) conceive two kinds of knowledge where really there is only one. If (b), the issue is one of human frailty, the widespread inability to pursue stable, fundamental knowledge simultaneously with pursuing the unstable apprehension of the beloved (including unstable apprehensions of oneself and of the relationship), resulting in the mistaken belief that there are two kinds of knowledge itself. But the prescription for that incapacity is dialectical philosophy, which would result in the recognition that knowledge is stable, and that unstable apprehensions gained through passion—however independently valuable—are not instances of knowledge. It is a result short of what Nussbaum seeks, but it leaves intact a truth that will carry over into the discussion of Lear's Socrates below: we humans are deeply affected by our closest relationships and should thus exercise great care in how we treat those with whom we are intimate.

But let us also consider (a), which is Nussbaum's position: there are in fact two incompatible, discrete kinds of *knowledge*, strictly so called.[37] In Nussbaum's view, *literature* has epistemological value of the Alcibiades-poetic-personal type. Because "we cannot all live, in our own overt activities, through all that we ought to know in order to live well" (1986:186), literature offers a kind of compensation. Literature provides knowledge that is required for living well.[38] But if literature extends only personal knowledge, blocking out the objective, we are left with no account of gaining objective knowledge as the result of reading the philosophical literature we call Platonic dialogues. Further, without objective knowledge from somewhere, I cannot assess the value of the instances of personal knowledge that I am supposed to be learning through my unique experience of another person (or at least my reading

---

[37] Cf. the innocuous "pieces of knowledge" (αἱ ἐπιστῆμαι, 207e6) and knowings or "kinds of knowledge" (τὰς ἐπιστήμας ... ἐπιστημῶν, 210c7–8).

[38] Since she says "ought" we are all duty-bound to read literature, if she is right.

about such unique experiences that others are having or imagining). I cannot know whether I've got it right. On the other hand, if knowledge from literature bridges personal and objective knowledge, even if the latter is not now on my mind, then personal apprehensions are not incompatible with objective knowledge after all, and the demand that one choose between them is deprived of force. One can have both, and nothing prevents one's moving from one to the other and back again repeatedly.

Regardless of whether literature extends personal knowledge, or bridges the personal to the objective, we are obliged to take the next step and ask the kinds of questions Socrates asks about the poet's epistemic authority. Did Plato experience personally what he writes about Alcibiades, or did he learn from literature, or did he extrapolate from someone else's account? In Nussbaum's own example, one person, Plato, is the master of both the personal and the objective, implying what seems the correct view: no choice is required. Plato is pulling the strings when, "through a lover's intimacy," Alcibiades "can produce accounts (stories) that are more deeply and precisely true" than those of Socrates (1986:191). We are left without an account under which these experiences of imagination, emotion, and so on are instances of knowledge (rather than what they seem to be—and what Socrates in other contexts argues that they are—volatile ephemera). Even if Alcibiades and Socrates were freaks at opposite ends of some knowledge scale, it does not follow without additional premises that choosing a life of passionate commitment to another person renders one's life unsuitable for seeking absolute knowledge, or seeking absolute knowledge passionately, for that matter. If absolute knowledge were as Diotima describes life at the top of the ladder of love—exclusive, pristine (211e1–2) contemplation of divine beauty (e4)—then, indeed, passionate commitment to another individual would be impossible, but it is far from clear that Socrates embraced the mystical initiation talk that occurred after Diotima said she did not know whether Socrates could follow her.

Diotima goes on to describe the promise of the difficult ascent, the seeker's pay-off as "bringing to birth ... true virtue, because he is grasping the truth" (212a2–5).[39] As a result, he will enjoy the love of the gods and such immortality as is available to a human being (d5–7). Even if the ascent leads to virtue, knowledge, and happiness, for I acknowledge close connections among these, it would not be necessary to take *Diotima's* path. I, for one, would prefer a different route, even if it were longer or more dangerous. The life "worth

---

[39] Although I would prefer 'excellence' for ἀρετή, the secondary literature for *Symposium* opts almost universally for 'virtue'.

living for a human being" according to the mystic priestess Diotima, is *pure* contemplation of the beautiful (*to kalon* 211d2–3); the philosopher Socrates, as we know, had a different conception of the only life worth living for a human being: the examined life (*Apology* 38a5–6), and he spells out what that means in relation to the lives of his fellow human beings.[40]

Nussbaum seems to have conflated philosophy and mystery religion, then drawn conclusions about Socrates; and she has thereby denied that the philosopher can enjoy the varied and rich life that no mystic can touch. The *Symposium* has had the same odd effect on other scholars, obscuring the divide between philosophy and religion. Dover, for example, praises Aristophanes' view as more Christian than Diotima's (citing 1 John 4.8, ὁ Θεὸς ἀγάπη ἐστίν, 1966:48), as does Kosman 1976:67, citing the mystery of incarnation.

In my view, such confusion and conflation are the "mortal nonsense" (φλυαρίας θνητῆς, 211e3) we would do better to avoid if we can. But it is all too common: a species of it relevant here is the notion that there is some transcendent, supernatural realm of forms, a "Platonic heaven" not only distinct but *separate* from the particulars that can be perceived and measured. I concede that such a "two worlds" view of Plato, divine and human, opens the way for interpretations that sever beautiful particulars from the beautiful itself. According to Diotima, reaching the peak enables the initiate to see that what he previously thought were beautiful particulars were all along mere *phluarias thnētēs*. Contrast this with Socrates' statement, "I simply, naively and perhaps foolishly cling to this, that nothing else makes it [a thing] beautiful other than the presence of (παρουσία), or the sharing in (κοινωνία), or however you may describe its relationship to that Beautiful we mentioned, for I will not insist on the precise nature of the relationship, but that all beautiful things are beautiful by the Beautiful" (*Phaedo* 100d4–9, trans. Grube). Whereas the analogy of the divided line provides for deduction from the first principle, by way of formulae (forms), down to conclusions about particulars (*Republic* 511b6–c2), the ascent in the *Symposium ends* at the summit with exclusive contemplation of *to kalon*. Formal knowledge of the beautiful,[41] apparently implying the clarity, truth, and reality of the top segment of the divided line, fails to enhance the ability of the knower—in Diotima's account—to recognize the beauty in particulars. Rather, at the pinnacle of the ascent, the knower looks back on the particu-

---

[40] The phrases βιωτὸν ἀνθρώπῳ at *Symposium* 211d3 and οὐ βιωτὸς ἀνθρώπῳ at *Apology* 38a6 are too similar not to recall one another, and the phrase does not appear elsewhere in Plato.

[41] For reasons not especially important to the current argument, I prefer this way of expressing what others would call "knowledge of the form of the beautiful."

lars as a lot of worthless stuff. I would not wish to overstate the point, but the two passages invite comparison between theoretical science and religion, knowledge of the theory of everything (TOE, as it is affectionately known to some physicists),[42] vs. mystical contemplation of the beautiful and the good. Insofar as such a vision distracts one from the higher passage to the first principle and consequent deduction—which Diotima knows nothing about—it is inferior. In any case, the other-worldly view attributed to Plato does nothing to turn images, feelings, and appetites—Nussbaum's personal data—into what she calls personal *knowledge*.

Jonathan Lear (1998:148–166) shares Nussbaum's concern for the tender feelings of the young Alcibiades, explicitly taking Socrates' *indifference* to Alcibiades as the tragic focus of the dialogue. With the rich theoretical apparatus of psychoanalysis at Lear's disposal, however, he does not require Nussbaum's bifurcated epistemology. Instead, he looks at the dialogue in its historical context and, following a suggestion of Blanckenhagen's,[43] accuses Socrates of failing to prevent Alcibiades from betraying Athens, with consequences for all of western civilization.[44] Lear takes Diotima to have counseled, "beautiful individuals have only instrumental value: they are to be used, stepped on, like rungs on a ladder ... after one has climbed the ladder, the best thing would be to kick it away" (1998:163). An attraction of Lear's analysis of the *Symposium* is his indignation on behalf of the *erōmenos* that the *erastēs* has failed him. Correct *paiderastia* in Diotima's sense (211b5–6) almost always ended with an *erōmenos* of fading beauty left behind, an *erastēs* attracted to something new. None of that human pain, however, is of concern to a priestess for whom beautiful boys are interchangeable with beautiful statues—just so long as the ultimate result is contemplation of the beautiful. Lear takes Socrates to have followed Diotima's counsel in his relationship with Alcibiades, and therein lies the blame. In particular, when Alcibiades attempted to seduce

---

[42] Others call it the GUT, grand unified theory.

[43] Referring to Alcibiades' attempt to seduce Socrates, Blanckenhagen 1992:67 says, "A rather good case could be made for the theory that the trauma of that night set the pattern of Alcibiades' neurotic, destructive, and catastrophic character and life."

[44] I do not pursue here the sense of 'agency' required to underpin a claim that Socrates is even in part to blame for actions taken by Alcibiades at such a remove, but I believe it suggests another important problem in the Lear-Nussbaum view. I also do not discuss whether Alcibiades could in fact have succeeded in Sicily, thereby preventing the oligarchy of 411, the resumption of the war, and the events of 404; there are too many variables. Nussbaum mentions the historical context but, on what I regard as inadequate grounds (unsubstantiated fourth-century opinion), privileges fiction, literature, by returning insistently to the desecration of herms, in which Alcibiades had no role (see below n64).

Socrates, Socrates was already too abstracted from real life to respond physically, so Alcibiades became the spurned lover who tragically—and some fifteen years later—turned traitor to Athens. As if semen could itself educate,[45] Blanckenhagen (1992:67) had already complained, "Had Socrates slept with Alcibiades not 'like a father or older brother' but as a true *erastēs*, he might well have channeled the manifold gifts of this most gifted of all Athenians in a classical, a 'Periclean', direction and would have made him the best statesman Athens ever had." Let us then look more closely at the case of Alcibiades.

The seduction described in the *Symposium* (217a2–219d2) would have been attempted at just about the time of the *Protagoras*,[46] or a little before, to judge from the description in the opening scene, when Hippocrates assumed Alcibiades was Socrates' beloved (*Protagoras* 309a1–b4). Very soon afterwards, if not already, Alcibiades would be too old to make a play for Socrates because a bearded man was an implausible *erōmenos*. So, was Socrates in fact following Diotima's advice to kick the ladder away? Lear does not claim that Socrates deliberately set out to use Alcibiades, just that Socrates resisted the youth from *indifference*. But if this is so, it was a reckless and careless indifference: "insofar as Alcibiades is trapped in the human-erotic, he can, from Socrates' perspective, go fuck himself. It does not matter to Socrates what the human consequences are" (1998:164). A powerful reason to doubt that this could be so—and it is incidentally a reason to decouple Diotima from the Socrates familiar in Plato—is Socrates' principle of doing no harm. If Socrates understood that horses become worse when they are mistreated, and he did, he could hardly have thought that humans could be stepped on, or kicked away, without suffering harm (*Apology* 25a13–b6); and his life of examining others in an effort to improve their psyches is further evidence that he took his mission seriously. Moreover, in Alcibiades' account of the night, Socrates treated him like a son or younger brother (*Symposium* 219d1–2), not like a stranger, not with indifference. It was at least three years after the dramatic date of the *Protagoras*, after the siege at Potidaea had ended and the troops were returning home in 429 (Thucydides 2.79.1–7) that Socrates risked his own life to save Alcibiades (220d5–e2, Scott 2000:36). That too tells against indifference.

Not long after saving Alcibiades in battle, however, Charmides became Socrates' favorite and, according to Alcibiades, was spurned as others were

---

[45] For evidence that this was a myth of the time, and that it is alluded to repeatedly in the dialogue, see Luc Brisson's and David Reeve's contributions to this volume. See also Sheffield 2001a:17–18.

[46] I.e. before the war began in earnest, about 433/2.

(222b1–2), providing ammunition for Lear's view that "Socrates kills them all softly, with his words. Socrates is a traumatizing seducer ... if one substitutes intellectual prowess for overtly sexual activity" (2000:102).[47] A different explanation for Socrates' treatment of his favorites and the other youths—one more compatible with Socrates' mission of examining himself and others—is not correct *paiderastia*, nor even correct pedagogy, but the correct *psychagogia*, 'soul guiding', attributed to Socrates.[48]

Teaching construed in the osmosis (*Symposium* 175d4–8), transmitter-receiver (*Meno* 73c6–8), or pitcher-and-empty-vessel (*Protagoras* 314b) models cannot work for the philosophical project of seeking wisdom and truth dialectically, thus Socrates repeatedly says of himself that he is not a teacher.[49] Thus he has no "teachings" to pass on to "pupils" or "disciples." Socrates does not truck with the transfer of information, but with the use of a method that increases its respondents' intellectual freedom, and therefore their chance of achieving both virtue and happiness by increasing their power to distinguish good from bad.[50] Despite his love of the beautiful itself, or as expressed by beautiful Alcibiades, despite his physical attraction, Socrates may plausibly think gratification of Alcibiades' erotic appetite will not make Alcibiades better and might well make him worse. Beware the soul-doctor who has sex with patients, or the professor with students, for the patient or student's *erōs* is thereby directed not to the proper objects of knowledge but to the pedagogue or *mystagogue* personally—not in addition, but instead. Something Plato apparently understood about the educational process is that it is difficult to know what really is good, and easy to be misled, making "do no harm" a high standard indeed. Often enough even now, the love of wisdom begins with a crush on Socrates. Plato's dialogues manipulate that emotional bond, affect in the service of formal knowledge, much like the *Symposium*'s ladder of love, for one's *erōs*, one's investment of emotion or psychic energy, must be redirected and transformed. So, for example, Plato's Socrates tells Agathon it is truth "that you can't argue with, since there's nothing difficult about arguing

---

[47] Belfiore 1980:136–137 argues on the contrary that Alcibiades was improved by his beloved Socrates.

[48] See Teloh 1986:2. Sheffield's 2001a:17–25 account of the process of education in the dialogue is acute, nuanced, and positive about prospects. See now also Rawson 2006.

[49] I.e. not a 'teacher' in the sense that term was understood by Athenians (see e.g. *Meno* 81e3–82a3 and *Apology* 33a3–b8). Plato's dialogues illustrate and pass on the dialectical practices Socrates used, and with the same positive results in prospect, as I have argued elsewhere (Nails 1995:213–235).

[50] See, again, Sheffield 2001a; cf. Gagarin 1977.

against Socrates" (201c8–9).[51] The psychagogical relationship—Socrates as dialectical guide to Alcibiades, Charmides, and others—is a stage that should be outgrown, not abandoned.[52] The erotic arrow must glance off Socrates and strike toward truth.

Plato's dialogues operate on the whole psyche, primarily on the intellect, but without neglecting the emotions. His longer road, his graduate-level course, depends entirely on the reader's or listener's yearning for wisdom rather than for Socrates, craving truth, not a person. When *erōs* is directed to wisdom and truth, Socrates' active participation, or even his presence in the dialogues, can diminish ... and disappear. That Plato can guide so many people in that direction is the mark of his own genius as a philosopher, an educator, and a literary author.

Blanckenhagen had called Alcibiades, "the human sacrifice on the altar of Socratic doctrine" (1992:67). For Alcibiades' plight to appear so tragic, it is necessary for both Nussbaum and Lear to suppress features of Socrates' life and personality that are familiar to us from the dialogues and were familiar to everyone in Plato's audience as well—a methodologically suspect move for anyone who invokes an understanding of historical circumstances. One such suppressed feature is given by Diotima at 208e3–6: there are some men who "turn their attention more toward women"—a phrase that accurately describes the Socrates of Plato and Xenophon. No *argument* is adduced to support the view that Socrates feels no *erōs* toward Xanthippe, for example, though it has been widely assumed. There is not much basis for arguments either way, but a few premises might be mentioned. First, it is not necessary to deny Socrates' attraction to Charmides (*Charmides* 155d3–e2) or his frequent remarks about beautiful boys and young men, to hold that his erotic drive embraced women *more* than men, as Diotima puts it. It is not only Alcibiades and Charmides, but Euthydemus and others (*Symposium* 222b1–2) whose amorous overtures were declined by Socrates. The second bears on the nature of his attraction to Alcibiades, with whom he was associated in the popular imagination well into the fourth century.[53] In *Protagoras*, Socrates measures

---

[51] "Give but little thought to Socrates and much to truth" (*Phaedo* 91c1–2). The point is made often in the dialogues, and not always by Socrates. Cf. *Phaedrus* 275b, *Republic* I 349a–b, *Gorgias* 473b.

[52] So with the transference relationship in psychoanalysis.

[53] *Alcibiades* I, a dialogue written not by Plato but very likely in the days of the initial Academy, shows the early interest in Socrates' relationship with Alcibiades: Socrates calls himself Alcibiades' *erastēs* (103a2). The dialogue is "Platonic" in the sense that the earliest accretion of academic writing around a core of genuine texts is interesting in illuminating the preoccupations of the Academy at that time. Cf. Thesleff 1982:85.

their relationship by the standard of Alcibiades' success at argument, and admits to being distracted from Alcibiades by Protagoras' wisdom (309b7–9). The description is confirmed by Alcibiades at *Symposium* 216d7–e6.[54] Third, Plato provides no support for Xenophon's view that Xanthippe was unlovable; rather, he represents her sympathetically in the *Phaedo* (her remark at 60a5–8 is selfless). Historically, it can be added that Socrates was still sexually active and begetting children as he approached the age of seventy. Thus Lear (1998:159) and Nussbaum (1986:195) need not be so concerned that Socrates was not sexually aroused when Alcibiades was. It is not as if Socrates was an ascetic, some celibate moralist; we know that he was not. Nor, judging from Socrates' active social life and the enthusiasm with which others sought his company, does it seem justified to call him a rational stone. Rather, Socrates appears to have been the happiest of men, thoroughly enjoying even the relationships that were not consummated physically; he grew old with dear fellow demesmen and friends from childhood, surrounded by many newer friends, with a wife and children; and he faced death with a tranquility that was a wonder to them all. The philosopher's life really does seem to be the best of all lives and Socrates the happiest of men because what he really wanted, and what he thought he wanted, really was good. He was not the philosopher of the digression in the *Theaetetus*.

By paraphrasing the philosopher of the digression (173e2–5) in his description of the indifferent Socrates, Lear makes the fault line in his account clearer.[55] He says Socrates "has become as divine as humanly possible, and though he remains in the human realm, he is no longer part of it" (1998:164). This would be the Socrates misunderstood and seemingly defective in the eyes of Athenians—like Nussbaum's freak—a philosopher at odds with practical life in the real world, perhaps at odds with his own body as he pursues death. But this is not the human Socrates of Plato's dialogues. "In contrast to the philosopher of the digression," Ruby Blondell (2002:299–300) argues, Socrates

---

[54] If Alcibiades were impartial in the matter, these same lines might be persuasive evidence that the *real* Socrates was like Diotima or an initiate into the higher mysteries in his attitude toward beautiful young men. But it would simultaneously raise questions why e.g. Socrates reports in a dialogue he narrates (*Charmides* 155d3–e2) that he *does* feel overwhelming erotic attraction. If one takes the *Symposium* as an aesthetic unity that recommends mystery religion as a route to virtue and knowledge—as the *Phaedrus* recommends rhetoric and the *Theaetetus* mathematics—one does not thereby deny that metaquestions about the dialogues can be addressed.

[55] Reading Lear 1998, in particular his emphasis on what happens after the dialogue ends, prompted my inquiry into what is tragic about the *Symposium* and my writing of this paper. Even when one disagrees with Lear, his provocations and insights make potent sparks.

serves as an embodied exemplar for other embodied persons. His ideal is unattainable precisely because it is detached from the circumstances of human life as actually lived. Sokrates therefore resembles his own *paradeigma* not through superficial slavish imitation (which would be impossible for any embodied human being), but by pursuing the same central values in a manner that is both possible and appropriate for a person whose concrete situation diverges radically, and fundamentally, from that of the ideal in question—that is, by means of structural imitation. Unlike the philosopher, he can speak about the material and social world.

The life of the real-world philosopher, according to this view, does not inevitably cause tragedy, nor must it *be* tragic. It may seem so, however, if the ends of Platonic philosophy are conflated with those of mysticism (Nussbaum), or if the philosophical paradigm is conflated with a flesh-and-blood philosopher (Lear). I suspect, however, that there is rather more going on than mere conflation, that a deeper concern draws the attention of not only the two contemporary scholars, but Plato's in the central section of *Theaetetus*. What is at stake is nothing less than how we philosophers ought to live our lives, and why.

Is it not inevitable that the person who responds to the desire to know the highest truths will seem ridiculous to other people and will risk both personal animosity and injustice?[56] Philosophers of the Socratic sort will indeed seem ridiculous to the great majority of people but will rarely give it a thought. Approbation and honors awarded by cave dwellers, the great majority of the great majority, are utterly worthless—despite the great worth of each individual cave dweller. The harder case arises from the philosopher's attachments to other people who, try as they might, cannot fathom the life of the philosopher.[57] That less common, but more poignant, case is seen in *Crito* where Socrates' childhood friend continues to urge Socrates to escape, despite the most sustained argument we ever hear from Socrates: that it is never right

---

[56] This is the problem Jim Lesher set for me in 2004 and that has been the stone in my boot ever since. I am all too aware that I have not yet met his challenge adequately.

[57] The notion of attachment, together with the commitment to education that will emerge below, reflects the broad sense of *erōs* found in the writings of the Russian anarchist (and prince), Peter Kropotkin (1924:94): "Plato understood by Eros not only a mutual attachment of two beings, but also the sociality based on the accord between the desires of the individual and the desires of all the other members of society. His Eros was also what we now call *sociability, mutual sympathy*, the feeling which, as can be seen from the previously mentioned facts taken from the life of animals and of human beings, *permeates the whole world of living creatures and which is just as necessary a condition of their lives as is the instinct of self-preservation*."

to do wrong. Some philosophers will be impelled by their knowledge of good and bad to take risks because the results of ignorance are so often disastrous, education is our defense against ignorance, and philosophical education (the elenchus, dialectics) is the most effective form of moral education. Others may simply calculate that responding to the desire to know the highest truths is a surer path to right action and thus to *eudaimonia* than any proffered alternative. The degree of risk philosophers face is usually a matter of political and social circumstances over which an individual has little influence. The greater the role a philosopher takes in the education of the young, perhaps, the greater the risk of animosity and injustice, but fear of retaliation does not motivate the real-world philosopher. Both Socrates and Plato put the education of the young first in their activist philosophical lives, and although both suffered, neither gave up. Even if it were absolutely certain that philosophers would always be misunderstood, despised, and treated unjustly, *erōs* aimed at truth is not satisfied with simulacra. Philosophy is thus the *only* way of life for the real-world philosopher, who is as bound to truth-seeking as to drawing breath.

Off-Stage Tragedy: Profanation of the Mysteries

The tragedy of the *Symposium* is not *in* the *Symposium*; it is not Agathon's speech[58] or that of Pausanias,[59] not Aristophanes' folktale,[60] not Alcibiades' disappointment at having failed to consummate his attraction to Socrates, not ours from being forced to choose between incommensurable types of knowledge, not played out off-stage as the result of Socrates' mistreatment of Alcibiades, and not Alcibiades' having betrayed Athens—or so I have tried to show. The two tragedies of the *Symposium* correspond to its two dramatic dates, the events of the months after 416 (religious hysteria) and 399 (reli-

---

[58] The tragedian Agathon's speech (194e4–197e8) is tragic in style, having the rhetorical structure of an encomium, embellishments, and studied poetic meters, even while it adds something playful (παιδιᾶς combined with σπουδῆς μετρίας). Dover 1980:123–124 catalogues the variety of meters in Agathon's peroration (197d1–e5); cf. Hunter 2004:73.

[59] Corrigan 1997:61 remarks on the "terrifying reality of Pausanias' speech" with its "thorough-going immoralism." What immoralism? Corrigan goes on to say that all the speeches before Socrates' have "prismatic, deconstructive ambiguity"—which sounds scary, but not tragic.

[60] Waterfield 1994:81, 95 remarks on the "sadness of Aristophanes' doctrine," a "tragic tale of man's original sin and its consequences." The human condition is "unfulfilled and unfulfillable longing" for "wholeness" through sex which, by its nature, offers only a sporadic, partial, and temporary respite. Wardy 2002:20 expresses some sympathy when he locates the tragedy of the *Symposium* in the fact that "All lovers would immediately take up Hephaestus' offer to weld them together inseparably, realizing that permanent unification was what they had desired all along (192e5–6)." This view seems better characterized as pathetic.

gious backlash).[61] Thoughtless religious fervor is dangerous, a persistent and insidious kind of ignorance that leads to error and that can be perpetuated by priests and priestesses. In this context, Diotima is an ambiguous character.

In the summer after Agathon's celebration, Alcibiades—always in quest of honors and glory—set an unprecedented Olympic record, entering seven teams in the chariot race, and finishing first, second, and fourth.[62] As spring rolled around again, he had determined that he should lead Athens on an invasion of Sicily and persuaded the Assembly of it over Nicias' objections.[63] Both men were elected to lead, with a third general as well, Lamachus, to settle disagreements between Alcibiades and Nicias. The story becomes complicated at just this point (see Figure 2) when it becomes important to understand the sequence of events. Preparations for the invasion began. When nearly complete, almost all the city's herms were desecrated in a single night. Hermes being the god of travel, the act was viewed as a terrible omen, and rumors spread that there was a plot against the democracy. A commission was appointed that offered rewards for information about any act of *asebeia*. When the fleet was at the point of embarking, a slave named Andromachus accused Alcibiades and nine others of having profaned the Eleusinian mysteries in a private home some time before. One of the accused was caught and executed, eight escaped capture by fleeing the city and forfeiting their property and citizenship. Alcibiades demanded a trial, but his enemies prevailed.[64] The fleet sailed. The commission then heard testimony, provided by the metic Teucrus, that Phaedrus and others had profaned the mysteries. Teucrus also testified that Eryximachus and others had desecrated herms;[65] all fled the city.[66]

---

[61] See Furley 1996. Halperin (2005:56) says, "We read the *Symposium* possessed of a tragic knowledge that is denied the characters at the moment of their speaking. They are surrounded by deep shadows of which they are unaware."

[62] It was in all the papers: Thucydides 6.16.2, Isocrates *On the Team of Horses* (fr. 16) 34, Demosthenes *Against Meidias* 21 145; but his son was still being sued in 397 because Alcibiades did not own one of the teams he had entered. See Nails 2002:s.v. and Excursus 1.

[63] Thucydides 6.8–26. The Sicilian invasion was to be the most complete and disastrous failure of the war, costly of men and morale, and toppling the democracy briefly in 411.

[64] Our source for the claim that eight men fled is Andocides 1.16, who provides the evidence in 400. As Dover 1970:280n1 points out, citing Thucydides 6.53.1, some of them (e.g. Alcibiades' three known comrades) may in fact have remained free under Alcibiades' protection until they all fled together from Thurii.

[65] See Mark McPherran's contribution to this volume for a number of insights into Eryximachus' important role in the dialogue as a whole.

[66] Teucrus also implicated himself, but in exchange for the immunity granted all who testified; he was later honored with a reward at the Panathenaea. Phaedrus was never accused of desecrating herms, though the erroneous view that he did has spun out of control since Dover 1970 (see Nails 2002:233–234).

Figure 2. Historical incidents in the aftermath of Plato's *Symposium*: central story, 416, and dramatic frame, 399.

Celebrating Agathon's victory	Later accused of	Accused by	Outcome
AGATHON, son of Tisamenus			
PAUSANIAS of Cerameis*			
PHAEDRUS of Myrrhinus, son of Pythocles*	profaning the mysteries	Teucrus, metic	fled into exile
(Acumenus, Eryximachus' father)	desecrating herms	Teucrus, metic	unknown
ERYXIMACHUS, son of Acumenus*	profaning the mysteries	Lydus, slave	fled into exile
ALCIBIADES of Scambonidae, son of Clinias*	profaning the mysteries	Andromachus, slave	trial postponed, embarked to Sicily†
	profaning the mysteries	Agariste, wife of Damon	recalled, defected to Sparta
SOCRATES of Alopece, son of Sophroniscus*	impiety (asebeia)	Meletus, Anytus, Lycon	executed
ARISTODEMUS of Cydathenaeum			
ARISTOPHANES of Cydathenaeum, son of Philippus			

Usually in Alcibiades' company	Later accused of	Accused by	Outcome
ADEIMANTUS of Scambonidae, son of Leucolophides*	profaning the mysteries	Agariste, wife of Damon	shared exile with Alcibiades
AXIOCHUS of Scambonidae, son of Alcibiades	profaning the mysteries	Agariste, wife of Damon	shared exile with Alcibiades
ALCIBIADES of Phegous	fraud	Dioclides, blackmailer	shared exile with Alcibiades
Spurned by Socrates, 222b1–2			
CHARMIDES, son of Glaucon*	profaning the mysteries	Agariste, wife of Damon	fled into exile, returned by 404
EUTHYDEMUS, son of Diocles			

* Present also in *Protagoras*, set c. 433/2 at the house of Callias of Alopece, son of Hipponicus.
† Alcibiades assisted the Spartans and Persians until the oligarchy of 411 collapsed; he then accepted command of the Athenian fleet in the Hellespont and returned to Athens for four months in 407, but was dismissed that year from his command and was killed in 404. Adeimantus was chosen (not elected) general in 407/6 and served again in 406/5 and 405/4. Axiochus was active in Athenian politics again in 407.

Phaedrus' house was occupied by Diogiton and three orphans, and his new wife went back to her family. Tensions rose. A third accuser, Agariste (wife of Damon, known from *Republic* and *Laches*) charged Alcibiades and two of his companions with profaning the mysteries in the house of Charmides, Plato's uncle; swift state triremes were sent to bring Alcibiades back to Athens for trial, so he jumped ship at Thurii and defected to the Spartans, giving them useful advice for defeating the Athenians in Sicily and at home. Eryximachus' father, Acumenus, was accused of profaning the mysteries by the slave Lydus; and a third of Alcibiades' friends was accused of aiding blackmail. Finally, the real herm-smashers were identified (a drinking club) and executed,[67] so some prisoners awaiting trial (including Plato's cousin Critias), were released.

That period of months was a time of mass religious hysteria in Athens. In addition to tortures and summary executions in the early days (some in error), and regular executions later, there were about fifty men who fled Athens and were sentenced to death *in absentia*. All lost their property and citizenship, all their families were affected, and none returned before 407, if then. Moreover, it cost Athens Alcibiades' leadership, to which the Athenian defeat in Sicily is sometimes attributed and for which Socrates has sometimes been blamed.

I focus on the profanations because the *Symposium* does, explicitly illustrating how the accusations could have come about from slaves and a woman, and foreshadowing what will happen to the happy party in the following months. To profane the mysteries, punishable by death, was to give away secrets about them, whether by acting them out, parodying them, or talking about the parts that only initiates were allowed to hear. Agathon's slaves were coming and going at their tasks, catching bits of what was going on, and the women were elsewhere in the house—probably in an adjacent room. Two particular speeches are telling. Diotima's of course. She not only tells about the higher mysteries, she first announces that she will (209e5–210a3), and then uses the appropriate technical vocabulary as she does so. The other is Alcibiades'. Half drunk, he says exactly what would cause any slave or woman overhearing the men to pay closer attention: "you wouldn't have heard it from me, if first of all—as the saying goes—the truth weren't in the wine, whether without slaves present or with them" (217e2–4), and "You slaves—and anyone else here who's uninitiated [βέβηλος] and a boor—fit some biggish doors to your ears" (218b6–8). Plato makes it easy to imagine that this is something

---

[67] See Thucydides 6.60–61, 6.88–93. Dover argues that, while Thucydides seems skeptical of Andocides' testimony, the Athenian jury was in a position to know and to confirm what he claimed.

Alcibiades may have said on other occasions. But when there is a reward for reporting what one has overheard, or if one thinks the gods will punish Athens if those guilty of *asebeia* are not rooted out, there is a motivation to accuse.

Who escaped unscathed? Socrates for a while. Agathon and Pausanias, but they left Athens together permanently and joined the court at Macedonia in about 408. Aristophanes was unscathed, and his *Frogs* of 406 updated the subject, lamenting the city's loss of Agathon's poetry (83–85), and bringing onto the stage a whole chorus of Eleusinian initiates (from line 316). The play was first performed following the naval disaster at Aegospotami, when the Athenians feared the Spartans would sail into the harbor and massacre them all; Aristophanes adapts a line from tragedy to describe how the Athenians even then pinned their hopes on Alcibiades, banished but still alive: the city "yearns for him, detests him, and wants to have him" (1425).[68] But even then Aristophanes was still assaulting Socrates,[69] the only other guest from Agathon's celebration still known to be in the city besides Aristophanes himself:

> So what's stylish is not to sit
> beside Socrates and chatter,
> casting the arts aside
> and ignoring the best
> of the tragedian's craft.
> To hang around killing time
> in pretentious conversation
> and hairsplitting twaddle
> is the mark of a man who's lost his mind.
>
> Aristophanes *Frogs* 1491–1499, trans. Henderson

Off-Stage Tragedy: Socrates' Execution

The *Symposium* frame shows a flurry of interest in the story of that long-ago banquet, probably precipitated by news of Socrates' indictment: the spring of 399, between the preliminary hearing Socrates attended after the *Euthyphro*, but before his trial, is the dramatic date of the frame.[70] Some months were required between Meletus' initial accusation and Socrates' execution, almost

---

[68] Dionysus, speaking to Aeschylus in the underworld, ποθεῖ μέν, ἐχθαίρει δέ, βούλεται δ ' ἔχειν, adapted from Ion *Guards* fr. 44.

[69] He had attacked Socrates in 414 in *Birds* too (1280–1283, 1553–1555).

[70] No sooner had I committed myself to the vague dramatic date of about 400 for the *Symposium* frame (Nails 2002:314), than David O'Connor persuaded me of this more precise date.

all of the period after notice of the accusation against Socrates had been published on whitened tablets in the agora and a date set for the pre-trial examination (ἀνάκρισις). Both the *Theaetetus* and the *Symposium* mention fact-checking with Socrates to get stories straight during that interim.[71]

Other things had been going on in Athens, things overshadowed by—though also brought on by—defeat in Sicily, revolt of the subject allies, rule of the Four Hundred, Spartan victory, rule of the Thirty, civil war, and the failed reconciliation agreement. A commission established in 410 had completely rewritten the laws by 404, for example, and a board established in 403 was assisted by the Council in adding new laws in response to the city's recent history. A new legal era was proclaimed from the archon year 403/2, at the same time an official religious calendar was adopted and inscribed, and after which all litigation was limited to laws inscribed 410–403. Proposing any change to them was criminalized, so Socrates had no legal standing to challenge the one-day trial law (*Apology* 37a7–b2), much less the *asebeia* law under which he was charged. His accusers had only to prove that Socrates had at some time in his seventy years committed *asebeia*.

The rise in the number of *asebeia* cases in Athenian courts at the turn of the century resulted from a religious backlash against what many Athenians saw as the insidious effects of sophists and natural philosophers who had caused the city's youths to question tradition and the role of the gods in Athens' affairs. Aristophanes' *Clouds* had illustrated it: chop-logic and hair-splitting instead of respect for custom, naturalistic explanations for divine phenomena. But so do Plato's dialogues illustrate Socrates' naturalistic explanations and interests (*Theaetetus* 152e, 153c–d, 173e–174a; *Phaedo* 96a–100a); Socrates says outright that he doesn't accept the poets' stories of the gods' wrongdoing (*Euthyphro* 6a–c) although the quarreling gods of the poets *were* the gods of Athens; Socrates' questioning of Meletus would not be easy for the average juryman to distinguish from cross-questioning by sophists or those trained by sophists to win court cases whether innocent or guilty (*Apology* 26e6–27a7); and Socrates' defense of his *daimonion* (31d1) and claim that Apollo commanded his practice (20e–23b) appear only to have intensified the jury's misunderstanding of who he was. It would have been one thing if Socrates had kept it all to himself while performing his religious civic obligations as always, but youths found him irresistible.[72] In an anti-intellectual climate of religious

---

[71] This is evidence in the dialogues for the composition of Socratic *logoi* before the death of Socrates.

[72] Socrates diagnoses his predicament correctly at *Euthyphro* 3c7–d2; cf. 2c–d.

intolerance, things become worse for such philosophers. What was harmlessly ridiculous in 416 was criminally impious by 399.

The *Symposium* is one of the dialogues in the series, beginning with the death of Socrates' look-alike in the *Theaetetus* and moving with the Greek tragic sense of inevitably to Socrates' death in the *Phaedo*. We don't see that at first. With an emotional attachment to Socrates, most of us blame the Athenians and consider Socrates innocent when we first read the dialogues. In the longer run, foreknowledge of that cup of hemlock refines and heightens our intellectual response along with our emotional attachment, and we finally see all the condemning evidence against Socrates laid out before us in the dialogues themselves. Socrates does not blame the Athenians, however, and for a familiar reason: they did not willingly do wrong. As we know, Socrates says he should be taken aside and instructed, not dragged into court, for corrupting the youth because, if he corrupted them, he did so unwillingly (*Apology* 25e6–26a4, 30b5–7). Likewise, he says of the Athenians, "Whatever word it [the state] applies to it [the good], that's surely what a state aims at when it legislates" (*Theaetetus* 177e4–6, tr. McDowell). The Athenians thus ought not to be blamed, but to be understood and instructed. Their instruction was Socrates' life's work. There was no evil conspiracy against the good Socrates. More profound and more tragic, his ordeal resulted from a catastrophic mistake, a misunderstanding that could not be reconciled in the single day the law allowed for his trial.[73]

[73] This paper is shorter and clearer than the version I presented at the Center for Hellenic Studies Conference on Plato's *Symposium* in August 2005. I deeply appreciate the participants' comments and conversations, which benefited my understanding as well as my paper; but I feel a special debt—a joyful one—to Ruby Blondell, Jim Lesher, William Levitan, Frisbee Sheffield, and the Center's anonymous readers for their telling criticism and helpful suggestions. A later version of part of the paper was presented to the Department of Philosophy at the University of Ottawa in April of 2006.

Nine

The Virtues of Platonic Love

Gabriela Roxana Carone

SOCRATES' SPEECH ON LOVE IN THE *SYMPOSIUM* (201–212), reporting his conversation with the Mantinean priest Diotima, stands as prima facie counterintuitive. First, it is not clear that it has anything to say about interpersonal love at all; and even if it does, it might seem to offer a view that conforms pretty well to our popular notion of "Platonic Love," one that does not involve any personal commitment, and that is spiritual rather than physical. How, if at all, is the speech supposed to help us understand ordinary love in our practical lives?[1] In this paper I wish to argue, by considering various objections, that the speech can be seen as providing useful tools for enhancing our understanding of love, both from a descriptive and a normative perspective.

We may start by briefly summarizing the main claims of the speech: (1) love is a state of mind directed towards beauty; (2) love is a state of mind expressing the yearning of humans for happiness;[2] (3) Love is a desire for perpetual possession of the beautiful, and thus for procreation as a means of perpetuation; (4) procreation through the soul or spirit is of higher value than physical procreation, and thus guarantees a higher or larger share in the Beautiful; (5) the highest manifestation of Beauty—the Form of Beauty—is to be reached after a process involving several steps—usually called the "Ladder of Love"—of which the individual physical body is only the first, and ultimately shown to be severely lacking in the property we all strive for.

While (2) might seem intuitively right—after all, few people would disagree that in searching for an object of love, one is searching for happiness—the other claims seem vulnerable to objections. For example:

---

[1] Christopher Rowe, for example, doubts that one can extract from this work much in the way of "general messages about personal relationships" (1998a:7).

[2] Talk of "states of mind" is here intended in a non-committal way. For love as a *diathesis* see e.g. 207b1, c1.

(1) seems to imply that when we love, what we love is a universal property, beauty, rather than an individual. This may appear problematic for various reasons: First, it seems to overlook a uniqueness in the person we love that cannot be reduced to her being a particular instantiation of a universal property (let us call it the "Uniqueness Problem"). Second, it could be thought that one may be drawn to, and love, precisely the ugly aspects of a person, so it is just wrong to claim that beauty is the aspect of something to which all love is directed. At least, it is not immediately clear that we are all attracted to Beauty and only to Beauty (call this the "Attraction to Beauty Problem").

(4) might also be resisted if it is taken to imply, first, that a life devoted e.g. to intellectual endeavors or artistic creativity (procreating in beauty through books, education, or works of art) is to be preferred to a life devoted to procreating children, and second, that one can be as much "in love" with art, philosophy or one's career as one is with a human being one is attracted to.

(5) is probably the greatest target of criticism, insofar as it seems to imply, first, that Platonic love at its summit excludes love of individuals, and second, that the individual that one loves can at most have value as a means—or rung in the ladder—and not as an end in itself.

While I agree that in many of these areas the text seems to be challenging our intuitions, I believe it deserves more credit than one might be inclined to give it at first sight. For, even where Diotima says something that does not sit well with our ordinary preconceptions about love, I wish to show that she has the resources to respond to our objections. The force of the speech, I contend, consists in working partly with preconceptions that we may share but showing us from there that, if we are to be utterly consistent, the conclusions that flow from them may differ markedly from many of the ordinary conceptions about love with which we began.

Love and Beauty

The *Charmides* had suggested a view about the individuation of mental acts that seems to be present also in the *Symposium*. According to this view, an act is defined, and individuated, by being directed at a distinctive kind of object.[3] Thus, fear is of the dreadful, hearing is of sound, love (*erōs*) is of beauty (cf. *Charmides* 167d–168a). This latter claim receives further elaboration in the *Symposium*, where Socrates, playing with the personification of *erōs* as a *daimōn*

---

[3] See here my 1998:273–274 and 2001:118.

or demigod, maintains that "*erōs* is love of Beauty, not of Ugliness" (201a9–10).[4] Thus, we have the joint claims that (1) *erōs* is "about" something; and (2) *erōs* is for something insofar as it is beautiful. Let us analyze each in turn.

The view that at least some emotions are about something has its contemporary resonances. Thus, Gabriele Taylor speaks of the "determinable" quality of the object of an emotion, by which the emotion is directed to that object in the first place:[5] fear, for example, exists insofar as its object is felt to be dangerous, even though "dangerous" admits of further determination (e.g. it is a determinate quality of this particular object of my fear that it has sharp claws and is aggressive). The ability to specify a determinable quality, according to Taylor, enables us to assess whether our emotions are reasonable or unreasonable (if the thing after all does not possess the quality that I believe it to have, then the emotion is unjustified): to this extent, it is possible to apply some rational scrutiny to our emotions. Yet Taylor fails to find a determinable quality that "love" is about, in a way that seems to make this emotion prima facie more intractable than others.

By these lights, Diotima's speech in the *Symposium* would seem to offer a more optimistic response to the question about the determinable quality of the object of love by telling us that it is *beauty*. Whether this answer is satisfactory, however, is a different matter, and we might wonder to what extent we are allowed to relate her remarks on *erōs* to the emotion we ordinarily call 'love'.

To be sure, the Greek term *erōs* seems rather more restricted in meaning than our English "love." What is distinctive of *erōs*, and need not be present in the other kinds of love, is the notion of a lack that triggers the desire for a fulfillment of that lack. Sexual desire is the most basic manifestation of *erōs*, but *erōs* would also encompass any striving for something stemming from a lack. Thus, when Peter is in love with Mary, part of his feeling (the one corresponding to *erōs*) consists in feeling that he *needs* Mary for his life to be fuller; he misses her insofar as that latter state is not achieved. (To this point, one could also feel *erōs* for, say, reading, if that desire stems from a lack and represents reading as the object that would render satisfaction. Thus conceived, my love of reading would also be a case of *erōs*, and we shall see later how Diotima exploits this.) By contrast, when Peter cares for Mary's well being, he may not be in a state of need; he may spontaneously and generously feel inclined to help her and protect her. Insofar as Peter is in the latter state of mind, we can say he is in a state of *philia* (of the sort Alcestis displayed in dying

---

[4] All translations are my own.
[5] Cf. Taylor 1979:165.

for her husband, *Symposium* 179b–c)[6] or in a state of *agapē*. Thus, the word the Christians chose to refer to God's "love" was *agapē*—they could not, obviously, choose *erōs*, insofar as *erōs* would have conveyed a desire and an attraction stemming from a need that a superior being like God could not feel for his inferior creatures. Similarly, Diotima contends in the *Symposium* that god, insofar as he is perfect, lacks nothing, which implies he feels no *erōs* (cf. 202c–d, 203e–204a).[7]

Thus the English "love" only partially overlaps with the ancient Greek *erōs*. But, despite this restriction, the speech still has many enlightening things to say about the "erotic" part of our love, where *erōs* need not be exclusively sexual, even though sexual desire is not excluded from it.

A definition of *erōs* is presented in the *Symposium* (199e–200b, 204d–e), as part of an argument that may be reconstructed as follows:

1. *Erōs* is a wanting, or longing for, the beautiful.
2. If A wants, or longs for, B that means that: (i) A does not have B, though (ii) A desires to have B, or make B its own.
3. Thus, *erōs* desires to make the beautiful its own.

Premises 1 and 2 express constitutive features of *erōs*: Premise 2 indicates that *erōs* pertains to the generic kind of "desire" (*epithumia*, cf. 200a–b), and, as such, involves a lack that seeks for its satisfaction; premise 1 adds that *erōs* is, specifically, a desire for the *beautiful*. (This specific difference is worth highlighting by contrast with other kinds of desire, which can also be individuated by their specific objects: thirst, for example, is desire for drink, and hunger for food.[8] Of course these objects may overlap. If, for example, I feel *erōs* for food,[9] that would occur, according to the *Symposium*, insofar as I find food beautiful. That is, beauty is the property that everything must possess in order for one to feel *erōs* for it.) While premise 2 seems unproblematic—particularly if one accepts the Greek usage of the word *erōs* as described above, in contrast e.g. with other forms of love—it is 1 that looks more difficult to grasp.

Diotima claims, in fact, that *erōs* "is love for beautiful things" (204d), but immediately proceeds to add that one can put "good" in place of "beautiful,"

---

[6] Even though *erōs* can also be a component of this experience, as explicitly attested: cf. 179c; also Nehamas and Woodruff 1989:xiv.

[7] On *erōs* and *philia* in the *Symposium* see also Ludwig 2002:212–220; on the triad *erōs, philia* and *agapē* (a noun which as such does not occur in Plato) see Santas 1988:8–9; on *agapē* in the Christian Bible see Nygren 1953 and Osborne 1994:24–51.

[8] Cf. *Republic* IV 437d–e.

[9] At e.g. *Republic* IX 573d *erōs* (as grows in the tyrannical soul) is associated with feasts and luxuries. On "*erōs* for food and drink" in Homer see e.g. Hunter 2004:16.

so that love can be rendered as a desire to make *good things* one's own (204e). The ease with which "beautiful" and "good" are interchanged may baffle us (after all, the *Charmides* had claimed that the good is the distinctive object of another faculty, namely wish, *boulēsis*, 167e). Yet the *Symposium* is very far from detaching moral from aesthetic value. It uses *kalon* (beautiful) and *agathon* (good) as words that can jointly help to describe the *valuable* aspect of an object that triggers our attraction to it.[10] According to this view, for example, crime is repulsive not only because it is morally reprehensible but also because it is aesthetically ugly. (After all, in English we can also call a good theory a beautiful theory, and a bad act an ugly act.) The interesting implication underlying this claim, however, is that Plato seems to believe that *erōs* for any object, whatever it may be (Mary or philosophy) is for that object *qua* beautiful; *erōs* could never be for an object *qua* ugly. In a similar way, Plato had Socrates claim in the early dialogues that one's wish is—only—for the *good*.[11] If this theory is maintained in the *Symposium*, and if it equates "good" with "beautiful," there is an implication that all the *erōs* one feels—however irrational it may seem—involves wishing for the good.

Now, this—let us call it—"teleological" view of erotic desire[12] may certainly be the target of criticism, as it could be argued that desire need not be for any good or beautiful at all, and it is here that Taylor's point might seem particularly poignant. In cases of infatuation, for example (which Plato would surely count as a type of *erōs*), a person may be drawn to another while recognizing that such a drive is bad or irrational. Further, a masochistic kind of personality may feel attraction towards abusive people, while finding their treatment not only bad and painful, but also ugly. Along these lines, in the eponymous dialogue, Meno had objected to Socrates that it is possible for people to wish and pursue the bad rather than the good. Socrates, however, had countered that if someone wishes the bad (which is also harmful), it must be because she finds it good in some way, as no one wishes to be harmed and miserable (cf. *Meno* 77b–78b). Similar reflections could be applied to the *Symposium*: if one loves something ugly, it must be insofar as one finds it beautiful.

---

[10] Cf. Nussbaum 1986:178n: "The *kalon* is meant to include ... everything that is valuable in the world," so that it might be more accurate to render it as "valuable"; also Price 1997:16 on subtle distinctions between the two notions. On the force of Plato's objectivist assumption here see Gentzler 2004.

[11] See e.g. *Gorgias* 466b–468d, *Meno* 78b, and cf. *Protagoras* 358c–d; also my 2004:61–67.

[12] *Erōs* in the *Symposium* can be said to be teleological in many ways: (1) insofar as Love is directed to the good; (2) insofar as Love has a purpose in nature (206–207); (3) insofar as Love is of use for humans (204c).

To illustrate this point, let us consider the following two scenarios:

1. Tom is attracted to Mary who is indeed ugly-and-bad, even though he finds her beautiful-and-good.
2. Tom is attracted to the ugly aspects of Mary.

The *Symposium* would allow 1, along the lines presented above, but deny that Tom is attracted to the ugly aspects of Mary *qua* ugly. Rather, Tom is attracted to the ugly aspects of Mary insofar as he finds those ugly aspects beautiful. That is, Mary may either be found ugly by most, even though Tom finds her beautiful, or Mary may indeed be ugly. In this latter scenario, it would again be denied that Tom could be attracted to Mary, who is really bad and ugly, insofar as he finds her so; rather, 2 would be treated as a case of 1: Tom must find Mary beautiful somehow or other if he is attracted to her. This introduces a distinction between the *subjective* and the *objective* aspects of good/beautiful, and betrays a commitment to some form of realism (aesthetic and/or moral) about properties such as the beautiful, a theory which precludes any sort of reduction of the beautiful to one's own perceptions of it. Controversial as this commitment may be, certain rewards are apparent. For, as we shall see, it is precisely because the reduction cannot be performed that one may have grounds for changing one's perceptions: one who starts being attracted to the "wrong" kind of person (say an abusive one), has potential for growth if she realizes that her value judgments guiding her original choice were mistaken. That is, however fashionable it may seem to say that "beauty" (and for that matter "goodness") is in the eye of the beholder, we come to see on close examination that, by postulating the existence of Beauty/Goodness as an objective value, the *Symposium* is providing us with *standards* by which to make our choices and assess their correctness or otherwise.[13]

Now, if this is so, a new problem might seem to arise: is Diotima claiming that one feels *erōs* for the (objective) Beautiful, or for what one believes to be beautiful? The latter might seem to undermine objectivism, depriving us of those standards that it seemed useful to have. On the other hand, if the claim is that we all feel *erōs* for the objective Beautiful, then we would be committing Diotima to denying that Tom really loves Mary (whose apparently beautiful side is actually ugly), even though he believes he does.

Maybe the latter problem can be resolved counterfactually: Tom would never be attracted to those sides of Mary if he knew better.[14] Now, it is possible

---

[13] See also n22.
[14] For an explanation of a similar problem in the early dialogues concerning our universal desire for the good cf. my 2004:61–67. And after all, if one finds out that a person doesn't have the

that Mary should (and indeed, I shall argue, according to Platonic meta-physics, Mary must) have also, side by side with her "bad" qualities (such as, say, the habit of invidious gossip) some "good" ones (such as, say, kindness to the poor): it may be that Tom loves her for her (even objectively) good side, not her bad one. What the theory would be denying is that Tom may love Mary for her "bad" qualities, unless he finds those qualities somehow or other (mistakenly or not) "beautiful." And this is, as we shall see later, the beginning of the "ladder of Love": one starts by loving an individual, perceptible sample of beauty, which admits of compresence of opposites (insofar as anything in the realm of particulars that admits of a property, also admits of the oppo-site property, so that it is beautiful in one way, ugly in another, or beautiful to some, not to others):[15] to this extent, there is room for subjectivity and differing tastes guiding one's choices. Yet the possibility of ascending to a more stable and uniform standard of Beauty will also mean the possibility of reevaluating, correcting or changing one's choices in the light of those newly acquired standards. Here, then, is a first response to the "Attraction to Beauty Problem," and to which I shall return.

Procreating in Beauty, the Scope of Love, and the Uniqueness Problem

Now, the claim that *erōs* expresses one's basic yearning for happiness seems to capture a common intuition. Even though we may think it is a matter of argument whether that yearning is common to all humans (Aristotle, for example, thought there might be exceptions),[16] it seems that, as we saw in the *Meno*, the claim that no one wishes to be miserable is axiomatic in this kind of philosophy. The interlocutors in both dialogues do not hesitate to agree with it. What is interesting in this regard, however, is not so much whether they should take it as axiomatic, but what consequences follow from its admission. Arguably, we are led to some pretty counterintuitive conclusions, as might be inferred from the following argument (204e–205a):

1. To have the beautiful and good is to be happy.
2. Everyone wishes to be happy.
3. To wish to have the beautiful and good is to be in love.
4. Therefore, everyone is in love!

---

qualities one used to believe she did, one may be willing to concede that one was not in love with that person but with the "idea" of her.

[15] Cf. *Symposium* 211a and below, n21.
[16] See *Nicomachean Ethics* 1.4.1095a17–19.

There are many factors that might make us question the soundness of this argument. First, to make our desire to share in the beautiful and good coextensive with "being in love" seems too broad. Second, if all of us have that desire, the conclusion that we are all in love seems disconcerting. If we are all in love already, why do some people feel that they would love so strongly to be in love? (After all, even Diotima concedes that in colloquial usage "we say that some people love and others don't," 205b.)

It is possible, though, that through this claim Diotima may be trying to show that the experience of *erōs* is less distant to us than it may seem: as long as we feel passion for something (call it a person, or sports, philosophy, an ideal), we are lovers of some sort—all of us, whether for good or bad. For, without the fuel of motivation, we would be inert. It is *erōs*, precisely, that provides the motivational energy,[17] and beauty that is the common target of *erōs* in all its variegated forms. Later on, we are told that there is a "vast sea of Beauty" to behold, under whose aspect we'll realize the kinship of all those things that seem so disconnected and different in kind (210c–d).

But even this might seem hard to understand. Nussbaum (1986:180) expresses her reaction powerfully:

> Just try to think it seriously: this body of this wonderful beloved person is exactly the same in quality as that person's mind and inner life. Both, in turn, the same in quality as the value of Athenian democracy; of Pythagorean geometry; of Eudoxan astronomy. What would it be like to look at a body and to see in it exactly the same shade and tone of goodness and beauty as in a mathematical proof— *exactly* the same, differing only in amount and in location ...?

This opens up a new question, one which Vlastos raised,[18] and Nussbaum tries to address, about the fact that the *Symposium*, in the speech of Diotima, seems to suggest that our love is only for the repeatable properties in an individual, thus missing their "uniqueness and wholeness" (what I have labeled as "the Uniqueness Problem"). Now the *Symposium* gives us an answer as to why love is not of the whole: "Love is neither of half or whole, unless, my friend, it happens to be good" (205e). Aristophanes, a previous speaker in the *Symposium*, had represented picturesquely what it is to yearn for someone,

---

[17] See here the *Republic*, where desire is attached to all parts of the soul, but where *erōs* can also be seen as a single source of motivation that can be diverted to different channels (IX 580d, VI 485a–e), as I have argued in my 2004:69–71.

[18] See Vlastos 1973b.

through the myth of those who were originally round wholes and, by punishment of Zeus, were cut in half, thereafter seeking their irreplaceable "other half" (189d–191d). While this myth may well capture a recognizable experience (we can have the sense of meeting, or even yearning to meet, "the one," that person who makes us complete),[19] Diotima seems to demystify the yearning by telling us that indeed it is the beauty, the property, that we yearn for, rather than the "other half" as such. Even granting the intuitive appeal of Aristophanes' speech, the point here is that no other human half as such, even if we meet it, can possibly satisfy our fundamental desire for completion; to understand that is to become initiated in the ladder of love:

> This is the correct way of approaching matters of love or being led by another: beginning with the beautiful things here and using them as steps, one always goes up for the sake of that Beauty, from one body to two, and from two to all the beautiful bodies, and from beautiful bodies to beautiful pursuits (or forms of behavior, *epitēdeumata*), and from pursuits to beautiful pieces of knowledge, and from pieces of knowledge one ends at this piece of knowledge, which is nothing other than knowledge of that very beauty, until finally one recognizes what is beautiful. Here, if anywhere in life ... is human life worth living: in contemplation of Beauty Itself ... unalloyed, pure and unmixed.
>
> *Symposium* 211b–e

It is the third transition that marks an important shift between stages, which can also be described in terms of different sorts of procreation resulting from one's basic desire for immortality, or for perpetual possession of the beautiful: what the *Symposium* had previously described as pregnancy of soul rather than pregnancy of body (208e–209c, cf. esp. *epitēdeumata* at 211c5 with 209c1). The drive to procreate in beauty explains why people seek to leave behind carnal children, but it also explains the desire to leave a spiritual legacy. Certainly, the step concerning love for ethical behavior (and thus for the soul) is presented as higher than the one concerning love for the body, and accordingly procreation in the former will have higher value than procreation in the latter. This need not exclude carnal procreation, but can simply be seen as emphasizing the right order of priorities—for one would not want to procreate in the body

---

[19] A similar thought seems to underlie talk of "merging of identities" and "ontological dependence" between lovers as found in modern studies of love such as Solomon 1988. Cf. also Scruton 1986, Hunter 1980, Fisher 1977 and 1990, Nozick 1989, Delaney 1996.

if one were to know in advance, for example, that one's children are fated to become incurable criminals. Further, much as the *Symposium* exalts procreation in the soul, special stress is laid on how one cherishes beauty of both body and soul in another person, even when the soul has priority of value: "So he welcomes beautiful bodies more than ugly ones insofar as he is pregnant, and if he encounters a fine, noble and gifted soul, he warmly embraces the combination (*sunamphoteron*)," 209b. That is, the *Symposium* teaches us to honor the people that we love as wholes rather than as objects of merely physical attraction.[20]

Certainly, if one's *erōs* is towards beauty, then one will be inclined to embrace the most beauty one can get. Nussbaum goes on to remark: "So, in each stage of the ascent, the aspiring lover, aided by his teacher, sees relationships between one beauty and another, acknowledges that these beauties are comparable and intersubstitutable" (180).

Should we really take the text to mean that the beauties we encounter are "intersubstitutable"? Here we must pause and reflect briefly on Platonic metaphysics. In the first place, it is true that all singular beauties in the realm of particulars are instances, or exemplifications, of Beauty. At the end of the ladder we shall see them as "images" of it (cf. 212a4). But images are not necessarily intersubstitutable, since the combination of beautiful properties that a particular sample embodies will most likely be unique in each case (let us just imagine making a list of the beautiful properties in the person we love: how complex a task, and how absurd the thought would seem to us that we might just encounter another person with exactly that same complex combination!).

At the same time, Beauty appears to be an all-pervasive property, at least to the extent that, since particulars suffer from compresence of opposites, everything in that realm that is not beautiful in one way will also be beautiful in another. The contrast between these and the Form of Beauty is made clear later on, when we read that: "First, it [the Form] always is and neither comes to be nor passes away, nor does it increase or decrease; next, it is not beautiful in one way and ugly in another, nor beautiful at one time and not at another,

---

[20] Certainly, it could still be argued that the whole we honor is the combination of the beautiful bodily and psychological properties of the person, to the exclusion of her ugly ones. Does this mean not having respect for the person as such? Much depends on our (or, for that matter, Plato's) notion of the person. After all, it might not seem unreasonable to identify a person with her better side, if identity, as Plato believes, is normative, that is, something to aspire to: in this regard, being loved for our good properties would work as an incentive for us to achieve our higher selves and thus grow further in virtue. For an argument along these lines see Price 1981.

nor beautiful in one respect and ugly in another, nor beautiful here and ugly there, as being beautiful to some and ugly to others" (211a).[21] It is, then, the fact that no particular can bear beauty unqualifiedly that makes it incomplete and imperfect in many ways, including the fact that particulars lend themselves to different perspectives. So, I may be attracted to someone because I rightly see the respect in which the person is beautiful (which you may miss, by focusing on her non-beautiful sides), or even because (unlike you) I wrongly take some aspects of her to be beautiful. To some extent, then, it is the ontological makeup of particulars that explains the phenomenology of love (why we tend to be attracted to different people and make the most diverse choices); it even leaves room for some sort of perspectivism based on our perceptions, as it is part of the various senses in which particulars appear beautiful and not beautiful that I may find a particular person beautiful (and thus be attracted to him or her) while the perceived lack of beauty in the same person keeps you away. Of course, this is not tantamount to saying that all perspectives matter the same; for, as was argued above, knowing the correct standards can serve to correct possibly distorted perspectives.[22] But it is the fact that individual beauty is in flux that explains our propensity to perspectivism.[23]

Perspectivism, then, together with the fact that to some extent beauty is everywhere, explains the variegatedness of our choices and attractions, and why there is always some beauty to be discovered even in the most apparently repellent person. The fact that there is beauty everywhere may in fact be seen as a consolation to the person who has suffered a particular loss, were she to

---

[21] I believe that here the various forms of compresence (of which the Form of Beauty is said to be free) must be understood as applying to tokens, and not just to types, as indicated by the context, which has just contrasted the Form of Beauty with the beauty of particulars such as "a certain young boy or man or single pursuit" 210d2–3, and which presents Beauty Itself as the top of a ladder whose first step is precisely an individual beautiful body (cf. *henos*, 211c3).

[22] Thus, a person who knew the correct standards of beauty would not fall back into inaccurate valuations of beauty when returning to the realm of particulars. Rather, the person who has reached a grasp of objective beauty would align her own valuations with objective standards. To the extent that a thing participates in beauty, and I recognize the exact degree or respect of such participation, my valuation is objectively correct, and it is precisely the grasp of the Form (what beauty is) that provides the criterion for assessing the correctness or otherwise of that valuation. The philosopher who has reached the top of the ladder can thus use the Forms as correct standards precisely insofar as grasping their essence will allow one to tell accurately whether or to what extent other things participate in it (just as the liberated prisoner in the Cave will be better able, after seeing the Forms, to discern their images, since he will know "the images and of what they are images," *Republic* VII 520c). More precisely, knowing what beauty is will allow one to distinguish correctly a person's beautiful and ugly aspects – and this is how one will be able to correct possibly distorted perspectives.

[23] For flux understood as compresence of opposites see e.g. Irwin 1977b.

climb higher in the ladder. But would that mean that a particular instantiation of beauty that was lost—and that was bound to be lost, cf. *Symposium* 211a—can easily be interchanged with another?

To think so would be a tremendous leap of logic, one that Diotima is careful not to make. Not only can people embody beautiful properties in complex combinations that may be very hard to duplicate; in addition, particulars can participate in Beauty to a *greater or lesser extent*. Presumably, the reason why Socrates was found so attractive to many, as the speech of Alcibiades will later on make vivid, is that he instantiated beauty as no other did. He, so to speak, made the Form shine through him to such an extent that, by the less philosophically trained, like Alcibiades, he could easily be confused with the paradigm of Beauty, that is, the Form itself.[24] And even the writer of the *Symposium* presumably found Socrates sufficiently irreplaceable that he felt drawn to compose dialogues after his powerful inspiration, thus perpetuating the beauty that he had seen in him and begetting in it by leaving behind "children of the soul." Neither is it denied that a complete relation with another which includes *erōs* will also include other aspects of love for one's companion that might be closer to an emotion such as *philia*; and it is because of *philia* (together with one's *erōs* for higher values) that one may be drawn to help one's partner grow. Let us elaborate this point by looking into the issue of personal commitment.

Personal Commitment and the Goal of One's Erotic Initiation

Does not the *Symposium* convey the thought that reaching the top of the ladder (contemplating beauty) would be the very end of one's erotic pursuits, so that interaction with other people turns out to be a mere instrument (or step in the ladder)?[25] From that perspective, does the theory of the *Symposium* leave room for personal commitment at all, if by comparison with the Form of Beauty all bodies and the like could be perceived as "mortal nonsense" (211e)?

First of all, it is true that we are told that contemplating Beauty is the end (*hou heneken*) of our previous toil (*ponois*, 210e), and it is suggested that its contemplation will give us sufficient detachment to realize the smallness of the things (the mortal things, *thnēta*, 211e3) that uninitiated lovers agonize about—just as the scientist who contemplates the vastness of the

---

[24] See n33.

[25] The concern about treating people as means towards some larger ethical goal is not confined to the *Symposium*. Michael Stocker 1997 finds a similar problem posed by the constraints of modern ethical theories such as consequentialism and deontology.

universe comes to realize the narrow dimensions of his own life within it. And it is Beauty more than anything else that makes our lives worth living (*biōton*, 211d2), if it is ideals and values more than anything else that give meaning to them; values without which we wouldn't even be able to recognize the goodness of other objects of our choice. But we still want to "beget true virtue" (212a)[26] and thus come back to the realm of particulars with an altered perspective—just as the liberated prisoner in the *Republic* (VII 520c) goes back to the cave after contemplation of the Good. To this extent, at least, it is not the Form, but the others to whom we come back in our practical lives that are the final destination of our erotic initiations,[27] which are prefaced precisely as targeted to making us understand "the correct love of boys," 211b5–6.[28]

At the same time, the right choice of companion may be viewed as a way of sustaining the *erōs* for that beauty which can now be seen more lastingly and fully instantiated in that individual than in others:

> For by being in contact with the beautiful and associating with such, one begets and generates those things which one has long been pregnant with, and whether present or absent he remembers. And jointly with the beloved he nurtures the offspring, so that such people have much more to share between them than they would with children and a firmer friendship (*philian bebaioteran*).
>
> *Symposium* 209c

[26] *Pace* Strauss 2001:239, who claims that here, given the interrogative mode in which Plato presents the issue to us, "he is not concerned with generating true virtue, he is only concerned with beholding beautiful things and beauty itself." As a matter of fact, the grammatical form of the Greek at 212a3–5 most likely indicates endorsement by the speaker.

[27] Begetting true virtue would result from spiritual pregnancy, of the sort described at 209a, which is said to "beget virtue" in a context where the "biggest and finest part of wisdom (*phronēsis*)" includes no less than the administration of cities, and is called moderation and justice; in a similar practical manner, at 209b8 the discussion of virtue is related to how the good man should be and what pursuits (*epitēdeumata*) he should practice. Certainly, one could argue that the "true virtue" of 212a is supposed to supersede the virtue discussed in 209a–b, since that passage comes before the "biggest mysteries" of 210a–212a, so that "begetting true virtue" is a merely contemplative affair (after all, we had been told about "begetting thoughts" at 210d5–6, which suggests the begetting needn't be practical). The burden of proof, however, lies in this opposing view, and I shall argue that a more interesting reading of the text results if we take Diotima's speech as a consistent whole rather than have one section (the one about the "highest mysteries") nullify the other, much as the ascent is undoubtedly supposed to give a theoretical foundation to our ethical lives.

[28] I am not here addressing the pederastic assumptions of the *Symposium* and its reflection of its own historical context (for a discussion, see Dover 1989 and the paper in the present volume by Luc Brisson); I take it that many of its claims can be applied to both heterosexual and homosexual love in our own age.

Thus, just after we are told that everything is in flux and nothing stays the same in the mortal realm (cf. 207d–208b), it is now insinuated that *erōs*, when directed to a beautiful whole including above all the soul, can precisely bring some stability to our lives, a stability in turn supported by *philia*. It is worth noting to this effect that the *Symposium* does not contain any theory about the preexistence or postmortem survival of the soul; rather, the only (*monon*, 207d2) form of immortality envisaged is through reproduction or leaving a legacy, either carnal or spiritual. But, without assuming a theory of recollection of the *Phaedo* sort,[29] we still find how important it is to have constant reminders of the value or values that ground the meaning of our lives.[30] And it is precisely that personal bond alluded to at *Symposium* 209a that helps one sustain the communing with the Form envisaged at the end of Diotima's speech (cf. *theōmenou kai sunontos autōi*, 212a2). If, as in other dialogues, also in the *Symposium* philosophy remains not a solipsistic but a communal affair (recall here Socrates' crowning his report of Diotima's speech by declaring that he has been "persuaded" by its truth, and that he feels a desire to "persuade others too" about it [cf. *pepeismenos de peirōmai kai tous allous peithein*, 212b2–3] as well as to exhort them [cf. *tois allois parakeleuomai*, b6–7]),[31] reaching the top of the ladder must be seen not as excluding but as grounding and enriching the practical dimension of our lives (*erōs* being a *sunergon*, 212b3–4), as it provides the scenario where the enlightened lover not only communes with the Form but is also able to use it to inform his practical existence. And this will in turn have the consequence that, once we have grasped the correct standards of beauty, there is more of a guarantee that our love choices will be the right ones, and thus more enduring.[32]

---

[29] For a recent discussion of its absence in the *Symposium* see Sheffield 2001a.

[30] It is suggestive that the Greek *tou kalou* at 209c2 (in the expression "by being in contact with the beautiful and associating with such") is ambiguous, as it can be either neuter or masculine. While the latter reading may suggest remembering one's beautiful companion, the former would proleptically suggest something like the Forms—after all, the language used for communing with it (*haptomenos, homilōn*, ibid.) is used, later in the *Symposium* and elsewhere, in relation to the Forms: cf. *ephatomenōi Symposium* 212a5, *homilein Republic* VI 500c, *haptesthai Phaedo* 65b, *ephaptesthai Timaeus* 90a.

[31] Cf. e.g. *Gorgias* 527e, *Republic* 531e–532b, 534b–c. Even Diotima herself, whom we can take as an example of someone who has presumably "seen" the Forms and grounds her report on such a vision (whether or not this is the case with Socrates himself) feels the desire to "instruct" Socrates: see 201d–e, 207c, 210a.

[32] According to Price (1981:28) companionship of this sort "first reminds the lover of Beauty itself, which is the apex of the ascent" (210e–211a); but I suggest that whether or not there is recollection *à la Phaedo* triggered before knowledge of the Form, such a companionship in any case provides the constant stimulus to keep recollection alive after communion with the Form itself, or even to preserve that very communion to the extent that it is possible for

Now, there are still issues concerning commitment and attachment. Does an enlightened understanding of the nature of Beauty liberate us from all contingencies, or, as Nussbaum would put it, "our bondage to luck" (1986:181)? To some extent, yes. For it is clear that, at some point in our ascent, there occurs, so to speak, an "internalization" of Beauty: now the beauty to be found need not be outside us, as *we* can become instantiations of fine forms of behavior, virtues, or knowledge by the love that draws us to them. In that sense, we have gained some self-sufficiency and detachment from this or that external instantiation of Beauty; we know that we can have fulfillment even if we are not attached to a particular person, as we have not only the beauty that we have internalized, but also the "vast sea of beauty" (210d4) that surrounds us. We understand that happiness is not just about this or that particular companionship, but a higher order experience. Is such experience of detachment, however, only, or mainly, therapeutic, as Nussbaum contends? That is, is it aimed at making one "abandon his or her cherished human belief in irreplaceability in the service of his inner need for health" (1986:181)?

To answer this question, it is useful to see the speech of Diotima side by side with the speech of Alcibiades. Nussbaum contends that, while the former tries to "describe the passion or its object in general terms," the latter describes precisely the particularity of it, "because his experience of love has happened to him only once" (1986:187). According to Nussbaum, the latter then captures an aspect of the experience that the former misses, even though, at the end of the day, the two speeches are put in front of us rather dilemmatically, as two "mutually exclusive varieties of vision" insofar as "we must choose: one sort of understanding blocks the other" (1986:198). Socrates gives us recipes to get away from the vulnerability and volatility that we all fear; but Alcibiades makes us realize "the deep importance unique passion has for ordinary human beings; we see its irreplaceable contribution to understanding."

---

humans to do so (cf. Diotima's qualifications and hypothetical mode in this regard: *ei tōi genoito auto to kalon idein*, 211d8–212a1, *dunaito* 211e4)—just as in the *Republic* dialectic is an activity of dialogue rooted in the *elenchos*: cf. VII 531e–532a, 534b. One might still wonder whether this sort of scenario is not ultimately based on self-interest rather than interest in the other person's good. I believe the question is misguided, as it is clear that "the good" (or "the beautiful"), to the extent that it subordinates and grounds all other things that we call "good," subordinates and grounds both one's own and one's companion's good. Thus even if, at the beginning of the ascent, one may be motivated by a selfish quest for immortality or possession of the beautiful, it will be part of the transformative effect of grasping the Form that one will put not only the other person, but also oneself in the right perspective, and realize the importance of promoting the good in others no less than in oneself. For further discussion of this large issue in Platonic philosophy, see e.g. Kraut 1973, Kosman 1976, Irwin 1995:308–311.

Rather than meant to juxtapose two attitudes on love, however, I believe that the addition of Alcibiades' speech after Diotima's can be read in an alternative way—that is, as providing a practical illustration of the risks one runs if one avoids philosophizing about love, and of the kind of confusion that a person who does not have a proper understanding of love is bound to experience. This is the confusion of Alcibiades, who arrives after Socrates' speech is over (212d), and who, so to speak, mistakes Socrates for the Form itself (just as the cave dwellers in the *Republic* mistake images for the realities that cause them).[33] Even though this section of the dialogue does have a positive side—showing us, through the image of Socrates, what it is like to be ascending the ladder[34]—it is not, in reality, a choice between a particularized experience of *erōs* and the apprehension of a Form (for we have shown that in a sense the latter is not even the ultimate end of the speech of Diotima—there is clearly a practical reward after the ascent). It is the choice between having an unenlightened experience of particulars and the transformed approach to them that one can gain ultimately through grasp of the Form. Socrates refuses to sleep with Alcibiades, but not because getting higher on the ladder has killed every sort of sexual attraction in him.[35] Indeed he is far from minimizing his feelings towards him: on the contrary, he describes his love (*erōs*) for Alcibiades to Agathon as "no trivial matter" (*ou phaulon pragma*, 213c).[36] It is rather that, one could say, the fact that his *erōs* is also directed towards a higher standard of beauty helps him realize that sex with that man would not be fulfilling, or (as he puts it) a fair exchange (cf. 218a), if the spiritual values that Alcibiades

[33] Alcibiades, like the sight-lovers in the *Republic*—who (unlike the philosophers, cf. VII 520c) "think that what is similar to something is not similar but that thing itself which it is like," V 476c—does not see the difference between the copy and the original, and that is why he is prone to confusion. For this, of course, he does not need to know the original; on the contrary, because of his uninformed view about what it is to embody beauty fully and unqualifiedly, he misidentifies the latter with particular instances such as Socrates (hence his obsession with him). For other ways in which Alcibiades misunderstands Socrates, cf. Reeve's paper in this volume.

[34] On this many scholars agree: see e.g. Bury 1932:lx, Dover 1980:164, Rowe 1998a:206. See also Sheffield 2001b:196–198 for a summary of many parallels between Alcibiades' portrait of Socrates and the description of philosophical *erōs* in Diotima's speech.

[35] *Pace* e.g. Scott 2000, who claims that Socrates does not feel *erōs* but only affection for Alcibiades.

[36] Further, Alcibiades refers to Socrates as "always in the company of beautiful boys and thunderstruck" (or "drawn out of his senses," *ekpeplēktai*) by them" (216d2–3; the same verb that he uses to describe his reaction to Charmides at *Charmides* 154c3, cf. *Symposium* 211d5), which suggests that these boys have a physical effect on him (just as at *Charmides* 155d), even though he refrains from acting on his desire—and that's why in the *Symposium* he is described as temperate (211d7), resilient, and brave (219d)—as mentally "looking down" on that physical beauty by which he is stricken (as at 216d7–8).

professes to lack (216a–c) are supposed to be present in a sexual exchange that honors the beauty of the person as a whole (recall here the *sunamphoteron* of 209b7); instead, Socrates, exemplifying a point previously made in the speech of Diotima, spends a good part of his time trying to bring forth virtue in his beloved (cf. 216a). (And after all, Socrates himself is far from being portrayed as a man who would shun bodily pleasures in the *Symposium*, as he is, for example, the man who can drink as much as it pleases him [cf. *pros hēdonēn*, 176e3], albeit without getting drunk, 220a4–5, and "enjoys" [*apolauein*] feasting, not like any other, but uniquely so [*monos*, 220a2]; other dialogues reveal that he has been sexually active in old age.)[37]

But this then leads to another philosophical question: if equipped with the correct standards, it appears that we shall be able to make better choices, and that we are lucky if, even deprived of those standards (as in principle Alcibiades would be), we come across a person with the capacity to draw others to them. But then, would this have the consequence that, despite the variegated and multiform mass of images of Beauty, we should all be drawn to the one that embodies it best? For example, assuming that Plato intends to represent Socrates as the "best" instantiation available, should then everyone around him be infatuated with him above all mortals?

To an extent, Plato might perhaps be willing to grant the point. How could one fail to be drawn to an individual of exceptional charisma, and how could one deny the rightness of such attraction if it promises significantly to improve the quality of our lives? At the same time, we must not forget that *we* are finding this or that other individual attractive; however high we have climbed on the ladder, we are after all human; and insofar as we are human we have needs that continue to be particular precisely in that we ourselves embody beauty in one sense but not in another. The sense in which we don't creates a lack, and it is the desire to fulfill that particular lack, distinct from one individual to another, that may draw us to different persons instead of necessarily the same one in all cases. And even in cases where we are attracted to, and seek the companionship of, a person embodying properties that we ourselves have, Plato would argue that, as one does not embody that property in its whole perfection, such companionship may make one's experience of beauty fuller and thus be a suitable channel for its enhanced instantiation.

This certainly does not mean that I will, or should, be bound with that person for ever—needs change, and so may one as one grows. So this view of

---

[37] See here *Phaedo* 116b and *Apology* 34d describing Socrates, at the age of seventy, as having small children, with Woolf 2004:104–105.

Love is no consolation for one who is looking for the security of a commit-ment as often understood and dreamt of today, the life-long contract that will shelter one against any eventuality. Rather, it teaches us how much delu-sion there may be in that idea. It is a category mistake to confuse the fleeting other—which itself changes, as we ourselves do—with the stable Form; it enables us to see the misplacement of our obsessions, and of the unreason-able demands that un-philosophical partners usually put on their beloved, from whom they expect to receive a completion that by definition they cannot provide. By liberating us from those obsessions, and by seeing the particular others for what they really are, Platonic Love—understanding love as Plato would have us understand it—enables us to treat them with more, not less, respect. And, ironically enough, it may thus promise something more long-lasting or—in the *Symposium*'s words—a "more stable friendship,"[38] as our rela-tion will be based on true apprehension of the facts rather than a fantasy, and thus liberate us from the disappointment that so often follows infatuation and is such a common cause of the dissolution of a bond.

The *Symposium* does not tell us much about what exactly it means to know the Form of Beauty, beyond the quasi-mystical description of the experience. This part of the theory must remain rather mysterious to us. It is conceivable that the essence it talks about is that which we are still searching for, through all forms of art and ethical enquiry; but the essence must be there, and justi-fies our search for it, as Plato's realist commitments indicate. To that extent, the *Symposium* invites us to continue searching for that property, which means continuing to discuss what qualifies as valuable, both in our aesthetic and moral choices. Certainly, at points it looks like Diotima's theory, while trying to accommodate the phenomenology of love at one level, is at another level highly normative: we are constantly reminded of what we "must" do in the ascent.[39] But should this be a subject of criticism? Even where one might be tempted to glorify one's privacy and the elusive nature of love, Diotima dili-gently reminds us that the theory of love we endorse is directly relevant to morality. We would certainly criticize a person who loves a criminal in his criminality:[40] not because she loves, but because her love is misplaced. By

---

[38] It may be objected that there are many couples that stay and die together without being philo-sophical about their love. The point here, however, is not about the fact of their love, but the grounds for it. It is one thing to say that a relationship can happen to last, and another that it was inherently stable in the sense of being well-grounded.

[39] Cf. 210a–212a. The point is noted in Nussbaum 1986:179.

[40] It could be objected that the thought of "loving someone *qua*" is contrary to our experience of love. However, common usage reveals it all the time: "I love you for your generosity." Likewise, one may find an object attractive precisely because of its illicitness.

contrast, when our love is given properly we have a better chance, as Diotima would say, of begetting true virtue rather than images.[41]

[41] The germinal ideas of this paper originated in many undergraduate philosophy lectures on the *Symposium* that I have given over the years. The research was furthered while I was holding a Rockefeller Fellowship at the Center for Human Values at Princeton University, and subsequently a Fellowship at the Harvard University Center for Hellenic Studies, Washington, DC. I should like to thank both institutions for their support, and the other conference participants, an anonymous referee, and especially Jim Lesher, for their helpful comments on the penultimate version.

Part Three

THE *SYMPOSIUM*, SEX, AND GENDER

Ten

Agathon, Pausanias, and Diotima in Plato's *Symposium*: *Paiderastia* and *Philosophia*

Luc Brisson

M Y GOAL IN THIS CONTRIBUTION[1] is to shift the center of interest of Plato's magnificent dialogue the *Symposium* on two points. First, by showing that the dialogue develops a critique of a specific form of education within the framework of *paiderastia*,[2] a social convention which appears as a response to the quest for knowledge (*philosophia*),[3] and how this critique of *paiderastia* naturally involves sexuality, opposing a type of education that associates the transmission of knowledge from one man to another to that of a seminal fluid. According to me,[4] this image is formulated in the following passage from the beginning of the dialogue, where Agathon, who wants Socrates to come and recline on his couch, addresses him:

> "Socrates, come lie down next to me. Who knows, if I touch you, I may catch a bit of the knowledge that came to you under my neighbor's porch" ... Socrates sat down next to him and said: "How wonderful it would be, dear Agathon, if what is empty were filled with what is full simply by touching the wise. If only wisdom were like water, which always flows from a full cup into an empty one when we connect them with a piece of yarn—well, then I would

---

[1] I thank Denis O'Brien and Debra Nails for their remarks, several of which have been integrated into the text.

[2] *Paiderastia* is a social convention that must not be interpreted in the narrow sense of 'pederasty', as we shall see below. In its contemporary meaning, 'pederasty' differs from *paiderastia* on the following three points: (1) it has no other finality than sex; (2) it involves no age limit; (3) because of the great inequality (on many levels) between an adult and a child, it always takes place, if not in a climate of violence, then at least in a relation of coercion.

[3] I take *philosophia* in its etymological sense of an 'quest' (*philos*) for 'knowledge' (*sophia*).

[4] See Brisson 1999. English translations are those in Cooper 1997, usually slightly modified.

consider it the greatest prize to have the chance to lie down next to you. I would soon be overflowing with your wonderful knowledge."

Symposium 175d–e

The image is suggestive in itself,[5] but in a Greek context and within the framework of *paiderastia*, it raises a number of problems. Agathon, who is not the older partner, plays the dominant role that should by rights be that of Socrates. However, is this not, on Socrates' part, an expression of his irony? At the end of the dialogue, we find a similar reversal of roles between Alcibiades and Socrates. Alcibiades, who also wants to lie down beside Socrates gives a detailed description of his attempts to seduce Socrates:

What I thought at the time was that what he really wanted was the bloom of my beauty (ἐπὶ τῇ ἐμῇ ὥρᾳ), and that seemed to me the luckiest coincidence: all I had to do was to let him have his way with me (χαρισαμένῳ), and he would teach me everything he knew— believe me, I had a lot of confidence in the blooming of my beauty (ἐπὶ τῇ ὥρᾳ).

Symposium 217a1–6

Here I will limit myself to Plato's critique of *paiderastia*, praised in the speeches of Pausanias and Agathon, but criticized in that of Diotima,[6] who considers the acquisition of knowledge as childbirth, implying the experiences of pregnancy and giving birth. Consequently, while I concede that the first subtitle of this dialogue is *On love*, I would like to show that for Plato, the point is above all to raise questions about *paiderastia*, a social convention which, implying sexual relations among males, played an important part in education at Athens in the highest social classes.

1. Sexuality in Ancient Greece in the Classical Period[7]

The Greeks of the archaic and classical period did not consider sexual desire and the behavior it inspires as a function of the resemblance or difference of the anatomical gender of the persons involved. In fact, they accorded to the sexual act a value that depended on the act's conformity to the norms of conduct fixed by society as a function of age and social status, among other

---

[5] Especially for modern readers, who are familiar with psychoanalysis.
[6] Halperin 1990:113–151, abridged in Halperin et al. 1990:257–308.
[7] On this subject, see Halperin 1990:53–71; Halperin et al. 1990; and Winkler 1990.

things. Consequently, we must exercise the greatest prudence when we use the terms 'homosexuality' and 'heterosexuality' to designate a reality and an opposition assumed to be valid both for classical antiquity and for the contemporary period.[8] A naïve use of these terms quickly leads to anachronism, since the distinctions established between the various types of behavior were not the same as those generally accepted today.

In ancient Greece, sexual relations were usually evaluated on a purely anatomical level, in terms of phallic penetration (real or symbolic).[9] The sexual act is thus polarized by the distinction between the person who penetrates and the person who is penetrated; or, in ancient Greece, between the person playing the active role and the person playing a passive role. These roles are, moreover, associated with a social status that is superior or inferior as a function of the oppositions: masculine/feminine; adult/adolescent. Phallic penetration manifests a man's superiority over a woman, that of an adult over an adolescent, or of one man over another man, which superiority is generally associated with an economic, social, or political domination. At the level of sexuality, then, the distinction between activity and passivity enables the evaluation of acts and actors. In other words, all sexual relationships that imply the penetration (real or symbolic) of a human being inferior from a social viewpoint (that is, from the viewpoint of age, sex, or status) is generally conceived as normal for a male, whatever the anatomical gender of the penetrated individual may be, whereas the fact of being penetrated may be considered as a shameful act. It is as a function of this presupposition that we must try to understand how sexual relations between women, between men, and between men and women were perceived in Ancient Greece.

2. An Inventory of Sexual Behaviors according to Aristophanes

In Plato's *Symposium*, we find a passage (191d–192e) in which Aristophanes proposes an inventory of sexual behaviors. The passage ends with some very fine lines that describe the wish expressed by a lover and his beloved never to be separated from one another, in life or in death, because they will have been fused into a single being by Hephaestus (192e).

---

[8] It is not illegitimate to utilize a modern vocabulary and concepts to speak of sexuality in antiquity; however, when we do so, it is appropriate to take particular care not to force contemporary categories and ideologies onto attitudes and modes of behavior from the past.

[9] Since problems obviously arise for the case of sexual relations between women, and even, as we shall see, for the case of intercrural penetrations.

2.1 Between men and women

When apprehended in terms of phallic penetration, sexual relations between a man and a woman are unproblematic for an adult citizen, since, in ancient Greece, women occupied a lower level than men in all fields, economic, social, and political, in which they were virtually insignificant. Difficulties really appear only with marriage, where everything was centered on the question of adultery.[10] Indeed, the relation between a man and a woman, once sanctioned by marriage, constitutes the privileged instrument that enables an adult male to transmit his genetic, economic, social, and political patrimony. Adultery is thus condemned because it introduces an element of confusion in this system of transmission.[11] It goes without saying that the problem also arises *earlier*, with daughters of marriageable age, whom the head of the family must supervise in order to ensure that confusion does not set in even before marriage.

2.2 Between women

The mention by Aristophanes (*Symposium* 191e) is practically the only one from this period to evoke sexual relations between women (with the exception of *Laws* I 636a–d and VIII 835d–836e).[12] This extreme discretion on the subject could be explained by the following two reasons: (1) we have to do with a world in which the evidence that has come down to us was produced in a specific ideological context, and (2) it is very difficult to find a place for this type of relation in a context where sexuality is apprehended in classical Greece in terms of phallic penetration (real or symbolic).[13]

2.3 Between men

Before we discuss the type of permanent attachment between men that would correspond to what would today be qualified as a homosexual union, it is appropriate to insist on the "convention" that the Greeks of the archaic and classical period called *paiderastia*, which obeyed quite specific constraints of age and social behavior.[14]

---

[10] On which Aristophanes insists, perhaps because adultery was one of the favorite themes of the comic poets.

[11] On the punishments inflicted on adulterers, see Hoffmann 1990. On the significance of these punishments, see Dover 1989:105–109.

[12] On this subject, see the remarkable Boehringer 2003, whose jury included David Halperin.

[13] On this subject, see Dover 1989:171–184.

[14] There is a description of the background of *paiderastia* in Sergent 1996.

2.3.1 Paiderastia

In order to bring forth the specificity of what was called *paiderastia*[15] in archaic and classical Greece, which had the status of a social convention in the higher circles of Athenian society, we must mention the following five particularities.

(1) *Paiderastia* implies a relation not between two adult males, but between a male citizen and a *pais* in the proper sense of "boy" who was in an age class that began around the age of puberty, until the appearance of the first beard;[16] i.e. roughly between 12 and 18.[17] In the context envisaged here, the term *pais*[18] conventionally designated a young male capable of becoming the object of sexual desire on the part of an adult male. It should be noted that *pais* also means 'slave', which indicates the inferior status[19] that the young boy has in his relation with an adult; he is younger and plays the passive role.

(2) The appearance of fuzz on a boy's cheeks represents the summit of his sexual attractiveness, which lasts until the arrival of the first beard.[20] At a transitional phase, a young boy can play both an active and a passive role in a sexual relation, but with different partners (Dover 1989:196–203). A grown man who, after his first beard, continues to play a passive role in a sexual relation with a male citizen is always mocked,[21] which is never the case for the man playing an active role (Dover 1989:139).

(3) Since it is restricted to one period of life for the young boy, and since it is not associated with an inclination for one particular individual, *paiderastia* is not exclusive to one individual: it is expected that young males will marry (*Symposium* 192a7–b5), after having played the passive role in the context of a homosexual relation, and at the same time as they continue to play an active role in such relations.[22]

---

[15] On this convention, see Halperin 1990:53–71 on Patzer 1982.

[16] Xenophon *Anabasis* 7.4.7.

[17] Some representations (see Dover 1989) might allow us to think of younger men, but from the viewpoint of its definition, it is difficult to imagine that *paiderastia* could mean anything before the age of twelve.

[18] In Plato, we also find *neaniskos* (*Charmides* 154d) as an equivalent. Clinias is qualified either as *neaniskos* (*Euthydemus* 271a, 275a) or as *meirakion* (*Euthydemus* 273a–b). At *Lysis* 205b–c, *pais* and *neaniskos* have the same referent.

[19] Because of his age. On this subject, see Golden 1985.

[20] See *Protagoras* 309a; Plutarch *Dialogue on Love* 770b–c. Compare the sordid side of the sexual activity of the sausage merchant (Aristophanes *Knights* 1242) who has passed this age.

[21] This seems to have been the case for Agathon in particular, despite his fame, as we shall see.

[22] Nevertheless, within the framework of *paiderastia*, the *erastēs* is often a relatively young man, between twenty and thirty years old, who is not yet married or whose wife is very young.

(4) Even when *paiderastia* relations are characterized by affection and tenderness, an emotional and erotic asymmetry subsists which the Greeks distinguish by speaking of the lover's *erōs* and the beloved's *philia*.[23] This asymmetry has its source in the very division of "sexual labor." A young boy (*pais*), who is not moved by passionate desire as his lover is, must therefore not play an active sexual role.[24]

(5) The older male is qualified as an *erastēs*, whereas the younger one is called his *erōmenos* (the present passive participle of *eran*), or his *paidika* (a neuter plural that literally means "what concerns young boys").[25] The amorous language found in Greek literature of a certain level, and in Plato in particular, always remains discreet, but the reader should not be fooled. Terms like *hupourgein*, 'to do someone a service'[26] and *kharizesthai* 'to accord a favor'[27] must often be interpreted in a specifically sexual meaning: the service expected or the favor requested by the older male is equivalent, in the final analysis, to physical contact leading to an ejaculation, even if, according to the context, a smile or a pleasant word may be all is needed to keep a lover happy. Society encouraged attempts at seduction undertaken by the *erastēs*, but did not tolerate those made by the *erōmenos*.[28] An older man, inspired by love, pursued with his advances a younger man who, if he yielded, was led to do so out of affection, gratitude, and admiration, feelings that are grouped together under the term *philia*; an honorable *erōmenos* should not seek pleasure in his case.[29]

---

[23] Dover 1989:52–53. Xenophon, *Memorabilia* 2.6.8; *Symposium* 8.16 and 8.19. There is in classical Greek no common term for the passion felt by the *erastēs* and the *philia* felt by the *erōmenos*.

[24] This could explain why, according to the vase painters, the lover inserts his penis between the boy's thighs, rather than in his anus or his mouth, which was the most condemned act. This sexual practice in fact preserved the beloved's physical integrity; however, it must be admitted that this holds for public behavior (in word and deed) and that nothing allows us to know what went on in private, either in bed or elsewhere. On all this, see Dover 1989:42–54; 91–100. In the postscript to the 1989 edition, Dover is less affirmative than in 1978, and thinks "that the fact that comedy assumes anal penetration to be the normal mode of homosexual intercourse suggests that the painter's overwhelming preference for the intercrural mode is highly conventional."

[25] On the sexual meaning of these terms, see Dover 1989:16.

[26] Dover 1989:44. See *Symposium* 184d.

[27] *Ibid.* See *Symposium* 182a, b, d, 183d, 185b, 186b, c, 187d, 188c, 218c, d.

[28] See Aristophanes *Clouds* 963–983; *Symposium* 183d–184a.

[29] Xenophon *Symposium* 8.21 and Plato *Phaedrus* 255d. It is surprising to note that the hierarchical model, based on age difference, governed the qualifications of all relations between males in ancient Greece. This model seems to have lasted from the Minoan period until the end of the Western Roman Empire. The *Iliad* does not say explicitly that Achilles and Patroclus maintained amorous relations, but it remains sufficiently vague on the subject for all authors of the classical

Outside of the satisfaction of sexual desire and the search for a certain affection or tenderness, of what use could *paiderastia* in ancient Greece possibly be? It seems that in classical Athens, sexual relations between a male citizen and an adolescent had, directly or indirectly, a social role, where the adult had the task of facilitating the adolescent's entry into the masculine society that led the city on the economic and political level. *Paiderastia* thus had a social and educative role. This is the origin of most of many remarks and passages on the usefulness (*khreia*) of erotic relations between males, which we find in Plato, particularly in the *Phaedrus*[30] and the *Symposium*.

All that has just been said about *paiderastia* might allow us to think that sexual relations between males in archaic and classical Greece were limited to this context of social conventions, obeying very strict rules, and from which desire and pleasure were supposedly banished at least for the younger male; and that these rules excluded permanence. Yet such was not the case. In his speech, Aristophanes insists on the existence of very powerful relations, which are long lasting, between individuals of the same sex. Agathon and Pausanias are examples of this. Yet this constancy and fidelity, since they violated the rule of *paiderastia* stipulating that one should abandon exclusive passive sexual relationships with men in order to get married and have children, brought upon them the social blame expressed with great violence by Aristophanes' lower-class characters in the *Thesmophoriazusae* (*Women at the Thesmophoria*).

2.3.2 An enduring homosexual couple

The following is what can be known about Agathon and Pausanias, who formed a couple for at least thirty years.

2.3.2.1 *Agathon.*[31] Agathon, an Athenian, son of Tisamenes of Athens,[32] was less than thirty years old when, as we learn in Plato's *Symposium*, he won the tragedy contest in 416 BCE. I shall enumerate the principal dates of his life.

a. He must have been born around 448/7, because in 432/1, Agathon was already linked to Pausanias, in a context that might be that of *paiderastia*. In the *Protagoras* (315d6–e3), we read: "Seated on couches next to Prodicus

---

period to be able to affirm that this was the case. This is why an attempt has been made to connect *paiderastia* with a ritual of initiation supposed to be mentioned by Strabo (10.4.21). On this subject, see Bethe 1907:438–475; Sergent 1996.

[30] On this aspect of the matter, that is, the uselessness and even the danger of love, see the paradoxical speeches of Phaedrus and Socrates in the *Phaedrus*, first at 230e–234b, then 237a–241d.

[31] On Agathon, see Lévêque 1955, and Nails 2002:8–10.

[32] In Nails 2002. See the scholium to *Symposium* 172 (i.e. scholium to Lucian *Rhetorum praeceptor* 2 in Cramer 1963:269).

of Ceos were Pausanias of Cerameis, and with Pausanias a fairly young boy (νέον τι ἔτι μειράκιον), well-bred I would say, and certainly good-looking. I think I heard his name is Agathon, and I wouldn't be surprised if he were Pausanias' young love (*paidika*)." If we consider that the term *meirakion* designates an age class that goes from 14–21, and therefore that Agathon may have been about 16, and if we situate the dramatic date of the *Protagoras* around 432/1,[33] we can place Agathon's birth around 448/7.

b. In 416, at the beginning of the year, Agathon was celebrating his first victory as a tragic author, and the *Symposium* alludes to this victory.[34] The speech he then pronounces reveals the influence of Gorgias, as Socrates points out to him before he himself begins to speak.[35] Agathon is then about thirty, and is still linked to Pausanias. Three passages in the *Symposium*[36] allude to the intimacy of their relations.

c. In 411, according to Aristotle,[37] Agathon congratulated Antiphon on his defense, which seems to indicate that his preferences did not tend towards democracy.[38] This political gesture may have focused upon Agathon the disapproval manifested by the *Thesmophoriazusae*. In that year, Aristophanes' characters mocked Agathon with unparalleled violence by presenting him as a passive homosexual and an effeminate man.[39] This was less than five years after Agathon's victory as a tragic poet.

---

[33] According to Morrison 1941.

[34] The testimony of Athenaeus of Naucratis (on 217a–b) does not seem to be beyond all suspicion (see Lévêque 1955:56–58). We must therefore remain prudent with regard to the date of the events and the age of the *dramatis personae*. At *Symposium* 223a, Alcibiades calls Agathon an 'adolescent' (*meirakion*), an age group that extends from 14 to 21. How is this to be interpreted: as flattery, as a veiled insult, or as an indication of the falsity of the date given for the event?

[35] See n56 below.

[36] The speakers are Socrates (177d), Aristophanes (193b), and Eryximachus (193e).

[37] Aristotle *Eudemian Ethics* 3.5.1232b8–9.

[38] Thucydides 8.68.2. The Attic orator Antiphon belonged to the group, which, in 411, took part in the conspiracy of the Four Hundred. He was arrested, judged, condemned to death, and executed. At his trial, he pronounced a speech of exceptional quality that earned him Agathon's congratulations.

[39] Aristophanes' characters violently targeted Agathon in the *Thesmophoriazusae*; Agathon is insulted and ridiculed in this comedy, which represents him as a passive and effeminate man. The plot of the play is as follows. As they do every year in the month of Pyanepsion (October), the women are celebrating the Thesmophoria, in honor of Demeter and her daughter Persephone, in mysteries that are forbidden to men. They must take advantage of the fact that they are among themselves to decide the fate of Euripides, on whom they want to take vengeance, because he has spoken ill of them in his tragedies. Euripides knows this, and considers that he is lost unless someone takes his defense in the Assembly. He thinks of the tragic poet Agathon, who dresses like a woman and who, because of his effeminate appearance and habits, can pass

d. Around 407, Agathon left for the court of Archelaus, king of Macedonia.[40] He seems to have remained with Archelaus, who had also invited the painter Zeuxis, the musician Timotheus of Miletus, the tragic poet Choerilus of Samos, and above all Euripides, to his court at Pella. Pausanias accompanied him.[41]

e. Agathon died in all probability at the end of the fifth century, when he was not yet 50 years old.[42]

2.3.2.2. Pausanias. We know practically nothing about this Pausanias[43] outside of the *corpus platonicum.* In his *Symposium* (8.32), Xenophon describes Pausanias as an ardent defender of *paiderastia.*[44]

a. In 432/1, in the *Protagoras* (315d–e), that is, 16 years before the date in which the event recounted in the *Symposium* is supposed to take place, we find Pausanias and Agathon side by side near the couch of the Prodicus of Ceos. Pausanias must be older than Agathon, who is his beloved (*erōmenos*). One might imagine an age difference of 15 or 20 years: Pausanias will then

---

for a woman. He therefore goes to Agathon, but the latter refuses to do him this favor. Euripides is desperate; fortunately, a relative by marriage offers to take charge of this maneuver. Euripides disguises the relative, to whom Agathon agrees to lend a female disguise. The scene in which the relative talks to Agathon constitutes a particularly violent attack against the tragic poet's homosexuality (*Thesmophoriazusae* 130–167), which must already have been famous at the time.

[40] Aristophanes *Frogs* 83–85; Plato *Symposium* 172c.

[41] Aelian *Varia Historia* 2.21.

[42] This can be deduced from a scholium to Aristophanes' *Frogs* (85). On the interpretation of this scholium, see Lévêque 1955:73–77. In the *Frogs* (83–85), Dionysus explains to Heracles that he must go to Hades to look for a good tragic author. The latter questions him on the fate of the illustrious poets of the last years: "*Heracles:* And Agathon, where is he? *Dionysus:* He left me and went away; he was a good poet, missed by his friends. *Heracles:* Where did he go, the miserable fellow? *Dionysus:* To the festival of the Blessed." The answer, εἰς μακάρων εὐωχίαν, leaves one porplexed. A scholiast mentions the following two interpretations: either Agathon has died and has left for the Isles of the Blessed, or else he is at Pella, feasting. This opposition continues, with support going now to one, now to the other of these hypotheses. A possible solution would be to accept the ambiguity, in the view that Aristophanes means that even if he is physically alive, Agathon has died to poetry, for he no longer produces at Athens, but is leading a life of debauch with Archelaus. A reply by Apollodorus to Glaucon in the *Symposium* (172d) tends in this direction: "Don't you know that it's been several years that Agathon doesn't live here any more?" Since the *Frogs* was produced in 405, we must place Apollodorus' declaration in 406 at the latest, if we admit that Agathon was dead when the *Frogs* was produced; and since Agathon left Athens around 411, he would have been absent for five years at the most.

[43] See Nails 2002:222.

[44] It may be of interest to note that in order to praise erotic relations between men, Pausanias here mentions the courage of the Sacred Band of Thebes, which Phaedrus had already mentioned at 178e–179a.

have been between 30 and 40.[45] He must therefore have been born between 470–460, and would be a contemporary of Socrates.

b. In 416, Pausanias was a guest at the celebration Plato's *Symposium* was supposed to recount. At the time of Agathon's victory, Pausanias was in his fifties, as were Socrates and Acumenus. He gives a speech in praise of Eros that is partly critical with regard to Athenian morals concerning homosexuality. In Pausanias, we observe a defense and illustration of *paiderastia* that is presumably related to the permanence of the couple he formed with Agathon, the man who was his "beloved." It seems, moreover, that, in the speech he is supposed to have given in the *Symposium*, Pausanias alludes to Agathon in at least two passages[46] in his description of the ideal lover.

c. Around 407, Pausanias accompanies Agathon to the court of Archelaus, king of Macedonia.

Pausanias, who seemingly came to know Agathon in the context of *paiderastia*, thus prolonged this relation until the death of his "beloved". Such permanence in an amorous relationship seems to be the expression, first, of an idealization of *paiderastia*, and, on the other hand, of the exclusivity of relations between "lover" and "beloved." In addition, there is no doubt about the "visibility" of this couple; it seems to have attracted both praise and blame in classical Athens.

2.3.3. Social blame

Despite the institutionalized form assumed by *paiderastia*, and despite the praise showered on the right sort of sexual relations between men, which

---

[45] Debra Nails asks me the following question *in litteris*: "are you quite sure you want to retain an age difference of 15–20 years between Pausanias and Agathon, although a difference of 5–8 years would better fit history, as well as the circumstances of the *Protagoras* (i.e. all other men, named as grouped around Protagoras, Hippias, and Prodicus, thirteen in all [omitting "others" at 315a, c, and e], are young men of an age to seek further education). If Pausanias was an exception, can you explain why that was not remarked? The only other older man, though still much younger than Socrates, was Critias, but Plato has him arriving separately." The point is well taken, but it is difficult to answer, since it takes for granted that Pausanias is there to learn, whereas he could have come to present Agathon, or simply to keep an eye on him.

[46] In *Symposium* 181c-d: "I am convinced that a man who falls in love with a young man of this age is generally prepared to share everything with the one he loves—he is eager, in fact, to spend the rest of his own life with him" (this anticipates what Aristophanes will say). And in *Symposium* 183d-e: "I'll tell you: it is the common, vulgar lover, who loves the body rather than the soul, the man whose love is bound to be inconsistent; since what he loves is itself mutable and unstable. The moment the body is no longer in bloom, 'he flies off and away' (*Iliad* II 71), his promises and vows in tatters behind him. How different from this is a man who loves the right sort of character, and who remains its lover for life, attached as he is to something that is permanent."

occupy the foreground particularly in the context of the banquet given by Agathon, this kind of relationship inspired resistance and blame in society.

It is possible, and even likely, that Pausanias is thinking of the young Agathon who was his "beloved" in the context of *paiderastia*, when, in his speech in the *Symposium*, he complains about the Athenians' ambiguous attitude towards this convention, of which Xenophon tells us that Pausanias was an ardent defender. Moreover, Aristophanes seems to anticipate the *Thesmophoriazusae* as he ends his speech in the *Symposium* (193b).

From this point, we may draw three conclusions, which we may generalize with some degree of probability. Despite the semi-institutional practice of *paiderastia*, the existence of couples formed by adult males was known at Athens. These couples laid claim to a genuine exclusivity, for they excluded any relation, in or out of marriage, with women. Above all, they featured an undeniable visibility and permanence.

3. The Speeches of Pausanias, Agathon, and Diotima in the *Symposium*

In the *Symposium*, only six of the speeches in praise of Eros are mentioned by Aristodemus:[47] they are given respectively by the following six characters: Phaedrus, Agathon, Pausanias, Eryximachus, Aristophanes, and Socrates, who speaks in the name of Diotima. These six speeches in praise of Eros may be subdivided into three groups, in which each speech is opposed to another. For Phaedrus and Agathon, there is only a single Eros. However, whereas Phaedrus holds that Eros is the eldest god, Agathon maintains, on the contrary, that he is the youngest. In addition, Pausanias and Eryximachus consider that there are two gods Eros, who correspond to the two Aphrodites, Celestial and Vulgar. Yet whereas Pausanias examines the consequences of this duality only in the case of men, Eryximachus extends his inquiry to the totality of beings. Finally, Aristophanes and Socrates raise the problem at another level. For Aristophanes, Eros is the only god who can enable us to realize that towards which all human beings tend: the union with that half of himself from which he has been separated by Zeus. For Socrates, who reports the words of Diotima, a foreigner from Mantinea, Eros is not a god, but a *daimōn*, who, in view of his function as an intermediary, enables the transformation of the aspiration towards the beautiful and the good that every man feels into a perpetual possession, by means of procreation according to the body and according to the soul.

---

[47] There were others, if we can believe Aristodemus at *Symposium* 180c.

These speeches are pronounced in the house of Agathon (174d), which may have been that of Pausanias as well.[48] In the room in which the scene unfolds, Agathon and Pausanias are stretched out on couches, one opposite the other along a diagonal.[49]

3.1 Pausanias' speech (180c–185c)[50]

Pausanias' speech is less sophisticated than Agathon's, but it displays a highly elaborate use of the turns of phrase taught is the schools of rhetoric and sophistics: paronomasia,[51] rhythmic correspondence between phrases and periods, whose invention Aristotle attributes to Thrasymachus,[52] and which characterizes the style of Isocrates.[53] One will note the use of *prōton* (at first) and of *epeita* (secondly, then) to give rhythm to the periods.[54] Finally, the remark by Apollodorus, who is recounting the scene to Glaucon, after Pausanias' speech, is particularly interesting: "When Pausanias finally came to a pause (*Pausaniou ... pausamenou*)[55]—I've learned this sort of fine figure from our clever rhetorician—, it was Aristophanes' turn, according to Aristodemus" (185d). This could be a "device" deriving from Gorgias,[56] the master and model of Agathon (and perhaps of Pausanias as well).

Pausanias gives a highly articulate speech based on two postulates: the first concerns mythology and more precisely Eros, while the second deals with the social evaluation of a particular type of behavior.

As far as mythology is concerned, Pausanias reasons as follows. Since there are two Aphrodites, the Celestial (Uranian) Aphrodite,[57] and the other,

---

[48] This is, of course, a mere hypothesis, with which Debra Nails expresses her disagreement in this volume.

[49] See the illustration in my 1999:248.

[50] On several points, my analysis is inspired by that of Görgemanns 2000. Dover 1989 has analyzed lengthy passages from this speech: 182a–184b and 184d–185a.

[51] For instance, ἔργα ἐργαζομένῳ, 182e3; δουλείας δουλεύειν, 183a6–7; πράττειν οὕτω τὴν πρᾶξιν, 183a, cf. 181a.

[52] Aristotle *Rhetoric* 3.9.1409a25.

[53] *Symposium* 180e–181a, 184d–e, 185a–c. For instance in *Helen* 17.

[54] I give *sophoi* the same meaning as above, at 182b.

[55] Such an expression, which includes both assonance and symmetry, is qualified by the technical expression ἴσα λέγειν.

[56] Gorgias, considered as one of the experts (*sophoi*), that is, 'sophists' mentioned here, exerted considerable influence on the composition of *epideictic* ('demonstrative') speeches at the end of the fifth and beginning of the fourth century BCE. In Gorgias' *Encomium of Helen* (2), we find a "device" similar to the one found here.

[57] Who is born from the sperm that flows from the severed testicles of Uranus, according to Hesiod *Theogony* 178–196.

the Vulgar Aphrodite,[58] each of whom had their temple and cult at Athens,[59] we must distinguish two gods Eros (180d4–e3). The Eros who pertains to Vulgar Aphrodite, whose birth implied the involvement of a male and a female principle, features three characteristics: it deals with women as well as with men; it is interested more in the body than in the soul; and it is more attached to the realization of the sexual act than to the way it is carried out (181a7–c2). The Eros who pertains to Celestial Aphrodite—who is older and whose birth depends only upon a male principle—presents three characteristic features opposed to those that determine the Eros pertaining to Vulgar Aphrodite: it deals exclusively with men; it is interested not in the body, but in the soul; and it is more concerned with the way the act is carried out than with its actual realization (181c2–d7). From this first part of his speech, it is clear that Pausanias accords the first place to the Eros that presides over sexual relations between men. What is more, Pausanias specifies that this masculine homosexuality must be understood either as love for young boys (*paiderastia*)[60] or a love that begins when the beard grows (181d1–3), but lasts all one's life (181d3–7).

Sexual relations between men are not, however, the object of unqualified approval: its realization must be good, insofar as its object must be the soul. Hence the second theme of Pausanias' speech (180e3–181a6). In this context, *paiderastia* is considered as a sexual behavior (*praxis*) that may be subject to evaluation in the context of popular morality. By 'beautiful' (*kalon*) we must understand what is suitable, and by 'ugly' (*aischron*), what is unseemly.[61] We can thus understand that an action is beautiful if it inspires praise (*epainos*, 182e3) and ugly if it entails blame (*oneidos*, in 182a1 and b4; *psogon* in 182a5). These reactions, moreover, imply the existence of a rule of conduct, or a law (*nomos*)[62] in the minimal sense of the term.

---

[58] Who is the daughter of Zeus and Dione, see *Iliad* V 370.

[59] On this subject, see Pirenne-Delforge 1988 and, on Aphrodite Urania, 1994:15–25, on Aphrodite Pandemos, 1994:26–34.

[60] The word appears at 181c7, but it was announced at 181c3–4 by what might be an interpolated gloss: καὶ ἔστιν οὗτος ὁ τῶν παίδων ἔρως.

[61] Dover 1974:69–73: "*Kalos* and *aiskhros* are applied very freely indeed by the orators to any action, behaviour or achievement which evokes any kind of favourable reaction and praise or incurs any kind of contempt, hostility or reproach (e.g. Aiskhines 1.127, Andokides 2.17–18, Demosthenes 58.37, Isokrates 19.4, Lykourgos 111). *Kalos* most often corresponds to our 'admirable', 'creditable, honourable', and *aiskhros* to 'disgraceful', 'shameful', 'scandalous'; they are among the most important tools of manipulative language" (70). One should compare the *Meno* (88d–e), and the *Euthydemus* (281d–e) as well as what we find a bit further on in the *Symposium* (183d).

[62] As Dover 1974 rightly points out, the Athenians understand "under the single term *nomos*, 'law', what we divide into separate categories, 'constitutional', 'legal', 'religious', 'moral', and

Pausanias justifies the rule of conduct (*nomos*) current in Attica, concerning the problem of whether it is good for a boy who is beloved to accord his favors to lovers (182a7–b1). This rule takes on an absolute character both in Lacedaemonian Elis and in Boeotia, where to accord one's favors is considered a fine and good thing (182b1–6), and in Ionia and among the barbarians (182b6–c7), where it is considered ugly and bad. We should note the association of this condemnation with a tyrannical regime (182b6–d4), which could be interpreted as a *captatio benevolentiae* with regard to Athens and its political leaders. In Attica, by contrast, the rule features nuances, according to whether the Eros involved pertains to Celestial or to Vulgar Aphrodite. In the former case, it is ugly and bad for the beloved boy to accord his favors to lovers; and in the latter case, it is fine and good. We thus return to the axiom formulated above (180e3–181a6).

Three modes of behavior indicate that, for a boy, the fact of according favors to one's lovers was something accepted at Athens. It is fitting to love openly and not in hiding (182d5–7). He who is in love receives encouragements (182d7–e1). In those who are in love, modes of behavior towards men and gods are tolerated that would be condemned in another context (182e1–183c2); to adopt conduct that even a slave would not accept[63] to seduce one's beloved, or even to break one's oaths. Yet matters are not so simple, for Pausanias notes the existence of people who oppose the modes of behavior that have just been enumerated. Fathers give pedagogues[64] the order to prevent them from meeting their lover (183c4–7). Their friends of the same age—who may become beloved—censure them (183c7–8); and those who are older—who may become lovers—, and who should protect the younger ones (183c8–d3) do not oppose this denunciation. To explain this apparent contradiction, Pausanias returns to his initial thesis (183d3–e6), which he develops in order to make explicit what must be the rule of conduct to follow. By adopting this rhetorical strategy, Pausanias becomes the defender of ancient tradition against the criticisms of his time.

The lover who is not worthy (*ponēros*)[65] is interested in the body more than the soul (183d8–e1). He has no more constancy (*monimos*) than the object of his desire, that is, the body (183e1–5). On the other hand, the lover who

---

'conventional', with the consequence that open defiance of usage could be exploited as ground for allegations of treason and conspiracy."

[63] The matter is particularly serious for a citizen who adopts a slave's behavior.

[64] Slaves whose task was to accompany their master's sons to the gymnasium, and to bring them back home, see *Lysis* 208b–c.

[65] The terms *agathos* and *khrēstos* are opposed to the terms *kakos* and *ponēros*, see Dover 1974.

is worthy is interested primarily in the beloved's character (183e5), and he remains faithful to him all his life (183e5–6). This, according to Pausanias, is why the rule at Athens intends to submit the lover to the test of time, so that the beloved may know whether he should give in or run away (183e6–184a2). Hence the following two rules. The beloved must not yield right away (184a5–7), thereby showing that he is not after wealth and advantages, either because he seeks them or because he fears failing to obtain them (184a–b3). The desperate search for wealth and power cannot bring constancy (184b3–5). The conclusion that ensues is as follows: there is only one way to follow the Athenian custom: lover and beloved must have excellence as their objective (184b5–6). In this perspective, the two laws must coincide: the one concerning the love of young boys (*paiderastia*) and the one concerning the love of knowledge (*philosophia*). The beloved must accord his favors to the lover (184b6–d3), who, for his part, must have as his goal the encouragement of excellence (*aretē*), in the form of knowledge or something else (184d3–e5). If one is the victim of deceit, this is not dishonorable (184e5). Either the beloved's baseness appears, when he abandons his poor lover (184e5–185a), or else his intentions were pure if he sought for knowledge from his lover, whereas the latter had no knowledge (185a–b) to give, and the beloved will show himself "the kind of person who will do anything in any circumstance[66] for the sake of becoming better" (185b1–3). As Dover points out, this is a euphemism to indicate that the boy will accept to have sexual relations with his lover, either to thank him for having transmitted his knowledge to him, or else to express his admiration for him. However, the beloved must never take the initiative in this area.[67] The passage on trickery is interesting, for trickery is also twofold. The victim is condemned if his aim is money, and forgiven if his goal is wisdom and virtue.

The heart of Pausanias' argumentation is to be found in this last section, where the synthesis is made between the rule of conduct that must guide love for young boys (*paiderastia*) and that which must govern the love for wisdom (*philosophia*). In fact, Pausanias' speech is a programmatic praise of *paiderastia*.

(1) This unequal relationship in which the beloved (*erōmenos*), a young boy, is the slave of his older lover (*erastēs*) must have as its goal not only the pleasure of the body, but also the improvement of the beloved's soul.

(2) Love for young boys implies sexual relations.

---

[66] I consider *panti* as a neuter, rather than a masculine.
[67] See Dover 1989:91.

(3) It is impossible to know what Pausanias understands by "soul", but we should note that he gives the term "character"[68] as a synonym for it. This is why the beloved must not seek wealth and power above all else in his lover, who, for his part, must have as his goal the search for excellence in general and more specifically of wisdom in particular in his beloved.

(4) For this reason, *paiderastia* is justified by *philosophia*,[69] and it presents itself as a means given to a boy to exercise his intelligence.

(5) The link between the educative character of *paiderastia* and its sexual aspect appears clearly in the following passage:

> Both these principles (τὼ νόμω τούτω)—that is, both the principle governing the proper attitude toward the lover of boys or young men (τόν τε περὶ τὴν παιδεραστίαν) and the principle governing the quest for knowledge (καὶ τὸν περὶ τὴν φιλοσοφίαν) and all other forms of excellence (καὶ τὴν ἄλλην ἀρετήν)—must be combined if a boy or a young man (παιδικὰ) is to grant his favors (τὸ χαρίσασθαι) to a lover (ἐραστῇ) in an honorable way. When an older lover (ἐραστής) and a boy or a young man (παιδικά) come together and each obeys the principle (νόμον) appropriate to him—when the lover realizes that he is justified in rending any service (ὑπηρετῶν)[70] to a beloved boy or young man who grants him favors (χαρισαμένοις παιδικοῖς), and when the boy or the young man understands that he is justified in performing any service (ὁτιοῦν δικαίως ἂν ὑπηρετεῖν) for a lover who can make him wise (σοφόν) and good (ἀγαθὸν)—and when the lover *is* able to have the boy or young man become wiser (εἰς φρόνησιν) and better (καὶ τὴν ἄλλην ἀρετὴν), when the boy or the young man *is* eager to be taught (εἰς παίδευσιν) and improved (καὶ τὴν ἄλλην σοφίαν) by his lovers—then, and only then, when these two principles (τῶν νόμων) coincide absolutely, is it ever honorable for a boy or a young man to accept a lover.
>
> *Symposium* 184c7–e4

[68] In ancient Greek, ἔθος, see *Symposium* 183e5.

[69] Pausanias uses the term *philosophia* twice: at 182c1 and at 184d1; at 183a1, I reject *philosophias* as did Schleiermacher and Bury. In the first case (182c1), we find an attack against tyrants who are opposed to *philosophia* and *philogumnastia*: note that the association of these words implies practices that promote the development of the soul and the body. We find this association once again in Diotima's speech at 205d5, where an allusion to functional tripartition filters through: love of wealth, of physical exercise and of wisdom. In the second case (184d1), the association is between *philosophia* and *paiderastia*.

[70] On the sexual meaning (similar to the sexual meaning of χαρισαμένοις παιδικοῖς and of ὑπουργεῖν) of this term, see Dover 1989:44–45.

The existence of sexual relations, clearly alluded to, between a young boy and his lover are justified in an educative context where the boy is led towards wisdom and all other forms of excellence by his lover.

(6) Yet it is precisely by means of education, it seems to me, that Pausanias tries to justify the fact that the lover may prolong amorous relations after the appearance of the first beard on his beloved. The emphasis on constancy in the amorous relation between two men demands the transcendence of the limits admitted in the context of *paiderastia*. This plea does not prevent the characters in Aristophanes' *Thesmophoriazusae* from reflecting views of Athenian society in denouncing Agathon's attitude in the violation of this rule of conduct.

3.2 Agathon's speech (194e–197e)

Agathon's speech is indissociable from that of Pausanias, for Agathon uses his praise of Eros to place implicitly himself on stage, by presenting the qualities he attributes to Eros as those that he himself so obviously possesses. Moreover, we may suppose him to attribute the qualities of character and intellect, as distinct from the advantages given by age and beauty, to this relationship with Pausanias.

In its style, Agathon's speech, empty but magnificently constructed, manifests the influence of the school of Gorgias, which was characterized in particular by the use of assonance and alliteration. Here we find short, parallel phrases, featuring an abundance of assonances and similarity in inflexions. These rhetorical turns of phrase are particularly numerous in the conclusion, which gives rise to Socrates' sarcastic comment: "I was afraid that Agathon would end by sending the terrifying Gorgias' head of eloquence in his speech against my speech, and turn me to stone, unable to utter a word" (198c). Finally, Agathon has a great love of poetic citations,[71] and has a tendency to make poetry out of his prose.

For Agathon, Eros is the youngest god (195a–c). His body is the most delicate (195c–196a) and the most beautiful (196a–b). Since his soul is also just (196b–c), temperate (196c–d), courageous (196d) and wise (196d–197b) in the field of poetry (196d–e) and in every other area (196e–197b), he promotes these virtues by way of benefits in all people (197c–e). We cannot get much out of this brilliant but empty speech. As in his relationship with Pausanias, Agathon is the beloved (*erōmenos*), and he describes an Eros who is young; in

---

[71] *Symposium* 196c, e, 196a, 197c.

addition, his Eros possesses all the virtues and can transmit them to everyone. On this level, at least, his speech echoes to that of Pausanias, which is intended as a defense and illustration of *paiderastia* as an educative instrument that enables the achievement of excellence in all its forms, particularly in the area of poetry.[72]

Agathon's speech, and especially that of Pausanias, seem to me to cause the appearance in the *Symposium* of something like a critique launched by Socrates against the association of *paiderastia* with *philosophia* in the framework of an Athenian convention associating the provisional acceptance of sexual relations between a boy or a young man and an older man with the transmission of material, political, and even intellectual values. Through his example and his speech, Agathon provides proof of the vacuousness of this education, limited as it is to the learning of rhetoric.

3.3 Diotima's speech (201e–209e)

It is here that Socrates begins to speak. With great courtesy, since Agathon is his host, Socrates begins by subjecting him to an *elenchos*.[73] Agathon has just asserted that Eros is "the most beautiful and the best" (197e2–3); but Eros seeks the beautiful and the good, which he consequently does not yet possess (199c–201c). To attenuate this refutation, however, Socrates explains that he used to maintain a position similar to that of Agathon on Eros, before he himself was refuted (*Symposium* 201d–e) by Diotima.[74] Socrates dilutes the criticism he has directed to his host Agathon, by taking it upon himself; above all, by reversing the representation of Eros shared by the other male guests, he engages, in a radical critique, placed under the authority of a woman, of *paiderastia* and of *philosophia*, in the context of a speech of praise which, like that given by Agathon,[75] deals with the nature of Eros and the benefits he accords.

Eros (Love) is always desire, not for nothing, but for something (199c–e). What one desires, however, one does not possess (200a–e). Since love's object is the beautiful and the good, it must be deficient in beauty and goodness (200e–201c). Agathon was therefore wrong to declare that Eros is a great god, endowed with every quality (201d–e). This does not mean that Eros is ugly and bad, but that he is an intermediary being (201e–202d).

---

[72] See *Symposium* 197a–b.

[73] Dorion 1990.

[74] On the question of the degree of historical reality that can be attributed to Diotima, see Halperin 1990:113–151.

[75] "So now, in the case of Love, it is right for us to praise (ἐπαινέσαι) him first for what he is (οἷός ἐστιν), and afterwards for his gifts (τὰς δόσεις)" (195a3–5).

Eros is a *daimōn*, that is, a being intermediary, on every level, between man and god (202e–203a). His father is Poros (Resource) and his mother Penia (Poverty) (203a–c). The nature (*phusis*) of Eros is explained by his origins. He occupies the midpoint of all things (203c–e), and particularly between knowledge and ignorance: "Wisdom is actually one of the most beautiful things, and Love (Eros) is love in relation with what is beautiful, so that love is necessarily a lover of wisdom (*philosophos*), and a lover of wisdom is necessarily between wisdom and ignorance" (204b).[76] This is why Eros is a philosopher: This definition of *philosophos* and consequently of *philosophia* will inspire the whole of the remaining argumentation.

Now that Eros's nature has been defined, one can enquire into the benefits he brings to men, and his usefulness (see *khreia* at 204c) in the context of *paiderastia*. Above all, however, a specification must be added that places Agathon's speech, once again, in question. Because Eros is not endowed with all beauties, but is rather in search of them, he is not the beloved (*erōmenos*), but the lover (*erastēs*) (203d–204c).

In fact, Eros leads men to seek the possession of the beautiful and the good for their own sake, and forever (204c–206a). In this way, Eros can be associated with an activity that deserves the most serious attention, and with an effort manifested in an occupation or a task (206a–210d): that of procreation, which ensures immortality for humans. This procreation may be according to the body or according to the soul: the former variety implies union between a man and a woman in order to produce, while the latter involves *paiderastia*.

The lover (*erastēs*) is the one primarily concerned. This viewpoint is found once again in a passage (208e–209e) which opens with the opposition between procreation according to the body and procreation according to the soul:

> For those who are fecund (ἐγκύμονες) by the body, this mode of being in love (ἐρωτικοί) consists in turning preferably toward women, in order to engender children (παιδογονίας), thereby ensuring a relative immortality. As far as the soul is concerned, by contrast, there is an engenderment of thought (φρόνησίν) and of every other form of virtue or excellence (τε καὶ τὴν ἄλλην ἀρετήν), which express themselves in the acts and discourses that are their genuine offspring (ἔκγονα).
>
> *Symposium* 208e2–209a3

---

[76] See *Phaedrus* 278d, where the qualification of *sophos* is reserved for the god, since man can only be *philosophos*.

These discourses may be, as tradition would have it, those of poets like Homer and Hesiod, of legislators like Lycurgus and Solon, and even of inventors (209c7–e3). Yet the highest part of thought is situated in justice and moderation (209a7–b1). Men who seek to be fruitful in this area become educators. They then seek out a young man whose body, and above all whose soul, shine with beauty, and they speak to him of virtue, that is, of the duties and occupations of a worthy man (209b2–c2). Upon contact (ἁπτόμενος) with a beautiful object, and by means of assiduous presence (ὁμιλῶν) near him, they engender and procreate (τίκτει καὶ γεννᾷ) what they long had within them (ἃ πάλαι ἐκύει, c2–3). It is interesting to note that it is the older man who is pregnant (κυῶν), who gives birth and procreates (τίκτει καὶ γεννᾷ), and who therefore reaps the benefit of the relation, while the young man represents that beauty which, as we have just seen, presides over the childbirth or the soul, as Moira and Eilithuia do for the body (206b–d). The procedure is as follows: because he teaches a young man, the older man brings forth to the light of day the beautiful children he bore within him, which then appear in the form of fine discourses and fine actions. It should also be noted that that to which he gives birth (τὸ γεννηθὲν) was already within him (ἃ πάλαι ἐκύει), which, it seems to me, is an allusion to reminiscence. This process does not stop at birth, for the child, whether discourse or action, is nourished (συνεκτρέφει) by the two protagonists, with the one who has given birth nourishing him both when the young man is present and when he is absent, for in this case the child remembers him. In other words, both the educator and the person being educated develop the fine discourses and perpetuate the fine actions that are their children. "This makes the relation (κοινωνίαν) between such men far more intimate than that which consists in having children together (τῶν παίδων) according to the body, and these children they have in common are more beautiful and more assured of immortality than children according to the body." This long passage (208e–209e) is surprising, for it describes the pregnancy (a phenomenon that is in principle feminine) of a man, who, once he has given birth, raises the children he has given to another man, who is his beloved (*erōmenos*).

In my view, the image of pregnancy applied to the soul of the lover (*erastēs*) refers to what is said of the human soul in the central part of the *Phaedrus*. Before it falls into a human body, the soul, in the company of other souls, ascends with the troop of gods and demons to contemplate the intelligible, situated somewhere beyond the sphere in which the body of the world consists. Here, it contemplates Beauty in particular (*Phaedrus* 250c–d). Once it has fallen into an earthly body, the human soul can rediscover the cognitive experiences that subsist within it in the form of memory only through the intermediary of reminiscence (*Phaedrus* 249c–d).[77] This, it seems, is the sense in which the image of the educator's pregnancy must be interpreted: as referring to reminiscence.[78]

The theme of reminiscence is, moreover, in perfect agreement with that of the Mysteries (*Symposium* 209e–210d). The lover (*erastēs*) can only reactualize the knowledge he already possesses in a virtual mode in a relation with the beautiful body of his beloved (*erōmenos*), which relation must then move on to his soul, and culminate in the vision of Beauty (210e–212a). Thus, *paiderastia*, henceforth described by terms borrowed from the Mysteries, is completely reinterpreted. Although she is a woman, Diotima is aware of the social convention known as *paiderastia*. Yet she wants to transform it:

> So when someone rises by these stages, through loving boys correctly (διὰ τὸ ὀρθῶς παιδεραστεῖν), and begins to see this beauty, he has almost grasped his goal. This is what it is to go aright, or be led by another, from one lovable thing to the other (ἐπὶ τα ἐρωτικὰ): one goes always upwards for the sake of this Beauty, starting out from beautiful things (ἀπὸ τῶνδε τῶν καλῶν) and using them like rising stairs: from one body to two and from two to all beautiful bodies (ἐπὶ πάντα τὰ καλὰ σώματα), then from beautiful bodies to beautiful customs (ἐπὶ τὰ καλὰ ἐπιτηδεύματα), and from customs to learning beautiful things (ἐπὶ τὰ καλὰ μαθήματα), and from these lessons he arrives[79] in the end at this lesson, which is learning of this very Beauty (αὐτοῦ ἐκείνου τοῦ καλοῦ), so that in the end he comes to know just what it is to be beautiful (ὅ ἐστι καλόν).
>
> *Symposium* 211b5–c8

This passage, which takes up what was said at 210a–211b, while replacing *epistēmai* (210c–e) by *mathēmata* (211c d), develops an idea similar to the one found at *Phaedrus* 250a. What love is searching for is beauty, which manifests

---

[77] 'Reminiscence' considered in a technical sense appears only in three dialogues, the *Meno* (81b–84a), the *Phaedo* (72e–77a), and the *Phaedrus* (249b–d). In all three cases, the point is to re-appropriate a knowledge, and therefore a discourse, which was already present within a man's soul. At least in the last two cases, it is clear that the knowledge that is to be recovered is that which the soul has acquired while contemplating the Forms when it was separated from all earthly bodies. This effort at reappropriation is the art of "maieutics," which consists in making the pregnant soul give birth.

[78] On reminiscence in general, see Huber 1964. For the most recent interpretation, with which I disagree, because it does not involve the intelligible, see Scott 1995.

[79] Reading τελευτῆσαι.

itself at various levels of reality: hence the interest of explaining how it is possible to pass from the sensible to the intelligible by way of the Mysteries.[80]

As in the case of the social convention known as *paiderastia*, we have here a relation between two men. We cannot rule out the existence of sexual relations between the lover and his beloved, but these relations must be transcended, and desire must be transferred to such incorporeal objects as the soul or the Forms. It is the older partner who is pregnant, while the younger one, through the beauty of his body and especially of his soul, plays the role of trigger with regard to him. In order to educate the younger partner, the older one brings into the world and into broad daylight the fine discourses and actions he already carried within him. The divinity that presides over this birth that involves the two men is Beauty, who must be assimilated to a divinity who plays the role, in the world of generation, that is the appendage of the Moirai and of Eilithuia.

The image of pregnancy implies that of birth, and points in the direction of maieutics[81] which favors birth; that is, in this context, the re-appropriation of the knowledge that was already present in the soul, but only in a virtual way. Here, a difficulty could be raised. At first, it is the beloved (*erōmenos*), or the younger partner, who plays the part of midwife for the older lover (*erastēs*) (209c–d). In what follows, however (210a–d), the relation may be generalized.

An analysis of the speeches of Pausanias and Agathon, on the one hand, and of that of Diotima on the other, makes the following three oppositions stand out. (1) On the level of education, a representation of education as the transmission of a knowledge from master to disciple in a hierarchical relation is opposed to a way of thinking about education as the rediscovery of a knowledge which is already present in the soul of the lover and which must be

---

[80] On this subject, for the *Symposium*, see Riedweg 1987:2–29, and for the *Phaedrus*, 1987:30–67.

[81] The art of maieutics is mentioned only in a single passage of the *corpus platonicum*, in the *Theaetetus* (148d–151). However, it is obvious that the idea is found here as well, through the intermediary the term ὠδίς 'the pangs of childbirth' and the verb ὠδίνω to 'suffer the pangs of childbirth', which is found not only in the aforementioned passage from the *Theaetetus*, but also in the *Republic* (VI 490b), and the *Phaedrus* 255e, 262d. Yet the question arises whether the image of maieutics does not refer to reminiscence, as mentioned in the *Meno* (81b–84a). The souls which education enables to give birth are "great" with the knowledge and discourses they have obtained in their journey beyond the cosmic sphere, and which they have forgotten on the occasion of their fall. The fact of presenting maieutics as a divine mission also points in this direction: "And the reason of it is this, that god compels me to attend the travail of others, but has forbidden me to procreate. So that I am not in any sense a wise man; I cannot claim as the child of my own soul any discovery worth the name of wisdom. But with those who associate with me it is different" (*Theaetetus* 150c–d). I subscribe to the position of Dorion 2004:66–69, who opposes Burnyeat 1977.

brought to light, as in the act of giving birth, in the form of fine discourses and fine actions handed over to the loved one, who has first the role of a midwife and must take care of the offspring. (2) On the level of sexuality, which serves to illustrate these two representations of education, two models confront one another: that of the transmission of the seminal liquid, in the context of *paiderastia*, where, in an institutionalized relationship (of masculine homosexuality), an older lover has sexual relations with a younger beloved who becomes his slave in order to benefit from his knowledge, his power, or his wealth, and that of conception in a woman, who must be delivered by bringing to light the embryo she carries; the image of pregnancy (pregnancy being related in antiquity and in our societies to the woman's role) seems to be linked, on an epistemological level, to the themes of reminiscence and maieutics. (3) Finally, on the level of reality, we note an opposition between physical beauty, which is an object of consumption, and incorporeal beauty (intelligible Beauty and that of the soul), which presides over the birth of fine discourses and fine actions, thereby making this birth possible; the transition from the sensible to the intelligible is described in the terms of the Mysteries. We witness here a complete reversal of perspective at all three levels, as is generally the case in Plato.

Trans. Michael Chase

Eleven

Female Imagery in Plato

Angela Hobbs

The Image of the Pregnant Philosopher

A T *SYMPOSIUM* 206C–E DIOTIMA TELLS US that all humans (*anthrōpoi*) are pregnant (*kuousin*) in both body and soul, and require contact with the beautiful in order to be able to relieve their pangs and give birth to their physical or spiritual children. She also makes it very clear that the virtues which constitute the spiritual children, and which can take the ascending forms of heroic acts, works of art and law, and various branches of learning right up to knowledge of the Form of Beauty, are decidedly superior to physical children: they are "more beautiful (*kallionōn*) and more immortal (*athanatōterōn*)" and "everyone would choose to produce children such as these rather than the human sort" (209c–d). She also makes it clear in 209a that some people are *more* pregnant in soul than in body. Indeed, despite the wording of 206, the remainder of her speech at least allows for the possibility that some humans will concentrate on spiritual pregnancy to the exclusion of physical pregnancy (and vice versa). It is certainly notable that, again despite 206, she never discusses an example of someone who is pregnant in both senses *qua* their double pregnancy, although some of the psychologically creative people she mentions undoubtedly had physical children too. In any event, it is plain that the best kind of pregnancy is the highest kind of spiritual pregnancy, and this is the pregnancy of the philosopher. Such a pregnancy paradoxically results in a transcendent version of sexual union, a "being with" the Form of Beauty itself (212a): "in this existence above all others is life livable for a human being" (211d).[1] In the *Symposium*, Diotima's philosophic contri-

---

[1] The term translated 'being with' (*sunontos*) can carry sexual overtones: 'have intercourse with'. See *Laws* 773a and LSJ s.v. *suneimi* (4).

bution notwithstanding,[2] the main representative of philosophy is a male, Socrates: not only is he the empirical voice of philosophy at the banquet, just as other characters are voices for comic and tragic drama, medicine, rhetoric, and public life, but he is described by Plato in ways which are clearly meant to recall the depiction of the wisdom-loving (204a–b) Eros in Diotima's speech.[3] As the philosopher-par-excellence, therefore, we are presumably meant to think of Socrates as spiritually[4] pregnant, walking barefoot about Athens in search of the young men, such as Alcibiades, whose spiritual and physical beauty can help him give birth to the fine and educative words which constitute his *phronēsis* and *aretē*. Indeed this image of Socrates as pregnant is reinforced in Alcibiades' speech at 215a–b where Alcibiades speaks of Socrates as a Silenus statue, containing figures of gods inside.[5]

It is an undeniably startling introduction of a female bodily process into a text which until this point has focused on men far more than on women. Women are excluded from the dramatic setting of the symposium (even the customary flute-girl is dismissed at 176e and told to pipe either to herself or to the women within), and the earlier speeches do not greatly concern themselves either with the love of women or love for women, though Phaedrus does mention Alcestis' love for her husband at 179b–c and Aristophanes includes women who love men and women who love women in his mythological account of the origins and aim of love (189c–193d, especially 191d–

---

[2] Even if Diotima is based on a historical figure (and I have yet to see convincing evidence of this, though I take Nails' caution (2002:137) about the danger of arguing largely *ex silentio*), she is still a dramatic construct in the *Symposium*: witness her (aptly) prophetic allusion to a remark that Aristophanes has just made in his speech, an allusion that Aristophanes himself points out (205d–e and 212c). However, the point about her philosophical contribution is that she is not just a character invented by Plato; she is also a character wholly or partly invented by the character of Socrates within the fiction of the banquet. The other characters are taking part in a fictional symposium; Diotima is physically absent even from that fiction. Nevertheless, the fact that even an invented and absent woman has her views reported (albeit by a man) at a male institution such as a symposium is still important and will be discussed below. For a judicious appraisal of Diotima's historicity, see Halperin 1990:119–122.

[3] Like wisdom-loving, "philosophic" Eros, Socrates is poor, barefoot and stands in doorways. (These attributes are assigned to Eros at 203c–d; Socrates is said by Alcibiades to have regularly walked barefoot in the ice on campaign in Potidaea at 220a–b (see also 174a), and Aristodemus recounts at 175a how Socrates stood in a doorway reflecting on a problem while on his way to the banquet.) It is also notable that Eros is categorized by Diotima as a *daimōn* (202d–e), while at 219c Alcibiades calls Socrates *daimonios*.

[4] There is no mention in the text of Socrates also being physically "pregnant," even in the metaphorical sense in which men can become "pregnant" in body which is discussed below.

[5] This reinforcement is unwitting on Alcibiades' part, as he was absent for Socrates' speech; but it is not unwitting of Plato.

192c).[6] Yet Aristophanes also emphasizes (191e–192b) that the "best" and "most manly" males will be involved in male pederastic relationships, and this is also the message of Pausanias' speech, in which men who love women are dismissed as 'paltry', *phauloi*, and are consigned to the domain of the inferior "popular" Aphrodite, who partakes of both male and female (181a–c). "Heavenly" Aphrodite, by contrast, partakes only of the male and is the source of love between males: indeed, the male in general is described by Pausanias as more robust by nature and in possession of a greater intellect (181c). Even in Diotima's own speech, and despite the gender-neutral *anthrōpos* of 206c and 211d,[7] the superior spiritually pregnant lovers of 209a–211d are mainly[8] spoken of as male: *ek neou* 209a–b; *ton andra* 209c; *tous neous* 210c; *tous kalous paidas te kai neaniskous* 211d. Indeed, at 211b they are explicitly said to be engaged in the "correct method of boy-loving" (*to orthōs paiderastein*). Diotima herself, of course, may be imagined as spiritually pregnant, and needing contact with the spiritual beauty of the young Socrates in order to relieve herself of her pedagogic offspring, but she does not refer to herself as such. The explicit emphasis of 209a–211d is in general on the male lover and the male beloved,[9] though we should keep in mind the uses of *anthrōpos* that we have already noted, as there will be more to come. Nevertheless, whatever else Diotima may be doing, she is certainly inviting us to see the older male *erastēs* as "pregnant"; and whatever else he may be doing, Plato is both placing his discussion of *erōs* at least partly within the Athenian upper-class convention of pederasty and at the same time radically revising that convention.[10] Finally, the impact of the

---

[6] Halperin (1990:128–129) is eloquent on the exclusion and downgrading of females and female experience from the *Symposium*, although he somewhat overstates the case. I hope to show why I think it matters so much to be accurate on this point.

[7] Unless stated otherwise, I use 'gender' in this paper to cover both cultural gender and biological sex and all reworkings of the two.

[8] Mainly, but not exclusively. Again, I intend to show why this point is so important.

[9] It is true that a little earlier (208d) she rather unfairly cites Alcestis as an example of a person prepared to sacrifice life through a desire to create an immortal name, but though this may be an instance of spiritual pregnancy, it is clearly not intended as the highest kind of spiritual pregnancy, which occurs only after 209.

[10] If an unspoken image of a spiritually pregnant Diotima is hovering in the background of this male social institution, then this would be another way in which the institution is being reworked by Plato. Similarly, if Diotima is also supposed to possess a spiritual beauty which in turn inspires Socrates to give birth, then this would be yet a further form of subversion on Plato's part. In his contribution to this volume, Brisson highlights the point that Pausanias' "heavenly" form of pederasty, in which *erōs* is based on spiritual qualities and can last throughout life rather than ending when the *erōmenos* first grows a beard, already constitutes an initial revision of the institution by Plato (and one which Plato illustrates through his depiction of the relation between Pausanias and Agathon).

pregnancy image is heightened still further if, in addition to love, we consider the concomitant models of education discussed earlier in the dialogue: as well as the educative element central to male pederasty and piously emphasized by Pausanias, we also have Socrates' allusion to the notion of education as a pouring of liquid from the fuller to the emptier (175d), which for Brisson and others is reminiscent of the ejaculation of seminal fluid.[11]

Responses to the Image

This metaphor of spiritual pregnancy has aroused a wide spectrum of reactions, ranging from the intrigued (Halperin 1990), through the ambivalent (Plass),[12] to the openly critical or even hostile. In this paper I wish in particular to consider one type of negative response, which focuses on whether Plato is morally justified in describing male practices and institutions through use of a female bodily function. Du Bois (1988:182–183), for example, has written with some passion about Plato's supposed "appropriation" of the female role in reproduction. Through the image of spiritual pregnancy, she claims, Plato is taking away from women the one act that is their sole biological provenance: "she teaches him that the philosophical intercourse, conception, pregnancy and delivery of male lovers are superior to the corporeal acts of human women ... the male philosopher becomes the site of metaphorical reproduction, the subject of philosophical generation; the female ... becomes a defective male, defined by lack." Pender (1992:86), too, in her stimulating discussion of spiritual pregnancy in the *Symposium*, argues that Plato deliberately conceals the origins of the image: "the whole of the 'female' experience of pregnancy and giving birth to a child has been suppressed"; "... that Plato has used the overtly female image of pregnancy and at the same time has obscured the female role in procreation is no small achievement." Cavarero (1995:92) expresses herself yet more strongly. Although she maintains that "the works of Plato ... seem marked by a mimetic desire for female experience" and "there is ... no trace of misogyny here," she nevertheless argues that the use of the pregnancy image ultimately brings about a situation where "maternal power is annihilated by offering its language and vocabulary to the power that will triumph over it" (1995:94). Such criticisms may seem to receive some support from *Republic*

---

[11] See Brisson's chapter in this volume. It should be stressed that Socrates makes it clear that he does not believe that this model is a true one.

[12] " ... the notion of pregnancy does seem in some respects rather awkward in defense of pederasty" (Plass 1978:48).

395d–e, where Socrates is adamant that the young guardians (at this stage of the work tellingly envisaged only as male) should on no account ever represent a woman in sickness or love or—apparently the climax of disgrace—childbirth. The charges may also bring to mind the apparent downplaying of female biological functions and traditional activities in *Republic* V: while Socrates acknowledges that women are distinguished from men by their capacity to bear children (454d–e), he appears to accord little value to the unique bond between mother and child and indeed emphasizes that, in the case of guardian women, they will not breastfeed or raise their own children, but must submit them to the care of a state nursery run by male and female officers (460b–c).[13] Indeed, some commentators have accused Socrates here of turning the female guardians into distasteful parodies of men, obliged to hunt and go to war.[14]

One may wish to go even further. One may be tempted to link this downplaying of female bodily functions and traditional nurturing roles with the significant number of passages in the dialogues in which Socrates contemptuously dismisses women in general and contemporary Athenian women in particular.[15] To take just four examples, the first three also from the *Republic*: at 469d he remarks that desecrating an enemy's corpse is the mark of a "small and womanish" mind, while at 431b–c the lower appetites are said to exist chiefly in "children and women and slaves and the base multitude." At 605d–e, private outbursts of wild grief are also derided as "womanish"; the manly thing to do is to endure in silence. Most damning of all, perhaps, is the stipulation in the *Timaeus* (42b–c) that the man who is unable to govern his emotions

---

[13] Tuana 1992:22 emphasizes this point: "... no guardian, male or female, would participate in the rearing of children. Thus we hear no mention of the guardians developing nurturing qualities or the types of wisdom needed for the raising of small children."

[14] See Annas 1981:185: "In most of Book V Plato spends his time claiming, irrelevantly and grotesquely, that women can engage in fighting and other 'macho' pursuits nearly as well as men." Blundell (1995:185) holds that "[Plato] ascribes such low value to ... women's traditional functions and qualities that he sees no reason why their role should not—within the guardian class—be abolished ... he turns them into 'honorary men'." A similar position is put forward by Tuana 1992:22: "Women, then, can serve as guardians only to the extent that they are capable of being like men." Saxonhouse 1994:68 (1976) expresses herself even more forthrightly, if not altogether consistently, claiming that in *Republic* V Socrates "attempts to turn women into men," and that the female guardians are "de-sexed and unnatural." It is worth noting that the Amazons have often received similar treatment: the *Shorter Oxford English Dictionary* (1973) revealingly gives for "Amazon" a "strong, tall, or masculine woman." All such attitudes, of course, depend on particular, if not always acknowledged, views concerning which attributes and activities are "appropriate" for women. They therefore tell us at least as much about Plato's critics (and modern lexicographers) as they do about Plato.

[15] See Wender 1973 for a balanced consideration of some of the more hostile comments about women in the Platonic corpus.

is to be punished by being reborn as a woman.[16] In the *Symposium* itself, as we have seen, the dismissal of women may be thought to be symbolized by the banishment of the flute-girl at 176e and the low value that Pausanias and others place on the love of and for women. If one does make this link between the deployment of the pregnancy image and the attitude of Socrates and other characters to women in general, then Du Bois' charge might be rephrased thus: Plato appropriates what is useful to him from female experience and discards the rest.[17]

A Different Response

Such responses are valid but they are not, I think, finally persuasive. In this paper I wish to offer a different interpretation of the pregnancy image and what it reveals about Plato's attitude to gender in general and women in particular. I wish to locate the image within an overall educative project of Plato in which he sees gender as both inevitably important in the everyday world of becoming (and thus an apt resource for rhetorical and pedagogic purposes), and at the same time as ultimately irrelevant in the eternal and unchanging realm of being to which inhabitants of the world of becoming should aspire.[18] Thus gender will vary in its significance to both student and (Platonic) teacher depending on which stage of his[19] intellectual and emotional education the student has reached (in the language of the *Symposium*, which rung of the ladder of love he has attained); in consequence, the function of gendered images will similarly vary for the educationalist depending on the level (and perhaps also mood) of the student that she or he is trying to influence.

The use of gendered images and themes will thus be of great value for an educator attempting to reach out to students in the earlier stages of their education (and on the lowest one or two rungs of the ladder);[20] yet the same

---

[16] See also *Timaeus* 90e–91a.

[17] Halperin 1990:118 and n21 gives a helpful survey of some of the vast secondary literature on attitudes to women in the dialogues, and inferences concerning Plato's own views. See also Tuana 1994.

[18] See *Symposium* 212a. Philosopher-Rulers are explicitly encouraged to model both themselves and their states and citizens on the order and divinity of the realm of the Forms at *Republic* 500c–e.

[19] I raise the question below of whether this project is intended to apply to future female students as well. As Plato employs both Diotima and Socrates as educators, I see no such difficulty about referring to the Platonic educator as "he or she."

[20] The point certainly holds for the lowest rung, in which the lover is fixated on one particular body. Whether it also applies to the next rung, in which the lover turns his attention to the beauty of

educator will also need to move his or her students towards an understanding of the irrelevance of gender to the ideal of the virtuous human,[21] and the ultimate inconsequentiality of gender and the body in general in the realm of the transcendent Forms. I shall therefore argue that we should not try to delineate a single, consistent approach of Plato towards gender and gendered images; on the contrary, I shall maintain that there is no such single approach to be found. All depends on the nature, mood and, above all, educational stage of both the interlocutor addressed by Socrates (or the Eleatic or Athenian Strangers) and the reader that Plato particularly has in mind in a given passage. He cannot, of course, control the make-up of his future readership or control the order in which the dialogues are read (though by means of certain stylistic techniques he can hope to attract certain readers more than others and make certain dialogues more likely to be read earlier or later). He can, however, through the judicious deployment of images and other literary devices, hope to speak in the same dialogue to different readers at different stages of their intellectual and emotional development. As this development progresses, so certain passages will resonate with them more forcibly than others, and some of these passages will even come to be understood quite differently: students will come to appreciate that their earlier understanding of a gendered image was dependent on an immature and limited (though temporarily inevitable) perspective drawn from the world of becoming. In short, I shall argue that gendered images are one of the main devices that Plato deploys when trying to confront the challenge of how to teach immutable truths in a mutable world, a world in which his students themselves are in a process of constant change. In the course of this argument, I shall consider some of the detailed implications of the thesis for the *Symposium* itself.

The Pregnancy Image in Context

Let us return to the image of spiritual pregnancy and the hostility it has sometimes provoked. In considering both image and hostile response, we need to apply some perspective, and there are four perspectives in particular that I

---

all bodies, depends on whether (a) the 'all' (*pasi* 210b) really does mean *all*, i.e. both male and female; and (b) even if it does apply to both male and female bodies, whether the gender of the beautiful beloveds is truly of no significance whatsoever to the lover (gender can still be important to those attracted to both sexes, even if they have no preference for one sex over the other).

[21] *Meno* 73a–c, discussed below.

wish to bring to bear. Firstly, the metaphor of pregnancy is not the only "female" image employed by Plato: there are, amongst others, the images of midwifery and weaving, and we need to reflect on these too.[22] Secondly, the "female" images need to be viewed in conjunction with the apparently "male" images used to describe the practice of philosophy in, for example, the *Laches*, *Gorgias* and *Republic*: images drawn from war, hunting and athletics.[23] Thirdly, we need to reflect on both sets of gendered images in conjunction with what Socrates says about the ideal roles of ideally educated guardian men and women in *Republic* V. Finally, we must consider all the above in the light of the ungendered, incorporeal, eternal Forms, and especially in the light of the Form of Beauty in the *Symposium*. It is only then that we shall be in a position to view the image of the pregnant philosopher in its full Platonic context.

This is not to say that the *Symposium* has to be placed in these wider contexts in order to make sense, or to be enjoyed; I strongly believe that all Plato's dialogues work as organic wholes in their own right, according to the model laid out in the *Phaedrus*.[24] Yet it is also an undeniable fact that Plato is well aware that many, probably the majority, of his readers are not going to confine themselves to just one of his works, and a significant number will study all or most of them. So while the *Symposium* can certainly be viewed as an independent unit, I believe that our appreciation of the dialogue can be greatly enriched by placing it in these wider settings.

"Female" Images in Plato

Let us begin by considering our chosen trio of "female" images. In the *Theaetetus*, the metaphor at 148e–151d and elsewhere[25] is not of a pregnant Socrates, but Socrates as a midwife (*maia*),[26] helping others—and in the

---

[22] For the midwife image, see *Theaetetus* 148e–151d; 157c–d; 160e–161b; 161e; 184b; 210b–d. For weaving, see e.g. *Statesman* 305e–311c and *Republic* 500d. These three images of pregnancy, midwifery and weaving are not the only images drawn from female experience in the dialogues, but they will suffice for the present discussion.

[23] In the *Republic*, doing philosophy is compared to battle: 534c; hunting and tracking: 432b–d; swimming, often against mighty waves: 453d, 457b–d, 472a–473c; wrestling: 554b, 583b; mountain-climbing: 445c. See Hobbs 2000:passim, but especially 243–249.

[24] *Phaedrus* 264c. This principle strikes me as true even for the explicitly linked *Theaetetus*, *Sophist* and *Statesman*.

[25] See n22 above.

[26] We are told at *Theaetetus* 149b that women only become midwives when they can no longer bear children of their own: hence the images of pregnancy and midwifery cannot, in the *Theaetetus* at least, be represented by the same person simultaneously.

context of the *Theaetetus* this means other men[27]—give birth to their ideas and test which ones are healthy and sound. Turning to the *Statesman*, the Eleatic Stranger tells us at 305e–311c that true statesmanship is the expertise which weaves (*sumplokē* and cognates) everything together in the correct way. In practice this means weaving together the apparently opposing virtues of *andreia* and *sōphrosunē* and the two classes of people who embody them; such interweaving is to be achieved by a twin policy of "divine" and "human" bonds, the divine bonds comprising true and secure beliefs concerning fine, just and good things, and the human ones being largely formed by a state-controlled policy of eugenics. Intermarriage between the two basic types will check the tendency of the one to descend into savagery and madness, and of the other to degenerate into sluggish passivity. In these ways, the citizen body will become a well-woven fabric of resolute warp and softer woof.

We have, then, three striking and memorable images, drawn on the face of it from female bodily functions and traditional female activities. These images can be approached (and have been so approached in the scholarly literature) in two main ways. Firstly, one can ask what such comparisons tell us about Plato's conception of the practice, purpose and value of philosophy and philosophic statesmanship; in particular, one can ask what the images of pregnancy and midwifery tell us about his theories of knowledge and education and what the image of weaving tells us about the art and function of ruling.[28] Furthermore, this approach can be taken either with respect to a single image or single dialogue (the latter considered as an independent unit), or by considering the images together, perhaps in the hope of building up some kind of developmental picture (a somewhat unfashionable hope at the moment in Platonic studies, but certainly not to be rejected on that account).[29] Do Plato's theories of knowledge and education, for instance, change between the *Symposium* and the *Theaetetus*? Is the picture of the pregnant Socrates of the former philosophically different from the midwife Socrates of the latter?

Secondly, one can approach the images specifically from the point of view of their apparent *femaleness*. Are their female connotations merely contingent—even irrelevant—to Plato's purposes, or does Plato exploit such female

---

[27] At *Theaetetus* 150b and 210c Socrates makes it clear that his midwifery is practiced upon men, not women.

[28] It is this approach which is mostly dominant in the fine studies of Burnyeat 1977, Sheffield 2001a, and Lane 1998.

[29] Many of the arguments both for and against developmentalist interpretations of Plato in general (although without specific reference to gendered images) are ably discussed in Annas and Rowe 2002.

associations for some particular rhetorical or philosophic goal or goals? And even if he does not deploy the gendered associations deliberately, does the "femaleness" of these images tell us something important nevertheless? Does it, for example, tell us something more about Plato's view (whether conscious or not) of the nature and role of women—both actual, contemporary Athenian women and the hypothetical female guardians of *Republic* V–VII, who have been trained and educated according to the ideals that Socrates lays out? What are the effects of the images on the minds of readers?

It is this second approach with which I am principally concerned here, though I hope to show that in any case this second approach leads us back to the question of how Plato views philosophy. To begin with, we need to consider an issue which has hitherto gone largely unexplored, namely the extent to which such images really are "female" in the first place.[30] Let us start with midwifery, because it is the most straightforward. The *Oxford Classical Dictionary* states that all—or almost all—midwives in Greece at this time were women: it admits that male midwives cannot be entirely ruled out, but points out that the evidence is very difficult to interpret, as male doctors not surprisingly sometimes delivered babies (a point made clear in inscriptions).[31] In any case, the critical point for our purposes is that the term *maia* would without doubt have had female associations for Plato's audience. However, the possibility that there might have been the occasional male midwife—and the certainty that male doctors sometimes delivered babies—is still important, as it allows Plato room to maneuver and to invite his readers to rethink the association between midwifery and women. In this context, it is helpful to turn to the proposals for occupational equality put forward by Socrates in *Republic* V and to ask whether they entail that midwives will be both female and male. At *Republic* 454d–e we are told that the only essential difference between men and women is that the female bears (*tiktein*) and the male begets (*ocheuein*), and this difference is not a sufficient basis for the assignation of different occupations to each: in consequence, there is no state-related function (*epitēdeuma ... pros dioikēsin poleōs*) peculiar to women (455a–b and 455d), though in general women will not perform as well as men. It is true that in *Republic* V this argument for occupational equality is only applied explicitly to the guardian class (457b–c, though see 455e discussed below), and midwifery is presumably an occupation of the producer class. Yet this does not stop the principle of 454d–

---

[30] An exception is Blondell, who briefly discusses the relation between gender and weaving in her thoughtful treatment of these images (2002:141n143). See below n34.

[31] See H. K. King "Midwives" in OCD ed. 3.

e and 455a–b from being applicable to the producers, even if it is not here applied. It may also be significant that at 460b it is stated that the officers who run the state nurseries will be both male and female;[32] the nurses themselves are described as female (460c), but as one of their main tasks is to breastfeed, this is hardly surprising. We are also told at 455e that a woman may possess a natural ability for medicine, which presumably means that Socrates envisages female doctors (a possible exception to the limitation of occupational equality to the guardian class of 457b–c), and if female doctors are permissible, then why not male midwives? In any event, the basic inference is clear: if consistently applied, then the principle of 454d–e would indeed have to allow for male midwives. In short, though the associations of *maia* in the *Theaetetus* are predominantly female, they are not necessarily exclusively so, either in contemporary Greece or in Plato's imaginary state.

A similar picture emerges from a study of weaving. The spinning and weaving of wool[33] was in this period of Greek history almost exclusively a female task and area of expertise, a point made by Plato himself at *Republic* 455c. Its archetypal exponent in myth was Penelope and its deity Athena. Indeed, the association between women and weaving is so strong that to accuse a man of weaving is to accuse him of being effeminate: witness the jibe at Cleisthenes at Aristophanes *Birds* 831. However, in contrast to our sketchy knowledge surrounding the possibility of male midwives, we do know for certain that some men did weave: the same passage at *Republic* 455c acknowledges this when Socrates says that women are mocked if a man can weave better than they; further evidence comes from *Republic* 369d, *Phaedo* 87b, *Cratylus* 388c and *Gorgias* 490d.[34] Once again, these exceptions are important, because they make it easier for Plato to rework the relations between occupation and gender in the ideal society; at the same time, the fact that they *are* exceptions and not the rule allows Plato (as we shall see) to appeal to weaving's mainly female associations for rhetorical purposes.

After the slight ambivalence about midwifery and weaving, pregnancy might appear the most unequivocally "female" image of the three, as it is the only one to refer not to a potentially transferable occupation but to a biological function: indeed, we have already seen how Socrates states at *Republic*

---

[32] These officers are presumably auxiliaries, who act in an executive as well as a military capacity (414b).

[33] According to I. Jenkins 2003:71, this was also true of the weaving of flax.

[34] See also Blondell 2002:141n143. I. Jenkins (2003:75) writes that "In addition to the 'amateur' female weavers of the self-sufficient household, there were also the professional artisans, both male and female."

454d–e that the only essential difference between women and men is that the female bears and the male begets. However, it is in fact the "femaleness" of the pregnancy image above all which some commentators have questioned. A few, such as Plass (1978:47–55), have argued that *kuousin* at *Symposium* 206c just means 'fertile', 'fecund': hence the applicability of the verb to all humans (*anthrōpoi*). A greater number, including Morrison, Dover, Stokes and Pender,[35] claim that Diotima's language shows that she is actually not much interested in female pregnancy at all, and is instead mostly talking about male arousal and ejaculation, which she views as a kind of male pregnancy and giving birth. To this end, such commentators adduce the *Timaeus*, particularly 86c, as proof that Plato could and did speak of male arousal and orgasm in such a way. Morrison and Pender in particular argue that, taken together, *Timaeus* 73b–c, 86c and 91c–d show that Plato is inclined to this view because he believed that the human seed originates in the brain and marrow of the male, and that both the male and female sexual organs serve as first receptacle and then outlet for this seed.

These are challenging ideas and I believe that they are partly correct. I agree that Diotima is chiefly, though certainly not exclusively (as we shall see), interested in both spiritual and physical procreation from a male perspective: witness 208e, which talks of the men who turn to women in order to beget physical children, and 209a–b, which discusses the case of a young male whose soul is pregnant with virtue and who, on attaining manhood, seeks a beautiful male through whom he may bring these conceptions forth. I also agree that *Timaeus* 86c shows that Plato does seem to view male arousal and orgasm as at least analogous to pregnancy and giving birth. I am a little less sure whether this is because he thinks that the mother's womb simply provides a receptacle for the father's seed (whether that seed originates in the brain and marrow of the male or not), and that the father is therefore the real parent: in my view, the *Timaeus* passages cited above make this view probable, but do not prove it conclusively. It is true that at *Republic* 454d–e, as we have seen, Socrates claims that the woman bears (*tiktein*) and the male begets (*ocheuein*), but again I am not clear that this conclusively rules out the possibility of a female seed as well. It is certainly the case that Plato would have been well acquainted with the common belief that only a male seed is involved, as such a belief is regularly expressed by the tragic poets, with whose works Plato was familiar: Apollo's words at Aeschylus *Eumenides* 657–663 are the *locus classicus* here.[36]

---

[35] Morrison 1964:42–55; Dover 1980:147; Stokes 1986; Pender 1992:72–86.

[36] See also Aeschylus *Septem* 753–754; Sophocles *Oedipus Rex* 1257; Euripides *Orestes* 551–556.

Yet Plato may also have been aware of an alternative view which postulated both a male and female seed, which is aired in the Hippocratic Corpus.[37] We simply do not know for certain what Plato's views were on the woman's role in reproduction.

In any event, Diotima's tendency to view physical and spiritual procreation from a male perspective is still only half the story. What the interpretations of Plass, Morrison, Pender and the others do not properly acknowledge is Diotima's careful choice of *kuousin* at 206c; in the Hippocratic Corpus, Aristotle and Galen, *kuō* in the present and imperfect tenses always refers to the woman's experience of conception or being with child.[38] Diotima could have used *tiktein* or *gennan*, which can apply to either sex, but she does not. There is no escaping the fact that she—Plato—has selected a term which the other symposiasts and Plato's readers would have associated with women, despite the fact that it is here applied to all humans (*anthrōpoi*). Nor should we overlook the fact that Plato has chosen to put these words into the mouth of a woman, which again would incline his audience to think of female pregnancy, even though, as a (probable)[39] prophetess, it is likely though by far from necessary that Diotima is childless, at least officially.[40] In short, the language of 206c

---

[37] See Dean-Jones 1994:chap. 3.

[38] See LSJ s.v. *kuō* (*sic*): the entry under *kuō* makes the point about the present and imperfect tenses being used of the female more clearly than the entry under *kueō*. The point is also emphasized by Sheffield 2001a.

[39] We are never told precisely what Diotima is: she is referred to as *xenē* (201e), which links her to the Eleatic Stranger of the *Sophist* and *Statesman* and the Athenian Stranger of the *Laws*. However, specifying that she comes from Mantinea is probably meant to suggest that she is some kind of *mantis*, 'seer', and the claim that, by advising sacrifices, she helped the Athenians delay the onset of the plague for ten years indicates a woman of special, though clearly not unlimited, spiritual powers (and perhaps function too). Her closest associates in Plato are the priestesses of *Meno* 81a (though there are also parallels with the secular Aspasia in *Menexenus*, a connection illuminated by Halperin 1990:122–124).

[40] Most commentators assume that Diotima is chaste (Halperin calls her "presumably chaste" 1990:199n102), but there was no uniformity of either regulation or practice concerning the virginity or chastity (or lack of them) of Greek priestesses and seers during this or any period: in a few instances chastity was an official requirement of office, but generally there seems to have been no such stipulation (and in some cases, such as on Samos, the obligation appears to have been spectacular lack of chastity). And if Diotima is simply to be viewed as some kind of religious expert (perhaps assisting in rituals and cults), then she could well have had a child: according to Demosthenes, Aeschines' mother offered initiation into a minor mystery-cult (18.259–260). At 201d Diotima is referred to as *gunē* (woman) and not *parthenos* (maiden), which may indicate that she is not a virgin, though it is not conclusive. Nor should we forget that Socrates, with teasing ambiguity, says that she is wise on the matter of *erōs*, and that she taught him *ta erōtika* (201d). For the role of women and girls within Greek religion generally see Dillon 2001 and Blundell 1995.

conjures up, and is supposed to conjure up, an image of both men and women pregnant and swelling in both body and mind in the way that a woman's body swells with child. Nevertheless, the point that female pregnancy and birth can be used as metaphors for male arousal and orgasm (which I am not denying) once more allows Plato room for maneuver in the use he makes of female imagery and will again prove helpful when we gather our conclusions on Plato's attitude towards the significance and function of gender.

Female Imagery and Pedagogy

In the images of pregnancy, midwifery and weaving, therefore, we have three metaphors which would have held mainly, but importantly not exclusively, female connotations for Plato's readers, at any rate to begin with. The question now is: does Plato put such female associations to any deliberate rhetorical, pedagogic or philosophical purpose? And—a separate question—do such female connotations produce any particular rhetorical, pedagogic or philosophic effects, whether Plato intended them or not?

To gain some purchase on this issue, it will be helpful to consider briefly Plato's deployment of ostensibly "male" imagery (imagery drawn, for example, from war, hunting and athletics) to describe the practice of philosophy in other dialogues. As I have written extensively about such imagery elsewhere,[41] I shall only point to my main conclusions here. The immediate rhetorical purpose of such vigorous images, I suggest, is to help counter the charges of critics such as Callicles that the serious pursuit of philosophy, particularly beyond a certain age, makes one feeble, impotent and generally "unmanly" (*Gorgias* 485c): it is part of a general project to show that the traditionally male virtue of *andreia* (literally 'manliness', though often 'courage') can be manifest in the academy as well as on the battlefield. In the *Republic* alone, as we have seen, the practice of philosophy is variously compared to making an assault, tracking, swimming against huge waves, wrestling and mountain-climbing: a pentathlon of the mind.

Yet such images also raise complex problems, of which one in particular concerns us: to what extent are the male connotations of *andreia*, war and sport really significant in these comparisons? What, again, of *Republic* V, where we are told that properly trained guardian women will also practice athletics and go to war (456a–b)? In the ideal state, many of the activities traditionally associated with males will be practiced just as much by guardian females, and

---

[41] See n23 above.

the virtue of *andreia* required for the excellent performance of these often risky activities will presumably be displayed by females too:[42] in short, neither *andreia* nor sporting and military pursuits are essentially male preserves at all. Yet this does not alter the fact that such images would have "manly" connotations for at least the majority of Plato's audience (certainly at first hearing or reading) and Plato cannot plausibly claim to be unaware of such reactions.

In response to this puzzle, my suggestion is as already outlined:[43] namely, that Plato's position is deliberately ambivalent, designed to accommodate both the ideals to which his students should aspire and the reality that his immediate audience is almost entirely male and living in a world of becoming in which gender (and the body generally) is inevitably important. On the one hand, he genuinely wishes to convince them of the originally Socratic theory, first voiced in the *Meno* 73a–c, that the virtues are gender-neutral.[44] Indeed, we have seen how, in the *Republic*, the *Meno* position is given a theoretical underpinning: beyond the roles men and women play in biological reproduction, there are no essentially male and female activities, and hence no essentially male and female excellences. What matters is the human subject. In time, Plato wishes to educate his students to another level again, a level where the ideal is the realm of ungendered and human-transcendent Forms (*Republic* 500c–e; *Symposium* 212a). Yet he is also acutely aware that some of the young males in his audience are deeply suspicious of higher philosophical studies, believing that the pursuit of philosophy in adulthood would be tantamount to abrogating their manhood. If he simply ignores their fears, he will lose them.

One of Plato's solutions to this conundrum is, I propose, as follows: namely to deploy images for the philosophic enterprise which his (predominantly male) students in the early stages of their education will perceive as "masculine" and find attractive, but which they will later, when they are ready, come to view as not really "masculine" at all. He is happy to exploit the fact that his depiction of philosophy in robustly active terms is likely, initially at least, to be misinterpreted by many of the young male students, new to the subject, and will thus alleviate their concerns. It is true that there is no formal separation of rhetorical tactic from rational teaching in any of the dialogues

---

[42] At 456a Socrates says that some women are naturally thumoeidic, and *andreia* is the particular virtue of the thumoeidic part of the *psychē* (441d).

[43] See "A Different Response" above.

[44] Aristotle criticizes the historical Socrates for holding that the temperance and courage and justice of a man and a woman are the same at *Politics* 1.13.1260a20–24, and a similar view is attributed to Socrates at Xenophon *Symposium* 2.9 (though here there is the qualification that women are still lacking in judgment and strength).

which uses such apparently gendered imagery, but this need not count as an argument against the theory: what one appreciates from a first reading of a work at eighteen is very different from what one understands from a tenth reading at forty, and its forty-something author may easily write with this knowledge of human emotional and intellectual development in mind.

The question, of course, is whether this approach, intended to accommodate the different needs and capabilities of students at different stages in their education,[45] will actually work in practice. There is surely a danger of readers feeling tricked when they appreciate Plato's technique and rejecting the work, and even philosophy altogether, in consequence: they could end up like the *misologoi* of *Phaedo* 89c–90d, who put their faith in unsound arguments and come to hate arguments altogether. In this paper, however, I shall not focus on these dangers:[46] here I simply wish to see whether Plato deploys "female" imagery in the same or a similar way, i.e. a way which aims to speak differently to readers at different developmental stages.

One point immediately strikes us: there certainly does not appear to be any comparable move to persuade young students that by pursuing philosophy they can still be "real women," or become more "womanly"—even though, if we are to take *Republic* V seriously, Plato must presumably be hoping for a time when many more women will be able to study his dialogues with more freedom than is the case in his Athens.[47] Plato understands his current young audience, and the concerns that he has to soothe. In this respect it is worth noting that Plato generally only deploys such female imagery when Socrates, and the Eleatic Stranger in the *Statesman*, are comfortably amongst friends, men who are not accusing philosophy of compromising their manhood.[48] In the *Symposium* the only character who might perhaps feel threatened by an image of a pregnant male philosopher is Alcibiades, and he notably does not arrive in time to hear Diotima's speech; besides, it is not obvious that he would be upset by it anyway: it is Alcibiades, after all, who likens Socrates to

---

[45] And perhaps also principally aimed at different parts of their *psychē*, respectively the *thumos* and *logistikon*.

[46] For more detailed discussion, see Hobbs 2000:247–249.

[47] This strikes me as another example of the *Republic* V discussion not being fully integrated with the rest of the work; the fact that the education program of II and III appears to be directed solely at male trainee guardians (see above) is a further instance.

[48] The use of weaving imagery at *Republic* 500d may be thought to be an exception, but by this point Thrasymachus is no longer an active opponent and if his capitulation is specious rather than genuine, Socrates is no longer particularly concerned. It could be argued that Aristophanes' lampooning of Socrates in the *Clouds* is hardly an act of friendship, but such hostility is at most only hinted at in the *Symposium* (e.g. 221b).

a statue with models of gods inside (215a–b), and it is Alcibiades who arrives crowned with violets and ribbons, conjuring up an image of the often androgynous Dionysus. Within such mostly friendly surroundings Plato is relaxed about depicting male philosophers engaged in activities and processes usually associated by his contemporaries with women. This relaxed attitude, however, does not mean that the "pregnant" male philosopher (or, indeed, intellectually pregnant female philosopher) is viewed as being a "real woman."

However, despite the fact that there is no parallel move to emphasize the potential "womanliness" of engaging in philosophy, it may still be thought that Plato exploits the predominantly female associations of the images of pregnancy, midwifery and weaving in a number of ways. For my present argument, I need only list four possible candidates. Firstly, in a culture where texts are mainly written by and for men, such images are plainly startling, memorable and thought-provoking, and thus an excellent pedagogic tool: witness the fact that they are still causing debate nearly 2,400 years later. They are another manifestation of Socrates' radicalism. Secondly, the images of pregnancy and midwifery are arguably used to appeal to the reader's protective instincts towards pregnant women and their unborn children, or children in the process of being born: precisely the attitude that is needed to nurture vulnerable young philosophers and their embryonic or newborn ideas.[49] Just as critically, these images illustrate Plato's belief that the process of achieving wisdom is a creative one, rather than the passive imbibing of knowledge that Socrates discredits at *Symposium* 175d.[50] Conversely, the mostly female connotations of weaving may be intended to soften and palliate—at any rate they have the effect of palliating—the image's decidedly troubling implications, namely that the statesman's subjects are inanimate wool to be spun and woven at will. Their passivity (only the statesman-philosopher remains a creative figure in this scenario) is thus in marked contrast to the creative potential ascribed to all humans by Diotima, and to a significant number of

---

[49] Both Plato (*Laws* 788d–790a) and Aristotle (*Politics* 7.16.1334b29–1335b20) show concern for the well-being of the fetus and newborn baby, and emphasize how important it is to provide the right conditions both within the womb and without for their development. Golden (1990:89–94) provides substantive, detailed and compelling evidence that both parents in classical Athens cared for their offspring, often deeply; he argues persuasively that the practice of exposure of newborns did not diminish the care bestowed by parents on the children they did raise, and in some cases may even have intensified it. The *Theaetetus* itself provides evidence of parental attachment: Socrates not only refers to the custom of exposure, but also mentions the distress of parents, when their newborn child is taken away (151c and 161a).

[50] See above. Both Halperin (1990:137–142) and Brisson (in this volume) emphasize the creative nature of Plato's conception of learning.

younger males by Socrates in the *Theaetetus*; whether this inconsistency presents a problem for Plato is something we shall discuss shortly.

Female, Male, and Human

All these possible uses relate to the "female" images when examined individually, within the context of individual dialogues. While still keeping these particular functions in mind, it is now time to explore the "femaleness" of the images when they are considered together, and also when they are, as a group, placed in the contexts both of the "male" imagery we have noted and of the proposals for idealized gender roles in *Republic* V. The results of such an exercise are striking, and do not support the view (at least not straightforwardly) that Plato is simply appropriating female functions and activities for male ends. If we take all the apparently "gendered" images together, and in addition view them in the light of *Republic* V, we can see that, at a higher level than that of appealing to initially wary young male students, or even of appealing to protective instincts towards pregnant women and their growing children, Plato is equally happy for the philosopher to appear as male or female, masculine or feminine. In the *Theaetetus* Socrates is implicitly presented as Theaetetus' father-figure as well as his midwife (Theaetetus is even said to look like Socrates 143e),[51] and Alcibiades' comparison of Socrates to a Silenus-statue containing images of gods inside (*Symposium* 215b) significantly combines the images of the pregnant female with the vigorously erect male. Socrates is also, of course, the voice of the female Diotima. Now some of the reasons for this cavalier approach towards gender will of course be *ad hoc*—whatever suits the purposes of a particular passage in a particular dialogue best; but I wish to suggest that, taken together and in conjunction with *Republic* V, the overall effect of the images is to suggest to the more reflective and informed reader that it really is ultimately of little consequence whether the philosopher is male or female. Nor is it ultimately of much consequence whether a male or female philosopher is described in terms traditionally associated with the opposite gender. At this level, talking of a male philosopher as pregnant, or as a midwife or weaver, does not mean that he is turning into a "real woman"; nor does talk of female philosophers hunting or going to war mean that they are turning into "real men." Taken together, the images can be seen as contributing to Plato's project of emulating his mentor, the historical Socrates, and

---

[51] Blondell also suggests that Plato plays with the idea of Socrates as Theaetetus' male *erastēs* (2002:271).

moving away from notions of gender towards an ideal of the human, an ideal which we have seen articulated eloquently by the character of Socrates at *Meno* 73a–c.[52] For Socrates in the *Meno* and his historical source, the goal is to become not a virtuous man or woman but a virtuous human, as both men and women are virtuous in the same way.

Diotima's choice to use *anthrōpoi* at 206 (despite the female-related verb) and *anthrōpoi* at 211d now takes on a deeper significance. Though it remains true, as we have seen, that she mostly speaks of love from a male perspective, it is still notable how often she pointedly talks of her erotic subjects as "human": as well as 206c and 211d, *anthrōp*- words also appear at 208c and 211e and twice in the rousing climax of 212a when she describes what it would be like to live in contemplation of the Form of Beauty: "do you call it a paltry life for a human to lead, to be looking in that direction, gazing on it by the appropriate means and in intercourse with it? ... if anyone is, such a human is immortal."[53]

It is at this higher level that Plato can exploit the fact that, though the images of pregnancy, midwifery and weaving have predominantly "female" connotations, each can in certain cases be applied to males too: even in Plato's Athens, men can and do occasionally weave and at any rate act as midwives; if we extend the principles of *Republic* V to the producer class, then they would do so in the ideal state as well. In the *Timaeus*, and perhaps also in the *Symposium*, male arousal and ejaculation are in some ways depicted as at least analogous to pregnancy and giving birth.[54] Such exceptions to the general rule help Plato to break down distinctions between the male and the female, and the masculine and the feminine. He has room to play. Such playfulness, furthermore, does not only manifest itself in to whom "gendered" images apply, but *how* they are made to apply: this is why it does not particularly matter that the creative subjects implied by the pregnancy and midwifery images appear at odds with the mostly passive subjects implied by the metaphor of weaving. Plato can afford to be relaxed in his used of gendered imagery because, from the perspective of the wise and virtuous human, gender really does not matter very much.

---

[52] See above and n44.

[53] Translation mine. It is interesting to compare *Apology* 38a5–6; Debra Nails has helpfully pointed out to me that the *Apology* contains forty-one instances of *anthrōp*- words.

[54] The connection may be even stronger if, as Morrison and Pender think, Plato does believe that both the male and the female sexual organs serve as receptacle and outlet for the seed that originates in the brain and marrow of the male. But see the discussion above for a counter-view.

Female Imagery and the Forms

There is another perspective, however, that as we have already seen matters even more, and this is most powerfully expressed by Diotima. Those who can gaze upon the Form of Beauty itself, she says, pure and unalloyed, would no longer have any interest in "human flesh and colors and all the rest of mortal trash."[55] Diotima bids us to transcend, as far as possible, not just our gender but, ultimately, even our humanity itself, in an attempt to have intercourse with and perhaps emulate, as far as we can, the non-human and non-gendered Forms.[56] Biological sex and cultural gender and all permutations of their relation are part of the corporeal world of becoming and impermanence: the final goal is the incorporeal, eternal realm of being manifest in the Forms. This is the ultimate context in which Plato's use of female imagery should be viewed. Now, the actions and words of both the character of Socrates in the *Symposium*, and Plato its author, partly undercut Diotima's contemptuous dismissal of humanity in 211e: both Socrates and Plato manifest a profound concern with how humanity fares, and Plato's masterly composition radiates an exuberant delight in the vividness and variety of its colors and flesh. Indeed, Diotima herself expresses a passionate interest in the welfare of humanity in the lines that immediately follow 211e. Yet this deep concern and delight can perfectly well be accompanied by an awareness of the smallness of humans in the greater scheme of things and an acknowledgement of the ultimate irrelevance of gender, which is contingent on our temporary incarnation and will not survive our death.[57] The enjoyment of playing with, transgressing and utilizing concepts of gender is possible precisely because, finally, they are of no lasting importance. The *Symposium* is not so much a rejection of the female as gaily cavalier in its attitude towards the embodied. I submit, therefore, that Plato is chiefly concerned not with "appropriating the feminine" but with liberating men and women alike from inessential bodily and cultural constraints.[58]

---

[55] 211e (translation mine).

[56] We have seen an open exhortation to emulate the Forms at *Republic* 500c.

[57] See *Republic* 486a8–10 and 604b–c for an acknowledgement of the small significance of human affairs when viewed from the perspective of "all time and all reality." Yet no one could seriously charge the author of the *Republic* with being indifferent to human concerns.

[58] I am indebted to comments made at the Center for Hellenic Studies in Washington, DC, and Warwick University, where earlier versions of this paper appeared. Particular thanks must go to Debra Nails, my main editor, and also to the anonymous readers for the Center, to Christine Battersby, Ruby Blondell, Jim Lesher, and Frisbee Sheffield.

Twelve

Plato in the Courtroom: The Surprising Influence of the *Symposium* on Legal Theory

Jeffrey Carnes

IT IS NOT OFTEN THAT CLASSICISTS FIND THEMSELVES in the middle of public policy debates, at least not in this day and age; yet this is precisely what has happened in recent years in the ongoing public battle over gay rights, in which proponents of both sides have invoked Plato to strengthen their positions. To some extent, this has been an outgrowth of traditional attempts to re-interpret and appropriate the Greek and Roman past: to argue that these societies, forming the largest non-Judeo-Christian component of our intellectual heritage, provide a model of plurality and tolerance; or a non-religious moral precedent for the condemnation of homosexuality; or a stern warning about the dangers of excessive personal liberty. More surprising, perhaps, is the extent to which theorizing about the past—including views on sexuality as a social construct, developed in large part based on classical models—has influenced the courts, in particular in the case of the U.S. Supreme Court's 2003 decision in *Lawrence v. Texas*, which declared state sodomy laws unconstitutional. The most abstract, theoretical, and apparently purely academic aspects of our work have, in fact, had a direct impact on the lives of millions of Americans.

This paper explores the background to this surprising turn of events. I begin with an examination of the well-known intervention of Platonic scholarship in *Romer v. Evans*, the case that began in 1993 as a challenge to the constitutionality of Colorado's anti-gay Amendment 2. The next section of the paper backtracks to the U.S. Supreme Court's 1986 *Bowers v. Hardwick* decision, in which a 5-4 majority upheld the constitutionality of Georgia's sodomy law, basing its decision in part on what it viewed as the "ancient roots" of proscriptions against homosexuality. Finally, I examine the Court's broad reversal of *Bowers* in *Lawrence*, in which the majority expressed a radically different view of human sexuality, including an acceptance of social constructionist theory, which was argued for—and against—on the basis of certain key texts, including Plato's *Symposium.*

1. Romer v. Evans

The first serious intervention of classics into the realm of laws concerning sexuality came in 1993, in the case of *Evans v. Romer* (known as *Romer v. Evans* on appeal).[1] In 1992, the voters of Colorado passed a ballot initiative known as Amendment 2, which stated that neither "the State of Colorado," nor any of its individual municipalities, could "adopt or enforce any statute, regulation, ordinance or policy" that prohibited discrimination on the grounds of "homosexual, lesbian or bisexual orientation, conduct, practices or relationships."[2]

Challenges to the constitutionality of the amendment were immediately launched in a lawsuit filed by a number of plaintiffs, including various municipalities whose anti-discrimination ordinances would have been nullified. The suit claimed that the "'moral judgment" expressed by Amendment 2 is nothing more than irrational hostility toward lesbians, gay men, and bisexuals. Amendment 2 does not serve any legitimate purpose." That is, they challenged the constitutionality of the amendment to withstand the rational basis test, under which a government entity passing laws that will deliberately disadvantage a particular group must demonstrate some legitimate government purpose in so doing.

One of the arguments used by the plaintiffs—and in fact one of the ones deemed least likely to succeed—was that Amendment 2 should be thrown out because it was in violation of the establishment of religion clause of the First Amendment. That is, prejudice against gays and lesbians is derived from Christianity (and ultimately from Judaism as well), and is therefore not a legit-

---

[1] *Evans v. Romer*, 854 P. 2d 1270 Colorado District Court (1993); *Romer v. Evans*, 882 P. 2d 1335 Colorado Supreme Court (1994); *Romer v. Evans*, 517 U.S. Supreme Court 620 (1996). Full texts of these and other major decisions are easily locatable on websites such as <findlaw.com> and a variety of university and advocacy websites such as <lambdalegal.org>.

[2] The full text of the amendment, passed by voter referendum in November, 1992, reads as follows: "No Protected Status Based on Homosexual, Lesbian, or Bisexual Orientation. Neither the State of Colorado, through any of its branches or departments, nor any of its agencies, political subdivisions, municipalities or school districts, shall enact, adopt or enforce any statute, regulation, ordinance or policy whereby homosexual, lesbian or bisexual orientation, conduct, practices or relationships shall constitute or otherwise be the basis of or entitle any person or class of persons to have or claim any minority status quota preferences, protected status or claim of discrimination."

imate reason for discriminatory legislation. Enter Plato—in this case, in the person of his interpreters, beginning with the Oxford moral philosopher John Finnis, who was brought in by the defense to argue that disdain for homosexuality has, in fact, roots in other Western, non-Christian traditions; and, further, that such disdain forms part of "natural law," providing a wholly legitimate moral ground for disliking, and therefore discouraging, homosexual behavior.[3] If the Greeks (arguably the most identifiable non-Judeo-Christian part of our cultural tradition) despised homosexuality, then this part, at least, of the case will fail; and the natural law arguments will go a long way toward providing something to pass the "rational basis" test, and might help meet the standard of strict scrutiny which was in fact applied in this case.

Finnis, then, had the task of showing that the Greeks disapproved of homosexuality. Questions relating to defining the category of homosexuality don't arise, of course: natural law, along with common sense and most pre-1980 scholarship, sees categories of sexuality as essentially invariant (or invariably essential). Now, the casual observer might point out that if the Greeks disapproved of homosexuality, they had a funny way of showing it. Finnis gets around this difficulty in two ways: first, by narrowing the scope of his inquiry to include only philosophical texts, in particular those by Plato and Aristotle; second, by carefully distinguishing between same-sex affection, or inclination, or desire, on the one hand; and its actual physical fulfillment on the other. By focusing on acts rather than inclinations, any questions of the commensurability of ancient and modern sexual categories were taken out of play; and more importantly, it become possible to explain away the large amount of homoerotic material in the philosophical texts as pertaining only to desire, not to its consummation.

This is a line of reasoning few, if any, classicists would pursue today, and in fact Finnis's status as outsider came to play a large role in the controversy, particularly in regard to his ability to read Greek. He is a Catholic natural law philosopher whose arguments seem to imply, in Thomistic fashion, that Plato and Aristotle to some extent presaged Christian morality:

> Marriage, with its double blessing—procreation and friendship—is a real common good. Moreover, it is a common good which can be both actualized and experienced in the orgasmic union of the reproductive organs of a man and a woman united in commitment to that good. Conjugal sexual activity, and—as Plato and Aristotle, and Plutarch and Kant all argue—*only* conjugal activity is free from

---

[3] Finnis's arguments, set out in his affidavit, are expanded in Finnis 1994a.

the shamefulness of instrumentalization which is found in mastur-
bating and in being masturbated or sodomized.[4]

In particular, Finnis held that only non-contracepted sex by a married couple
may be free of such instrumentalization (although he did make an exception
for those married couples who are infertile)—all else is regarded as sodomy
and masturbation.

Finnis's arguments concerning Plato and Aristotle sound curiously old-
fashioned, insensitive to context, and anachronistic. While citing certain
passages in the *Laws* that actually do seem to condemn same-sex activity
(although even here context makes it far from certain how to read Plato's
intentions), he vastly over-generalizes: "To know or tell Plato's views on the
morality, and the immorality, of all such non-marital conduct as homosexual
sex acts, one need go no further than these unmistakably clear passages in
the *Laws*, texts with which every other text of Plato can readily be seen to be
consistent."[5] Classicists might object that the *Symposium* contains precious
little about marriage, and that Finnis seems not to have read the *Republic* on
the communal family arrangements to be imposed on the Guardian class. Yet
elsewhere he seems to realize that this is over-statement, referring to the
"*mature* Plato of the *Laws*" (emphasis mine) as the source to be taken as authoritative, in contrast, I suppose, to the "*immature*" Plato of the erotic dialogues
and the *Republic*. Worthy of note here are two tendencies in the interpretation
and invocation of Plato: first, a desire to make Platonic doctrine seem more
unified than it actually is (a tendency to which professional classicists are typically less prone than other academics and pundits); second, a preference for
Plato the Censor—the stern lawgiver and moral authority of the *Republic* and
the *Laws*, who speaks across the ages with an authoritative Voice of Reason.
These tendencies are perhaps not surprising in a context in which Plato is
being invoked as part of the history of Western thought; but as we shall see,
this is hardly the only way in which he may be brought into the debate.

From a classicist's perspective, Finnis proved to be, in effect, a weak
advocate, one who should be easily trounced by any competent philolo-
gist—especially one as learned and formidable as his actual opponent, Martha
Nussbaum. And in fact she *did* trounce him, at least so far as the published
arguments go. Her affidavit, as reconstructed in her *Virginia Law Review*
article, effectively undercuts almost all of Finnis's specific claims concerning

[4] Finnis, affidavit, p. 46, quoted in Nussbaum 1994:1585.
[5] Finnis 1994a:1061.

Plato, Aristotle, and other philosophers. In particular, she deals very effectively with those situations in which Plato does, in fact, demonstrate some aversion to same-sex sexual activity, pointing out that Plato was in general suspicious of all bodily appetites (not just of sex, much less homosexuality) and that his finding bodily appetites and their fulfillment *inferior to* spiritual pleasures is not at all the same as his saying that such appetites and pleasure are "shameful, depraved, and depraving," as Finnis claimed. In addition, she distinguishes in key passages—particularly those in the *Nicomachean Ethics* and the *Gorgias*—between the Greeks' general approbation of, or sympathy toward, active, penetrative males and their fear of and contempt for the figure of the habitually passive *kinaidos*. Where Finnis spoke of attitudes toward homosexuality *tout court*, Nussbaum points out that to do so is at best over-generalization, at worst a complete misreading of the Greeks' categorization of sexuality.

Better still is her treatment of the implications of scholarship, and the question of why reading ancient texts should have any relevance for the modern legal system. Her *Virginia Law Review* article begins with a story of the conservative jurist and legal theorist Richard Posner reading Plato's *Symposium* and finding himself "surprised to discover that it was a defense, and as one can imagine a highly interesting and articulate one, of homosexual love. It had never occurred to me that the greatest figure in the history of philosophy, or for that matter any other respectable figure in the history of thought, had attempted such a thing."[6] Posner, in his book *Sex and Reason*, attempted to remedy the ignorance about homosexuality he found throughout the legal profession, claiming that the *Bowers v. Hardwick* decision evidenced "irrational fear and loathing" of homosexuality, and that judges, in their ignorance of sexual issues, are "likely ... to vote their prejudices."[7] Nussbaum whole-heartedly agrees with Posner's educational project, and the conclusion to her affidavit makes a plea for reason and greater understanding of sexuality.

Obviously, Nussbaum will have the Greeks teach us a rather different lesson from the one Finnis had in mind. Rather than showing us a set of universal principles that take the form of natural law, and are instantiated with varying degrees of perfection in various legal systems, they will provide us with a contrasting world-view—one in which sexuality is less central, more equated with other appetites. Examining the Greeks (and here she quotes Foucault) will "free our thought from what it silently thinks, and so enable it to think differently" (1994:1598). Attacking Finnis on his own ground, she

---

[6] Posner 1992:1, quoted at Nussbaum 1994:1516.
[7] Posner, ibid.

invokes the Catholic branch of the natural law tradition against him: if it was possible for the Greeks, a culture we in general admire as one of our moral and intellectual forebears, "to hold that same-sex relationships are not only not per se shameful, but potentially of high spiritual and social value," then it cannot simply be claimed that all rational persons will despise same-sex relationships. It will be necessary, if one follows the Catholic natural law tradition, "which claims to derive its conclusions from reason, not from authority," to "be sure that we have distinguished between reasoned argument and prejudice" (ibid).

If Finnis had an unenviable task—that of showing that the Greeks disapproved of same-sex activity—Nussbaum took on, for reasons that are easy to sympathize with, a task nearly equally difficult: that of explaining away virtually *every* negative reference to same-sex activity in the Greek world. It's an odd variation on the old sophistic theme: trying to make the Better case appear the Airtight; and in fact Nussbaum wound up making the Better case appear the Worse, at least in some circles. This is due in large part to the *tolmēma* controversy, in which it would appear that Nussbaum cited an earlier edition of Liddell and Scott in order to avoid having the definition "daring or shameless act" appear as one of the word's possible meanings when considering how best to render a passage in the *Laws*.

Finnis seized on this inconsistency and ran with it. Rather than being a minor oversight, or even a deliberate but small trick to present her case in the best possible light, he viewed Nussbaum's testimony as "a wholesale abuse of her scholarly authority and attainments." His article in *Academic Questions* (a journal published by the National Association of Scholars) begins with a condemnation of the historical inaccuracies he alleges existed in testimony before the Court in various abortion cases, and goes on to see Nussbaum as a further practitioner of "law office history," a sort of scholarship that is an "attempt to get the American people to constitute themselves around conceptions of their own past, and the past of their civilization, that are profoundly untrue" (Finnis 1994b:35).

In his thoughtful analysis of the case, Daniel Mendelsohn suggests that there is perhaps a problem in the very nature of the competing discourses involved—those of the scholar and the lawyer. Perhaps, he muses, "the gap that separates law and scholarship may well be as unbridgeable as the gap that distinguishes tragedy from comedy" (Mendelsohn 1996:45). After all, courtroom testimony is designed to provide some specific answer, not to raise further interesting questions for study: "the narrow requirements of legal discourse as it actually proceeds may ultimately be incompatible with the expansive nature of serious humanistic inquiry."[8] Although the Solicitor General of Colorado was quoted as saying: "This is not just an academic issue— our courts make decisions based on this material" (Mendelsohn 1996:37), it seemed unlikely that there would be any real effect of anyone's testimony on Plato or the ancient world. It was instead an interesting sideshow, one that the scholarly community was dragged into by the plaintiffs' long-shot establishment of religion argument. It's all very well and good to speak of educating the court, but how many judges are as inquisitive as Richard Posner? And after all, the court decisions, including that of the U.S. Supreme Court, made no direct reference to this material, and decided the issue on grounds of Due Process, not establishment of religion.

There is some irony in the fact that Plato could be brought in as a champion of liberties—religious and social—that accord ill with his large parts of his philosophical corpus; and that Plato's voice should be used to champion democratic decision-making. Also ironic is the notion that Greek ideas about sexuality should be seen as a liberating force, a counterweight to our own prejudices. Yes, same-sex behavior and affection were given greater leeway in Greece than they traditionally have been in the Judeo-Christian world—but only if they conformed to certain rigid notions of masculinity, in which grown men were expected to be active, dominant, penetrating partners, and were subject to severe disapproval if they varied from this norm. Further, if we are to use the Greeks as models of enlightenment concerning homosexuality, does this imply acceptance of their entire misogynistic gender system? For classicists to testify in court about the Greeks' philosophy, their loves, their ideas of friendship and the common good, yet passing over in silence the seclusion and denigration of women that were a contributing, and perhaps a necessary, precondition for the glories of their masculinist culture, seems at best bitterly ironic, at worst a betrayal of our scholarship and our personal moral principles.

While it might have been useful to acknowledge the Greeks' faults and limitations neither side in the *Romer* case adopted this approach. Both Finnis and Nussbaum revere the Greeks: as founders of some of our most cherished intellectual traditions, and, for Finnis, as the earliest Western example of natural law; while for Nussbaum, they serve as a diachronic example of cultural diversity, giving us an *autres temps, autres moeurs* lesson in tolerance. For Finnis, the key texts were the *Republic* and the *Laws*, texts that position

---

[8] Mendelsohn 1996:46. At the time of reading Mendelsohn's article, I was very much in sympathy with this particular argument, but am less so now, for reasons explained below.

Plato as a serious and stern moral authority. For Nussbaum, the key text was the *Symposium* (and to a lesser extent the *Phaedrus*): texts that not only focus on sexuality and desire, but in which one could view Plato's thought as open and radically incomplete, and to discern different voices speaking through the Platonic mask of authority.[9] But if modern scholarship tends in this direction—what we might call the *Symposium* approach to interpretation—we might well ask whether this can provide a useful tool for legal analysis, which after all looks for certainty and precedent, not the endlessly regenerating eroticism of the text.

Further, the reading of the *Symposium* espoused by Nussbaum (and more explicitly by Posner) seems to validate Foucault's repressive hypothesis, in that we now celebrate our own openness and tolerance in regard to sexual matters, and pride ourselves on having thrown off the shackles of Victorian prudishness. Thus we proclaim our liberation, and are pleased to find that people in the more distant past may have been liberated as well. Yet to celebrate Plato as a champion of "gay rights" and to see the *Symposium* as a "defense of ... homosexual love" is profoundly ahistorical: not only would Plato probably fail to recognize the categories employed in the debate, but the notion that same-sex affection or sexuality needed defending in the first place remakes Plato in our own image. He becomes, like ourselves, a modern, liberal thinker. A better approach—at least in the scholarly world, if not in the courts—might be to leave aside case-by-case arguments about whether Greek philosophers approved of same-sex attraction, kissing, or intercourse, and to argue instead that the Greeks' sexual system was so different from our own as to be for all practical purposes useless as a basis for comparison.[10] If the ancient world did not recognize the concept of the homosexual, or recognize homosexuality as a category that classified individuals in a meaningful way, then how can we legitimately speak of their attitude toward these phenomena?

Nussbaum takes up this argument near the conclusion of her article. While conceding that such an approach might say "important things about the two cultures," she alludes to two speeches in the *Symposium* as proof that the Greeks *did*, in fact, have sexual categories similar to our own. Further, she points out that Finnis's arguments were based on acts rather than dispositions, and so anti-essentializing arguments would have little countervailing force. Nussbaum, then, might be viewed as a "loose constructionist": that is,

---

[9] David Halperin (esp. 1990 and 1992) has been at the forefront of this trend.
[10] For those unfamiliar with the constructionist/essentialist debate, a good and balanced introduction to the controversy may be found in Skinner 2005.

one who believes that sexual identity is socially constructed, but also believes that—for the Greek world at least—our basic categories of straight and gay have some justification, even though they may be defined differently in practice (and even though other categories may exist as well).[11] As for Finnis's distinction between acts and dispositions, this is probably due to a certain strategic difficulty on his part: that the only way around the Greeks' obvious approval of certain same-sex affects is to divide mind and body, affect and practice, and demonize the latter member of each dichotomy. But in fact this does little to speak to the issue at hand: the language of Amendment 2 specifically targeted individuals for their status or orientation (as well as for their conduct, although we must imagine that this is secondary, given the purpose of the legislation). Further, the *Bowers* and *Lawrence* cases show that regulation of conduct and of status go hand in hand, so the creation of a Plato who approves of some version of homosexual status, while condemning homosexual conduct, fails to make Plato an effective advocate for anti-gay legislation.

Neither side, then, presented an uncontroversial view of ancient sexual categories and their possible relevance to modern civil liberties. Yet suppose Nussbaum *had* wanted to make the strict constructionist, anti-essentialist argument outlined above—could she have done so? After all, this would involve explaining the history of scholarship: the fact that scholars up until about 1980 accepted certain categories as unproblematic and universal, but now believed quite the opposite. Such an argument would, in fact, be subject to easy "refutation," if by refutation is meant finding eminent scholars (quite likely, even a majority of the reputable sources on the subject) to affirm essentialism. Explaining to a court a lot of details about Greek sexual practices and attitudes, talking about Foucault, trying to get them to accept a proposition that is on the face of it seriously counter-intuitive—all this certainly seemed an ill-advised and quixotic project. Add to this the fact that constructionism is sometimes viewed with disdain or embarrassment within the gay community, in part

---

[11] My own view is closer to that of the "strict constructionists," who hold that there is little evidence for a trans-historical gay or straight identity, at least not for one that encompasses fifth-century Athens and twenty-first-century America. Ironically, it is the *Symposium* that provides the ideological litmus test for separating strict and loose constructionists: namely, whether Aristophanes' taxonomic division of proto-humans into male, female, and hermaphroditic wholes is evidence that such categories were common in Greek thought. As I have argued elsewhere (Carnes 1997), the context of Aristophanes' speech makes it extremely likely that this was a nonce construct, readily intelligible insofar as variations in sexual object preference were discernible among individuals, yet unlikely to reflect any deeper and more lasting categorization analogous to the ones in use today.

because it can be seen as undermining a hard-won identity and giving ammunition to cultural conservatives who view homosexuality as a conscious choice.

2. Bowers v. Hardwick

Several of the issues we have identified resurfaced in the U.S. Supreme Court's decision on *Lawrence v. Texas* in June, 2003. But first, a recap of the notorious earlier case, *Bowers v. Hardwick*, that was overturned by *Lawrence* (after having been seriously damaged by *Romer v. Evans*). The *Bowers* case started in 1982, when Michael Hardwick was charged with violating a Georgia statute criminalizing sodomy, the text of the act reading as follows:

(a) A person commits the offense of sodomy when he performs or submits to any sexual act involving the sex organs of one person and the mouth or anus of another ...

(b) A person convicted of the offense of sodomy shall be punished by imprisonment for not less than one nor more than 20 years.[12]

Hardwick was arrested in the bedroom of his own home, when a roommate directed the police (who were looking for him on an unrelated matter) to open his closed bedroom door. Although the sodomy charges were soon dropped, he brought suit, asserting that, as a practicing homosexual, the statute, "as administered by the defendants, placed him in imminent danger of arrest, and that the statute for several reasons violates the Federal Constitution."[13] Since the statute was gender-neutral, the original action also included as plaintiffs a straight couple, John and Mary Doe, who claimed that they wished to engage in the sexual activity forbidden by the statute, but had been "chilled and deterred" from doing so by the statute itself and by Hardwick's arrest. The trial court, however, found that they had not sustained, nor were likely to sustain, any direct injury from the enforcement of the statue, and therefore lacked the proper standing to sue. This had significant consequences, since it allowed the court to focus on same-sex activities only, and to "express no opinion on the constitutionality of the Georgia statute as applied to other acts of sodomy" (*Bowers* ibid.).

The decision—one of the most controversial of the past generation—was handed down in 1986, one of the last of the Burger court. Joining the Chief Justice in a 5-4 opinion were Powell, Rehnquist, O'Connor, and Byron White,

---

[12] *Georgia Code Annotated* §16-6-2 (1984).
[13] *Bowers v. Hardwick*, 478 U.S. Supreme Court 186 (1986).

who wrote for the majority. Pointing out at the beginning that the Court makes no judgment on whether sodomy laws are "wise or desirable," White framed the issue as one concerning the "judgment(s) about the limits of the Court's role in carrying out its constitutional mandate" (*Bowers* 190). The most serious of Hardwick's claims was that any such law should be invalidated as unnecessarily infringing upon the right of privacy implicit in the Due Process clauses of the Fifth and Fourteenth Amendments.[14] The right of privacy had been rapidly expanding with a series of decisions relating to marriage and sex: *Griswold v. Connecticut,* and *Eisenstadt v. Baird,* which struck down laws banning the sale of contraceptives; *Loving v. Virginia,* which invalidated anti-miscegenation laws; and of course the 1973 abortion decision in *Roe v. Wade.* White drew a line in the sand with *Hardwick*: "No connection between family, marriage, or procreation on the one hand and homosexual activity on the other has been demonstrated ... Precedent aside, however, respondent would have us announce, as the Court of Appeals did, a fundamental right to engage in homosexual sodomy. This we are quite unwilling to do" (*Bowers* 191).

The question as White framed it was this: what is the nature of the rights that are said to qualify for heightened judicial protection? Defining "fundamental liberties," White quoted a pair of cases to the effect that such rights are "implicit in the concept of ordered liberty ... (such that) neither liberty nor justice would exist if [they] were sacrificed," and that these liberties are those that are "deeply rooted in this Nation's history and tradition." He continued: "It is obvious to us that neither of these formulations would extend a fundamental right to homosexuals to engage in acts of consensual sodomy. Proscriptions against that conduct have ancient roots ... to claim that a right to engage in such conduct is 'deeply rooted in this Nation's history and tradition' or 'implicit in the concept of ordered liberty' is, at best, facetious" (*Bowers* 191–192).

---

[14] The text of the Fifth Amendment of the Constitution of the United States reads as follows: "No person shall be held to answer for a capital, or otherwise infamous crime, unless on a presentment or indictment of a grand jury, except in cases arising in the land or naval forces, or in the militia, when in actual service in time of war or public danger; nor shall any person be subject for the same offense to be twice put in jeopardy of life or limb; nor shall be compelled in any criminal case to be a witness against himself, nor be deprived of life, liberty, or property, without due process of law; nor shall private property be taken for public use, without just compensation."

The Fourteenth Amendment of the Constitution of the United States: Section 1. "All persons born or naturalized in the United States, and subject to the jurisdiction thereof, are citizens of the United States and of the state wherein they reside. No state shall make or enforce any law which shall abridge the privileges or immunities of citizens of the United States; nor shall any state deprive any person of life, liberty, or property, without due process of law; nor deny to any person within its jurisdiction the equal protection of the laws."

White then launched a manifesto against judicial activism (*Bowers* 194–195):

> Nor are we inclined to take a more expansive view of our authority to discover new fundamental rights imbedded in the Due Process Clause. The Court is most vulnerable and comes nearest to illegitimacy when it deals with judge-made constitutional law having little or no cognizable roots in the language or design of the Constitution ... There should be, therefore, great resistance to expand the substantive reach of those Clauses, particularly if it requires redefining the category of rights deemed to be fundamental. Otherwise, the Judiciary necessarily takes to itself further authority to govern the country without express constitutional authority. The claimed right pressed on us today falls far short of overcoming this resistance.

Finally, the Court rejected the possibility of overturning the law under the easier-to-pass rational basis test: the fact that there is a "presumed belief of a majority of the electorate in Georgia that homosexual sodomy is immoral and unacceptable" (*Bowers* 196) is sufficient; the law, White points out, is frequently based on notions of morality.

Chief Justice Warren Burger weighed in with a concurrence of particular significance for us here, emphasizing the "ancient roots" of the proscriptions against sodomy. "Condemnation of those practices is firmly rooted in Judeo-Christian moral and ethical standards. Homosexual sodomy was a capital crime under Roman law ... To hold that the act of homosexual sodomy is somehow protected as a fundamental right would be to cast aside millennia of moral teaching" (*Bowers* 196–197).

It was at this point where historians began to come in to the story, as well as psychologists. First, the Court was taking the "ancient roots" quite seriously, going back as far as late antiquity: the citations to sodomy as capital crime under Roman law were to the law codes of Theodosius and Justinian, and there were subsequent citations to the law codes enacted under Henry VIII. Further, there were references to the sodomy laws prevailing in the original thirteen colonies at the time of Independence (so we see that the historicist arguments used ten years later in *Romer v. Evans* were already present in the debate over sodomy laws). Clarifying whether or not all ancient societies held similar judgments would, in fact, be relevant to this Court.

Other issues are worthy of mention. First, Blackmun outlined the limits of deference to tradition, which will prove to be a key factor in *Lawrence*: "Like Justice Holmes, I believe that it is revolting to have no better reason for a rule of law than that so it was laid down in the time of Henry IV. It is still more revolting if the grounds upon which it was laid down have vanished long since, and the rule simply persists from blind imitation of the past" (*Bowers* 199). Second, he referred to the Court's "almost obsessive focus on homosexual activity"—after all, Burger's brief concurrence added no new doctrine or interesting dicta, and was merely an attack on sodomy *per se*—and in particular the ways in which this obsessive view of the Court misstated the apparent intent of the Georgia law, which is gender neutral. Third, and perhaps most interesting from a classicist's perspective, is the analysis of whether or not homosexuality is a condition. Recognizing changing attitudes, Blackmun pointed out that homosexuality is no longer viewed as a disease by mental health professionals, but is also not a matter of deliberate choice. "Homosexual orientation may well form part of the very fiber of an individual's personality ... an individual's ability to make constitutionally protected decisions concerning sexual relations ... is rendered empty indeed if he or she is given no real choice but a life without any physical intimacy" (*Bowers* 203). The question adumbrated here was to what extent gays can be protected under the Equal Protection Clause without having to face the additional burden of proving that they are a suspect class; that is, one that has experienced a history of past purposeful discrimination or unequal treatment, and which is defined by a characteristic that is "obvious, immutable or distinguishing," and whether it has met with systematic exclusion from redress via the normal political process. That is, the Court (or rather, a substantial minority of it) accepted that homosexual identity is a category that exists and is immutable for given individuals, and that these individuals are unduly burdened by sodomy laws.

3. Romer v. Evans Redux

Hardwick was, of course, one of the most controversial decisions of the Burger Court, one attacked not only by liberals and gay activists, but also by conservatives of a libertarian bent. It was reported soon afterward that Lewis Powell, the swing vote on the case, had changed his vote after intense lobbying from the Chief Justice, and within a few years Powell himself made it known that he regretted this vote more than any other. In addition, as was revealed in his 1994 biography, Powell was operating in near-total ignorance of homosexuality, claiming that he had never to his knowledge met a homosexual—despite the fact that one of his clerks at the time was gay, but closeted. (We may recall Posner's 1992:346 remarks about "the narrowness of legal learning," and his assertion that "what lawyers and judges mainly know is their own prejudices plus what is contained in judicial opinions.") The Court itself seemed rather embarrassed by the *Hardwick* decision: as some scholars have pointed out, it was not always relied upon for precedent, and a mere ten years later it was partly overturned by the verdict in *Romer*.

It was not entirely overturned, of course—that didn't happen until *Lawrence*—but it was weakened as regards its key implications. The Court's finding in *Romer v. Evans* was based on the Equal Protection Clause of the Fourteenth Amendment. Writing for the majority, Justice Anthony Kennedy quoted with approval the 1973 decision *Department of Agriculture v. Moreno* (413 U.S. 528): "[I]f the constitutional conception of 'equal protection of the laws' means anything, it must at the very least mean that a bare ... desire to harm a politically unpopular group cannot constitute a legitimate governmental interest" (*Romer* 1632). And the Court does in fact find that this was the intent of Amendment 2, rejecting the notion that the amendment merely "deprives homosexuals of special rights ... to the contrary, it imposes a special disability upon those persons alone. (They) are forbidden the safeguards that others enjoy or may seek without constraint" (*Romer* 1626–1627). Since gays and lesbians do not constitute a suspect class, heightened scrutiny is not warranted; instead, the State must pass the simpler rational basis test, of the law bearing "a rational relation to some legitimate end." Indeed, the Court finds this sort of deliberate, broad-based singling out of a group for hardship rare and unjustifiable.

Yet in his dissent Antonin Scalia found a rationale. Opening with the salvo "The Court has mistaken a Kulturkampf for a fit of spite," he defends the amendment as "a modest attempt by seemingly tolerant Coloradans to preserve traditional sexual mores against the efforts of a politically powerful minority to revise those mores through use of the laws." And he continues with a point whose logic is hard to deny (*Romer* 1631):

> The case most relevant to the issue before us today is not even mentioned in the Court's opinion: In *Bowers v. Hardwick* ... we held that the Constitution does not prohibit ... making homosexual conduct a crime. That holding is unassailable, except by those who think that the Constitution changes to suit current fashions ... If it is constitutionally permissible for a State to make homosexual conduct criminal, surely it is constitutionally permissible for a State to enact other laws merely disfavoring homosexual conduct.

Not entirely coincidentally, at the time the Court was reviewing *Romer*, Congress was busily engaged in crafting the Defense of Marriage Act in response to the possibility that Hawaii would soon recognize same-sex marriages. The Act, which was passed overwhelmingly by both Houses, and signed into law by President Clinton, defined marriage as a union between opposite-sex couples only, and further granted states an exemption from the "full faith and credit" provision of the Constitution so that marriages from one state need not be recognized in another. Here, too, classics played a role, although in the more usual way: the field was mined for specious precedent and example rather than being called upon as a source of expert testimony.[15]

4. Lawrence v. Texas

On one evening in 1998 the petitioners in this case, John Lawrence and Tyron Garner, were engaged in anal sex in Lawrence's apartment. The Houston police, apparently not realizing that *delicto* is normally a dead metaphor, responding to a call regarding a man with a weapon, broke into the apartment and found Lawrence and Garner *in flagrante delicto*. The police arrested the pair, who spent a day in jail before being released on bond. They sought, at the level of the Harris County criminal court, to have the charges dismissed on constitutional grounds; when this failed, they pleaded *nolo contendere* to the charges, were fined $200 plus $141 in court costs, and pursued the case to the Court of Appeals; when this was unfruitful, to the Supreme Court.

This was, in many respects, a better test case than *Hardwick*: first of all, the petitioners suffered actual harm: the conviction could debar them from or restrict their entry into a variety of professions in Texas. Further, after such a conviction they would have to register as sex offenders if they moved to certain states. The arguments that made *Hardwick* seem less compelling— no real prosecution; "no real harm" clearly did not apply here. Further, the fact that the Texas statute applied only to same-sex sodomy allowed the petitioners to raise an Equal Protection claim, since they were in fact members of a class being singled out, as they maintained, for its unpopularity, and therefore the precedent established by *Romer* was much more on point than it would be for a gender-neutral law. And, oddly enough, the fact that the petitioners were engaged in anal rather than oral sex also made it a better test case, since some recent Constitutional scholarship has argued that oral sex is not generally prohibited by pre-twentieth century sodomy laws, and was not therefore the

---

[15] See, for example, the speech by West Virginia Senator Robert Byrd in which selections from various classical authors are marshaled in defense of the institution of marriage (*Congressional Record—U.S. Senate*, September 10, 1996).

object of a proscription that had "ancient roots." This particular dodge would not work, and the Court would have to face squarely the question of whether such ancient proscriptions were to be overthrown.

The petitioners sought to have the case examined under both the Due Process and Equal Protection Clauses, and to have *Bowers* invalidated. The majority opinion, again written by Kennedy, concluded that the Due Process Clause was the relevant section of the Constitution, and that *Bowers* needed reconsideration. The Equal Protection Clause was not considered entirely sufficient for the Court's ends, although it was invoked in Sandra Day O'Connor's concurrence.

The main issue was substantive due process, and the opinion sketches out the development of certain privacy and spatial rights, including the *Griswold, Eisenstadt,* and *Roe* decisions. Then comes the key paragraph that dismisses the central claim of the *Bowers* decision—that is, that the right to engage in homosexual sodomy is not a fundamental one:

> That statement, we now conclude, discloses the Court's own failure to appreciate the extent of the liberty at stake. To say that the issue in *Bowers* was simply the right to engage in certain sexual conduct demeans the claim the individual put forward, just as it would demean a married couple were it to be said marriage is simply about the right to have sexual intercourse. The laws involved in *Bowers* and here are, to be sure, statutes that purport to do no more than prohibit a particular sexual act. Their penalties and purposes, though, have more far-reaching consequences, touching upon the most private human conduct, sexual behavior, and in the most private of places, the home. The statutes do seek to control a personal relationship that, whether or not entitled to formal recognition in the law, is within the liberty of persons to choose without being punished as criminals.
>
> This, as a general rule, should counsel against attempts by the State, or a court, to define the meaning of the relationship or to set its boundaries absent injury to a person or abuse of an institution the law protects. It suffices for us to acknowledge that adults may choose to enter upon this relationship in the confines of their homes and their own private lives and still retain their dignity as free persons. When sexuality finds overt expression in intimate conduct with another person, the conduct can be but one element in a personal bond that is more enduring. The liberty protected by

the Constitution allows homosexual persons the right to make this choice.[16]

Instead of focusing on "homosexual sodomy" the court spoke of dignity, choice, and bonding. Yet even when the decision had been made to regard private, in the home, sexual conduct as a liberty interest, protected by the doctrine of substantive Due Process, two loose threads remained: first, how to deal with the objection that "proscriptions against this conduct have ancient roots"; and second, how to overcome the principle of *stare decisis*, in which a Court is loath to overturn the decisions of its predecessors.

In fact, the Court adopted a version of the social construction theory of sexuality to explain why sodomy laws used to be gender neutral, and to try to get at the original intent of the framers of those laws. First, Kennedy noted that "there is no longstanding history in this country of laws directed at homosexual conduct as a distinct matter" (*Lawrence* 7). That is to say, beginning with the Reformation Parliament of 1533 and continuing through the nineteenth century, sodomy laws were thought to prohibit certain types of acts between men and women, or between men and men. Why the change? "The absence of legal prohibitions focusing on homosexual conduct may be explained in part by noting that according to some scholars the concept of the homosexual as a distinct category of person did not emerge until the late 19th century." Kennedy then quoted from Jonathan Katz' *The Invention of Heterosexuality*: "the modern terms homosexuality and heterosexuality do not apply to an era that had not yet articulated these distinctions" and concluded: "Thus early American sodomy laws were not directed at homosexuals as such but instead sought to prohibit non-procreative sexual activity more generally. This does not suggest approval of homosexual conduct. It does tend to show that this particular form of conduct was not thought of as a separate category from like conduct between heterosexual persons" (*Lawrence* 7–8).

Continuing further in his history of sodomy laws, Kennedy (*Lawrence* 10) suggests that,

> far from possessing 'ancient roots', American laws targeting same-sex couples did not develop until the last third of the 20th century … it was not until the 1970s that any State singled out same-sex relations for criminal prosecution … In summary, the historical grounds relied upon in *Bowers* are more complex than the majority opinion and the concurring opinion by Chief Justice Burger indicate. Their

---

[16] *Lawrence v. Texas*, 539 U.S. Supreme Court 558 (2003).

historical premises are not without doubt and, at the very least, are overstated.

Several things are worth noting here. First, the rhetoric of possibility and uncertainty: the Court was seeking a way to get around the earlier proscriptions of sodomy, a way to deflect their relevance for this particular case. The fact that the situation is not so simple as had been claimed, that many scholars now argue that there were no recognizable homosexuals before 1892, provided a window of opportunity. The kind of reading now favored by literary critics in which openness, lack of closure, and dialogue are valued above certainty and structure (what might be termed the "*Symposium*" approach), has come to prominence in legal discourse as well. The second noteworthy point is the irony that ancient theories concerning sexuality should be triumphing in their most radical form: while the sources cited are not classical, they clearly depend on Foucault's *History of Sexuality* and its problematization of sexual categories (and, to a lesser extent, on the work of followers of Foucault such as David Halperin and Jack Winkler). The constructionist view of sexuality is brought in as a way of silencing the strict constructionist, original intent, approach to the interpretation of law. Third, the construction of the gay subject comes at precisely the right historical moment for the Court's purposes (the straight subject is constructed, too, of course, but heterosexuality is, as always, viewed as unproblematic). That is, for the Court's reasoning to work, categories of homosexuality and heterosexuality cannot exist during the formative period for sodomy laws, which lasts up until the end of the nineteenth century. And yet that category must exist now, since it is being subject to attempts at discrimination, and is an identity that marks out a class of citizens deserving of equal protection under the laws. Ironically, one of the reasons I mentioned earlier for resistance to constructionist theories of sexuality—that, whatever their truth value, they might lead to discrimination on the grounds that a constructed sexual identity is infinitely mutable, and a conscious choice—seems not to apply here at all. In what must be seen as the most important decision ever relating to gay rights in the United States, constructionism played a crucial role.

Of course, our sexualities, constructed as they are, are real, just as the sexual categories of the nineteenth century, or of fifth-century Athens, were real to those who inhabited them. But now we have seen them reified by the Court, in what we may view as the latest step in a long process of the construction of the modern subject. The Court's own analysis mentions the evolution of sodomy laws from being directed at sexual predators, on the one hand, and those who shirked their reproductive duties, on the other. In this analysis it is possible to see the well-known evolution of sexual categories, the move from the earlier equation of same-sex activity with pederasty and infertility, to its construction as a medical and legal condition: the mobilization of the juridico-medical regime that Foucault spoke of.

The Court's logic concerning the construction of sexuality is, of course, by no means unassailable. Suppose that the Framers of the Constitution, and the legislators of the various states as they were admitted to the Union, *had* believed in homosexuality as a category and deliberately disadvantaged homosexual status and behavior with their legislation. The Court would then have to take those legal and moral strictures more seriously; but at the same time it felt free to override the express will of the current majority of actually existing citizens in such cases as *Romer v. Evans*, and to do so more freely because they lacked the aura of tradition. That is, the Court's particular line of logic may be seen as a sop to foundationalism, as a way of making a rather radical departure from precedent seem less radical.

After establishing the basis for finding a liberty interest that would be violated by the sodomy statue, the Court moved on to deal with the questions of *stare decisis*. Having dismissed the "ancient roots" argument, Kennedy continued by saying "In all events we think that our laws and traditions in the past half century are of most relevance here. These references show an emerging awareness that liberty gives substantial protection to adult persons in deciding how to conduct their private lives in matters pertaining to sex. 'History and tradition are the starting point but not in all cases the ending point of the substantive due process inquiry.'"[17]

At this point the Court in essence issued an apology for its earlier decision, citing the 1955 Model Penal Code of the American Law Institute (which recommended removing criminal penalties for consensual sex), and even referring to the practices of the European Court of Human Rights (a very inclusive gesture, and one that nods as well towards the more liberal branches of natural law that underlie the human rights movement and much international legal theory). The Court continued by citing its own decision in *Romer*, reiterating that a "provision 'born of animosity toward the class of persons affected' has no rational relation to a legitimate government purpose." Other criticism of *Bowers* is said to have weakened it (here Posner is cited, among others), and in essence turns John Paul Stevens' dissent in that earlier case into a majority

---

[17] *Lawrence* 11 (quoting *County of Sacramento v. Lewis*, 523 U.S. Supreme Court 833, 857 [1998]).

opinion: "Justice Stevens' analysis, in our view, should have been controlling in *Bowers* and should control here." The opinion concludes with the following words (*Lawrence* 18):

> Had those who drew and ratified the Due Process Clauses of the Fifth Amendment or the Fourteenth Amendment known the components of liberty in its manifold possibilities, they might have been more specific. They did not presume to have this insight. They knew times can blind us to certain truths and later generations can see that laws once thought necessary and proper in fact serve only to oppress. As the Constitution endures, persons in every generation can invoke its principles in their own search for greater freedom.

A text consists not only of itself but also of the readings of it made throughout its history, and needs interpreters to bring out its true meaning, whether that text be Plato's *Symposium* or the United States Constitution. All judges are, by necessity, reception theorists.

Part Four

THE RECEPTION OF PLATO'S *SYMPOSIUM*

Thirteen

Plato's *Symposium* and the Traditions of Ancient Fiction

Richard Hunter

MONG THE MOST STRIKING PRODUCTS of the literature of the Roman empire are large-scale fictional narratives in prose, or occasionally a mixture of prose and verse. Such "novels"—the validity of the term is much debated but its usefulness seems undeniable—appear in both Greek and Latin, and cover a remarkable range of tone, style and milieu.[1] At the heart of most of these narratives lies a pair of lovers, usually but not always (cf. Petronius *Satyrica*) heterosexual, who eventually find happiness and each other after the most extraordinary adventures. In different ways, through both allusion and direct reference, most of the extant novelists acknowledge Plato as one of their authorizing models, second in importance perhaps only to Homer. In this paper I wish to explore two particular instances of that acknowledgement in the Latin novel, in both of which Plato, and particularly, though not exclusively, the *Symposium*, is indeed combined with Homer in scenes in which, through the figure of Socrates, the novelists seem to reflect upon their literary heritage and upon the business of creating fiction.

Critical interest in the links between Plato's *Symposium* and later traditions of fictional narrative has, broadly speaking, concentrated in two areas. The first is how Plato's work itself foreshadows these later developments. Many critics, including Nietzsche and Bakhtin, have seen the dialogues as foreshadowing the later novel and/or providing a paradigm for it and/or (to simplify a complex argument) as themselves the first novels (cf. further

---

[1] The Greek material is most accessible in translation in Reardon 1989, and in Stephens and Winkler 1995. The Latin novels of Petronius and Apuleius have been translated many times, but Walsh 1994, and Branham and Kinney 1996 are good places to start. There is now a huge bibliography on the ancient novel, but Schmeling 2003 offers a helpful way into the whole subject.

below).[2] Alongside (and in part stimulated by) this, the very obvious concern of the *Symposium*, as also of (say) the *Phaedo*, with its own status as a fiction, i.e. with the historicity of what is reported within it,[3] can with hindsight be seen to foreshadow a similar (and much discussed) feature of some of the novels of later antiquity, which display a partly playful and partly anxious concern with the "truth status" of their fictional narratives (is this *logos* or is this *muthos*?);[4] it is a small step from noting this similarity to seeing in these concerns a move by the later novelists to trace their literary genealogy back to Plato and/or to claim the philosopher as "one of them." I will return presently to another way in which Apuleius seems to claim Plato as "the father of the *logos*."

The second principal area of scholarly interest has been with the actual influence of the *Symposium* in the later novels, both in terms of intertextual echoes and, more broadly, with how later fiction reproduces and varies Platonic paradigms of *erōs*, particularly those of the *Symposium*.[5] Interest has centered on the apparent similarity between the mutual obsession with each other shown by Aristophanes' "separated halves" in the *Symposium* and the devotion and constant searching of the central couples at the heart of the novels of later antiquity, though other patterns, such as the reversal of "Pausaniac" *erōs* in Petronius' famous story of the sex-mad "Pergamene boy," have not been neglected. In this paper I will to some extent be pursuing these same paths, although this essay should also be seen within the broader context of an investigation of the interest of the novelists, one they inherited from (*inter alios*) Plato himself,[6] in contemporary interpretative practices. In an earlier contribution to this theme,[7] I put the matter (not very elegantly) as follows:

> When ... novelists themselves—to put it very crudely—overtly write "interpretation" into their own works, they are not merely challenging the scholastic hierarchy, they are also challenging us to have the critical courage and/or naïveté to take them seriously. The history of the interpretation of—to use the strongest case—

---

[2] See Nietzsche 1956:87–88, Bakhtin 1981:21–26, and the discussions of e.g. Gold 1980, Corrigan and Glazov-Corrigan 2005. For Bakhtin and the ancient novel more generally, cf. Branham 2002b, Branham 2005, in one sense, at least, the *Symposium* is a limit case of "polyglossia."

[3] Cf. e.g. Hunter 2004:20–29, Corrigan and Glazov-Corrigan 2005.

[4] For this distinction in the novels and further bibliography, cf. Hunter 1994 and 1997.

[5] For bibliography and discussion, cf. Hunter 1996 and (more briefly) Hunter 2004:125–129; cf. further Branham 2002b:173–174.

[6] For the *Symposium* as a key text for the history of "interpretation," cf. Hunter 2004:11–12, 128–130.

[7] Hunter 2005b:125.

Apuleius' *Metamorphoses* shows that the interpretative community ... is far from making up its mind on this matter. This critical uncertainty arises in large part precisely from the fact that, as the novelists (and, we may assume, at least many of their readers) knew only too well, the practice and modes of interpretation to which they direct us arose from and were designed for texts which occupied a very different cultural position.

This unsettling gap is in fact crucial to the literary effects of these techniques. All of our extant novels lay claim, with varying degrees of explicitness and persistence, to the Homeric mantle, and as Homer is the privileged font and subject of all interpretative practice, so an internal discourse of interpretation must be considered as a (ludic or otherwise) part of those generic and cultural claims.

Of rather more interest is a passage of Origen which all but certainly has Plato's *Symposium* in mind, in which the Christian scholar finds pagan parallels for the *Song of Songs*—parallels for that work's subject (love), for the fact that it can be (and has been) "misread," and for its form (dialogue):[8]

> Among the Greeks, indeed, many of the sages, desiring to pursue the search for truth in regard to the nature of love, produced a great variety of writings in this dialogue form, the object of which was to show that the power of love is none other than that which leads the soul from earth to the lofty heights of heaven, and that the highest beatitude can only be attained under the stimulus of love's desire. Moreover, the disputations on this subject are represented as taking place at meals (*conuiuia*), between persons whose banquet, I think, consists of words and not of meats.[9] And others also have left us written accounts of certain arts, by which this love might be generated and augmented in the soul. But carnal men have perverted these arts to foster vicious longings and the secrets of sinful love.
>
> *Prologue* 63.6–16 Baehrens, trans. Lawson (1957:23–24)

Plato's *Symposium* is indeed a text which, in Origen's terms, has a very great deal invested in the distinction between "carnal" and "higher" love, between bodies and souls, and in the various ways in which erotic texts can be read.

---

[8] For Origen's debt to the *Symposium* here and elsewhere, cf. Rist 1964:195–212, Osborne 1994:164–184.

[9] For this topos cf. e.g. Lucian *Symposium* 2.

Of the surviving ancient novels, it is the *Metamorphoses* of Apuleius which is perhaps most called to mind by Origen's words. This novel, probably composed near the middle of the second century AD, tells the story of Lucius, who, through misplaced curiosity about magic, is transformed into an ass and thus witnesses and experiences terrible cruelty and "carnality" until he is finally saved by the grace of the great goddess Isis, whose priest he becomes. Apuleius was steeped in the works of Plato and the trends of second-century Platonism, and the debt of the *Metamorphoses* to Plato, and particularly to the *Symposium*, is very obvious;[10] it is particularly felt in the central books of the novel in which Lucius listens to the famous tale of "Cupid and Psyche," in which the beautiful young Psyche ('Soul') is indeed finally led by Love "from earth to the lofty heights of heaven," as Origen puts it. Moreover, the whole plot of the *Metamorphoses* seems structured around the opposition between two forms of pleasure, the slavish and carnal on one side and the higher pleasure of true knowledge on the other, and we are at least invited to ponder throughout the work how much seriousness (*spoudaion*) lies concealed beneath the humor (*geloion*), as Alcibiades famously describes the *logoi* of the silenic Socrates.[11] Behind the *Metamorphoses* lies a Greek novel which survives in a version ascribed to Lucian, the *Onos* ('Ass').[12] Apuleius is, then, not just, as is his own Isis-priest (*Metamorphoses* 11.15), a self-conscious reader and interpreter of his own gloriously metaliterary *Metamorphoses*, he is also the first reader and exegete, of whom we know, of the Greek *Onos*, and he revels in displaying the operations of, in his own words, a *lector scrupulosus* 'busybody reader' confronted with that remarkable tale; the shifting and multi-faceted relationship between translation and interpretation is one to which Apuleius himself draws attention in the prologue. The very addition of an introductory prologue to the Greek model suggests "intentionality" in the narrative, i.e. that it is being told for a particular purpose, while simultaneously teasing us with the story's (alleged) lack of seriousness.[13]

The Greek *Onos* can be read—as Apuleius' transformation of the tale above all proves—as a parody of the philosopher's progress. Lucius feels a powerful 'desire' (ἐπιθυμεῖν, chaps. 4, 5, 11, 12) to see or 'learn' (μαθεῖν, chap. 11) paradoxical things; he in fact feels *erōs* for such knowledge (chaps. 4, 5).

---

[10] Cf. (briefly) Hunter 2004:128–129; further bibliography and discussion in Münstermann 1995:16–23 and Dowden 2006.

[11] Cf. e.g. Schlam 1970:486–487, who compares Alcibiades' words to Lucius' plea at *Metamorphoses* 1.3 for "close examination" of what at first seems absurd.

[12] Translation by J. P. Sullivan in Reardon 1989:589–618.

[13] For the prologue of the *Metamorphoses,* cf. Kahane and Laird 2001.

Lucius wanders about aimlessly, "at a loss (ἀπορῶν) as to where to begin the search" (*Onos* 4, cf. *Metamorphoses* 2.1-2), like the aimless philosopher without a guide (Plato *Symposium* 173a1-2);[14] the Luciuses of both the *Onos* and the *Metamorphoses* are indeed afflicted with the obsessive "desire to know" (cf. *Metamorphoses* 1.2) of which Apollodorus is so conscious in the *Symposium* (172e5-6, cf. further below). The desire to see metamorphosis (*Onos* 4, 11) would seem, however, to be the parodic opposite of the philosopher's ascent in the *Symposium* where, through the beneficent effects of *erōs* and a guide, the philosopher may catch sight of eternal, unchanging Beauty. Apuleius' Lucius at any rate imagines the Thessalian town of Hypata as a kind of Platonic limit-case, a site of Heraclitean flux in which everything visible is both changeable and indeed changed (*Metamorphoses* 2.1). It is against this background that we must consider the name of the central character of the opening story in the *Metamorphoses*, Socrates, a name which has, of course, not gone unremarked.[15]

In the opening pages of the *Metamorphoses*, Lucius (not yet transformed) listens to his traveling companion, Aristomenes, telling how a friend of his called Socrates was killed by a vengeful witch, Meroe, with whom Socrates had lived and slept but whom he had then left. That Aristomenes' story both fore-shadows many of the themes of the work which it introduces and acts as some-thing of a microcosmic taster of that work is well recognized, and it is made explicit in Lucius' farewell to a more skeptical traveling companion, who has also listened to Aristomenes' tale; Lucius' words echo the prologue, and thus draw an analogy between the whole work and the tale of Socrates: *sed ego huic credo hercule et gratas gratias memini quod lepidae fabulae festiuitate nos auocauit*, "for my part I believe him and I am very grateful to him for having distracted us with a charming and pretty tale" (1.20). As the adventures of both Socrates, another pursuer (like Lucius) of 'pleasure' (*uoluptas*, 1.7),[16] and Aristomenes (cf. the *curiositas* of 1.8.1 and 1.12) to some extent parallel those of Lucius, so Meroe foreshadows "the witch" Pamphile, who fascinates Lucius in Hypata, and acts as a warning to the listening Lucius; Lucius even claims that his horse enjoyed the story of Socrates (1.20), as he himself is soon to have to listen to a great

[14] Cf. Hunter 2004:24-25.

[15] Cf. e.g. O'Brien 2002:27-31, Smith and Woods 2002:185-191, Keulen 2003, 2004. Most scholars limit themselves to observing that the name is ironical, though the reasons for that irony may differ, cf. e.g. Walsh 1994:242, Harrison 1990:194. Münstermann 1995:22 sees the Apuleian Socrates as a *Zerrbild* of the Platonic character. The most elaborate "Platonic" reading of the episode is that of Thibau 1965:104-117, but the direction of that reading is at least problem-atic.

[16] For Aristomenes' Socrates foreshadowing Lucius, cf. e.g. Tatum 1969:493-501, Smith and Woods 2002:185-187, Keulen 2003:108-109, citing further bibliography.

many such stories in the shape of an ass.[17] The ambivalent relationship between the narrator "Lucius" and the author "Apuleius"—a relationship upon which so much Apuleian bibliography is founded—may even find a parallel in the unsurprising fact that the Platonic Socrates was one of the many classical models after whom "the real" Apuleius fashioned himself (cf. Apuleius *Florida* 2).

That the central character of Aristomenes' story is called "Socrates" suggests philosophical parody at more than one level (the *Phaedrus*, for example, is very obviously prominent in *Metamorphoses* 1.19—the Apuleian Socrates dies beside a plane-tree); both Plato's and Aristomenes' Socrates end their life with a drink, though Plato's stress on his Socrates' unchanged complexion and demeanor in the face of death (*Phaedo* 117b) resonates curiously against the deathly pallor of the Apuleian Socrates as death approaches (*Metamorphoses* 1.19.1). Whatever intertextual echoes there may be, Apuleius chooses to begin his novel with a story about (the death of) Socrates, and in such a way as to make clear that this story is emblematic for the longer narrative we are about to read and for the possibilities of interpretative reading which it is to offer. The death of Socrates is in fact the beginning of fiction, as Plato's Socrates himself is a figure of myth and fiction.[18] What is at issue is not how overtly fictional Plato's own account of his Socrates' death is,[19] but rather how "stories about Socrates" act as paradigms of fiction.

Most obviously, perhaps, we may wish to compare the paraded concern with historicity at the opening of the *Phaedo* and, even more so, the *Symposium* with the obtrusive concern with truth, fiction, and gullibility with which Aristomenes' tale is framed. That the introduction to the *Symposium* makes it very clear that we are not to be overly concerned with its documentary historicity is very familiar critical territory and it is also to be remarked that both Apollodorus' story in Plato and Aristomenes' in Apuleius are "repeats": Apollodorus had told his tale to Glaukon a couple of days earlier and Aristomenes had told (all or some of) his tale to his skeptical companion before Lucius intervenes and asks him to begin again.[20] The repeated telling of oral tales inevitably foregrounds—as both Plato and Apuleius make explicit—the role of the audience, and this too carries its own familiar implications for fictionality; Plato's Aristodemus (himself hardly an impartial narrator) found as receptive an audience in Apollodorus as Apollodorus then found in

---

[17] Cf. Winkler 1985:36–37.

[18] For some brief remarks and bibliography, cf. Hunter 2004:28, 110–112.

[19] Cf. e.g. Gill 1973, Bloch 2002.

[20] Cf. Van Der Paardt 1978:82, who directly links Apollodorus' telling of Socrates *chez* Agathon with Aristomenes' tale of his friend Socrates.

Glaukon, and as Aristomenes found in Lucius. At the heart of ancient notions about fiction lies precisely the attitude of the teller to his tale (the prologue of Lucian's *True Histories* makes this very clear), the attitude with which the audience receive it, and the effect of the tale upon them; whether what is told is, in a historical sense, strictly true or not is—as often as not—of secondary importance. A "true" tale can in this sense be fictional.[21]

The telling of the story of Agathon's symposium beguiled a "journey to town (εἰς ἄστυ)" for Apollodorus and Glaukon (173b7–8), just as Aristomenes' tale brought Lucius very pleasantly "to the very gates of the city" (*Metamorphoses* 1.2, 20). Pleasure, of course, is crucial here—it is what the *Metamorphoses* promises, what "Cupid and Psyche" quite literally delivers (the last phrase of the tale tells of the birth of their child Voluptas, *Metamorphoses* 6.24), and the state in which Lucius finishes his narrative (*Metamorphoses* 11.30); it, along with benefit (τὸ ὠφελεῖσθαι), is what Apollodorus derives from telling or listening to "*logoi* about philosophy" (*Symposium* 173c2–5). This last passage of the *Symposium* seems a remarkable foreshadowing of the Hellenistic concern with the *utile* and the *dulce* in literature; we may wonder to what extent Apollodorus' remarkable enthusiasm (ὑπερφυῶς ὡς χαίρω) marks him as someone who is never going to get very far in philosophy, but it certainly makes him of a piece with Apuleius' Lucius. Apollodorus should perhaps have been doing and listening to "philosophy" rather than "*logoi* about philosophy," if he wishes to make progress, but this phrase, together with the idea of benefit mixed with pleasure, strongly suggests a form of *literature* (a term here used, I hope, neutrally) such as we enjoy every time we read the *Symposium*. So too does Alcibiades' account of the effect of the *logoi* of Socrates/Marsyas: "when we hear you speaking, or listen to even a second-rate report of one of your arguments, then it doesn't matter who we are—woman, man or child—we're all overwhelmed and spellbound" (215d2–6, trans. Waterfield). This description of the effect of Socrates' *logoi*, which are in non-musically accompanied prose (215c7), ἐκπεπληγμένοι ἐσμὲν καὶ κατεχόμεσθα "we are overwhelmed and spellbound," is of course dictated by the context of ecstatic music (cf. 215c5), but it also looks both forwards and backwards in "literary theory": if the former word makes us think of *ekplēxis*, that quality of high poetry, particularly epic and tragedy, which "knocks out" the audience with its powerful clarity,[22] the latter recalls the whole idea of poetry as *thelxis*, 'echantment', an idea which has a powerful hold in the Greek tradition from the *Odyssey*

---

[21] Cf. further, though with very different concerns, Gill 1993, esp. 66–69.

[22] Cf. Heinze 1915:466–467 (i.e. 1993:384–385), Russell on "Longinus" 15.2.

onwards.[23] Neither critical notion, of course, suggests the literal truth of what is being represented, and often indeed the very opposite. Again, then, we may wonder whether the terms in which Alcibiades describes the effect of Socrates' *logoi* reveal the lack of depth of his own philosophical nature (and cf. 215e1–4),[24] but the idea that Socrates' *logoi* could be related by someone else—as indeed Apollodorus and Plato relate the *Symposium*—shows again how these *logoi* now have a life and circulation of their own, quite independent of Socrates himself. Yet another testimony to this idea is Phaedo's willingness to tell the story of the great man's death: "for remembering Socrates, whether by speaking myself or listening to another, brings me the greatest pleasure in the world (πάντων ἥδιστον)" (*Phaedo* 58d5–6). Here then is the blueprint for Aristomenes' tale.

In the *Poetics* Aristotle famously makes a distinction between poetry and history:

> ... the historian speaks of events which have occurred, the poet of the sort of events which could occur. It is for this reason that poetry is both more philosophical and more serious than history, since poetry speaks more of universals, history of particulars. A "universal" comprises the *kind* of speech or action which belongs by probability or necessity to a certain *kind* of character—something which poetry aims at while adding particular names. A "particular," by contrast, is what Alcibiades did or experienced.

> Aristotle *Poetics* 1451b4–11, trans. Halliwell, adapted

Although Aristotle's focus is utterly different, this passage can with hindsight be seen as (directly or indirectly) a significant step along the path of the justification of higher interpretation. Poetry can be seen as "more philosophical" because it is not tied to the historicity of what it relates, a claim which—if taken in ways which Aristotle did not apparently intend—also frees the interpreter to consider the "value" and real "meaning" of what is written, rather than just the surface literal meaning. The language of "doing and suffering," together with the idea of detailed completeness which Aristotle identifies as the hallmark of historiography, find (perhaps paradoxically) a striking parallel in the language used in epic poetry and then in the later novel (cf. Xenophon of Ephesus 5.15.2) to describe such extended (fictional) narratives them-

---

[23] [Plutarch] *De Homero* 2.5 sees a combination of ψυχαγωγία and ἔκπληξις in Homer's use of the gods conversing with men.

[24] Cf. e.g. Hunter 2004:101.

selves.[25] Against this background, Apollodorus' claim that he now takes care "every day to know what [Socrates] says or what he does" (*Symposium* 172e5–6) points in more than one direction. Apollodorus, of course, is interested in the "historical record," as his concern to check his source (*Symposium* 173b4–6) shows; for him the tale he tells, *his* "Symposium," is not just "*logoi* about philosophy," it is also *historia*.[26] We, on the other hand, will wonder whether these things are compatible. Once, however, we have been alerted to the problems with using "historicity" as a criterion, we will be looking for alternative interpretative strategies to help us with the fact that, in Aristotle's terms (and one imagines he would have agreed with the sentiment), Plato's *Symposium*, as opposed to Apollodorus', is "more philosophical and more serious" than historiography.

Here, then, is another way in which the death of Socrates is the beginning of fiction, particularly for a writer such as Apuleius. The large body of Socratic dialogues to which Socrates' death gave birth can be seen as the first major prose genre (and one very largely in the first person) which deliberately re-creates a past and asks us to read it with "philosophical" strategies. If we concern ourselves with whether or not the *Phaedo* is a literally "historical" account of Socrates' last hours, we will probably have missed much of the point; similarly, if we concern ourselves with the "historicity" of Aristomenes' tale we will have also missed the point, as surely as we would do so if we read "Cupid and Psyche" with such an attitude.

Socrates is not, of course, the only, nor indeed the most famous, originary hero of fiction. Plato's Alcibiades makes Socrates himself a latter-day Odysseus in the *Symposium* (220c),[27] and the paradigmatic role of the *polutropos* hero and of the *Odyssey* as a whole in the ancient novel (and particularly in Apuleius' *Metamorphoses*) requires no demonstration. In Aristomenes' tale, his Socrates is compared by Meroe to the cunning Odysseus who deserted Calypso (*Metamorphoses* 1.12), and it is clear that much about this Socrates recalls the Homeric hero.[28] When we first meet Socrates in Aristomenes' tale (1.6) he is shabbily dressed and very obviously down on his luck: "he was sitting on

---

[25] Cf. Hunter 2005a:157–162.

[26] The influence of Plato's depiction of Apollodorus is also visible in the characterization of Damis, Philostratus' alleged principal source in the *Life of Apollonius of Tyana*. Apollonius is of course another "Socrates" (e.g. 1.2.2, 4.25.1 etc.), as also another Pythagoras, and Damis was a follower who is said to have written a complete account of all of Apollonius' doings and sayings so that "nothing about Apollonius would not be known" (1.19.3, cf. 1.3.1, 7.28.1).

[27] Cf. Hunter 2004:109. There is much relevant material in Montiglio 2000, and see also Lévystone 2005.

[28] A useful discussion in Münstermann 1995:8–26, who does not, however, catch everything.

the ground, half-covered in a torn cloak, almost unrecognizable in his pallor and wretched emaciation, like those who beg at the public crossroads" (*humi sedebat scissili palliastro semiamictus, paene alius lurore, ad miseram maciem deformatus, qualia solent fortunae †deterrimat† stipes in triuiis erogare*). This description has been referred to particular features of "the" Socrates and the Socratic tradition,[29] but we may here rather recall the beggarly state to which Athena reduces Odysseus for the purposes of disguise (*Odyssey* xiii 429–38);[30] moreover, both Odysseus and the Apuleian Socrates are hard to recognize, both are believed dead in their homelands, their wives given to extremes of weeping and the pressure to re-marry,[31] both cover their heads for shame (αἴδετο, *prae pudore*) at crucial moments of recollection (cf. *Odyssey* viii 83–86),[32] and a bath does both of them a lot of good. More generally, Socrates is a victim of the twists and turns of fortune no less than Homer's *polutropos* hero (cf. *Metamorphoses* 1.6 "the dangerous twists, unsteady assaults and winding changes of our fortunes," *fortunarum lubricas ambages et instabiles incursiones et reciprocas uicissitudines*),[33] and no less than Lucius himself, who endured "the winding twists of most terrible journeys," *asperrimorum itinerum ambages reciprocae* (11.15), and whose debt to the figure of Odysseus requires no demonstration; Socrates' lament in 1.6. is echoed and varied in the Isis-priest's famous words of consolation to Lucius in 11.15, as for example at the beginning of his speech: "having endured many and varied tribulations and driven by the great storms and terrible blasts of Fortune, you have at last come, Lucius, to the altar of pity," *multis et uariis exanclatis laboribus magnisque Fortunae tempestatibus et maximis actus procellis ad portum quietis et aram misericordiae tandem, Luci, uenisti*. Here too, we can hardly fail to think of the hero who "endured in his heart many sufferings upon the sea" (*Odyssey* i 4).[34] Finally we may note

[29] Cf. e.g. Keulen 2003:111–112.

[30] Cf. James 1987:48.

[31] Cf. James 1987:48, Münstermann 1995:9–11.

[32] In doing so, Socrates reveals the lower part of his body, including the genitals (discussed by Keulen 2003:114–116); cf. perhaps *Odyssey* xviii 66–69, a famous passage in antiquity, and one which Apuleius may recall at 7.5.2, cf. Harrison 1990:199–200. The Apuleian Socrates' covering of his head is usually taken as recalling familiar gestures of his Platonic namesake (cf. e.g. Thibau 1965:106, Van Der Paardt 1978:82, Keulen 2003:112–113), but the gesture is, at the very least, both Odyssean and Socratic.

[33] Cf. e.g. Keulen 2003:121.

[34] Apuleius' verb, *exanclare*, should be allowed its full weight here; cf. also Horace's translation of the opening verses of the *Odyssey* at *Epistle* 1.2.21–22. Book 10 ends with Lucius "oppressed by sweet sleep" (*dulcis somnus oppresserat*) at Cenchreae: he has found a harbor which is, literally, a "very safe anchorage for ships" (*tutissimum nauium receptaculum*, 10.35), but which—in a paradigmatic example of "interpretation"—he will learn is, at a higher level of reality, a "harbor of quiet" in which he has been "received into the protection of the Fortune which has sight" (*in*

that the Apuleian Socrates tells his story over food and drink, preceding it, as does Odysseus (cf. *Odyssey* viii 535, 540, ix 13), with the noise of sadness, "drawing up a tortured sigh from the depths of his chest," *imo de pectore cruciabilem suspiritum ducens.*

It is of course no surprise that the long-suffering Apuleian Socrates is an Odysseus figure, particularly as his "Calypso" is very obviously a "Circe,"[35] but the fusion of these two originary figures of fiction at the head of Apuleius' novel deserves more attention than it has received.[36] Such self-conscious concern with the history of the form in which Apuleius is writing is very much of a piece with the concerns and self-positioning of the prologue of the *Metamorphoses*, but—like the prologue itself—the appeal to the models of Odysseus and Socrates is also an appeal to an interpretative tradition and a nudge to us as to how we should read this text; how misleading that nudge is may, of course, be another question.

2.

Petronius' *Satyrica* wears its "culturedness" very openly; it strokes our self-importance as knowledgeable readers/interpreters, but the "low realism" of the text works to close down its educational value, by leaving very little (no?) room for interpretability of a moralizing or even quasi-allegorical kind, such as flourished in ancient school-rooms and with which the poet Eumolpus introduces his "Capture of Troy" (*Satyrica* 88) and which is written into his own epic "The Civil War" (*Satyrica* 119–124). There is apparently nothing you can do with this text, which it has not already done to itself; this has not, of course, stopped modern scholarship. This aspect of the text is, for example, made very obvious by a comparison between the *Satyrica* and the most ambitious and complex of all surviving Greek novels, Heliodorus' *Aithiopika*; both works are laden with cultural knowledge of all kinds, but whereas the *Satyrica* dares us to "interpret," to "know" things (if you like) at our peril, the *Aithiopika* rather

---

tutelam ... receptus Fortunae ... uidentis, 11.15). Very obviously, the sleeping Lucius embodies (once more, cf. esp. 9.13) the figure of Odysseus, 'overcome' (δεδμημένον *Odyssey* xiii 119) by sweet sleep (cf. *Odyssey* xiii 79–80), first on the Phaeacian ship and then subsequently at the harbor of Phorkys on the shore of Ithaca, itself a safe haven for ships (*Odyssey* xiii 100–101); Odysseus has, like Lucius, safely arrived "home," did he but know it. Cf. further Dowden 1998:13–14.

[35] Cf. e.g. Harrison 1990:194–195.

[36] It is tempting to suggest that in Meroe's sister, Panthia, we have another acknowledgment of generic affiliation: this is the name of the "heroine" of Xenophon's romantic novella in the *Cyropaideia* (and of Leucippe's mother in the novel of Achilles Tatius). Griffiths 1975:140 associates the name "Panthia" with the worship of the cosmic Isis.

invites us to wallow in interpretative excess.[37] With this preliminary warning, I want to look at the episode of the *Satyrica* in which Encolpius, pretending to be a slave called Polyaenus ('much praised', an epithet of Odysseus),[38] becomes involved at Croton with a rich woman called "Circe"; one reason for choosing this episode in the current context is that it forms part of an elaborate fiction of role-playing staged by Encolpius and his companions, and part of that fiction is explicitly a rewriting of the *Odyssey*. Here perhaps we are being nudged as Apuleius was later to do.[39]

At Croton Encolpius' persistent impotence disappoints not merely Circe, but also his boyfriend Giton, whose sarcastic response is preserved: "I am grateful to you for loving me in the manner of Socrates: Alcibiades was not so untouched when he lay in his teacher's bed," *itaque hoc nomine gratias ago, quod me Socratica fide diligis. non tam intactus Alcibiades in praeceptoris sui lecto iacuit* (*Satyrica* 128.7). The barb reminds us of how little of the ideal "Pausaniac" relationship there is between Encolpius and Giton, his 'brother' (*frater*), in the terminology of the *Satyrica*;[40] Petronius may here be pointing (by the familiar technique of "window reference") to the (real or constructed) model of verses from the Ovidian poem which is so important to these Petronian scenes, namely *Amores* 3.7, in which Ovid relates how he too proved impotent at a crucial moment:

---

[37] Bibliography and discussion in Hunter 1998b. A third path is followed in the novel of Achilles Tatius: many of his moralizing and generalizing disquisitions form a kind of commentary upon the narrative, which explains why, in their particular cultural context, the characters behave as they do (weep, fear, fall in love etc.), cf. Morales 2004:106–130. This is very different from the mode of both Heliodorus and the Roman novels; Achilles in fact is very resistant to any form of "higher interpretation" beyond moralising disapproval (cf. e.g. Photius *Bibliotheca* 87 i.e. 2.11 Henry, 94 i.e. 2.34 Henry), and it is the very superstructure of explanation which shuts out our "desire to know."

[38] It is relevant that the epithet is only used in the *Odyssey* by the Sirens, as they offer Odysseus knowledge, cf. *Satyrica* 127.5. In view of the Epicurean material reflected in this episode (cf. further below), it is at least curious that one of Epicurus' closest followers was Polyainos of Lampsacus, the town which also gave Priapus to the world, cf. Usener 1887:415–416, K. Ziegler, *RE* 21.1431; a connection of that philosopher with Petronius was suggested by Knaack 1883:33. The anecdotal tradition presented Polyainos as, like Epicurus himself, the teacher and/or *erastēs* of Pythocles, Epicurus' "star pupil," cf. Usener 1887:402, Alciphron *Letters of Courtesans* 2.2.3 (i.e. 4.17.3 Benner-Fobes), "Epicurus ... wants to be a Socrates ... and he considers Pythocles to be an Epicurean."

[39] I pass over on this occasion the familiar echoes of the *Symposium* in our best preserved part of the *Satyrica*, the "dinner party of Trimalchio" (cf. Hunter 2004:126, with bibliography), and cf. above for other well-known links. It is worth noting that Judith Perkins has recently tried to draw (perhaps surprising) structural and other parallels between Diotima and Trimalchio (Perkins 2005:148).

[40] Cf. Hunter 1996:200.

> sic flammas aditura pias aeterna sacerdos
> surgit et a caro fratre uerenda soror

Thus does a virgin priest rise to approach the holy flames, or a modest sister from beside her dear brother.

Ovid Amores 3.7.21–22

Petronius has in mind, of course, Alcibiades' famous words: "I rose up after having slept with Socrates no differently than if I had slept with my father or an older brother" (*Symposium* 219c7–d2); it is indeed with "an older brother (*frater*)" that Giton has slept (just as 'sister' [*soror*] Circe also is disappointed with her "brother's" performance in bed [cf. *Satyrica* 127.1–2]). At the heart of these scenes lies a very obvious Homeric parody: Odysseus must fear that Circe will make him 'unmanned' (ἀνήνωρ, *Odyssey* x 341), but in Petronius Encolpius is already in that state and thus no good to Circe at all. Giton's remark, however, suggests that Socrates too, that other paradigmatic hero of fiction with which we are concerned, may have left Alcibiades *intactus*, not because of some high philosophical attitude, but simply because he was impotent; as so often, the alluding text makes us read the model with new eyes—allusion is interpretation. The final mystery (Plato *Symposium* 218b5–8) revealed by Alcibiades, the new Dionysus, which corresponds to Diotima's "epoptic" vision, turns out to have been of an impotent teacher; if some Dionysiac mysteries revealed an erect phallus to initiates,[41] here the revelation, the "what Alcibiades saw" and the "what *phantasia* allows us to see," is somewhat less exciting.

Socrates is also important elsewhere in these scenes. Circe warns Encolpius in a letter of the mortal danger in which he finds himself: "if that same chill attacks your knees and hands, you might as well send for the funeral trumpeters," *quod si idem frigus genua manusque temptauerit tuas, licet ad tubicines mittas* (*Satyrica* 129.7). Here again we seem to have both Ovid and Plato. In *Amores* 3.7 the poet blames his tools for missing a golden opportunity:

> tacta tamen ueluti gelida mea membra cicuta
> segnia propositum destituere meum.

My lifeless limbs, as though I had drunk chill hemlock, could not perform as I wished.

Ovid Amores 3.7.13–14

---

[41] Cf. Burkert 1987:95–96.

The reference to the coldness induced by hemlock can hardly fail to recall Plato's account of the final hours of Socrates, as the cold numbness moves up from the feet to the legs and lower abdomen (*Phaedo* 117e–118a8). The prison-warder's observation that "when the coldness reached Socrates' heart, he would die" (*Phaedo* 118a4) is all but translated in Circe's warning to Encolpius (*Satyrica* 129.7 above).

If Apuleius' Socrates resembles Odysseus, Petronius' Odysseus resembles (the Platonic) Socrates. This ought to make us look again at how we are encouraged to read the Circe-scenes of the *Satyrica*. The most common ancient interpretation of the Homeric Circe-episode, as of course also (*inter alia*) of the land of the Lotus-eaters and of the Sirens (with whom Encolpius compares his "Circe," *Satyrica* 127.5), was that it was a story about the dangers of the pursuit of irrational pleasure;[42] in such interpretations Circe is often portrayed as a hetaira (cf. Horace *Epistles* 1.2.25) who controlled men "because of the desires which irrationally inclined them towards pleasure" ("Heraclitus" *De incredibilibus* 16), whereas Odysseus overcomes her by reason, education, and through the aid of Hermes and/or his *mōly*, i.e. rational *logos* (cf. e.g. "Heraclitus" *Homeric Problems* 72). Such a reading, which has roots as early as Plato's *Cratylus* (407e–408a)[43] and which was apparently promoted by Cleanthes (*SVF* I 526), in fact makes an explicit appearance at the close of Apuleius' "On the god of Socrates" (chap. 178), in a passage which associates Socrates and Odysseus and suggests that there was a great deal more such material available which has been lost to us. Be that as it may, this reading was by no means universal: thus, for example, the Homeric scholia preserve remnants of a moralizing interpretation in which Circe invites Odysseus into her bed "not for pleasure, but as a pledge of good faith" (Σ on *Odyssey* x 334) or "not out of wantonness, but because, on the basis of what Hermes had told her, Odysseus was dear to the gods" (Σ on *Odyssey* x 296). Nevertheless, it is usually of the dangers of Circe of which the interpreters warn. Of particular interest is the set of interpretations preserved in the Homeric commentary of the twelfth-century bishop of Thessaloniki, Eustathius, which certainly draw on much earlier material. Here Circe is, as usual, pleasure (1656.6 on *Odyssey* x 231, 1656.41–55 on *Odyssey* x 241), and particularly the irrational pleasures of appetite and of the flesh, by

---

[42] There is much relevant material in Buffière 1956:289–296 and Kaiser 1964:201–203; cf. Schlam 1992:15, 68–69 on the "Circe model" in Apuleius. A more philosophical version of the "reason v. pleasure" reading is to be found at Porphyry fr. 382 Smith and [Plutarch] *De Homero* 2.126, cf. Buffière 1956:506–516; cf. further below.

[43] Cf. also Xenophon, *Memorabilia* 1.3.7–8, Cornutus, *Theologiae Graecae Compendium* 16, p20.18–20 Lang.

which men become beasts; these are, however, short-lived pleasures which "flatter us with the appearance (φαντασία) of good" (1656.30–31 on *Odyssey* x 241).[44] According to Eustathius, Circe's own character (if read outside the allegory) is base: she likes sex far too much and she shows the cowardice of a woman (1659.62–1660.2 on *Odyssey* x 323). As for Hermes, he is *logos* and the *mōly* is education: its root is black because for those who set out on the path of education the end is obscure, hard to grasp, and not pleasant (ἡδύ) to reach, but its flower is white, because the end of education is of a brilliant purity, both pleasant and nourishing; armed with these weapons Odysseus "the philosopher" conquers the pleasures of the flesh (1658.25–40 on *Odyssey* x 277, 1660.26 on *Odyssey* x 337). Odysseus extracts from Circe an oath that she will do him no harm, thus guaranteeing "like a philosopher" that he can sleep with her "with *sōphrosynē* and without suffering harm" (1660.32–36 on *Odyssey* x 343).

In the fiction which he creates, Encolpius is indeed a "slave to pleasure": the fact that he plays the role of a slave (*Satyrica* 126.5) makes the point forcefully. Nevertheless, it is perhaps his very control of *logos*, his "culture" and education, his knowledge of how narratives such as the Homeric Circe are to be read, which keeps him impotent in the face of Circe's charms; he lives out the Odyssean nightmare, a fate with which Ovid's disappointed mistress also charges her useless lover ("either the witch of Aia has pierced woolen dolls to put a spell on you or you come tired after lovemaking with another," *aut te traiectis Aeaea uenefica lanis / deuouet, aut alio lassus amore uenis'*, *Amores* 3.7.79–80). If "the ancients depicted the older bearded Hermes with an erect penis ... because in men of advanced years *logos* is productive and complete (γόνιμος καὶ τέλειος)" (Cornutus *Theologiae Graecae Compendium* 16, p23.16–21 Lang), in the case of Encolpius *logos* has produced the very opposite effect; education here is truly disempowering. Fortunately for Encolpius, however, the god who takes away can also restore (*Satyrica* 140.12).[45] Be that as it may, the

---

[44] It is worth noting in regard to the Apuleian Lucius' dalliance with the sexy slave-girl Fotis that the Homeric Circe's drugs were designed to make men forget their homeland (*Odyssey* x 236), a fate which Eustathius ascribes to the hold of pleasure: "for pleasure makes the pleasure-seeker entirely her own possession and leads him away from more serious matters" (1656.22 on *Odyssey* x 236), cf. *Onos* 11, *Metamorphoses* 3.19 (Lucius to Fotis) "I am bound and given to you like a willing slave; I no longer seek my home or want to depart, and spending the night with you is the most important thing in the world," *in seruilem modum addictum atque mancipatum teneas uolentem: iam denique nec Larem requiro nec domuitionem paro et nocte ista nihil antepono.*

[45] The importance of an ithyphallic Hermes is seen by, e.g. Conte 1996:98–102, though he does not connect this with Homeric interpretation. My discussion is not, of course, intended to deny the role of Priapus, but rather to see how the "novel within the novel" carries its own interpretative logic: it is always ahead of its readers.

Eustathian account of Circe may again recall the Platonic Socrates to us. After his night of chastity, Alcibiades immediately expresses his wonderment at Socrates' *"physis*[46] and *sōphrosynē* and *andreia*," for he had never imagined that he would meet a man so distinguished for *phronēsis* and *karteria*, "intelligence and endurance" (*Symposium* 219d3–7). Socrates' *sōphrosynē*, that quality which, in the Eustathian reading, allowed Odysseus to enter Circe's bed, has become in Petronius impotence, *andreia* ('the quality of a man') has become *anandria*, and we will not, I think, accuse Encolpius of sharing in *phronēsis* and *karteria*, which are again the hallmarks of the Eustathian Odysseus. In the interpretation of [Plutarch] *De Homero*, the wise Odysseus was not metamorphosed by Circe because "he had received impassivity (τὸ ἄπαθες) from Hermes, that is from *logos*" (2.128); impotence is not what a Skeptic or a Stoic normally meant by *apatheia*, but that is certainly what this Odysseus enjoyed (or, rather, did not).[47]

If Odysseus and Socrates are the "beginning" of fiction, what is its end (τέλος)? The answer is sex, both in the Alexandrian "end" of the *Odyssey* (*Odyssey* xxiii 296) and in a prominent part of the ancient novel tradition (note the end of Longus' *Daphnis and Chloe* and the reversal of the idea at the end of Apuleius' *Metamorphoses* which celebrates chastity); the famous elegiacs of *Satyrica* 132.15 adduce the authority of Epicurus for sex as the *telos* of all life.[48] More broadly, perhaps, texts such as "Cupid and Psyche" suggest that the end of fiction, as of life, is pleasure, ἡδονή, and this is not without interest in the context of the interpretative tradition of the Circe-episode which we have been tracing and of the parodic *mise-en-abîme* of the "novel within a novel" which the charade at Croton represents.[49] Moreover, this idea seems to be thematized in what survives of the text: Circe and Encolpius sport on the grass "seeking more robust pleasure" (*quaerentes uoluptatem robustam*, *Satyrica* 127.10), and when Circe flounces off, Encolpius is left to ponder "whether I had been

---

[46] I forebear from suggesting that readers of Petronius may be tempted to take this in the sense 'genitals'; Circe was certainly amazed, though not pleased, at this part of Encolpius' nature.

[47] Eustathius notes that when Odysseus expresses his fear to Circe that she will make him "wretched and unmanned" κακὸν καὶ ἀνήνορα (*Odyssey* x 341), he means that he will become a coward, because cowards are "without weapons at critical times" οἱ ἐν δεινοῖς ἄοπλοι (1660.42 on *Odyssey* x 341); "I was ready to serve but had no weapons" (*paratus miles arma non habui*) pleads Encolpius (*Satyrica* 130.4), and even here there may be an Odyssean tinge.

[48] The reference is to Epicurus περὶ τέλους; cf. fr. 67 Usener i.e. 21L L-S. It is perhaps worth remarking that Epicurus fr. 2 Usener (i.e. 21R L-S), ἡ δὲ χαρὰ καὶ ἡ εὐφροσύνη κατὰ κίνησιν ἐνεργείᾳ [or ἐνέργειαι] βλέπονται would very readily lend itself to *double entendre*; ἐνεργεῖν is one thing which Encolpius cannot do.

[49] For Circe as a "novel heroine" cf. e.g. Hunter 1994:1074–1075, Conte 1996:91.

cheated of genuine pleasure" (*an uera uoluptate fraudatus essem*, *Satyrica* 128.5). It looks as though Petronius' comedy overturns not just Homeric models, but also models of Homeric interpretation: the end of life (as of fiction) really *is* sexual pleasure, that very lesson which the Homeric Circe-episode was read as disproving. On his side of the argument, Petronius/Encolpius musters some powerful allies: Homer himself, for one. The foreplay of Circe and Encolpius (*Satyrica* 127.9) rewrites the very end of the Iliadic "Deception of Zeus," in which Hera tricks her husband into making love so that he will be distracted from the battle at Troy, to "set the reader up for the failure of Encolpius to perform with Circe";[50] the parody allows us to see Circe's words at 127.7 "there is no need to fear any busybody [seeing us]," *neque est quod curiosum aliquem extimescas*, as a rewriting of *Iliad* XIV 342–3, "have no fear that a god or any man will see this" (with a typical move from simple "sight" to the voyeuristic *curiositas* of the Roman novel tradition). Zeus and Hera lend powerful authority to any argument.[51]

There was of course one great philosophical school devoted to ἡδονή and *uoluptas*, namely the Epicureans. The Epicurean resonances which surface in many places in the *Satyrica* have long been catalogued, and it is familiar that 'genuine pleasure' (*uera uoluptas*) in 128.5 takes us immediately to Lucretius and his master.[52] The poem which follows, on how we take pleasure in what we possess only in dreams and regret its loss when we awake, may fairly be described as sub-Lucretian, and it is, as Marina Di Simone noted,[53] precisely the famous passage of Lucretius 4 on the frustrating pursuit of sexual *uoluptas* to which we are directed:[54]

---

[50] Slater 1990:174.

[51] Connors 1998:42 makes the attractive suggestion that *rosae* in the poem at 127.9 reflects ancient discussion of the Iliadic passage (cf. Σ on XIV 347). We might also add that *concesso ... amori*, which seems certain for the transmitted *confesso ... amori*, may also reflect the ancient observation (Σ on XIV 342–343) that "any place is a proper chamber for lawful (i.e. married) sex." I suspect that the very close of the *Dios apatē*, 'the glistening dew came down' (*Iliad* XIV 351), had been parodically read as a reference to ejaculation; perhaps as early as the "Cologne Epode" of Archilochus?

[52] Cf. e.g. Di Simone 1993:98–99.

[53] It is not clear to me, *pace* Di Simone, that *uera uoluptas* (128.5) need refer to the Epicurean distinction between kinetic and catastematic pleasure. Encolpius' point is that Circe's sudden disappearance suggests to him that the whole love-making might have been a figment of his imagination, cf. Lucretius 4.1057 *uoluptatem praesagit muta cupido*; it is, however, correct that his language lets us see how philosophical issues and ideas are here being abused. On the philosophical flavor of 128.6 cf. also Kragelund 1989:444.

[54] Note especially verse 4.1101 *Venus simulacris ludit amantis*, 4.1103–1104 *manibus ... errantes*, 4.1128 *Veneris sudorem*, 4.1135 *conscius ipse animus*. The same passage of Lucretius 4 lies behind Petronius fr. 30 Müller on the relation between our dreams and our daytime activities.

nocte sporifera ueluti cum somnia ludunt
errantes oculos effossaque protulit aurum
in lucem tellus: uersat manus improba furtum
thesaurosque rapit, sudor quoque perluit ora
et mentem timor altus habet, ne forte grauatum
excutiat gremium secreti conscius auri:
mox ubi fugerunt elusam gaudia mentem
ueraque forma redit, animus quod perdidit optat
atque in praeterita se totus imagine uersat.

As when in the deep sleep of night dreams deceive our wander-ing eyes and the earth is exposed to reveal gold; a wicked hand turns over what it has stolen and grabs the treasure; sweat bathes the face and a deep fear grips the mind, lest someone who knows about our secret gold robs our bursting pocket. When such joys have aban-doned our minds which have been tricked and true appearances have been restored, our hearts long for what they have lost and are completely absorbed in the image which has gone.

Petronius *Satyrica* 128.6

The pleasure and excitement of sudden riches is as short-lived as the pleasure and relief which sex with a desired partner brings. Even without the Lucretian resonances, it is clear that Petronius' poem paints the illicit pleasure of unex-pected wealth in sexual terms: dreams in the night, the wicked hand (*manus improba*), sweat, the fear which attends adultery as much as secret riches (cf. Horace *Satires* 1.2.127–131), fleeting joys. Thus, whereas "philosophy," as embodied in the wisdom of Odysseus, is normally opposed to the life of plea-sure which Circe represents, here philosophy, as represented by the self-defensive Encolpius, fights on Circe's side; so would Socrates have done, if his manhood had been up to it.

14

Some Notable Afterimages of Plato's *Symposium*[1]

J. H. Lesher

FROM THE FOURTH CENTURY BCE DOWN TO THE PRESENT DAY, Plato's *Symposium* has provided a stimulus to reflection on the nature of love.[2] Among the earliest known responses to the dialogue are portions of Xenophon's *Symposium*, Petronius' *Satyrica*, Plutarch's *Dialogue on Love*, Tacitus' *Dialogue Concerning Oratory*, and Apuleius' *Metamorphoses*.[3] Aristotle composed a symposium-style dialogue on drunkenness, Epicurus wrote one on wine and sex, Heraclides of Pontius one on the effects of food and drink, Maecenas one on the effects of wine, and both Menippus and Lucian wrote philosophical symposia. *The Symposium* of St. Methodius, although it features ten virgins speaking in praise of chastity, is still a recognizable instance of the same genre. Clearly, the

---

[1] An earlier version of this paper was presented at the conference on Plato's *Symposium* held at the Center for Hellenic Studies in Washington, DC in August of 2005. For sources of the images mentioned but not displayed in the text, see the following notes.

[2] As Reginald Allen has observed, "The *Nachleben* of the dialogue, as the Germans call it, its afterlife and influence, is very nearly as broad as the breadth of humane letters in the West; in the matter of *Quellenstudien*, it is not a spring, but a mighty river" (Allen 1991:2, vii). Allen discusses several later responses to the dialogue. Novotny 1977 provides a general survey of the Platonic legacy. Bury 1932:xlix–li cites several later writers to show "how the doctrines of Plato, and of the *Symposium* in special, have permeated the mind of Europe." There have also been accounts comparing the view of love put forward in the *Symposium* with those of later eras: Gould 1963, D'Arcy 1954, Singer 1966, and Paz 1997. Most recently, Richard Hunter has surveyed a number of the literary traditions and psychoanalytic notions that can be traced back to the dialogue (see Hunter 2004, especially chap. 4, The Morning After). See also Lesher 2004 and 2006.

[3] For echoes of the *Symposium* in works by Petronius and Apuleius see the discussion by Richard Hunter in the present volume. For a defense of the view that Socrates' speech in Xenophon's *Symposium* 8 was composed in imitation of Plato's *Symposium*, see Thesleff 1978 and Bowen 1998:8–9.

format of "after dinner conversations of illustrious individuals" struck many later writers as an attractive framework within which to work.[4]

Near the end of the third century of the common era the philosopher Plotinus elected to read Plato's *Symposium* not merely as an account of the nature of *erōs*—'love' or 'passionate desire'[5]—but also as an allegorical representation of the different levels of reality and the process by which the human soul, inspired by its perception of physical beauty, ascends from the material world to the realm of intelligible form. Following Plotinus' lead, many early Christian writers borrowed from the language of the *Symposium* in describing the process by which the human soul ascends from earth to heaven.

Toward the end of the fifteenth century the Florentine scholar Marsilio Ficino translated the *Symposium* (first into Latin and later into Italian) and coined the phrase *amor Platonicus* to refer to the special bond of affection between two men Plato had highlighted in the dialogue.[6] The publication in 1484 of Ficino's commentary on the *Symposium*, popularly known as the *De Amore*, sparked the creation of no fewer than thirty-three "treatises on love" in Italy during the next century alone—works such as the *Platonic Discourse upon Love* by Pico della Mirandola, the *Dialogue on Love* by Leo Hebraeus, and the novel *Gli Asolani* by Pietro Bembo.

Bembo's view of a "good kind of love"—now strictly heterosexual—was spread to a far wider audience as a result of the publication in 1528 of Castiglione's *Book of the Courtier*. During the sixteenth and seventeenth centuries European poets alternately praised and questioned the merits of a distinctly spiritual or "Platonick love." In the eighteenth century the translation of the *Symposium* by Floyer Sydenham, later revised by Thomas Taylor,

---

[4] For a discussion of the development of the symposium genre as well as the influence of the Greek *symposion* on the Christian dinner celebration and the Jewish *seder,* see Smith 2003:280 who observes that: "Plato's *Symposium* alone was of enormous importance as a model for the form and ideology of the banquet as well as for the literary form in which a banquet was to be described."

[5] Greek *erōs* may be rendered either as 'love' or 'desire' but it is more precisely passionate love or desire, typically sexual in character. Prodicus the sophist described *erōs* (D-K B7) as "desire (*epithumia*) multiplied by two," while "*erōs* multiplied by two," he added, "is madness." One can feel *erōs* toward different sorts of things—objects and activities as well as persons—just as we might speak of politics, chess, or philosophy as "the ruling passion in one's life"—and this feature of the term plays a key role in Plato's account.

[6] In the *De Amore* Ficino speaks only of "Socratic love," but both expressions signify a love focused on the beauty of a person's character and intelligence rather than on physical charms.

spread Plato's philosophy to a wide circle of readers of English. Plato's view of natural beauty as merely an imperfect shadow of a Beauty existing in an ideal realm also influenced the thinking of leading figures in the German and English Romantic movements.

During the twentieth century themes and images in the *Symposium* appear in novels or plays written by Thomas Mann (*Death in Venice*), T. S. Eliot (*The Cocktail Party*), E. M. Forster (*Maurice*), Virginia Woolf (*To the Lighthouse*), and Yukio Mishima (*Forbidden Colors*); in essays by the American social reformer Jane Addams; and in explorations of the nature of sexual desire by Sigmund Freud, Jacques Lacan, and Michel Foucault.

Among the works of art inspired at least in part by Plato's *Symposium* are sketches by Peter Paul Rubens, Jacques-Louis David, and Hans Erni; and paintings by Anselm Feuerbach and John La Farge, among others. Among musical works there is Erik Satie's *Socrate* Suite for Voices and Small Orchestra (the text for part I is drawn from Alcibiades' speech in the *Symposium*), and Leonard Bernstein's Serenade *After Plato's Symposium* for Violin, Strings, Harp, and Percussion—each of whose six movements bears the name of a character in Plato's dialogue. Bernstein's Serenade has served in turn as the basis for ballets by Jerome Robbins, *Serenade for Seven,* and Christopher Wheeldon, *Corybantic Ecstasies.*

In recent years the *Symposium* has been adapted for performance on stage or television on at least six occasions, including the "musical version of Plato's *Symposium*" called *All about Love,* performed in Colorado Springs, Colorado, in 1997. There was also a 1969 BBC production, *The Drinking Party,* with Leo McKern as Socrates. Most recently, John Cameron Mitchell's rock musical *Hedwig and the Angry Inch* borrows elements of Plato's *Symposium* to tell the story of Hedwig's search for love and happiness after suffering a botched sex-change operation. In the song "The Origin of Love" (written by Stephen Trask) Hedwig draws on Aristophanes' story of the original race of globular creatures to tell "the sad story of how we became lonely two-legged creatures."

In what follows I will largely ignore the dialogue's many literary offspring and focus on a number of its most notable visual aftereffects. After we have reviewed a number of these "afterimages" we will consider what it was about the dialogue that inspired so rich and varied a set of responses.

Perhaps the best-known artistic recreation of Plato's *Symposium* is *Das Gastmahl des Platon* by the nineteenth century German artist Anselm Feuerbach (Figure 1):

Figure 1. Anselm Feuerbach (1829–1880), *Das Gastmahl des Platon*, 1869. Staatliche Kunsthalle, Karlsruhe, Germany, inv. no. 813. Photo, Bildarchiv Preussischer Kulturbesitz / Art Resource, NY.

When Feuerbach displayed *Das Gastmahl* in the 1869 Great International Art Exhibition in Munich, its larger-than-life dimensions, grey under-layering, and muted tones provoked much negative comment. One critic wrote that that the painting reminded him of "a sea of ice that had forced itself undesired into a perfume shop." Another called it "an extreme of ugliness in form and color which borders on vulgarity and filth ... as if Feuerbach had put his paint brush into ink and calcium water instead of color" (Bratke and Schimpf 1980:9). When the painting was purchased and disappeared into a private collection, Feuerbach decided to create a far more colorful and ornate version that since 1878 has been in the collection of the National Gallery in Berlin, now the Old National Gallery.[7]

In the earlier, 1869 version, generally considered the superior of the two works, Feuerbach captures the moment at which Alcibiades enters the dining chamber dressed like the god Dionysus and accompanied by a band of Bacchic revelers. A cherubic figure to Alcibiades' right holds up the wreath Alcibiades is about to bestow on Agathon, who stands at center stage, extending his right hand in welcome. The identities of the other persons shown in the painting are a matter of debate, but if we assume (as suggested by Heinrich Meier in the introduction to Benardete 1993) that spatial proximity betokens some degree of personal attachment, then the person seated behind Agathon would be his lover Pausanias. Similarly, Eryximachus the physician, identifiable by the cadu-

---

[7] See http://gastmahl-des-plato-ii-1888.gemaelde-webkatalog.de.

ceus wrapped around the lamp, would be seated near his friend Phaedrus. Two individuals appear in overlapping images, one facing away from the viewer absorbed in conversation, the other with his gaze fixed intently upon him—almost certainly Socrates with his devoted follower Aristodemus. This would leave only someone sufficiently distinguished looking to be Aristophanes engaged in conversation with Socrates and, at the far right, three other individuals, perhaps the other unnamed guests Plato mentions were in attendance, but perhaps (so Meier suggests) one of them is Plato himself, who would have been about nine at the time the event is supposed to have taken place. If so, then Phaedrus, Aristodemus, and Plato, if that is who it is, would create an isosceles triangle of admirers around Socrates, as opposed to the ragged arrangement of Alcibiades' cohort. The wall paintings in the background (one depicting the marriage of Dionysus and Ariadne, the other Maenads and a satyr) were perhaps inspired by Feuerbach's 1866 visit to Naples and Pompeii.

According to his biographer, Julius Allgeyer, in *Das Gastmahl* Feuerbach was seeking to depict the two contrasting impulses at work in the human psyche—the sensualism represented by Alcibiades and his cohort on the left, and the cool rationalism of Socrates, over on the right. On this reading Feuerbach may be said to have given visual expression to a kind of Dionysian-Apollonian contrast, two years before the publication of Nietzsche's *Birth of Tragedy*. But this is probably not the whole story. Feuerbach revealed in one of his letters that he completed the left hand side of the work at an early date and only much later conceived of the grouping on the right hand side: "Certain forms I have carried in me for years before they became useful." Feuerbach wrote, "At the symposium the group of bacchants of Alcibiades had been present for a long time, only while searching for a suitable counterweight to it, I remembered, through a sudden intuition, Plato's *Symposium*" (Bratke and Schimpf 1980:2).

We may also note, since this is not the last time we will see this happen, that Feuerbach provides a somewhat idiosyncratic version of the event. In the description he wrote for the inaugural exhibition he mistook Pausanias for Glaucon; the rather Italianate decor and seating arrangement accord neither with Plato's description nor the typical configuration of couches in an Athenian dining chamber of the classical period; and the prominence accorded to Agathon in the painting has struck more than one observer as reflecting an exalted view of the poet as someone honored for bringing beauty into being, in much the same way, I suspect, that Feuerbach hoped to be honored for his monumental painting.

The contrast between Alcibiades and Socrates highlighted by Feuerbach appeared more than two centuries earlier in a 1648 etching by Pietro Testa,

The Drunken Alcibiades, which depicts a naked Alcibiades, this time holding the wreath, set off against the argumentative Socrates, who continues to try to make a point while everyone else is looking in the other direction (Figure 2):

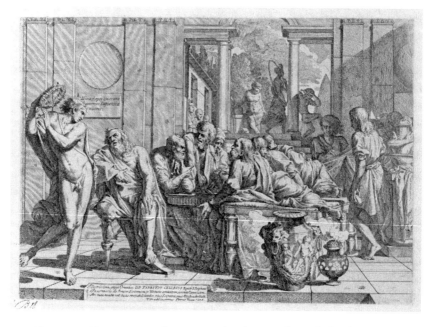

Figure 2. Pietro Testa (1612–1650), *The Drunken Alcibiades*, 1648. Kupferstichkabinett, Staatliche Museen zu Berlin, inv. no. 353–21. Photo, Bildarchiv Preussischer Kulturbesitz / Art Resource, NY.

Perhaps by way of a reference to Xenophon's *Symposium*, a hoop dancer is shown in the background leaving the celebration (the image of the marriage of Dionysus and Ariadne in Feuerbach's *Gastmahl* also recalled the ending of Xenophon's *Symposium*). In her study of Testa's work, Elizabeth McGrath (1983:233–234) sees the drawing as a celebration of the kind of youthful naked beauty that can serve both as a contrast and springboard for the ascent to a higher and more profound understanding of love.

A number of later works were inspired by "the wreath incident" recounted at 212a–b. Alcibiades announces that he has come to award a garland to Agathon, "the wisest and most beautiful man," and removes some of the ivy and violets on his own head to place them on Agathon's. But when he spots Socrates reclining just behind Agathon, Alcibiades attempts to retrieve some of the ribbons to award them instead to Socrates. A somewhat simplistic 1793 drawing by Asmus Jakob Carstens[8] depicts the moment at which Alcibiades places the wreath on Socrates' head while an elderly Agathon looks on.

A sketch by Peter Paul Rubens from around 1602, now badly faded, offers a more complex image (Figure 3):

Figure 3. Peter Paul Rubens (1577–1640), *The Drunken Alcibiades Interrupting the Symposium*, c. 1602. The Metropolitan Museum of Art, New York; gift of Harold K. Hochschild, 1940; inv. no. 40.91.12. Photo, all rights reserved, The Metropolitan Museum of Art.

In *The Drunken Alcibiades Interrupting the Symposium* Rubens depicts Alcibiades wearing one wreath on his head, holding above a second wreath above extended toward Socrates, while at the same time pulling back a third wreath, the one he previously awarded to Agathon. In effect, Rubens has telescoped the entire "wreath incident" into a single image. The result is an ambiguous message, perhaps a reflection of the quicksilver here-today-gone-tomorrow quality of Alcibiades' sense of loyalty. The motivation behind Rubens' creation

---

[8] See *Alkibiades kränzt den Sokrates beim Gastmahl* in Runes 1959:84 labeled as "One of the Famous Platonic Banquets." The work is now in the collection of the Thorvaldsen Museum in Copenhagen.

of the image is unknown, but one possibility, also suggested by McGrath (1983:234), is that the sketch was created as a gift for a friend, perhaps in remembrance of some memorable occasion during which both love and Platonic philosophy had been in the air.

The nineteenth century "American impressionist," John La Farge, explored the wreath image in two separate works. La Farge had read widely in Plato and studied in Europe with Thomas Couture—who had been one of Feuerbach's teachers. In a work La Farge created in 1861 entitled *Agathon to Erosanthe* we see a multicolored wreath of flowers with the inscription *Erosanthē Kalē*—"Beautiful love-blossom" or "Love-blossom is beautiful"—barely visible below the wreath and scratched in with reddish-brown ink (Figure 4).

The word *kalē* evokes the similar inscriptions of *KALOS* on the ancient cups and drinking bowls members of the Athenian elite bestowed on their favorites. Given the feminine form *kalē*, the violets, and the natural association of the poet Agathon with the poetic painter La Farge, we might conjecture that in this work La Farge drew on the imagery of Plato's *Symposium* to

express his love (for Margaret Perry, one assumes, whom he had married the year before). A second La Farge wreath painting entitled *Wreath of Flowers* dates from 1866 and bears the Greek inscription *THEREOS NEON HISTAMENOIO*—"as summer was just beginning" (Shields 1997:86). La Farge scholars regard both paintings as highly enigmatic, but I think we can see at least *Agathon to Erosanthe* as an example of the way in which a particular feature of the *Symposium* lived on the work of a later artist.

Another memorable feature of the dialogue for many artists was

Figure 4. John La Farge (1835–1910), *Agathon to Erosanthe (Votive Wreath)*, 1861. Private Collection, New England. Photo, courtesy of Thomas Colville Fine Art, LLC.

the relationship Plato described between Socrates and Alcibiades. One influential depiction was *Socrates Leading Alcibiades away from the Dangers of a Sensual Life* by Jean-François-Pierre Peyron (Figure 5):

Figure 5. Jean-François-Pierre Peyron (1744–1814), *Socrates Leading Alcibiades away from the Dangers of a Sensual Life*, after 1785. Ackland Art Museum, The University of North Carolina at Chapel Hill, The William A. Whitaker Foundation Art Fund; inv. no. 69.18.1.

The ancient literary sources for Peyron's depiction are uncertain (Gillham and Wood 2001:119). As Plato tells the story, Alcibiades rejected Socrates' attempt to recruit him into the philosophical life and fell back, with a palpable sense of shame and failure, into the pursuit of political power and popularity. At *Symposium* 216b Alcibiades confesses that: "I'm carried away by the people's admiration, so I act like a runaway slave and escape from him; and whenever I see him I'm ashamed because of what he's made me agree to." The image of Alcibiades as a runaway slave also appears in Plutarch's *Life of Alcibiades*: "He would sometimes abandon himself to flatterers, when they proposed to him varieties of pleasures, and would desert Socrates, who then would pursue him as if he had been a fugitive slave" (6.1). Plutarch tells also how Alcibiades consorted with courtesans ("giving himself up to every sort of luxury and excess among the courtesans of Abydos and Ionia," 36.2), although he does not say that Socrates actually rescued Alcibiades from a group of them. Udolpho van de Sandt has also linked Peyron's choice of subject with Homer's account of Hector's visit to the tent of Paris in *Iliad VI*, and to an article written by Diderot for his *Encyclopedia* in which he suggested that artists turn to Plato's *Symposium* for suitable subjects (Van de Sandt 2001).

The two male figures shown in Peyron's drawing appear to be modeled on the ancient statue known as the Apollo Belvedere, with the entire grouping bearing some resemblance to a Hellenistic relief in the collection of the National Museum in Naples, traditionally entitled *Youth among the Courtesans* (Figure 6):[9]

Figure 6. Hellenistic marble relief, *Youth among the Courtesans*, late second–early first century BCE. Naples, Museo Archeologico Nazionale, inv. no. 6688. Photo, Soprintendenza per i Beni Archeologici delle province di Napoli e Caserta.

So Peyron appears to have drawn on both artistic and literary precedents to fashion an image of ancient virtue, or more precisely, to contrast one ancient paragon of virtue with a classic example of the misspent life.

Among the many later re-workings of this theme are *Socrates Tearing Alcibiades from the Arms of a Courtesan* (1791) by Jean-Baptiste Regnault (Figure 7), *Socrates Seeking Alcibiades in the House of Aspasia* (1861) by Jean-Leon Gerome

---

[9] See also Bieber 1955:153, Figure 654.

Figure 7. Jean-Baptiste Regnault (1754–1829), *Socrates Tearing Alcibiades from the Arms of a Courtesan*, 1791. Paris, Musée du Louvre, inv. no. R.F. 1976.9. Photo, Erich Lessing / Art Resource, NY.

Figure 8. Jean-Leon Gerome (1824–1904), *Socrates Seeking Alcibiades in the House of Aspasia*, c. 1861. The Snite Museum of Art, The University of Notre Dame, on loan from Mr. and Mrs. Noah L. Butkin; inv. no. L1980.027.011.

(Figure 8), and *Socrates Discovers Alcibiades in the Women's Quarters* by Francesco Hayez (Figure 9):

Figure 9. Francesco Hayez (1791–1882), *Socrates Discovers Alcibiades in the Women's Quarters*. Palazzo Papadopoli, Venice, Italy. Photo, Cameraphoto / Art Resource, NY.

On a similar theme, based on the incident described at *Symposium* 220e and in Plutarch's *Lives*, is Antonio Canova's *Socrates Rescuing Alcibiades at the Battle of Potidaea* (1797) (Figure 10):

Figure 10. Antonio Canova (1757–1822), *Socrates Rescuing Alcibiades at the Battle of Potideia*, 1797. Gipsoteca Canoviana, Veneto, Italy. Photo, Conway Library, Courtauld Institute of Art.

There is also a set of sketches done by Inigo Jones, the English architect and artist, that shows Socrates with Alcibiades (Figure 11) :

Figure 11. Inigo Jones (1573–1652), *Heads of Socrates and Alcibiades.* Chatsworth, Devonshire Collection, vol. x, 74, no. 382. Reproduced by permission of the Duke of Devonshire and the Chatsworth Settlement. Photo, courtesy of the Photographic Survey, Courtauld Institute of Art.

Another memorable aspect of the dialogue was the relationship between Socrates and the mysterious priestess Diotima. Among the earliest of these images may be this bronze relief, part of a decoration on a wooden treasure box found in 1832 in the House of the Decorated Arches in Pompeii (and now in the collection of the National Archeological Museum in Naples) (Figure 12):

Figure 12. Bronze relief, Socrates and Diotima. Naples, Museo Archeologico Nazionale. Photo, Soprintendenza per i Beni Archeologici delle province di Napoli e Caserta.

Within a decade after the box had been found one scholar (O. Jahn) observed that it reminded him of the scene in Plato's *Symposium* in which Diotima instructs Socrates in the ways of love. In his recent study of the image of the intellectual in antiquity Paul Zanker states that the decoration "probably depict[s] Socrates' initiation into the mysteries of love by Diotima" (Zanker 1996:37). But others have challenged this interpretation, noting the oddity of an object bearing a scene from a Platonic dialogue appearing as early as the second half of the fourth century BCE as well as the correspondence on a number of points between the female figure and images of the goddess

Aphrodite on a number of small bronze mirrors (discussed in Schwarzmaier 1997). On this alternative reading, we see Aphrodite looking on as a Silenus teaches Erōs to read. Others have focused on what appears to be a necklace in the hand of the female figure, suggesting that it is an image of a *hetaira*, perhaps Aspasia, with Erōs and an unidentified observer.

From more recent times is a sketch by Jacques-Louis David, recently purchased by the National Gallery of Art in Washington, which unambiguously depicts Diotima instructing Socrates (Figure 13):[10]

Figure 13. Jacques-Louis David (1748–1825), *Socrates and Diotima*, 1775/80. National Gallery of Art, Washington, DC, Patrons' Permanent Fund; inv. no. 1998.105.1.e. Photo, © Board of Trustees, National Gallery of Art.

That this is David's Socrates is made evident by a comparison with the image of the Socratic torso in David's well-known *Death of Socrates* (Figure 14):

---

[10] David's images of Socrates and Diotima bear unmistakable resemblances to the figures depicted at both ends of the Sarcophagus of the Muses, now in the Louvre (see the two profile views available on the Museum's website at http://cartelfr.louvre.fr/cartelfr/visite?srv=car_not_frame&idNotice=2859).

Figure 14. Jacques-Louis David, *The Death of Socrates*, 1787. The Metropolitan Museum of Art, Catharine Lorillard Wolfe Collection, Wolfe Fund, 1931; inv. no. 31.45. Photo, all rights reserved, The Metropolitan Museum of Art.

There is also a set of sketches of Socrates with Diotima by the contemporary Swiss artist Hans Erni (Erni 1971).

Diotima's speech to Socrates, as one would expect, inspired imitation on several points, especially as the ascent passage was read and reinterpreted by a series of Neoplatonic thinkers. In his reformulation of Plato's account, Plotinus described love and beauty as cosmic powers locked into a continuous cycle of emanation and return as divine love first imparts beauty to the world, and then created beauty draws us up and back to our divine source. Plotinus writes:

> The born lover ... has a certain memory of beauty but, severed from it now, he no longer comprehends it: spellbound by visible loveliness he clings amazed about that. His lesson must be to fall down no longer in bewildered delight before some one embodied form; he must be led, under a system of mental discipline, to physical beauty everywhere and made to discern the One Principle underlying all ... he must learn to recognize the beauty in the arts, sciences, virtues; then these severed and particular forms must be brought together under the one principle by the explanation of their origin. From

the virtues he is to be led on to the Intellectual Principle, to the Authentic-Existent; thence onward, he treads the upward way.

Plotinus *Enneads* 1.3.2

As the historian Anders Nygren showed, this vision of the soul inspired by love of divine beauty to ascend a celestial ladder pervades much of early Christian thought: "For a thousand years ... the ladder-symbolism characteristic of *Eros* piety sets its mark almost without question upon the general conception of Christian fellowship with God" (Nygren 1953:594). One image of the ladder to heaven appears in an early fourteenth-century manuscript based on the writings of the sixth-century hermit Johannes Climacus or St. John of the Ladder (Figure 15):

Figure 15. Miniature, *St. John Mounting the Ladder to the Opened Doors of Heaven*, from an Anglo-Norman manuscript of the early fourteenth century. British Library, Royal MS 19 B. XV, f. 5v. Photo by permission of the British Library.

The simile of the celestial ladder of love and beauty also appears in the writings of Gregory of Nyssa, St. Augustine, Pseudo-Dionysius the Areopagite, Boethius, and St. Bonaventure, among others. It can also be found in Books 21 and 22 of Dante's *Il Paradiso* when another female spiritual guide, Beatrice, leads the poet from the sphere of Saturn up to the realm of the fixed stars:

> I saw—the color of gold as it reflects
> The sun—a ladder gleaming in the sky,
> Stretching beyond the reaches of my sight.

Dante *Il Paradiso* 1984:28, 21.28–30[11]

---

[11] While there is no evidence that Dante had any direct knowledge of Plato's *Symposium* or *Phaedrus*, there is also no need to establish that fact. As Etienne Gilson once observed, "If, in the

Images of the celestial ladder appear in a series of illustrations done for *Il Paradiso* by Sandro Botticelli (Figure 16), as well as in a painting by Giovanni di Paolo from about the same period (Figure 17).

Figure 16. Sandro Botticelli (1444–1510), *The Seventh Sphere: Saturn,* after 1480. Kupferstichkabinett, Staatliche Museen zu Berlin, inv. no. Cim.33, Paradiso 21. Photo, Bildarchiv Preussischer Kulturbesitz / Art Resource, NY.

Perhaps the most influential feature of Diotima's account turned out to be the basic distinction between physical and spiritual love—i.e. between love of a beautiful body and love of a beautiful soul. Many later readers—from Plotinus to Ficino and beyond, extracted the same distinction from the contrast drawn by Pausanias between the Heavenly and Common Aphrodites. Pausanias had introduced the distinction in his defense of love on the classic pederastic model,[12] but in his commentary on the *Symposium* Ficino repre-

---

Middle Ages in Western Europe, Plato was virtually nowhere, Platonism was everywhere, in the fathers, in Cicero, in the Arab philosophers, and indeed in Aristotle" (Mazzeo 1958:2). Mazzeo adds: "... the scattered elements of platonic doctrines of love were everywhere present awaiting a synthesis. The vocabulary awaited a man who had a platonic experience and had the need and ability to express it. Dante, I think, was such a man."

[12] For a brief but informative discussion of the pederastic model, see Pickett 2002 who writes, in part: "The central distinction in ancient Greek sexual relations was between taking an active

Figure 17. Giovanni di Paolo (fl. 1420–1482), *The Heaven of Saturn,* c. 1445. British Library, Yates-Thompson MS 36, f. 165r. Photo by permission of The British Library.

sented Pausanias' distinction as a contrast between any desire for physical union fueled by our senses of smell, taste, and touch, and the enjoyment of a person's mental and moral qualities acquired through sight and conversation. Ficino's version of the two forms of love surfaces in the novel *Gli Asolani of Pietro Bembo* when, after previous speakers have alternately praised and censured love, the gentleman Lavinello asks: "Who can fail to see that if I love some gallant, gentle lady, and love her more for her wit, integrity, good breeding, grace, and other qualities, than for her bodily attractions, and love

---

or insertive role, versus a passive or penetrated one. The passive role was acceptable only for inferiors, such as women, slaves, or male youths who were not yet citizens. Hence the cultural ideal of a same-sex relationship was between an older man, probably in his twenties or thirties, known as the *erastēs,* and a boy whose beard had not yet begun to grow, the *erōmenos* or *paidika.* In this relationship there was courtship ritual, involving gifts (such as a rooster), and other norms. The *erastēs* had to show that he had nobler interests in the boy, rather than a purely sexual concern. The boy was not to submit too easily, and if pursued by more than one man, was to show discretion and pick the more noble one. There is also evidence that penetration was often avoided by having the *erastēs* face his beloved and place his penis between the thighs of the *erōmenos,* which is known as intercrural sex. The relationship was to be temporary and should end upon the boy reaching adulthood (Dover 1989). To continue in a submissive role even while one should be an equal citizen was considered troubling, although there certainly were many adult male same-sex relationships that were noted and not strongly stigmatized. While the passive role was thus seen as problematic, to be attracted to men was often taken as a sign of masculinity."

those attractions not for themselves but as adornments of her mind—who can fail to see that my love is good because the object of my love is likewise good?" (Bembo 1954:158). This contrast between, essentially, physical and spiritual love found its way into the visual arts where, according to Kenneth Clark, it "formed the justification for the female nude." Clark (1956:71) explains:

> ... because it symbolized a deep-seated human feeling, this passing allusion [made by Pausanias] was never forgotten. It became an axiom of medieval and Renaissance philosophy. It is the justification of the female nude. Since the earliest times the obsessive, unreasonable nature of physical desire has sought relief in images, and to give these images a form by which Venus may cease to be vulgar and become celestial has been one of the recurring aims of European art. The means employed have been symmetry, measurement, and the principle of subordination [i.e. of part to whole].

Among early examples of the Heavenly Venus/Aphrodite cited by Clark are the Knidian Aphrodite of Praxiteles, from around 330 BCE (known to us only through later copies), and the famous Aphrodite of Melos—the Venus de Milo—from around 100 BCE (illustrated in Clark 1956). Art historian Erwin Panofsky (1969:109–138) has also linked the distinction between the two Aphrodites to the work of Titian traditionally called *Sacred and Profane Love*, arguing that the unclothed woman represents the "naked truth" or Heavenly Venus, while the clothed or "worldly" figure is her natural twin, though this reading has been challenged by others.

Another relevant image is provided by one of the most famous works in the permanent collection of the (American) National Gallery of Art, Leonardo's *Ginevra de' Benci*, completed at some point in the late 1470s.[13] There is some uncertainty about the exact date of the painting and the occasion for which it was created, but the inscription on the back of the painting, *Virtutem Forma Decorat*—"Beauty Adorns Virtue"—provides a helpful clue. The wreath of laurel and palm, which surrounds the inscription, was the personal emblem of Bernardo Bembo, the Venetian ambassador who came to Florence in the late 1470s and, during his visit, proclaimed Ginevra de' Benci to be his "*Platonic love*." What Leonardo created, then, was essentially a visual representation of Platonic love—of physical form as the outward show of an inner, spiritual beauty.[14]

[13] For images of Leonardo's painting, see the paper by Diskin Clay included in this volume.

[14] Ficino himself described it as "A picture of a beautiful body and a beautiful mind." See the discussions in Brown 2001:142–145, and the paper by Clay in this volume.

Many scholars have linked the distinction between the two Aphrodites to Botticelli's famous works *Primavera* (Figure 18) and *The Birth of Venus* (Figure 19).

Figure 18. Sandro Botticelli (1444–1510), *Primavera*, 1477. Galleria degli Uffizi, Florence, Italy, inv. no. 8360. Photo, Scala / Art Resource, NY.

In *Primavera* or *Fiorenza* created around 1477, Botticelli presents a tapestry of earthly delights presided over by a richly-clothed Venus/Aphrodite figure, with Cupid/Eros firing his darts of love down from above. On the right side of the painting Zephyr pursues Chloris who is transformed into Flora, the goddess of vegetative growth, with the three graces and Mercury over on the left. On one level, Botticelli gives us a visual image of the ancient *carmen rusticum* or "country song," drawing on accounts of the first appearance of spring in Lucretius' *De rerum natura*, Ovid's *Fasti*, and the *Odes of Horace*.[15] But on a more symbolic level *Primavera* may be seen to reflect the process through which love and desire beget natural beauty, which in turn draws the mind upwards toward the more rational forms of which they are reminiscent.[16]

---

[15] For a detailed analysis of the literary sources on which Botticelli may have drawn for his *Primavera*, see the account in Dempsey 1992, especially chap. 1.

[16] See, for example, the account in Cheney 1985. For a contrasting account, see Dempsey 1992 and Ames-Lewis 2002.

In the *Birth of Venus*, created around 1486, we find the Common Aphrodite's naked counterpart, the Heavenly Venus/Aphrodite arriving on the Italian shore, transported by divine powers from her oceanic birthplace (Figure 19):

Figure 19. Sandro Botticelli, *Birth of Venus*, 1486. Galleria degli Uffizi, Florence, Italy, inv. no. 878. Photo, Scala / Art Resource, NY.

This is clearly the Aphrodite born from the foam created when the severed genitals of Kronos were cast into the sea. Her modesty—as revealed by the arrangement of her arms—and her elegantly balanced stance mark her as a direct descendant of the Heavenly Aphrodites of antiquity.

For several centuries European poets created an array of sonnets, plays, songs, and masques that explored and sometimes ridiculed the "Platonic" notion that men and women should seek a spiritual rather than physical union. In the 1630s the English playwright William D'Avenant created entertainments such as *The Temple of Love* and *The Platonic Lovers* for the amusement of the lords and ladies of the court of Queen Henrietta Maria, in performances in the magnificent Banqueting House designed by Inigo Jones. One observer of the London scene wrote to a friend that, "... there is a Love called Platonick Love which much sways here of late. It is a Love abstracted from all corporeal, gross impressions and sensual appetite, but consists in contemplations and ideas of the mind, not in any carnal fruition" (James Howell in Jacobs 1982:1:317–318).

Jones explained that he designed a costume for Queen Henrietta's appearance in one of her Platonic masques "so that corporeal beauty, consisting in symmetry, colour, and certain inexpressible graces, shining in the Queen's Majesty, may draw us to the contemplation of the beauty of the soul, unto which it hath an analogy" (Strong 1973:159).

With the masques of the Stuart court we come face to face with an aspect of the *Symposium* that has been in the background all along—namely, the dialogue's *dramatic* character. Other dialogues of Plato feature the occasional dramatic *moment*—the death scene in the *Phaedo* and Thrasymachus' outburst in *Republic* I come to mind—but the *Symposium* is, and was intended to be, a philosophical *drama* rich in scenes that could be readily visualized in the mind's eye.

After an introductory framing narrative, the drama proper opens with Socrates and Aristodemus walking together toward the house of Agathon—we might compare the image of arriving symposiasts in the mural in the Tomb of the Diver at Paestum (Figure 20a):

although at 175a Plato gives the additional striking detail that Socrates has stopped lost in thought on the porch of the house next door. We are then told that the group "poured libations, sang a hymn, and performed all the customary rituals" (176a, as again depicted in the Paestum mural, Figure 20b):

Figures 20a and 20b. Fresco, arriving symposiasts and funerary banquet, early fifth century BCE. From the Tomb of the Diver, Paestum; now in the Museo Archeologico Nazionale, Paestum. Photo, Scala / Art Resource, NY.

While the speeches of Phaedrus, Pausanias, and Eryximachus contain few dramatic moments, the tone changes abruptly when we come to Aristophanes' memorable account of the race of original round creatures of three types—double men, double women, and the man-woman or *androgyne*—Zeus decided to slice in half when they threatened to occupy the domain of the gods. An image of these remarkable creatures appears on a medal coined in honor of the Paduan philosopher Marcantonio Passeri, with the caption "With philosophy leading, we retrace our steps" (Figure 21):[17]

Figure 21. Woodcut after the reverse of a portrait medal by Giovanni da Cavino (1500–1570) of the Aristotelian philosopher Marcantonio Passeri. After Jacopo Tomasini, *Iacobi Philippi Tomasini Patavini illustrium elogio* (Padua, 1630), p104.

[17] The caption reflects the then current view of the image as a symbol of man's original unified (physical and spiritual) nature. An image of the *androgyne* also appears as a device on Gargantua's hat (in Rabelais' *Gargantua and Pantagruel*), along with a quotation from St. Paul.

An image of the "children of the sun" also appears in the rock musical *Hedwig and the Angry Inch* (Figure 22):

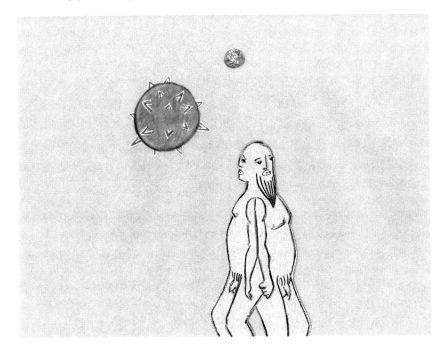

Figure 22. Emily Hubley, *Children of the Sun*, from the film *Hedwig and the Angry Inch*, copyright MMI, New Line Productions, Inc. All rights reserved. Photo appears courtesy of Emily Hubley and New Line Productions, Inc.

Even something so abstract as the process of abstraction is effectively dramatized through the importation of the language of the Mysteries and the visual simile of the ladder of love. Next comes the dramatic entrance of the drunken Alcibiades, his accounts of his failed attempt to seduce Socrates and of Socrates' various military exploits, and the final breakdown of order upon the arrival of an uninvited mob. In the drama's final scene, Socrates sets out with Aristodemus in tow for another day of the philosophical life.

The dramatic character of the *Symposium* has made it a natural choice for performance on stage or on television (see the recent performances mentioned at the outset of the paper). In 1969 the BBC broadcast a version of the *Symposium* written for television by Leo Aylen, directed by Jonathan Miller, and featuring Leo McKern in the role of Socrates. Aylen has explained how he came to be involved in the production: "Jonathan started talking about how he wanted to put dialogues on TV and asked me about Plato. I said very quickly that Plato's dialogues were excellently dramatic—quite as dramatic as some Shaw plays, and that the obvious dialogue to start with was the *Symposium*, because of the vividness of its characters."[18] The classicist Kenneth Reckford has argued that T. S. Eliot modeled his play, *The Cocktail Party*, on Plato's *Symposium*. Reckford notes that both titles mean "drinking party," both involve "libations" and both describe a merry scene in ways that mask deeper philosophical and religious concerns. Reckford identified Sir Henry Harcourt-Reilly who provides spiritual therapy and moral insight, as Socrates, and Julia Shuttlethwaite as Diotima. Reckford also notes the similarity in overall narrative structure: both works "move inward from a convivial, secular periphery to a philosophical or religious center of meaning and vitality, and then out again" (Reckford 1991:303–312).

In his conversation with Agathon at 194a–b Socrates likens their present speeches to a theatrical performance; at 222d he likens Alcibiades' speech to a satyr play; and the concluding conversation between Socrates, Aristophanes, and Agathon suggests that the dialogue itself should be seen as a kind of philosophical drama. In any case, the dialogue's many memorable scenes and incidents would have encouraged those of an artistic bent to seek to represent one or more of them in some visual medium.

One other feature of the *Symposium* that significantly enhanced its appeal to later artists was the absence of a single clear and dominant message. By this I do not mean that the *Symposium* had no dominant message or set of messages. I believe, along with some others, that one of Plato's main aims in the *Symposium* was to present a case for the philosophical life as the best possible kind of life for a human being—drawing on a distinction between originals and their inferior images that lay at the heart of Platonic metaphysics as well as on the example provided by Socrates' life—while at the same time displaying the limitations inherent in various other, then-popular approaches to wisdom. As Christopher Rowe has written: "The *Symposium* as a whole is (no doubt among other things) an extended protreptic—an invitation to philosophy, on the Socratic model" (Rowe 1998a:4). Plato makes the case for the superiority of the philosophical life by offering a series of "lessons in love" from various popular perspectives—relying upon the teachings of the poets, adopting the language and kinds of argument taught by the sophists, employing the language and explanatory categories of "the new natural science," resorting

---

[18] Correspondence with the author, 2005.

to popular myths and folk tales, etc. In the end, however, each perspective on love, save one, is shown to provide merely a parochial view of the true nature of *erōs*. Like the proverbial blind men who had different conceptions of an elephant because they had touched different parts, each of the participants in the symposium describes *Erōs* in different terms because, with the exception of Socrates, each has seen only a part of the whole. Only from Socrates, armed with Diotima's comprehensive account of love and beauty, do we learn, as she puts it at 210e, "what all those earlier labors were really aiming at."

The complex structure of the narrative, however, tended to obscure this important point. Not only were later readers confronted with a multiplicity of perspectives from which to choose, it was no longer obvious (if it ever had been) which speech enshrined the truth. One might normally suppose that Socrates served as "Plato's mouthpiece," but the frequent references to the shortcomings in Socrates' grasp of *erōs* made that approach difficult here.[19] Moreover, as Gregory Vlastos argued in a famous paper (1973b:3–42), the view of *erōs* championed by Socrates—focused as it is on the pursuit of an abstract ideal of beauty—seems poorly suited to the kind of affection human beings feel for one another. Both Martha Nussbaum (1979:131–172) and Jacques Lacan (1977, 2002)[20] concluded that the real moral of the dialogue was that one must choose between being a Socrates and being an Alcibiades—that is to say, between pursuing an abstract ideal and forging ties of affection with other persons. Others have felt that the dialogue's deepest insight was provided by Aristophanes' view of love as a yearning for completion and wholeness, while still others maintain that by offering multiple perspectives on *erōs* Plato was really just saying that all forms of sexual desire are natural and therefore equally good. In the notes he wrote for his *Serenade,* Bernstein even characterized Agathon's speech as "the most moving in the entire dialogue."

In short, in the absence of a single clear and dominant message, readers of the *Symposium* have been able to treat the dialogue as a kind of smorgasbord from which to select the most appealing idea or image. Many later readers treasured the *Symposium* because, as Richard Hunter has put it, "Plato offered almost the only available language in which homosexual feelings could seriously be discussed" (2004:116). Those fascinated by human drama could focus their attention on the story of Socrates and Alcibiades; those more interested in religious education tended to view the dialogue as a guide to the spiritual

---

[19] Frisbee Sheffield (2001a:10n) has argued that these references apply to Socrates in some earlier period rather than as an indictment of his current state of understanding, but this would not be evident to many readers.

[20] See also Chiesa (n.d.).

life; while those with an aesthetic sensibility responded most strongly to the dialogue's poetic and dramatic qualities. Philosophers have generally focused their attention on the nature of the intellectual process described by Diotima and Socrates—sometimes to the complete neglect of the rest of the dialogue. We might regret that the lesson or lessons Plato sought to impart were so often ignored or misunderstood, but we can hardly regret the way in which the *Symposium* was able to acquire new life and meaning, indeed to gain a kind of immortality, through the efforts of so many later writers and artists with agendas of their own.[21]

---

[21] Earlier versions of this paper were read at the College of Charleston, Washington and Lee University, the University of Maryland, the University of Mary Washington, the University of North Carolina at Chapel Hill, and the University of North Carolina at Greensboro. I am indebted to many individuals for helpful comments and criticisms, especially Patrick Miller, Debra Nails, Francis Newton, David Reeve, Eleanor Rutledge, Frisbee Sheffield, Peter Smith, Michael Trapp, and Cecil Wooten.

Fifteen

The Hangover of Plato's *Symposium* in the Italian Renaissance from Bruni (1435) to Castiglione (1528)

Diskin Clay[1]

IT IS NOT THAT SOCRATES DID NOT DRINK with his companions at symposia; he did. The strange thing about the man is that no one ever saw him drunk. In Plato's *Symposium* he leaves the company who had remained at the second day of celebration for Agathon's victory in the tragic competitions of the Lenaia of 416 asleep and heavy with wine. He goes out with Aristodemus to face a new day and returns to his wife sober, only with evening. As we know from the opening scene of the dialogue, the memory of what was said and done at Agathon's symposium is of great interest years later, but vague and faulty. As vague and faulty as this memory was, the *Symposium* has been recalled for nearly twenty-four centuries in imitation, emulation, constatation, and transformation not only in the dialogues of Xenophon, Plutarch, and Lucian but in the visual arts. I think of the bronze relief on a chest from Pompei showing Diotima and Socrates and Anselm Feuerbach's painting of the company at Agathon's (Karlsruhe, State Museum, 1869). In these fixed images there is none of the animation and accident of the moving sequence of the seven speeches of the *Symposium* and no reflection of its opening or its close, only "clichés." Feuerbach chooses the most dramatic moment of Agathon's

---

[1] I will not repeat the thanks rendered by the organizers of this memorable conference on Plato's *Symposium* to all those who made it possible and then the success it was. I endorse them heartily. I do have three idiosyncratic debts that I must acknowledge: to James Lesher for the inspiration of his "Afterimages of Plato's *Symposium*," images I saw in Durham, North Carolina, long before I heard him present them at the Center for Hellenic Studies in August of 2005; to Lawrence Richardson, Jr., who commented on the Latinity of Cristoforo Landino; and to Charles Fantazzi, who, I think, helped me solve an enigma in a notation Bernardo Bembo entered into his autograph copy of Ficino's *De Amore* (for these contributions, see my acknowledgements in the Epilogue).

symposium, its disruption by the drunken and Dionysiac Alcibiades to represent the *Symposium* as a whole.

The *Symposium* was remembered selectively in Italy of the fourteenth and early fifteenth centuries. Its history in the humanist and Christian culture of the Italian Renaissance in Florence, Asolo in the Veneto, and the court of Urbino is a story of selective attention and amnesia that I cannot tell fully. This very partial report is appropriate to my theme, for the *Symposium* is fragmented in its refracted images in Italy, even as it is melded into a Platonic whole. I begin with the Latin translation of the speech of Alcibiades that Leonardo Bruni sent to Cosimo de' Medici in 1435 and I end with Pietro Bembo's speech in the fourth book of Castiglione's *Il Cortegiano* (*The Book of the Courtier*, finished in 1516, printed in 1528). One of the courtiers present during these conversations was Giulano de' Medici, the youngest son of Lorenzo and, like his father, called *il Magnifico*.

We traverse then a period of four generations of the Medicis. It is fitting that Cardinal Pietro Bembo is buried in Santa Maria Sopra Minerva between the two Medici popes, Leo X and Clement VII. Before we begin with Bruni's long career as a translator of Plato, we should note a transformation in Italian culture. Bruni translated the speech of Alcibiades in Plato's *Symposium* into Latin. Marsilio Ficino's *De Amore* (set on November 7, 1468 and written in 1469) is a brilliant attempt to recreate the *Symposium* in a Florence that for some had come to think of itself as the Athens of Italy. All of the speakers who assemble at the Medicean villa at Careggi speak Latin. But in the next century, the speakers of Pietro Bembo's *Gli Asolani* (of 1505) and Castiglione's *Il Cortegiano* speak less learnedly in the vernacular and under the influence not only of Ficino's Platonism but of Boccaccio's *Decamerone*. And, after Ficino, the printing press disseminates in Aldine octavos works once laboriously copied and illuminated. We owe the Bembo font to Pietro Bembo's close association with Aldus Manutius.

In the case of these four humanists, we are dealing with a form of "translation." In learned Latin or in the vernacular the *Symposium* was assimilated into the culture shared and created by the Florentines Bruni and Ficino, the Venetian Bembo, and Castiglione, who was active in Milan, Mantua, Urbino, and Rome. What was Greek was made Latin or Italian in a cultural translation.[2] Plato's *Symposium* was remembered only imperfectly—as if a haze of forgetfulness had overtaken it. If it had lost its original integrity, it gained another in Italy. But such was the fate of the banquet offered by Agathon and created by Plato in the *Symposium*.

[2] For the manuscripts that arrived in Florence in the age of Ficino see Gentile et al. 1984.

What these Italian humanists found fascinating about the dialogue is obvious. They all moved in aristocratic circles and appreciated the ennobling prototype of their own societies in the Athens of Socrates and Plato. Plato had brought together the most brilliant Athenians of his youth. Of special fascination were the figures of Socrates, Aristophanes, Agathon, and Alcibiades (*Symposium* 172a–b). Then there is the unparalleled virtuoso rhetoric of the seven speeches of the *Symposium*, with all of their variety and drama and Plato's stunning brilliance in creating the characters of his seven speakers. Then, for the Christian reader, Diotima's speech seemed a faint reflection of Jacob's ladder and a pagan anticipation of the ascent of the mind to God. *Erōs* is translated with no cultural hesitation into *amor Dei*.

But there were some essential features of the dialogue and its culture that were queasy to be touched.[3] One of these was the theme of pederasty that is so conspicuously present in a conversation of Greek males about love. In Ficino's *De Amore* the nine guests at Careggi are addressed *o convive castissimi*.[4] Two features of the *Symposium* that none of our authors seems to have appreciated are the drama and the plan of the dialogue. In a history of the reenactments and appropriations of the *Symposium* what is omitted is as important as what is preserved, if transformed. The beginning (or setting) and the strange and seemingly unconnected end of the dialogue are of no interest to our nodding authors. Nor were Aristophanes' hiccough and the disruption of the movement of praise around the banquet room. As a consequence there is no appreciation of Plato's signature in the tragic and comic poet envisaged by Socrates at the end of the dialogue or the relevance of the opening scene of the dialogue to the theme of a philosophical praise of Socrates as the human embodiment of *Erōs*.[5]

Leonardo Bruni (1370–1444)

Bruni, called Leonardo Aretino, became a Florentine citizen when he returned to Florence (in 1414) after nearly a decade in Rome serving in the papal Curia.

---

[3] So Ben Jonson, *Sejanus* act 1, line 82.

[4] By Tommaso Benci as Socrates (60r/199 [6.1]) and Cristoforo Landino as Alcibiades (114v/251 [7.6]). I cite this text from Marcel's edition (Ficino 1956). For ease of reference I give first the page (recto or verso) of the Vatican autograph (7.705) followed by the page number and square brackets enclosing the book and chapter. The homoerotic epigrams of Plato are recognized by Ficino, but Dicaearchus' criticism of Plato's libido (to be found in Cicero, *Tusculans* 4.34.71, 8r/143 [1.4]) is indignantly repudiated.

[5] As I have argued in Clay 1975.

As a young Aretine in the Florence of Coluccio Salutati, he had translated
Plato's *Phaedo, Apology*, and *Crito*. Inspired by Cicero's *De Oratore* he composed
his own Latin *Dialogi* (Book 1 in 1401 and Book 2 in 1406). In Rome he went on
to translate Plato's *Gorgias* (1404–1409), a work he dedicated to Pope John XXIII,
soon to be deposed as Pope by the Council of Constance (whose sarcophagus,
the joint work of Donatello and Michelozzo, is the only burial in the Baptistry
of Florence). It would be more than a decade after his return to Florence
that Bruni returned to translating Plato. He first produced a compilation of
passages excerpted from the *Phaedrus*. Two last translations remained, both
of which he dedicated to Cosimo de' Medici: the Platonic letters and, oddly, a
version of Alcibiades' speech in the *Symposium*, perhaps to defend the memory
of Socrates against the criticisms of Ambrigio Traversari.[6] This he sent Cosimo
with a dedicatory epistle in 1435.

In the case of Alcibiades' speech in the *Symposium*, Bruni confronted
the delicate problem he had faced years before in translating the *Gorgias*: the
frank and unabashed recognition of pederasty. His solution was simply to
blink, look away, and leave the offending passages untranslated and, thus, to
prepare for Ficino's chaste conception of *amor Socraticus* in the next generation of Florentine Platonism. Another strange gift for Cosimo was to arrive in
Florence from Milan. This was a poem in the vernacular with the Latin title
Hermaphroditus, sent by the soon to be notorious Antonio Beccadelli (known
as Panormita, 1394–1471). If Cosimo ever read these two manuscripts or
Panormita's epistle to Poggio Bracciolini citing Plato and his epigrams as an
authority to legitimate his interest in homoerotic love, he would have been
greatly puzzled. In Bruni's translation of Alcibiades' speech in the *Symposium*
he could have found no trace of such a thing. Bruni discretely transformed
Alcibiades' account of his attempt to seduce Socrates and reverse the roles of
erastēs and *erōmenos* (218b–219d) into an admirable confession of his pursuit
of Socrates in search of wisdom. Bruni had, indeed, closed the door on the
bedroom scene revealed by Alcibiades (*Symposium* 218b), just as he had closed
the door on the flute girls who broke into Agathon's sober banquet in the
company of the drunken Alcibiades. In another age, Benjamin Jowett was to
perform the same castigation of homosexual love in his Victorian "parody"
of the praise of a philosophical pederasty in the *Phaedrus*. Pederasty translates into Victorian English as the sanctioned but eventually Platonic love of
a married couple. This is one mode of translation: bowdlerization in commentary. Bruni practiced another tactic: truncation or the excision of the offending

---

[6] For this see Hankins 1990:80–81 and his Appendix 3D.

parts of the dialogue. In this Bruni's nemesis, Ambrigio Traversari, was of one mind with his enemy. When faced with the pederastic poems attributed to Plato in Diogenes Laertius 3, Traversari left them untranslated. Or rather he first translated them with a notation on the margin of his manuscript: *Platonis amor* and then cancelled his translation.[7] This cancellation of *Platonis amor* is a theme we will follow in Ficino's *De Amore*, in Bembo's *Gli Asolani*, and in Castiglione's *Il Cortegiano*.

Marsilio Ficino (1433–1499)

Marsilio Ficino's "commentary" or commemoration of Plato's *Symposium* carried the subtitle, *sive De Amore*. It is not a translation like Bruni's, which itself is not a translation; it is a reenactment of Plato's *Symposium*. Its occasion is the banquet celebrated in the Medici villa at Careggi to commemorate the day of Plato's birth on November 7, 1468. We have moved from the age of Cosimo de' Medici to that of his grandson, Lorenzo, properly called *il Magnifico*. It was Lorenzo who reinstated the feast day of this pagan saint. The list of those present and their roles is as follows:

Plato's *Symposium*	Ficino's *De Amore*
Plato	Marsilio Ficino (1433–1499)
Phaedrus	Giovanni Cavalcanti (c. 1444–509)
Pausanias	Antonio Agli (1400–1477)
Eryximachus	Diotifeci Ficino (1402–1479)
Agathon	Carlo Marsuppini (son of Carlo 1399–1453)
Aristophanes	Cristoforo Landino (1424–1498)
Socrates/Diotima	Tommaso Benci (1427–1470)
Alcibiades	Cristoforo Marsuppini (son of Carlo)

To this guest list should be added some distinguished *umbrae*, or uninvited guests: Orpheus, Hermes Trismegistus, Dionysius the Areopagite, the spirit if not the letter of other works of Plato (including the second letter), and the only female presence at the banquet, the graceful and saving spirit of Allegoresis. There are empty places for Bernardo Bembo (1443–1519), born on the same day in the same year as Ficino, and Bembo's son soon to be born, Pietro (May 20, 1470–January 18, 1547). Pietro would continue the tradition of Ficino's *De Amore* in his *Gli Asolani*. His statesman father, Bernardo Bembo, owned and annotated the manuscript of Ficino's *De Amore* now in Oxford and

---

[7] The erotic epigrams cited are concentrated in Diogenes Laertius 3.29–32.

was the recipient of many of Ficino's letters.[8] There is also a place not only for Phaedrus but for the *Phaedrus*, a text that is as much a presence at Careggi as was the *Symposium*. We will see at the end of this brief sketch that *Phaedrus* and *Symposium* are melded in Bembo's speech in the *Cortegiano*. And, under the sign of Scorpio, the speeches of Ficino's *De Amore* are filled with contemporary astrology and theory of the humors, a subject that introduces a note of melancholy.

The master of ceremonies is Francesco Bandini. There are nine other guests, significantly the number of the Muses. Appropriately, only seven of these nine guests speak. Although he casts his father, Diotifeci, in the appropriate role of Eryximachus, Ficino confines his own role to presenting the seven speeches introduced by Bernardo Nuzzi's reading of the sacred text of the *Symposium*, whether in Greek or in Latin we do not know. Because of his silence in the dialogue as its author, we could cast Ficino in the role of Plato, but he might not be suited to this role. As narrator he pays no attention to the beginning or end of the *Symposium* and thus makes it impossible to connect Socrates' odd behavior in this opening scene with Alcibiades' praise—not of *Erōs* but of Socrates as Plato's subtle tribute to Socrates' *erōs*.[9] At the same time he erases the Platonic signature at the end of the *Symposium* that can be deciphered in Socrates' paradox of the unheard of possibility of a poet who could write both tragedy and comedy.

Ficino's *Commentarium* cannot rival the drama and *ethopoiia* of Plato's *Symposium*. At times he fails to preserve the illusion that we are hearing a speech actually delivered, and, in the case of Bishop Antonio Agli's rendition of the dangerously homosexual speech of Pausanias (the *erastēs* of the young poet Agathon),[10] the Latin *oratio* has virtually no contact with Plato's Greek. But we could interpret this incongruity as Ficino's attempt to characterize a guest he calls a *theologus* (1v/137[1.1]). In the case of the poet Cristoforo Landino, we find a speech well suited to his character as a poet and the allegorist of Dante's

---

[8] One piece of evidence for the close association of Bernardo Bembo and the circle assembled at Careggi is the dialogue held by Florentine humanists at Regnano in the Florentine countryside in which Giovanni Gavalcanti, Cristoforo Landino, Bernardo Nuzzi, and Bernardo Bembo were present (Ficino 2002:VII.1).

[9] Impressively, though, Ficino is the first modern author that I know of to connect Plato's praise of *Erōs* with his praise of the erotic Socrates, as is abundantly clear from Cristoforo Marsuppini's rendition of Alicibiades' speech, 105r–108v/242–245 [7.2]. He was anticipated by Maximus of Tyre, *Philosophoumena* 18.

[10] *Pausanias hactenus. Nunc Eryximachi orationem interpretamur*, 22v/160 [3.1]. These are not the words of a speaker but the reporter, named in the speech of Cristoforo Marsuppini, 103r/240 [7.1].

Commedia and Virgil's *Aeneid* (and, therefore, out of character for the role of Plato's Aristophanes). The same can be said of the speech of Carlo Marsuppini, whom Ficino casts as Agathon. His Christian and "Platonic" rhetoric overwhelms the Gorgianic performance of Agathon's speech in the *Symposium*, a performance Marsuppini describes as lengthy and diffuse. I reckon that his speech is at least three times as long as Agathon's.[11]

The guests at Careggi comment on the speeches just read by the rhetor Bernardo Nuzzi, although their performances are described as *orationes*. They are also commentaries, and, as commentaries, they resemble Ficino's commentary on Plato's *Phaedrus* in their general tendencies.[12] In the Alexandrian mode of explaining Homer from Homer (Ὅμηρος ἐξ Ὁμήρου), they interpret Plato from Plato and authors who are described as *Platonici* and they reconcile Platonism with Christianity by the charitable device of allegoresis.[13] My exhibit is the speech that will take us to Bembo's *Gli Asolani*—Cristoforo Landino's explication of Aristophanes' speech. Landino was a poet—Ficino calls him "an Orphic and Platonic poet" (28r/167 [4.1]). We will encounter his Platonic poem addressed to Bernardo Bembo describing Bernardo's Platonic love for Ginevra de' Benci as we introduce Pietro Bembo (Epilogue). Perhaps more than any of Dante's Quattrocento commentators, Landino read Dante's *Commedia* in the then fashionable manner of allegoresis. His perspective on Dante has now dimmed in the distance of what C. S. Lewis called "the discarded vision," but this vision is relevant to Ficino and to the speeches of Carlo Marsuppini and Tommaso Benci. Landino describes Aristophanes' meaning as "obscure and involved" (*obscuram et implicatam*, 28r/167 [4.1]). There is an indelicacy in Aristophanes' myth. The hermaphrodite represents the seemingly normal union of male and female, but it is abnormal if both are combined into one. Landino clothes it in silence. For Aristophanes there were originally three sexes compounded into three rotund creatures: male and male, female and female, and male and female. Landino avoids the offensive word ἀνδρόγυνον (*Symposium* 189e) and translates *promiscuum*. And his astral allegoresis recognizes but does away with the problems Bruni faced a generation earlier. This passage is revealing of Ficino's manner of reading, as it is of Landino's (29v/168–31r/169 [4.2]):

---

[11] *Symposium* 194e–197e vs. 39r/178–59r/198 [5.1–13]. The complaints come in 40v/179 [5.2] and 53v/191 [5.7].

[12] Well presented by Allen 1984.

[13] In commenting on Pietro Bembo's "Hymn to St. Stephen," Chatfield (Bembo 2005:xiv) discovers "a peculiar phenomenon of humanist mentality: how easily permeable was the membrane between classical myth and the Christian religion."

Hec Aristophanes et alia narrat per multa, monstris portentibusque similia, sub quibus quasi velaminibus quibusdam divina mysteria latere putandum. Mos enim erat veterum theologorum sacra ipsorum puraque arcana, ne a prophanis et impuris polluerentur, figurarum umbraculis tegere. Nos autem que in figuris superioribus et aliis describuntur singula exacte ad sensum pertinere non arbitramur. Nam et Aurelius Augustinus non omnia inquit, que in figuris finguntur, significare aliquid putanda sunt. Multa enim propter illa que significant ordinis et connexionis gratia sunt adiuncta. Solo vomere terra proscinditur sed, ut hoc fieri possit, | cetera quoque huic aratri membra iunguntur. Que igitur nobis exponenda proponitur, hec est summa.

Homines quondam tres sexus habebant, masculum, feminum, promiscuum, solis, terre, luneque filios. Erant et integri. Sed propter superbiam, cum deo equare se vellent, scissi in duo sunt, iterum si superbiant, bifariam discindendi. Sectione facta, dimidium amore ad dimidium trahitur, ut integritatis restitutio fiat. Qua completa, beatum genus humanum est futurum.

Summa vero nostre interpretationis erit huiusmodi. *Homines*, id est hominum anime. *Quondam*, id est, quando a deo creantur. *Integre sunt*, duobus sunt exornate luminibus, ingenito et infuso. Ut ingenito equalia et inferiora, infuso superiora conspicerent. *Deo equare se voluerunt*. Ad unicum lumen ingenitum se reflexerunt. *Hinc divise sunt*. Splendorem infusum amiserunt, quando ad solum ingenitum sunt converse statimque in corpora cecidere. *Superbiores facte iterum dividentur*, id est, si naturali | nimium confidant ingenio, lumen illud ingenitum et naturale quod restitit quondammodo extinguetur. *Tres sexus habebant. Mares sole, femine terra, promiscuum luna genite.* Dei fulgorem alie secundum fortitudinem que mascula est, alie secundum temperantiam que femina, alie secundum iustitiam que promiscua, susceperunt. He tres in nobis virtutes aliarum trium quas deus habet sunt filie. Sed in duo tres ille, sol, luna, terra, in nobis mas, femina, promiscuum, nuncunpantur. *Sectione facta, dimidium amore ad dimidium trahitur.* Anime enim divise et immerse corporibus, cum primum ad annos adolescentie venerint, naturali et ingenito lumine quod servarunt, ceu sui quodam dimidio excitantur ad infusum illud divinumque lumen olim ipsarum dimidium, quod cadentes amisere, studio veritatis recipiendum. Quo recepto iam integre erunt et dei visione beate. Hoc igitur erit inter|pretationis nostre compendium.

This is the speech of Aristophanes; he has more to say with many strange and bizarre illustrations. We should think that lurking under these, as if under the cover of veils, sacred mysteries lie hidden. It was the practice of the ancient theologians to conceal their sacred and pure secret doctrines with the shadows (*figurae*) of allegory to prevent their being sullied by the profane and the impure. It is not our object, however, to claim that what is revealed by these allegories to be discovered in this speech and elsewhere have a precise correspondence to an allegorical meaning. Even Augustine says that not everything represented in symbolic form should be thought to have some deeper meaning. Many details are included for the sake of the sequence and connection of what they are meant to convey. The soil is broken only by the plow, but for it to be broken by the plough the parts of the plough must be joined together for it to operate.

Once human beings were of three sexes: male, female, and a mixture of both male and female. These were the offspring of the sun, the earth, and the moon. They were at one time whole. But, because of the pride that inspired them to be the equal of god, they were cut into two halves. And, should they wax proud once again, they would be drawn and quartered. Once divided, one half was drawn by its love for its other half to restore its original unity. Once reunited, the human race would in the future have a blessed life.

The essence of our interpretation is as follows: *Human beings*: meaning the souls of human beings. *Once*: meaning when they are created by god. *At one time they were whole*: meaning adorned by two lights, the innate light and the infused light so that they might contemplate [by the innate light] what is their equal and what is below them and, the light infused, so that they might contemplate what is above them. *They wanted to make themselves equal to god*: they turned to their innate light alone. *For this reason they were divided*: meaning that they lost the illumination of the light infused within them, and, when they first turned only to the inborn light within them, they immediately fell into bodies. *If once again they wax proud they will be quartered*: meaning that, if they place too much confidence in human intelligence, the inborn and natural light that remains will to some degree be extinguished. *They were of three sexes: males the offspring of the sun, women the offspring of the moon, the mixed sex the offspring of the earth*: some received the brilliant light of the sun, because of their courage, which is a masculine trait; others moderation from the light of the moon, which is a feminine characteristic; others the light of the two, because of their moderation, which combined both lights, which is a feminine characteristic. These three virtues are the daughters of three others which god possesses. But in god these three virtues are called: the sun, the moon, and the earth; in us, they are called male, female, and mixed. *Once divided, one half is drawn by love to its other half.* For souls are divided and immersed in bodies. When they first arrive at the age of adolescence, the innate and natural light which they had received at birth, that is a half of themselves, prompts them to recover it to discover the truth: that is, the light infused within them that is divine. At one time this light was their other half, a half they lost when they fell. If they should recover this light, they will immediately be made whole and will find their final blessedness in the vision of God. This then, is a short summary of our interpretation.

Strangely, Ficino invokes St. Augustine's doctrine that not all allegorical discourse (*figurae*) involves a deeper meaning and then begins to excavate a deeper meaning. A figurative interpretation of a text was reserved for interpretations of the Bible.[14] Landino does not propose to reveal the meaning of all the bizarre details of Aristophanes' speech, but only the *figura* lurking under his account of the original condition of human kind. *Figura* we recall is one of the key terms of Biblical exegesis, not the interpretation of the sacred and abstruse teachings of the ancient theologians (*veterum theologorum sacra ... puraque arcana*, 29v/168 [4.2]).[15] Landino's exegesis proceeds in a series of *lemmata* and their commentary. By men (*homines*) Plato means souls. In invoking the doctrine of twin lights, one innate, the other infused or inspired in us, Landino brings Plato into the sphere of Ficino's Platonic theology and produces a symbolic version of man's fall from a union with God. The severing

---

[14] The texts of Augustine he has in mind are *De Vera Religione* 1.50–51 and *De Trinitate* 15.9; also relevant for the Augustinian "charity" involved in allegorical reading are *De Doctrina Christiana* 2.6 and *De Civitate Dei* 17.20. Ficino's project of Christianizing Plato, "the Moses who spoke Attic," is clear from the Introduction dedicating his *Theologia Platonica* to Lorenzo de' Medici (1482). For the background of the striking term *mysteria*, there is the revealing commentary of Edgar Wind 1968:201–204.

[15] For which there is the fundamental introduction of Auerbach 1984:chap. 1.

of the two lights has as a consequence man's fall and separation from his Creator. It is in the reunion of these lights that men are *healed* (Aristophanes' term) and blessed. The concept of the fall is nowhere to be found in Aristophanes' speech, but one does not have far to go to find it in Plato. Ficino found it in the *Phaedrus* and Socrates' description of the fall of men from their winged state and companionship with the gods.[16]

Pietro Bembo (1470–1547)

In moving to the deeply erotic Pietro Bembo, who wrote in Italian and not Latin, one must recall his more Platonic father, the Venetian statesman Bernardo Bembo, who was purely enamored with a young Florentine woman, Ginevra de' Benci. Leonardo da Vinci's portrait of Ginevra (a distant relative of Tommaso de' Benci) is on display in the National Gallery in Washington, DC. It is Leonardo's first secular painting (dated to around 1474). Pietro's father, who was twice the Venetian ambassador to Florence is believed to have commissioned the painting.[17] In a mysterious marginal note to Landino's speech in Bernardo Bembo's manuscript of Ficino's *De Amore*, the Venetian ambassador speaks of the close contacts he had with the poet Landino and Ginevra de' Benci, "the most lovely of married women." Landino composed a poem dedicated to Bernardo Bembo on his Platonic relation with Ginevra, named after the juniper (*ginepro*), a symbol of chastity. Leonardo painted a sprig of juniper on the back panel of the portrait. The enclosing wreath of laurel and palm on the simulated porphyry back of the painting were Bernardo Bembo's own device, to which Leonardo added the juniper and the motto: *Virtutem Forma Decorat*.

The setting of Bembo's *Gli Asolani* is the castle of Caterina Cornaro in Asolo in the north of the Veneto looking up to the distant heights of the Dolomites, but he was writing the dialogue in the court of Ercole d'Este during his stay in Ferrara. Appropriately, Caterina was at the time the queen of Cyprus, and love is the subject of a three-day conversation in the gardens of her court on the occasion of the marriage of a lady in waiting. The setting and form of the conversations is clearly indebted to Boccaccio's *Decamerone*, a book (known as *Il Cento*) that the young Pietro Bembo presented to his Venetian lover, Maria

---

[16] *illum divinum lumen ... quod cadentes amisere ...* 30v/169 [4.2]). The Platonic equivalent of the fall is to be discovered in *Phaedrus* 248c.

[17] A suggestion made by Fletcher 1989:811–816 and now generally accepted, for example, by Zöllner 2004:35 (Catalogue VII) among others. The scroll is framed by a branch of laurel and palm. I endorse this suggestion in an Epilogue.

Savorgnan.[18] Bembo dedicated *Gli Asolani* not to the Queen of Cyprus but to Lucrezia Borgia, the recipient of many of his amatory poems.[19] Asolo seems a world away from the Florence of Marsilio Ficino. Plato is never mentioned by any of the speakers, but his *Symposium* is a minor and silent presence in the Queen's garden, as is the passage in the *Phaedo* describing the "true earth" (108c–115a).[20] In *Gli Asolani* Bembo recognizes Aristophanes and Diotima. This might seem a strange pairing, but it is made already in the *Symposium* (212c) and, indeed, at the end of Tommaso Benci's speech in Ficino's *De Amore*.[21] Aristophanes' conception of our original unity surfaces in the speech Gismondo delivers to counter Perottino's (a mask for Bembo himself) hostile conception of love as "bitter." The connection between *amore* and *amaro* is facile, as is the connection between *amore* and *morte*. Gismondo offers a praise of love and seems to recognize Diotima's third step in the ascent to beauty—the love one has for one's country and its institutions.[22] In the presence of the ladies of the court, Gismondo is inspired with a fervor that leads him into poetry and fable. He attempts to unite man and woman by appealing to Greek myth and asks Perottino if he has not heard of the tale of our aboriginal double and rotund unity. If Bembo had heard Landino's speech in Ficino's *De Amore*, Gismondo has not. Gismondo speaks of one union, that of man and woman, not three. But, in a tribute to Aristophanes, he compares our present segments—not to a flat fish but to a nut.[23] Bembo was to return to this image in *Le Stanze*, a carnival and juvenile poem of the future cardinal that was placed on the Index.[24]

Bembo transforms Diotima into the ancient hermit (*romito*) who instructs Lavinello on true love. There is much to comment on this the last reported speech of *Gli Asolani* (3.9–22). It mimics the speech of Socrates in the *Symposium* in that it is a dialogue (begun in 3.15). Lavinello's teacher is not a prophet from Mantinea but a holy man who was prophetically expecting Lavinello as he left the Queen's gardens for the wilderness to meditate on what he could say about

---

[18] For their correspondence (which came to light in the Vatican in 1974), see Kidwell 2004:chap. 3.

[19] Now elegantly published as Bembo 1987.

[20] A version of this starling cosmology is given by the hermit in *Gli Asolani* 3.20 and reflected in *Il Cortegiano* 3.58.

[21] In the conclusion that returns to the theme of our aboriginal "mutilation" and our "healing," 102v/239 [6.19].

[22] I cite *Gli Asolani* from the edition of Dilemmi 1991 (Bembo 1505). The allusion to Diotima's speech in Plato's *Symposium* comes in 2.10 (139.65–70). Diotima will also play her part in *Il Cortegiano*.

[23] *Gli Asolani* 2.11 (140.6–141.173).

[24] In Bembo 1525:651–671, the edition of Dionisotti 1989; Kidwell 2004:134–135.

love (3.11). The hermit is an old man dressed in rags that look like bark (and therefore resembles contemporary images of John the Baptist) and he stresses his age when he speaks of himself and "the ancient masters of things sacred" (*gli antichi maestri delle sante cose*, 3.18). In this description he acknowledges the ancient theologians of Ficino's *De Amore*.[25] Two passages of the hermit's speech deserve notice. The first seems to have nothing to do with either Ficino or Plato. This is the hermit's tale of the ever-virgin Queen of the Islands of the Blest (*La Reina delle Fortunate Isole*, 3.18) and her courtiers and suitors. She examines their dreams as they become visible on their foreheads by day and decides whether they are bestial or worthy of her. It is a parable Lavinello has never heard of and Bembo's happy invention. The second passage derives from Socrates' description of the "true earth" in the *Phaedo* (a dialogue translated into Latin by Leonardo Bruni and then by Ficino). There are many other reflections and refractions of Plato in this final speech of *Gli Asolani*, but in this mirror one can also make out the dim reflection of Cicero's *Somnium Sciopinis* and Dante, a poet Bembo saw into print with Aldus Manutius.[26]

Baldessarre Castiglione (1478–1529)

We now come to the final day of this brief history, the last of the four days of Castiglione's *Il Cortegiano*. Castiglione created a courtly dialogue set in the court of Urbino (a court he inhabited from 1504–1513). His subject is not love (the subject of Ficino and Bembo), but the ideal (*la idea*) of the Courtier. The dramatic date is March 1507. Castiglione makes it clear that he is attempting to approach an ideal of a human reality, like that perhaps Plato attempted to describe in the *Republic* or the *Statesman*.[27] It is also a reality, like that of Plato's *Symposium*, that was long past. Castiglione was in England and the court of Henry VII at the date of the conversations. He has an anonymous infor-

---

[25] *De Amore* 8r/143 [1.4] *theologi veteres* by contrast to Christian theologians (*posteriores theologi*) and 11r/147 [2.2].

[26] In 1502 in octavo, Lowry 1979:144, 147–148. Bembo recognizes both Cicero's *Somnium* in 3.19 and, in the description of our small and distant earth as a "small garden of God's temple" (3.10.43–45) and Dante's Ciceronian prospect on the distant earth in *Paradiso* 22.151.

[27] I cite Castiglione from the edition of Missier 1968 (Castiglione 1528). The aspiration to attain the "Platonic" ideal is expressed in the Dedication to Michel de Silva (14) and 1.53 with the notorious example of Zeuxis' Platonic ideal of beauty collected from five of the beauties of Croton, Pliny's *Historia Naturalis* 35.64. Leone Battista Alberti had adopted it in his treatise *Della Pictura* (*On Painting* 1436), a treatise well presented by Erwin Panofsky 1968:56–59. Socrates' dialogue with the painter Parrhesius is also relevant to the concept of ideals in the Renaissance, Xenophon *Memorabilia* 3.10.1–6; cf. Pliny *Historia Naturalis* 35.68.

mant for his knowledge of what was done and said in the court of Urbino. As a courtly compliment to the ladies present during these four days and, as a close friend of Castiglione, the future cardinal, Pietro Bembo, is introduced and given two speeches. Bembo is now at the age of thirty-seven and an older man than the slight youth who might be the subject of Bellini's portrait in the Royal Collection of Hampton Court.

The friend of Castiglione since Bembo's arrival in Urbino (in 1506) and the now famous author of *Gli Asolani*, Bembo is briefly involved in the conversation of the first day of *Il Cortegiano*, as he, the author of the influential treatise on *Prose della lingua volgare*, argues that the principal virtue of the courtier is not arms but that arms are the ornament of the more fundamental culture of letters: *l'e arme ... ornamento delle lettere* (1.45). One could revise the motto on the scroll on the device of Bernardo Bembo on the back of Leonardo's portrait of Ginevra de' Benci (for which see the Epilogue) and inscribe: *ARMA VIRTUTEM ADORNANT*. Pietro Bembo gives the final speech of *Il Cortegiano*. It has many connections with Bembo's *Gli Asolani*,[28] and is Castiglione's studied version of Diotima's speech in the *Symposium*, but his *Symposium* is not Plato's; it is Ficino's. Like Ficino's *De Amore* it melds the *Phaedrus* and the *Symposium*. It recalls Diotima's *Erōs* as binding and mediating heaven and earth, represents her mysteries and the ladder of love, and recalls Socrates' vision in the *Phaedrus* of the ascent of the soul to the celestial realm of nectar and ambrosia. Bembo concludes with his own prayer to Amor (transforming Socrates' prayer in *Phaedrus* 257a–b).[29] He then falls silent, transported by a sacred madness (*sacro furore*). But he is brought to earth by a gesture of Emilia Pia, the sister-in-law of Elisabetta Gonzaga. The light of dawn is streaming in through the narrow windows of the castle. Venus is the only star still visible in the heavens. Mt. Catria stands starkly on the horizon. Emilia Pia pulls at the hem of his garment, and Bembo returns to earth, much as Socrates did at the end of the *Symposium* when he left the inebriated and sleeping survivors of Agathon's banquet, returned to the marketplace of Athens and, at evening, to his wife.

---

[28] The connections between Bembo and Castiglione are set out by Floriani 1976. There are evident connections between Bembo's last speech in *Il Cortegiano* and Lavinello's in his *Gli Asolani* (*Il Cortegiano* 4.50 where Bembo's Lavinello is recalled), *Il Cortegiano* 4.55 (love as a dream, *Gli Asolani* 3.15), the fabric of the world, *Il Cortegiano* 4.58 (*Gli Asolani* 3.19), the happiness of the old as contrasted with the misery of the young, *Il Cortegiano* 4.60 (*Gli Asolani* 3.16). The long dispute over the end of *Il Cortegiano* (planned or adventitious) is surveyed by Ryan 1972. More recently Hankins 2002 has examined the presence of philosophy in Bembo's concluding speech.

[29] As well as his Stesichorean palinode, *Il Cortegiano* 4.57 and *Phaedrus* 243e–244a.

Epilogue: Bernardo Bembo's manuscript of Ficino's *De Amore*, Leonardo's *Portrait of Ginevra de' Benci*, and the Poetry of Cristoforo Landino

Figure 1. Leonardo da Vinci (1452-1519), *Ginevra de' Benci*, obverse, c. 1474/1478. National Gallery of Art, Washington, DC, Ailsa Mellon Bruce Fund, inv. no. 1967.6.1a. Photo, © Board of Trustees, National Gallery of Art.

Figure 2. Leonardo da Vinci, *Ginevra de' Benci*, reverse. National Gallery of Art, Washington, DC, Ailsa Mellon Bruce Fund, inv. no. 1967.6.1b. Photo, © Board of Trustees, National Gallery of Art.

It has been argued that Leonardo's portrait of Ginevra (Figure 1), now in the National Gallery in Washington, was commissioned by her Platonic admirer, Bernardo Bembo, who served twice as the Venetian ambassador to Florence (1475–1476 and 1478–1480), most recently and persuasively by Fletcher (1989), who identifies the emblem on the "porphyry" back of the portrait as that of Bernardo Bembo. The device shows a laurel and palm branch framing a scroll bearing the inscription *Virtutem Forma Decorat* (Figure 2). Bembo was well known to Marsilio Ficino, as is attested by the thirty letters to him in Ficino's epistolary. Of particular interest are two: that praising him as a poet and devotee of the Muses and that offering Bembo his reflections on an ideal symposium, translated in Ficino 1975– (1978:18, 42). There is also another letter of Ficino to Bembo in which he associates him with the circle in which these men moved and thrived and, as a poet, with Critoforo Landino 14 June 1477 (1981:20). Ficino styles the unmusical name Bembo as "a name musical to the Graces and most gratifying to the Muses, those in whom he most delights: Cristoforo Landino, a man worthy of Minerva and the Muses" (1981:51). Bembo owned an autograph copy of Ficino's *De Amore* now in the Bodleian Library, Oxford. It is identified as his by his personal device (shown in Fletcher 1989:812). He was also praised by Landino (1970:46, 48) in his *De Vera Nobilitat.*

Bembo's annotation to *Christophorus Landinus, vir doctrina excellens* (Ficino 1956:167n1) Codex Oxoniensis Bodleianus (Canonicianus Latinus 156) folio 21r is both revealing and, in one of its phrases, difficult to interpret:

> Quod nos itidem plurimo usu celebrem agnovimus, dum Florentie legatum ageremus. Is qui nos in Bernardi filii de sacro fonte sublati compaternitatem adsciverit. Atque in ibi Ginevram Benciam Matronarum pulcherriman. Atque etiam virtute moribusque illustrem ellegantissimis carminibus coequarit.

> Something we came to know as we became acquainted with this famous man from frequent contacts when we served as ambassador [of the Venetian senate] to Florence. It was he who invited us to become part of his family at the baptism of his son Bernardo. And in this same city he introduced us to Ginevra de' Benci, the most beautiful of married women. It was Landino who matched the virtue and character of this renowned woman by his surpassingly elegant poems.

Fletcher notes Bembo's personal reminiscence of Landino in her argument that he commissioned Leonardo's painting (1989:811n3), but she does not reproduce the full text. The words *Bernardi filli de sacro fonte sublati* given here, are a puzzle. But my colleague Charles Fantazzi has suggested that they must refer to Bernardo's role in the baptism of Landino's son Bernardo. This suggestion is born out by the fact that Landino's second son (of four children) was baptized Bernardo; see Simone Foà, 2004:429. The poem of Landino that seems to describe Leonardo's portrait best is his *Ad Ginevra* (no. 26 in Landino 1939:159–160):

Flavis crinibus aureisque pulchra
    et nigris oculis, gena nitenti,
et tota facie nimis superba,
    incedis tetrico, Ginevra, vultu.

Lovely with your golden locks,
    your black eyes, your radiant cheeks,
and proud, too proud, in all your countenance,
    you move in triumph with your forbidding look.

Ad Ginevram (or *Ad Leandram*) 26.1–4

Landino's poem on Ginevra and Bernardo Bembo is long and rhetorical, and not to every Latinist's taste. My colleague, Lawrence Richardson, Jr., offers the following comment on the poem: "It seems to me that Landino's poem is not simply fustian, but almost bordering on doggerel. There is not a single trope in it that merits admiration, and the stock comparisons amount to an inventory." Yet it seems that it was acceptable to and appreciated by the cultured circle in which Bembo and Landino moved. I give a further sample from the poem with a prose translation:[30]

Qui nuper Veneta missus ab urbe venis,
    sensibus amplectans imis et pectore firmo
10   cantarem laudes, maxime Bembe, tuas,
Bembe decus nostri, Musarum dulcis alumne,
    delitiae Charitum, Palladiumque caput.

. . .

sed curtis elegis Erato me iussit amantum
    usta cupidinea ludere corda face.
25   Quapropter Bembi castos ludere amores
    versibus ut surgat Bencia nota meis.
Bembus, pulchra, tuam miratur, Bencia, formam,
    caelestes valeas qua superare deas.
Quae magnus Veneris Mavors praeponere amori,
30   quam missa Europa Iuppiter ipse velit.
Sed magis antiquos mores pectusque pudicum
    M iratur stupidus Palladiasque manus.
Semper amore pio calet hic, contagia tetrae
    nec possunt illum tangere luxuriae.

. . .

---

[30] He wrote other poems to Bembo on Bencia (in Landino 1939:161–172).

51　Pulchrior at Ledae partu iam, Bencia, cunctis
　　　gentibus es rara nota pudicitia.

8　you come to us as an envoy from Venice, I would sing your praise, greatest Bembo, embracing you with deepest affection and a stout heart.

25　So, Bembo. Let us celebrate chaste loves, so that Ginevra will be exalted in my verse. Ginevra, Bembo is captivated by your great beauty, a beauty that gives you the power to surpass the goddesses of heaven, a beauty mighty Mars would prefer to his beloved Venus, a beauty for which Jove himself would leave Europa in his desire for you. Even more does Bembo in his awe admire your pristine character, your chaste heart, and Minerva's hands. Bembo's love is ardent and chaste. He is ever immune to the poison of bitter lust.

51　Lovelier now than Leda's daughter, you Ginevra are known among all nations for your rare purity.

Sixteen

Platonic Selves in Shelley and Stevens

David K. O'Connor

R ALPH WALDO EMERSON, who certainly knew a thing or two about essays, said in "History" that the best of them describe to their readers our "unattained but attainable self" (1983:239). Our reading shows us how the self we have so far attained is estranged from the self we can be. The self we are is deficient, lacking, less than real or true. This is a provoking discovery. It is no wonder if we hide in shame, and shift the blame. But it is also possible to acknowledge the deficiency of one's life, and seek a better self as one's vocation. The instinct to hide and deny, to hunker down into that attained self we hold so dear, is strong. But strong too is the taste for the knowledge and the wandering made possible only when we leave that charmed circle.

As Emerson read him, Plato was the master provocateur: "Before I began to converse with Socrates, and to observe each day all his words and actions, I wandered about wherever it might chance, thinking that I did something, but being, in truth, a most miserable wretch, not less than you are now, who believe that you ought to do anything rather than practice the love of wisdom" (Shelley trans.). Apollodorus' words near the beginning of Plato's *Symposium* (172c–173a) are addressed to Glaucon, Plato's brother, but the reader hears the same call to conversion. It is what, in "Plato; Or, The Philosopher" (1983:636), Emerson called Plato's "perpetual modernness."

That Plato's call to conversion is "perpetual" means it is never heard once and for all. Apollodorus did not stop wandering after he met Socrates; he wandered all the more, albeit in search of Socrates rather than by chance. The self that is "unattained but attainable" is the only self we will ever have; the attainment will never end. In "Circles," Emerson finds "the moral fact of the Unattainable, the flying Perfect" (1983:403) to be the living core of a Plato without Platonism. Emerson knows this is an unsettling claim. Are we to be so fond of Plato's provocations that we can dispense with all his convictions?

"Plato was born to behold the self-evolving power of spirit, generator of new ends; a power which is the key at once to the centrality and the evanescence of things," replied Emerson in "Plato: New Readings." "Plato is so centered, that he can well spare all his dogmas" (1983:658). To be centered means to see all one's expressions as transitory, as the moving circumference. For all Emerson cared, Plato can be as reticent about expressing his own opinion as his Socrates was. What counts is that he helped Emerson find the way to his own opinion, and then find the way away from it again.

In this appreciation of Plato, Emerson was part of a tradition of reading also carried on by other Romantic poets and their heirs. Such poets love Plato for his vertical energies, and envy his escape from the weary staleness to which the prosy world is prone. They value ascent, and are grateful to Plato for it. But they value freedom more. Such poets can't confide in a changeless end or a standing heaven. Better to court a demoniacal flux than concede an angelic fixity. Not that they want to be devils. It is just that they value departures as much as arrivals, and are suspicious of any arrival that seems to leave nothing more to be attained. They suffer a Platonic desire that refuses a Platonic satisfaction.

An aspect of the poets' mixed motives is the importance of obscurity for them. I do not mean that their writing is obscure. It is rather that they see the essential resistance of words to lucidity as both a frustration (of ascent) and as a blessing (for freedom). They would write anything before a catechism. Wallace Stevens, heir to Emerson, put his mixed motives into a longing for ascent to the ideal that yet left room for "the desire of the artist." Platonism, including that Platonism for the people, Christianity, would make the world inhospitable to this desire.

> one confides in what has no
> Concealed creator. One walks easily
>
> The unpainted shore, accepts the world
> As anything but sculpture.
> "So-and-So Reclining on Her Couch" (Stevens 1997:263)

Platonism excludes the intimacy that accepting and confiding in the world express. A bare world, a barren world, is more inviting than a decorated one, if you seek a home where you can carve and color.

If it is inevitable that poetic ascent be figured as a bird, the Platonic bird these poets trust most is the phoenix, "neither mortal nor immortal, on the same day at one time flourishing, and then dying away, and then again reviving"

(*Symposium* 203e). This phoenix is, of course, Socrates' image of himself, and it would take no great effort to find more Platonic reflection on the resistance of words to final lucidity. There is always rewriting to be done. What Plato figured as eroticized defect or lack, the poets' tradition takes up as freedom.

But this freedom provokes an anxiety of its own. Given their Platonic sympathies and envies, the poets in this tradition also want to ascend from eccentricity (individuality, egoism) to an impersonal or universal perspective, call it an ecstasy from self. But what would a poet who lost himself have left to say? The impersonal aspiration seems to require, as the title of a Stevens poem has it, a "description without place." But the scribe's scribblings must come from somewhere. The poets' open freedom—the stubbornness of words and the incompleteness of ascent—is inconsistent with this impersonal ecstasy. If the poet escapes private whim to make his perception impersonal, must the escape become fatal to poetic freedom, as Emerson almost says in "Self-Reliance" (Emerson 1983:269)?

Percy Shelley, whom Emerson says in his journals he found "wholly unaffecting," was nonetheless his predecessor into this territory of the soul. Shelley's "To a Sky-Lark" (2002b:306) is riven by the competing aspirations of freedom and impersonality. The title bird sings beyond human sight of super-human pleasures.

> I have never heard
>> Praise of love or wine
> That panted forth a flood of rapture so divine.

The bird's song is untainted by the pain or defect that the attained self of human poetry always bears. Which praise of love and praise of wine does the bird transcend? Perhaps Plato's *Symposium* itself, that drinking party where love is said to be the offspring of Plenty and Poverty (203c), neither human nor divine, demoniacal, between.

Shelley goes on to identify himself with Hamlet. Hamlet is the opposite of impersonal, focused as he is on the terrible question of how to be Hamlet. The prince's frustration that a "god-like reason," "looking before and after," should "fust in us unused" (*Hamlet* 4.4) is Shelley's emblem for human poetry:

> We look before and after,
>> And pine for what is not—
> Our sincerest laughter
>> With some pain is fraught—
> Our sweetest songs are those that tell of saddest thought.

Hamlet's frailties keep him all too human, despite his divine capacity. But finally Shelley accepts this human eccentricity:

> Yet if we could scorn
>> Hate and pride and fear;
> If we were things born
>> Not to shed a tear,
> I know not how thy joy we ever should come near.

The untainted bird must remain an unattained self. Our nearest approach to the skylark's impersonal and therefore painless joy requires pain, is called for by deficiency. Stevens (1997:55) subscribes to the same sentiment in "Sunday Morning": "Death is the mother of beauty"; and again with "The imperfect is our paradise" in "The Poems of Our Climate" (1997:179).

Shelley's invocation of Hamlet is not accidental. Shakespeare's most imaginative hero is tortured by the suspicion that all the gaudiness of love and the world is no more than a narcissistic projection, a wish fulfillment. "There is nothing either good or bad, but thinking makes it so," says Hamlet, "I could be bounded in a nutshell and count myself a king of infinite space." An exhilarating prospect, but his consciousness of this imaginative power also enervates the prince, when he suspects that all ambition, including his to revenge his father, is merely "a fantasy and a trick of fame" (*Hamlet* 2.2 and 4.4).

Like Emerson, Percy Shelley and Wallace Stevens both worked out their sense of these aspirations and anxieties by thinking about Plato. Shelley's engagement was much more extensive, but Stevens' late prose reflections on poetry and the imagination show he too found in Plato a voice to be heard.

In July of 1818, Shelley translated Plato's *Symposium*. The translation was not the employment of idle hours, either. In the fours years he had left to live, Shelley continued to use the translation, to work from it, rewriting passages from it into some of his most mature and moving poetry. Finding words for Plato's, finding that Plato's words could be his words, was the most important prose writing Shelley ever did. In the *Symposium*, Shelley found himself more truly and more strange.

Mary Shelley considered her husband's congeniality with Plato as the defining feature of his personality. "He loved to idealize reality; and this is a taste shared by few. ... Few of us understand or sympathize with the endeavour to ally the love of abstract beauty ... with our sympathies for our own kind. ... Shelley resembled Plato; both taking more delight in the abstract and the ideal than in the special and the tangible." Mary wanted to avoid giving the impression, however, that Shelley was a mere student or enthusiast of Plato. She insisted that Shelley's love of idealizing "did not result from imitation." It existed long before "he made Plato his study" in July of 1818 by translating the *Symposium* (Shelley 1839:viii–ix). The *Symposium* recalled Shelley to the erotic themes of his earlier work, rather than inspiring him with a wholly new interest. In particular, Mary thought, the translation had returned Shelley to a view of the ideal self and its problems "a good deal modelled on *Alastor*" (1839:176n).

"Alastor: Or, The Spirit of Solitude" (1815) was Shelley's first fully accomplished poem, and in a way he kept rewriting it. The subject of the poem is the spiritual quest of a Poet whose mind "thirsts for intercourse with an intelligence similar to itself." In the poem's epigraph from St. Augustine (*Confessions* 3.1), the self-involvement of love is enacted in self-involving language: "*Nondum amabam, et amare amabam, quaerebam quid amarem, amans amare.*" ("Not yet did I love, though I loved to love; I sought something to love, loving to love.") Within the poem, Shelley's rough magic conjures forth a vision of the ideal lover in an atmosphere of apparent narcissism, even of autoeroticism. Phrase and image play together to intensify the atmosphere of Augustinian narcissism. St. Augustine, of course, presented erotic self-involvement as sinful, and suggested that our love of loving could find rest only when reoriented away from self toward its ultimate satisfaction in God. But for Shelley, erotic satisfaction must be sought elsewhere, in what the preface of "Alastor" calls the "prototype" (2002b:73). Accepting Augustine's problem while rejecting his solution, Shelley asks whether an ideal self can provide the focal point.

The prototype is the Poet's idealized beloved. "The vision in which [the Poet] *embodies his own imaginations* unites all of wonderful, or wise, or beautiful, which the poet, the philosopher, or the lover could depicture" (ibid.). In a vision, the Poet "images to himself the Being whom he loves" (ibid.):

> He dreamed a veilèd maid
> Sate near him, talking in low solemn tones.
> Her voice was like the voice of his own soul
>
> "Alastor" lines 151–153

This "veilèd maid" is an idealization of the Poet's own aspirations. The music of her voice speaks to his own "inmost sense" (line 156) of "thoughts the most dear to him" (line 160). These lines describe the culmination of what the preface to the poem calls the intense and passionate search of "the pure and tender-hearted" for "human sympathy" (2002b:70). Shelley uses "sympathy" where we might say "intimacy" or "mutual understanding." But the intimacy sought is not, or at least not primarily, with another person. It is the longing for the unattained but attainable self, for an overcoming of the estrangement Emerson diagnosed.

Three years after writing this, immediately after translating the *Symposium*, Shelley returned to this idea in language that shows the clear influence of the translation. "The ideal prototype," he wrote in "On Love," is "a miniature ... of our entire self, yet deprived of all that we condemn or despise," uniting "everything excellent or lovely we are capable of conceiving, ... a soul within our soul" (2002b:504). In other words, the prototype is a standard by which we measure how far we ourselves have escaped from "all that we condemn or despise." The conception of the prototype as a "miniature" within us derives from *Symposium* 215a–b, where Alcibiades says Socrates is like a statue of a satyr filled inside with figurines of the gods. Shelley was so taken with the idea that he made it the title of a later *Symposium*-influenced poem, "Epipsychidion," again about an idealized lover. This title is clearly intended, I believe, to mean "miniature soul within," though Shelley's Norton editors take it to mean "On the Subject of the Soul."

It is true that the love of the prototype is a species of self-love. But it is not mere self-indulgent narcissism, since it requires an idealization of the self as well as of the beloved. This sort of self-love is a vehicle for shame at one's own faults, as well as for disappointment in the faults of others whom we love.

The communication between Poet and vision climaxes in the self-kindled "warm light of their own life" (line 175). With her "beamy bending eyes" and "parted lips ... quivering eagerly" (lines 179–180), the maid yields "to the irresistible joy" of their embrace (line 185), echoed in "On Love" (2002b:503). The Poet rises to the elevation of consummation. But then the vision dissipates, and he sinks into dispirited languor:

> His wan eyes
> Gaze on the empty scene as vacantly
> As ocean's moon looks on the moon in heaven.
>
> "Alastor" lines 200–202

This beautiful passage inverts the myth of Narcissus, who lost himself in rapt contemplation of his own reflection. The Poet of "Alastor" loses himself when he no longer can see himself as a reflection of an ideal beauty. He becomes the empty earthbound shadow ("ocean's moon") of an absent ethereal reality ("the moon in heaven"). The Poet's sympathetic identification with his ideal love, this projection of his own ideal self, is eclipsed in "sudden darkness" when "the vacancy" of his spirit "suddenly makes itself felt" (2002b:73). The Poet loses his grasp on the vision, and "the insatiate hope" awakened by the maid stings his brain "even like despair" (lines 221–222).

So long as the prototype was present to his imagination, the Poet was filled with "visitations of the divinity in man," and could see the possibility of divinity in himself. But our condition is not so handsome as these "best and happiest moments of the happiest and best minds" make it appear. The experience of these moments and visitations, he says in *A Defence of Poetry*, proves to be "evanescent" (2002b:532), a favorite word of Shelley's as it was of Emerson's.

Evanescence brings a despairing grief as surely as presence brought a divine delight. When the loss of this higher sympathy plunges the vision into "sudden darkness," the lover mourns the compromised reality of his own perfection. The lover's grief, then, comes only in part from his failure to achieve a sympathetic communion with the imagined beloved. The loss is equally of the lover's access to his own higher self. On this view, the vacancy provoked by the inconstancy of the prototype redoubles the pain of failed communion with the shame of humiliated aspiration.

Shelley found the experience of the Poet of "Alastor" again in a novel form when he translated Alcibiades' ambivalence toward Socrates. The intoxicated Alcibiades irrupts into the decorous speech making, bearing about him the emblems of Dionysus (212e). He is torn between a desire to praise Socrates and a desire to censure him (214e, 222a). In the extremity of his ambivalence, he contemplates Socrates' death, and oscillates between considering it as his most fervent wish and his most painful fear: "Often and often have I wished that he were no longer to be seen among men. But if that were to happen, I well know that I should suffer far greater pain; so that where I can turn, or what I can do with this man, I know not" (216c). What delight and grief entangle Alcibiades in this violent ambivalence?

He begins with delight. Alcibiades praises Socrates for having within himself "images of the Gods," or more precisely little statues or figurines of them (215a–b). The full significance of this conception of Socrates becomes apparent only when Alcibiades returns to it in his peroration: "If any one should ... get within the sense of [Socrates'] words, he would then find ... that they were most divine; and that they presented to the mind innumerable images of every excellence, and that they tended ... towards all, that he who seeks the possession of what is supremely beautiful and good, need regard as essential to the accomplishment of his ambition" (222a).

In the poem's terms, these passages treat Socrates as the prototype of Alcibiades' own idealized self. Socrates' virtues are a perpetual provocation to Alcibiades' own ambition to seek "the possession of what is supremely beautiful and good."

But Socrates' inward divinity is also obscure, to be glimpsed rarely and with difficulty, and often not at all. The divine images are not visible to everyone or at every time. They show forth only in moments of sudden epiphany: "I know not if any one of you have ever seen the divine images which are within, when he has been opened and is serious. I have seen them, and they are so supremely beautiful, so golden, so divine, and wonderful, that every thing which Socrates commands surely ought to be obeyed" (216e–217a). This evanescence is the source of Alcibiades' ambivalence: his admiration seeks an intimacy that Socrates appears both to offer and to deny.

Alcibiades' delight in Socrates is analogous to the delight of the Poet in the "veilèd maid" of his vision. Alcibiades is also exposed to the evanescence and obscuring "sudden darkness" that provokes the Poet's redoubled grief. He suffers the pain of failed intimacy or sympathy when he tries to convince Socrates to become his lover. He suffers the shame of humiliated aspiration when the divine images of virtue he sees in Socrates no longer seem accessible to him as images of his own idealized self.

In thrall to his vision of idealized intimacy, Alcibiades casts himself wholly into its pursuit: "I lay the whole night with my arms around this truly divine and wonderful being" (219c). But for Alcibiades as for Shelley's Poet, the humiliating truth only becomes clear in "the cold white light of morning" (line 193): "He despised and contemptuously neglected that beauty which I had thus exposed to his rejection ... I swear that I awoke and arose from as unimpassioned an embrace as if I had slept with my father or my elder brother" (219c–d).

The consummating embrace with the "truly divine and wonderful being" proves itself a most fleeting visitation of the divine, if not an outright illusion.

When the Poet of "Alastor" awakes from his vision, he pursues "beyond the realms of dream that fleeting shade" (line 206) his veilèd maid, and "wildly he wandered" (line 244) in the pursuit. This "wandering" (another favorite word of Shelley's) is the fated condition of the erotic idealist. Shelley builds up this theme throughout the *Symposium*. Apollodorus at the dialogue's beginning tells us he had "wandered about," a "miserable wretch," before devoting himself to Socrates (173a). Socrates later reports that Diotima said the young man pregnant in soul must be "wandering about" in his urgent search for "the beautiful in which he may propagate what he has conceived" (209b). Finally, Alcibiades "wandered about disconsolately" in Socrates' company after their failed embrace, in restless pursuit of that evanescent glimpse of those divine images. His sudden vacancy left him "the prey of doubt and trouble," and he became "enslaved to [Socrates] far more than any other was ever enslaved" (219e). Shelley could see in the wanderings of these Socratics the image of his own struggles against evanescence and vacancy.

Simply to be alienated from the intimacy of Socrates was disorienting enough for Alcibiades. But the pain of loss was redoubled by his shame at falling short of his own aspirations to excellence:

> This man has reduced me to feel the sentiment of shame, which I imagine no one would readily believe was in me; he alone inspires me with remorse and awe. For I feel in his presence my incapacity of refuting what he says, or of refusing to do that which he directs. ...
> I hide myself from him, and when I see him I am overwhelmed with humiliation, because I have neglected to do what I have confessed to him ought to be done. (216b)

Alcibiades finds his failed intimacy with Socrates to be at the same time an alienation from his own idealized self. Socrates is Alcibiades' prototype of "what is supremely beautiful and good" and of everything to which Alcibiades' "ambitions" drive him (218a, 222d). When he loses Socrates, Alcibiades loses more than what he loves. He also loses his sense of himself as the lover of what he loves. He suffers the redoubled grief of every divorce, for it is one thing to give up a spouse, and quite another to give up being a spouse. This Augustinian labyrinth holds Alcibiades in its wandering mazes. Such is the shame of humiliated aspiration.

Does the poet's pursuit of an ideal self move him toward a satisfying substitute for a Platonic or Augustinian reality, or is all the beauty he finds no more than a trick of strong imagination? Shelley's culminating statement in *A Defence of Poetry* hovers around this issue in perfect ambivalence: "Whether [poetry] spreads its own figured curtain or withdraws life's dark veil from before the scene of things, it equally creates for us a being within our being" (2002b:533). The disputed question is left undetermined, and with it the fate of the erotic quest. The "being within our being" whose status is left undecided is precisely the prototype sought by Shelley's lovers, a self-idealization. Shelley is here returning to the language we have already seen in the fragment "On Love," language derived from the *Symposium*: the prototype is "a miniature

... of our entire self, yet deprived of all that we condemn or despise, ... a soul within our soul" (2002b:504).

What the *Symposium* presents as an incomplete but nonetheless real human openness to the divine, Shelley fears may be an enclosure within the self's imaginative power. For Shelley, there always lurked within love's wandering mazes the awful vacancy of self-involvement. What accounts for this difference between Plato's confidence in the openness of erotic love and Shelley's fear of enclosure?

Shelley was the sort of poet who felt he needed a philosophy, and he played at grounding his fear in an empiricist skepticism derived from Locke and Hume. But Shelley's true emblems of erotic self-enclosure are literary rather than philosophical, and he interpreted self-enclosure by alluding to Milton's Satan and Shakespeare's Hamlet. This is where he learned the views of creative will and melancholy reflection that served to counterbalance Platonic confidence in erotic ascent.

Both heroes exemplify Shelley's ambivalence to imagination's tendency to invention rather than insight. "There is nothing either good or bad, but thinking makes it so" (*Hamlet* 2.2); "The mind is its own place, and in itself can make a heav'n of hell, a hell of heav'n" (*Paradise Lost* 1.254–255): these brave claims to imaginative self-sufficiency reveal their aspect as curses, too. Hamlet cannot spur his "dull revenge" because his inwardness makes his cause feel to him but "a fantasy and trick of fame" (*Hamlet* 4.4). And Satan's self-glorifying vaunt is echoed back in an abyss of self-despair:

> Which way I fly is hell; myself am hell;
> And in the lowest deep a lower deep
> Still threat'ning to devour me opens wide,
> To which the hell I suffer seems a heav'n.
>
> *Paradise Lost* 4.73–78

Hamlet and Satan are for Shelley illustrations of the self-consuming isolation suffered by the Poet of "Alastor" at the hands of his own erotic idealism.

When Shelley thought most directly about the erotic prototype and our evanescent vision of it, his skeptical impulse drew him particularly to King Theseus in *A Midsummer Night's Dream*. Theseus famously derides the idealizations of love and poetry:

> Lovers and madmen have such seething *brains*,
> Such shaping fantasies, that apprehend
> More than cool reason ever comprehends.

> The lunatic, the *lover*, and the *poet*
> Are of imagination all compact.
> ...
> And as *imagination bodies forth*
> The forms of things unknown, the poet's pen
> Turns them to shapes, and gives to *airy nothing*
> A local habitation and a name.
>
> *A Midsummer Night's Dream* 5.1

Shelley used Shakespeare's italicized words himself in the Preface to "Alastor" to describe the erotic ideal: "The vision in which he *embodies his own imaginations* unites all of wonderful, or wise, or beautiful, which the poet, the philosopher, or the lover could depicture" (2002b:73). When Shelley wrote "On Love," revisiting the "prototype" of the "Alastor" preface fresh from translating the *Symposium*, he once again turned to Theseus' famous speech: "If we imagine, we would that *the airy children of our brain* were born anew within another's" (2002b:504).

Much as he appreciated Plato's vertical energies, Shelley also felt the strong pull of Theseus' sober skepticism. He felt himself a kind of Alcibiades, suspended in the demoniacal intermediate of a vulgar humanity and an evanescent divinity. Every apprehension of ideal love served to increase Shelley's anguished comprehension of the lower deeps of his vacancy.

In 1936, Wallace Stevens, at the age of 56, wrote the first extended prose reflection of his life on poetry and thought. In "The Irrational Element in Poetry," he identified himself as a kind of Platonist (1997:786, 788):

> While it can lie in the temperament of very few of us to write poetry in order to find God, it is probably the purpose of each of us to write poetry to find the good which, in the Platonic sense, is synonymous with God ... The poet who wishes to contemplate the good in the midst of confusion is like the mystic who wants to contemplate God in the midst of evil. There can be no thought of escape.

God does not draw Stevens, but Plato's good does. Stevens' word "temperament" here is the marker for the narcissism or egoism of the imagination. The depersonalizing ascent to the good does not free itself from the individual. It remains, as Stevens' called it (in "A Primitive Like an Orb"), a "fated eccentricity," responsive to the individual. Stevens found Plato's version of the ascent described his own longing too.

Yet Stevens could not believe in Plato. In 1941, he wrote a second reflection on the imagination's power that began, surprisingly enough, by quoting a long section from the charioteer myth in Plato's *Phaedrus*. He quoted it both in homage and in elegy. The charioteer was exemplary for Stevens of a nobility still observable in Plato's image, but no longer accessible:

> We have scarcely read the passage before we have identified ourselves with the charioteer, have, in fact, taken his place and, driving his winged horses, are traversing the whole heaven. Then suddenly we remember, it may be, that the soul no longer exists and we droop in our flight and at last settle on the solid ground … We recognize, even if we cannot realize, the feelings of the robust poet clearly and fluently noting the images of his mind and by means of his robustness, clearness, and fluency communicating much more than the images themselves. Yet we do not quite yield. We cannot. We do not feel free.
>
> "The Noble Rider and the Sound of Words" (1997:643, 644)

Why cannot Stevens yield? Something in his own motives made him reject the ascent of the charioteer. It was too loud, too indiscreet, too assured that its lucidities were final. Stevens wrote poetry of pleasures more obscure.

Stevens could have been made more comfortable with other sides of Plato. Aristotle, serpent-like, told philosophers to go beyond merely human thoughts and be like gods (*Nicomachean Ethics* 10.7.1177b31–34). Plato had learned enough from Socrates to have his doubts. "None of the gods philosophizes"; philosophy is the entirely human response to lack of wisdom (*Symposium* 204a), not the enjoyment of achieved wisdom. Here Plato lets his wings droop, too, like the wings of the phoenix must in its oscillations between heaven and earth.

But then what sort of enjoyment does writing so conceived provide, if it must bear the mark of our human exclusion from Aristotle's paradise? Stevens was deeply exercised by what could motivate poetry in the face of what he saw as its cognitive limitations. If the twentieth century could produce a Socratic poet, it was Stevens. How is one to go on, whether as poet or philosopher, when all one knows is that one knows nothing? "The lapses and failures of idealization," in Helen Vendler's (1984:28) apt formulation, are the stuff of Stevens' poetry.

Two early poems, "The Snow Man" and "Tea at the Palaz of Hoon," first published in *Harmonium* (1923), express two competing aspects of Stevens' motives for poetry.

The Snow Man

One must have a mind of winter
To regard the frost and the boughs
Of the pine-trees crusted with snow;

And have been cold a long time
To behold the junipers shagged with ice,
The spruces rough in the distant glitter

Of the January sun; and not to think
Of any misery in the sound of the wind,
In the sound of a few leaves,

Which is the sound of the land
Full of the same wind
That is blowing in the same bare place

For the listener, who listens in the snow,
And, nothing himself, beholds
Nothing that is not there and the nothing that is.

Snow Man enjoys a kind of inhuman purity of vision, one that exposes to himself his own nothingness as just another entity in the nothingness of the natural world. The motive for this vision, this beholding, is hard to articulate, but there is clearly an exhilaration about this kind of self-evacuation, about getting out of the way of one's perception of the real world. The impersonal purification of the vision is Stevens' way of living at the top of Diotima's ladder, which "you will esteem far beyond gold and rich garments, and even beyond those lovely persons whom you and many others now gaze on with astonishment, ... the supreme beauty itself, simple, pure, uncontaminated with the intermixture of human flesh and colors" (*Symposium* 211d–e).

But I think there is also a macho motive here, as if seeing the world as cold and inhospitable is a way to show how tough one is. What Vendler (1984:chap. 1) describes as Stevens' brutality toward himself, a function of self-loathing, seems to me more ambiguous. It is enjoyable to "rough it" sometimes. It makes you feel like a real man. A camp without running water will not stand empty even if nearby there is an inexpensive hotel. I think Stevens enjoys roughing it, thinking of the world as really a cold place that he needs great courage to see in its purity. Nietzsche says somewhere that the man who holds himself in contempt is still proud of himself as a contemner. That is how I see Stevens when he gets into the Snow Man persona.

Hoon is Snow Man's alter ego. Hoon is responding to a challenge, as if from Snow Man, that runs something like this: Who do you think you're fooling with the extravagance of your colors; you're nothing but a setting sun. The ointment someone sprinkled in your beard, the hymns someone was singing for you, the sea itself which bore you up, all are nothings, illusions and delusions of grandeur. You are nothing but an inhabitant of the loneliest air, afraid to confront that loneliness.

Tea at the Palaz of Hoon

Not less because in purple I descended
The western day through what you called
The loneliest air, not less was I myself.

What was the ointment sprinkled on my beard?
What were the hymns that buzzed beside my ears?
What was the sea whose tide swept through me there?

Out of my mind the golden ointment rained,
And my ears made the blowing hymns they heard.
I was myself the compass of that sea:

I was the world in which I walked, and what I saw
Or heard or felt came not but from myself;
And there I found myself more truly and more strange.

Hoon's answer to his challenger in the last two stanzas is assertive and expansive. I even hear it as rather indignant, and as said in the kind of voice intended to convince oneself as much as the questioner. He takes possession of the beauty that surrounds him and declares himself its source. Where Snow Man enjoyed the macho toughness of pure vision and self-reduction, Hoon insists on the gaudy beauties of purple, of ointments, of songs, and the magnitude of ocean. What's more, he does not merely celebrate these natural beauties, as if merely resisting Snow Man's austere preference for winter landscapes. Instead he shows that once he acknowledges that he is himself the source of these beauties—he is himself even as he descends in purple—the beauties take on an intensity far beyond what the challenger can see: ointment no longer is sprinkled, but rains; hymns no longer buzz, but blow like trumpets; and Hoon does not passively ride the tide, he encompasses the whole sea as its agent force. And as Snow Man's triumph is to achieve selflessness, Hoon's is to find himself, more truly and more strange.

One thread to follow through the labyrinth of Stevens' poetry is his attempts to combine the nobility of Snow Man with the pleasures of Hoon. It is his closest approach to the difficulty in the *Symposium* of holding together the phoenix image of Socratic incompleteness and restlessness with the image of completed ascent. For Stevens, unchanging completion is something to be actively avoided, even though it is so beautiful. Better an earthy Socrates than a heavenly Form.

In "The Poems of Our Climate," a poem written at about the same time as "The Noble Rider and the Sound of Words," Stevens achieved an especially memorable statement of this theme. The first stanza is a more tranquil accomplishment of the Snow Man mood. Clarity, a whiteness that takes away other outlines, simplification: the tranquility is real.

> Clear water in a brilliant bowl,
> Pink and white carnations. The light
> In the room more like snowy air,
> Reflecting snow. A newly-fallen snow
> At the end of winter when afternoons return.
> Pink and white carnations—one desires
> So much more than that. The day itself
> Is simplified: a bowl of white,
> Cold, a cold porcelain, low and round,
> With nothing more than the carnation there.

But this tranquil simplicity comes at the price of a desire. Give "complete simplicity" all the credit it deserves, as Stevens does in the second stanza. Simplicity removes our "torments" and refreshes us by getting us away from the narcissism pain induces. We feel the snowy pull toward impersonality. Yet the self, that temperamental necessity, is only "concealed," not transcended:

> Say even this complete simplicity
> Stripped one of all one's torments, concealed
> The evilly compounded, vital I
> And made it fresh in a world of white,
> A world of clear water, brilliant-edged,
> Still one would want more, one would need more,
> More than a world of white and snowy scents.

In a stanza that is pure Stevens, no less for being so Emersonian, the poem ends with a celebration of the freedom ("never-resting mind") that final lucidity would exclude:

There would still remain the never-resting mind,
So that one would want to escape, come back
To what had been so long composed.
The imperfect is our paradise.
Note that, in this bitterness, delight,
Since the imperfect is so hot in us,
Lies in flawed words and stubborn sounds.

"The imperfect is our paradise": the resistance of words, stubborn and flawed, is what makes them the fit stuff of the never-resting mind. There is a beautiful play here on "carnations" of the first stanza. They turn out in the end not to be the indistinct white blurs of the first stanza, but flowers of flesh and blood, incarnations. They were made emblems of purity and simplicity in a way that is challenged by their stubborn name. The bitterness that motivates escape—from torment and imperfection—is the condition of delight, in our hot erotic enjoyment of the imperfect obscurities we count as a poem. Shelley's sky-lark provokes the same reflection. I am tempted to say that both are versions of Socrates' claim to ignorance.[1]

[1] I am grateful to the Dean's Office of the College of Arts and Letters of the University of Notre Dame for supporting a special leave that allowed me to work on this essay.

The Contributors

RUBY BLONDELL is Professor of Classics at the University of Washington, Seattle.

LUC BRISSON is Directeur de Recherche at the Centre National de la Recherche Scientifique.

JEFFREY CARNES is Associate Professor of Languages, Literature, and Linguistics at Syracuse University.

GABRIELA ROXANA CARONE is an independent scholar.

DISKIN CLAY is R. J. R. Nabisco Professor of Classical Studies at Duke University.

LLOYD P. GERSON is Professor of Philosophy at the University of Toronto.

ANGELA HOBBS is Lecturer in Philosophy at the University of Warwick.

RICHARD HUNTER is Regius Professor of Greek at the University of Cambridge.

GABRIEL RICHARDSON LEAR is Assistant Professor of Philosophy at the University of Chicago.

J. H. LESHER is Professor of Philosophy at the University of Maryland.

MARK L. MCPHERRAN is Professor of Philosophy at Simon Fraser University.

DEBRA NAILS is Professor of Philosophy at Michigan State University.

DAVID K. O'CONNOR is Associate Professor of Philosophy at the University of Notre Dame.

C. D. C. REEVE is Delta Kappa Epsilon Distinguished Professor of Philosophy at the University of North Carolina at Chapel Hill.

CHRISTOPHER ROWE is Professor of Greek at the University of Durham.

FRISBEE C. C. SHEFFIELD is Lecturer in Philosophy at King's College London.

Works Cited

Plato Texts and Translations

Adam, J. 1902. *The Republic of Plato.* Cambridge.

Allen, R. E., trans. 1991. *The Dialogues of Plato.* Vol. 2 *The Symposium.* New Haven.

Benardete, Seth, trans. 1993. *Plato's Symposium.* Introduction by Heinrich Meier. 2nd ed. 2001 with commentary by Allan Bloom. Chicago.

Brisson, Luc, trans. 1999. *Platon, Le Banquet.* Collection GF 987. Paris. 3rd ed. 2004.

Bury, R. G., ed. 1932. *The Symposium of Plato.* 2nd ed. Cambridge. 1st ed. 1909.

Cooper, John M., ed. 1997. *Plato, Complete Works.* With Douglas S. Hutchinson. Indianapolis.

Dover, Kenneth J., ed. 1980. *Plato: Symposium.* Cambridge.

Gill, Christopher, trans. 1999. *Plato The Symposium.* London.

Grube, G. M. A., trans. 1992. *Plato, Republic.* Revised by C. D. C. Reeve. Indianapolis. Also in Cooper 1997:971–1223.

Lombardo, Stanley, trans. 1997. *Plato, Lysis.* In Cooper 1997:687–707.

McDowell, John, trans. 1973. *Plato Theaetetus.* Oxford.

Nehamas, Alexander, and Woodruff, Paul, trans. 1989. *Plato, Symposium.* Indianapolis. Also in Cooper 1997:457–505.

———, trans. 1995. *Plato, Phaedrus.* Indianapolis. Also in Cooper 1997:506–556.

Robin, Léon. 1958. *Platon. Oeuvres completes,* t. IV.2: *Le banquet.* Paris.

Rowe, Christopher J., trans. 1986. *Plato: Phaedrus.* Warminster.

———, trans. 1998a. *Plato: Symposium.* Warminster.

Shelley, Percy Bysshe. 2002a. *The Symposium of Plato: The Shelley Translation.* Ed. David K. O'Connor. South Bend, IN.

Shorey, Paul, trans. 1937. *Plato Republic.* 2 vols. Loeb Classical Library. Cambridge, MA.

Waterfield, Robin, trans. 1994. *Plato Symposium.* Oxford.

Other Works Cited

Allen, Michael J. B. 1984. *The Platonism of Marsilio Ficino: A Study of the "Phaedrus" Commentary, Its Sources and Genesis.* Berkeley and Los Angeles.

Allen, Michael J. B., and Rees, Valery. 2002. *Marsilio Ficino: His Theology, His Philosophy, His Legacy.* Boston.

Amden, Bettina, Flensted-Jensen, Pernille, Nielsen, Thomas Heine, Schwartz, Adam, and Tortzen, Chr. Gorm. 2002. *Noctes Atticae: 34 Articles on Graeco-Roman Antiquity and its Nachleben: Studies Presented to Jørgen Mejer on his Sixtieth Birthday March 18, 2002.* Copenhagen.

Ames-Lewis, F. 2002. "Neoplatonism and the Visual Arts at the Time of Marsilio Ficino." In Allen and Rees 2002:327–338.

Anderson, Daniel E. 1993. *The Masks of Dionysos: A Commentary on Plato's Symposium.* Albany.

Annas, Julia. 1981. *An Introduction to Plato's Republic.* Oxford.

Annas, Julia, and Rowe, Christopher, eds. 2002. *New Perspectives on Plato, Modern and Ancient.* Center for Hellenic Studies Series 6. Washington, DC.

Anton, John P. 1974. "The Secret of Plato's *Symposium.*" *Southern Journal of Philosophy* 12:277–293.

Anton, John P., and Kustas, G. L. 1971. *Essays in Ancient Greek Philosophy.* vol. I. Albany.

Arieti, James A. 1991. *Interpreting Plato: The Dialogues as Drama.* Savage, MD.

Auerbach, Erich. 1984. "Figura." *Scenes from the Drama of European Literature.* Minneapolis. 1st ed. 1944:chap. 1.

Bacon, Helen. 1959. "Socrates Crowned." *Virginia Quarterly Review* 35:415–430.

Bakhtin, Mikhail M. 1981. *The Dialogic Imagination: Four Essays.* Austin, TX.

Barnes, Jonathan. 1981. "Aristotle and the Methods of Ethics." *Revue Internationale de la Philosophie* 34:490–511.

Bartsch, Shadi, and Bartscherer, Thomas, eds. 2005. *Erotikon: Essays on Eros, Ancient and Modern.* Chicago.

Belfiore, Elizabeth. 1980. "*Elenchus, Epode,* and Magic: Socrates as Silenus." *Phoenix* 34:128–137.

———. 1984. "Dialectic with the Reader in Plato's *Symposium.*" *Maia* 36:137–149.

Bembo, Pietro. 1505. *Gli Asolani.* 1991 ed. Giorgio Dilemmi. Florence.

———. 1525. *Prose della volgare lingua; Gli Asolani; Rime.* 1989 ed. Carolo Dionisotti. Milan.

———. 1954. *Gli Asolani.* Trans. R. Gottfried. Bloomington, IN.

———. 1987. *The Prettiest Love Letters in the World: Letters between Lucrezia Borgia and Pietro Bembo 1503-1519.* Trans. Hugh Shankland. Boston.

———. 2005. *Lyric Poetry, Etna.* Ed. Mary P. Chatfield. Cambridge, MA and London.

Bergquist, Birgitta. 1990. "Sympotic Space: A Functional Aspect of Greek Dining-Rooms." In Murray 1990a:37–65.

Bernstein, Leonard. 1956. Serenade *After Plato's Symposium* for Solo Violin, Strings, Harp and Percussion. New York.

Bethe, H. 1907. "Die dorische Knabenliebe; ihre Ethik und ihre Idee." *Rheinisches Museum für Philologie* 62:438–475.

Bieber, M. 1955. *The Sculpture of the Hellenistic Age.* New York.

Blanckenhagen, Peter H. von. 1992. "Stage and Actors in Plato's *Symposium.*" *Greek, Roman, and Byzantine Studies* 33(1):51–68.

Bloch, Enid. 2002. "Hemlock Poisoning and the Death of Socrates; Did Plato Tell the Truth." In Brickhouse and Smith 2002:255–278.

Blondell, Ruby. 2002. *The Play of Character in Plato's Dialogues.* Cambridge.

Blundell, Mary Whitlock. 1992. "Commentary on Reeve." *Proceedings of the Boston Area Colloquium in Ancient Philosophy* 8:115–133.

Blundell, Sue. 1995. *Women in Ancient Greece.* London.

Boehringer, Sandra. 2003. *L'homosexualité féminine dans l'Antiquité.* Thesis, EHESS/Centre Louis-Gernet.

Boersma, J., ed. 1976. *Festoen. Opgedragen aan A. N. Zadoks-Josephus Jitta bii haar zevenstige verjaardag.* Groningen.

Bolton, Robert. 1990 "The Epistemological Basis of Aristotelian Dialectic." In Devereux and Pellegrin 1990:185–236.

———. 1993. "Aristotle's Account of the Socratic Elenchus." *Oxford Studies in Ancient Philosophy* 11:121–152.

Boudouris, K. J. ed. 1998. *Philosophy and Medicine* vol. 2. Athens.

Bowen, A. 1998. *Xenophon: Symposium.* Warminster.

Branham, R. Bracht, ed. 2002a. *Bakhtin and the Classics.* Evanston, IL.

———. 2002b. "A Truer Story of the Novel?" In Branham 2002a:161–186.

———, ed. 2005. *The Bakhtin Circle and Ancient Narrative. Ancient Narrative* supp. 3. Groningen.

Branham, R. Bracht, and Kinney, D. 1996. *Petronius. Satyrica.* London.

Brandwood, Leonard. 1976. *A Word Index to Plato.* Leeds.

Bratke, Elka, and Schimpf, Hans. 1980. *Anselm Friedrich Feuerbach: 1829-1880.* Koblenz-Ehrenbreitstein.

Bremmer, J. 1990. "Adolescents, *Symposion,* and Pederasty." In Murray 1990a: 135–148.

Brickhouse, Thomas C., and Smith, Nicholas D. 2002. *The Trial and Execution of Socrates: Sources and Controversies.* New York.

Brown, David Alan. 2001. *Virtue and Beauty: Leonardo's Ginevra de' Benci and Renaissance Portraits of Women.* Princeton and Washington, DC.

Buchner, Hartmut. 1965. *Eros und Sein.* Bonn.

Buffière, F. 1956. *Les mythes d'Homère et la pensée grecque.* Paris.

Burkert, Walter. 1985. *Greek Religion.* Cambridge, MA.

————. 1987. *Ancient Mystery Cults.* Cambridge, MA.

Burnet, John. 1928. *Greek Philosophy. Part I. Thales to Plato.* London.

Burnyeat, Myles F. 1977. "Socratic Midwifery, Platonic Inspiration." *Bulletin of the Institute of Classical Studies* 24:7–17.

————. 1986. "Good Repute." *London Review of Books* 8(19):11.

Burnyeat, Myles F., and Honderich, Ted, eds. 1979. *Philosophy As It Is.* London.

Cairns, Douglas L., ed. 2001. *Oxford Readings in Homer's Iliad.* Oxford.

Carnes, Jeffrey. 1997. "This Myth Which is Not One." In Larmour et al. 1997:104–121.

Carone, Gabriela Roxana. 1988. "Socrates' Human Wisdom and *Sophrosune* in *Charmides.*" *Ancient Philosophy* 18:267–286.

————. 2001. "*Akrasia* in the *Republic*: Does Plato Change His Mind?" *Oxford Studies in Ancient Philosophy* 20:107–148.

————. 2004. "Calculating Machines or Leaky Jars? The Moral Psychology of Plato's *Gorgias.*" *Oxford Studies in Ancient Philosophy* 26:55–96.

Castiglione, Baldassarre. 1528. *Il Corteggiano.* ed. Silvano del Messier. Novara.

Cavarero, A. 1995. *In Spite of Plato: A Feminist Rewriting of Ancient Philosophy.* Trans. S. Anderlini-D'Onofrio and A. O'Healy. Cambridge.

Cavina, Anna Ottani, ed. 2001. *Mélanges en hommage à Pierre Rosenberg.* Paris.

Chantraine, P. 1968. *Dictionnaire étymologique de la lange grecque.* Paris.

Chapman, John Jay. 1931. *Lucian, Plato, and Greek Morals.* Oxford.

Chen, L. C. H. 1983. "Knowledge of Beauty in Plato's *Symposium.*" *Classical Quarterly* 33:66–74.

Cheney, Liana. 1985. *Quattrocento Neoplatonism and Medici humanism in Botticelli's Mythological Paintings.* Lanham, MD. Reissued 1993 as *Botticelli's Neoplatonic Images.*

Cherniss, Harold F. 1944. *Aristotle's Criticism of Plato and the Academy.* Baltimore.

————. 1945. *The Riddle of the Early Academy.* New York.

Chiesa, Liana. (n.d.) "Le resort de l'amour: Lacan's Theory of Love in His Reading of Plato's *Symposium.*" http://www.janvaneyck.nl/~clicM/documents/Leressortdelamour.doc.

Clark, Kenneth. 1956. *The Nude: A Study in Ideal Form.* Princeton.

Clay, Diskin. 1975. "The Tragic and Comic Poet of the *Symposium*." *Arion* 2:238–261.

Cleary, John J., and Gurtler, Gary M., eds. 1998. *Proceedings of the Boston Area Colloquium in Ancient Philosophy* 14. Leiden.

Cleary, John J., ed. 1999. *Traditions of Platonism. Essays in Honour of John Dillon.* Aldershot and Brookfield, VT.

Cohen, J. M., trans. 1955. *François Rabelais: Gargantua and Pantagruel.* London.

Connors, Catherine M. 1998. *Petronius the Poet.* Cambridge.

Conte, Gian Biagio. 1996. *The Hidden Author: An Interpretation of Petronius's Satyricon.* Berkeley.

Cooper, J. M. 1982. "The *Gorgias* and Irwin's Socrates." *Review of Metaphysics* 35:577–587.

———. 1999a. *Reason and Emotion: Essays on Ancient Moral Psychology and Ethical Theory.* Princeton.

———. 1999b. "Socrates and Plato in Plato's *Gorgias*." In Cooper 1999a:29–75.

Cornford, F. M. 1971. "The Doctrine of *Eros* in Plato's *Symposium*." In Vlastos 1971:119–131.

Corrigan, Kevin. 1997. "The Comic-Serious Figure in Plato's Middle Dialogues: The *Symposium* as Philosophical Art." *Laughter Down the Centuries* 3:55–64.

Corrigan, Kevin and Glazov-Corrigan, Elena. 2004. *Plato's Dialectic at Play: Argument, Structure, and Myth in the Symposium.* University Park, PA.

———. 2005. "Plato's *Symposium* and Bakhtin's Theory of the Dialogical Character of Novelistic Discourse." In Branham 2005:32–50.

Cramer, J. A. 1963. *Anecdota Graeca e coddices manuscriptis Bibliothecarum Oxoniensium.* Amsterdam.

Crisp, Roger, and Slote, Michael, eds. 1997. *Virtue Ethics.* New York.

Dancy, R. M. 2004. *Plato's Introduction of Forms.* Cambridge.

Dante Alighieri. 1984. *Paradise.* Trans. Mark Musa. Bloomington, IN.

D'Arcy, Martin C. 1954. *The Mind and Heart of Love.* London.

Davidson, James N. 1997. *Courtesans and Fishcakes: The Consuming Passions of Classical Athens.* New York. London ed., 1998.

Dean-Jones, Lesley Ann. 1994. *Women's Bodies in Classical Greek Science.* Oxford.

DeHart, Scott M. 1999. "Hippocratic Medicine and the Greek Body Image." *Perspectives on Science.* 7:349–382.

Delaney, N. 1996. "Romantic Love and Loving Commitment: Articulating a Modern Ideal." *American Philosophical Quarterly* 33:375–405.

Dempsey, Charles. 1992. *The Portrayal of Love.* Princeton.

Derda, T., Urbanik, J., and Wecowski, M. 2002. *Euergesias Charin: Studies Presented to Benedetto Bravo and Ewa Wipszycka by Their Disciples*. Warsaw.

Des Places, Édouard. 1964. "Platon et la langue des mystères." *Annales de la Faculté des Lettres et Sciences Humaines Aix* 38(1):9–23.

Devereux, Daniel, and Pellegrin, Pierre, eds. 1990. *Biologie, Logique et Meta-physique chez Aristote*. Paris.

Dillon, Matthew. 2001. *Girls and Women in Classical Greek Religion*. London.

Di Simone, Marina. 1993. "I fallimenti di Encolpio, tra esemplarità mitica e modelli letterari: una ricostruzione" (Sat. 82, 5; 132, 1)." *Materiali e Discussioni* 30:87–108.

Dodds, E. R. 1951. *The Greeks and the Irrational*. Berkeley.

Dorion, Louis-André. 1990. "La subversion de l'*elenchos* juridique dans l'*Apologie de Socrate*." *Revue Philosophique de Louvain* 88:311–344.

———. 2004. *Socrate*. Paris.

Dover, Kenneth J. 1966. "Aristophanes' Speech in Plato's *Symposium*." *Journal of Hellenic Studies* 86:41–50.

———. 1970. "Excursus: The Herms and the Mysteries." In *A Historical Commentary on Thucydides*, ed. A. W. Gomme et al., 4:264–288.

———. 1974. *Greek Popular Morality in the Time of Plato and Aristotle*. Oxford.

———. 1989. *Greek Homosexuality*. London and Cambridge, MA. 1st ed., 1978.

Dowden, K. 1998. "Cupid and Psyche: A Question of the Vision of Apuleius." In Zimmerman 1998:1–22.

———. 2006. "A tale of two texts: Apuleius' *sermo Milesius* and Plato's *Symposium*." In Keulen et al. 2006:42-58.

Du Bois, Page. 1988. *Sowing the Body: Psychoanalysis and Ancient Representations of Women*. Chicago.

Dyson, M. 1986. "Immortality and Procreation in Plato's *Symposium*." *Antichthon* 20:59–72.

Edelstein, Ludwig. 1937. "Greek Medicine in its Relation to Religion and Magic." In Temkin and Temkin 1987:205–246.

———. 1945. "The Role of Eryximachus in Plato's *Symposium*." *Transactions of the American Philological Association* 76:85–103.

Edelstein, Emma L. and Edelstein, Ludwig. 1945. *Asclepius, Collection and Interpretation of the Testimonies*. 2 vols. Baltimore, MD.

Edmonds, Radcliffe G. 2004. *Myths of the Underworld Journey: Plato, Aristophanes, and the 'Orphic' Gold Tablets*. Cambridge.

Eijk, P. J. van der. 1990. "The 'Theology' of the Hippocratic Treatise on the Sacred Disease." *Apeiron* 23:87–119.

Eliade, Mircea. 1972. *Zalmoxis, The Vanishing God*. Chicago.

Emerson, Ralph Waldo. 1983. *Ralph Waldo Emerson: Essays and Lectures*. Ed. Joel Porte. New York.

Entralgo, Pedro Laín. 1970. *The Therapy of the Word in Classical Antiquity*. Ed. and trans. L. J. Rather and J. M. Sharp. New Haven.

Erde, Edmund L. 1976. "Comedy and Tragedy and Philosophy in the *Symposium*: An Ethical Vision." *Southwest Journal of Philosophy* 7:161–167.

Erni, Hans. 1971. *Catalogue Raisonné de L'Oeuvre Lithographié et Gravé de Hans Erni*, vol. 2. Geneva.

Ferrari, Giovanni R. F. 1992. "Platonic Love." In Kraut 1992:248–276.

———, ed. forthcoming. *The Cambridge Companion to Plato's Republic*. Cambridge.

Ficino, Marsilio. 1956. Raymond Marcel, ed. *De Amore, Marsile Ficin: Commentaire sur le Banquet de Platon*. Paris.

———. 1975–(1978, 1981). *The Letters of Marsilio Ficino*. Trans. members of the Language Department of the School of Economic Science. London.

———. 1985. *Commentary on Plato's Symposium on Love*. Trans. Sears Reynolds Jayne. Woodstock, CN.

———. 2001, 2002. *Theologia Platonica de Immortalitate Animorum* (Florence 1482). Vol. 1:I–IV, vol. 2:V–VIII. Trans. Michael J. B. Allen. Ed. James Hankins. Cambridge, MA and London.

Fine, Gail. 2003a. *Plato on Knowledge and Forms*. Oxford.

———. 2003b. "Inquiry in the *Meno*." In Fine 2003a:44–65.

———, ed. forthcoming. *The Oxford Handbook on Plato*. Oxford.

Finnis, John. 1994a. "Law, Morality, and 'Sexual Orientation'." *Notre Dame Law Review* 69:1049–1076.

———. 1994b. "'Shameless Acts' in Colorado: Abuse of Scholarship in Constitutional Cases." *Academic Questions* 7(4):10–41.

Fisher, Mark. 1977. "Reason, Emotion, and Love." *Inquiry* 20:189–203.

———. 1990. *Personal Love*. London.

Fletcher, Jennifer. 1989. "Bernardo Bembo and Leonardo's Portrait of Ginevra de' Benci." *Burlington Magazine* (December) 811–816.

Floriani, Piero. 1976. *Bembo e Castiglione*. Rome.

Foà, Simone. 2004. "Landino, Cristoforo." *Dizionario Biografico degli Italiani* 63:428–433.

Foucault, Michel. 1978. *History of Sexuality*. New York.

Friedländer, Paul. 1969a. *Plato*. vol. 1. ed. 2. Trans. H. Meyerhoff. Princeton.

———. 1969b. *Plato*, vol. 3. Trans. H. Meyerhoff. Princeton.

Furley, William D. 1996. *Andokides and the Herms: A Study of Crisis in Fifth-Century Religion. Bulletin of the Institute of Classical Studies* supp. 65. London.

Gagarin, Michael. 1977. "Socrates' *Hybris* and Alcibiades' Failure." *Phoenix* 31:22–37.

Gallop, David. 1971. "Dreaming and Waking in Plato." In Anton and Kustas 1971:187–201.

Garland, Robert. 1990. *The Greek Way of Life: From Conception to Old Age.* Ithaca, NY.

———. 1992. *Introducing New Gods: the Politics of Athenian Religion.* London.

Gentile, S., Niccoli, M., and Viti, P. 1984. *Marsilio Ficino e il ritorno di Platone: Mostra di Manoscritti Stampe e Documenti 17 Maggio–16 giugno 1984.* Florence.

Gentzler, Jill. 2004. "The Attractions and Delight of Goodness." *Philosophical Quarterly* 54:353–367.

Gerber, Douglas E., ed. 1984. *Greek Poetry and Philosophy: Studies in Honour of Leonard Woodbury.* Chicago.

Gerson, Lloyd P. 1997. "Socrates' Absolutist Prohibition of Wrongdoing." In McPherran 1997:1–11.

———. 2004. "Platonism in Aristotle's Ethics." *Oxford Studies in Ancient Philosophy* 27:217–248.

———. 2005a. "What is Platonism." *Journal of the History of Philosophy* 43:253–276.

———. 2005b. *Aristotle and Other Platonists.* Ithaca.

Gill, Christopher. 1973. "The Death of Socrates." *Classical Quarterly* 23:25–28.

———, ed. 1990a. *The Person and the Human Mind: Issues in Ancient and Modern Philosophy.* Oxford.

———. 1990b. "Platonic Love and Individuality." In Loizou and Lesser 1990:69–88.

——— 1993 "Plato on Falsehood—Not Fiction." In Gill and Wiseman 1993:38–87.

———, ed. 2005. *Virtue, Norms, and Objectivity: Issues in Ancient and Modern Ethics.* Oxford.

Gill, Christopher, and Wiseman, T. P. 1993. *Lies and Fiction in the Ancient World.* Exeter.

Gillham, C., and Wood, C. 2001. *European Drawings: from the Collection of the Ackland Art Museum.* Chapel Hill, North Carolina.

Gold, Barbara K. 1980. "A Question of Genre: Plato's *Symposium* as Novel." *Modern Language Notes* 95:1353–1359.

Golden, Mark. 1985. "*Pais*, Child and Slave." *Antiquité classique* 54:91–104.

———. 1990. *Childhood in Classical Athens*. Baltimore, MD.

Gonzales, Francisco J., ed. 1995. *The Third Way*. Lanham, MD.

Görgemanns, Herwig. 2000. "Die Rede des Pausanias in Platons *Symposion*." In Haltenhoff and Mutschler 2000:177–190.

Gosling, J. C. B. and Taylor, C. C. W. 1982. *The Greeks on Pleasure*. Oxford.

Gould, Thomas. 1963. *Platonic Love*. London.

Griffith, Mark. 1999. *Sophocles: Antigone*. Cambridge.

Griffiths, J. Gwyn. 1975. *Apuleius of Madauros: The Isis Book (Metamorphoses Book XI)*. Leiden.

Grmek, Mirko D., ed. 1998. *Western Medical Thought from Antiquity to the Middle Ages*. Trans. A. Shugaar. Cambridge, MA.

Grube, G. M. A. 1935. *Plato's Thought*. Boston.

Hackforth, R. 1950. "Immortality in Plato's Symposium." *Classical Review* 64:43–45.

Hadot, Pierre. 2002. *What is Ancient Philosophy?* Trans. M. Chase. Cambridge, MA.

Halperin, David M. 1985. "Platonic Eros and What Men Call Love." *Ancient Philosophy* 5:161–204.

———. 1986. "Plato and Erotic Reciprocity." *Classical Antiquity* 5:60–80.

———. 1990. *One Hundred Years of Homosexuality: and Other Essays on Greek Love*. New York.

———. 1992. "Plato and the Erotics of Narrativity." In Klagge and Smith 1992:93–130.

———. 2005. "Love's Irony: Six Remarks on Platonic Eros." In Bartsch and Bartscherer 2005:48–58.

Halperin, David M., Winkler John J., and Zeitlin, Froma I., eds. 1990. *Before Sexuality: The Construction of Erotic Experience in the Ancient Greek World*. Princeton.

Haltenhoff, Andreas, and Mutschler, Fritz-Heiner. 2000. *Hortus litterarum antiquarum: Festschrift für Hans Armin Gärtner zum 70*. Heidelberg.

Hankins, James. 1990. *Plato in the Italian Renaissance*. 2 vols. Leiden.

———. 2002. "Renaissance Philosophy in Book IV of *Il Cortegiano*." In Javitch 2002:377–388.

Harrison, S. J. 1990. "Some Odyssean Scenes in Apuleius' *Metamorphoses*." *Materiali e Discussioni* 25:193–201.

Harrison, Stephen, Paschalis, Michael, and Frangoulidis, Stavros, eds. 2005. *Metaphor and the Ancient Novel. Ancient Narrative* supp. 4. Groningen.

Heinze, R. 1915. *Virgils epische Technik*. 3rd ed. Leipzig and Berlin. Trans. Fred Robertson, *Virgil's Epic Technique*, London. 1993.

Henderson, Jeffrey, ed. and trans. 1998a, 1998b, 2000, 2002. *Aristophanes* 1, 2, 3, 4. Loeb Classical Library 178, 488, 179, 180. Cambridge, MA.

Hijmans, B. L., and Van Der Paardt, R. Th., eds. 1978. *Aspects of Apuleius'* Golden Ass. Groningen.

Hobbs, Angela. 2000. *Plato and the Hero: Courage, Manliness and the Personal Good.* Cambridge.

Hoffmann, G. 1990. *Le châtiment des diamants dans la Grèce classique.* Paris.

Holford-Strevens, L., and Vardi, A., eds. 2004. *The Worlds of Aulus Gellius.* Oxford.

Holowchak, M. A. 2001. "Interpreting Dreams for Corrective Regimen: Diagnostic Dreams in Greco-Roman Medicine." *Journal of the History of Medicine and Allied Sciences* 56:382–399.

Huber, C. E. 1964. *Anamnesis bei Platon.* Pullacher philosophische Forschung 6. Munich.

Hunter, J. F. M. 1980. *Thinking about Sex and Love.* New York.

Hunter, Richard. 1994. "History and Historicity in the Romance of Chariton." *Aufstieg und Niedergang der römischen Welt* II.34.2:1055–1086. Berlin and New York.

———. 1996. "Response to J. R. Morgan." In Sommerstein and Atherton 1996:191–205.

———. 1997. "Longus and Plato." In Picone and Zimmerman 1997:15–28.

———, ed. 1998a. *Studies in Heliodorus.* Cambridge.

———. 1998b. "The *Aithiopika* of Heliodorus: Beyond Interpretation?" In Hunter 1998a:40–59.

———. 2004. *Plato's Symposium.* Oxford.

———. 2005a. "Generic Consciousness in the *Orphic Argonautica?*" In Paschalis 2005:149–168.

———. 2005b. "'Philip the Philosopher' on the *Aithiopika* of Heliodorus." In Harrison et al. 2005:122–138.

Irwin, Terence. 1977a. *Plato's Moral Theory: The Early and Middle Dialogues.* Oxford.

———. 1977b. "Plato's Heracliteanism." *Philosophical Quarterly* 27:1–13.

———. 1988. *Aristotle's First Principles.* Oxford.

———. 1995. *Plato's Ethics.* Oxford.

Jacobs, J., ed. 1982. *Epistolae Ho-Eliane.* London.

James, Paula. 1987. *Unity in Diversity.* Hildesheim.

Javitch, Daniel, ed. 2002. Baldesar Castigione: *The Book of the Courtier.* Trans. Singleton. New York and London.

Jenkins, D., ed. 2003. *The Cambridge History of Western Textiles.* Cambridge.

Jenkins, I. 2003. "The Greeks." In Jenkins, D. 2003:71–76.

Jouanna, J. 1998. "The Birth of Western Medical Art." In Grmek 1998:22–71.

Kahane, Ahuvia, and Laird, Andrew, eds. 2001. *A Companion to the Prologue of Apuleius' Metamorphoses.* Oxford.

Kahn, Charles H. 1996. *Plato and the Socratic Dialogue: The Philosophical Use of a Literary Form.* Cambridge.

Kaiser, E. 1964. "Odyssee-Szenen als Topoi." *Museum Helveticum* 21:109–136, 197–224.

Karasmanis, V. ed. 2004. *Socrates: 2400 Years Since His Death.* Delphi.

Katz, Jonathan Ned. 1995. *The Invention of Heterosexuality.* New York.

Keulen, W. H. 2003. "Comic Invention and Superstitious Frenzy in Apuleius' *Metamorphoses:* The Figure of Socrates as an Icon of Satirical Self-Exposure." *American Journal of Philology* 124:107–135.

———. 2004. "Gellius, Apuleius, and Satire on the Intellectual." In Holford-Strevens and Vardi 2004:223–245.

Keulen, W. H., Nauta, R. R., and Panayotakis, S., eds. 2006. *Lectiones Scrupulosae.* Groningen.

Kidwell, Carol. 2004. *Pietro Bembo: Lover, Linguist, Cardinal.* Montreal.

Kierkegaard, Søren. 1941. *Concluding Unscientific Postscript.* Princeton.

Kihara, S. 1998. "Heraclitus and Greek Medicine in Corpus *Hippocraticum.*" *Methodos* 30. In Japanese; English summary http://www.bun.kyoto-u.ac.jp/ancphil/methodos/methodos30.html#kihara.

———. 2002. "Eryximachus' Doctrine of *Erôs.*" *Methodos* 34. In Japanese; English summary http://www.bun.kyoto-u.ac.jp/ancphil/methodos/methodos34.html#kihara.

Konstan, David E., and Young-Bruehl, Elisabeth. 1982. "Eryximachus' Speech in the *Symposium.*" *Apeiron* 16:40–46.

Klagge, James C., and Smith, Nicholas D., eds. 1992. *Methods of Interpreting Plato and his Dialogues. Oxford Studies in Ancient Philosophy* supp. vol. Oxford.

Knaack, G. 1883. "Analecta." *Hermes* 18:28–33.

Kosman, L. A. 1976. "Platonic Love." In Werkmeister 1976:53–69.

Kragelund, P. 1989. "Epicurus, Priapus and the Dreams in Petronius." *Classical Quarterly* 39:436–450.

Kraut, Richard. 1973. "Egoism, Love, and Political Office." *Philosophical Review* 82:330–344.

———. 1992. *The Cambridge Companion to Plato.* Cambridge.

———. forthcoming. "Plato on Love." In Fine forthcoming.

Kropotkin, Prince [Peter]. 1924. *Ethics: Origin and Development.* Trans. Louis S. Friedland and Joseph R. Piroshnikoff. New York.

Lacan, Jacques. 1977. *Ecrits: A Selection.* New York.

————. 2002. *Le seminaire, livre VIII: Le transfert*, 1960–61. Paris.

Landino, Cristoforo. 1939. *Carmina Omnia*. Ed. Alessandro Perosa. Florence.

————. 1970. *De vera nobilitate*. Ed. Manfred Lentzen. Geneva.

Lane, Melissa S. 1998. *Method and Politics in Plato's Statesman*. Cambridge.

Langholf, V. 1990. *Medical Theories in Hippocrates*. Berlin.

Larmour, D. H. J., Miller, P. A., and Platter, C., eds. 1997. *Rethinking Sexuality: Foucault and Classical Antiquity*. Princeton.

Lawson, R. P. 1957. *Origen. The Song of Songs, commentary and homilies*. Westminster MD and London.

Lear, Gabriel Richardson. 2004. *Happy Lives and the Highest Good: An Essay on Aristotle's Nicomachean Ethics*. Princeton.

————. 2006. "Plato on Learning to Love Beauty." In Santas 2006:104–124.

Lear, Jonathan. 1998. *Open Minded: Working out the Logic of the Soul*. Cambridge.

————. 2000. *Happiness, Death, and the Remainder of Life*. Cambridge.

————. 2004. *Therapeutic Action*. New York.

Lesher, James H. 2004. "The Afterlife of Plato's *Symposium*." *Ordia Prima* 3:89–105.

————. 2006. "Later Views of the Socrates of Plato's *Symposium*." In Trapp 2006:59–76.

Lévêque, Pierre. 1955. *Agathon*. Paris.

Levy, D. 1979. "The Definition of Love in Plato's *Symposium*." *Journal of the History of Ideas* 40:285–291.

Lévystone, D. 2005. "La figure d'Ulysse chez les Socratiques: Socrate polutropos." *Phronesis* 50:181–214.

Lissarague, F. 1990. *The Aesthetics of the Greek Banquet*. Princeton.

Lloyd, G. E. R. 1975a. "The Hippocratic Question." *Classical Quarterly* 25:171–192.

————. 1975b. "Aspects of the Interrelations of Medicine, Magic, and Philosophy in Ancient Greece." *Apeiron* 9:1–16.

————. 1979. *Magic, Reason, and Experience*. Cambridge.

Lloyd-Jones, Hugh. 1979. *Aeschylus: Eumenides*. London.

Loizou, A., and Lesser, H., eds. 1990. *Polis and Politics: Essays in Greek Moral and Political Philosophy*. Aldershot.

Lowenstam, S. 1985. "Paradoxes in Plato's *Symposium*." *Ramus* 14:85–104.

Lowry, Martin. 1979. *The World of Aldus Manutius: Business and Scholarship in Renaissance Venice*. Ithaca, NY.

Luce, J. V. 1952. "Immortality in Plato's *Symposium*." *Classical Review* 66:137–141.

Ludwig, Paul W. 2002. *Erôs and Polis*. Cambridge.

Mahoney, T. 1996. "Is Socratic *Eros* in the *Symposium* Egoistic?" *Apeiron* 29:1–18.

Maraguianou, Évangélie. 1985. "L'amour, objet d'initiation chez Platon." *Philosophia* (Athens) 15/16:240–253.

Martin, Dale B. 2004. *Inventing Superstition: From the Hippocratics to the Christians.* Cambridge, MA.

Mazzeo, J. 1958. *Structure and Thought in the Paradiso.* Ithaca, NY.

McGrath, E. 1983. "'The Drunken Alcibiades': Rubens's Picture of Plato's *Symposium*." *Journal of the Warburg and Courtauld Institutes* 46:228–235 (Plates on 42–44).

McPherran, Mark. 1996. *The Religion of Socrates.* University Park, PA. Paper ed., 1999.

———, ed. 1997. *Wisdom Ignorance and Virtue.* Edmonton.

———. 2000. "Piety, Justice, and the Unity of Virtue." *Journal of the History of Philosophy* 38:299–328.

———. 2004. "Socrates and Zalmoxis on Drugs, Charms, and Purification." *Apeiron* 37:11–33.

Mendelsohn, Daniel. 1996. "The Stand: Expert Witnesses and Ancient Mysteries in a Colorado Courtroom." *Lingua Franca* 6.6:34–46.

Mikalson, J. D. 1983. *Athenian Popular Religion.* Chapel Hill.

Miller, Mitchell. 1995. "The Choice Between the Dialogues and the 'Unwritten Teachings': A Scylla and Charybdis for the Interpreter?" In Gonzales 1995:225–244.

Montiglio, Silvia. 2000. "Wandering Philosophers in Classical Greece." *Journal of Hellenic Studies* 120:86–105.

———. 2005. *Wandering in Greek Culture.* Chicago.

Morales, Helen. 2004. *Vision and Narrative in Achilles Tatius' Leucippe and Clitophon.* Cambridge.

Morgan, Michael L. 1990. *Platonic Piety.* New Haven.

Morrison, John S. 1941. "The Place of Protagoras in Athenian Public Life." *Classical Quarterly* 25:1–16.

———. 1964. "Four Notes on Plato's *Symposium*." *Classical Quarterly* 14:42–55.

Moravcsik, J. M. E. 1971. "Reason and Eros in the 'Ascent' Passage of the *Symposium*." In Anton and Kustas 1971:285–302.

Münstermann, Hans. 1995. *Apuleius. Metamorphosen literarischer Vorlagen.* Stuttgart and Leipzig.

Murdoch, Iris. 1970. *The Sovereignty of Good.* London.

Murphy, David J. 2000. "Doctors of Zalmoxis and Immortality in the *Charmides*." In Robinson and Brisson 2000:287–295.

Murray, Oswyn. 1990a. *Sympotica: A Symposium on the Symposion.* Oxford.

———. 1990b. "The Affair of the Mysteries: Democracy and the Drinking Group." In Murray 1990a:149–161.

Murray, Oswyn, and Tecuşan, Manuela, eds. 1995. *In Vino Veritas*. London.

Murray, Penelope, ed. 1996. *Plato on Poetry*. Cambridge.

Nails, Debra. 1995. *Agora, Academy, and the Conduct of Philosophy*. Dordrecht.

———. 2001. "Seduced by Prodicus." *Southwest Philosophy Review* 17(2):129–139.

———. 2002. *The People of Plato*. Indianapolis.

Nehamas, Alexander. 1998. *The Art of Living: Socratic Reflections from Plato to Foucault*. Berkeley and Los Angeles.

Neumann, H. 1965. "Diotima's Concept of Love." *American Journal of Philology* 86:33–59.

Nietzsche, Friedrich. 1956. *The Birth of Tragedy; and The Genealogy of Morals*. Trans. Francis Golffing. New York. Reprinted 1990.

———. 1967. *The Birth of Tragedy* (1872). Trans. Walter Kaufmann. New York.

Nightingale, Andrea Wilson. 1993. "The Folly of Praise: Plato's Critique of Encomiastic Discourse in the *Lysis* and *Symposium*." *Classical Quarterly* 43:112–130.

———. 1995. *Genres in Dialogue: Plato and the Construct of Philosophy*. Cambridge.

———. 2004. *Spectacles of Truth in Classical Greek Philosophy*. Cambridge.

Novotny, F. 1977. *The Posthumous Life of Plato*. The Hague.

Nozick, Robert. 1989. *The Examined Life*. New York.

Nussbaum, Martha Craven. 1979. "The Speech of Alcibiades: A Reading of Plato's *Symposium*." *Philosophy and Literature* 3:131–172. Reprinted in Nussbaum 1986:165–199.

———. 1986. *The Fragility of Goodness: Luck and Ethics in Greek Tragedy and Philosophy*. Cambridge.

———. 1994. "Platonic Love and Colorado Law: The Relevance of Ancient Greek Norms to Modern Sexual Controversies." *Virginia Law Review* 80(7):1515–1643.

Nygren, Anders. 1953. *Agape and Eros*. Trans. Philip S. Watson. Philadelphia.

O'Brien, Maeve C. 2002. *Apuleius' Debt to Plato in the Metamorphoses*. Lewiston, NY.

O'Brien, Michael J. 1984. "Becoming Immortal in Plato's *Symposium*." In Gerber 1984:185–205.

O'Connor, David K. forthcoming. "Rewriting the Poets in Plato's Characters." In Ferrari forthcoming.

Osborne, Catherine. 1994. *Eros Unveiled: Plato and the God of Love*. Oxford.

Owen, G. E. L. 1968. *Aristotle on Dialectic: The Topics*. Oxford.

————. 1986. *Logic, Science and Dialectic: Collected Papers in Greek Philosophy*. Ed. Martha Nussbaum. Ithaca, NY.

Panofsky, Erwin. 1968. *Idea: A Concept in Art Theory (A Study of the Changes in the Definition & Conception of the Term "Idea," from Plato to the 17th Century, when the Modern Definition Emerged)*. Trans. Joseph J. S. Peake. Columbia, SC.

————. 1969. *Problems in Titian*. New York.

Parfit, Derek. 1984. *Reasons and Persons*. Oxford.

Parker, Robert. 1996. *Athenian Religion: A History*. Oxford.

Paschalis, Michael, ed. 2005. *Roman and Greek Imperial Epic*. Heraklion, Crete.

Patterson, Richard A. 1982. "The Platonic Art of Comedy and Tragedy." *Philosophy and Literature* 6:76–93.

————. 1991. "The Ascent in Plato's *Symposium*." *Proceedings of the Boston Area Colloquium in Ancient Philosophy* 7:193–214.

Patzer, H. 1982. *Die Griechische Knabenliebe*. Wiesbaden.

Paz, Octavio. 1997. *La Llama Doble: Amor y Erotismo*. Barcelona.

Pender, Elizabeth. 1992. "Spiritual Pregnancy in Plato's *Symposium*." *Classical Quarterly* ns 42:72–86.

Penner, Terry, and Rowe, Christopher. 2005. *Plato's Lysis*. Cambridge.

Penwill, J. L. 1978. "Men in Love: Aspects of Plato's *Symposium*." *Ramus* 7:143–175.

Perkins, Judith. 2005. "Trimalchio: Naming Power." In Harrison et al. 2005:139–162.

Peters, W. 1976. "The Sileni of Alcibiades. An Archeological Commentary on Plato *Symposium* 215a–b." In Boersma 1976:475–485.

Pickett, Brent. 2002. "Homosexuality." *Stanford Encyclopedia of Philosophy*, ed. Edward N. Zalta. http://plato.stanford.edu/entries/homosexuality.

Picone, M. and Zimmermann, B., eds. 1997. *Der antike Roman und seine mittelalterliche Rezeption*. Basel.

Pirenne-Delforge, V. 1988. "Épithètes cultuelles et interprétation philosophique: À propos d'Aphrodite Ourania et Pandémos à Athènes." Antiquité Classique 57:142–157.

————. 1994. *L'Aphrodite grecque*. *Kernos* supp. 4. Athens and Liege.

Plass, P. 1978. "Plato's Pregnant Lover." *Symbolae Osloenses* 53:47–55.

Posner, Richard A. 1992. *Sex and Reason*. Cambridge, MA.

Poulakos, J. 1998. "Philosophy and Medicine in Plato's *Symposium*." In Boudouris 1998:164–170.

Press, Gerald A. 1995. "Plato's Dialogues as Enactments." In Gonzales 1995:133–152.

————, ed. 2000. *Who Speaks for Plato? Studies in Platonic Anonymity*. Lanham, MD.

Price, A. W. 1981. "Loving Persons Platonically." *Phronesis* 26:25–34.

————. 1991. "Martha Nussbaum's Symposium." *Ancient Philosophy* 11:285–299.

————. 1995. *Mental Conflict*. London.

————. 1997. *Love and Friendship in Plato and Aristotle*. Oxford. 1st ed., 1989.

Race, W. 1997. *Pindar: Olympian Odes, Pythian Odes*. Loeb Classical Library. Cambridge, MA.

Rawson, Glenn. 2006. "Platonic Recollection and Mental Pregnancy." *Journal of the History of Philosophy* 44(2):137–155.

Reardon, B. P., ed. 1989. *Collected Ancient Greek Novels*. Berkeley.

Reckford, K. 1991. "Eliot's Cocktail Party and Plato's *Symposium*." *Classical and Modern Literature* 11:303–312.

Reeve, C. D. C. 1992a. *Practices of Reason: Aristotle's Nicomachean Ethics*. Oxford.

————. 1992b. "Telling the Truth About Love: Plato's *Symposium*." *Proceedings of the Boston Area Colloquium in Ancient Philosophy* 8:89–114.

————. 2004. "*Sôkratês Erôtikos*." In Karasmanis 2004:94–106.

Riedweg, Christoph. 1987. *Mysterienterminologie bei Platon, Philon und Klemens von Alexandrien*. Untersuchungen zur antiken Literatur und Geschichte 26. Berlin.

Rist, John M. 1964. *Eros and Psyche: Studies in Plato, Plotinus, and Origen*. Toronto.

Robin, Léon. 1908. *La Théorie platonicienne de l'amour*. Paris. 3rd ed. 1964.

Robinson, Thomas M. and Brisson, Luc, eds. 2000. *Plato: Euthydemus, Lysis, Charmides: Proceedings of the V Symposium Platonicum*. Sankt Augustin, Germany.

Rosen, Stanley. 1987. *Plato's Symposium*. New Haven. 1st ed. 1968.

Rösler, Wolfgang. 1990. "*Mnemosyne* in the *Symposion*." In Murray 1990:230–238.

————. 1995. "Wine and Truth in the Greek *Symposium*." In Murray and Tecuşan 1995:106–112.

Rowe, Christopher J. 1990. "Philosophy, Love, and Madness." In Gill 1990a:227–246.

————. 1998b. "Socrates and Diotima: Eros, Immortality, and Creativity." In Cleary and Gurtler 1998:239–259.

————. 1999. "The Speech of Eryximachus in Plato's *Symposium*." In Cleary 1999:53–64.

————. 2005. "What Difference Do Forms Make to Platonic Epistemology?" In Gill 2005:215–232.

————. 2006. "The Literary and Philosophical Style of the *Republic*." In Santas 2006:7–24.

Runes, Dagobert. 1959. *Pictorial History of Philosophy*. New York.

Rutherford, R. B. 1995. *The Art of Plato: Ten Essays in Platonic Interpretation*. Cambridge, MA.

Ryan, Lawrence V. 1972. "Book IV of Castiglione's *Courtier*: Climax or Afterthought?" *Studies in the Renaissance* 19:156–179.

Santas, Gerasimos X. 1988. *Plato and Freud: Two Theories of Love*. New York.

————, ed. 2006. *Blackwell Guide to the Republic*. Oxford.

Saxonhouse, Arlene W. 1976. "The Philosopher and the Female in the Political Thought of Plato." *Political Theory* 4(2):195–212. Reprinted in Tuana 1994:67–85.

Schein, Seth. 1974. "Alcibiades and the Politics of Misguided Love in Plato's *Symposium*." *Theta-Pi* 3:158–167.

Schlam, C. 1970. "Platonica in the *Metamorphoses* of Apuleius." *Transactions of the American Philological Association* 101:477–487.

————. 1992. *The Metamorphoses of Apuleius*. London.

Schmeling, Gareth. 2003. *The Novel in the Ancient World*. 2nd ed. Boston and Leiden.

Schmitt-Pantel, Pauline. 1990. "Sacrificial Meal and *Symposion*: Two Models of Civic Institutions in the Archaic City?" In Murray 1990a:14–33.

Schwarzmaier, A. 1997. "Wirklich Sokrates und Diotima?" *Archaologischer Anzeiger* 1:79–96.

Scott, Dominic. 1995. *Recollection and Experience. Plato's Theory of Learning and Its Successors*. Cambridge.

————. 2000. "Socrates and Alcibiades in the *Symposium*." *Hermathena* 168:25–37.

Scott, Gary Alan and Welton, William A. 2000. "Eros as Messenger in Diotima's Teaching." In Press 2000:147–159.

Scruton, Roger. 1986. *Sexual Desire*. New York.

Sedley, David. 2004. *The Midwife of Platonism*. Oxford.

Sergent, B. 1996. *Homosexualité chez les peuples indo-européens*. 1st ed. in 2 vols. 1984, 1986. Paris.

Sheffield, Frisbee C. C. 2001a. "Psychic Pregnancy and Platonic Epistemology." *Oxford Studies in Ancient Philosophy* 20:1–33.

————. 2001b. "Alcibiades' Speech: A Satyric Drama." *Greece & Rome* 48:193–209.

————. 2006. *Plato's Symposium: The Ethics of Desire*. Oxford.

Shelley, Percy Bysshe. 1839. *The Complete Poems of Percy Bysshe Shelley.* Ed. Mary Shelley. 2nd ed. 1994. New York.

————. 2002b. *Shelley's Poetry and Prose.* 2nd ed. Donald H. Reiman and Neil Fraistat. New York.

Shields, S. 1997. "Memorable Wreaths: Love, Death, and the Classical Text in La Farge's *Agathon to Erosanthe* and *Wreath of Flowers.*" *American Art* 11:82–105.

Shorey, Paul. 1933. *What Plato Said.* Chicago.

Sider, David. 1980. "Plato's *Symposium* as a Dionysian Festival." *Quaderni Urbinati di Cultura Classica* 33:41–56.

————. 2002. "Two Jokes in Plato's *Symposium.*" In Amden et al. 2002:260–264.

Sier, Kurt. 1997. *Die Rede der Diotima: Untersuchungen zum platonischen Symposion.* Stuttgart and Leipzig.

Singer, Irving. 1966. *The Nature of Love: Plato to Luther.* New York.

Skinner, Marilyn. 2005. *Sexuality in Greek and Roman Culture.* Malden, MA.

Slater, Niall W. 1990. *Reading Petronius.* Baltimore and London.

Smith, Dennis E. 2003. *From Symposium to Eucharist: the Banquet in the Early Christian World.* Minneapolis.

Smith, Warren S., and Woods, Baynard. 2002. "Tale of Aristomenes: Declamation in a Platonic Mode." *Ancient Narrative* 2:172–195.

Solmsen, Friedrich. 1968. "Dialectic Without the Forms." In Owen 1968:49–68.

Solomon, Robert C. 1988. *About Love: Reinventing Romance for Our Times.* New York.

Sommerstein, Alan H. 1989. *Aeschylus, Eumenides.* Cambridge.

Sommerstein, Alan H., and Atherton, Catherine, eds. 1996. *Education in Greek Fiction.* Nottingham Classical Lecture Series 4. Bari.

Staden, H. von. 1998. "*Dynamis:* The Hippocratics and Plato." In Boudouris 1998:262–279.

Stannard, J. 1959. "Socratic Eros and Platonic Dialectic." *Phronesis* 4:120–134.

Stehle, Eva. 1997. *Performance and Gender in Ancient Greece: Nondramatic Poetry in its Setting.* Princeton.

Stephens, S. A., and Winkler, John J. 1995. *Ancient Greek Novels. The Fragments.* Princeton.

Stevens, Wallace. 1997. *Wallace Stevens: Collected Poetry and Prose.* Ed. Frank Kermode and Joan Richardson, eds. New York.

Stocker, Michael. 1997. "The Schizophrenia of Modern Ethical Theories." In Crisp and Slote 1997:453–466.

Stokes, Michael C. 1986. *Plato's Socratic Conversations: Drama and Dialectic in Three Dialogues.* Baltimore.

Strauss, Leo. 2001. *On Plato's Symposium.* Ed. Seth Benardete. Chicago.

Strong, R. 1973. *Splendor at Court: Renaissance Spectacle and the Theater of Power.* Boston.

Tatum, J. 1969. "The Tales in Apuleius' *Metamorphoses.*" *Transactions of the American Philological Association* 100:487–527.

Taylor, A. E. 1960. *Plato: The Man and his Work.* 7th ed. London.

Taylor, Gabriele. 1979. In Burnyeat and Honderich 1979:165–182.

Tecuşan, Manuela. 1990. "*Logos Sympotikos:* Patterns of the Irrational in Philosophical Drinking: Plato outside the *Symposium.*" In Murray 1990a:238–260.

Tejera, Victorino. 2000. *Plato's Dialogues One by One.* Washington. 1st ed. 1983.

Teloh, Henry. 1986. *Socratic Education in Plato's Early Dialogues.* Notre Dame, IN.

Temkin, O. and Temkin, C. L., eds. 1987. *Ancient Medicine.* Baltimore, MD.

Thesleff, Holger. 1978. "The Interrelation and Date of the *Symposia* of Plato and Xenophon." *Bulletin of the Institute for Classical Studies* 25:157–170.

———. 1982. *Studies in Platonic Chronology.* Commentationes Humanarum Litterarum 70. Helsinki.

Thibau, R. 1965. "Les Métamorphoses d'Apulée et la théorie platonicienne de l'Erôs." *Studia Philosophica Gandensia* 3:89–144.

Trapp, Michael, ed. 2006. *Socrates in the Nineteenth and Twentieth Century.* Centre for Hellenic Studies Conference Series. London.

Tsekourakis, D. 1991–1993. "Plato's *Phaedrus* and the Holistic Viewpoint in Hippocrates' Therapeutics." *Bulletin of the Institute of Classical Studies of the University of London* 38:162–173.

Tuana, Nancy. 1992. *Woman and the History of Philosophy.* New York.

———, ed. 1994. *Feminist Interpretations of Plato.* Pennsylvania.

Usener, H. 1887. *Epicurea.* Leipzig.

Van Der Paardt, R. Th. 1978. "Various Aspects of Narrative Technique in Apuleius' *Metamorphoses.*" In Hijmans and Van Der Paardt 1978:75–94.

Van de Sandt, Udolpho. 2001. "Un tableau de Pierre Peyron commandé par le comte d'Angiviller: Socrate détachant Alcibiade des charmes de la volupté." In Cavina 2001:410–416.

Vendler, Helen. 1984. *Words Chosen Out of Desire.* Cambridge, MA.

Verga, Giovanni. 2003. *Life in the Country.* London.

Vernant, Jean-Pierre. 1990. "One... Two... Three: Erôs." In Halperin et al. 1990:465–478.

———. 1991. *Mortals and Immortals.* Princeton.

———. 2001. "A 'Beautiful Death' and the Disfigured Corpse in Homeric Epic." In Cairns 2001:311–341.

Vlastos, Gregory. 1949. "Religion and Medicine in the Cult of Asclepius: A Review Article." *Review of Religion* 13:269–290.

——, ed. 1971. *Plato: A Collection of Critical Essays.* vol. 2. *Ethics, Politics, and Philosophy of Art and Religion.* Garden City, NY.

——. 1973a. *Platonic Studies.* Princeton.

——. 1973b. "The Individual as Object of Love." In Vlastos 1973a:3–34.

——. 1991. *Socrates: Ironist and Moral Philosopher.* Ithaca, NY.

Vries, G. J. des. 1973. "Mystery Terminology in Aristophanes and Plato." *Mnemosyne* 26:1–8.

Wardy, Robert. 2002. "The Unity of Opposites in Plato's *Symposium.*" *Oxford Studies in Ancient Philosophy* 23:1–61.

Waithe, Mary Ellen, ed. 1987a. *A History of Women Philosophers.* Dordrecht.

——. 1987b. "Diotima of Mantinea." In Waithe 1987:chap 6.

Walsh, P. G. 1994. *Apuleius: The Golden Ass.* Oxford.

Warner, M. 1979. "Love, Self, and Plato's *Symposium.*" *Philosophical Quarterly* 29:329–339.

Wecowski, Marek. 2002. "Towards a Definition of the Symposion." In Derda et al. 2002:337–361.

Wellman, R. R. 1969. "Eros and education in Plato's *Symposium.*" *Paedogica Historica* 9:129–158.

Wender, Dorothea. 1973. "Plato: Misogynist, Paedophile and Feminist." *Arethusa* 6(1):75–90.

Werkmeister, W. H. 1976. *Facets of Plato's Philosophy.* Assen.

White, F. C. 1989. "Love and Beauty in Plato's *Symposium.*" *Journal of Hellenic Studies* 109:149–157.

——. 2004. "Virtue in Plato's *Symposium.*" *Classical Quarterly* 54:366–378.

White, Nicholas. 2002. *Individual and Conflict in Greek Ethics.* Oxford.

Wind, Edgar. 1960. *Pagan Mysteries in the Renaissance.* Enlarged ed. 1968. London.

Winkler, John J. 1985. *Auctor & Actor. A Narratological Reading of Apuleius's The Golden Ass.* Berkeley.

——. 1990. *The Constraints of Desire: The Anthropology of Sexual Gender in Ancient Greece.* New York.

Woolf, Raphael. 2004. "The Practice of a Philosopher." *Oxford Studies in Ancient Philosophy* 26:97–129.

Zaidman, L. B., and Pantel, P. S. 1992. *Religion in the Ancient Greek City.* Trans. P. Cartledge. Cambridge.

Zanker, P. 1996. *The Mask of Socrates: The Image of the Intellectual in Antiquity.* Berkeley, Los Angeles, and Oxford.

Zimmerman, M., Hunink, V., McCreight, T. D., Mal-Maeder, D. van, Panayotakis, St., Schmidt, V., and Wesseling, B., eds. 1998. *Aspects of Apuleius' Golden Ass.* vol. 2. Groningen.

Zöllner, Frank. 2004. *Leonardo da Vinci 1452–1519: The Complete Paintings and Drawings.* Cologne.

Index of Passages

Slight variations in line numbers of Plato's texts may be noticed; these result from the use of different editions of the Greek text by the various authors.

Index

Achilles, 35, 98n2, 108, 234n29

Achilles Tatius, 305n36, 306n37

Acumenus, 74n10, 182, 202, 204

Adam, J., 131n12

Adamson, Peter, 23n1

Addams, Jane, 315

Adeimantus of Scambonidae, 184n15, 203

Admetus, 35

Adonis, garden of, 130–131

Aegospotami, Battle of, 205

Aeschines, 264n40

Aeschylus, 20, 205n68. *See also* Index of Passages

agalmata (figurative statues), 3–4, 124–146, 157, 366–367

agapē, 211

Agariste wife of Damon, 202, 203, 204

Agathon son of Tisamenus, 163; historical, 39, 181–183, 187, 202, 205, 233n21, 235–237, 240; represented in visual arts, 316, 318–320; speech of, 15n14, 26, 27n6, 28, 32–33, 42n24, 89, 151n16, 170, 172, 200, 229–230, 245–246, 339, 347

Agli, Antonio, 345, 346

Ahmed, Arif, 23n1

Ajax, 140

Alberti, Leone Battista: *Della Pictura*, 353n27

Alcestis, 99n5, 108, 253, 254n9

Alcibiades of Scambonidae, son of Clinias, 6; actions of, in *Symposium*, 15, 114, 366–368; as tragic figure, 189, 190–191, 192, 194–197; as witness of Socrates, 158, 164–165; historical, 78n21, 166n83, 181–182, 183–184, 201–205; in later representations, 316–319, 321–325, 342; Plato's view of, 141; speech of, 3–4, 119–120, 124–127, 132, 133, 135–136, 140–141, 204–205, 219, 222–224, 230, 267–268, 301–302, 315, 344

Alcibiades of Phegous, 184n15, 203

Alcibiades I, 56, 65, 166, 168n92. *See also* Index of Passages

Alcibiades II, 166n81

Alcmaeon, 74

All about Love, 1, 315

Allegoresis (personification of allegory), 345, 346

Allen, Michael J. B., 347n12

Allen, Reginald E., 51–52n11, 55n22, 59n40, 63n57, 88, 124n2, 128,

426

This book was composed by Ivy Livingston
and manufactured by Edwards Brothers, Ann Arbor, MI

The typeface is Gentium, designed by Victor Gaultney
and distributed by SIL International

CPSIA information can be obtained at www.ICGtesting.com
Printed in the USA
BVOW071837150712

295173BV00001B/8/P